Roger Norris, Lawrie Ryan
and David Acaster

Cambridge International AS and A Level

Chemistry

Coursebook

CAMBRIDGE
UNIVERSITY PRESS

CAMBRIDGE UNIVERSITY PRESS
Cambridge, New York, Melbourne, Madrid, Cape Town,
Singapore, São Paulo, Delhi, Mexico City

Cambridge University Press
The Edinburgh Building, Cambridge CB2 8RU, UK

www.cambridge.org
Information on this title: www.cambridge.org/9780521126618

First published 2011
6th printing 2013

Printed in Dubai by Oriental Press

A catalogue record for this publication is available from the British Library

ISBN 978-0-521-12661-8 Paperback with CD-ROM for Windows and Mac

Cambridge University Press has no responsibility for the persistence or
accuracy of URLs for external or third-party internet websites referred to in
this publication, and does not guarantee that any content on such websites is,
or will remain, accurate or appropriate.

Contents

Introduction

Cambridge CIE AS and A Level Chemistry

This new Cambridge AS/A Level Chemistry course has been specifically written to provide a complete and precise coverage for the Cambridge International Examinations syllabus 9701. The language has been kept simple, with bullet points where appropriate, in order to improve the accessibility to all students. Principal Examiners have been involved in all aspects of this book to ensure that the content gives the best possible match to both the syllabus and to the type of questions asked in the examination.

The book is arranged in two sections. Chapters 1–17 correspond to the AS section of the course (for examination in Papers 1, 2 and 31/32). Chapters 18–30 correspond to the A level section of the course (for examinations in papers 4 and 5). Within each of these sections the material is arranged in the same sequence as the syllabus. For example in the AS section, Chapter 1 deals with atoms, molecules and stoichiometry and Chapter 2 deals with atomic structure. The A level section starts with lattice energy (Chapter 18: syllabus section 5) then progresses to redox potentials (Chapter 19: syllabus section 6).

Nearly all the written material is new, although some of the diagrams have been based on material from the endorsed *Chemistry for OCR* books 1 and 2 (Acaster and Ryan, 2008). There are separate chapters about nitrogen and sulfur (Chapter 12) and the elements and compounds of Group IV (Chapter 22), which tie in with the specific syllabus sections. Electrolysis appears in Chapter 7 and quantitative electrolysis in Chapter 19. The chapter on reaction kinetics (Chapter 21) includes material about catalysis whilst the organic chemistry section has been rewritten to accommodate the iodoform reaction and to follow the syllabus more closely. The last three chapters have been developed to focus on the applications of chemistry (Paper 4B). These chapters contain a wealth of material and questions which will help you gain confidence to maximise your potential in the examination. Important definitions are placed in boxes to highlight key concepts.

Several features of the book are designed to make learning as effective and interesting as possible.

- **Objectives** for the chapter appear at the beginning of each chapter. These relate directly to the statements in the syllabus, so you know what you should be able to do when you have completed the chapter.
- **Important definitions** are placed in boxes to highlight key concepts.
- **Check-up questions** appear in boxes after most short sections of text to allow you to test yourself. They often address misunderstandings that commonly appear in examination answers. The detailed answers can be found at the back of the book.
- **Fact files** appear in boxes at various parts of the text. These are to stimulate interest or to provide extension material. They are not needed for the examination.
- **Worked examples**, in a variety of forms, are provided in chapters involving mathematical content.
- **Experimental chemistry** is dealt with by showing detailed instructions for key experiments, e.g. calculation of relative molecular mass, titrations, thermochemistry and rates of reaction. Examples are also given of how to process the results of these experiments.
- A **summary** at the end of each chapter provides you with the key points of the chapter as well as key definitions.
- **End-of-chapter questions** appear after the summary in each chapter. Many of these are new questions and so supplement those to be found on the Cambridge Students' and Teachers' websites. The answers to these questions, along with exam-style mark schemes, can be found on the CD-ROM.
- **Examiner tips** are given with the answers to the end-of-chapter questions on the CD-ROM.
- A full **glossary** of definitions is provided at the back of the book.

A student CD-ROM is also provided. In addition to the summaries and glossary, this contains:

- **animations** to help develop your understanding
- **test-yourself questions** (multiple choice) for Chapters 1–17. These are new questions and will help you with Paper 1
- **study skills** guidance to help you direct your learning so that it is productive
- **advice on the practical examination** to help you achieve the best results.

1 Moles and equations

Learning outcomes

Candidates should be able to:

- [ ] define the terms **relative atomic**, **isotopic**, **molecular** and **formula masses** based on the ^{12}C scale
- [ ] analyse mass spectra in terms of isotopic abundances (no knowledge of the working of the mass spectrometer is required)
- [ ] calculate the relative atomic mass of an element given the relative abundances of its isotopes or its mass spectrum
- [ ] define the term **mole** in terms of the Avogadro constant
- [ ] define the terms **empirical** and **molecular formulae**
- [ ] calculate empirical and molecular formulae using combustion data or composition by mass

- [ ] write and/or construct balanced equations
- [ ] perform calculations, including use of the mole concept involving
  - reacting masses (from formulae and equations)
  - volumes of gases (e.g. in the burning of hydrocarbons)
  - volumes and concentrations of solutions
- [ ] perform calculations taking into account the number of significant figures given or asked for in the question
- [ ] deduce stoichiometric relationships from calculations involving reacting masses, volumes of gases and volumes and concentrations of solutions.

1.1 Introduction

For thousands of years, people have heated rocks and distilled plant juices to extract materials. Over the past two centuries, chemists have learnt more and more about how to get materials from rocks, from the air and the sea and from plants. They have also found out the right conditions to allow these materials to react together to make new substances, such as dyes, plastics and medicines. When we make a new substance it is important to mix the reactants in the correct proportions to ensure that none is wasted. In order to do this we need to know about the relative masses of atoms and molecules and how these are used in chemical calculations.

1.2 Masses of atoms and molecules

Relative atomic mass, A_r

Atoms of different **elements** have different masses. When we perform chemical calculations, we need to know how heavy one atom is compared with another. The mass of a single atom is so small that it is impossible to weigh it directly. To overcome this problem, we have to weigh a lot of atoms. We then compare this mass with the mass of the same number of 'standard' atoms. Scientists have chosen to use the isotope carbon-12 as the standard. This has been given a mass of exactly 12 units. The mass of other atoms is found by comparing their mass with the mass of carbon-12 atoms. This is called the **relative atomic mass**, A_r.

> The **relative atomic mass** is the weighted average mass of naturally occurring atoms of an element on a scale where an atom of carbon-12 has a mass of exactly 12 units.

Figure 1.1 A titration is a method used to find the amount of a particular substance in a solution.

From this it follows that

$A_r[\text{element } Y]$

$$= \frac{\text{average mass of one atom of element } Y \times 12}{\text{mass of one atom of carbon-12}}$$

We use the average mass of the atom of a particular element because most elements are mixtures of isotopes. For example, the exact A_r of hydrogen is 1.0079. This is very close to 1 and most Periodic Tables give the A_r of hydrogen as 1.0. However, some elements in the Periodic Table have values that are not whole numbers. For example, the A_r for chlorine is 35.5. This is because chlorine has two isotopes. In a sample of chlorine, chlorine-35 makes up about three-quarters of the chlorine atoms and chlorine-37 makes up about a quarter.

Relative isotopic mass

Isotopes are atoms which have the same number of protons but different numbers of neutrons (see page 28). We represent the **nucleon number** (the total number of neutrons plus protons in an atom) by a number written at the top left-hand corner of the atom's symbol, e.g. ^{20}Ne, or by a number written after the atom's name or symbol, e.g. neon-20 or Ne-20.

We use the term **relative isotopic mass** for the mass of a particular isotope of an element on a scale where an atom of carbon-12 has a mass of exactly 12 units. For example, the relative isotopic mass of carbon-13 is 13.00. If we know both the natural abundance of every isotope of an element and their isotopic masses, we can calculate the relative atomic mass of the element very accurately. To find the necessary data we use an instrument called a mass spectrometer.

Relative molecular mass, M_r

The **relative molecular mass** of a **compound** (M_r) is the relative mass of one molecule of the compound on a scale where the carbon-12 isotope has a mass of exactly 12 units. We find the relative molecular mass by adding up the relative atomic masses of all the atoms present in the molecule.

For example, for methane:

formula	CH_4
atoms present	$1 \times C; 4 \times H$
add A_r values	$(1 \times A_r[C]) + (4 \times A_r[H])$
M_r of methane	$= (1 \times 12.0) + (4 \times 1.0)$
	$= 16.0$

Relative formula mass

For compounds containing ions we use the term **relative formula mass**. This is calculated in the same way as for relative molecular mass. It is also given the same symbol, M_r. For example, for magnesium hydroxide:

formula	$Mg(OH)_2$
ions present	$1 \times Mg^{2+}; 2 \times (OH^-)$
add A_r values	$(1 \times A_r[Mg]) + (2 \times (A_r[O] + A_r[H]))$
M_r of magnesium hydroxide	$= (1 \times 24.3) + (2 \times (16.0 + 1.0))$
	$= 58.3$

Check-up

1 Use the Periodic Table on page **497** to calculate the relative formula masses of the following:
   a calcium chloride, $CaCl_2$
   b copper(II) sulfate, $CuSO_4$
   c ammonium sulfate, $(NH_4)_2SO_4$
   d magnesium nitrate-6-water, $Mg(NO_3)_2.6H_2O$

   Hint: for part **d** you need to calculate the mass of water separately and then add it to the M_r of $Mg(NO_3)_2$.

1.3 Accurate relative atomic masses

Mass spectrometry

A **mass spectrometer** (Figure **1.2**) can be used to measure the mass of each isotope present in an element. It also compares how much of each isotope is present – the relative abundance. A simplified diagram of a mass spectrometer is shown in Figure **1.3**. You will not be expected to know the details of how a mass spectrometer works, but it is useful to understand how the results are obtained.

The atoms of the element in the vaporised sample are converted into ions. The stream of ions is brought to a detector after being deflected (bent) by a strong magnetic field. As the magnetic field is increased, the ions of heavier and heavier isotopes are brought to the detector.

Figure 1.2 A mass spectrometer is a large and complex instrument.

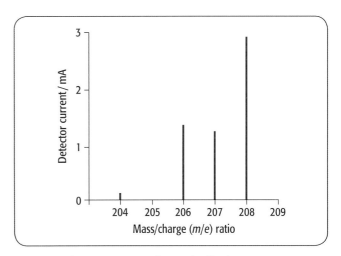

Figure 1.4 The mass spectrum of a sample of lead.

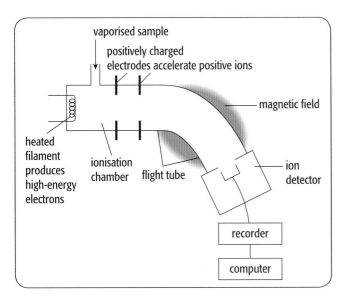

Figure 1.3 Simplified diagram of a mass spectrometer.

Isotopic mass	Relative abundance / %
204	2
206	24
207	22
208	52
total	100

Table 1.1 The data from Figure 1.4.

Fact file

Laser-microprobe mass spectrometry can be used to confirm that a pesticide has stuck to the surface of a crop plant after it has been sprayed.

The detector is connected to a computer which displays the mass spectrum.

The mass spectrum produced shows the relative abundance on the vertical axis and the mass to ion charge ratio (m/e) on the horizontal axis. Figure 1.4 shows a typical mass spectrum for a sample of lead. Table 1.1 shows how the data is interpreted.

For singly positively charged ions the m/e values give the nucleon number of the isotopes detected. In the case of lead, Table 1.1 shows that 52% of the lead is the isotope with an isotopic mass of 208. The rest is lead-204 (2%), lead-206 (24%) and lead-207 (22%).

Determination of A_r from mass spectra

We can use the data obtained from a mass spectrometer to calculate the relative atomic mass of an element very accurately. To calculate the relative atomic mass we follow this method:
- multiply each isotopic mass by its percentage abundance
- add the figures together
- divide by 100.

We can use this method to calculate the relative atomic mass of neon from its mass spectrum, shown in Figure 1.5.

The mass spectrum of neon has three peaks: ^{20}Ne (90.9%), ^{21}Ne (0.3%) and ^{22}Ne (8.8%).

A_r of neon
$$= \frac{(20.0 \times 90.9) + (21.0 \times 0.3) + (22.0 \times 8.8)}{100} = 20.2$$

Note that this answer is given to 3 significant figures, which is consistent with the data given.

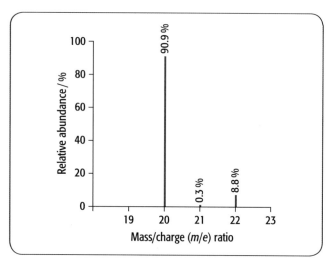

Figure 1.5 The mass spectrum of neon, Ne.

Check-up

2   Look at the mass spectrum of germanium, Ge.

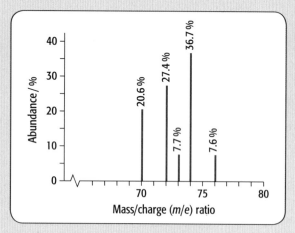

Figure 1.6 The mass spectrum of germanium.

   a   Write the isotopic formula for the heaviest isotope of germanium.

   b   Use the % abundance of each isotope to calculate the relative atomic mass of germanium.

Fact file

A high-resolution mass spectrometer can give very accurate relative isotopic masses. For example $^{16}O = 15.995$ and $^{32}S = 31.972$. Because of this, chemists can distinguish between molecules such as SO_2 and S_2 which appear to have the same relative molecular mass.

1.4 Amount of substance

The mole and the Avogadro constant

The formula of a compound shows us the number of atoms of each element present in one formula unit or one molecule of the compound. In water we know that two atoms of hydrogen ($A_r = 1.0$) combine with one atom of oxygen ($A_r = 16.0$). So the ratio of mass of hydrogen atoms to oxygen atoms in a water molecule is $2:16$. No matter how many molecules of water we have, this ratio will always be the same. But the mass of even 1000 atoms is far too small to be weighed. We have to scale up much more than this to get an amount of substance which is easy to weigh.

The relative atomic mass or relative molecular mass of a substance in grams is called a **mole** of the substance. So a mole of sodium ($A_r = 23.0$) weighs $23.0\,g$. The abbreviation for a mole is mol. We define the mole in terms of the standard carbon-12 isotope (see page **1**).

> One mole of a substance is the amount of that substance which has the same number of specific particles (atoms, molecules or ions) as there are atoms in exactly 12 g of the carbon-12 isotope.

We often refer to the mass of a mole of substance as its **molar mass** (abbreviation M). The units of molar mass are $g\,mol^{-1}$.

The number of atoms in a mole of atoms is very large, 6.02×10^{23} atoms. This number is called the **Avogadro constant** (or Avogadro number). The symbol for the Avogadro constant is L. The Avogadro constant applies to atoms, molecules, ions and electrons. So in 1 mole of sodium there are 6.02×10^{23} sodium atoms and in 1 mole of sodium chloride (NaCl) there are 6.02×10^{23} sodium ions and 6.02×10^{23} chloride ions.

It is important to make clear what type of particles we are referring to. If we just state 'moles of chlorine', it is not clear whether we are thinking about chlorine atoms or chlorine molecules. A mole of chlorine molecules, Cl_2, contains 6.02×10^{23} chlorine molecules but it contains twice as many chlorine atoms since there are two chlorine atoms in every chlorine molecule.

Figure 1.7 Amedeo Avogadro (1776–1856) was an Italian scientist who first deduced that equal volumes of gases contain equal numbers of molecules. Although the Avogadro constant is named after him, it was left to other scientists to calculate the number of particles in a mole.

Fact file

The Avogadro constant is given the symbol L. This is because its value was first calculated by Johann Joseph Loschmidt (1821–1895). Loschmidt was Professor of Physical Chemistry at the University of Vienna.

Moles and mass

The Système International (SI) base unit for mass is the kilogram. But this is a rather large mass to use for general laboratory work in chemistry. So chemists prefer to use the relative molecular mass or formula mass in grams (1000 g = 1 kg). You can find the number of moles of a substance by using the mass of substance and the relative atomic mass (A_r) or relative molecular mass (M_r).

$$\text{number of moles (mol)} = \frac{\text{mass of substance in grams (g)}}{\text{molar mass (g mol}^{-1})}$$

Worked example

1 How many moles of sodium chloride are present in 117.0 g of sodium chloride, NaCl?
(A_r values: Na = 23.0, Cl = 35.5)

continued ⋯⟶

$$\text{molar mass of NaCl} = 23.0 + 35.5$$
$$= 58.5 \, \text{g mol}^{-1}$$
$$\text{number of moles} = \frac{\text{mass}}{\text{molar mass}}$$
$$= \frac{117.0}{58.5}$$
$$= 2.0 \, \text{mol}$$

Figure 1.8 From left to right, one mole of each of copper, bromine, carbon, mercury and lead.

Check-up

3 **a** Use these A_r values (Fe = 55.8, N = 14.0, O = 16.0, S = 32.1) to calculate the amount of substance in moles in each of the following:
   i 10.7 g of sulfur atoms
   ii 64.2 g of sulfur molecules (S_8)
   iii 60.45 g of anhydrous iron(III) nitrate, $Fe(NO_3)_3$
  b Use the value of the Avogadro constant (6.02×10^{23} mol^{-1}) to calculate the total number of atoms in 7.10 g of chlorine atoms. (A_r value: Cl = 35.5)

To find the mass of a substance present in a given number of moles, you need to rearrange the equation

$$\text{number of moles (mol)} = \frac{\text{mass of substance in grams (g)}}{\text{molar mass (g mol}^{-1})}$$

$$\text{mass of substance (g)}$$
$$= \text{number of moles (mol)} \times \text{molar mass (g mol}^{-1})$$

Worked example

2 What mass of sodium hydroxide, NaOH, is present in 0.25 mol of sodium hydroxide? (A_r values: H = 1.0, Na = 23.0, O = 16.0)

molar mass of NaOH = 23.0 + 16.0 + 1.0
$$= 40.0\,\mathrm{g\,mol^{-1}}$$

mass = number of moles × molar mass
$$= 0.25 \times 40.0\,\mathrm{g}$$
$$= 10.0\,\mathrm{g\ NaOH}$$

Check-up

4 Use these A_r values: C = 12.0, Fe = 55.8, H = 1.0, O = 16.0, Na = 23.0
Calculate the mass of the following:
 a 0.20 moles of carbon dioxide, CO_2
 b 0.050 moles of sodium carbonate, Na_2CO_3
 c 5.00 moles of iron(II) hydroxide, $Fe(OH)_2$

1.5 Mole calculations

Reacting masses

When reacting chemicals together we may need to know what mass of each reactant to use so that they react exactly and there is no waste. To calculate this we need to know the chemical equation. This shows us the ratio of moles of the reactants and products – the **stoichiometry** of the equation. The balanced equation shows this stoichiometry. For example, in the reaction

$$Fe_2O_3 + 3CO \rightarrow 2Fe + 3CO_2$$

1 mole of iron(III) oxide reacts with 3 moles of carbon monoxide to form 2 moles of iron and 3 moles of carbon dioxide. The stoichiometry of the equation is 1:3:2:3. The large numbers that are included in the equation (3, 2 and 3) are called stoichiometric numbers.

Fact file

The word 'stoichiometry' comes from two Greek words meaning 'element' and 'measure'.

Figure 1.9 Iron reacting with sulfur to produce iron sulfide. We can calculate exactly how much iron is needed to react with sulfur and the mass of the products formed by knowing the molar mass of each reactant and the balanced chemical equation.

In order to find the mass of products formed in a chemical reaction we use:
• the mass of the reactants
• the molar mass of the reactants
• the balanced equation.

Worked example

3 Magnesium burns in oxygen to form magnesium oxide.

$$2Mg + O_2 \rightarrow 2MgO$$

We can calculate the mass of oxygen needed to react with 1 mole of magnesium. We can calculate the mass of magnesium oxide formed.

Step 1 Write the balanced equation.

Step 2 Multiply each formula mass in g by the relevant stoichiometric number in the equation.

$2Mg$	+	O_2	$\rightarrow$	$2MgO$
$2 \times 24.3\,\mathrm{g}$		$1 \times 32.0\,\mathrm{g}$		$2 \times (24.3\,\mathrm{g} + 16.0\,\mathrm{g})$
$48.6\,\mathrm{g}$		$32.0\,\mathrm{g}$		$80.6\,\mathrm{g}$

From this calculation we can deduce that
• 32.0 g of oxygen are needed to react exactly with 48.6 g of magnesium
• 80.6 g of magnesium oxide are formed

continued ⋯⋯⟶

If we burn 12.15 g of magnesium (0.5 mol) we get 20.15 g of magnesium oxide. This is because the stoichiometry of the reaction shows us that for every mole of magnesium burnt we get the same number of moles of magnesium oxide.

In this type of calculation we do not always need to know the molar mass of each of the reactants. If one or more of the reactants is in excess, we need only know the mass in grams and the molar mass of the reactant which is not in excess (the limiting reactant).

Worked example

4   Iron(III) oxide reacts with carbon monoxide to form iron and carbon dioxide.

$$Fe_2O_3 + 3CO \rightarrow 2Fe + 3CO_2$$

Calculate the maximum mass of iron produced when 798 g of iron(III) oxide is reduced by excess carbon monoxide.
(A_r values: Fe = 55.8, O = 16.0)

Step 1 $Fe_2O_3 + 3CO \rightarrow 2Fe + 3CO_2$

Step 2   1 mole iron(III) oxide $\rightarrow$ 2 moles iron
$(2 \times 55.8) + (3 \times 16.0)$ 2×55.8
159.6 g Fe_2O_3 $\rightarrow$ 111.6 g Fe

Step 3   798 g $\dfrac{111.6}{159.6} \times 798$

                                          = 558 g Fe

You can see that in step **3**, we have simply used ratios to calculate the amount of iron produced from 798 g of iron(III) oxide.

Check-up

5 **a** Sodium reacts with excess oxygen to form sodium peroxide, Na_2O_2.

$$2Na + O_2 \rightarrow Na_2O_2$$

continued ···>

Calculate the maximum mass of sodium peroxide formed when 4.60 g of sodium is burnt in excess oxygen.
(A_r values: Na = 23.0, O = 16.0)

b Tin(IV) oxide is reduced to tin by carbon. Carbon monoxide is also formed.

$$SnO_2 + 2C \rightarrow Sn + 2CO$$

Calculate the mass of carbon that exactly reacts with 14.0 g of tin(IV) oxide. Give your answer to 3 significant figures.
(A_r values: C = 12.0, O = 16.0, Sn = 118.7)

The stoichiometry of a reaction

We can find the stoichiometry of a reaction if we know the amounts of each reactant that exactly react together and the amounts of each product formed.

For example, if we react 4.0 g of hydrogen with 32.0 g of oxygen we get 36.0 g of water. (A_r values: H = 1.0, O = 16.0)

hydrogen (H_2) + oxygen (O_2) $\rightarrow$ water (H_2O)

$$\dfrac{4.0}{2 \times 1.0} \qquad \dfrac{32.0}{2 \times 16.0} \qquad \dfrac{36.0}{(2 \times 1.0) + 16.0}$$
$$= 2\ mol \qquad = 1\ mol \qquad = 2\ mol$$

This ratio is the ratio of stoichiometric numbers in the equation. So the equation is:

$$2H_2 + O_2 \rightarrow 2H_2O$$

We can still deduce the stoichiometry of this reaction even if we do not know the mass of oxygen which reacted. The ratio of hydrogen to water is 1:1. But there is only one atom of oxygen in a molecule of water – half the amount in an oxygen molecule. So the mole ratio of oxygen to water in the equation must be 1:2.

Check-up

6 56.2 g of silicon, Si, reacts exactly with 284.0 g of chlorine, Cl_2, to form 340.2 g of silicon(IV) chloride, $SiCl_4$. Use this information to calculate the stoichiometry of the reaction.
(A_r values: Cl = 35.5, Si = 28.1)

Significant figures

When we perform chemical calculations it is important that we give the answer to the number of significant figures that fits with the data provided. The examples show the number 526.84 rounded up to varying numbers of significant figures.

rounded to 4 significant figures = 526.8
rounded to 3 significant figures = 527
rounded to 2 significant figures = 530

When you are writing an answer to a calculation, the answer should be to the same number of significant figures as the least number of significant figures in the data.

Percentage composition by mass

We can use the formula of a compound and relative atomic masses to calculate the percentage by mass of a particular element in a compound.

% by mass

$$= \frac{\text{atomic mass} \times \text{number of moles of particular element in a compound}}{\text{molar mass of compound}} \times 100$$

Figure 1.10 This iron ore is impure Fe_2O_3. We can calculate the mass of iron that can be obtained from Fe_2O_3 by using molar masses.

Empirical formulae

The **empirical formula** of a compound is the simplest whole number ratio of the elements present in one molecule or formula unit of the compound. The **molecular formula** of a compound shows the total number of atoms of each element present in a molecule.

 Table 1.2 shows the empirical and molecular formulae for a number of compounds.

• The formula for an ionic compound is always its empirical formula.
• The empirical formula and molecular formula for simple inorganic molecules are often the same.
• Organic molecules often have different empirical and molecular formulae.

Fact file

An organic compound must be very pure in order to calculate its empirical formula. Chemists often use gas chromatography to purify compounds before carrying out formula analysis.

Compound	Empirical formula	Molecular formula
water	H_2O	H_2O
hydrogen peroxide	HO	H_2O_2
sulfur dioxide	SO_2	SO_2
butane	C_2H_5	C_4H_{10}
cyclohexane	CH_2	C_6H_{12}

Table 1.2 Some empirical and molecular formulae.

Check-up

8 Write the empirical formula for:
   a hydrazine, N_2H_4
   b octane C_8H_{18}
   c benzene, C_6H_6
   d ammonia, NH_3

The empirical formula can be found by determining the mass of each element present in a sample of the compound. For some compounds this can be done by combustion.

Worked examples

7 Deduce the formula of magnesium oxide. This can be found as follows:
   • burn a known mass of magnesium (0.486 g) in excess oxygen
   • record the mass of magnesium oxide formed (0.806 g)
   • calculate the mass of oxygen which has combined with the magnesium (0.806 − 0.486 g) = 0.320 g

continued ···▶

• calculate the mole ratio of magnesium to oxygen (A_r values: Mg = 24.3, O = 16.0)

$$\text{moles of Mg} = \frac{0.486\,g}{24.3\,g\,mol^{-1}} = 0.0200\,mol$$

$$\text{moles of oxygen} = \frac{0.320\,g}{16.0\,g\,mol^{-1}} = 0.0200\,mol$$

The simplest ratio of magnesium : oxygen is 1 : 1. So the empirical formula of magnesium oxide is MgO.

8 When 1.55 g of phosphorus is completely combusted 3.55 g of an oxide of phosphorus is produced. Deduce the empirical formula of this oxide of phosphorus. (A_r values: O = 16.0, P = 31.0)

		P	**O**
Step 1	note the mass of each element	1.55 g	3.55 − 1.55 = 2.00 g
Step 2	divide by atomic masses	$\frac{1.55\,g}{31.0\,g\,mol^{-1}}$ = 0.05 mol	$\frac{2.00\,g}{16.0\,g\,mol^{-1}}$ = 0.125 mol
Step 3	divide by the lowest figure	$\frac{0.05}{0.05} = 1$	$\frac{0.125}{0.05} = 2.5$
Step 4	if needed, obtain the lowest whole number ratio to get empirical formula		P_2O_5

An empirical formula can also be deduced from data that give the percentage composition by mass of the elements in a compound.

Worked example

9 A compound of carbon and hydrogen contains 85.7% carbon and 14.3% hydrogen by mass. Deduce the empirical formula of this hydrocarbon. (A_r values: C = 12.0, O = 16.0)

continued ···▶

		C	H
Step 1	note the % by mass	85.7	14.3
Step 2	divide by A_r values	$\frac{85.7}{12.0} = 7.142$	$\frac{14.3}{1.0} = 14.3$
Step 3	divide by the lowest figure	$\frac{7.142}{7.142} = 1$	$\frac{14.3}{7.142} = 2$

Empirical formula is CH_2

Check-up

9 The composition by mass of a hydrocarbon is 10% hydrogen and 90% carbon. Deduce the empirical formula of this hydrocarbon. (A_r values: C = 12.0, H = 1.0)

Molecular formulae

The molecular formula shows the actual number of each of the different atoms present in a molecule. The molecular formula is more useful than the empirical formula. We use the molecular formula to write balanced equations and to calculate molar masses. The molecular formula is always a multiple of the empirical formula. For example, the molecular formula of ethane, C_2H_6, is two times the empirical formula, CH_3.

In order to deduce the molecular formula we need to know:
• the relative formula mass of the compound
• the empirical formula.

Worked example

10 A compound has the empirical formula CH_2Br. Its relative molecular mass is 187.8. Deduce the molecular formula of this compound. (A_r values: Br = 79.9, C = 12.0, H = 1.0)

Step 1 find the empirical formula mass:
$12.0 + (2 \times 1.0) + 79.9 = 93.9$

Step 2 divide the relative molecular mass by the empirical formula mass: $\frac{187.8}{93.9} = 2$

Step 3 multiply the number of atoms in the empirical formula by the number in step 2: $2 \times CH_2Br$, so molecular formula is $C_2H_4Br_2$

Check-up

10 The empirical formulae and molar masses of three compounds, A, B and C, are shown in the table below. Calculate the molecular formula of each of these compounds. (A_r values: C = 12.0, Cl = 35.5, H = 1.0)

Compound	Empirical formula	M_r
A	C_3H_5	82
B	CCl_3	237
C	CH_2	112

1.6 Chemical formulae and chemical equations

Deducing the formula

The electronic structure of the individual elements in a compound determines the formula of a compound (see page 51). The formula of an ionic compound is determined by the charges on each of the ions present. The number of positive charges is balanced by the number of negative charges so that the total charge on the compound is zero. We can work out the formula for a compound if we know the charges on the ions. Figure 1.11 shows the charges on some simple ions related to the position of the elements in the Periodic Table.

For a simple metal ion, the value of the positive charge is the same as the group number. For a simple non-metal ion the value of the negative charge is 8 minus the group number. The charge on the ions of transition elements can vary. For example, iron forms two types of ions, Fe^{2+} and Fe^{3+} (Figure 1.12).

Group I	II		H⁺			III	IV	V	VI	VII	0
											none
Li^+	Be^{2+}								O^{2-}	F⁻	none
Na^+	Mg^{2+}					Al^{3+}			S^{2-}	Cl⁻	none
K^+	Ca^{2+}	transition elements				Ga^{3+}				Br⁻	none
Rb^+	Sr^{2+}									I⁻	none

Figure 1.11 The charges on some simple ions is related to their position in the Periodic Table.

Ions which contain more than one type of atom are called compound ions. Some common compound ions that you should learn are listed in Table **1.3**. The formula for an ionic compound is obtained by balancing the charges of the ions.

Ion	Formula
ammonium	NH_4^+
carbonate	CO_3^{2-}
hydrogencarbonate	HCO_3^-
hydroxide	OH^-
nitrate	NO_3^-
phosphate	PO_4^{3-}
sulfate	SO_4^{2-}

Table 1.3 The formulae of some common compound ions.

Figure 1.12 Iron(II) chloride (left) and iron(III) chloride (right). These two chlorides of iron both contain iron and chlorine but they have different formulae.

Worked examples

11 Deduce the formula of magnesium chloride.
Ions present: Mg^{2+} and Cl^-.
For electrical neutrality, we need two Cl^- ions for every Mg^{2+} ion. $(2 \times 1-) + (1 \times 2+) = 0$
So the formula is $MgCl_2$.

12 Deduce the formula of aluminium oxide.
Ions present: Al^{3+} and O^{2-}.
For electrical neutrality, we need three O^{2-} ions for every two Al^{3+} ions. $(3 \times 2-) + (2 \times 3+) = 0$
So the formula is Al_2O_3.

The formula of a covalent compound is deduced from the number of electrons needed to complete the outer shell of each atom (see page **52**). In general, carbon atoms form four bonds with other atoms, hydrogen and halogen atoms form one bond and oxygen atoms form two bonds. So the formula of water, H_2O, follows these rules. The formula for methane is CH_4, with each carbon atom bonding with four hydrogen atoms. However, there are many exceptions to these rules.

Compounds containing a simple metal ion and non-metal ion are named by changing the end of the name of the non-metal element to -ide.

sodium + chlorine → sodium chloride
zinc + sulfur → zinc sulfide

Compound ions containing oxygen are usually called -ates. For example, the sulfate ion contains sulfur and oxygen, the phosphate ion contains phosphorus and oxygen.

11 a Write down the formulae of each of the
following compounds:
   i magnesium nitrate
   ii calcium sulfate
   iii sodium iodide
   iv hydrogen bromide
   v sodium sulfide
  b Name each of the following compounds:
   i Na_3PO_4
   ii $(NH_4)_2SO_4$
   iii $AlCl_3$
   iv $Ca(NO_3)_2$

Balancing chemical equations

When chemicals react, atoms cannot be either created
or destroyed. So there must be the same number of each
type of atom on the reactants side of a chemical equation
as there are on the products side. A symbol equation is a
shorthand way of describing a chemical reaction. It shows
the number and type of the atoms in the reactants and
the number and type of atoms in the products. If these
are the same, we say the equation is balanced. Follow
these examples to see how we balance an equation.

Worked examples

13 Balancing an equation

   Step 1 Write down the formulae of all the
   reactants and products. For example:

   $$H_2 \quad + \quad O_2 \quad \rightarrow \quad H_2O$$

   Step 2 Count the number of atoms of each
   reactant and product.

   $$H_2 \quad + \quad O_2 \quad \rightarrow \quad H_2O$$
   $$2\,[H] \qquad 2\,[O] \qquad 2\,[H] + 1\,[O]$$

   Step 3 Balance one of the atoms by placing
   a number in front of one of the reactants or

continued ⋯▸

products. In this case the oxygen atoms on the
right-hand side need to be balanced, so that they
are equal in number to those on the left-hand side.
Remember that the number in front multiplies
everything in the formula. For example, $2H_2O$ has
4 hydrogen atoms and 2 oxygen atoms.

$$H_2 \quad + \quad O_2 \quad \rightarrow \quad 2H_2O$$
$$2\,[H] \qquad 2\,[O] \qquad 4\,[H] + 2\,[O]$$

Step 4 Keep balancing in this way, one type of
atom at a time until all the atoms are balanced.

$$2H_2 \quad + \quad O_2 \quad \rightarrow \quad 2H_2O$$
$$4\,[H] \qquad 2\,[O] \qquad 4\,[H] + 2\,[O]$$

Note that when you balance an equation you
must not change the formulae of any of the
reactants or products.

14 Write a balanced equation for the reaction of
iron(III) oxide with carbon monoxide to form
iron and carbon dioxide.

Step 1	formulae	$Fe_2O_3 + CO$		$\rightarrow Fe$	$+ CO_2$
Step 2	count the number of atoms	$Fe_2O_3 + CO$		$\rightarrow Fe$	$+ CO_2$
		$2[Fe] + 3[O]$	$1[C] + 1[O]$	$1[Fe]$	$1[C] + 2[O]$
Step 3	balance the iron	$Fe_2O_3 + CO$		$\rightarrow 2Fe$	$+ CO_2$
		$2[Fe] + 3[O]$	$1[C] + 1[O]$	$2[Fe]$	$1[C] + 2[O]$
Step 4	balance the oxygen	$Fe_2O_3 + 3CO$		$\rightarrow 2Fe$	$+ 3CO_2$
		$2[Fe] + 3[O]$	$3[C] + 3[O]$	$2[Fe]$	$3[C] + 6[O]$

In step 4 the oxygen in the CO_2 comes from two
places, the Fe_2O_3 and the CO. In order to balance
the equation, the same number of oxygen atoms
(3) must come from the iron oxide as come from
the carbon monoxide.

Check-up

12 Write balanced equations for the following reactions.
   a Iron reacts with hydrochloric acid to form iron(II) chloride, $FeCl_2$, and hydrogen.
   b Aluminium hydroxide, $Al(OH)_3$, decomposes on heating to form aluminium oxide, Al_2O_3, and water.
   c Hexane, C_6H_{14}, burns in oxygen to form carbon dioxide and water.

Using state symbols

We sometimes find it useful to specify the physical states of the reactants and products in a chemical reaction. This is especially important where chemical equilibrium and rates of reaction are being discussed (see pages **128** and **154**). We use the following **state symbols**:

• (s) solid
• (l) liquid
• (g) gas
• (aq) aqueous (a solution in water).

State symbols are written after the formula of each reactant and product. For example:

$$ZnCO_3(s) + H_2SO_4(aq) \rightarrow ZnSO_4(aq) + H_2O(l) + CO_2(g)$$

Check-up

13 Write balanced equations, including state symbols, for the following reactions.
   a Solid calcium carbonate reacts with aqueous hydrochloric acid to form water, carbon dioxide and an aqueous solution of calcium chloride.
   b An aqueous solution of zinc sulfate, $ZnSO_4$, reacts with an aqueous solution of sodium hydroxide. The products are a precipitate of zinc hydroxide, $Zn(OH)_2$, and an aqueous solution of sodium sulfate.

Figure 1.13 The equation for the reaction between calcium carbonate and hydrochloric acid with all the state symbols: $CaCO_3(s) + 2HCl(aq) \rightarrow CaCl_2(aq) + CO_2(g) + H_2O(l)$

Balancing ionic equations

When ionic compounds dissolve in water, the ions separate from each other. For example:

$$NaCl(s) + aq \rightarrow Na^+(aq) + Cl^-(aq)$$

Ionic compounds include salts such as sodium bromide, magnesium sulfate and ammonium nitrate. Acids and alkalis also contain ions. For example $H^+(aq)$ and $Cl^-(aq)$ ions are present in hydrochloric acid and $Na^+(aq)$ and $OH^-(aq)$ ions are present in sodium hydroxide.

Many chemical reactions in aqueous solution involve ionic compounds. Only some of the ions in solution take part in these reactions.

The ions that play no part in the reaction are called **spectator ions**.

An ionic equation is simpler than a full chemical equation. It shows only the ions or other particles that are reacting. Spectator ions are omitted. Compare the full equation for the reaction of zinc with aqueous copper(II) sulfate with the ionic equation.

full chemical equation: $Zn(s) + CuSO_4(aq)$
$\rightarrow ZnSO_4(aq) + Cu(s)$

with charges $Zn(s) + Cu^{2+}SO_4^{2-}(aq)$
$\rightarrow Zn^{2+}SO_4^{2-}(aq) + Cu(s)$

cancelling spectator ions $Zn(s) + Cu^{2+}\cancel{SO_4^{2-}(aq)}$
$\rightarrow Zn^{2+}\cancel{SO_4^{2-}(aq)} + Cu(s)$

ionic equation $Zn(s) + Cu^{2+}(aq)$
$\rightarrow Zn^{2+}(aq) + Cu(s)$

In the ionic equation you will notice that:
• there are no sulfate ions – these are the spectator ions as they have not changed
• both the charges and the atoms are balanced.

The next examples show how we can change a full equation into an ionic equation.

Worked examples

15 Writing an ionic equation

Step 1   Write down the full balanced equation.

$$Mg(s) + 2HCl(aq) \rightarrow MgCl_2(aq) + H_2(g)$$

Step 2   Write down all the ions present. Any reactant or product that has a state symbol (s), (l) or (g) or is a molecule in solution such as chlorine, $Cl_2(aq)$, does not split into ions.

$$Mg(s) + 2H^+(aq) + 2Cl^-(aq)$$
$$\rightarrow Mg^{2+}(aq) + 2Cl^-(aq) + H_2(g)$$

Step 3   Cancel the ions that appear on both sides of the equation (the spectator ions).

$$Mg(s) + 2H^+(aq) + \cancel{2Cl^-(aq)}$$
$$\rightarrow Mg^{2+}(aq) + \cancel{2Cl^-(aq)} + H_2(g)$$

Step 4   Write down the equation omitting the spectator ions.

$$Mg(s) + 2H^+(aq) \rightarrow Mg^{2+}(aq) + H_2(g)$$

16 Write the ionic equation for the reaction of aqueous chlorine with aqueous potassium bromide. The products are aqueous bromine and aqueous potassium chloride.

Step 1   The full balanced equation is:

$$Cl_2(aq) + 2KBr(aq) \rightarrow Br_2(aq) + 2KCl(aq)$$

Step 2   The ions present are:

$$Cl_2(aq) + 2K^+(aq) + 2Br^-(aq)$$
$$\rightarrow Br_2(aq) + 2K^+(aq) + 2Cl^-(aq)$$

Step 3   Cancel the spectator ions:

$$Cl_2(aq) + \cancel{2K^+(aq)} + 2Br^-(aq)$$
$$\rightarrow Br_2(aq) + \cancel{2K^+(aq)} + 2Cl^-(aq)$$

Step 4   Write the final ionic equation:

$$Cl_2(aq) + 2Br^-(aq) \rightarrow Br_2(aq) + 2Cl^-(aq)$$

Check-up

14 Change these full equations to ionic equations.
  a $H_2SO_4(aq) + 2NaOH(aq)$
$$\rightarrow 2H_2O(l) + Na_2SO_4(aq)$$
  b $Br_2(aq) + 2KI(aq) \rightarrow 2KBr(aq) + I_2(aq)$

Chemists usually prefer to write ionic equations for precipitation reactions. A precipitation reaction is a reaction where two aqueous solutions react to form a solid – the precipitate. For these reactions the method of writing the ionic equation can be simplified. All you have to do is:
• write the formula of the precipitate as the product
• write the ions that go to make up the precipitate as the reactants.

Worked example

17 An aqueous solution of iron(II) sulfate reacts with an aqueous solution of sodium hydroxide. A precipitate of iron(II) hydroxide is formed, together with an aqueous solution of sodium sulfate.
• Write the full balanced equation:

$$FeSO_4(aq) + 2NaOH(aq)$$
$$\rightarrow Fe(OH)_2(s) + Na_2SO_4(aq)$$

• The ionic equation is:

$$Fe^{2+}(aq) + 2OH^-(aq) \rightarrow Fe(OH)_2(s)$$

Check-up

15 Write ionic equations for these precipitation reactions.
  a $CuSO_4(aq) + 2NaOH(aq)$
$$\rightarrow Cu(OH)_2(s) + Na_2SO_4(aq)$$
  b $Pb(NO_3)_2(aq) + 2KI(aq)$
$$\rightarrow PbI_2(s) + 2KNO_3(aq)$$

1.7 Solutions and concentration

Calculating the concentration of a solution

The concentration of a solution is the amount of solute dissolved in a solvent to make $1\,dm^3$ (one cubic decimetre) of solution. The solvent is usually water. There are $1000\,cm^3$ in a cubic decimetre. When 1 mole of a compound is dissolved to make $1\,dm^3$ of solution the concentration is $1\,mol\,dm^{-3}$.

$$\text{concentration (mol dm}^{-3}) = \frac{\text{number of moles of solute (mol)}}{\text{volume of solution (dm}^3)}$$

We use the terms 'concentrated' and 'dilute' to refer to the relative amount of solute in the solution. A solution with a low concentration of solute is a dilute solution. If there is a high concentration of solute, the solution is concentrated.

When performing calculations involving concentrations in $mol\,dm^{-3}$ you need to:
- change mass in grams to moles
- change cm^3 to dm^3 (by dividing the number of cm^3 by 1000).

Figure 1.14 The concentration of chlorine in the water in a swimming pool must be carefully controlled.

We often need to calculate the mass of a substance present in a solution of known concentration and volume. To do this we:
- rearrange the concentration equation to:

  number of moles = concentration × volume

- multiply the moles of solute by its molar mass

  mass of solute (g)
  = number of moles (mol) × molar mass $(g\,mol^{-1})$

Worked example

18 Calculate the concentration in $mol\,dm^{-3}$ of sodium hydroxide, NaOH, if $250\,cm^3$ of a solution contains $2.0\,g$ of sodium hydroxide. (M_r value: NaOH = 40.0)

Step 1 change grams to moles:

$$\frac{2.0}{40.0} = 0.050\,mol\ NaOH$$

Step 2 change cm^3 to dm^3:

$$250\,cm^3 = \frac{250}{1000}\,dm^3 = 0.25\,dm^3$$

Step 3 calculate concentration:

$$\frac{0.050\,(mol)}{0.25\,(dm^3)} = 0.20\,mol\,dm^{-3}$$

Worked example

19 Calculate the mass of anhydrous copper(II) sulfate in $55\,cm^3$ of a $0.20\,mol\,dm^{-3}$ solution of copper(II) sulfate.
(A_r values: Cu = 63.5, O = 16.0, S = 32.1)

Step 1 change cm^3 to dm^3:

$$\frac{55}{1000} = 0.055\,dm^3$$

Step 2 moles = concentration $(mol\,dm^{-3})$ × volume of solution (dm^3)

$$0.20 \times 0.055 = 0.011\,mol$$

Step 3 mass (g) = moles × M
$$= 0.011 \times (63.5 + 32.1 + (4 \times 16.0))$$
$$= 1.8\,g\ \text{(to 2 significant figures)}$$

16 a Calculate the concentration, in mol dm^{-3}, of the following solutions:
(A_r values: C = 12.0, H = 1.0, Na = 23.0, O = 16.0)

    i a solution of sodium hydroxide, NaOH, containing 2.0 g of sodium hydroxide in 50 cm^3 of solution

    ii a solution of ethanoic acid, CH_3CO_2H, containing 12.0 g of ethanoic acid in 250 cm^3 of solution.

b Calculate the number of moles of solute dissolved in each of the following:

    i 40 cm^3 of aqueous nitric acid of concentration 0.2 mol dm^{-3}

    ii 50 cm^3 of calcium hydroxide solution of concentration 0.01 mol dm^{-3}

Carrying out a titration

A procedure called a titration is used to determine the amount of substance present in a solution of unknown concentration. There are several different kinds of titration. One of the commonest involves the exact neutralisation of an alkali by an acid (Figure 1.15).

Figure 1.15 a A funnel is used to fill the burette with hydrochloric acid. **b** A graduated pipette is used to measure 25.0 cm^3 of sodium hydroxide solution into a conical flask. **c** An indicator called litmus is added to the sodium hydroxide solution, which turns blue. **d** 12.5 cm^3 of hydrochloric acid from the burette have been added to the 25.0 cm^3 of alkali in the conical flask. The litmus has gone red, showing that this volume of acid was just enough to neutralise the alkali.

If we want to determine the concentration of a solution of sodium hydroxide we use the following procedure.
- Get some of acid of known concentration.
- Fill a clean burette with the acid (after having washed the burette with a little of the acid).
- Record the initial burette reading.
- Measure a known volume of the alkali into a titration flask using a graduated (volumetric) pipette.
- Add an indicator solution to the alkali in the flask.
- Slowly add the acid from the burette to the flask, swirling the flask all the time until the indicator changes colour (the end-point).
- Record the final burette reading. The final reading minus the initial reading is called the **titre**. This first titre is normally known as a 'rough' value.
- Repeat this process, adding the acid drop by drop near the end-point.
- Repeat again, until you have two titres that are no more than $0.10\,cm^3$ apart.
- Take the average of these two titre values.

Your results should be recorded in a table, looking like this:

	Rough	**1**	**2**	**3**
final burette reading / cm^3	37.60	38.65	36.40	34.75
initial burette reading / cm^3	2.40	4.00	1.40	0.00
titre / cm^3	35.20	34.65	35.00	34.75

You should note:
- all burette readings are given to an accuracy of $0.05\,cm^3$
- the units are shown like this '/ cm^3'
- the two titres that are no more than $0.10\,cm^3$ apart are 1 and 3, so they would be averaged
- the average titre is $34.70\,cm^3$.

Fact file

The first 'burette' was developed by a Frenchman called Frances Descroizilles in the 18th century. Another Frenchman, Joseph Gay-Lussac, was the first to use the terms 'pipette' and 'burette', in an article published in 1824.

In every titration there are five important pieces of knowledge:
1 the balanced equation for the reaction
2 the volume of the solution in the burette (in the example above this is hydrochloric acid)
3 the concentration of the solution in the burette
4 the volume of the solution in the titration flask (in the example above this is sodium hydroxide)
5 the concentration of the solution in the titration flask.

If we know four of these five things, we can calculate the fifth. So in order to calculate the concentration of sodium hydroxide in the flask we need to know the first four of these points.

Calculating solution concentration by titration

A titration is often used to find the exact concentration of a solution. Worked example 20 shows the steps used to calculate the concentration of a solution of sodium hydroxide when it is neutralised by aqueous sulfuric acid of known concentration and volume.

Worked example

20 $25.0\,cm^3$ of a solution of sodium hydroxide is exactly neutralised by $15.10\,cm^3$ of sulfuric acid of concentration $0.200\,mol\,dm^{-3}$.

$$2NaOH + H_2SO_4 \rightarrow Na_2SO_4 + 2H_2O$$

Calculate the concentration, in $mol\,dm^{-3}$, of the sodium hydroxide solution.

Step 1   calculate the moles of acid

moles = concentration ($mol\,dm^{-3}$)
$\qquad\qquad\qquad$ × volume of solution (dm^3)

$$0.200 \times \frac{15.10}{1000} = 0.003\,02\,mol\ H_2SO_4$$

Step 2   use the stoichiometry of the balanced equation to calculate the moles of NaOH

moles of NaOH = moles of acid (from step 1) × 2

$0.003\,02 \times 2 = 0.006\,04\,mol\ NaOH$

continued ⋯⇢

Step 3 calculate the concentration of NaOH

concentration (mol dm^{-3})

$$= \frac{\text{number of moles of solute (mol)}}{\text{volume of solution (dm}^3)}$$

$$= \frac{0.006\,04}{0.0250}$$

$$= 0.242\,\text{mol dm}^{-3}$$

Note 1 In the first step we use the reagent for which the concentration and volume are **both** known.

Note 2 In step **2**, we multiply by 2 because the balanced equation shows that 2 mol of NaOH react with every 1 mol of H_2SO_4.

Note 3 In step **3**, we divide by 0.0250 because we have changed cm^3 to dm^3 $(0.0250 = \frac{25.0}{1000})$.

Note 4 The answer is given to 3 significant figures because the smallest number of significant figures in the data is 3.

17 a The equation for the reaction of strontium hydroxide with hydrochloric acid is shown below.

$$Sr(OH)_2 + 2HCl \rightarrow SrCl_2 + 2H_2O$$

25.0 cm^3 of a solution of strontium hydroxide was exactly neutralised by 15.00 cm^3 of 0.100 mol dm^{-3} hydrochloric acid. Calculate the concentration, in mol dm^{-3}, of the strontium hydroxide solution.

b 20.0 cm^3 of a 0.400 mol dm^{-3} solution of sodium hydroxide was exactly neutralised by 25.25 cm^3 of sulfuric acid. Calculate the concentration, in mol dm^{-3}, of the sulfuric acid. The equation for the reaction is:

$$H_2SO_4 + 2NaOH \rightarrow Na_2SO_4 + 2H_2O$$

Deducing stoichiometry by titration

We can use titration results to find the stoichiometry of a reaction. In order to do this, we need to know the concentrations and the volumes of **both** the reactants. The example below shows how to determine the stoichiometry of the reaction between a metal hydroxide and an acid.

Worked example

21 25.0 cm^3 of a 0.0500 mol dm^{-3} solution of a metal hydroxide was titrated against a solution of 0.200 mol dm^{-3} hydrochloric acid. It required 12.50 cm^3 of hydrochloric acid to exactly neutralise the metal hydroxide. Deduce the stoichiometry of this reaction.

Step 1 Calculate the number of moles of each reagent.

moles of metal hydroxide
= concentration (mol dm^{-3}) × volume of solution (dm^3)

$$0.0500 \times \frac{25.0}{1000} = 1.25 \times 10^{-3}\,\text{mol}$$

moles of hydrochloric acid
= concentration (mol dm^{-3}) × volume of solution (dm^3)

$$0.200 \times \frac{12.50}{1000} = 2.50 \times 10^{-3}\,\text{mol}$$

Step 2 Deduce the simplest mole ratio of metal hydroxide to hydrochloric acid.

1.25×10^{-3} moles of hydroxide : 2.50×10^{-3} moles of acid

= 1 hydroxide : 2 acid

Step 3 Write the equation.

$$M(OH)_2 + 2HCl \rightarrow MCl_2 + 2H_2O$$

One mole of hydroxide ions neutralises one mole of hydrogen ions. Since one mole of the metal hydroxide neutralises two moles of hydrochloric acid, the metal hydroxide must contain two hydroxide ions in each formula unit.

18 20.0 cm³ of a metal hydroxide of concentration 0.0600 mol dm⁻³ was titrated with 0.100 mol dm⁻³ hydrochloric acid. It required 24.00 cm³ of the hydrochloric acid to exactly neutralise the metal hydroxide.

   a Calculate the number of moles of metal hydroxide used.

   b Calculate the number of moles of hydrochloric acid used.

   c What is the simplest mole ratio of metal hydroxide to hydrochloric acid?

   d Write a balanced equation for this reaction using your answers to parts **a**, **b** and **c** to help you. Use the symbol **M** for the metal.

1.8 Calculations involving gas volumes

Using the molar gas volume

In 1811 the Italian Scientist Amedeo Avogadro suggested that equal volumes of all gases contain the same number of molecules. This is called Avogadro's hypothesis. This idea is approximately true as long as the pressure is not too high or the temperature too low. It is convenient to measure volumes of gases at room temperature (20 °C) and pressure (1 atmosphere). At room temperature and pressure (r.t.p.) one mole of any gas has a volume of 24.0 dm³. So, 24.0 dm³ of carbon dioxide and 24.0 dm³ of hydrogen both contain one mole of gas molecules.

We can use the molar gas volume of 24.0 dm³ at r.t.p. to find:

• the volume of a given mass or number of moles of gas

• the mass or number of moles of a given volume of gas.

Worked examples

22 Calculate the volume of 0.40 mol of nitrogen at r.t.p.

$$\text{volume (in dm}^3) = 24.0 \times \text{number of moles of gas}$$

$$\text{volume} = 24.0 \times 0.40$$
$$= 9.6\,\text{dm}^3$$

continued ⋯→

23 Calculate the mass of methane, CH₄, present in 120 cm³ of methane.
(M_r value: methane = 16.0)

$$120\,\text{cm}^3 \text{ is } 0.120\,\text{dm}^3 \; (\frac{120}{1000} = 0.120)$$

$$\text{moles of methane} = \frac{\text{volume of methane (dm}^3)}{24.0}$$

$$= \frac{0.120}{24.0}$$

$$= 5 \times 10^{-3}\,\text{mol}$$

$$\text{mass of methane} = 5 \times 10^{-3} \times 16.0$$
$$= 0.080\,\text{g methane}$$

19 a Calculate the volume, in dm³, occupied by 26.4 g of carbon dioxide at r.t.p. (A_r values: C = 12.0, O = 16.0)

   b A flask of volume 120 cm³ is filled with helium gas at r.t.p. Calculate the mass of helium present in the flask. (A_r value: He = 4.0)

Figure 1.16 Anaesthetists have to know about gas volumes so that patients remain unconscious during major operations.

Fact file

A large room (4 m × 4 m × 4 m) contains about 2600 moles of gas, which is about 60 kg of nitrogen and 17 kg of oxygen!

Gas volumes and stoichiometry

We can use the ratio of reacting volumes of gases to deduce the stoichiometry of a reaction. If we mix $20\,cm^3$ of hydrogen with $10\,cm^3$ of oxygen and explode the mixture, we will find that the gases have exactly reacted together and no hydrogen or oxygen remains. According to Avogadro's hypothesis, equal volumes of gases contain equal numbers of molecules and therefore equal numbers of moles of gases. So the mole ratio of hydrogen to oxygen is 2:1. We can summarise this as:

	hydrogen	+	oxygen	$\rightarrow$	water
	(H_2)		(O_2)		(H_2O)
	$20\,cm^3$		$10\,cm^3$		
ratio of moles	2	:	1		
equation	$2H_2$	+	O_2	$\rightarrow$	$2H_2O$

We can extend this idea to experiments where we burn hydrocarbons. The example below shows how the formula of propane and the stoichiometry of the equation can be deduced. Propane is a hydrocarbon – a compound of carbon and hydrogen only.

Worked example

24 When $50\,cm^3$ of propane reacts exactly with $250\,cm^3$ of oxygen, $150\,cm^3$ of carbon dioxide is formed.

	propane	+	oxygen	$\rightarrow$	carbon dioxide	+	water
			(O_2)		(CO_2)		(H_2O)
	$50\,cm^3$		$250\,cm^3$		$150\,cm^3$		
ratio of moles	1		5		3		

Since 1 mole of propane produces 3 moles of carbon dioxide, there must be 3 moles of carbon atoms in one mole of propane.

$$C_3H_x + 5O_2 \rightarrow 3CO_2 + yH_2O$$

continued ⋯⟶

The 5 moles of oxygen molecules are used to react with both the carbon and the hydrogen in the propane. 3 moles of these oxygen molecules have been used in forming carbon dioxide. So $5 - 3 = 2$ moles of oxygen molecules must be used in reacting with the hydrogen to form water. There are 4 moles of atoms in 2 moles of oxygen molecules. So there must be 4 moles of water formed.

$$C_3H_x + 5O_2 \rightarrow 3CO_2 + 4H_2O$$

So there must be 8 hydrogen atoms in 1 molecule of propane.

$$C_3H_8 + 5O_2 \rightarrow 3CO_2 + 4H_2O$$

Check-up

20 $50\,cm^3$ of a gaseous hydride of phosphorus, PH_n reacts with exactly $150\,cm^3$ of chlorine, Cl_2, to form liquid phosphorus trichloride and $150\,cm^3$ of hydrogen chloride gas, HCl.
   a How many moles of chlorine react with 1 mole of the gaseous hydride?
   b Deduce the formula of the phosphorus hydride.
   c Write a balanced equation for the reaction.

Summary

- [ ] Relative atomic mass is the weighted average mass of naturally occurring atoms of an element on a scale where an atom of carbon-12 has a mass of exactly 12 units. Relative molecular mass, relative isotopic mass and relative formula mass are also based on the ^{12}C scale.
- [ ] The type and relative amount of each isotope in an element can be found by mass spectrometry.
- [ ] The relative atomic mass of an element can be calculated from its mass spectrum.
- [ ] One mole of a substance is the amount of substance that has the same number of particles as there are in exactly 12 g of carbon-12.
- [ ] The Avogadro constant is the number of a stated type of particle (atom, ion or molecule) in a mole of those particles.
- [ ] Empirical formulae show the simplest whole number ratio of atoms in a compound.
- [ ] Empirical formulae may be calculated using the mass of the elements present and their relative atomic masses or from combustion data.
- [ ] Molecular formulae show the total number of atoms of each element present in one molecule or one formula unit of the compound.
- [ ] The molecular formula may be calculated from the empirical formula if the relative molecular mass is known.
- [ ] The mole concept can be used to calculate:
    - reacting masses
    - volumes of gases
    - volumes and concentrations of solutions.
- [ ] The stoichiometry of a reaction can be obtained from calculations involving reacting masses, gas volumes, and volumes and concentrations of solutions.

End-of-chapter questions

1 a i What do you understand by the term **relative atomic mass**? [1]

   ii A sample of boron was found to have the following % composition by mass:

   $^{10}_{5}B$ (18.7%), $^{11}_{5}B$ (81.3%)

   Calculate a value for the relative atomic mass of boron. Give your answer to 3 significant figures. [2]

   b Boron ions, B^{3+}, can be formed by bombarding gaseous boron with high-energy electrons in a mass spectrometer. Deduce the number of electrons in one B^{3+} ion. [1]

   c Boron is present in compounds called borates.

   i Use the A_r values below to calculate the relative molecular mass of iron(III) borate, $Fe(BO_2)_3$.
   (A_r values: Fe = 55.8, B = 10.8, O = 16.0) [1]

   ii The accurate relative atomic mass of iron, Fe, is 55.8. Explain why the accurate relative atomic mass is not a whole number. [1]

   Total = 6

2 This question is about two transition metals, hafnium (Hf) and zirconium (Zr).

   a Hafnium forms a peroxide whose formula can be written as $HfO_3.2H_2O$. Use the A_r values below to calculate the relative molecular mass of hafnium peroxide.
   (A_r values: Hf = 178.5, H = 1.0, O = 16.0) [1]

   b A particular isotope of hafnium has 72 protons and a nucleon number of 180. Write the isotopic symbol for this isotope, showing this information. [1]

c The mass spectrum of zirconium is shown below.

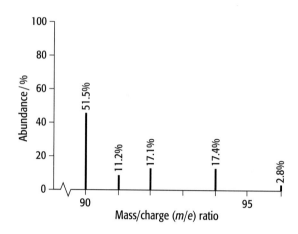

i Use the information from this mass spectrum to calculate the relative atomic mass of zirconium. Give your answer to 3 significant figures. [2]

ii High-resolution mass spectra show accurate relative isotopic masses. What do you understand by the term **relative isotopic mass**? [1]

Total = 5

3 Solid sodium carbonate reacts with aqueous hydrochloric acid to form aqueous sodium chloride, carbon dioxide and water.

$$Na_2CO_3 + 2HCl \rightarrow 2NaCl + CO_2 + H_2O$$

a Rewrite this equation to include state symbols. [1]

b Calculate the number of moles of hydrochloric acid required to react exactly with 4.15 g of sodium carbonate.
(A_r values: C = 12.0, Na = 23.0, O = 16.0) [3]

c Define the term **mole**. [1]

d An aqueous solution of $25.0\,cm^3$ sodium carbonate of concentration $0.0200\,mol\,dm^{-3}$ is titrated with hydrochloric acid. The volume of hydrochloric acid required to exactly react with the sodium carbonate is $12.50\,cm^3$.

i Calculate the number of moles of sodium carbonate present in the solution of sodium carbonate. [1]

ii Calculate the concentration of the hydrochloric acid. [2]

e How many moles of carbon dioxide are produced when 0.2 mol of sodium carbonate reacts with excess hydrochloric acid? [1]

f Calculate the volume of this number of moles of carbon dioxide at r.t.p. (1 mol of gas occupies $24\,dm^3$ at r.t.p.) [1]

Total = 10

4 Hydrocarbons are compounds of carbon and hydrogen only. Hydrocarbon **Z** is composed of 80% carbon and 20% hydrogen.
  a Calculate the empirical formula of hydrocarbon **Z**.
  (A_r values: C = 12.0, H = 1.0) [3]
  b The molar mass of hydrocarbon **Z** is $30.0 \, \mathrm{g \, mol^{-1}}$. Deduce the molecular formula of this hydrocarbon. [1]
  c When $50 \, \mathrm{cm^3}$ of hydrocarbon **Y** is burnt, it reacts with exactly $300 \, \mathrm{cm^3}$ of oxygen to form $200 \, \mathrm{cm^3}$ of carbon dioxide. Water is also formed in the reaction. Deduce the equation for this reaction. Explain your reasoning. [4]
  d Propane has the molecular formula C_3H_8. Calculate the mass of $600 \, \mathrm{cm^3}$ of propane at r.t.p.
  (1 mol of gas occupies $24 \, \mathrm{dm^3}$ at r.t.p.) (A_r values: C = 12.0, H = 1.0) [2]

  Total = 10

5 When sodium reacts with titanium chloride ($TiCl_4$), sodium chloride (NaCl) and titanium (Ti) are produced.
  a Write the balanced symbol equation for the reaction. [2]
  b What mass of titanium is produced from $380 \, \mathrm{g}$ of titanium chloride? Give your answer to 3 significant figures (A_r values: Ti = 47.9, Cl = 35.5). [2]
  c What mass of titanium is produced using $46.0 \, \mathrm{g}$ of sodium? Give your answer to 3 significant figures (A_r values: Na = 23.0) [2]

  Total = 6

6 In this question give all answers to 3 significant figures.
  The reaction between NaOH and HCl can be written as:

  $$HCl + NaOH \rightarrow NaCl + H_2O$$

  In such a reaction, $15.0 \, \mathrm{cm^3}$ of hydrochloric acid was neutralised by $20.0 \, \mathrm{cm^3}$ of $0.0500 \, \mathrm{mol \, dm^{-3}}$ sodium hydroxide.
  a What was the volume in $\mathrm{dm^3}$ of:
  i the acid?
  ii the alkali? [2]
  b Calculate the number of moles of alkali. [1]
  c Calculate the number of moles of acid and then its concentration. [2]

  Total = 5

7 Give all answers to 3 significant figures.
  Ammonium nitrate decomposes on heating to give nitrogen(I) oxide and water as follows:

  $$NH_4NO_3(s) \rightarrow N_2O(g) + 2H_2O(l)$$

  a What is the formula mass of ammonium nitrate? [1]
  b How many moles of ammonium nitrate are present in $0.800 \, \mathrm{g}$ of the solid? [2]
  c What volume of N_2O gas would be produced from this mass of ammonium nitrate? [2]

  Total = 5

8   Give all answers to 3 significant figures.
    a $1.20\,dm^3$ of hydrogen chloride gas was dissolved in $100\,cm^3$ of water.
       i   How many moles of hydrogen chloride gas are present?   [1]
       ii What was the concentration of the hydrochloric acid formed?   [2]
    b $25.0\,cm^3$ of the acid was then titrated against sodium hydroxide of concentration $0.200\,mol\,dm^{-3}$
       to form NaCl and water:

       $$NaOH + HCl \rightarrow H_2O + NaCl$$

       i   How many moles of acid were used?   [2]
       ii Calculate the volume of sodium hydroxide used.   [2]
                                                                                       Total = 7

9   Give all answers to 3 significant figures.
    $4.80\,dm^3$ of chlorine gas was reacted with sodium hydroxide solution. The reaction taking place
    was as follows:

    $$Cl_2(g) + 2NaOH(aq) \rightarrow NaCl(aq) + NaOCl(aq) + H_2O(l)$$

    a How many moles of Cl_2 reacted?   [1]
    b What mass of NaOCl was formed?   [2]
    c If the concentration of the NaOH was $2.00\,mol\,dm^{-3}$, what volume of sodium hydroxide solution
       was required?   [2]
    d Write an ionic equation for this reaction.   [1]
                                                                                       Total = 6

10 Calcium oxide reacts with hydrochloric acid according to the equation:

    $$CaO + 2HCl \rightarrow CaCl_2 + H_2O$$

    a What mass of calcium chloride is formed when $28.05\,g$ of calcium oxide reacts with excess
       hydrochloric acid?   [2]
    b What mass of hydrochloric acid reacts with $28.05\,g$ of calcium oxide?   [2]
    c What mass of water is produced?   [1]
                                                                                       Total = 5

11 When ammonia gas and hydrogen chloride gas mix together, they react to form a solid called
    ammonium chloride.
    a Write a balanced equation for this reaction, including state symbols.   [2]
    b Calculate the molar masses of ammonia, hydrogen chloride and ammonium chloride.   [3]
    c What volumes of ammonia and hydrogen chloride gases must react at r.t.p. in order to produce
       $10.7\,g$ of ammonium chloride? (1 mol of gas occupies $24\,dm^3$ at r.t.p.)   [3]
                                                                                       Total = 8

2 Atomic structure

2.1 Elements and atoms

Every substance in our world is made up from chemical elements. These chemical elements cannot be broken down further into simpler substances by chemical means. A few elements, such as nitrogen and gold, are found on their own in nature, not combined with other elements. Most elements, however, are found in combination with other elements as compounds.

Every element has its own chemical symbol. The symbols are often derived from Latin or Greek words. Some examples are shown in Table **2.1**.

Chemical elements contain only one type of atom. An atom is the smallest part of an element that can take part in a chemical change. Atoms are very small. The diameter of a hydrogen atom is approximately 10^{-10} m, so the mass of an atom must also be very small. A single hydrogen atom weighs only 1.67×10^{-27} kg.

Element	Symbol
carbon	C
lithium	Li (from Greek 'lithos')
iron	Fe (from Latin 'ferrum')
potassium	K (from Arabic 'al-qualyah' or from the Latin 'kalium')

Table 2.1 Some examples of chemical symbols.

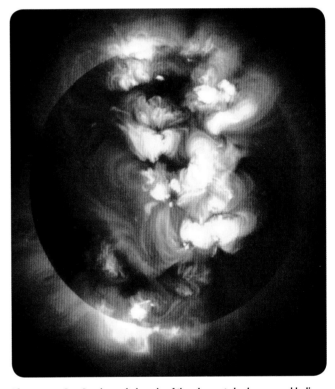

Figure 2.1 Our Sun is made largely of the elements hydrogen and helium. This is a composite image made using X-ray and solar optical telecopes.

2.2 Inside the atom

The structure of an atom

Every atom has nearly all of its mass concentrated in a tiny region in the centre of the atom called the **nucleus**. The nucleus is made up of particles called nucleons. There are two types of nucleon: **protons** and **neutrons**. Atoms of different elements have different numbers of protons.

Outside the nucleus, particles called **electrons** move around in regions of space called orbitals (see page 38).

Chemists often find it convenient to use a model of the atom in which electrons move around the nucleus in electron shells. Each shell is a certain distance from the nucleus at its own particular energy level (see page 37). In a neutral atom, the number of electrons is equal to the number of protons. A simple model of a carbon atom is shown in Figure 2.3.

Atoms are tiny, but the nucleus of an atom is far tinier still. If the diameter of an atom were the size of a football stadium, the nucleus would only be the size of a pea. This means that most of the atom is empty space! Electrons are even smaller than protons and neutrons.

Experiments with sub-atomic particles

We can deduce the electric charge of sub-atomic particles by showing how beams of electrons, protons and neutrons behave in electromagnetic fields. If we fire a beam of electrons past electrically charged plates, the electrons are deflected (bent) away from the negative plate and towards the positive plate (Figure 2.4). This shows us that the electrons are negatively charged.

A cathode-ray tube (Figure 2.5) can be used to produce beams of electrons. At one end of the tube is a metal wire (cathode) which is heated to a high temperature when a

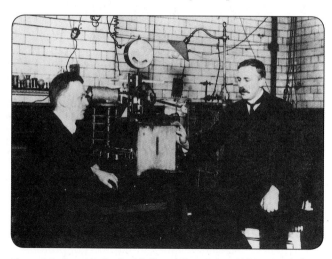

Figure 2.2 Ernest Rutherford (left) and Hans Geiger (right) using their alpha-particle apparatus. Interpretation of the results led to Rutherford proposing the nuclear model for atoms.

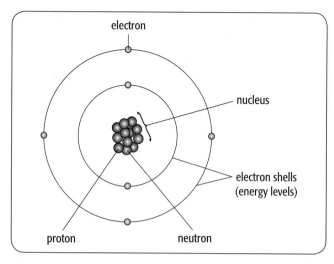

Figure 2.3 A model of a carbon atom. This model is not very accurate but it is useful for understanding what happens to the electrons during chemical reactions.

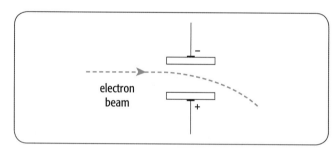

Figure 2.4 The beam of electrons is deflected away from a negatively charged plate and towards a positively charged plate.

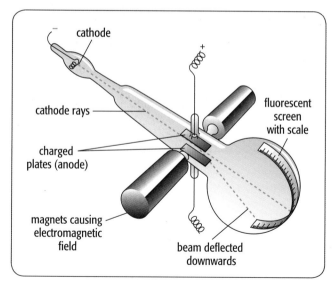

Figure 2.5 The electron beam in a cathode-ray tube is deflected (bent) by an electromagnetic field. The direction of the deflection shows us that the electron is negatively charged.

low voltage is applied to it. At the other end of the tube is a fluorescent screen which glows when electrons hit it.

The electrons are given off from the heated wire and are attracted towards two metal plates which are positively charged. As they pass through the metal plates the electrons form a beam. When the electron beam hits the screen a spot of light is produced. When an electromagnetic field is applied across this beam the electrons are deflected (bent). The fact that the electrons are so easily attracted to the positively charged anode and that they are easily deflected by an electromagnetic field shows us that:
- electrons have a negative charge
- electrons have a very small mass.

In recent years, experiments have been carried out with beams of electrons, protons and neutrons. The results of these experiments show that:
- a proton beam is deflected away from a positively charged plate; since like charges repel, the protons must have a positive charge (Figure 2.7)
- an electron beam is deflected towards a positively charged plate; since unlike charges attract, the electrons must have a negative charge
- a beam of neutrons is not deflected; this is because they are uncharged.

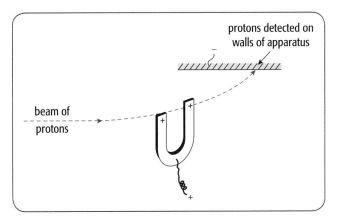

Figure 2.7 A beam of protons is deflected away from a positively charged area. This shows us that protons have a positive charge.

In these experiments, huge voltages have to be used to show the deflection of the proton beam. This contrasts with the very low voltages needed to show the deflection of an electron beam. These experiments show us that protons are much heavier than electrons. If we used the same voltage to deflect electrons and protons, the beam of electrons would have a far greater deflection than the beam of protons. This is because a proton is about 2000 times as heavy as an electron.

Check-up

1 A beam of electrons is passing close to a highly negatively charged plate. When the electrons pass close to the plate, they are deflected (bent) away from the plate.
   a What deflection would you expect, if any, when the experiment is repeated with beams of **i** protons and **ii** neutrons? Explain your answers.
   b Which sub-atomic particle (electron, proton or neutron) would be deviated the most? Explain your answer.

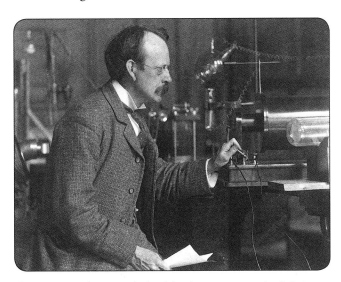

Figure 2.6 J. J. Thomson calculated the charge to mass ratio of electrons. He used results from experiments with electrons in cathode-ray tubes.

Fact file

Atomic scientists now believe that elementary particles called quarks and leptons are the building blocks from which most matter is made. They think that protons and neutrons are made up from quarks and that an electron is a type of lepton.

Masses and charges: a summary

Electrons, protons and neutrons have characteristic charges and masses. The values of these are too small to be very useful when discussing general chemical properties. For example, the charge on a single electron is -1.602×10^{-19} coulombs. We therefore compare their masses and charges by using their relative charges and masses. These are shown in Table 2.2.

Sub-atomic particle	Symbol	Relative mass	Relative charge
electron	e	$\dfrac{1}{1836}$	-1
neutron	n	1	0
proton	p	1	$+1$

Table 2.2 Comparing electrons, neutrons and protons.

Atom	Nucleon number	Proton number
vanadium	51	23
strontium	84	38
phosphorus	31	15

2.3 Numbers of nucleons

Proton number and nucleon number

The number of protons in the nucleus of an atom is called the proton number (Z). It is also known as the atomic number. Every atom of the same element has the same number of protons in its nucleus. It is the proton number which makes an atom what it is. For example an atom with a proton number of 11 must be an atom of the element sodium. The Periodic Table of elements is arranged in order of the proton numbers of the individual elements (see Appendix 1, page 497).

The **nucleon number** (A) is the number of protons plus neutrons in the nucleus of an atom. This is also known as the **mass number**.

How many neutrons?

We can use the nucleon number and proton number to find the number of neutrons in an atom. Since

nucleon number

= number of protons + number of neutrons

Then

number of neutrons

= nucleon number – number of protons

= $A - Z$

For example, an atom of aluminium has a nucleon number of 27 and a proton number of 13. So an aluminium atom has 27 – 13 = 14 neutrons.

Isotopes

All atoms of the same element have the same number of protons. However, they may have different numbers of neutrons. Atoms of the same element which have differing numbers of neutrons are called isotopes.

> **Isotopes** are atoms of the same element with different nucleon (mass) numbers.

Isotopes of a particular element have the same chemical properties because they have the same number of electrons. They have slightly different physical properties, such as small differences in density.

We can write symbols for isotopes. We write the nucleon number at the top left of the chemical symbol and the proton number at the bottom left.

The symbol for the isotope of boron with 5 protons and 11 nucleons is written:

nucleon number $\rightarrow$ $^{11}_{5}\text{B}$
proton number $\rightarrow$

Hydrogen has three isotopes. The atomic structure and isotopic symbols for the three isotopes of hydrogen are shown in Figure 2.8.

When writing generally about isotopes, chemists also name them by omitting the proton number and placing

Check-up

2 Use the information in the table to deduce the number of electrons and neutrons in a neutral atom of:
 a vanadium
 b strontium
 c phosphorus. *continued* ⋯➔

Fact file

Isotopes can be radioactive or non-radioactive. Specific radioisotopes (radioactive isotopes) can be used to check for leaks in oil or gas pipelines and to check the thickness of paper. They are also used in medicine to treat some types of cancer and to check the activity of the thyroid gland in the throat.

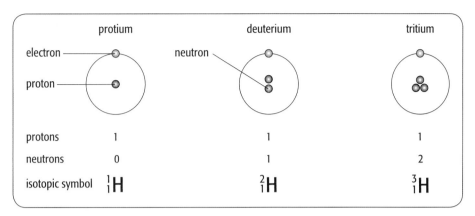

Figure 2.8 The atomic structure and isotopic symbols for the three isotopes of hydrogen.

the nucleon number after the name. For example, the isotopes of hydrogen can be called hydrogen-1, hydrogen-2 and hydrogen-3.

Check-up

3 Use the Periodic Table on page 497 to help you.
   a Write isotopic symbols for the following neutral atoms:
      i   bromine-81
      ii calcium-44
      iii iron-58
      iv palladium-110
   b What is the number of protons and neutrons in each of these atoms?

2.4 How many protons, neutrons and electrons?

In a neutral atom the number of positively charged protons in the nucleus equals the number of negatively charged electrons outside the nucleus. When an atom gains or loses electrons, ions are formed which are electrically charged. For example:

$$Cl \quad + \quad e^- \quad \rightarrow \quad Cl^-$$

chlorine atom	1 electron gained	chloride ion
17 protons		17 protons
17 electrons		18 electrons

The chloride ion has a single negative charge because there are 17 protons (+) and 18 electrons (–).

$$Mg \quad \rightarrow \quad Mg^{2+} \quad + \quad 2e^-$$

magnesium atom	magnesium ion	2 electrons removed
12 protons	12 protons	
12 electrons	10 electrons	

The magnesium ion has a charge of 2+ because it has 12 protons (+) but only 10 electrons (–).

The isotopic symbol for an ion derived from sulfur-33 is $^{33}_{16}S^{2-}$. This sulfide ion has 16 protons, 17 neutrons (because $33 - 16 = 17$) and 18 electrons (because $16 + 2 = 18$).

Check-up

4 Deduce the number of electrons in each of these ions:

   a $^{40}_{19}K^+$

   b $^{15}_{7}N^{3-}$

   c $^{18}_{8}O^{2-}$

   d $^{71}_{31}Ga^{3+}$

Summary

- ☐ Every atom has an internal structure with a nucleus in the centre and the negatively charged electrons arranged in 'shells' outside the nucleus.
- ☐ Most of the mass of the atom is in the nucleus, which contains protons (positively charged) and neutrons (uncharged).
- ☐ Beams of protons and electrons are deflected by electric fields but neutrons are not.
- ☐ All atoms of the same element have the same number of protons. This is the proton number (Z), which is also called the atomic number.
- ☐ The nucleon number, which is also called the mass number (A), is the total number of protons and neutrons in an atom.
- ☐ The number of neutrons in an atom is found by subtracting the proton number from the nucleon number ($A - Z$).
- ☐ In a neutral atom, number of electrons = number of protons. When there are more protons than electrons the atom becomes a positive ion. When there are more electrons than protons, a negatively charged ion is formed.
- ☐ Isotopes are atoms with the same atomic number but different nucleon numbers. They only differ in the number of neutrons they contain.

End-of-chapter questions

1 Boron is an element in Group III of the Periodic Table.

   a Boron has two isotopes.
     What do you understand by the term **isotope**? [1]

   b State the number of **i** protons, **ii** neutrons and **iii** electrons in one neutral atom of the isotope $^{11}_{5}B$. [3]

   c State the relative masses and charges of:
     i an electron [2]
     ii a neutron [2]
     iii a proton [2]

                                         Total = 10

2 Zirconium, Zr, and hafnium, Hf, are metals.
   An isotope of zirconium has 40 protons and 91 nucleons.

   a **i** Write the isotopic symbol for this isotope of zirconium. [1]
     ii How many neutrons are present in one atom of this isotope? [1]

   b Hafnium ions, $^{180}_{72}Hf^{2+}$, are produced in a mass spectrometer.
     How many electrons are present in one of these hafnium ions? [1]

c The sub-atomic particles present in zirconium and hafnium are electrons, neutrons and protons. A beam of protons is fired into an electric field produced by two charged plates, as shown in the diagram.

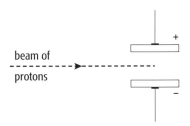

   i Describe how the beam of protons behaves when it passes through the gap between the charged plates. Explain your answer. [2]
   ii Describe and explain what happens when a beam of neutrons passes through the gap between the charged plates. [2]

Total = 7

3 a Describe the structure of an atom, giving details of the sub-atomic particles present. [6]
   b Explain the terms **atomic number** and **nucleon number**. [2]
   c Copy and complete the table:

Neutral atom	Atomic number	Nucleon number	Numbers of each sub-atomic particle present
Mg	12	24	
Al	13	27	

[2]

   d Explain why atoms are neutral. [1]
   e An oxygen atom has 8 protons in its nucleus. Explain why it cannot have 9 protons. [1]
   f When calculating the mass of an atom, the electrons are not used in the calculation. Explain why not. [1]

Total = 13

4 The symbols below describe two isotopes of the element uranium.

   $^{235}_{92}U$ $^{238}_{92}U$

   a State the meaning of the term **isotope**. [1]
   b i In what ways are these two isotopes of uranium identical? [2]
      ii In what ways do they differ? [2]
   c In a mass spectrometer uranium atoms can be converted to uranium ions, U^{2+}.
      State the number of electrons present in one U^{2+} ion. [1]

Total = 6

5   The table below shows the two naturally occurring isotopes of chlorine.

   a   Copy and complete the table.

	$^{35}_{17}\text{Cl}$	$^{37}_{17}\text{Cl}$
number of protons		
number of electrons		
number of neutrons		

[3]

   b   The relative atomic mass of chlorine is 35.5. What does this tell you about the relative abundance of the two naturally occurring isotopes of chlorine? [2]

   c   Magnesium chloride contains magnesium ions, Mg^{2+}, and chloride ions, Cl^-.

   i   Explain why a magnesium ion is positively charged. [1]

   ii Explain why a chloride ion has a single negative charge. [2]

Total = 8

3 Electrons in atoms

Learning outcomes

Candidates should be able to:

- describe the number and relative energies of the s, p and d orbitals for the principal quantum numbers 1, 2 and 3 and also the 4s and 4p orbitals
- describe the shapes of s and p orbitals
- state the electronic configuration of atoms and ions given the proton number (and charge)
- explain and use the term **ionisation energy**
- explain the factors influencing the ionisation energies of elements

- explain the trends in ionisation energies across a period and down a group of the Periodic Table
- deduce the electronic configurations of elements from successive ionisation energy data
- interpret successive ionisation energy data of an element in terms of the position of that element within the Periodic Table.

3.1 Simple electronic structure

On page **26** we saw that electrons are arranged outside the nucleus in energy levels or quantum shells. These

Figure 3.1 Electrons moving between energy levels are the source of this light energy. Chemicals in the tube are said to be 'chemiluminescent'.

principal **energy levels** or **principal quantum shells** (symbol n) are numbered according to how far they are from the nucleus. The lowest energy level, $n = 1$, is closest to the nucleus, the energy level $n = 2$ is further out, and so on. The electrons in quantum shells further away from the nucleus have more energy and are held less tightly to the nucleus.

The arrangement of electrons in an atom is called its electronic structure or **electronic configuration**. The electronic configurations of lithium, carbon and neon are shown in Figure **3.2**, together with a shorthand way of writing this structure.

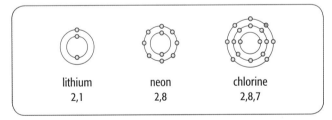

Figure 3.2 The simple electronic structures of lithium, neon and chlorine. The nuclei of the atoms are not shown.

Table **3.1** shows the number of electrons in each of the principal quantum shells (energy levels) for the first 11 elements in the Periodic Table. Each principal quantum shell can hold a maximum number of electrons:

- shell 1 – up to 2 electrons
- shell 2 – up to 8 electrons
- shell 3 – up to 18 electrons
- shell 4 – up to 32 electrons.

	Atomic number	Number of electrons in shell		
		$n = 1$	$n = 2$	$n = 3$
H	1	1		
He	2	2		
Li	3	2	1	
Be	4	2	2	
B	5	2	3	
C	6	2	4	
N	7	2	5	
O	8	2	6	
F	9	2	7	
Ne	10	2	8	
Na	11	2	8	1

Table 3.1 Simple electronic configurations of the first 11 elements in the Periodic Table.

Check-up

1 Write the simple electronic configuration of the following atoms, showing the principal quantum shells only:
   a sulfur; the atomic number of sulfur, $Z = 16$
   b magnesium, $Z = 12$
   c fluorine, $Z = 9$
   d potassium, $Z = 19$
   e carbon, $Z = 6$

3.2 Evidence for electronic structure

Ionisation energy, ΔH_i

By firing high-speed electrons at atoms, scientists can work out how much energy has to be supplied to form an ion by knocking out one electron from each atom.

The energy change which accompanies this process is called the **ionisation energy**.

The 1st **ionisation energy** of an element is the energy needed to remove one electron from each atom in one mole of atoms of the element in the gaseous state to form one mole of gaseous 1+ ions.

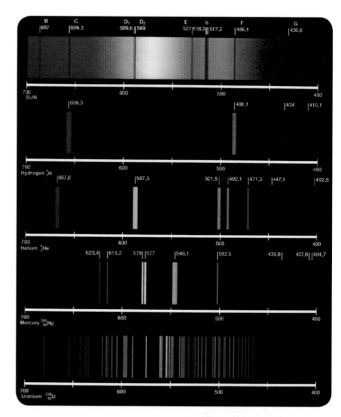

Figure 3.3 The frequencies of the lines in an atomic emission spectrum can be used to calculate a value for the ionisation energy.

Ionisation energies are measured under standard conditions. The general symbol for ionisation energy is ΔH_i. Its units are $kJ\,mol^{-1}$.

The symbol for the 1st ionisation energy is ΔH_{i1}. Using calcium as an example:

1st ionisation energy: $Ca(g) \rightarrow Ca^+(g) + e^-$

$\Delta H_{i1} = 590\,kJ\,mol^{-1}$

If a second electron is removed from each ion in a mole of gaseous 1+ ions, we call it the 2nd ionisation energy, ΔH_{i2}. Again, using calcium as an example:

2nd ionisation energy: $Ca^+(g) \rightarrow Ca^{2+}(g) + e^-$

$\Delta H_{i2} = 1150\,kJ\,mol^{-1}$

Removal of a third electron from each ion in a mole of gaseous 2+ ions is called the 3rd ionisation energy. Again, using calcium as an example:

3rd ionisation energy: $Ca^{2+}(g) \rightarrow Ca^{3+}(g) + e^-$

$\Delta H_{i3} = 4940\,kJ\,mol^{-1}$

We can continue to remove electrons from an atom until only the nucleus is left. We call this sequence of ionisation energies, **successive ionisation energies**.

Element		Electrons removed										
		1	2	3	4	5	6	7	8	9	10	11
1	H	1310										
2	He	2370	5250									
3	Li	519	7300	11800								
4	Be	900	1760	14850	21000							
5	B	799	2420	3660	25000	32800						
6	C	1090	2350	4620	6220	37800	47300					
7	N	1400	2860	4580	7480	9450	53300	64400				
8	O	1310	3390	5320	7450	11000	13300	71300	84100			
9	F	1680	3370	6040	8410	11000	15200	17900	92000	106000		
10	Ne	2080	3950	6150	9290	12200	15200	20000	23000	117000	131400	
11	Na	494	4560	6940	9540	13400	16600	20100	25500	28900	141000	158700

Table 3.2 Successive ionisation energies for the first 11 elements in the Periodic Table.

The successive ionisation energies for the first 11 elements in the Periodic Table are shown in Table 3.2. The data in Table 3.2 shows us that:

- For each element, the successive ionisation energies increase. This is because the charge on the ion gets greater as each electron is removed. As each electron is removed there is a greater attractive force between the positively charged protons in the nucleus and the remaining negatively charged electrons. Therefore more energy is needed to overcome these attractive forces.
- There is a big difference between some successive ionisation energies. For nitrogen this occurs between the 5th and 6th ionisation energies. For sodium the first big difference occurs between the 1st and 2nd ionisation energies. These large changes indicate that for the second of these two ionisation energies the electron being removed is from a principal quantum shell closer to the nucleus.

For example, for the 5th ionisation energy of nitrogen, the electron being removed is from the 2nd principal quantum shell. For the 6th ionisation energy of nitrogen, the electron being removed is from the 1st principal quantum shell.

Check-up

2 a Write equations which describe:
   i   the 1st ionisation energy of calcium
   ii the 3rd ionisation energy of potassium

continued ┈┈>

   iii the 2nd ionisation energy of lithium
   iv the 5th ionisation energy of sulfur
 b The 2nd ionisation energy of nitrogen is $2860 \, kJ \, mol^{-1}$. The 3rd ionisation energy of nitrogen is $4590 \, kJ \, mol^{-1}$. Explain why the 3rd ionisation energy is higher.

Three factors that influence ionisation energies

1 The size of the nuclear charge

As the atomic number (number of protons) increases, the positive nuclear charge increases. The bigger the positive charge, the greater the attractive force between the nucleus and the electrons. So, more energy is needed to overcome these attractive forces if an electron is to be removed.

- In general, ionisation energy increases as the proton number increases.

2 Distance of outer electrons from the nucleus

The force of attraction between positive and negative charges decreases rapidly as the distance between them increases. So, electrons in shells further away from the nucleus are less attracted to the nucleus than those closer to the nucleus.

- The further the outer electron shell is from the nucleus, the lower the ionisation energy.

3 Shielding effect of inner electrons

Since all electrons are negatively charged, they repel each other. Electrons in full inner shells repel electrons in outer shells. Full inner shells of electrons prevent the full nuclear charge being felt by the outer electrons. This is called **shielding**. The greater the shielding of outer electrons by the inner electron shells, the lower the attractive forces between the nucleus and the outer electrons.

- The ionisation energy is lower as the number of full electron shells between the outer electrons and the nucleus increases.

Interpreting successive ionisation energies

Figure 3.4 shows a graph of successive ionisation energies against the number of electrons removed for sodium. A logarithmic scale (to the base 10) is used because the values of successive ionisation energies have such a large range.

We can deduce the following about sodium from Figure 3.4:

- The first electron removed has a low 1st ionisation energy, when compared to the rest of the data. It is very easily removed from the atom. It is therefore likely to be a long way from the nucleus and well shielded by inner electron shells.

- The second electron is much more difficult to remove than the first electron. There is a big jump in the value of the ionisation energy. This suggests that the second electron is in a shell closer to the nucleus than the first electron. Taken together, the 1st and 2nd ionisation energies suggest that sodium has one electron in its outer shell.
- From the second to the ninth electrons removed there is only a gradual change in successive ionisation energies. This suggests that all these eight electrons are in the same shell.
- The 10th and 11th electrons have extremely high ionisation energies, when compared to the rest of the data. This suggests that they are very close to the nucleus. There must be a very great force of attraction between the nucleus and these electrons and there are no inner electrons to shield them. The large increase in ionisation energy between the 9th and 10th electrons confirms that the 10th electron is in a shell closer to the nucleus than the 9th electron.

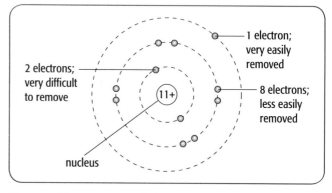

Figure 3.5 The arrangement of electrons in an atom of sodium can be deduced from the values of successive ionisation energies.

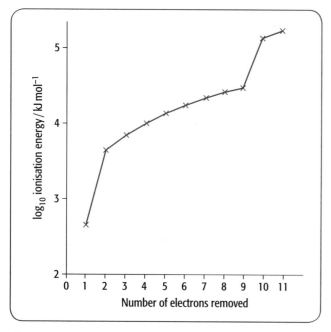

Figure 3.4 Graph of logarithm ($\log_{10}$) of ionisation energy of sodium against the number of electrons removed.

Check-up

3 a The successive ionisation energies of boron are shown in Table 3.3.

Ionisation	1st	2nd	3rd	4th	5th
Ionisation energy / kJ mol^{-1}	799	2420	3660	25 000	32 800

Table 3.3 Successive ionisation energies of boron.

continued ⋯⟶

continued ⋯⟫

i Why is there a large increase between the third and fourth ionisation energies?

ii Explain how these figures confirm that the electronic structure of boron is 2, 3.

b For the element aluminium ($Z = 13$), draw a sketch graph to predict the $\log_{10}$ of the successive ionisation energies (y-axis) against the number of electrons removed (x-axis).

We can use successive ionisation energies in this way to:
- predict or confirm the simple electronic configuration of elements
- confirm the number of electrons in the outer shell of an element and hence the group to which the element belongs.

Worked example

1 The successive ionisation energies, ΔH_i, of an element **X** are shown in Table **3.4**. Which group in the Periodic Table does **X** belong to?

We look for a large jump in the value of the ionisation energy. This occurs between the removal of the 6th and 7th electrons. So, six electrons have been removed comparatively easily. The removal of the 7th electron requires about three times the energy required to remove the 6th electron. So, there must be six electrons in the outer shell of **X**. So, element **X** must be in Group VI of the Periodic Table.

Check-up

4 a The first six ionisation energies of an element are 1090, 2350, 4610, 6220, 37 800 and 47 300 kJ mol^{-1}. Which group in the Periodic Table does this element belong to? Explain your decision.

b Draw a sketch graph to show the $\log_{10}$ values of the first four successive ionisation energies of a Group II element.

3.3 Sub-shells and atomic orbitals

Quantum sub-shells

The principal quantum shells, apart from the first, are split into **sub-shells** (sub-levels). Each principal quantum shell contains a different number of sub-shells. The sub-shells are distinguished by the letters s, p or d. There are also f sub-shells for elements with more than 57 electrons. Figure **3.6** shows the sub-shells for the first four principal quantum levels. In any principal quantum shell, the energy of the electrons in the sub-shells increases in the order s < p < d.

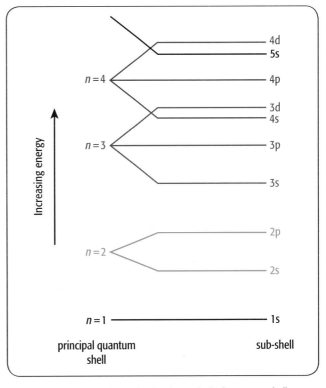

Figure 3.6 The sub-shells for the first four principal quantum shells.

	Number of electrons removed									
	1	**2**	**3**	**4**	**5**	**6**	**7**	**8**	**9**	**10**
ΔH_i / kJ mol^{-1}	1000	2260	3390	4540	7010	8500	27 100	31 670	36 580	43 140

Table 3.4 The successive ionisation energies of an element **X**. For Worked example **1**.

The maximum number of electrons that are allowed in each sub-shell is: s – 2 electrons, p – 6 electrons, d – 10 electrons.

- The first principal quantum level, $n = 1$, can hold a maximum of 2 electrons in an s sub-shell.
- The second principal quantum level, $n = 2$, can hold a maximum of 8 electrons: 2 electrons in the s sub-shell and 6 electrons in the p sub-shell.
- The third principal quantum level, $n = 3$, can hold a maximum of 18 electrons: 2 electrons in the s sub-shell, 6 electrons in the p sub-shell and 10 electrons in the d sub-shell.

You will also notice from Figure 3.6 that the order of the sub-shells in terms of increasing energy does not follow a regular pattern of s then p then d after the element argon. The order of sub-shells after argon appears to overlap. The next element after argon is potassium. Potassium's outer electron is in the 4s, not in the 3d sub-shell. The first element with an electron in the 3d sub-shell is element 21, scandium.

Fact file

When high-speed electrons hit gas particles at low pressure, coloured lines are seen through an instrument called a spectroscope. The letters s, p and d come from the terms used to describe these lines: s for 'sharp', p for 'principal' and 'd for 'diffuse'.

Atomic orbitals

Each sub-shell contains one or more **atomic orbitals**.

> An atomic orbital is a region of space around the nucleus of an atom which can be occupied by one or two electrons.

Since each orbital can only hold a maximum of two electrons, the number of orbitals in each sub-shell must be:

s – one orbital
p – three orbitals
d – five orbitals.

Shapes of the orbitals

Each orbital has a three-dimensional shape. Within this shape there is a high probability of finding the electron or electrons in the orbital. Figure 3.7 shows how we represent the s and p orbitals.

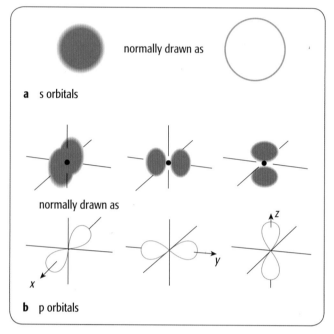

Figure 3.7 Representations of orbitals (the position of the nucleus is shown by the black dot): **a** s orbitals are spherical; **b** p orbitals, p_x, p_y and p_z, have 'lobes' along the x, y and z axes.

An s orbital has a spherical shape. The 2s orbital in the second principal quantum shell has the same shape as the 1s orbital in the first quantum shell. They are both spherical, but electrons in the 2s orbital have more energy than electrons in the 1s orbital. There are three 2p orbitals in the second quantum shell. Each of these has the same shape. The shape is like an hourglass with two 'lobes'. The three sets of 'lobes' are arranged at right angles to each other along the x, y and z axes. Hence the three 2p orbitals are named $2p_x$, $2p_y$ and $2p_z$. The three 2p orbitals have the same energy as each other. There are also three 3p orbitals in the third quantum shell. Their shapes are similar to the shapes of the 2p orbitals.

The d orbitals are more complex in shape and arrangement in space. You will not need to know these shapes for your AS chemistry exam.

Fact file

In 1925 Louis de Broglie suggested that electrons behaved like waves. This led to the idea of electron probability clouds. The electron probability cloud for one type of d orbital is very strange – it is like a modified p orbital with a ring around the middle! (Figure **3.8**)

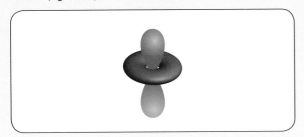

Figure 3.8 The shape of a dz^2 orbital.

Filling the shells and orbitals

The most stable electronic configuration (electronic structure) of an atom is the one that has the lowest amount of energy. The order in which the sub-shells are filled depends on their relative energy. The sub-shell with the lowest energy, the 1s, is therefore filled first, followed by those which are successively higher in energy. As we noted in Figure **3.6**, the order of the sub-shells in terms of increasing energy does not follow a regular pattern of s then p then d after argon, where the 3p sub-shell is full. Figure **3.9** shows the order of filling the sub-shells.

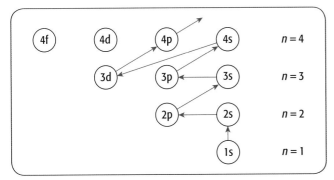

Figure 3.9 Diagram to show the order in which orbitals are filled up to shell $n = 4$.

Check-up

5 a Name the three types of orbital present in the third principal quantum shell.
  b State the maximum number of electrons that can be found in each sub-shell of the third quantum shell.

3.4 Electronic configurations

Representing electronic configurations

A detailed way of writing the electronic configuration of an atom which includes information about the number of electrons in each sub-shell is shown below for hydrogen.

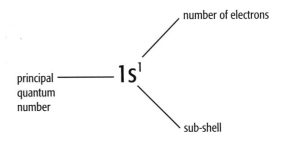

- Helium has two electrons. Both electrons can go into the 1s orbital since this can hold a maximum of two electrons. So, the electronic structure of helium is $1s^2$.
- Lithium has three electrons. The 1s orbital can only hold a maximum of two electrons so the third electron must go into the next highest sub-shell, the 2s. So, the electronic structure of lithium is $1s^2 2s^1$.

Electrons are added one by one for successive elements, filling each sub-shell in order of increasing energy. The electronic configurations of the first 18 elements are shown in Table **3.5**.

When an exam question wishes you to use this type of detailed notation it will often be stated like this: 'Use $1s^2$ notation to give the electronic configuration …'

Check-up

6 Use $1s^2$ notation to give the electronic configurations of the atoms with the following atomic numbers:
  a 16
  b 9
  c 20

Element number	Symbol	Electronic configuration
1	H	$1s^1$
2	He	$1s^2$
3	Li	$1s^2 2s^1$
4	Be	$1s^2 2s^2$
5	B	$1s^2 2s^2 2p^1$
6	C	$1s^2 2s^2 2p^2$
7	N	$1s^2 2s^2 2p^3$
8	O	$1s^2 2s^2 2p^4$
9	F	$1s^2 2s^2 2p^5$
10	Ne	$1s^2 2s^2 2p^6$
11	Na	$1s^2 2s^2 2p^6 3s^1$
12	Mg	$1s^2 2s^2 2p^6 3s^2$
13	Al	$1s^2 2s^2 2p^6 3s^2 3p^1$
14	Si	$1s^2 2s^2 2p^6 3s^2 3p^2$
15	P	$1s^2 2s^2 2p^6 3s^2 3p^3$
16	S	$1s^2 2s^2 2p^6 3s^2 3p^4$
17	Cl	$1s^2 2s^2 2p^6 3s^2 3p^5$
18	Ar	$1s^2 2s^2 2p^6 3s^2 3p^6$

Table 3.5 Electronic configurations for the first 18 elements in the Periodic Table.

Element number	Name (Symbol)	Electronic configuration
19	Potassium (K)	$[Ar] 4s^1$
20	Calcium (Ca)	$[Ar] 4s^2$
21	Scandium (Sc)	$[Ar] 3d^1 4s^2$
24	Chromium (Cr)	$[Ar] 3d^5 4s^1$
25	Manganese (Mn)	$[Ar] 3d^5 4s^2$
29	Copper (Cu)	$[Ar] 3d^{10} 4s^1$
30	Zinc (Zn)	$[Ar] 3d^{10} 4s^2$
31	Gallium (Ga)	$[Ar] 3d^{10} 4s^2 4p^1$
35	Bromine (Br)	$[Ar] 3d^{10} 4s^2 4p^5$
36	Krypton (Kr)	$[Ar] 3d^{10} 4s^2 4p^6$

Table 3.6 Electronic configurations for some of the elements 19 to 36, where [Ar] is the electronic structure of argon $1s^2 2s^2 2p^6 3s^2 3p^6$.

The electronic configuration of some of the elements after argon are shown in Table **3.6**. In this table part of the electronic configuration of each element is represented by [Ar]. This 'noble gas core' represents the electronic configuration of argon: $1s^2 2s^2 2p^6 3s^2 3p^6$. This method is a shorthand way of writing electronic structures of atoms with many electrons. However, in an exam you should be prepared to write out the full electronic configuration.

You should note the following:

- **Electronic configuration of potassium**
  Potassium has the electronic structure $1s^2 2s^2 2p^6 3s^2 3p^6 4s^1$. The outer electron goes into the 4s sub-shell rather than the 3d sub-shell because the 4s is below the 3d in terms of its energy.

- **Filling the 3d sub-shell**
  After calcium, a new sub-shell becomes occupied. The next electron goes into a 3d sub-shell rather than a 4p sub-shell. So scandium has the electronic configuration $[Ar] 3d^1 4s^2$. This is because electrons occupy the orbitals with the lowest energy – the 3d sub-shell is just above the 4s sub-shell but below the 4p sub-shell. This begins a pattern of filling the 3d sub-shell ending with zinc. Zinc has the electronic configuration $[Ar] 3d^{10} 4s^2$.

- **Chromium and copper**
  The electronic configurations of chromium and copper do not follow the expected pattern. Chromium has the electronic configuration $[Ar] 3d^5 4s^1$ (rather than the expected $[Ar] 3d^4 4s^2$). Copper has the electronic configuration $[Ar] 3d^{10} 4s^1$ (rather than the expected $[Ar] 3d^9 4s^2$). You will have to learn that these two elements are exceptions to the pattern.

- **Gallium to krypton**
  The electrons add to the 4p sub-shell because this is the next highest energy level above the 3d.

Check-up

7 Use $1s^2$ notation to give the electronic configurations for the following elements:
   a   vanadium ($Z = 23$)
   b   copper ($Z = 29$)
   c   selenium ($Z = 34$)

Orbitals and the Periodic Table

The arrangement of elements in the Periodic Table reflects the electronic structure of the elements. The Periodic Table can be split into blocks of elements (Figure **3.10**).

• Elements in Groups I and II have outer electrons in an s sub-shell.
• Elements in Groups III to 0 (apart from He) have outer electrons in a p sub-shell.
• Elements that add electrons to the d sub-shells are called the d-block elements. Most of these are transition elements.

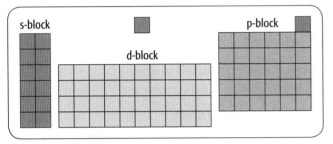

Figure 3.10 Some of the blocks of elements in the Periodic Table.

Filling the orbitals

A useful way of representing electronic configurations is a diagram which places electrons in boxes (Figure **3.11**).

• Each box represents an atomic orbital.
• The boxes (orbitals) can be arranged in order of increasing energy from bottom to top.
• An electron is represented by an arrow.
• The direction of the arrow represents the 'spin' of the electron. (We imagine an electron rotating around its own axis either in a clockwise or anticlockwise direction).
• When there are two electrons in an orbital, the 'spins' of the electrons are opposite so the two arrows in this box point in opposite directions.

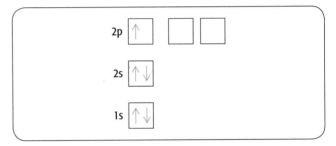

Figure 3.11 The electronic configuration of boron in box form.

Electrons in the same region of space repel each other because they have the same charge. So wherever possible, electrons will occupy separate orbitals in the same sub-shell to minimise this repulsion. These electrons have their 'spin' in the same direction. Electrons are only paired when there are no more empty orbitals available within a sub-level. The spins are then opposite to minimise repulsion. Figure **3.12** shows the electronic structures of carbon, nitrogen and oxygen to illustrate these points.

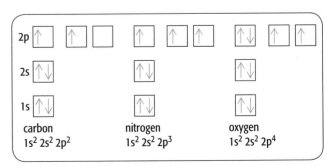

Figure 3.12 When adding electrons to a particular sub-shell, the electrons are only paired when no more empty orbitals are available.

Electronic configuration of ions

Positive ions are formed when electrons are removed from atoms. The sodium ion, Na^+ (proton number = 11) has 10 electrons. So, its electron configuration is $1s^2 2s^2 2p^6$. Note that this is the same as the electron configuration of neon, the element with 10 electrons in each atom.

Negative ions are formed when atoms gain electrons. The sulfide ion, S^{2-} (proton number = 16) has 18 electrons. Its electron configuration is $1s^2 2s^2 2p^6 3s^2 3p^6$, which is the same as argon, the element with 18 electrons in each atom.

Notice that, in general, it is the electrons in the outer sub-shell that are removed when ions are formed. However, the d-block elements behave slightly differently. Reading across the Periodic Table from potassium to zinc the 4s sub-shell fills before the 3d sub-shell. But when atoms of a d-block element lose electrons to form ions it is the 4s electrons which are lost first. For example:

Ti atom: $1s^2 2s^2 2p^6 3s^2 3p^6 3d^2 4s^2$
$\rightarrow Ti^{2+}$ ion: $1s^2 2s^2 2p^6 3s^2 3p^6 3d^2$

Cr atom: $1s^2 2s^2 2p^6 3s^2 3p^6 3d^5 4s^1$
$\rightarrow Cr^{3+}$ ion: $1s^2 2s^2 2p^6 3s^2 3p^6 3d^3$

Check-up

9 Write electronic configurations for the following ions:
  a Al^{3+} ($Z = 13$)
  b O^{2-} ($Z = 8$)
  c Fe^{3+} ($Z = 26$)
  d Cu^{2+} ($Z = 29$)
  e Cu^+ ($Z = 29$)

3.5 Patterns in ionisation energies in the Periodic Table

Patterns across a period

Figure 3.13 shows how the first ionisation energy, ΔH_{i1}, changes across the first two periods. We can explain the form of the graph mainly by referring to the three things that influence ionisation energies (see page 35).

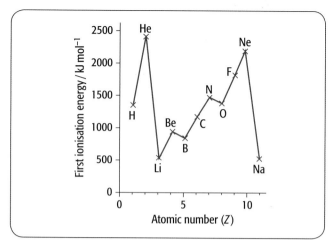

Figure 3.13 A graph of the first ionisation energies of the elements hydrogen to sodium plotted against atomic number.

1 There is a general increase in ΔH_{i1} across a period. This applies to Period 1 (hydrogen and helium), Period 2 (lithium to neon) and also to other periods. As you go across a period the nuclear charge increases. But the electron removed comes from the same shell. So, the force of attraction between the positive nucleus and the outer negative electrons increases across the period because:
  i the nuclear charge increases
  ii the distance between the nucleus and the outer electron remains reasonably constant
  iii the shielding by inner shells remains reasonably constant.
2 There is a rapid decrease in ionisation energy between the last element in one period and the first element in the next period. The ΔH_{i1} for lithium is much smaller than the ΔH_{i1} for helium. Helium has two electrons. These are in the first quantum shell. But lithium has three electrons. The third electron must go into the next quantum shell further away from the nucleus. So, the force of attraction between the positive nucleus and the outer negative electrons decreases because:
  i the distance between the nucleus and the outer electron increases
  ii the shielding by inner shells increases
  iii these two factors outweigh the increased nuclear charge.
3 There is a slight decrease in ΔH_{i1} between beryllium and boron. Although boron has one more proton than beryllium, there is a slight decrease in ΔH_{i1} on removal

of the outer electron. Beryllium has the electronic structure $1s^2 2s^2$ and boron has the electronic structure $1s^2 2s^2 2p^1$. The fifth electron in boron must be in the 2p sub-shell, which is slightly further away from the nucleus than the 2s sub-shell. There is less attraction between the fifth electron in boron and the nucleus because:

i the distance between the nucleus and the outer electron increases slightly
ii the shielding by inner shells increases slightly
iii these two factors outweigh the increased nuclear charge.

4 There is a slight decrease in ΔH_{i1} between nitrogen and oxygen. Oxygen has one more proton than nitrogen and the electron removed is in the same 2p sub-shell. So, you might think that ΔH_{i1} would increase. However, the spin-pairing of the electrons plays a part here. If you look back at Figure **3.12**, you will see that the electron removed from the nitrogen is from an orbital which contains an unpaired electron. The electron removed from the oxygen is from the orbital which contains a pair of electrons. The extra repulsion between the pair of electrons in this orbital results in less energy being needed to remove an electron. So, ΔH_{i1} for oxygen is lower, because of **spin-pair repulsion**.

These patterns repeat themselves across the third period. However, the presence of the d-block elements in Period 4 disrupts the pattern, since d-block elements have first ionisation energies which are relatively similar and fairly high.

Patterns down a group

The first ionisation energy decreases as you go down a group in the Periodic Table. For example, in Group I the values of ΔH_{i1} are:

- Li = $519\,kJ\,mol^{-1}$
- Na = $494\,kJ\,mol^{-1}$
- K = $418\,kJ\,mol^{-1}$
- Rb = $403\,kJ\,mol^{-1}$

As you go down the group, the outer electron removed is from the same type of orbital but from a successively higher principal quantum level – 2s from lithium, 3s for sodium and 4s for potassium. Although the nuclear charge is increasing down the group there is less attraction between the outer electron and the nucleus because

i the distance between the nucleus and the outer electron increases
ii the shielding by complete inner shells increases
iii these two factors outweigh the increased nuclear charge.

Check-up

10 a The first ionisation energies of four consecutive elements in the Periodic Table are:
sodium = $494\,kJ\,mol^{-1}$
magnesium = $736\,kJ\,mol^{-1}$
aluminium = $577\,kJ\,mol^{-1}$
silicon $786\,kJ\,mol^{-1}$
 i Explain the general increase in ionisation energies from sodium to silicon.
 ii Explain why aluminium has a lower first ionisation energy than magnesium.
b The first ionisation energy of fluorine is $1680\,kJ\,mol^{-1}$ whereas the first ionisation energy of iodine is $1010\,kJ\,mol^{-1}$. Explain why fluorine has a higher first ionisation energy than iodine despite it having a smaller nuclear charge.

Summary

- Electrons in an atom can exist only in certain energy levels (shells) outside the nucleus.
- The main energy levels (shells) are given principal quantum numbers $n = 1, 2, 3, 4$, etc. The lowest energy level ($n = 1$) is closest to the nucleus.
- The shells may be divided into sub-shells known as s, p and d sub-shells, which can hold a maximum of 2, 6 and 10 electrons respectively.
- The region of space where an electron is likely to be found is called an orbital. Each sub-shell has a number of orbitals which can each hold a maximum of two electrons. Sub-shells s, p and d have 1, 3 and 5 orbitals respectively.
- The s orbitals are spherical in shape. The p orbitals have two 'lobes'.
- When two electrons are present in an orbital they spin in opposite directions and are said to be paired.
- The electronic configuration of atoms is found by adding electrons to each orbital starting from those in the lowest energy level.
- When electrons are added to orbitals in the same sub-shell they go into separate orbitals if possible. Electrons pair up where this is not possible.
- The 1st ionisation energy of an element is the energy needed to remove one electron from each atom in one mole of atoms of the element in the gaseous state (to form gaseous 1+ ions).
- The ionisation energies needed to remove the first, second, third, fourth, etc., electrons from each atom or ion in a mole of gaseous atoms are called successive ionisation energies.
- The magnitude of the ionisation energy depends on these four factors:
  - the distance of the electron from the nucleus
  - the number of positive charges in the nucleus
  - the degree of shielding of outer electrons by inner electron shells
  - spin-pair repulsion.
- The trends in 1st ionisation energy of the elements across a period and down a group can be explained using the four factors above.
- Values of successive ionisation energies of atoms provide evidence for their electronic configuration.

End-of-chapter questions

1 The sketch graph shows the 13 successive ionisation energies of aluminium.

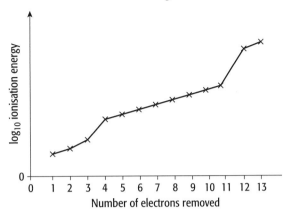

    a Define the term **1st ionisation energy**. [3]

    b How does the graph provide evidence for the existence of three electron shells in an aluminium atom? [6]

    c Write an equation, including state symbols, to represent the 2nd ionisation energy of aluminium. [2]

    d Write the electronic configuration of an aluminium ion, Al^{3+}, using $1s^2$ notation. [1]

                                                               Total = 12

2 The table below shows the 1st ionisation energies, ΔH_{i1}, in $kJ\,mol^{-1}$, of the elements in Period 3 of the Periodic Table.

Element	Na	Mg	Al	Si	P	S	Cl	Ar
ΔH_{i1}	494	736	577	786	1060	1000	1260	1520

    a Explain why there is a **general** increase in the value of ΔH_{i1} across the Period. [4]

    b Explain why aluminium has a lower value of ΔH_{i1} than magnesium. [4]

    c Write the electronic configuration for argon ($Z = 18$) using $1s^2$ notation. [1]

    d Copy and complete the diagram below for the 15 electrons in phosphorus by

       i adding labels for the other sub-shells [1]

      ii showing how the electrons are arranged. [3]

$$1s\quad \boxed{\uparrow\downarrow}$$

    e Predict a value for the 1st ionisation energy for potassium, which has one more proton than argon. [1]

                                                               Total = 14

3   **a** What do you understand by the term **atomic orbital**?   [1]
   b Draw diagrams to show the shape of:
      i an s orbital   [1]
      ii a p orbital.   [1]
   c Element **X** has the electronic configuration $1s^2 2s^2 2p^6 3s^2 3p^6 3d^8 4s^2$.
      i Which block in the Periodic Table does element **X** belong to?   [1]
      ii State the maximum number of electrons in a d sub-shell.   [1]
      iii Element **X** forms an ion of type **X**$^{2+}$.
        Write the full electronic configuration for this ion using $1s^2$ notation.   [1]
      iv Write the symbol for the sub-shell which begins to fill after the 3d and 4s are completely full.   [1]

                                                       Total = 7

4   The 1st ionisation energies of several elements with consecutive atomic numbers are shown in the graph below. The letters are not the symbols of the elements.

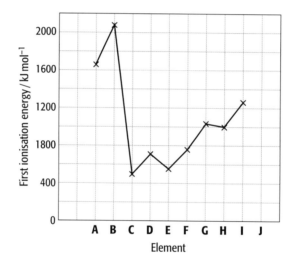

   a Which of the elements **A** to **I** belong to Group I in the Periodic Table? Explain your answer.   [3]
   b Which of the elements **A** to **I** could have the electronic configuration $1s^2 2s^2 2p^6 3s^2$?   [1]
   c Explain the rise in 1st ionisation energy between element **E** and element **G**.   [4]
   d Estimate the 1st ionisation energy of element **J**.   [2]

e The successive ionisation energies of element **A** are shown in the sketch graph.

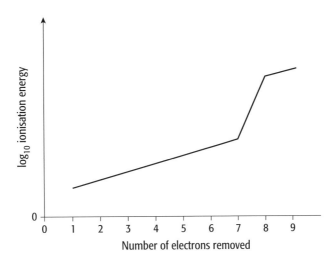

What information does this graph give about how the electrons are arranged in shells for element **A**?   [3]

Total = 13

5 **a** Define the following:
   i   1st ionisation energy   [3]
   ii 3rd ionisation energy.   [3]
   b Give the equations representing:
   i   the 1st ionisation energy of magnesium   [2]
   ii the 3rd ionisation energy of magnesium.   [2]
   c Which ionisation energies are represented by the equations below?
   i $Mg^{3+}(g) \rightarrow Mg^{4+}(g) + e^-$ [1]
   ii $Al^{5+}(g) \rightarrow Al^{6+}(g) + e^-$ [1]

Total = 12

6 The graph shows a sketch of $\log_{10}$ ionisation energy against number of electrons removed for magnesium. Use this sketch graph to answer the following questions.

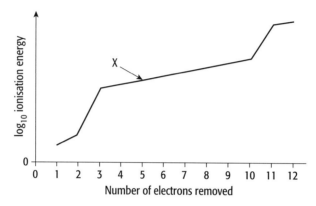

a Explain why the first two electrons are relatively easy to remove. [3]
b Why is there a sharp rise in ionisation energy when the third electron is removed? [3]
c What information does the graph give about the electron arrangement of magnesium? [3]
d Give the equation for the ionisation energy marked **X** (the 5th ionisation energy). [2]

Total = 11

7 a The table shows the first six ionisation energies for five elements (**A** to **E**). For each one state which group the element belongs to. [5]

Element	Ionisation energy / kJ mol^{-1}				
	1st	**2nd**	**3rd**	**4th**	**5th**
A	786.5	1577.1	3231.6	4355.5	16091
B	598.8	1145.4	4912	6491	8153
C	496	4562	6910	9543	13354
D	1087	2353	4621	6223	37831
E	578	1817	2744	11577	14842

b Explain your reasoning behind your answer for element **E**. [1]
c Draw a sketch graph to show how $\log_{10}$ ionisation energy for phosphorus (atomic number 15) varies when plotted against number of electrons removed. [6]

Total = 12

8 a Define the term **1st ionisation energy**. [3]
b Draw a sketch graph to show how $\log_{10}$ ionisation energy for chlorine (atomic number 17), varies when plotted against number of electrons removed. [6]
c Explain the shape of the graph you have drawn. [6]

Total = 15

Learning outcomes

Candidates should be able to:

- ☐ describe ionic (electrovalent) bonding, as in sodium chloride and magnesium oxide, including the use of 'dot-and-cross' diagrams
- ☐ describe covalent bonding, as in hydrogen, oxygen, chlorine, hydrogen chloride, carbon dioxide, methane and ethene, including the use of 'dot-and-cross' diagrams
- ☐ describe co-ordinate (dative covalent) bonding, as in the formation of the ammonium ion and in the Al_2Cl_6 molecule, including the use of 'dot-and-cross' diagrams
- ☐ explain the shapes of, and bond angles in, molecules by using the qualitative model of electron-pair repulsion (including lone pairs), using as simple examples: BF_3 (trigonal), CO_2 (linear), CH_4 (tetrahedral), NH_3 (pyramidal), H_2O (non-linear), SF_6 (octahedral)
- ☐ describe covalent bonding in terms of orbital overlap, giving σ and π bonds
- ☐ explain the shape of, and bond angles in, ethane and ethene
- ☐ predict the shapes of, and bond angles in, molecules similar to those stated above

- ☐ explain the terms bond energy, bond length and bond polarity and use them to compare the reactivities of covalent bonds
- ☐ describe intermolecular forces (including van der Waals' forces) based on permanent and induced dipoles, as in $CHCl_3(l)$, $Br_2(l)$ and the liquid noble gases
- ☐ describe hydrogen bonding, using ammonia and water as simple examples of molecules containing N—H and O—H groups
- ☐ describe metallic bonding in terms of a lattice of positive ions surrounded by mobile electrons
- ☐ describe, interpret and/or predict the effect of different types of bonding (ionic, covalent, metallic, hydrogen bonding and other intermolecular attractions) on the physical properties of substances
- ☐ deduce the type of bonding present from given information.

4.1 Introduction: types of chemical bonding

In Chapter 3 we looked at the electron configuration of individual atoms. We can use these electron configurations to help us understand what happens

Figure 4.1 This sodium chloride (salt) has been extracted from the ground. Sodium chloride is an ionic compound.

when atoms combine to form compounds. The complete **transfer** of one or more electrons from one atom to a different atom leads to the formation of an ionic bond. When outer electrons are **shared** a covalent bond is formed. The ionic or covalent bonds formed are usually very strong – it takes a lot of energy to break them. There is also a third form of strong bonding: metallic bonding.

Although the atoms within molecules are kept together by strong covalent bonds, the forces between molecules are weak. We call these weak forces, **intermolecular forces**.

There are several types of intermolecular forces:

- van der Waals' forces (also called 'dispersion forces' and 'temporary dipole–induced dipole forces')
- permanent dipole–dipole forces
- hydrogen bonds.

An understanding of these different types of chemical bonding and an understanding of intermolecular forces helps us to explain the structure and physical properties of elements and compounds.

4.2 Ionic bonding

How are ions formed?

Ions are formed when atoms lose or gain electrons.

- Positive ions are formed when an atom loses one or more electrons. Metal atoms usually lose electrons and form positive ions.
- Negative ions are formed when an atom gains one or more electrons. Non-metal atoms usually gain electrons and form negative ions.

The charge on the ion depends on the number of electrons lost or gained (see page **29**).

When metals combine with non-metals, the electrons in the outer shell of the metal atoms are transferred to the non-metal atoms. Each non-metal atom usually gains enough electrons to fill its outer shell. As a result of this, the metal and non-metal atoms usually end up with outer electron shells which are complete – they have an electron configuration of a noble gas.

In Figure 4.2 we can see that:

- the sodium ion has the electronic structure [2,8]$^+$, the same as that of neon
- the chloride ion has the electronic structure [2,8,8]$^-$, the same as that of argon.

Fact file

The idea that ions have a noble gas electron configuration was first put forward by the German physicist Walther Kossel in 1916. In the same year the American chemist Gilbert Lewis came up with the same idea independently.

The strong force of attraction between the oppositely charged positive and negative ions results in an **ionic bond**. An ionic bond is sometimes called an **electrovalent bond**. In an ionic structure, the ions are arranged in a regular repeating pattern (see Chapter 5). As a result of this, the force between one ion and the ions of opposite charge which surround it is very great. In other words, ionic bonding is very strong.

Dot-and-cross diagrams

You will notice that in Figure 4.2, we used dots and crosses to show the electronic configuration of the chloride and sodium ions. This helps us keep track of where the electrons have come from. It does not mean that the electron transferred is any different from the others. Diagrams like this are called **dot-and-cross diagrams**.

When drawing a dot-and-cross diagram for an ionic compound it is usually acceptable to draw the outer electron shell of the metal ion without any electrons. This is because it has transferred these electrons to the negative ion. Figure 4.4 shows the outer shell dot-and-cross diagram for sodium chloride.

A dot-and-cross diagram shows:

- the outer electron shells only
- that the charge of the ion is spread evenly, by using square brackets
- the charge on each ion, written at the top right-hand corner of the square brackets.

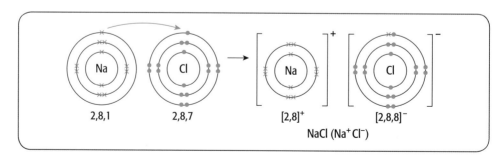

Figure 4.2 The formation of a sodium ion and chloride ion by electron transfer.

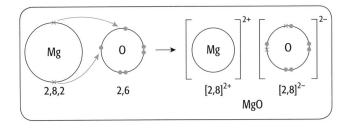

Figure 4.5 Dot-and-cross diagram for magnesium oxide.

Calcium chloride

Each calcium atom has two electrons in its outer shell and these can be transferred to two chlorine atoms. By losing two electrons, each calcium atom achieves the electron configuration [2,8,8] (Figure 4.6). The two chlorine atoms each gain one electron to achieve the electron configuration [2,8,8]. [2,8,8] is the electron configuration of argon; it is a 'noble-gas configuration'.

Figure 4.3 These crystals of salt are made up of millions of sodium ions and chloride ions.

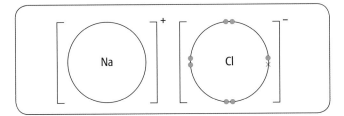

Figure 4.4 Dot-and-cross diagram for sodium chloride.

Some examples of dot-and-cross diagrams

Magnesium oxide

When magnesium reacts with oxygen to form magnesium oxide the two electrons in the outer shell of each magnesium atom are transferred to the incompletely filled orbitals of an oxygen atom. By losing two electrons, each magnesium atom achieves the electron configuration [2,8] (Figure 4.5). By gaining two electrons, each oxygen atom achieves the electron configuration [2,8]. [2,8] is the electron configuration of neon; it is a 'noble-gas configuration'.

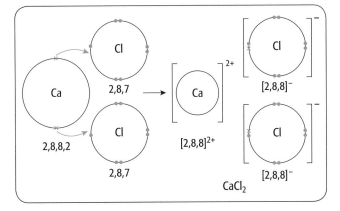

Figure 4.6 Dot-and-cross diagram for calcium chloride.

Check-up

1 Draw dot-and-cross diagrams for the following ionic compounds. Show only the outer electron shells.
   a Potassium chloride, KCl
   b Sodium oxide, Na_2O
   c Calcium oxide, CaO
   d Magnesium chloride, $MgCl_2$

4.3 Covalent bonding

Single covalent bonds

When two non-metal atoms combine, they share one, or more, pairs of electrons. A shared pair of electrons is called a single **covalent bond**, or a bond pair. A single covalent bond is represented by a single line between the atoms. For example, Cl–Cl.

You can see that when chlorine atoms combine not all the electrons are used in bonding. The pairs of outer-shell electrons not used in bonding are called **lone pairs**. Each atom in a chlorine molecule has three lone pairs of electrons and shares one bonding pair of electrons (Figure 4.8).

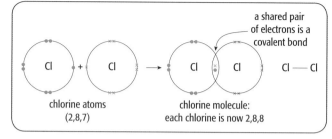

Figure 4.8 Atoms of chlorine share electrons to form a single covalent bond.

When drawing the arrangement of electrons in a molecule we
- use a 'dot' for electrons from one of the atoms and a 'cross' for the electrons from the other atom
- if there are more than two types of atom we can use additional symbols such as a small circle or a small triangle
- we draw the outer electrons in pairs, to emphasise the number of bond pairs and the number of lone pairs.

Some examples of dot-and-cross diagrams for simple covalently bonded molecules are shown in Figure 4.9.

There are some cases where the electrons around a central atom may not have a noble gas configuration. For example:
- boron trifluoride, BF_3, has only six electrons around the boron atom; we say that the boron atom is 'electron deficient'
- sulfur hexafluoride, SF_6, has twelve electrons around the central sulfur atom; we say that the sulfur atom has an 'expanded octet' (Figure 4.10).

Figure 4.7 (a) Bromine and (b) iodine are elements. They both have simple covalent molecules.

Fact file

One of the first people to suggest that particles of matter are fixed together by forces was the English scientist, Isaac Newton. He first suggested this in 1685.

Check-up

2 Draw dot-and-cross diagrams for the following covalently bonded molecules. Show only the outer electron shells. Note that in part **d** the beryllium atom is electron deficient and in part **e** the phosphorus atom has an expanded octet.
   a Tetrachloromethane, CCl_4
   b Phosphorus(III) chloride
   c Bromine, Br_2
   d Beryllium chloride, $BeCl_2$
   e Phosphorus(V) chloride, PCl_5

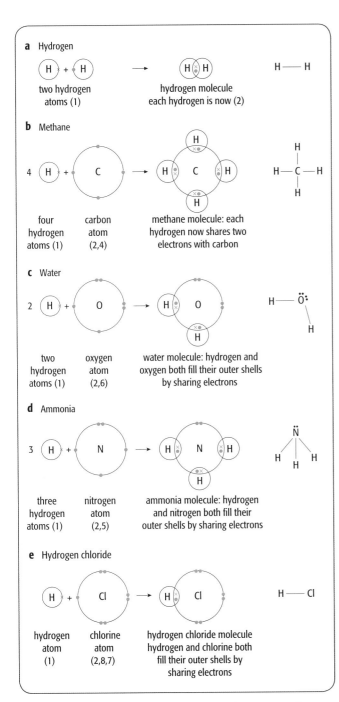

Figure 4.9 Dot-and-cross diagrams for some covalent compounds:
a hydrogen, H_2, **b** methane, CH_4, **c** water, H_2O, **d** ammonia, NH_3, and
e hydrogen chloride, HCl.

Multiple covalent bonds

Some atoms can bond together by sharing two pairs of
electrons. We call this a **double covalent bond**. A double
covalent bond is represented by a double line between the
atoms. For example, O=O. The dot-and-cross diagrams
for oxygen, carbon dioxide and ethene, all of which have
double covalent bonds, are shown in Figure 4.11.

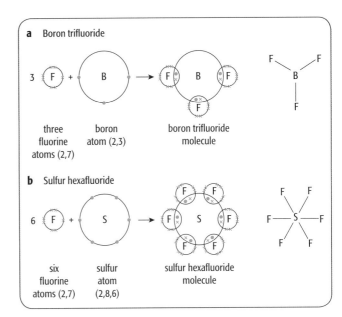

Figure 4.10 Dot-and-cross diagrams for **a** boron trifluoride, BF_3, and **b**
sulfur hexafluoride, SF_6.

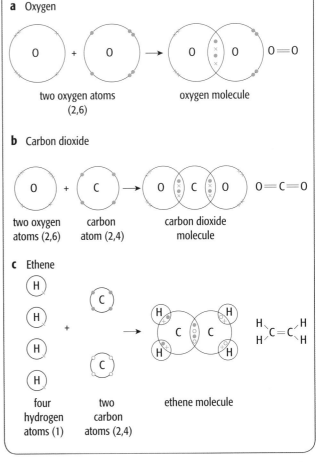

Figure 4.11 Dot-and-cross diagrams for **a** oxygen, O_2, **b** carbon dioxide,
CO_2, and **c** ethene, C_2H_4.

- In order to form an oxygen molecule, each oxygen atom needs to gain two electrons to complete its outer shell. So two pairs of electrons are shared and two covalent bonds are formed.
- For carbon dioxide, each oxygen atom needs to gain two electrons as before. But the carbon atom needs to gain four electrons to complete its outer shell. So two oxygen atoms each form two bonds with carbon, so that the carbon atom has eight electrons around it.
- In ethene, two hydrogen atoms share a pair of electrons with each carbon atom. This leaves each carbon atom with two outer shell electrons for bonding with each other. A double bond is formed.

Atoms can also bond together by sharing three pairs of electrons. We call this a **triple covalent bond**. Figure 4.12 shows a dot-and-cross diagram for the triple-bonded nitrogen molecule.

In order to form a nitrogen molecule, each nitrogen atom needs to gain three electrons to complete its outer shell. So three pairs of electrons are shared and three covalent bonds are formed.

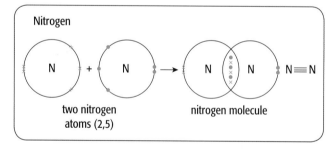

Figure 4.12 Dot-and-cross diagram for a nitrogen molecule, N_2.

Co-ordinate bonding (dative covalent bonding)

A **co-ordinate bond** (or **dative covalent bond**) is formed when one atom provides both the electrons needed for a covalent bond.

For dative covalent bonding we need:
- one atom having a lone pair of electrons
- a second atom having an unfilled orbital to accept the lone pair; in other words an electron-deficient compound.

An example of this is the ammonium ion, NH_4^+, formed when ammonia combines with a hydrogen ion, H^+. The hydrogen ion is electron deficient; it has space for two electrons in its shell. The nitrogen atom in the ammonia molecule has a lone pair of electrons. The lone pair on the nitrogen atom provides both electrons for the bond (Figure 4.13).

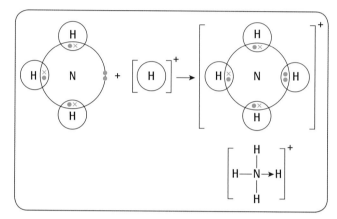

Figure 4.13 The formation of a co-ordinate bond in the ammonium ion.

In a displayed formula (which shows all atoms and bonds), a co-ordinate bond is represented by an arrow. The head of the arrow points away from the lone pair which forms the bond.

Another molecule which has co-ordinate bonds is aluminium chloride. At high temperatures aluminium chloride exists as molecules with the formula $AlCl_3$. This molecule is electron deficient; it still needs two electrons to complete the outer shell of the aluminium atom. At lower temperatures two molecules of $AlCl_3$ combine to form a molecule with the formula Al_2Cl_6. The $AlCl_3$ molecules are able to combine because lone pairs of electrons on two of the chlorine atoms form co-ordinate bonds with the aluminium atoms, as shown in Figure 4.14.

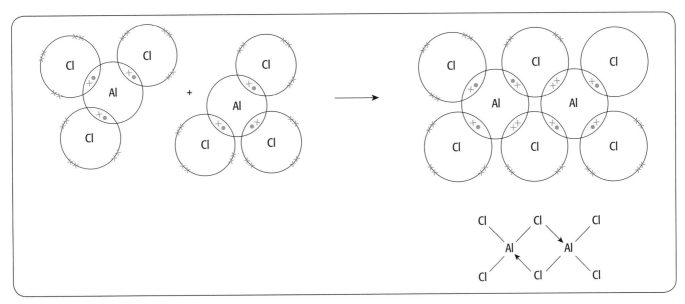

Figure 4.14 A dot-and-cross diagram for an aluminium chloride molecule, Al_2Cl_6.

Check-up

4 a Draw dot-and-cross diagrams to show the formation of a co-ordinate bond between the following:

    i boron trifluoride, BF_3, and ammonia, NH_3, to form the compound F_3BNH_3

    ii phosphine, PH_3, and a hydrogen ion, H^+, to form the ion PH_4^+.

b Draw the displayed formulae of the products formed in part **a**. Show the co-ordinate bond by an arrow.

Bond	Bond energy / kJ mol^{-1}	Bond length / nm
C—C	350	0.154
C=C	610	0.134
C—O	360	0.143
C=O	740	0.116

Table 4.1 Examples of values for bond energies and bond lengths.

Bond length and bond energy

In general, double bonds are shorter than single bonds. This is because double bonds have a greater quantity of negative charge between the two atomic nuclei. The greater force of attraction between the electrons and the nuclei pulls the atoms closer together. This results in a stronger bond. We measure the strength of a bond by its **bond energy**. This is the energy needed to break one mole of a given bond in a gaseous molecule (see also Chapter 6). Table 4.1 shows some values of bond lengths and bond energies.

Bond strength can influence the reactivity of a compound. The molecules in liquids and gases are in random motion so they are constantly colliding with each other. A reaction only happens between molecules when a collision occurs with enough energy to break bonds in either or both molecules. Nitrogen is unreactive because it has a triple bond, N≡N. It takes a lot of energy to break the nitrogen atoms apart; the bond energy required is 994 kJ mol^{-1}. Oxygen is much more reactive. Although it has a double bond, it only takes 496 kJ to break a mole of O=O bonds. However, bond strength is only one factor that influences the reactivity of a molecule. The polarity of the bond (see page **62**) and whether the bond is a σ bond (sigma bond) or a π bond (pi bond) (see page **58**) both play a large part in determining chemical reactivity.

5 The table lists bond lengths and bond energies of some hydrogen halides.

Hydrogen halide	Bond length / nm	Bond energy / kJ mol^{-1}
H—Cl	0.127	431
H—Br	0.141	366
H—I	0.161	299

a What is the relationship between the bond length and the bond energy for these hydrogen halides?
b Suggest why the bond energy values decrease in the order HCl > HBr > HI.
c Suggest a value for the bond length in hydrogen fluoride, HF.

4.4 Shapes of molecules

Electron-pair repulsion theory

Because all electrons have the same (negative) charge, they repel each other when they are close together. So, a pair of electrons in the bonds surrounding the central atom in a molecule will repel other electron pairs. This repulsion forces the pairs of electrons apart until the repulsive forces are minimised.

The shape and bond angles of a covalently bonded molecule depend on:
• the number of pairs of electrons around each atom
• whether these pairs are lone pairs or bonding pairs.

Lone pairs of electrons have a more concentrated electron charge cloud than bonding pairs of electrons. Their cloud charges are wider and slightly closer to the nucleus of the central atom. This results in a different amount of repulsion between different types of electron pairs. The order of repulsion is lone pair–lone pair (most repulsion) > lone pair–bond pair > bond pair–bond pair (least repulsion).

Figure 4.15 shows the repulsions between lone pairs (pink) and bonding pairs (white) in a water molecule.

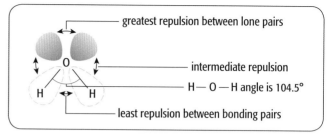

Figure 4.15 Repulsion between lone and bonding electron pairs in water.

Working out the shapes of molecules

The differences in electron-pair repulsion determine the shape and bond angles in a molecule. Figure 4.16 compares the shapes and bond angles of methane, ammonia and water. Space-filling models of these molecules are shown in Figure 4.17. Each of these molecules has four pairs of electrons surrounding the central atom. Note that in drawing three-dimensional diagrams, the triangular 'wedge' is the bond coming towards you and the dashed black line is the bond going away from you.

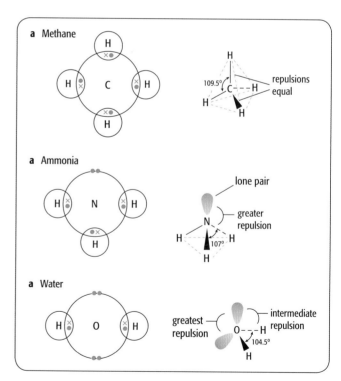

Figure 4.16 The bond angles in **a** methane, **b** ammonia and **c** water depend on the type of electron-pair repulsion.

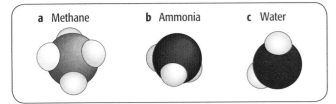

Figure 4.17 Shapes of molecules. These space-filling models show the molecular shapes of **a** methane, CH_4, **b** ammonia, NH_3, and **c** water, H_2O.

- Methane has four bonding pairs of electrons surrounding the central carbon atom. The equal repulsive forces of each bonding pair of electrons results in a tetrahedral structure with all H—C—H bond angles being 109.5°.

In ammonia and water, the tetrahedral arrangement of the electron pairs around the central atom becomes distorted.

- Ammonia has three bonding pairs of electrons and one lone pair. Since lone pair–bond pair repulsion is greater than bond pair–bond pair repulsion, the bonding pairs of electrons are pushed closer together. This gives the ammonia molecule a triangular pyramidal shape. The H—N—H bond angle is about 107°.

- Water has two bonding pairs of electrons and two lone pairs. The greatest electron pair repulsion is between the two lone pairs. This results in the bonds being pushed even closer together. The shape of the water molecule is a non-linear V shape. The H—O—H bond angle is 104.5°.

Check-up

6 a Predict the shapes of the following molecules, which you drew in Check-up 2 (page 52):
  i tetrachloromethane, CCl_4
  ii beryllium chloride, $BeCl_2$
  iii phosphorus(III) chloride.
  b Draw dot-and-cross diagrams for the following molecules and then predict their shapes:
  i hydrogen sulfide, H_2S
  ii phosphine, PH_3.

More molecular shapes

We can work out the shapes of other molecules by following the rules for electron-pair repulsion.

Boron trifluoride

Boron trifluoride is an electron-deficient molecule. It has only six electrons in its outer shell. The three bonding pairs of electrons repel each other equally, so the F—B—F bond angles are 120° (Figure 4.18). We describe the shape of the molecule as trigonal planar. 'Trigonal' means 'having three angles'.

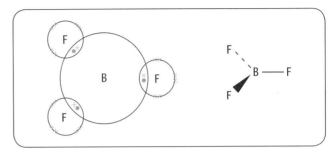

Figure 4.18 Boron trifluoride.

Carbon dioxide

Carbon dioxide has two carbon–oxygen double bonds and no lone pairs. The four electrons in each double bond repel other electrons in a similar way to the two electrons in a single bond (Figure 4.19). So, the O=C=O bond angle is 180°. We describe the shape of the carbon dioxide molecule as linear.

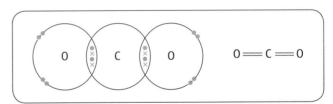

Figure 4.19 Carbon dioxide.

Fact file

A molecule of chlorine trifluoride, ClF_3, is described as trigonal pyramidal. This is because there are two lone pairs of electrons in each molecule, which repel each other more than the bond pairs do. The F—Cl—F bond angle is reduced to 87.5°:

Sulfur hexafluoride

Sulfur hexafluoride has six bonding pairs of electrons and no lone pairs. The equal repulsion between the electron pairs results in the structure shown in Figure 4.20. All F—S—F bond angles are 90°. We describe the shape as octahedral.

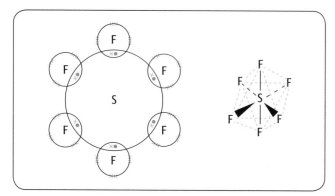

Figure 4.20 Sulfur hexafluoride.

Check-up

7 a Draw a dot-and-cross diagram for a molecule of selenium hexafluoride, SeF₆. A single selenium atom has six electrons in its outer shell.
  b Predict the shape of selenium hexafluoride.
  c Draw the shape of the phosphorus(V) chloride molecule that you drew as a dot-and-cross diagram in Check-up 2 (page 52).

σ bonds and π bonds

A single covalent bond is formed when two non-metal atoms combine. Each atom that combines has an atomic orbital containing a single unpaired electron. In the formation of a covalent bond the atomic orbitals overlap so that a combined orbital is formed, containing two electrons. We call this combined orbital a molecular orbital. The amount of overlap of the atomic orbitals determines the strength of the bond: the greater the overlap, the stronger the bond. Figure 4.21 shows how the s atomic orbitals of two hydrogen atoms overlap to form a covalent bond.

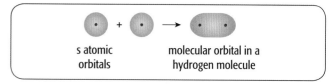

Figure 4.21 Two 1s atomic orbitals in hydrogen overlap to form a covalent bond.

The p atomic orbitals can also overlap to form covalent bonds. When p orbitals are involved in forming single bonds, they become modified to include some s orbital character. The orbital is slightly altered in shape to make one of the lobes of the p orbital bigger. When one of these modified p orbitals overlaps linearly (end-on) with an s orbital, or another modified p orbital, we call the bond a σ bond (**sigma bond**). Figure 4.22 shows the formation of σ bonds.

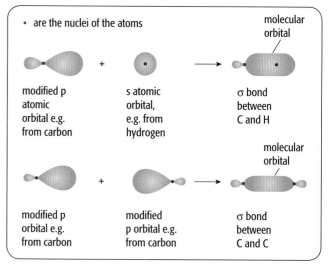

Figure 4.22 σ bonds are formed by the linear (end-on) overlap of atomic orbitals.

The electron density of each σ bond is symmetrical about a line joining the nuclei of the atoms forming the bond.

Bonds formed by the sideways overlap of p orbitals are called π bonds (**pi bonds**). A π bond is not symmetrical

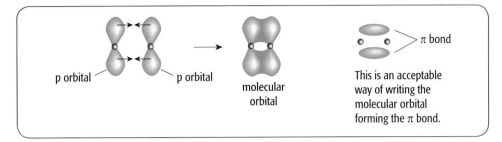

Figure 4.23 π bonds are formed by the sideways overlap of atomic orbitals.

about the axes joining the nuclei of the atoms forming the bond. Figure 4.23 shows how a π bond is formed from two p orbitals overlapping sideways.

We often draw a single π bond as two electron clouds, one arising from each lobe of the p orbitals. You must remember though, that the two clouds of electrons in a π bond represent one bond consisting of a total of two electrons.

The shape of some organic molecules

We can explain the shapes of molecules in terms of the patterns of electron density found in σ bonds and π bonds.

Ethane

The displayed formula for ethane is

```
      H   H
      |   |
  H — C — C — H
      |   |
      H   H
```

All the bonds in ethane are formed by linear overlap of atomic orbitals. They are all σ bonds.

Figure 4.24 shows the electron density distribution in ethane formed by these σ bonds. All the areas of electron density repel each other equally. This makes the H—C—H bond angles all the same (109.5°).

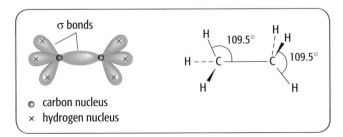

Figure 4.24 The electron density distribution in ethane.

Ethene

The displayed formula for ethene is

```
  H           H
   \         /
    C  ====  C
   /         \
  H           H
```

Each carbon atom in ethene uses three of its four outer electrons to form σ bonds. Two σ bonds are formed with the hydrogen atoms and one σ bond is formed with the other carbon atom.

The fourth electron from each carbon atom occupies a p orbital, which overlaps sideways with a similar p orbital on the other carbon atom. This forms a π bond. Figure 4.25 shows how this occurs.

The electron density distribution of both the σ and π bonds in ethene is shown in Figure 4.26.

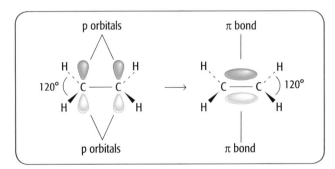

Figure 4.25 Overlap of p orbitals to produce a π bond in ethene.

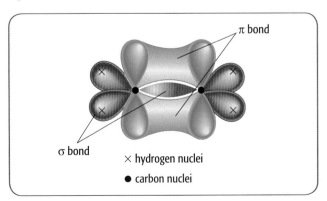

Figure 4.26 The electron density distribution in ethene.

Ethene is a planar molecule because this ensures the maximum overlap of the p orbitals which form the π bond. You will notice that the electron clouds which make up the π bond lie above and below the plane of the carbon and hydrogen nuclei. We would expect the H—C—H bond angle in ethene to be about 120° because the three areas of electron density of the σ bonds are equally distributed. However, because of the position of the π bond, this bond angle is actually 117°. This minimises the repulsive forces.

4.5 Metallic bonding

What is a metallic bond?

In a metal, the atoms are packed closely together in a regular arrangement called a lattice. Metal atoms in a lattice tend to lose their outer shell electrons and become positive ions. The outer shell electrons occupy new energy levels and are free to move throughout the metal lattice. We call these electrons **delocalised electrons**. Delocalised electrons are electrons which are not associated with any one particular atom or bond.

Metallic bonding is strong. This is because the ions are held together by the strong electrostatic attraction between their positive charges and the negative charges of the delocalised electrons (Figure 4.28). This electrostatic attraction acts in all directions. The strength of metallic bonding increases with:

- increasing positive charge on the ions in the metal lattice
- decreasing size of metal ions in the lattice
- increasing number of mobile electrons per atom.

Metallic bonding and the properties of metals

We can use our model of metallic bonding to explain many of the properties of metals.

Figure 4.27 Metals, clockwise from top left: sodium, gold, mercury, magnesium and copper.

Fact file

Why is mercury a liquid (Figure **4.29**)? Mercury atoms are bonded by metallic bonding – yet mercury is a liquid. This suggests that the metallic bonding is not particularly strong – but why? You can find out why mercury is a liquid by doing some research of your own. You could start by typing 'why is mercury a liquid' or 'relativistic contraction' into an internet search engine.

Most metals have high melting points and high boiling points

It takes a lot of energy to weaken the strong attractive forces between the metal ions and the delocalised electrons. These attractive forces can only be overcome at high temperatures.

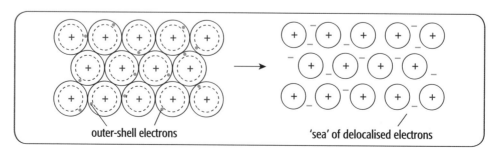

outer-shell electrons · 'sea' of delocalised electrons

Figure 4.28 Metallic bonding: there are strong attractive forces between the positively charged ions and the delocalised of electrons.

Figure 4.29 Mercury is a liquid at room temperature.

Metals conduct electricity

When a voltage is applied to a piece of metal, an electric current flows in it because the delocalised electrons are free to move. Metallic bonding is the only type of bonding that allows us to predict reliably that a solid will conduct electricity. Covalent solids cannot conduct electricity because none of their electrons are free to move, although graphite is an exception to this. Ionic solids cannot conduct because neither their electrons nor their ions are free to move.

Metals conduct heat

The conduction of heat is partly due to the movement of the delocalised electrons and partly due to the vibrations passed on from one metal ion to the next.

Check-up

8 Answer the following questions, giving a full explanation in terms of metallic bonding.
  a Explain why aluminium has a higher melting point than sodium.
  b The thermal conductivity of stainless steel is $82\,W\,m^{-1}\,K^{-1}$. The thermal conductivity

of copper is $400\,W\,m^{-1}\,K^{-1}$. Why do some stainless steel saucepans have a copper base?
  c Why does aluminium conduct electricity better than sodium?

4.6 Intermolecular forces

The forces within molecules due to covalent bonding are strong. However, the forces between molecules are much weaker. We call these forces **intermolecular forces**.

There are three types of intermolecular forces:
- van der Waals' forces (which are also called dispersion forces and temporary dipole–induced dipole forces)
- permanent dipole–dipole forces
- hydrogen bonding.

Table 4.2 compares the relative strength of these intermolecular forces and other bonds.

Type of bond	Bond strength / $kJ\,mol^{-1}$
ionic bonding in sodium chloride	760
O—H covalent bond in water	464
hydrogen bonding	20–50
permanent dipole–dipole force	5–20
van der Waals' forces	1–20

Table 4.2 Strength of different types of bond and intermolecular force.

In order to understand how intermolecular forces work, we first have to know about electronegativity and bond polarity.

Figure 4.30 The intermolecular forces in water allow some insects to skate over its surface.

Electronegativity

> **Electronegativity** is the ability of a particular atom, which is covalently bonded to another atom, to attract the bond pair of electrons towards itself.

The greater the value of the electronegativity, the greater is the power of an atom to attract the electrons in a covalent bond towards itself. For Groups I to VII the pattern of electronegativity is:
• electronegativity increases across a period from Group I to Group VII
• electronegativity increases up each group.
This means that fluorine is the most electronegative element.

For the most electronegative elements, the order of electronegativity is:

increasing electronegativity
$$\longrightarrow$$
Br < Cl < N < O < F

Carbon and hydrogen have electronegativities that are lower than those of most other non-metallic elements.

Polarity in molecules

When the electronegativity values of the two atoms forming a covalent bond are the same, the pair of electrons is equally shared. We say that the covalent bond is **non-polar**. For example, hydrogen (H_2), chlorine (Cl_2) and bromine (Br_2) are non-polar molecules.

When a covalent bond is formed between two atoms having different electronegativity values, the more electronegative atom attracts the pair of electrons in the bond towards it.

As a result:
• the centre of positive charge does not coincide with the centre of negative charge
• we say that the electron distribution is asymmetric
• the two atoms are partially charged
• we show
  – the less electronegative atom with the partial charge δ+ ('delta positive')
  – the more electronegative atom with the partial charge δ– ('delta negative')
• we say that the bond is **polar** (or that it has a **dipole**).

Figure 4.31 Hydrogen chloride is a polar molecule.

Figure 4.31 shows the polar bond in a hydrogen chloride molecule.

As the difference in electronegativity values of the atoms in a covalent bond increases, the bond becomes more polar. The degree of polarity of a molecule is measured as a dipole moment. The direction of the dipole is shown by the sign ⟼. The arrow points to the partially negatively charged end of the dipole.

In molecules containing more than two atoms, we have to take into account:
• the polarity of each bond
• the arrangement of the bonds in the molecule.
Trichloromethane, $CHCl_3$, is a polar molecule. The three C–Cl dipoles point in a similar direction. Their combined effect is not cancelled out by the polarity of the C–H bond. This is because the C–H bond is virtually non-polar. The electron distribution is asymmetric. The molecule is polar, with the negative end towards the chlorine atoms. This is shown in Figure 4.32a.

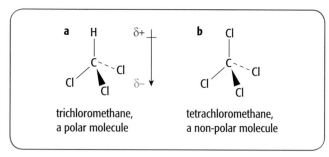

Figure 4.32 The polarity of **a** trichloromethane and **b** tetrachloromethane.

Some molecules contain polar bonds but have no overall polarity. This is because the polar bonds in these molecules are arranged in such as fashion that the dipoles cancel each other out. An example is tetrachloromethane, CCl_4 (Figure 4.32b). Tetrachloromethane has four polar C–Cl bonds pointing towards the four corners of a tetrahedron. The dipoles in each bond cancel each other. So, tetrachloromethane is non-polar.

Check-up

9   Are the following molecules polar or non-polar? In each case give a reason for your answer.
    (Electronegativity values: F = 4.0, Cl = 3.0, Br = 2.8, S = 2.5, C = 2.5, H = 2.1)
    a   Chlorine, Cl_2
    b   Hydrogen fluoride, HF
    c   The V-shaped molecule, sulfur dichloride, SCl_2
    d   The tetrahedral molecule, chloromethane, CH_3Cl
    e   The tetrahedral molecule tetrabromomethane, CBr_4

Polarity and chemical reactivity

Bond polarity influences chemical reactivity. For example, both nitrogen, $N\equiv N$, and carbon monoxide, $C\equiv O$, have triple bonds requiring a similar amount of energy to break them. Nitrogen is a non-polar molecule and is fairly unreactive. But carbon monoxide is a polar molecule and this explains its reactivity with oxygen and its use as a reducing agent. Many chemical reactions are started by a reagent attacking one of the electrically charged ends of a polar molecule. For example, chloroethane, C_2H_5Cl, is far more reactive than ethane, C_2H_6. This is because reagents such as OH^- ions can attack the delta positive carbon atom of the polarised C—Cl bond (see also page 233).

$$
\begin{array}{cccc}
& H & H & \\
& | & | & \\
H - & C - & C - & Cl \\
& | & | & \\
& H & H &
\end{array}
$$

(with $\delta+$ above the second C and $\delta-$ above the Cl)

Such an attack is not possible with ethane because the C—H bond is virtually non-polar. This helps to explain why alkanes, such as ethane, are not very reactive.

Van der Waals' forces

Noble gases such as neon and argon exist as isolated atoms. Noble gases can be liquefied, but at very low temperatures, so there must be very weak forces of attraction between their atoms. These weak forces keep the atoms together in the liquid state.

Bromine is a non-polar molecule that is liquid at room temperature. The weak forces of attraction are keeping the bromine molecules together at room temperature. These very weak forces of attraction are called **van der Waals' forces**. Van der Waals' forces exist between all atoms or molecules. So, how do van der Waals' forces arise?

The electron charge clouds in a non-polar molecule (or atom) are constantly moving. It often happens that more of the charge cloud is on one side of the molecule than the other. This means that one end of the molecule has, for a short moment, more negative charge than the other. A temporary dipole is set up. This dipole can set up (induce) a dipole on neighbouring molecules. As a result of this, there are forces of attraction between the $\delta+$ end of the dipole in one molecule and the $\delta-$ end of the dipole in a neighbouring molecule (Figure 4.33). These dipoles are always temporary because the electrons clouds are always moving. Van der Waals' forces are sometimes called temporary dipole–induced dipole forces.

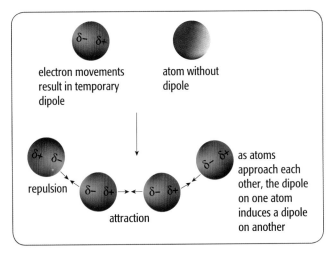

Figure 4.33 How van der Waals' forces arise.

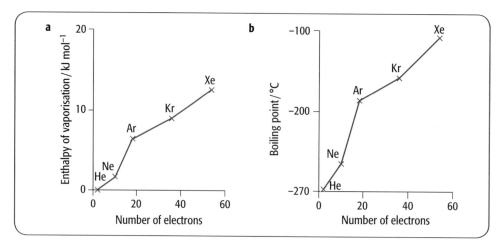

Figure 4.34 a Enthalpy changes of vaporisation and **b** boiling points of the noble gases plotted against the number of electrons present.

Van der Waals' forces increase with
- increasing number of electrons (and protons) in the molecule
- increasing the number of contact points between the molecules – contact points are places where the molecules come close together.

Differences in the size of the van der Waals' forces can be used to explain the trend in the enthalpy change of vaporisation and boiling points of the noble gases. Figure 4.34 shows how these vary with the number of electrons present. (The enthalpy change of vaporisation is the energy required to convert a mole of liquid into a mole of gas.)

You can see that both the enthalpy change of vaporisation and the boiling points of the noble gases increase as the number of electrons increases. This is because the van der Waals' forces between the atoms are increased with an increasing number of electrons. So, more energy is needed to change the liquid into vapour and the boiling point is higher.

The effect of increasing the number of contact points can be seen by comparing the boiling points of pentane (boiling point 36 °C) and 2,2-dimethylpropane (boiling point 10 °C) (Figure 4.35). These compounds have equal numbers of electrons in their molecules.

The molecules in pentane can line up beside each other so there are a large number of contact points. The van der Waals' forces are higher, so the boiling point is higher. The molecules of 2,2-dimethylpropane are more compact. The surface area available for coming into contact with neighbouring molecules is smaller. The van der Waals' forces are relatively lower, so the boiling point is lower.

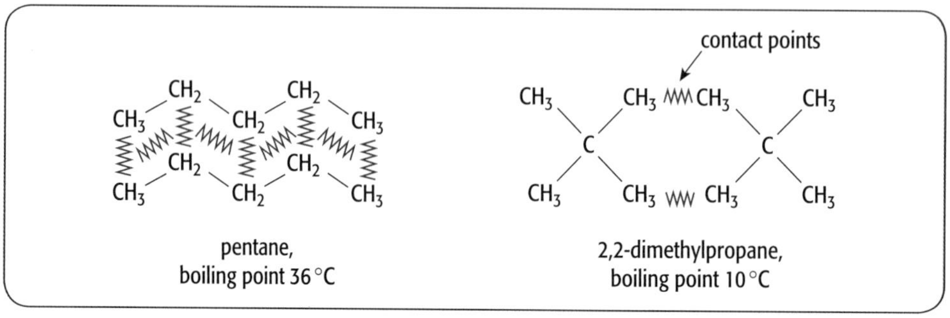

Figure 4.35 The difference in boiling points of pentane and 2,2-dimethylpropane can be explained by the strength of the van der Waals' forces.

The van der Waals' forces between individual atoms are very small. However, the total van der Waals' forces between very long non-polar molecules such as poly(ethene) molecules (see page 224) can be much larger. That is why poly(ethene) is a solid at room temperature.

Fact file

Two types of poly(ethene) are low-density poly(ethene), LDPE, and high-density poly(ethene), HDPE. Both have crystalline and non-crystalline regions in them (Figure **4.36**).

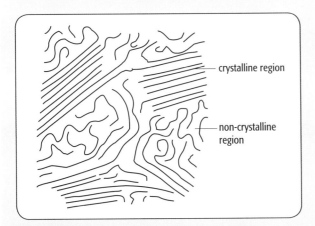

Figure 4.36 Crystalline and non-crystalline regions in poly(ethene).

HDPE has more crystalline regions where the molecules are closer together than LDPE. The total van der Waals' forces are greater in HDPE, so HDPE is the stronger of the two.

Check-up

10 a The boiling points of the halogens are:

fluorine   −188 °C
chlorine   −35 °C
bromine   +59 °C
iodine   +184 °C

  i Describe the trend in these boiling points going down Group VII.
  ii Explain the trend in these boiling points.

continued ⋯⋗

b The table lists the formulae and boiling points of some alkanes. Explain the trend in these boiling points.

Alkane	Structural formula	Boiling point / °C
methane	CH_4	−164
ethane	CH_3CH_3	−88
propane	$CH_3CH_2CH_3$	−42
butane	$CH_3CH_2CH_2CH_3$	0

Permanent dipole–dipole forces

In some molecules, the dipole is permanent. Molecules with a permanent dipole are called polar molecules. A fine jet of polar molecules will be attracted towards an electrically charged plastic rod or comb. (The rod can be charged by rubbing it with a woollen cloth.) Figure **4.37** shows the result of this experiment.

Figure 4.37 The deflection of water by an electrically charged nylon comb.

The molecules are always attracted to the charged rod, whether it is positively or negatively charged. This is because the molecules have both negatively and positively charged ends.

The forces between two molecules having permanent dipoles are called **permanent dipole–dipole forces**. The attractive force between the δ+ charge on one molecule and the δ– charge on a neighbouring molecule causes a weak attractive force between the molecules (Figure 4.38).

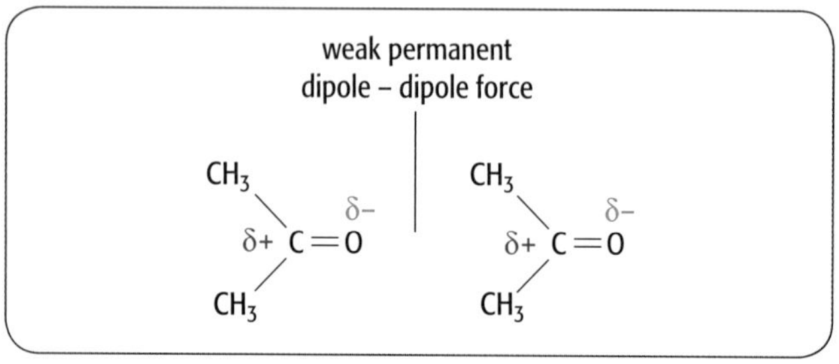

Figure 4.38 Dipole–dipole forces in propanone.

For small molecules with the same number of electrons, permanent dipole–dipole forces are often stronger than van der Waals' forces. For example, propanone (CH_3COCH_3, $M_r = 58$) has a higher boiling point than butane ($CH_3CH_2CH_2CH_3$, $M_r = 58$) (Figure 4.39). This means that more energy is needed to break the intermolecular forces between propanone molecules than between butane molecules.

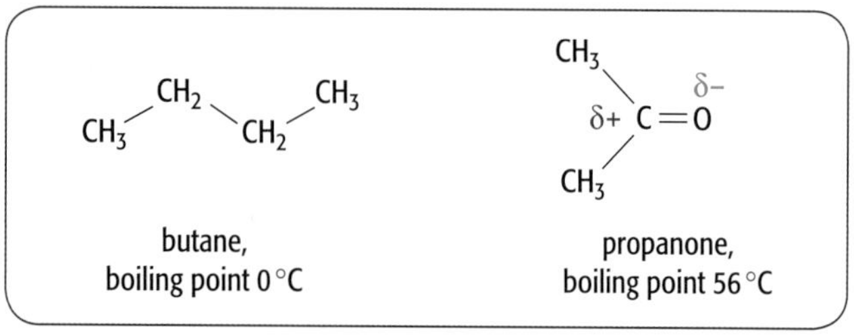

Figure 4.39 The difference in the boiling points of propanone and butane can be explained by the different types of intermolecular force between the molecules.

The permanent dipole–dipole forces between propanone molecules are strong enough to make this substance a liquid at room temperature. There are only van der Waals' forces between butane molecules. These forces are comparatively weak, so butane is a gas at room temperature.

Check-up

11 Bromine, Br_2, and iodine monochloride, ICl, have the same number of electrons. But the boiling point of iodine monochloride is nearly 40 °C higher than the boiling point of bromine. Explain this difference.

Hydrogen bonding

Hydrogen bonding is the strongest type of intermolecular force. For hydrogen bonding to occur between two molecules we need:
- one molecule having a hydrogen atom covalently bonded to F, O or N (the three most electronegative atoms)
- a second molecule having a F, O or N atom with an available lone pair of electrons.

When a hydrogen atom is covalently bonded to a very electronegative atom, the bond is very highly polarised. The δ+ charge on the hydrogen atom is high enough for a bond to be formed with a lone pair of electrons on the F, O or N atom of a neighbouring molecule (Figure 4.40). The force of attraction is about one-tenth of the strength of a normal covalent bond. For maximum bond strength, the angle between the covalent bond to the hydrogen atom and the hydrogen bond is usually 180°.

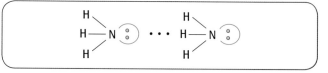

Figure 4.40 Hydrogen bonding between two ammonia molecules. A hydrogen bond is represented by a line of dots.

The average number of hydrogen bonds formed per molecule depends on:
- the number of hydrogen atoms attached to F, O or N in the molecule
- the number of lone pairs present on the F, O or N.

Water has two hydrogen atoms and two lone pairs per molecule (Figure 4.41). So water is extensively hydrogen bonded with other water molecules. It has an average of two hydrogen bonds per molecule.

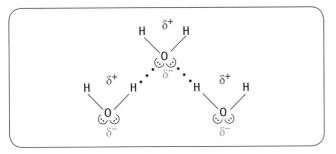

Figure 4.41 Water can form, on average, two hydrogen bonds per molecule.

Ammonia is less extensively hydrogen bonded than water (see Figure 4.40). It can form, on average, only one hydrogen bond per molecule. Although each ammonia molecule has three hydrogen atoms attached to the nitrogen atom, it has only one lone pair of electrons which can be involved in hydrogen bond formation.

Check-up

12 Draw diagrams to show hydrogen bonding between the following molecules:
  a ethanol, C_2H_5OH, and water
  b ammonia and water
  c two hydrogen fluoride molecules.

How does hydrogen bonding affect boiling point?

Some compounds may have higher boiling points than expected. This can be due to hydrogen bonding. Figure 4.42 shows a graph of the boiling points of the hydrogen halides, HF, HCl, HBr and HI, plotted against the position of the halogen in the Periodic Table.

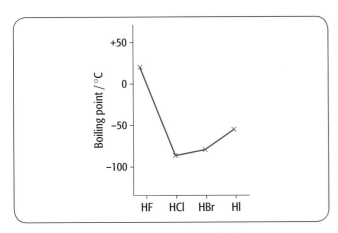

Figure 4.42 The boiling points of the hydrogen halides.

The rise in boiling point from HCl to HI is due to the increasing number of electrons in the halogen atoms as we go down the group. This leads to increased van der Waals' forces as the molecules get bigger. If hydrogen fluoride only had van der Waals' forces between its molecules, we would expect its boiling point to be about −90 °C. However, the boiling point of hydrogen fluoride is 20 °C, which is much higher. This is because of the stronger intermolecular forces of hydrogen bonding between the HF molecules.

Check-up

13 The table lists the boiling points of some Group V hydrides.

Hydride	Boiling point / °C
ammonia, NH_3	−33
phosphine, PH_3	−88
arsine, AsH_3	−55
stibine, SbH_3	−17

  a Explain the trend in the boiling points from phosphine to stibine.
  b Explain why the boiling point of ammonia does not follow this trend.

The peculiar properties of water

1 Enthalpy change of vaporisation and boiling point

Water has a much higher enthalpy change of vaporisation and boiling point than expected.

This is due to its extensive hydrogen bonding. Figure 4.43 shows the enthalpy changes of vaporisation of water and other Group VI hydrides.

The rise in enthalpy change of vaporisation from H_2S to H_2Te is due to the increasing number of electrons in the Group VI atoms as we go down the group. This leads to increased van der Waals' forces as the molecules get bigger. If water only had van der Waals' forces between its molecules, we would expect its enthalpy change to be about $17\,kJ\,mol^{-1}$. But the enthalpy change of vaporisation of water is much higher. This is because water is extensively hydrogen bonded. The boiling point of water is also much higher than predicted by the trend in boiling points for the other Group VI hydrides. This

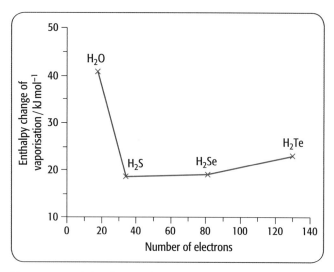

Figure 4.43 Enthalpy changes of vaporisation for Group VI hydrides plotted against number of electrons present.

Figure 4.44 Ice floats on water.

also indicates that much more energy is required to break the bonds between water molecules compared with other hydrides of Group VI elements.

2 Surface tension and viscosity

Water has a high surface tension and high viscosity.

Hydrogen bonding reduces the ability of water molecules to slide over each other, so the viscosity of water is high. The hydrogen bonds in water also exert a significant downward force at the surface of the liquid. This causes the surface tension of water to be higher than for most liquids.

Fact file

You can float a needle on water! Place a small piece of tissue paper on the surface of some water in a bowl. The water surface must be still. Place a needle on the tissue. The paper will sink slowly, leaving the needle to float. The hydrogen bonding in the water gives it a high surface tension. If you then add some detergent, the needle will sink.

3 Ice is less dense than water

Most solids are denser than their liquids. This is because the molecules are more closely packed in the solid state. But this is not true of water. In ice, there is a three-dimensional hydrogen-bonded network of water

molecules. This produces a rigid lattice in which each oxygen atom is surrounded by a tetrahedron of hydrogen atoms. This 'more open' arrangement allows the water molecules to be slightly further apart than in the liquid (Figure 4.45). So the density of ice is less than that of liquid water.

Figure 4.45 A model of ice. Oxygen atoms are red, hydrogen atoms are white, hydrogen bonds are lilac. This hydrogen-bonded arrangement makes ice less dense than water.

4.7 Bonding and physical properties

The type of bonding between atoms, ions or molecules influences the physical properties of a substance.

Physical state at room temperature and pressure

Ionic compounds

Ionic compounds are solids at room temperature and pressure. This is because:
- there are strong electrostatic forces (ionic bonds) holding the positive and negative ions together
- the ions are regularly arranged in a lattice (see Chapter 5), with the oppositely charged ions close to each other.

Ionic compounds have high melting points, high boiling points and high enthalpy changes of vaporisation. It takes a lot of energy to overcome the strong electrostatic attractive forces.

Metals

Metals, apart from mercury, are solids. Most metals have high melting points, high boiling points and high enthalpy changes of vaporisation. This is because it takes a lot of energy to overcome the strong attractive forces between the positive ions and the 'sea' of delocalised electrons.

Covalent compounds

Covalently bonded substances with a simple molecular structure, for example water and ammonia, are usually liquids or gases. This is because the forces between the molecules are weak. It does not take much energy to overcome these intermolecular forces, so these substances have low melting points, low boiling points and low enthalpy changes of vaporisation compared with ionic compounds. Some substances that have covalently bonded molecules may be solids at room temperature, for example iodine and poly(ethene). These are usually molecules where the van der Waals' forces are considerable. However, the melting points of these substances are still fairly low compared with ionic compounds or most metals.

Solubility

Ionic compounds

Most ionic compounds are soluble in water. This is because water molecules are polar and they are attracted to the ions on the surface of the ionic solid. These attractions are called ion–dipole attractions (see page 263). These attractions replace the electrostatic forces between the ions and the ions go into solution.

Metals

Metals do not dissolve in water. However, some metals, for example sodium and calcium, react with water.

Covalent compounds

Covalently bonded substances with a simple molecular structure fall into two groups.
- Those that are insoluble in water. Most covalently bonded molecules are non-polar. Water molecules are not attracted to them so they are insoluble. An example is iodine.
- Those that are soluble in water. Small molecules that can form hydrogen bonds with water are generally soluble. An example is ethanol, C_2H_5OH.

Some covalently bonded substances react with water rather than dissolving in it. For example, hydrogen chloride reacts with water to form hydrogen ions and chloride ions, and the ions are soluble. Silicon chloride reacts with water to form hydrogen ions, chloride ions and silicon dioxide. This reaction is called a hydrolysis reaction.

Electrical conductivity

Ionic compounds

Ionic compounds do not conduct electricity when in the solid state. This is because the ions are fixed in the lattice and are not free to move. When molten, an ionic compound conducts electricity because the ions are free to move.

Metals

Metals conduct electricity both when solid and when molten. This is because the delocalised electrons are free to move.

Covalent compounds

Covalently bonded substances with a simple molecular structure do not conduct electricity. This is because they have neither ions nor electrons which are free to move.

14 Explain the following differences in terms of the type of bonding present.

a Aluminium oxide has a melting point of 2980 °C but aluminium chloride changes to a vapour at 178 °C.

b Magnesium chloride conducts electricity when molten but not when solid.

continued ⋯⋗

c Iron conducts electricity when solid but the ionic solid iron(II) chloride does not conduct when solid.

d Sodium sulfate dissolves in water but sulfur does not.

e Propanol, $CH_3CH_2CH_2OH$, is soluble in water but propane, $CH_3CH_2CH_3$, is not.

f A solution of hydrogen chloride in water conducts electricity.

Summary

- [ ] Ions are formed when atoms gain or lose electrons.
- [ ] Ionic (electrovalent) bonding involves an attractive force between positively and negatively charged ions.
- [ ] A covalent bond is formed when atoms share a pair of electrons.
- [ ] When atoms form covalent or ionic bonds each atom or ion has a full outer electron shell of electrons. (Some covalent compounds may be electron deficient or have an 'expanded octet'.)
- [ ] Dot-and-cross diagrams can be drawn to show the arrangement of electrons in ionic and covalent compounds.
- [ ] In dative covalent bonding one atom provides both electrons in the formation of the covalent bond.
- [ ] The shapes and bond angles in molecules can be predicted using the idea that lone pairs of electrons repel other lone pairs more than bond pair electrons, and that bond pair to bond pair repulsion is least.
- [ ] σ bonds (sigma bonds) are formed by end-on overlap of atomic orbitals whereas π bonds (pi bonds) are formed by sideways overlap of p-type atomic orbitals.
- [ ] Three types of relatively weak intermolecular forces are hydrogen bonding, permanent dipole–dipole forces and van der Waals' forces.
- [ ] Electronegativity differences can be used to predict the type of weak intermolecular forces between molecules.
- [ ] Hydrogen bonding occurs between molecules that have a hydrogen atom covalently bonded to an atom of a very electronegative element (fluorine, oxygen or nitrogen).
- [ ] The reactivities of covalent bonds can be explained in terms of bond energy, bond length and bond polarity.
- [ ] Intermolecular forces are based on either permanent dipoles, as in $CHCl_3(l)$, or temporary induced dipoles (van der Waals' forces), as in $Br_2(l)$.
- [ ] Metallic bonding can be explained in terms of a lattice of positive ions surrounded by mobile electrons.
- [ ] The physical properties of substances may predicted from the type of bonding present.
- [ ] Substances with ionic bonding have high melting and boiling points, whereas simple molecules with covalent bonding have low melting points.
- [ ] The presence of hydrogen bonding in a molecule influences its melting point and boiling point.

End-of-chapter questions

1   The table shows the atomic number and boiling points of some noble gases.

Gas	helium	neon	argon	krypton	xenon
Atomic number	2	10	18	36	54
Boiling point / °C	–253	–246	–186	–152	–107

    a Use ideas about forces between atoms to explain this trend in boiling points.   [2]
    b Xenon forms a number of covalently bonded compounds with fluorine.
       i What do you understand by the term **covalent bond**?   [1]
       ii Draw a dot-and-cross diagram for xenon tetrafluoride, XeF_4.   [1]
       iii Suggest a shape for XeF_4. Explain why you chose this shape.   [3]
    c The structure of xenon trioxide is shown below.

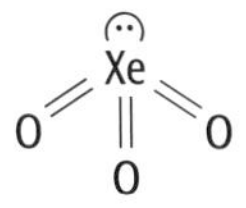

$$O = \overset{\displaystyle \overset{..}{Xe}}{\underset{\displaystyle O}{\|}} = O$$

       i By referring to electron pairs, explain why xenon trioxide has this shape.   [2]
       ii Draw the structure of xenon trioxide to show the partial charges on the atoms and the direction of the dipole in the molecule.   [2]

                                                                    Total = 11

2   Aluminium chloride, $AlCl_3$, and ammonia, NH_3, are both covalent molecules.
    a i Draw a diagram of an ammonia molecule, showing its shape. Show any lone pairs of electrons.   [3]

      ii State the bond angle $H—\overset{N}{\diagup \diagdown}—H$ in the ammonia molecule.   [1]
    b Explain why ammonia is a polar molecule.   [2]
    c An ammonia molecule and an aluminium chloride molecule can join together by forming a co-ordinate bond.
      i Explain how a co-ordinate bond is formed.   [1]
      ii Draw a dot-and-cross diagram to show the bonding in the compound formed between ammonia and aluminium chloride, H_3NAlCl_3.
        (Use a • for a nitrogen electron, a ∘ for an aluminium electron and an × for the hydrogen and chlorine electrons.)   [3]
    d Aluminium chloride molecules join together to form a compound with the formula Al_2Cl_6. Draw a displayed formula (showing all atoms and bonds) to show the bonding in one Al_2Cl_6 molecule. Show the dative covalent bonds by arrows.   [2]

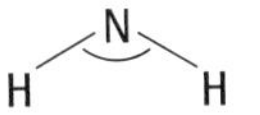

                                                                    Total = 12

3 Electronegativity values can be used to predict the polarity of bonds.

   a Explain the term **electronegativity**. [2]

   b The electronegativity values for some atoms are given below:

     H = 2.1, C = 2.5, F = 4.0, Cl = 3.0, I = 2.5

     Use these values to predict the polarity of each of the following bonds by copying the bonded atoms shown below and adding δ+ or δ– above each atom.

     i H—I

     ii F—I

     iii C—Cl [2]

   c The shape of iodine trichloride, ICl_3, is shown below.

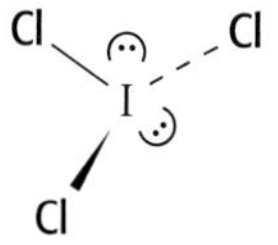

     i Describe the shape of this molecule. [2]

     ii Explain why the ICl_3 molecule has this shape. [2]

     iii Suggest a value for the Cl—I—Cl bond angle. [1]

   d The boiling points of the hydrogen halides are shown in the table.

Hydrogen halide	HF	HCl	HBr	HI
Boiling point / °C	+20	–85	–67	–35

     i Explain the trend in boiling points from HCl to HI. [2]

     ii Explain why the boiling point of HF is so much higher than the boiling point of HCl. [3]

   e Tetrachloromethane, CCl_4, is a non-polar molecule.

     i Draw a diagram to show the shape of this molecule. [2]

     ii Explain why this molecule is non-polar. [1]

                                        Total = 17

4 The diagram below shows part of a giant metallic structure.

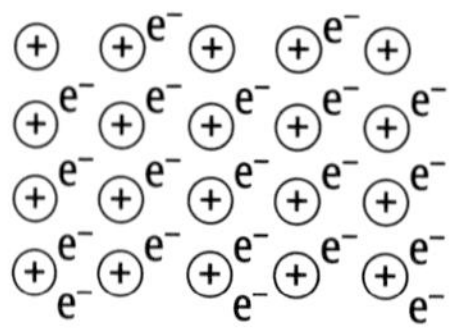

   a Use this diagram to explain the main features of metallic bonding. [3]

   b Explain why metals are good conductors of electricity. [2]

   c Explain why, in general, metals have high melting points. [2]

   d Suggest why potassium is a better conductor of electricity than lithium. [4]

                                        Total = 11

5 Methane, CH_4, is a gas at room temperature.

   a Explain why methane is a gas at room temperature. [2]

   b Draw a diagram to show the shape of a molecule of methane. On your diagram show a value for the

        C
       H   H   bond angle. [3]

   c Perfumes often contain molecules that have simple molecular structures. Explain why. [2]

   d When a negatively charged rod is held next to a stream of propanone, CH_3COCH_3, the stream of propanone is attracted to the rod.

      Draw the full structure of a molecule of propanone and use your diagram to explain why the stream of propanone is attracted to the rod. [3]

                                                        Total = 10

6 Sodium iodide and magnesium oxide are ionic compounds. Iodine and oxygen are covalent molecules.

   a Draw dot-and-cross diagrams for:

     i magnesium oxide

     ii oxygen. [2]

   b How do sodium iodide and iodine differ in their solubility in water? Explain your answer. [3]

   c Explain why molten sodium iodide conducts electricity but molten iodine does not. [2]

   d The boiling point of sodium iodide is 1304 °C. The boiling point of iodine is 184 °C. Explain this difference. [5]

                                                         Total = 12

7 Hydrogen sulfide, H_2S, is a covalent compound.

   a Draw a dot-and-cross diagram for hydrogen sulfide. [2]

   b Draw a diagram of a hydrogen sulfide molecule to show its shape. Show on your diagram:

     i the value of the   H   S   H   bond angle

     ii the partial charges on each atom as $\delta+$ or $\delta-$

     iii an arrow showing the exact direction of the dipole in the molecule as a whole. [4]

   c Oxygen, O, sulfur, S, and selenium, Se, are in the same group in the Periodic Table.

     i Explain why hydrogen selenide, H_2Se, has a higher boiling point than hydrogen sulfide, H_2S. [2]

     ii Explain why the boiling point of water is so much higher than the boiling point of hydrogen sulfide. [5]

                                                         Total = 13

8 The table shows the type of bonding in a number of elements and compounds.

Element or compound	Type of bonding
Fe, Na	metallic
NaCl, $MgCl_2$	ionic
CO_2, Br_2	covalent within the molecules

   a Draw a labelled diagram to show metallic bonding. [2]

   b Explain why magnesium chloride has a high melting point but bromine has a low melting point. [5]

c Explain why solid sodium conducts electricity but solid sodium chloride does not conduct electricity. [2]

d i Draw a dot-and-cross diagram for carbon dioxide. [1]

  ii Describe the shape of the carbon dioxide molecule. [1]

  iii Explain why a carbon dioxide molecule has this shape. [2]

e Bromine is a liquid at room temperature. Weak van der Waals' forces hold the bromine molecules together.

Describe how van der Waals' forces arise. [5]

Total = 18

9 Water is extensively hydrogen bonded. This gives it anomalous (peculiar) properties.

a Explain why ice is less dense than liquid water. [3]

b State two other anomalous properties of water. [2]

c Propanone has the structure shown below.

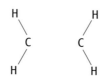

When propanone dissolves in water, it forms a hydrogen bond with water.

  i What features must water and propanone molecules posses in order to form a hydrogen bond? [2]

  ii Draw a diagram to show a propanone molecule and a water molecule forming a hydrogen bond. [2]

d Propanone has a double bond. One of the bonds is a σ bond (sigma bond). The other is a π bond (pi bond).

  i Explain the difference between a σ bond and a π bond in terms of how they are formed. [3]

  ii Copy the diagram, then complete it to show the shapes of the electron clouds in the σ bond and the π bond between the carbon atoms in ethene. Label your diagram. [3]

```
   H            H
    \            \
     C            C
    /            \
   H            H
```

Total = 15

States of matter

Learning outcomes

Candidates should be able to:

- [ ] state the basic assumptions of the kinetic theory as applied to an ideal gas
- [ ] explain qualitatively in terms of intermolecular forces and molecular size
  - the conditions necessary for a gas to approach ideal behaviour
  - the limitations of ideality at very high pressures and very low temperatures
- [ ] state and use the general gas equation $pV = nRT$ in calculations, including the determination of M_r
- [ ] describe, using a kinetic-molecular model, the liquid state, melting, vaporisation and vapour pressure
- [ ] describe in simple terms the lattice structure of a crystalline solid which is
  - ionic, as in sodium chloride, magnesium oxide
  - simple molecular, as in iodine
  - giant molecular, as in graphite, diamond, silicon(IV) oxide
  - hydrogen bonded, as in ice
  - metallic, as in copper (the concept of the 'unit cell' is not required)
- [ ] explain the strength, high melting point and insulating properties of ceramics in terms of their giant molecular structure
- [ ] relate the uses of ceramics based on magnesium oxide, aluminium oxide and silicon(IV) oxide to their properties, e.g. furnace linings, electrical insulators, glass, crockery
- [ ] describe and interpret the uses of the metals aluminium (including its alloys) and copper (including brass) in terms of their physical properties
- [ ] understand that materials are a finite resource and the importance of recycling processes
- [ ] suggest from quoted physical data the type of structure and bonding present in a substance.

5.1 States of matter

In the last chapter we looked at the types of forces which keep the particles in solids and liquids together and make it possible to liquefy gases. In this chapter, we shall also consider how the closeness and motion of the particles influences the properties of these three states of matter (Figure 5.1).

Gases have no fixed shape or volume. Gas particles:
- are far apart, therefore gases can be compressed
- are randomly arranged
- can move freely from place to place, in all directions.
  Liquids take the shape of the container they occupy.
Liquid particles:
- are close together, so liquids have a fixed volume and can only be compressed slightly

Figure 5.1 The three states of water are ice, water and steam. The 'steam' we see from the kettle is condensed droplets of water. The real gaseous water is in the area between this condensation and the spout of the kettle. We can't see it because it is colourless.

- are arranged fairly randomly
- have limited movement from place to place, in all directions.
  Solids have a fixed shape and volume. Solid particles:
- are touching each other, so solids cannot be compressed
- are usually in a regular arrangement
- cannot change positions with each other – they can only vibrate.

The state of a substance at room temperature and pressure depends on its structure and bonding. Five types of structure are found in elements and compounds:
- simple atomic, e.g. argon
- simple molecular, e.g. carbon dioxide
- giant ionic, e.g. sodium chloride
- giant metallic, e.g. iron
- giant molecular, e.g. silicon(IV) oxide.

The simple atomic structures found in the noble gases generally have similar physical properties to simple molecular gases.

5.2 The gaseous state

The kinetic theory of gases

The idea that molecules in gases are in constant movement is called the **kinetic theory of gases**. This theory makes certain assumptions:
- the gas molecules move rapidly and randomly
- the distance between the gas molecules is much greater than the diameter of the molecules so the volume of the molecules is negligible
- there are no forces of attraction or repulsion between the molecules
- all collisions between particles are elastic – this means no kinetic energy is lost in collisions (kinetic energy is the energy associated with moving particles)
- the temperature of the gas is related to the average kinetic energy of the molecules.

A theoretical gas that fits this description is called an **ideal gas**. In reality, the gases we encounter don't fit this

description exactly, although they may come very close. The gases we encounter are called **real gases**.

Noble gases with small atoms, such as helium and neon, approach ideal gas behaviour. This is because the intermolecular forces are so small.

Fact file

The durian fruit, found in Malaysia and Indonesia, has a very strong smell. It is so strong that many hotels will not allow the fruit on the premises. If it were not for the constant movement of molecules in the air, smells would not reach our noses.

Ideal gases

The volume which a gas occupies depends on
- its pressure; we measure pressure in pascals, Pa
- its temperature; we measure temperatures of gases in kelvin, K.

The kelvin temperature equals the Celsius temperature plus 273. For example, $100\,°C$ is $100 + 273 = 373\,K$

Fact file

The kelvin temperature scale was named after Lord Kelvin. Kelvin suggested that at a temperature of about $-273\,°C$, the particles in a gas will stop moving and the gas will have zero volume. Kelvin's original name was William Thomson. When he was made a Lord, he chose 'Kelvin' from the name of the river outside his laboratory in Glasgow, Scotland.

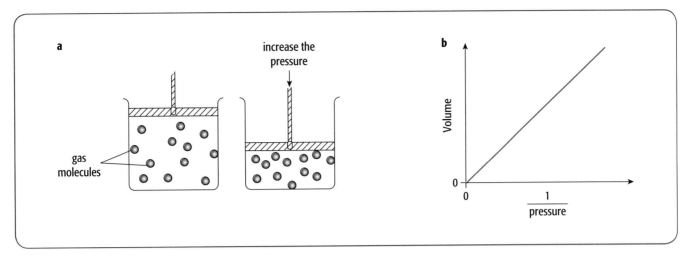

Figure 5.2 a As the volume of a gas decreases, its pressure increases due to the increased frequency of the gas molecules hitting the walls of the container.
b For an ideal gas a plot of the volume of gas against 1/pressure shows a proportional relationship.

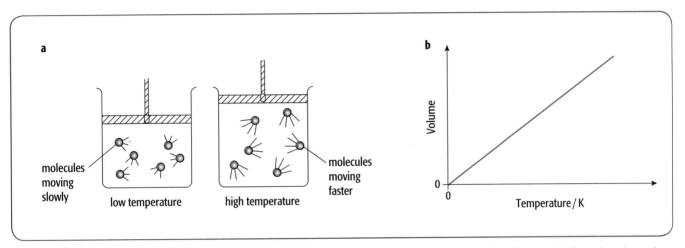

Figure 5.3 a As the temperature increases, the volume of a gas increases. Molecules hit the walls with increased force. **b** For an ideal gas, the volume of a gas is proportional to its kelvin temperature.

Gases in a container exert a pressure. This is because the gas molecules are constantly hitting the walls of the container. If we decrease the volume of a gas (at constant temperature) the molecules are squashed closer together and hit the walls of the container more often. So the pressure of the gas increases (Figure **5.2a**). A graph of volume of gas plotted against 1/pressure gives a proportional relationship (as shown by the straight line in Figure **5.2b**). We say that the volume is inversely proportional to the pressure.

When a gas is heated at constant pressure its volume increases (Figure **5.3a**). This is because the particles move faster and hit the walls of the container with greater force. If the pressure is to be constant the molecules must get further apart. The volume of a gas at constant pressure

is proportional to its temperature measured in kelvin (Figure **5.3b**).

An ideal gas will have a volume that varies exactly in proportion to its temperature and exactly in inverse proportion to its pressure.

Check-up

4 Some chemical reactions involving gases are performed in sealed glass tubes which do not melt at high temperatures. The tubes have thin walls and can easily break. Use the kinetic theory of gases to explain why the tubes should not be heated to high temperatures.

Limitations of the ideal gas laws

Scientists have taken accurate measurements to show how the volumes of gases change with temperature and pressure. These show us that gases do not always behave exactly as we expect an ideal gas to behave. This is because real gases do not always obey the kinetic theory in two ways:
- there is not zero attraction between the molecules
- we cannot ignore the volume of the molecules themselves.

These differences are especially noticeable at very high pressures and very low temperatures. Under these conditions:
- the molecules are close to each other
- the volume of the molecules is not negligible compared with the volume of the container
- there are van der Waals' or dipole–dipole forces of attraction between the molecules
- attractive forces pull the molecules towards each other and away from the walls of the container
- the pressure is lower than expected for an ideal gas
- the effective volume of the gas is smaller than expected for an ideal gas.

Check-up

5 a What is meant by the term **ideal gas**?
   b Under what conditions do real gases differ from ideal gases? Give reasons for your answer.

The general gas equation

For an ideal gas, we can combine the laws about how the volume of a gas depends on temperature and pressure. We also know from page 19, that the volume of a gas is proportional to the number of moles present. Putting all these together, gives us the **general gas equation**:

$$pV = nRT$$

p is the pressure in pascals, Pa
V is the volume of gas in cubic metres, m^3 ($1\,m^3 = 1000\,dm^3$)
n is the number of moles of gas $\left(n = \dfrac{m}{M_r}\right)$
R is the gas constant, which has a value of $8.31\,J\,K^{-1}\,mol^{-1}$
T is the temperature in kelvin, K.

Calculations using the general gas equation

If we know any four of the five physical quantities in the general gas equation, we can calculate the fifth.

Worked examples

1 Calculate the volume occupied by 0.500 mol of carbon dioxide at a pressure of 150 kPa and a temperature of 19 °C.
   ($R = 8.31\,J\,K^{-1}\,mol^{-1}$)

   Step 1 Change pressure and temperature to their correct units:

   $150\,kPa = 150\,000\,Pa$; $19\,°C = 19 + 273 = 292\,K$

   Step 2 Rearrange the general gas equation to the form you require:

   $$pV = nRT \qquad so \qquad V = \frac{nRT}{p}$$

   Step 3 Substitute the figures:

   $$V = \frac{nRT}{p}$$

   $$= \frac{0.500 \times 8.31 \times 292}{150\,000}$$

   $$= 8.09 \times 10^{-3}\,m^3$$
   $$= 8.09\,dm^3$$

2 A flask of volume 5.00 dm^3 contained 4.00 g of oxygen. Calculate the pressure exerted by the gas at a temperature of 127 °C.
   ($R = 8.31\,J\,K^{-1}\,mol^{-1}$; M_r oxygen = 32.0)

   Step 1 Change temperature and volume to their correct units and calculate the number of moles of oxygen.

   $127\,°C = 127 + 273 = 400\,K$;

   $5\,dm^3 = \dfrac{5.00}{1000}\,m^3 = 5.00 \times 10^{-3}\,m^3$

continued ⋯▸

$$n = \frac{m}{M_r}$$

$$= \frac{4.00}{32.0}$$

$$= 0.125 \text{ mol}$$

Step 2 Rearrange the general gas equation to the form you require:

$$pV = nRT \quad \text{so} \quad p = \frac{nRT}{V}$$

Step 3 Substitute the figures:

$$p = \frac{nRT}{V}$$

$$p = \frac{0.125 \times 8.31 \times 400}{5 \times 10^{-3}}$$

$$p = 8.31 \times 10^4 \text{ Pa}$$

Check-up

6 **a** Calculate the volume occupied by 272 g of methane at a pressure of 250 kPa and a temperature of 54 °C.
($R = 8.31 \text{ J K}^{-1} \text{mol}^{-1}$; M_r methane = 16.0)

b The pressure exerted by 0.25 mol of carbon monoxide in a 10 dm^3 flask is 120 kPa. Calculate the temperature in the flask in kelvin.

Calculating relative molecular masses

An accurate method of finding the relative molecular mass of a substance is to use a mass spectrometer (see Chapter 1). A less accurate method, but one that is suitable for a school laboratory, is to use the general gas equation to find the mass of gas in a large flask. Since the number of moles is the mass of a substance divided by its relative molecular mass, we can find the relative molecular mass of a gas by simply substituting in the general gas equation. Although weighing gases is a difficult process because they are so light and the buoyancy of the air has to be taken into account, the method can give reasonable results.

3 A flask of volume 2.0 dm^3 was found to contain 5.28 g of a gas. The pressure in the flask was 200 kPa and the temperature was 20 °C. Calculate the relative molecular mass of the gas. ($R = 8.31 \text{ J K}^{-1} \text{mol}^{-1}$)

Step 1 Change pressure, temperature and volume to their correct units and calculate the number of moles of oxygen.

$$200 \text{ kPa} = 2.00 \times 10^5 \text{ Pa};$$

$$20 °C = 20 + 273 = 293 \text{ K};$$

$$2.00 \text{ dm}^3 = \frac{2.00}{1000} \text{ m}^3 = 2.00 \times 10^{-3} \text{ m}^3$$

Step 2 Rearrange the general gas equation to the form you require:

$$pV = nRT \text{ and } n = \frac{m}{M_r}, \text{ so } pV = \frac{m}{M_r} RT,$$

which gives $M_r = \dfrac{mRT}{pV}$

Step 3 Substitute the figures:

$$M_r = \frac{mRT}{pV}$$

$$= \frac{5.28 \times 8.31 \times 293}{(2.00 \times 10^5) \times (2.0 \times 10^{-3})}$$

$$= 32.14$$

$$= 32 \text{ g mol}^{-1}$$

This method can also be applied to find the relative molecular mass of a volatile liquid. The volatile liquid is injected into a gas syringe placed in a syringe oven (Figure 5.4). The liquid vaporises and the volume of the vapour is recorded.

The procedure is:

1 put a gas syringe in the syringe oven and leave until the temperature is constant
2 record the volume of air in the gas syringe
3 fill a hypodermic syringe with the volatile liquid and find its total mass
4 inject a little of the liquid into the gas syringe then find the total mass of the hypodermic syringe again

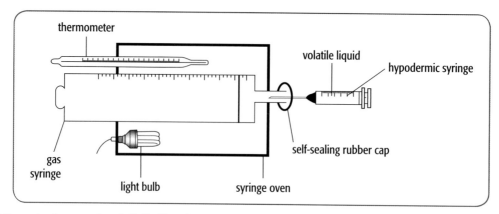

Figure 5.4 The relative molecular mass of a volatile liquid can be found using a syringe oven.

5 allow the liquid to vaporise in the gas syringe
6 record the final volume of vapour + air in the gas syringe
7 record the atmospheric temperature and pressure.

The calculation is carried out in the same way as Worked example **3**.

The volume of vapour produced is:

final gas syringe volume – initial gas syringe volume

The mass used in the calculation is:

initial mass of hypodermic syringe + liquid
          – final mass of hypodermic syringe + liquid

Check-up

7 When 0.08 g of liquid X was vaporised at 100 °C, 23 cm^3 of vapour was formed. The atmospheric pressure was 1.02×10^5 Pa. Calculate the relative molecular mass of liquid X. ($R = 8.31$ J K^{-1} mol^{-1})

5.3 The liquid state

The behaviour of liquids

When we heat a solid:
• the energy transferred to the solid makes the particles vibrate more vigorously
• the forces of attraction between the particles weaken
• the solid changes to a liquid when its temperature is sufficiently high.
We call this change of state melting.

For ionic compounds, a high temperature is needed because ionic bonding is very strong. For molecular solids, a lower temperature is needed, just enough to overcome the weak intermolecular forces between the particles.

The particles in a liquid are still close to each other but they have enough kinetic energy to keep sliding past each other in a fairly random way. They do not move freely as gas particles do. For brief periods, the particles in liquids are arranged in a slightly ordered way. But this order is always being broken up when the particles gain kinetic energy from neighbouring particles.

When we cool a liquid, the particles:
• lose kinetic energy so they do not move around so readily
• experience increasing forces of attraction
• stop sliding past each other when the temperature is sufficiently low; the liquid solidifies.
We call this change of state freezing.

Fact file

In 1827, the English Botanist Robert Brown noticed that pollen grains in water moved around randomly. The explanation for this did not come until many years later, when it was suggested that the random motion was due to bombardment of the pollen grains by the water molecules.

Vaporisation and vapour pressure

When we heat a liquid:
• the energy transferred to the liquid makes the particles move faster
• the forces of attraction between the particles weaken
• the particles with most energy are the first to escape from the forces holding them together in the liquid

- the liquid evaporates – this happens at a temperature below the boiling point
- the forces weaken enough for all the particles to become completely free from each other; they move fast and randomly and they spread out
- the liquid boils; this happens at the boiling point.

This change from the liquid state to the gas state is called **vaporisation**. The energy required to change one mole of liquid to one mole of gas is called the enthalpy change of vaporisation.

When we cool a vapour, the particles:
- lose kinetic energy so the molecules move around less quickly
- experience increasing forces of attraction
- move more slowly and become closer together when the temperature is sufficiently low; the gas liquefies.

We call this change of state **condensation**.

These changes in state are reversible. Water can be boiled to form steam, and steam can be condensed to form liquid water. These changes involve opposite energy transfers. For example: energy has to be transferred to water to boil it to form steam. But when steam condenses to form water, energy is transferred from the steam.

If we put some water in an open beaker, it evaporates until none is left. But what happens when we allow water to evaporate in a closed container?

At first, water molecules escape from the surface of the liquid to become vapour (Figure 5.5a). As more and more molecules escape, the molecules in the vapour become closer together. Eventually the molecules with lower kinetic energy will not be able to overcome the attractive forces of neighbouring molecules. The vapour begins to condense. So some water molecules return to the liquid (Figure 5.5b). Eventually, water molecules return to the liquid at the same rate as water molecules escape to the vapour. A position of equilibrium is reached (Figure 5.5c; see Chapter 8).

At equilibrium the concentration of water molecules in the vapour remains constant.

$$\text{water molecules in liquid} \underset{\text{equal rate of movement}}{\rightleftharpoons} \text{water molecules in vapour}$$

In this situation the pressure exerted by a vapour in equilibrium with its liquid is called its **vapour pressure**. The vapour pressure is caused by the gas particles hitting

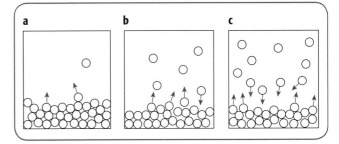

Figure 5.5 a Water molecules move from liquid to vapour. **b** As more molecules move from liquid to vapour, some begin to move back to the liquid. **c** An equilibrium is reached with molecules going from liquid to vapour at the same rate as from vapour to liquid.

the walls of the container. Vapour pressure will increase when the temperature increases because:
- the gas particles have more kinetic energy
- the gas particles move faster, so are able to overcome intermolecular forces of attraction more easily.

The temperature at which the vapour pressure is equal to the atmospheric pressure is the **boiling point** of the liquid.

Check-up

8 Bromine is a reddish-brown liquid. Some liquid bromine is placed in a closed jar. The bromine starts to evaporate. The colour of the vapour above the liquid bromine becomes darker and darker. After a time the bromine vapour does not get any darker.

   Use ideas about moving particles to explain these observations.

5.4 The solid state

Many ionic, metallic and covalent compounds are crystalline. The regular structure of crystals is due to the regular packing of the particles within the crystal. We call this regularly repeating arrangement of ions, atoms or molecules a crystal **lattice**.

Ionic lattices

Ionic lattices have a three-dimensional arrangement of alternating positive and negative ions. Compounds with ionic lattices are sometimes called giant ionic structures.

The type of lattice formed depends on the relative sizes of the ions present. The ionic lattices for sodium chloride and magnesium oxide are cubic. In sodium chloride, each sodium ion is surrounded by six oppositely charged chloride ions. The chloride ions are much larger than the sodium ions. The sodium ions fit into the spaces between the chloride ions so that they are as close as possible to them (Figure 5.6).

Magnesium oxide has the same lattice structure as sodium chloride. Magnesium ions replace sodium ions and the oxide ions replace the chloride ions.

The properties of ionic compounds reflect their structure as well as their bonding.

- They are hard. It takes a lot of energy to scratch the surface because of the strong attractive forces keeping the ions together.
- They are brittle. Ionic crystals may split apart when hit in the same direction as the layers of ions. The layers of ions may be displaced by the force of the blow so that ions with the same charge come together. The repulsions between thousands of ions in the layers, all with the same charge, cause the crystal to split along these cleavage planes.
- They have high melting points and high boiling points because the attraction between the large numbers of oppositely charged ions in the lattice acts in all directions and bonds them strongly together. The melting points and boiling points increase with the charge density on the ions. So magnesium oxide, $Mg^{2+}O^{2-}$, has a higher melting point (2852 °C) than sodium chloride, Na^+Cl^- (801 °C). This is because there is a greater electrostatic attraction between doubly charged ions than singly charged ions of similar size.
- Many of them are soluble in water (see page **263**).
- They only conduct electricity when molten or in solution (see page **69**).

Figure 5.7 Sapphires sparkle in the light when polished. They are cut by exerting a force on the cleavage planes between layers of ions in the crystal.

Metallic lattices

In Chapter 4, we learnt that a metallic lattice consists of ions surrounded by a sea of electrons. The ions are often packed in hexagonal layers or in a cubic arrangement. When a force is applied, the layers can slide over each other. But in a metallic bond, the attractive forces between the metal ions and the delocalised electrons act in all directions. So when the layers slide, new metallic bonds are easily re-formed between ions in new lattice positions and the delocalised electrons (Figure 5.8). The delocalised electrons continue to hold the ions in the lattice together. The metal now has a different shape. This explains why metals are malleable (they can be hammered into different shapes) and ductile (they can be drawn into wires). The high tensile strength and hardness of most metals is also due to the strong attractive forces between the metal ions and the delocalised electrons.

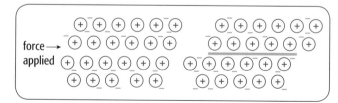

Figure 5.8 When a force is applied to a metallic structure, the layers slide over each other and re-form in new lattice positions.

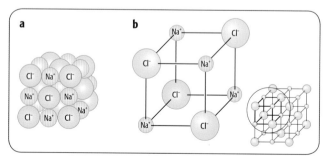

Figure 5.6 The arrangement of the ions in sodium chloride: **a** the actual packing of the ions; **b** an 'exploded' view so that you can see the arrangement of the ions clearly.

Fact file

Gallium has unusual properties for a metal. It can be melted by just the heat of your hand.

Figure 5.9 You can clearly see the metal crystals or 'grains' in this metal plate.

Alloys and their properties

An **alloy** is a mixture of two or more metals or a metal with a non-metal. The metal added to create the alloy becomes part of the crystal lattice of the other metal.

Brass is an alloy of copper (70%) with zinc (30%). It is stronger than copper but still malleable. For these reasons it is used for musical instruments, ornaments and household items such as door handles.

But why is brass stronger than pure copper?

Zinc ions are larger than copper ions. The presence of different-sized metal ions makes the arrangement of the lattice less regular. This stops the layers of ions from sliding over each other so easily when a force is applied (Figure **5.10**).

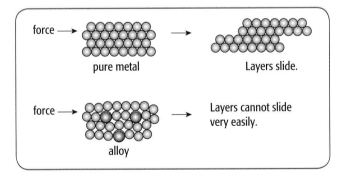

Figure 5.10 The layers of ions in an alloy slide less easily than in a pure metal because the structure of the lattice is less regular.

Pure aluminium is soft, ductile and has high electrical and thermal conductivity. Because of its low strength, pure aluminium is of little use in engineering. But its strength can be increased by addition of other elements such as

copper, magnesium, silicon and manganese. Many alloys of aluminium are lightweight, strong and resistant to corrosion. These are used for the bodies of aircraft, for the cylinder blocks of car engines and for bicycle frames, all situations where low density combined with strength and corrosion resistance is important.

Check-up

9 Explain the following:
   a why are most metals strong, but ionic solids are brittle?
   b why is an alloy of copper and tin stronger than either copper or tin alone?

Fact file

Bronze is an alloy of copper and tin. A 33-metre high bronze statue was built near the harbour in Rhodes (Greece) over 2000 years ago. The statue fell down after an earthquake and was eventually bought by a Syrian merchant. The bronze was recycled to make useful implements.

Simple molecular lattices

Substances with a simple molecular structure, such as iodine, can also form crystals (Figure **5.11**). This reflects the regular packing of the molecules in a lattice structure.

The distance between the nuclei of neighbouring iodine molecules is greater than the distance between the nuclei within the iodine molecule. This is because the forces between the molecules are weak van der Waals' forces whereas the forces between the atoms within the molecule

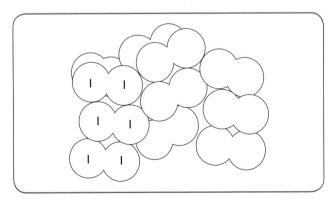

Figure 5.11 Iodine molecules are arranged in a lattice structure.

are strong covalent bonds. Very little energy is needed to overcome the weak van der Waals' forces between the molecules. The lattice is easily broken down when iodine crystals are heated; iodine has a low melting point.

Ice also forms a crystalline lattice. Ice and water have peculiar properties because of hydrogen bonding (see page 67).

(see page 67)

Check-up

10 The table shows some properties of four elements. Use the data to answer the following questions. (Assume that steel has similar properties to iron.)

Element	Density/ $g cm^{-3}$	Tensile strength / $10^{10} Pa$	Electrical conductivity/ $10^{8} S m^{-1}$
aluminium	2.70	7.0	0.38
iron	7.86	21.1	0.10
copper	8.92	13.0	0.59
sulfur	2.07	breaks easily	1×10^{-23}

a Why is aluminium with a steel core used for overhead electricity cables in preference to copper?

b Suggest why many car engine blocks are made from aluminium alloys rather than from steel.

c Explain the differences in tensile strength and electrical conductivity of iron and sulfur.

Giant molecular structures

Some covalently bonded structures have a three-dimensional network of covalent bonds throughout the whole structure. We call these structures **giant molecular structures** or giant covalent structures. They have high melting and boiling points because of the large number of strong covalent bonds linking the whole structure. Both elements, such as carbon (graphite and diamond), and compounds, such as silicon dioxide, can be giant molecular structures. Carbon and graphite are different forms of the same element. Different crystalline or molecular forms of the same element are called **allotropes**.

Graphite

In graphite, the carbon atoms are arranged in planar layers. Within the layers, the carbon atoms are arranged in hexagons. Each carbon atom is joined to three other carbon atoms by strong covalent bonds (Figure 5.12). The fourth electron of each carbon atom occupies a p orbital. These p orbitals on every carbon atom in each planar layer overlap sideways. A cloud of delocalised electrons is formed above and below the plane of the carbon rings. These electron clouds join up to form extended delocalised rings of electrons.

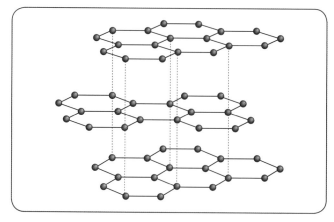

Figure 5.12 The structure of graphite.

The layers of carbon atoms are kept next to each other by weak van der Waals' forces.

The properties of graphite are related to its structure.

- High melting and boiling points: there is strong covalent bonding throughout the layers of carbon atoms. A lot of energy is needed to overcome these strong bonds.
- Softness: graphite is easily scratched. The forces between the layers of carbon atoms are weak. The layers of graphite can slide over each other when a force is applied. The layers readily flake off. This 'flakiness' is why graphite is used in pencil 'leads' and feels slippery.
- Good conductor of electricity: when a voltage is applied, the delocalised electrons can move along the layers.

Diamond

In diamond, each carbon atom forms four covalent bonds with other carbon atoms (Figure 5.13). The carbon atoms are tetrahedrally arranged around each other. The network of carbon atoms extends almost unbroken throughout the whole structure. The regular arrangement of the atoms gives diamond a crystalline structure.

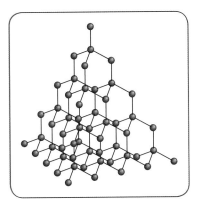

Figure 5.13 The structure of diamond.

The properties of diamond are related to its structure.
- High melting and boiling points: there is strong covalent bonding throughout the whole structure. A lot of energy is needed to break these strong bonds and separate the atoms.
- Hardness: diamond cannot be scratched easily because it is difficult to break the three-dimensional network of strong covalent bonds.
- Does not conduct electricity or heat: each of the four outer electrons on every carbon atom is involved in covalent bonding. This means that there are no free electrons available to carry the electric current.

Fact file
Artificial diamonds can be made by heating other forms of carbon under high pressure. Artificial diamonds are too small to be used for jewellery but they can be used for drill tips.

Silicon(IV) oxide

There are several forms of silicon(IV) oxide. The silicon(IV) oxide found in the mineral quartz (Figure 5.14) has a structure similar to diamond (Figure 5.15).

Figure 5.14 The shape of these quartz crystals reflects the regular arrangement of the silicon and oxygen atoms.

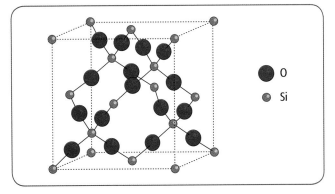

Figure 5.15 The structure of silicon(IV) oxide.

Each silicon atom is bonded to four oxygen atoms but each oxygen atom is bonded to only two silicon atoms. So the formula for silicon(IV) oxide is SiO_2. Silicon dioxide has properties similar to that of diamond. It forms hard, colourless crystals with high melting and boiling points and it does not conduct electricity.

Sand is largely silicon(IV)oxide.

Check-up

11 Explain the following properties of silicon(IV) oxide by referring to its structure and bonding.
   a It has a high melting point.
   b It does not conduct electricity.
   c It is a crystalline solid.
   d It is hard.

continued ⋯⟶

12 Copy and complete the table below to compare the properties of giant ionic, giant molecular, giant metallic and simple molecular structures.

	Giant ionic	Giant molecular	Metallic	Simple molecular
Two examples				
Particles present				
Forces keeping particles together				
Physical state at room temperature				
Melting points and boiling points				
Hardness				
Electrical conductivity				
Solubility in water				

5.5 Ceramics

What is a ceramic?

A **ceramic** is an inorganic non-metallic solid which is prepared by heating a substance or mixture of substances to a high temperature.

Many ceramics are giant molecular structures but some, such as magnesium oxide, contain metal ions in their structures.

Ceramics are often made by heating clay, which contains aluminium oxide, or sand, which contains silicon(IV) oxide, with other materials. Ceramics can be made into complex shapes.

Ceramics have characteristic properties.

- Very high melting and boiling points: they have giant molecular structures. It needs a high temperature to break the strong covalent bonds.

- Do not conduct electricity: they are electrical insulators. This is because they have no ions or electrons which are free to move.
- Do not conduct heat: there are no free electrons.
- Retain their strength at high temperatures (above 550 °C): materials with this property are called refractories. The network of strong covalent bonds cannot be broken, even at quite high temperatures.
- Hard: they cannot be scratched easily because it is difficult to break the three-dimensional network of strong covalent bonds.
- Chemically unreactive: electrons in atoms are responsible for chemical reactivity. In ceramics, the electrons are firmly held in strong covalent bonds and are not available for reaction.

Fact file
The word 'ceramic' come from a Greek word 'keramikos', meaning pottery.

Uses of ceramics

The uses of ceramics depend on the materials present in them.
- Ceramics containing magnesium oxide are used:
  – as electrical insulators in industrial electrical cables where magnesium oxide surrounds the copper wires
  – as a refractory in furnace linings
  – in fire-resistant wall boards.
- Ceramics containing aluminium oxide are used:
  – as a refractory in furnace linings
  – as an abrasive for grinding hard materials; they don't conduct heat or melt when heat is given off during grinding
  – in transparent aluminium oxide–scandium windows for furnaces and for military vehicles.
- Ceramics containing silicon(IV) oxide are used:
  – as a refractory in furnace linings
  – as an abrasive; for example in sandpaper
  – in the manufacture of glass.

Porcelain is a ceramic made by firing clay. Clay contains varying quantities of aluminium oxide and silicon(IV) oxide. Porcelain is used for making crockery (plates, dishes and cups). It is also an important electrical insulator used in high-voltage electricity pylons. The porcelain spacing insulators stop the wires from touching the pylon or other wires.

5.6 Conserving materials

Why conserve materials?

There is only a limited supply of metal ores in the Earth.
If we use them all up, they cannot be replaced. The
things we make from metals and other materials from
the Earth's crust are often thrown away. This leads to
huge waste dumps and landfill sites scarring the landscape
and problems with litter. Extracting metals from their
ores requires a lot of energy. Energy resources are also
limited and we need to conserve these as well. One
way to help conserve materials and energy is to recycle
metals (Figure 5.16).

Recycling materials

Large amounts of energy are needed to extract and purify
metals. It is often cheaper to collect used metals and
recycle them rather than extract them from their ores.
   Recycling has several advantages:
• it saves energy (this helps tackle global warming since
  we burn less fossil fuel)
• it conserves supplies of the ore
• landfill sites do not get filled up as fast and there is
  less waste
• it is cheaper than extracting the metal from the ore.
   It is not always easy to recycle metals. They have to
be collected and sorted and then transported to the
recycling plant. This takes energy and money. It may
be difficult to separate individual metals. For example
'tin' cans are made from steel coated with tin. The
two metals have to be separated before they can be
used again. Two metals that can be recycled easily are
copper and aluminium.

Copper

Most copper ores remaining in the Earth contain less
than 1% copper. Recycling copper is important because:

Figure 5.16 Remember to recycle your cans. As well as aluminium cans,
we can also save energy and resources by recycling steel cans.

• less energy is needed to recycle copper than is needed to
  transport copper ore to the smelting plant and extract
  copper from it
• less energy is needed to extract and refine the recycled
  copper so that it is pure enough to be electrolysed.
The copper used for water pipes and cooking utensils
does not have to be very pure, so little purification of
recycled copper is needed for these uses. The copper used
for electrical wiring has to be 99.99% pure. This has to be
purified by electrolysis.

Aluminium

Purifying and remoulding aluminium is much cheaper
than extracting aluminium from bauxite ore. Savings are
made because:
• it is not necessary to extract the aluminium ore from
  the ground or to transport it to the smelting plant; these
  processes require energy
• the treatment of bauxite to make pure aluminium oxide
  for electrolysis does not need to be carried out
• the aluminium scrap needs less energy to melt it,
  compared with melting aluminium oxide
• the expensive electrolysis of aluminium oxide does not
  need to be carried out (see Chapter 7).
There is a 95% saving in energy if we recycle aluminium
rather than extract it from its ore.

Summary

- [ ] The kinetic theory of gases states that gas particles are always in constant random motion at a variety of speeds.
- [ ] The volume of a gas increases when the temperature increases and decreases when the pressure increases.
- [ ] The volume of a gas under different conditions of temperature and pressure can be calculated using the ideal gas equation $pV = nRT$.
- [ ] The ideal gas equation can be used to determine the relative molecular mass of simple molecules.
- [ ] Gases do not obey the ideal gas equation at low temperatures and high pressures.
- [ ] The kinetic-molecular model can be used to describe the states of matter in terms of proximity and motion of the particles and to describe changes of state and vapour pressure.
- [ ] Ionic compounds such as sodium chloride and magnesium oxide form a giant three-dimensional lattice structure containing ions in a regularly repeating pattern.
- [ ] The strong ionic forces acting in all directions between the ions in the lattice cause ionic substances to have high melting and boiling points.
- [ ] Simple molecular solids with low melting points such as iodine have a regular arrangement of molecules; they are crystalline. There are weak intermolecular forces between the molecules.
- [ ] Giant covalent (giant molecular) structures such as diamond have a large number of covalent bonds arranged in a regularly repeating pattern.
- [ ] The strong covalent bonds between the atoms in giant molecular structures cause these substances to have high melting and boiling points.
- [ ] In metals, the atoms are closely packed in a giant lattice in which the outer electrons are free to move.
- [ ] Metals such as aluminium and copper and their alloys have a variety of uses, which can be related to their physical properties, e.g. density, malleability, conductivity, hardness.
- [ ] Physical data can be used to suggest the type of structure and bonding present in a substance.
- [ ] The strength, high melting point and insulating properties of ceramics are due to their giant molecular structure.
- [ ] Ceramics can be used as furnace linings, electrical insulators and in glass and crockery because of their high melting points and insulating properties.
- [ ] Recycling plays an important part in conserving finite resources such as metals.

End-of-chapter questions

1   Four types of structure are:

    giant molecular
    giant ionic
    giant metallic
    simple molecular

   a Give **two** examples of a giant ionic structure and **two** examples of a simple molecular structure.   [4]
   b Explain why substances with giant ionic structures are often brittle but metallic structures are malleable.   [6]
   c Explain why giant molecular structures have higher melting points than simple molecular structures.   [6]
   d Diamond and graphite are two forms of carbon with giant molecular structures. Explain why graphite conducts electricity but diamond does not.   [5]

   Total = 21

2   The structures of carbon dioxide and silicon dioxide are shown in the diagram below.

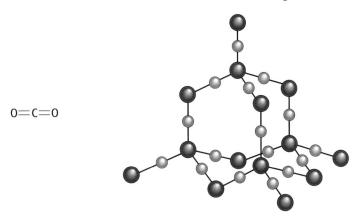

O=C=O

Use your knowledge of structure and bonding to explain the following:
a carbon dioxide is a gas at room temperature   [3]
b silicon(IV) oxide is a solid with a high melting point   [3]
c neither carbon dioxide nor silicon(IV) oxide conducts electricity.   [2]
                                                                               Total = 8

3   This question is about gases.
a What do you understand by the term **ideal gas**?   [1]
b Under what conditions does a gas **not** behave ideally? Explain your answer for one of these conditions.   [4]
c Helium is a noble gas. It exists as single atoms. Explain why:
   i   helium has a very low boiling point   [2]
   ii helium does not conduct electricity.   [1]
d A weather balloon contains 0.500 kg of helium. Calculate the volume of the gas in the balloon at a
   pressure of 0.500×10^5 Pa and a temperature of –20.0 °C.
   ($R = 8.31 \, \text{J K}^{-1} \, \text{mol}^{-1}$; A_r He = 4.0)   [5]
                                                                               Total = 13

4   Water and bromine are both simple molecular substances.
a Both water and bromine form a lattice structure in the solid state. What do you understand by the
   term **lattice**?   [2]
b The boiling point of water is 100 °C. The boiling point of bromine is 59 °C. Explain the reason
   for this difference in terms of intermolecular forces.   [4]
c Use ideas about the kinetic theory to explain what happens when liquid bromine evaporates to form
   bromine vapour.   [4]
d Some liquid bromine is allowed to evaporate in a closed glass jar until no further change is seen in the
   colour of the bromine vapour. Under these conditions the vapour pressure is constant.
   i   What do you understand by the term **vapour pressure**?   [1]
   ii Explain why the vapour pressure remains constant in the jar.   [2]
e When 0.20 g of a liquid, **Y**, with a simple molecular structure was evaporated it produced 80 cm^3
   of vapour. The temperature was 98 °C and the pressure 1.1×10^5 Pa. Calculate the relative molecular
   mass of **Y**.
   ($R = 8.31 \, \text{J K}^{-1} \, \text{mol}^{-1}$)   [5]
                                                                               Total = 18

5 The table gives data on the physical properties of five substances, **A** to **E**.
   a Copy the table and fill in the gaps.   [7]

Substance	Melting point	Electrical conductivity		Type of structure
		as a solid	**as a liquid**	
A	high	poor	good	**i**
B	low	**ii**	**iii**	**iv**
C	high	poor	poor	**v**
D	high	good	**vi**	giant metallic
E	high	poor	**vii**	giant covalent

   b Explain the melting point and electrical conductivity of substance **A**.   [6]
   c Explain the melting point and electrical conductivity of substance **B**.   [5]

   Total = 18

6 The uses of metals are often related to their properties.
   a Describe the structure of a typical metal.   [2]
   b Explain why metals are malleable.   [4]
   c Use the information in the table below to answer the questions which follow.

Element	Density / $g\,cm^{-3}$	Tensile strength / $10^{10}\,Pa$	Electrical conductivity / $10^8\,S\,m^{-1}$
aluminium	2.70	7.0	0.38
copper	8.92	13.0	0.59
steel	7.86	21.1	0.10

   i   Why is aluminium more suitable than steel for building aeroplane bodies?   [1]
   ii Explain why overhead electricity cables are made from aluminium with a steel core rather than
           just from copper.   [5]
   d The effect of alloying copper with zinc on the strength of the alloy is shown in the table below.

% copper	% zinc	Tensile strength / $10^8\,Pa$
100	0	2.3
80	20	3.0
60	40	3.6
0	100	1.4

    i Describe and explain the change in tensile strength as the percentage of zinc increases from
       0% to 40%. [5]
    ii State the name of the alloy of copper with zinc. [1]
  e Many metals, such aluminium, can be recycled. Give three reasons why about 90% of aluminium
    is made by recycling rather than extracting it from its ore. [3]
                                                 Total = 21

7 The diagram shows the structures of graphite and diamond.

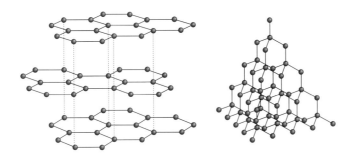

  Use the diagrams and your knowledge of structure and bonding to answer the following questions.
  a Explain why both diamond and graphite have high melting points. [2]
  b i Why is graphite used in making handles for tennis racquets? [3]
    ii Explain why graphite is used in pencil 'leads' for writing. [4]
  c i Explain why diamond is used on the tips of high-speed drills. [5]
                                                 Total = 14

8 Crystals of sodium chloride have a lattice structure.
  a Describe a sodium chloride lattice. [3]
  b Explain the following properties of sodium chloride.
    i Sodium chloride has a high melting point. [3]
    ii Sodium chloride conducts electricity when molten but not when solid. [3]
    iii Sodium chloride is hard but brittle. [5]
                                                 Total = 14

9 Ceramics are used in everyday life for furnace linings, for heat and electrical insulation and for crockery.
  a What do you understand by a **ceramic**? [2]
  b Use your knowledge of the structure and bonding in ceramics to explain why aluminium oxide is
    used as a furnace lining. [3]
  c Use the information in the table below to answer the following questions.

Type of ceramic	Density / g cm^{-3}	Tensile strength / GPa	Electrical conductivity/ W m^{-1} K^{-1}
earthenware	2.5	40	1.6
e-porcelain	2.5	70	1.6
high aluminium	3.7	310	19

    i Suggest why e-porcelain, rather than high aluminium, is used as an insulator between overhead
       power cables. [2]

   ii Suggest why high aluminium ceramic, rather than earthenware, can be used in the construction
       of military vehicles. [1]

d Magnesium oxide is used in the manufacture of high-voltage copper electricity cables, see the
diagram below.

    Explain, by referring to the structure of magnesium oxide, why this compound is used in these
high-voltage cables. [6]

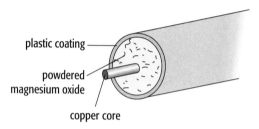

plastic coating

powdered
magnesium oxide

copper core

Total = 14

6 Enthalpy changes

Learning outcomes

Candidates should be able to:

- [ ] explain that some chemical reactions are accompanied by energy changes, mainly in the form of heat energy
- [ ] explain that energy changes can be exothermic (ΔH negative) or endothermic (ΔH positive)
- [ ] construct and interpret a reaction pathway diagram in terms of the enthalpy change of reaction
- [ ] explain and use the terms **enthalpy change of reaction** and **standard conditions** with reference to enthalpy changes of: formation, combustion, hydration, solution, neutralisation and atomisation
- [ ] explain and use the term **bond energy**

- [ ] calculate enthalpy changes from experimental results, including the use of the relationship: enthalpy change $= mc\Delta T$
- [ ] apply Hess's law to construct simple energy cycles and carry out calculations involving such cycles
- [ ] apply Hess's law to determine enthalpy changes that cannot be found by direct experiment
- [ ] show understanding of chemical reactions in terms of energy transfers associated with the breaking and making of chemical bonds
- [ ] calculate enthalpy change of reaction using average bond enthalpies.

6.1 Introduction: energy changes

When chemical reactions take place there is an energy change. Energy can take many forms, including heat, light, sound and electrical energy. The chemical energy in the atoms and bonds of a substance is also very important. One of the most obvious energy transfers in chemical reactions is the transfer of heat (Figure **6.1**). A car engine gets hot when the energy is transferred from the burning fuel. Fireworks release a lot of energy as heat (as well as light and sound) when they explode. Our bodies keep warm because of the continuous oxidation of the food we eat.

In some reactions energy is absorbed. Plants use the energy in sunlight to convert carbon dioxide and water into carbohydrates by the process of photosynthesis. Energy is needed to change a solid into a liquid.

Figure 6.1 The chemical reactions in this fire are releasing large quantities of energy.

6.2 What are enthalpy changes?

Exothermic or endothermic?

Chemical reactions which release energy to the surroundings are described as **exothermic**. In an exothermic reaction the temperature of the surroundings increases. For example, when magnesium reacts with sulfuric acid in a test tube the energy released is transferred to the surroundings and the temperature of the reaction mixture in the tube increases.

$$Mg(s) + H_2SO_4(aq) \rightarrow MgSO_4(aq) + H_2(g) \text{ (energy released)}$$

The **surroundings** include:

- the solvent (in this case water)
- the air around the test tube
- the test tube itself
- anything dipping into the test tube (e.g. a thermometer).

Other examples of exothermic reactions include:
• the combustion of fuels
• the oxidation of carbohydrates in the bodies of animals and plants (respiration)
• the reaction of water with quicklime (calcium oxide) (see page 178).

Chemical reactions which absorb energy from the surroundings are described as **endothermic**. In an endothermic reaction the temperature of the surroundings decreases (Figure 6.2). For example, when sodium hydrogencarbonate reacts with an aqueous solution of citric acid in a test tube the temperature of the reaction mixture in the tube decreases. The citric acid and sodium hydrogencarbonate are absorbing the heat energy from the solvent, the test tube and the air.

Other examples of endothermic reactions include:
• the decomposition of limestone by heating (all thermal decomposition reactions are endothermic)
• photosynthesis (where the energy is supplied by sunlight)
• dissolving certain ammonium salts in water

$$NH_4Cl(s) \quad + \quad aq \quad \rightarrow \quad NH_4^+(aq) \quad + \quad Cl^-(aq)$$

| ammonium chloride | water | ammonium ions | chloride ions |

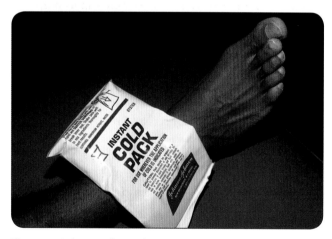

Figure 6.2 Using a cooling pack to treat a sports injury. When the pack is kneaded, water and ammonium chloride crystals mix. As the crystals dissolve, energy is transferred from the surroundings, cooling the injury.

Fact file

Self-heating food boxes can be used to heat up meals when camping. They use the exothermic reaction between anhydrous calcium chloride and water to heat the food.

Enthalpy changes and enthalpy profile diagrams

We call the energy exchange between a chemical reaction and its surroundings at constant pressure the **enthalpy change**. Enthalpy is the total energy associated with the materials which react. The symbol for enthalpy is H. We cannot measure enthalpy, but we can measure an enthalpy change when heat energy is exchanged with the surroundings. We can write this as:

$$\Delta H \quad = \quad H_{products} \quad - \quad H_{reactants}$$

| enthalpy change | enthalpy of products | enthalpy of reactants |

The symbol Δ is the upper case Greek letter 'delta'. This symbol is often used to mean a change in a quantity. For example, ΔT means a change in temperature and ΔH means the enthalpy change.

The units of enthalpy change are kilojoules per mole ($kJ\,mol^{-1}$).

We can draw **enthalpy profile diagrams** (also known as reaction pathway diagrams) to show enthalpy changes. The enthalpy of the reactants and products is shown on the y-axis. The x-axis shows the reaction pathway, with reactants on the left and products on the right.

For an exothermic reaction, energy is released to the surroundings. So the enthalpy of the reactants must be greater than the enthalpy of the products. We can see from the enthalpy profile diagram for the combustion of methane (Figure **6.3**) that $H_{\text{products}} - H_{\text{reactants}}$ is negative.

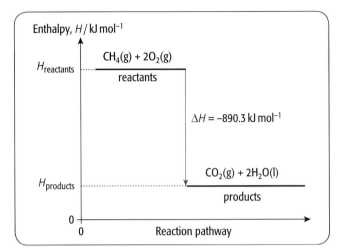

Figure 6.3 Enthalpy profile diagram for the combustion of methane.

We can include this information in the equation for the reaction:

$$CH_4(g) + 2O_2(g) \rightarrow CO_2(g) + 2H_2O(l)$$
$$\Delta H = -890.3 \, kJ \, mol^{-1}$$

The negative sign shows that the reaction is exothermic.

For an endothermic reaction, energy is absorbed from the surroundings by the chemicals in the reaction. So the enthalpy of the products must be greater than the enthalpy of the reactants. We can see from the enthalpy profile diagram for the thermal decomposition of calcium carbonate (Figure **6.4**) that $H_{\text{products}} - H_{\text{reactants}}$ is positive.

$$CaCO_3(s) \rightarrow CaO(s) + CO_2(g) \qquad \Delta H = +572 \, kJ \, mol^{-1}$$

The positive sign shows that the reaction is endothermic.

Check-up

2 Draw enthalpy profile diagrams for:
  a the combustion of sulfur to form sulfur dioxide
  b the endothermic reaction

  $$H_2O(g) + C(s) \rightarrow H_2(g) + CO(g)$$

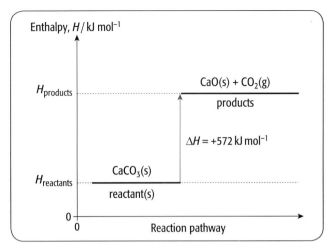

Figure 6.4 Enthalpy profile diagram for the decomposition of calcium carbonate.

6.3 Standard enthalpy changes

Standard conditions

To make any comparison of enthalpy changes a fair comparison, we must use the same conditions. These are called **standard conditions**:
- a pressure of 10^5 Pa (10^5 Pa is 100 kPa, approximately normal atmospheric pressure)
- a temperature of 298 K (25 °C) (add 273 to the Celsius temperature to convert a temperature into kelvin)
- each substance involved in the reaction is in its normal physical state (solid, liquid or gas) at 10^5 Pa and 298 K.

The symbol $\ominus$ indicates that the enthalpy change refers to a reaction carried out under standard conditions.

The information in the equation:

$$CH_4(g) + 2O_2(g) \rightarrow CO_2(g) + 2H_2O(l)$$
$$\Delta H^{\ominus} = -890.3 \, kJ \, mol^{-1}$$

shows us that when one mole of methane gas reacts with two moles of oxygen gas to form one mole of carbon dioxide gas and two moles of water in the liquid state the **standard enthalpy change** is $-890.3 \, kJ \, mol^{-1}$.

A variety of enthalpy changes

We can describe enthalpy changes according to the type of chemical reaction taking place. For example:
- enthalpy change of formation
- enthalpy change of combustion
- enthalpy change of neutralisation

- enthalpy change of solution
- enthalpy change of atomisation
- enthalpy change of hydration.

  In more general cases we can use the term:
- enthalpy change of reaction.

Standard enthalpy change of reaction, $\Delta H_r^{\ominus}$

> The standard enthalpy change of reaction is the enthalpy change when the amounts of reactants shown in the equation react to give products under standard conditions. The reactants and products must be in their standard states.

The symbol for standard enthalpy change of reaction is $\Delta H_r^{\ominus}$. Enthalpy changes of reaction can be exothermic or endothermic.

The equation which describes the reaction must be given. For example, the equation:

$$H_2(g) + \tfrac{1}{2}O_2(g) \rightarrow H_2O(l) \qquad \Delta H_r^{\ominus} = -286\,kJ\,mol^{-1}$$

shows us the enthalpy change when one mole of water is formed from hydrogen and oxygen. In this case 286 kJ of energy are released.

However, if we write the equation as

$$2H_2(g) + O_2(g) \rightarrow 2H_2O(l) \qquad \Delta H_r^{\ominus} = -572\,kJ\,mol^{-1}$$

two moles of water are formed from hydrogen and oxygen. In this case 572 kJ of energy are released.

Standard enthalpy change of formation, $\Delta H_f^{\ominus}$

> The standard enthalpy change of formation is the enthalpy change when one mole of a compound is formed from its elements under standard conditions. The reactants and products must be in their standard states.

The symbol for standard enthalpy change of formation is $\Delta H_f^{\ominus}$. Enthalpy changes of formation can be exothermic or endothermic. We write the formula of the compound in square brackets after $\Delta H_f^{\ominus}$ to help us when we do calculations involving enthalpy changes. Examples are:

$$2Fe(s) + 1\tfrac{1}{2}O_2(g) \rightarrow Fe_2O_3(s)$$
$$\Delta H_f^{\ominus}\,[Fe_2O_3(s)] = -824.2\,kJ\,mol^{-1}$$

$$C(graphite) + 2S(s) \rightarrow CS_2(l)$$
$$\Delta H_f^{\ominus}\,[CS_2(l)] = +89.7\,kJ\,mol^{-1}$$

Notice that the state symbol for carbon is shown as 'graphite'. This is because there are several forms of carbon but the most stable is graphite and we chose the most stable form when writing equations where enthalpy changes are shown.

By definition, the standard enthalpy change of formation of any element in its standard state is zero.

Standard enthalpy change of combustion, $\Delta H_c^{\ominus}$

> The standard enthalpy change of combustion is the enthalpy change when one mole of a substance is burnt in excess oxygen under standard conditions. The reactants and products must be in their standard states.

The symbol for standard enthalpy change of combustion is $\Delta H_c^{\ominus}$. Enthalpy changes of combustion are always exothermic. The substances combusted can be either elements or compounds.

$$S(s) + O_2(g) \rightarrow SO_2(g) \qquad \Delta H_c^{\ominus}\,[S(s)] = -296.8\,kJ\,mol^{-1}$$

$$CH_4(g) + 2O_2(g) \rightarrow CO_2(g) + 2H_2O(l)$$
$$\Delta H_c^{\ominus}\,[CH_4(g)] = -890.3\,kJ\,mol^{-1}$$

Notice that the first equation can be considered as either the enthalpy change of combustion of sulfur or the enthalpy change of formation of sulfur dioxide.

Standard enthalpy change of neutralisation, $\Delta H_n^{\ominus}$

The standard enthalpy change of neutralisation $(\Delta H_n^{\ominus})$ is the enthalpy change when one mole of water is formed by the reaction of an acid with an alkali under standard conditions.

For example:

$$HCl(aq) + NaOH(aq) \rightarrow NaCl(aq) + H_2O(l)$$
$$\Delta H_n^{\ominus} = -57.1\,kJ\,mol^{-1}$$

For any acid–alkali reaction the ionic equation is:

$$H^+(aq) + OH^-(aq) \rightarrow H_2O(l)$$

The other ions in solution (Cl^- and Na^+) are spectator ions and take no part in the reaction (see page 13).

Standard enthalpy change of solution, $\Delta H_{sol}^{\ominus}$

The standard enthalpy change of solution $(\Delta H_{sol}^{\ominus})$ is the enthalpy change when one mole of solute is dissolved in a solvent to form an infinitely dilute solution under standard conditions.

An infinitely dilute solution is one which does not produce any further enthalpy change when more solvent is added. An example is the addition of a small amount of solid sodium hydroxide to a large amount of water.

$$NaOH(s) + aq \rightarrow NaOH(aq)$$

We use known amounts of solute and solvent with the solvent in excess to make sure that all the solute dissolves.

Standard enthalpy change of atomisation, $\Delta H_{at}^{\ominus}$

The standard enthalpy change of atomisation, $\Delta H_{at}^{\ominus}$, is the enthalpy change when one mole of gaseous atoms is formed from its element under standard conditions.

The standard enthalpy change of atomisation of hydrogen relates to the equation:

$$\frac{1}{2}H_2(g) \rightarrow H(g) \qquad \Delta H_{at}^{\ominus}[\frac{1}{2}H_2(g)] = +218\,kJ\,mol^{-1}$$

Standard enthalpy change of hydration of an anhydrous salt

The standard enthalpy change of hydration of an anhydrous salt is the enthalpy change when one mole of a hydrated salt is formed from one mole of the anhydrous salt under standard conditions.

For example:

$$Na_2S_2O_3(s) + 5H_2O(l) \rightarrow Na_2S_2O_3.5H_2O\,(s)$$
$$\Delta H^{\ominus} = -55.0\,kJ\,mol^{-1}$$

This should not be confused with the standard enthalpy change of hydration of aqueous ions (see page 264).

6.4 Measuring enthalpy changes

Calorimetry

We can measure the enthalpy change of some reactions by a technique called calorimetry. The apparatus used is called a calorimeter. A simple calorimeter can be a polystyrene drinking cup (Figure 6.5), a vacuum flask or a metal can.

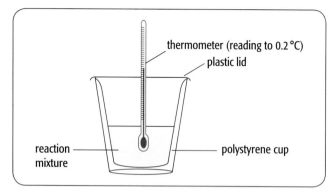

Figure 6.5 A polystyrene cup can act as a calorimeter for finding some enthalpy changes.

When carrying out experiments in calorimeters we use known amounts of reactants and known volumes of liquids. We also measure the temperature change of the liquid in the calorimeter as the reaction occurs. The thermometer should be accurate to 0.1 or 0.2 °C.

Calorimetry relies on the fact that it takes 4.18 J of energy to increase the temperature of 1 g of water by 1 °C. The energy required to raise the temperature of 1 g of a liquid by 1 °C is called the specific heat capacity, c, of the liquid. So, the specific heat capacity of water is $4.18 \, J \, g^{-1} \, °C^{-1}$.

The energy transferred as heat (the enthalpy change) is given by the relationship:

$$q = mc\Delta T$$

where:
q is the energy transferred, in J
m is the mass of water, in g
c is the specific heat capacity, in $J \, g^{-1} \, °C^{-1}$
ΔT is the temperature change, in °C

Since $1 \, cm^3$ of water weighs 1 g, we can substitute volume of water in cm^3 of water for mass of water in g in the equation. Aqueous solutions of acids, alkalis and salts are assumed to be largely water.

With solutions we make the assumptions that:
• $1 \, cm^3$ of solution has a mass of 1 g
• the solution has the same specific heat capacity as water.

Check-up

4 a Calculate the energy transferred when the temperature of $75 \, cm^3$ of water rises from 23 °C to 54 °C.
  b When 8 g of sodium chloride is dissolved in $40 \, cm^3$ of water the temperature falls from 22 °C to 20.5 °C. Calculate the energy absorbed by the solution when sodium chloride dissolves.
  c A student added $50 \, cm^3$ of sodium hydroxide to $50 \, cm^3$ of hydrochloric acid. Both solutions were at 18 °C to start with. When the solutions were mixed a reaction occurred. The temperature rose to 33 °C. Calculate the energy released in this reaction.

The enthalpy change of neutralisation by experiment

We can find the enthalpy change of neutralisation of sodium hydroxide with hydrochloric acid by mixing equal volumes of known equimolar concentrations of acid and alkali together in a polystyrene cup. A typical procedure for the reaction above is as follows.

1 Place $50 \, cm^3$ of $1.0 \, mol \, dm^{-3}$ hydrochloric acid in the cup and record its temperature.
2 Add $50 \, cm^3$ of $1.0 \, mol \, dm^{-3}$ sodium hydroxide (at the same temperature) to the acid in the cup.
3 Stir the reaction mixture with the thermometer and record the highest temperature.

In this experiment most of the heat is transferred to the solution since the polystyrene cup is a good insulator. Cooling of the warm solution is not a great problem: the reaction is rapid so the maximum temperature is reached before much cooling of the warm solution has occurred. However, there are still heat losses to the air and to the thermometer which make the result less exothermic than the data book value of $-57.1\,kJ\,mol^{-1}$.

Results and calculation

mass of solution	=	100 g (50 cm³ of acid plus 50 cm³ of alkali and assuming that 1.0 cm³ of solution has a mass of 1.0 g)
specific heat capacity	=	$4.18\,J\,g^{-1}\,°C^{-1}$ (assuming that the heat capacity of the solution is the same as the heat capacity of water)
starting temperature of reactant solutions	=	21.3 °C
final temperature of product solution	=	27.8 °C
temperature rise	=	6.5 °C
use the relationship q	=	$mc\Delta T$
heat energy released	=	$100 \times 4.18 \times 6.5 = 2717\,J$

At the start, the reaction mixture contained 50 cm³ of 1.0 mol dm⁻³ hydrochloric and 50 cm³ of 1.0 mol dm⁻³ sodium hydroxide. The number of moles of each (and of the water formed) is calculated using

$$\frac{\text{concentration} \times \text{volume (in cm}^3)}{1000} = \frac{1.0 \times 50}{1000}$$
$$= 0.050\,\text{moles}$$

So 2717 J of energy was released by 0.050 moles of acid.

Therefore for one mole of acid (forming one mole of water) the energy released was $\dfrac{2717}{0.050} = -54340\,J\,mol^{-1}$
$= -54\,kJ\,mol^{-1}$ (to 2 significant figures). The negative sign shows that the reaction is exothermic.

Enthalpy change of solution by experiment

The enthalpy change of solution of sodium hydroxide can be found using a polystyrene cup as a calorimeter. We use known amounts of solute and solvent with the solvent in excess to make sure that all the solute dissolves.

The procedure is:
1 Weigh an empty polystyrene cup.
2 Pour 100 cm³ of water into the cup and weigh the cup and water.
3 Record the steady temperature of the water with a thermometer reading to at least the nearest 0.2 °C.
4 Add a few pellets of sodium hydroxide (corrosive!) which have been stored under dry conditions.
5 Keep the mixture stirred continuously with a thermometer and record the temperature at fixed intervals, e.g. every 20 seconds.
6 Keep recording the temperature for 5 minutes after the maximum temperature has been reached.
7 Weigh the cup and its contents to calculate the mass of sodium hydroxide which dissolved.

Results and calculations

mass of polystyrene cup	=	23.00 g
mass of polystyrene cup + water	=	123.45 g
mass of water	=	100.45 g
mass of cup + water + sodium hydroxide	=	124.95 g
mass of sodium hydroxide that dissolved	=	1.50 g
initial temperature of water	=	18.0 °C
final temperature of water	=	21.6 °C
temperature rise	=	3.6 °C

From the results, 1.50 g of sodium hydroxide dissolved in 100.45 cm³ (100.45 g) of water and produced a temperature rise of 3.6 °C.

energy transferred as heat (in J)	=	mass of water (in g)	×	specific heat capacity (in $J\,g^{-1}\,°C^{-1}$)	×	temperature change (in °C)
	=	100.45	×	4.18	×	3.6
	=	\multicolumn{5}{l}{1511.57 J = 1.5 kJ (to 2 significant figures)}			

1.5 g of sodium hydroxide releases 1.5 kJ of energy on dissolving

1.0 mole of sodium hydroxide ($M_r = 40\,g\,mol^{-1}$)

releases $\dfrac{40}{1.5} \times 1.5\,kJ = 40\,kJ$

$\Delta H^{\ominus}_{sol} = -40\,kJ\,mol^{-1}$

In this experiment we are assuming that the specific heat capacity of the solution is the same as the specific heat capacity of water. The heat losses in this experiment, however, are likely to be considerable because the sodium hydroxide takes some time to dissolve. This means that the reaction mixture has a longer period of cooling.

Check-up

6 A student added 10 g (0.25 mol) of sodium hydroxide to 40 cm^3 of water to make a concentrated solution. All the sodium hydroxide dissolved. He measured the maximum temperature rise. He suggested that these results would give an accurate value for the standard enthalpy change of solution. Give two reasons why he is incorrect.

Finding the enthalpy change of combustion

Experiment: the enthalpy change of combustion of propan-1-ol

We can find the enthalpy change of combustion by burning a known mass of substance and using the heat released to raise the temperature of a known mass of water. The apparatus used for this consists of a spirit burner and a metal calorimeter (Figure 6.6).

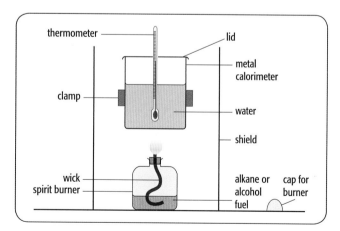

Figure 6.6 A simple apparatus used to find the enthalpy change of combustion of fuels.

The procedure is:
1 Weigh the spirit burner containing propan-1-ol. The cap on the burner must be kept on when the burner is not lit to avoid evaporation of the fuel.
2 Pour 100 cm^3 (100 g) of water into the calorimeter. For greater accuracy this should be weighed out.
3 Stir the water and record its temperature with a thermometer reading to at least the nearest 0.1 °C.
4 Place the spirit burner beneath the calorimeter, remove the cap and light the wick. The length of the wick should have been previously adjusted so that the material of the wick does not burn and the flame just touches the bottom of the calorimeter.
5 Keep stirring the water with the thermometer until there is a temperature rise of about 10 °C. Record this temperature.
6 Remove the spirit burner, place the cap on it and reweigh it.

Results and calculations

To find the standard enthalpy change of combustion we need to know:
• the mass of fuel burnt
• the temperature rise of the water
• the mass of the water
• the relative molecular mass of the fuel (propan-1-ol).

mass of water in calorimeter	= 100 g
mass of spirit burner and propan-1-ol at start	= 86.27 g
mass of spirit burner and propan-1-ol at end	= 86.06 g
mass of propan-1-ol burnt	= 0.21 g
initial temperature of water	= 30.9 °C
final temperature of water	= 20.2 °C
temperature rise of the water	= 10.7 °C

Using the relationship $q = mc\Delta T$ (mass of water × specific heat capacity of water × temperature rise)
energy released by burning 0.21 g propanol
$$= 100 \times 4.18 \times 10.7 = 4472.6 \text{ J}$$
the mass of 1 mole of propan-1-ol, C_3H_7OH, is 60 g
so for 60 g propan-1-ol the energy released

is $4472.6 \times \dfrac{60}{0.21}$
$= 1\,277\,885.7 \text{ J mol}^{-1}$
$= 1300 \text{ kJ mol}^{-1}$ (to 2 significant figures)

This is much less than the data book value of −2021 kJ mol^{-1}, mainly due to heat losses to the surroundings.

Check-up

7 A student calculated the standard enthalpy change of combustion of ethanol $\Delta H_c^{\ominus}$ [C₂H₅OH] by calorimetry as $-870\,\text{kJ}\,\text{mol}^{-1}$. The data book value is $-1367\,\text{kJ}\,\text{mol}^{-1}$. Explain the difference between these values.

6.5 Hess's law

Conserving energy

The Law of Conservation of Energy states that 'energy cannot be created or destroyed'. This is called the First Law of Thermodynamics.

This law also applies to chemical reactions. The total energy of the chemicals and their surroundings must remain constant. In 1840 Germain Hess applied the Law of Conservation of Energy to enthalpy changes.

> **Hess's law** states that 'the total enthalpy change in a chemical reaction is independent of the route by which the chemical reaction takes place as long as the initial and final conditions are the same'.

Fact file

One of the first people to suggest a 'perpetual motion machine' was Bhaskara II from India, who described a wheel which could run forever. People are still trying to make 'perpetual motion', even though it contradicts the Law of Conservation of Energy!

Enthalpy cycles

We can illustrate Hess's law by drawing enthalpy cycles (Hess cycles). In Figure **6.7**, the reactants A and B combine directly to form C. This is the direct route.

Two indirect routes are also shown. One other way of changing A + B to C is to convert A + B into different substances F + G (intermediates), which then combine to form C.

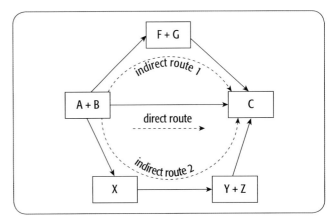

Figure 6.7 The enthalpy change is the same no matter which route is followed.

Hess's law tells us that the enthalpy change of reaction for the direct route is the same as for the indirect route. It does not matter how many steps there are in the indirect route. We can still use Hess's law.

We can use Hess's law to calculate enthalpy changes that cannot be found by experiments using calorimetry. For example, the enthalpy change of formation of propane cannot be found by direct experiment because hydrogen does not react with carbon under standard conditions.

Enthalpy change of reaction from enthalpy changes of formation

We can calculate the enthalpy change of reaction by using the type of enthalpy cycle shown in Figure **6.8**.

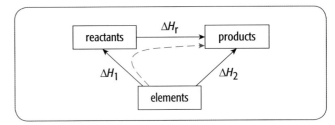

Figure 6.8 An enthalpy cycle for calculating an enthalpy change of reaction. The dashed line shows the indirect (two-step) route.

We use the enthalpy changes of formation of the reactants and products to calculate the enthalpy change of the reaction. We take note of the directions of the arrows to find the one-stage (direct) and two-stage (indirect) routes. When we use Hess's law we see that

$$\underset{\text{direct route}}{\Delta H_2} = \underset{\text{indirect route}}{\Delta H_1 + \Delta H_r}$$

So $\Delta H_r = \Delta H_2 - \Delta H_1$

To calculate the enthalpy change of reaction using this type of enthalpy cycle we use the following procedure:

- write the balanced equation at the top
- draw the cycle with elements at the bottom
- draw in all arrows, making sure they go in the correct directions
- apply Hess's law, taking into account the number of moles of each reactant and product.

If there are 3 moles of a product, e.g. $3CO_2(g)$, we must multiply the enthalpy change of formation by 3. Also remember that the standard enthalpy change of formation of an element in its standard state is zero.

Worked example

1 Calculate the standard enthalpy change for the reaction:

$$2NaHCO_3(s) \rightarrow Na_2CO_3(s) + CO_2(g) + H_2O(l)$$

The relevant enthalpy changes of formation are:
$\Delta H_f^\ominus [NaHCO_3(s)] = -950.8\,kJ\,mol^{-1}$
$\Delta H_f^\ominus [Na_2CO_3(s)] = -1130.7\,kJ\,mol^{-1}$
$\Delta H_f^\ominus [CO_2(g)] = -393.5\,kJ\,mol^{-1}$
$\Delta H_f^\ominus [H_2O(l)] = -285.8\,kJ\,mol^{-1}$

The enthalpy cycle is shown in Figure 6.9.

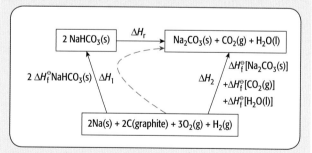

Figure 6.9 The enthalpy cycle for the decomposition of sodium hydrogencarbonate. The dashed line shows the two-step route.

continued ···▸

Using Hess's law
$$\Delta H_2 = \Delta H_1 + \Delta H_r$$
$$\Delta H_f^\ominus [Na_2CO_3(s)] + \Delta H_f^\ominus [CO_2(g)] + \Delta H_f^\ominus [H_2O(l)]$$
$$= 2\Delta H_f^\ominus [NaHCO_3(s)] + \Delta H_r$$

$$(-1130.7) + (-393.5) + (-285.8) = 2(-950.8) + \Delta H_r$$

$$-1810.0 = -1901.6 + \Delta H_r$$

So $\Delta H_r^\ominus = (-1810.0) - (-1901.6)$
$$= +91.6\,kJ\,mol^{-1} \text{ (for the equation shown)}$$

Note:
i the value for $\Delta H_f^\ominus NaHCO_3(s)]$ is multiplied by 2 because 2 moles of $NaHCO_3$ appear in the equation

ii the values for $\Delta H_f^\ominus [Na_2CO_3(s)]$, $\Delta H_f^\ominus [CO_2(g)]$ and $\Delta H_f^\ominus [H_2O(l)]$ are added together to give ΔH_2. Take care to account for the fact that some values may be positive and some negative.

Check-up

8 a Draw an enthalpy cycle to calculate $\Delta H_r^\ominus$ for the reaction

$$2Al(s) + Fe_2O_3(s) \rightarrow 2Fe(s) + Al_2O_3(s)$$

b Calculate $\Delta H_r^\ominus$ using the following information:

$$\Delta H_f^\ominus [Fe_2O_3(s)] = -824.2\,kJ\,mol^{-1}$$
$$\Delta H_f^\ominus [Al_2O_3(s)] = -1675.7\,kJ\,mol^{-1}$$

Enthalpy change of formation from enthalpy changes of combustion

We can calculate the enthalpy change of formation of many compounds by using the type of enthalpy cycle shown in Figure 6.10.

We use the enthalpy changes of combustion of the reactants and products to calculate the enthalpy change of formation. When we take note of the direction of

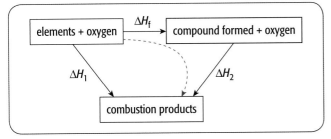

Figure 6.10 An enthalpy cycle for calculating an enthalpy change of formation from enthalpy changes of combustion. The dashed line shows the two-step route.

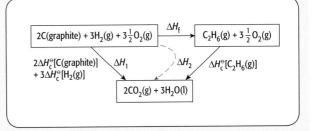

Figure 6.11 The enthalpy cycle to find the enthalpy change of formation of ethane using enthalpy changes of combustion. The dashed line shows the two-step route.

the arrows to find the one-stage (direct) and two-stage (indirect) routes and use Hess's law we see that

$$\underbrace{\Delta H_1}_{\text{direct route}} = \underbrace{\Delta H_f + \Delta H_2}_{\text{indirect route}}$$

So $\Delta H_f = \Delta H_1 - \Delta H_2$

To calculate the enthalpy change of formation using this type of cycle:
• write the equation for enthalpy change of formation at the top; add oxygen on both sides of the equation to balance the combustion reactions
• draw the cycle with the combustion products at the bottom
• draw in all arrows, making sure they go in the correct directions
• apply Hess's law, taking into account the number of moles of each reactant and product.

Worked example

2 Calculate the standard enthalpy change of formation of ethane, C_2H_6.
The relevant enthalpy changes of combustion are:

$C(graphite) + O_2(g) \rightarrow CO_2(g)$
$\qquad \Delta H_c^{\circ}[C(graphite)] = -393.5 \, \text{kJ} \, \text{mol}^{-1}$

$H_2(g) + \frac{1}{2}O_2(g) \rightarrow H_2O(l)$
$\qquad \Delta H_c^{\circ}[H_2(g)] = -285.8 \, \text{kJ} \, \text{mol}^{-1}$

$C_2H_6(g) + 3\frac{1}{2}O_2(g) \rightarrow 2CO_2(g) + 3H_2O(l)$
$\qquad \Delta H_c^{\circ}[C_2H_6(g)] = -1559.7 \, \text{kJ} \, \text{mol}^{-1}$

The enthalpy cycle is shown in Figure 6.11.

continued ⋯⟶

Using Hess's law

ΔH_1		$= \Delta H_f + \Delta H_2$
$2(-393.5) + 3(-285.8)$		$= \Delta H_f + (-1559.7)$
-1644.4		$= \Delta H_f + (-1559.7)$
So $\Delta H_f = -1644.4 - (-1559.7)$		$= -84.7 \, \text{kJ} \, \text{mol}^{-1}$

Check-up

9 a Draw an enthalpy cycle to calculate the enthalpy change of formation of ethanol, C_2H_5OH, using enthalpy changes of combustion.
   b Calculate a value for $\Delta H_f^{\circ}[C_2H_5OH(l)]$ using the following data:
   $\Delta H_c^{\circ}[C(graphite)] = -393.5 \, \text{kJ} \, \text{mol}^{-1}$
   $\Delta H_c^{\circ}[H_2(g)] = -285.8 \, \text{kJ} \, \text{mol}^{-1}$
   $\Delta H_c^{\circ}[C_2H_5OH(l)] = -1367.3 \, \text{kJ} \, \text{mol}^{-1}$

Calculating the enthalpy change of hydration of an anhydrous salt

Hydrated salts such as hydrated copper(II) sulfate, $CuSO_4.5H_2O$, contain water molecules surrounding their ions. It is very difficult to measure the enthalpy change when an anhydrous salt such as anhydrous sodium thiosulfate becomes hydrated.

$$Na_2S_2O_3(s) + 5H_2O(l) \rightarrow Na_2S_2O_3.5H_2O(s)$$

We can, however, use an enthalpy cycle to calculate this. We use the standard enthalpy changes of solution to complete the enthalpy cycle (Figure 6.12).

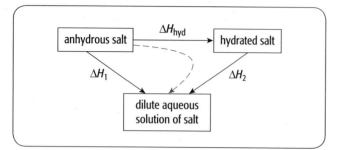

Figure 6.12 An enthalpy cycle to calculate the enthalpy change of hydration of an anhydrous salt. The dashed line shows the two-step route.

The enthalpy cycle for calculating the enthalpy of hydration of anhydrous sodium thiosulfate is shown in Figure 6.13.

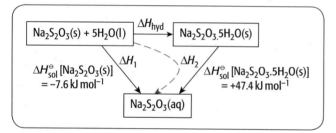

Figure 6.13 An enthalpy cycle to calculate the enthalpy change when anhydrous sodium thiosulfate is hydrated. The dashed line shows the two-step route.

Using Hess's law:

$$\Delta H_1 = \Delta H_{hyd} + \Delta H_2$$

$$(-7.6) = \Delta H_{hyd} + (+47.4)$$

So $\Delta H_{hyd} = (-7.6) - (+47.4) = -55.0 \, \text{kJ mol}^{-1}$

Check-up

10 Suggest why it is difficult to measure the enthalpy change directly when an anhydrous salt is converted to a hydrated salt.

6.6 Bond energies and enthalpy changes

Bond breaking and bond making

Enthalpy changes are due to the breaking and forming of bonds. Breaking bonds requires energy. The energy is needed to overcome the attractive forces joining the atoms together. Energy is released when new bonds are formed. Bond breaking is endothermic and bond forming is exothermic.

In a chemical reaction:

- if the energy needed to break bonds is less than the energy released when new bonds are formed the reaction will release energy and the reaction is exothermic.
- if the energy needed to break bonds is more than the energy released when new bonds are formed the reaction will absorb energy and the reaction is endothermic.

We can draw enthalpy level (reaction pathway) diagrams to show these changes (Figure 6.14). In reality not all the bonds in a compound are broken and then re-formed during a reaction. In most reactions only some of the bonds in the reactants are broken and then new bonds are formed in a specific sequence. The minimum energy required to break certain bonds in a compound to get a reaction to start is called the activation energy (see page 155).

Bond energy

The amount of energy needed to break a specific covalent bond is called the bond dissociation energy. We sometimes call this the **bond energy** or bond enthalpy. The symbol for bond energy is E. We put the type of bond broken in brackets after the symbol. So $E(\text{C}-\text{H})$ refers to the bond energy of a mole of single bonds between carbon and hydrogen atoms.

The bond energy for double and triple bonds refers to a mole of double or triple bonds. Two examples of equations relating to bond energies are:

$$\text{Br}_2(\text{g}) \rightarrow 2\text{Br}(\text{g}) \qquad E(\text{Br}-\text{Br}) = +193 \, \text{kJ mol}^{-1}$$

$$\text{O}=\text{O}(\text{g}) \rightarrow 2\text{O}(\text{g}) \qquad E(\text{O}=\text{O}) = +498 \, \text{kJ mol}^{-1}$$

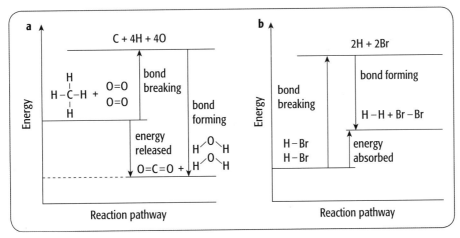

Figure 6.14 a An energy level diagram showing bond breaking and bond forming for the combustion of methane (exothermic). **b** An energy level diagram showing bond breaking and bond forming for the decomposition of hydrogen bromide (endothermic).

The values of bond energies are always positive because they refer to bonds being broken.

When new bonds are formed the amount of energy released is the same as the amount of energy absorbed when the same type of bond is broken. So, for the formation of oxygen molecules from oxygen atoms:

$$2O(g) \rightarrow O_2(g) \qquad E(O{=}O) = -498 \text{ kJ mol}^{-1}$$

Average bond energy

Bond energy is affected by other atoms in the molecule. The O—H bond in water has a slightly different bond energy value to the O—H bond in ethanol; in ethanol the oxygen is connected to a carbon atom rather than another hydrogen atom. The O—H bond is in a different environment. Identical bonds in molecules with two (or more) types of bond have different bond energies when we measure them. It takes more energy to break the first O—H bond in water than to break the second. For these reasons we use **average bond energies** taken from a number of bonds of the same type but in different environments.

We cannot usually find the value of bond energies directly so we have to use an enthalpy cycle. The average bond energy of the C—H bond in methane can be found using the enthalpy changes of atomisation of carbon and hydrogen and the enthalpy change of combustion or formation of methane.

The enthalpy cycle for calculating the average C—H bond energy is shown in Figure **6.15**. Using the enthalpy cycle shown in Figure **6.15**, the average C—H bond

energy can be found by dividing the value of ΔH on the diagram by four (because there are four C—H bonds in a molecule of methane).

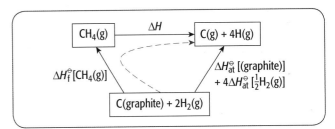

Figure 6.15 An enthalpy cycle to find the average bond energy of the C—H bond. The dashed line shows the two-step route.

Calculating enthalpy changes using bond energies

We can use bond enthalpies to calculate the enthalpy change of a reaction that we cannot measure directly.

For example, the reaction for the Haber process (see page 142):

$$N_2(g) + 3H_2(g) \rightleftharpoons 2NH_3(g)$$

The enthalpy cycle for this reaction is shown in Figure 6.16. The relevant bond energies are:
$E(N\equiv N) = 945 \, kJ \, mol^{-1}$
$E(H{-}H) = 436 \, kJ \, mol^{-1}$
$E(N{-}H) = 391 \, kJ \, mol^{-1}$

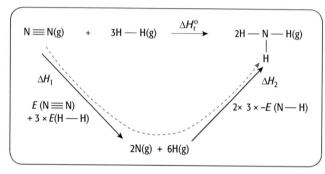

Figure 6.16 The enthalpy cycle for ammonia synthesis. The dashed line shows the two-step route.

It is often easier to set out the calculation as a balance sheet, as shown below.

Bonds broken ΔH_1 (kJ)	Bonds formed ΔH_2 (kJ)
1 × N≡N = 1 × 945 = 945	6 × N–H = 6 × 391
3 × H–H = 3 × 436 = 1308	
total = +2253	total = –2346

Notice in these calculations that:
• one triple bond in nitrogen is broken
• three single bonds in hydrogen are broken
• six single N–H bonds in hydrogen are formed (because each of the two ammonia molecules has 3 N–H bonds)
• values for bond breaking are positive since these are endothermic and values for bond forming are negative since these are exothermic.

From the enthalpy cycle in Figure 6.16:

$$\Delta H_r = \Delta H_1 + \Delta H_2$$

ΔH_r = enthalpy change for bonds broken
         + enthalpy change for bonds formed

$$\Delta H_r = 2253 + (-2346) = -93 \, kJ \, mol^{-1}$$

Check-up

12 The equation for the combustion of ethanol is

$$C_2H_5OH(l) + 3O_2(g) \rightarrow 2CO_2(g) + 3H_2O(l)$$

a Rewrite this equation to show all the bonds in the reactants and products.

b Use the following bond energies (in $kJ \, mol^{-1}$) to calculate a value for the standard enthalpy change of this reaction:
$E(C{-}C) = +347$
$E(C{-}H) = +410$
$E(C{-}O) = +336$
$E(O{=}O) = +496$
$E(C{=}O) = +805$
$E(O{-}H) = +465$

c The standard enthalpy change of combustion of ethanol is $-1367.3 \, kJ \, mol^{-1}$. Suggest why this value differs from the value obtained using bond energies.

Summary

☐ When a chemical reaction occurs, energy is transferred to or from the surroundings.

☐ In an exothermic reaction, heat is given out to the surroundings so the products have less energy than the reactants. In an endothermic reaction, heat is absorbed from the surroundings so the products have more energy than the reactants.

☐ Energy changes in chemical reactions which lead to heating or cooling are called enthalpy changes (ΔH).

☐ Exothermic enthalpy changes are shown as negative values (−).

☐ Endothermic enthalpy changes are shown as positive values (+).

☐ Standard enthalpy changes are compared under standard conditions of pressure, 10^5 Pa (100 kPa), and temperature, 298 K (25 °C).

☐ Enthalpy changes can be calculated experimentally using the relationship:

heat energy = mass of liquid × specific heat capacity × temperature change

$$q = mc\Delta T$$

☐ The standard enthalpy change of formation ($\Delta H_f^\ominus$) is the enthalpy change when one mole of a compound is formed from its elements under standard conditions.

☐ The standard enthalpy change of combustion ($\Delta H_c^\ominus$) is the enthalpy change when one mole of a substance is burnt in excess oxygen under standard conditions.

☐ The standard enthalpy change of atomisation ($\Delta H_{at}^\ominus$) is the enthalpy change when one mole of gaseous atoms is formed from the element in its standard state under standard conditions.

☐ The standard enthalpy changes of hydration and solution can be defined in terms of one mole of a specified compound reacting completely.

☐ The standard enthalpy change of neutralisation can be defined in terms of one mole of water formed when hydrogen ions and hydroxide ions react.

☐ Hess's law states that 'the total enthalpy change for a chemical reaction is independent of the route by which the reaction takes place'.

☐ Hess's law can be used to calculate enthalpy changes for reactions that do not occur directly or cannot be found by experiment.

☐ Hess's law can be used to calculate the enthalpy change of a reaction using the enthalpy changes of formation of the reactants and products.

☐ Hess's law can be used to calculate the enthalpy change of formation of a compound using the enthalpy changes of combustion of the reactants and products.

☐ Bond breaking is endothermic; bond making is exothermic.

☐ Bond energy is a measure of the energy needed to break a covalent bond.

☐ Average bond energies are often used because the strength of a bond between two particular types of atom is slightly different in different compounds.

☐ Hess's law can be used to calculate the enthalpy change of a reaction using the average bond energies of the reactants and products.

End-of-chapter questions

1 Copper(II) nitrate decomposes on heating. The reaction is endothermic.

$$2Cu(NO_3)_2(s) \rightarrow 2CuO(s) + 4NO_2(g) + O_2(g)$$

   a Draw an enthalpy level diagram (reaction profile diagram) for this reaction. [3]

   b Draw an enthalpy cycle diagram to calculate the standard enthalpy change for this reaction, using enthalpy changes of formation. [3]

   c Calculate the enthalpy change for this reaction using the following enthalpy changes of formation.
$\Delta H_f^\ominus [Cu(NO_3)_2(s)] = -302.9 \, kJ \, mol^{-1}$
$\Delta H_f^\ominus [CuO(s)] = -157.3 \, kJ \, mol^{-1}$
$\Delta H_f^\ominus [NO_2(g)] = +33.2 \, kJ \, mol^{-1}$ [3]

   d Copper(II) sulfate is soluble in water. A student dissolved 25.0 g of copper(II) sulfate in 100 cm³ of water in a polystyrene beaker stirring all the time. The temperature of the water fell by 2.9 °C.

     i Calculate the enthalpy change of solution of copper(II) sulfate.
(specific heat capacity of water = $4.18 \, J \, g^{-1} \, °C^{-1}$; relative molecular mass of copper(II) sulfate = 249.7 g mol⁻¹) [3]

     ii Suggest **one** source of error in this experiment and explain how the error affects the results. [2]

                                                    Total = 14

2 Propanone is a liquid. It has the structure

$$\begin{array}{ccccc} & H & O & H & \\ & | & || & | & \\ H - & C & - C & - C & - H \\ & | & & | & \\ & H & & H & \end{array}$$

The equation for the complete combustion of propanone is:

$$CH_3COCH_3(l) + 4O_2(g) \rightarrow 3CO_2(g) + 3H_2O(l)$$

   a Use the following bond energies (in kJ mol⁻¹) to calculate a value for the standard enthalpy change of this reaction:
$E(C-C) = +347$
$E(C-H) = +413$
$E(O=O) = +496$
$E(C=O) = +805$
$E(O-H) = +465$ [4]

   b Suggest why it would be more accurate to use bond energies which are not average bond energies in this calculation. [2]

   c The standard enthalpy change of combustion of propanone is –1816.5 kJ mol⁻¹. Suggest why this value differs from the value obtained using bond energies. [2]

   d The standard enthalpy change of formation of propanone is –248 kJ mol⁻¹.

     i Define the term **standard enthalpy change of formation**. [3]

     ii Write the equation which describes the standard enthalpy change of formation of propanone. [2]

     iii Explain why the enthalpy change of formation of propanone cannot be found by a single experiment. [1]

                                                    Total = 14

3 $240 \, cm^3$ of ethane (C_2H_6) was burned in a controlled way and found to raise the temperature of $100 \, cm^3$ of water by $33.5 \, °C$.

(specific heat capacity of water = $4.18 \, J \, g^{-1} \, K^{-1}$; 1 mol of gas molecules occupies $24.0 \, dm^3$ at r.t.p.)

    a How many moles of ethane were burned?   [1]

    b Calculate the heat change for the experiment.   [2]

    c Calculate the molar enthalpy change of combustion for ethane, as measured by this experiment.   [2]

    d Use the values below to calculate the standard molar enthalpy change for the complete combustion of ethane.

        $\Delta H_f^⦵ (CO_2) = -394 \, kJ \, mol^{-1}$

        $\Delta H_f^⦵ (H_2O) = -286 \, kJ \, mol^{-1}$

        $\Delta H_f^⦵ (C_2H_6) = -85 \, kJ \, mol^{-1}$ [4]

    e Give possible reasons for the discrepancy between the two results.   [2]

                                                    Total = 11

4   **a** Define **standard enthalpy change of combustion**.   [3]

    b When red phosphorus burns in oxygen the enthalpy change is $-2967 \, kJ \, mol^{-1}$. For white phosphorus the enthalpy change is $-2984 \, kJ \, mol^{-1}$. For both forms of phosphorus the reaction taking place is:

$$P_4(s) + 5O_2(g) \rightarrow P_4O_{10}(s)$$

      i Use this information to calculate the enthalpy change for the transformation: P_4(white) $\rightarrow P_4$(red)   [5]

      ii Represent these changes on an enthalpy profile diagram.   [3]

                                                      Total = 11

5   **a** Define **standard enthalpy change of formation**.   [3]

    b Calculate the standard enthalpy change of formation of methane from the following standard enthalpy changes of combustion:

      carbon = $-394 \, kJ \, mol^{-1}$

      hydrogen = $-286 \, kJ \, mol^{-1}$

      methane = $-891 \, kJ \, mol^{-1}$ [4]

    c Calculate the standard enthalpy change of combustion of methane using the following bond energies:

      $E(C-H) = +412 \, kJ \, mol^{-1}$

      $E(O-O) = +496 \, kJ \, mol^{-1}$

      $E(C=O) = +805 \, kJ \, mol^{-1}$

      $E(O-H) = +463 \, kJ \, mol^{-1}$ [4]

                                                         Total = 11

6   **a** Define **average bond enthalpy**.   [2]

    b Use the average bond enthalpies that follow to calculate a value for the enthalpy change for the reaction:

$$H_2 + I_2 \rightarrow 2HI$$

      $E(H-H) = +436 \, kJ \, mol^{-1}$

      $E(I-I) = +151 \, kJ \, mol^{-1}$

      $E(H-I) = +299 \, kJ \, mol^{-1}$ [3]

    c Represent these changes on an enthalpy profile diagram.   [3]

                                                         Total = 8

7 a Define **enthalpy change of solution**.   [3]
   b Given the enthalpy changes ΔH_1 and ΔH_2 below, construct a Hess's cycle that will enable you to find
      the enthalpy change, ΔH_r, for the reaction:

$$MgCl_2(s) + 6H_2O(l) \rightarrow MgCl_2.6H_2O(s) \qquad\qquad \Delta H_r$$

$$MgCl_2(s) + aq \rightarrow MgCl_2(aq) \qquad\qquad \Delta H_1$$

$$MgCl_2.6H_2O(s) + aq \rightarrow MgCl_2(aq) \qquad\qquad \Delta H_2$$

                                                                                                                [4]
                                                                                                    Total = 7

8 a Define **standard enthalpy change of reaction**.   [3]
   b Given the enthalpy changes ΔH_1 and ΔH_2 below, construct a Hess's cycle that will enable you to
      find the enthalpy change, ΔH_r, for the reaction:

$$MgCO_3(s) \rightarrow MgO(s) + CO_2(g) \qquad\qquad \Delta H_r$$

$$MgCO_3(s) + 2HCl(aq) \rightarrow MgCl_2(aq) + CO_2(g) + H_2O(l) \qquad\qquad \Delta H_1$$

$$MgO(s) + 2HCl(aq) \rightarrow H_2O(l) + MgCl_2(aq) \qquad\qquad \Delta H_2$$

                                                                                                                [4]
                                                                                                    Total = 7

9 In an experiment, a spirit burner is used to heat $250\,cm^3$ of water by burning methanol (CH_3OH).
   (A_r values: C = 12.0, H = 1.0, O = 16.0; specific heat capacity of water = $4.18\,J\,g^{-1}\,°C^{-1}$)
   Results:
   starting temperature of water = 20.0 °C
   starting mass of burner + fuel = 248.8 g
   final temperature of water   = 43.0 °C
   final mass of burner + fuel   = 245.9 g
   a How many joules of heat energy went into the water?   [2]
   b How many moles of fuel were burnt?   [2]
   c Calculate an experimental value for the enthalpy change of combustion of methanol from these results. [2]
   d Suggest three reasons why your answer is much smaller than the accepted standard enthalpy of
      combustion of methanol.   [3]
                                                                                                    Total = 9

Learning outcomes

Students should be able to:

☐ describe and explain redox processes in terms of electron transfer and/or of changes in oxidation number (oxidation state)

☐ explain, including the electrode reactions, the industrial processes of
  – the electrolysis of brine using a diaphragm cell
  – the extraction of aluminium from molten aluminium oxide/cryolite mixture
  – the electrolytic purification of copper.

7.1 What is a redox reaction?

A simple definition of **oxidation** is gain of oxygen by an element. For example, when magnesium reacts with oxygen, the magnesium combines with oxygen to form magnesium oxide. Magnesium has been oxidised.

$$2Mg(s) + O_2(g) \rightarrow 2MgO(s)$$

Figure 7.1 A redox reaction is taking place when the fuel in the Space Shuttle's rockets burns.

A simple definition of **reduction** is loss of oxygen. When copper(II) oxide reacts with hydrogen, this is the equation for the reaction:

$$CuO(s) + H_2(g) \rightarrow Cu(s) + H_2O(l)$$

Copper(II) oxide loses its oxygen. Copper(II) oxide has been reduced.

But if we look carefully at the copper oxide/hydrogen equation, we can see that oxidation is also taking place. The hydrogen is gaining oxygen to form water. The hydrogen has been oxidised. We can see that **red**uction and **ox**idation have taken place together.

Oxidation and reduction **always** take place together. We call the reactions where this happens **redox reactions**. Redox reactions are very important. For example, one redox reaction – photosynthesis – provides food for the entire planet, and another one – respiration – keeps you alive. Both are redox reactions.

We can also define reduction as addition of hydrogen to a compound and oxidation as removal of hydrogen from a compound. This is often seen in the reaction of organic compounds (see page **248**).

There are two other ways of finding out whether or not a substance has been oxidised or reduced during a chemical reaction:
• electron transfer
• changes in oxidation number.

Check-up

1 **a** In each of the following equations, state which reactant has been oxidised:
   i $PbO + H_2 \rightarrow Pb + H_2O$
   ii $CO + Ag_2O \rightarrow 2Ag + CO_2$
   iii $2Mg + CO_2 \rightarrow 2MgO + C$
   b In each of the following equations, state which reactant has been reduced:
   i $5CO + I_2O_5 \rightarrow 5CO_2 + I_2$
   ii $2H_2S + SO_2 \rightarrow 3S + 2H_2O$
   iii $CH_2{=}CH_2 + H_2 \rightarrow CH_3CH_3$

7.2 Redox and electron transfer

Half-equations

We can extend our definition of redox to include reactions involving ions.

> Oxidation **Is** Loss of electrons.
> Reduction **Is** Gain of electrons.
>   The initial letters shown in bold spell **OIL RIG**. This may help you to remember these two definitions!

Sodium reacts with chlorine to form the ionic compound sodium chloride.

$$2Na(s) + Cl_2(g) \rightarrow 2NaCl(s)$$

We can divide this reaction into two separate equations, one showing oxidation and the other showing reduction. We call these **half-equations**.

When sodium reacts with chlorine:
- Each sodium atom loses one electron from its outer shell. Oxidation is loss of electrons (OIL). The sodium atoms have been oxidised.

$$Na \rightarrow Na^+ + e^-$$

This half-equation shows that sodium is oxidised. It is also acceptable to write this half-equation as:

$$Na - e^- \rightarrow Na^+$$

- Each chlorine atom gains one electron to complete its outer shell. Reduction is gain of electrons (RIG). The chlorine atoms have been reduced.

$$Cl_2 + 2e^- \rightarrow 2Cl^-$$

This is a half-equation showing chlorine being reduced. There are two chlorine atoms in a chlorine molecule, so two electrons are gained.

In another example iron reacts with copper(II) ions, Cu^{2+}, in solution to form iron(II) ions, Fe^{2+}, and copper.

$$Fe(s) + Cu^{2+}(aq) \rightarrow Fe^{2+}(aq) + Cu(s)$$

- Each iron atom loses two electrons to form an Fe^{2+} ion. The iron atoms have been oxidised.

$$Fe \rightarrow Fe^{2+} + 2e^-$$

It is also acceptable to write this half-equation as:

$$Fe - 2e^- \rightarrow Fe^{2+}$$

- Each copper(II) ion gains two electrons. The copper ions have been reduced.

$$Cu^{2+} + 2e^- \rightarrow Cu$$

Balancing half-equations

We can construct a balanced ionic equation from two half-equations by balancing the numbers of electrons lost and gained and then adding the two half-equations together. The numbers of electrons lost and gained in a redox reaction must be equal.

Worked examples

1 Construct the balanced ionic equation for the reaction between nickel and iron(III) ions, Fe^{3+}, from the half-equations:

$$Ni(s) \rightarrow Ni^{2+}(aq) + 2e^-$$

$$Fe^{3+}(aq) + e^- \rightarrow Fe^{2+}(aq)$$

- Each Ni atom loses two electrons when it is oxidised. Each Fe^{3+} ion gains one electron when it is reduced.
- So two Fe^{3+} ions are needed to gain the two electrons lost when each Ni^{2+} ion is formed

$$2Fe^{3+}(aq) + 2e^- \rightarrow 2Fe^{2+}(aq)$$

$$Ni(s) \rightarrow Ni^{2+}(aq) + 2e^-$$

- The balanced ionic equation is

$$Ni(s) + 2Fe^{3+}(aq) \rightarrow Ni^{2+}(aq) + 2Fe^{2+}(aq)$$

Notice how the electrons have cancelled out.

2 Construct the balanced ionic equation for the reaction of iodide ions (I^-) with manganate(VII) ions (MnO_4^-) in the presence of hydrogen ions (H^+). Use the following two half-equations to help you:

$$2I^-(aq) \rightarrow I_2(aq) + 2e^- \qquad \text{(i)}$$

$$MnO_4^-(aq) + 8H^+(aq) + 5e^- \rightarrow Mn^{2+}(aq) + 4H_2O(l) \qquad \text{(ii)}$$

- When two iodide ions are oxidised, they lose two electrons. Each MnO_4^- ion gains five electrons when it is reduced.
- So we must multiply equation (i) by 5 and equation (ii) by 2 to balance the number of electrons:

$$10I^-(aq) \rightarrow 5I_2(aq) + 10e^-$$

$$2MnO_4^-(aq) + 16H^+(aq) + 10e^-$$
$$\rightarrow 2Mn^{2+}(aq) + 8H_2O(l)$$

- The balanced ionic equation is

$$2MnO_4^-(aq) + 10I^-(aq) + 16H^+(aq)$$
$$\rightarrow 2Mn^{2+}(aq) + 5I_2(aq) + 8H_2O$$

Check-up

2 a Write two half-equations for the following reactions. For each half-equation state whether oxidation or reduction is occurring.
   i $Cl_2 + 2I^- \rightarrow I_2 + 2Cl^-$
   ii $2Mg + O_2 \rightarrow 2MgO$
   iii $4Fe + 3O_2 \rightarrow 2Fe_2O_3$
 b Zinc metal reacts with IO_3^- ions in acidic solution. Construct a balanced ionic equation for this reaction, using the two half-equations below:

$$2IO_3^- + 12H^+ + 10e^- \rightarrow I_2 + 6H_2O$$

$$Zn \rightarrow Zn^{2+} + 2e^-$$

7.3 Oxidation numbers

What are oxidation numbers?

We can extend our definition of redox even further to include oxidation and reduction in reactions involving covalent compounds. We do this by using **oxidation numbers** (oxidation numbers are also called **oxidation states**). An oxidation number is a number given to each atom or ion in a compound which shows us its degree of oxidation. Oxidation numbers can be positive, negative or zero. The + or – sign must always be included. Higher positive oxidation numbers mean that an atom or ion is more oxidised. Higher negative oxidation numbers mean that an atom or ion is more reduced.

Oxidation number rules

We can deduce the oxidation number of any atom or ion by using oxidation number rules. It is important to note that an oxidation number refers to a single atom in a compound.

1 The oxidation number of any uncombined element is zero. For example, the oxidation number of each atom in S_8, Cl_2 and Zn is zero.
2 In compounds many atoms or ions have fixed oxidation numbers
   - Group I element are always +1
   - Group II elements are always +2
   - fluorine is always –1

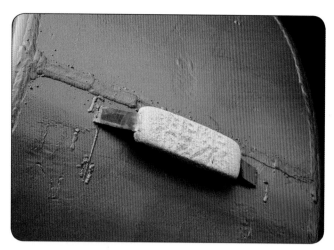

Figure 7.2 This is part of a ship's hull. It is made of iron protected by bars of magnesium metal. The magnesium atoms (oxidation number = 0) are oxidised to Mg^{2+} ions (oxidation number = +2) in preference to iron atoms changing to Fe^{3+}. This is called sacrificial protection.

- hydrogen is +1 (except in metal hydrides such as NaH when it is –1)
- oxygen is –2 (except in peroxides where it is –1 and in F_2O where it is +2).

3 The oxidation number of an element in a monatomic ion is always the same as the charge. For example, Cl^- is –1, Al^{3+} is +3.

4 The sum of the oxidation numbers in a compound is zero.

5 The sum of the oxidation numbers in an ion is equal to the charge on the ion.

6 In either a compound or an ion, the more electronegative element is given the negative oxidation number.

Applying the oxidation number rules

In the following examples we shall use 'ox. no.' as an abbreviation for oxidation number.

Compounds of a metal with a non-metal

The metal always has the positive ox. no. and the non-metal has the negative ox. no. For example in sodium oxide, Na_2O, Na = +1 and O = –2.

If we do not know the ox. no. of one of the atoms, we can often work it out using the invariable ox. nos. in rule 2. For example in sodium sulfide:

- ox. no. of each Na atom = +1
- for two sodium atoms = +2
- Na_2S has no overall charge, so the total ox. no. is zero (rule 4)
- ox. no. of S = –2

Compounds of a non-metal with a non-metal

In compounds containing two different non-metals, the sign of the ox. no. depends on the electronegativity of each atom (see page **62**). The most electronegative element is given the negative sign (rule 6).

Sulfur dioxide, SO_2
- ox. no of each O atom = –2
- for two oxygen atoms = $2 \times (-2) = -4$
- SO_2 has no charge, so the total ox. no. is zero (rule 4)
- ox. no. of S = +4

Iodine trichloride, ICl_3
- chlorine is more electronegative than iodine, so chlorine is – and iodine is +
- ox. no. of each Cl atom = –1
- for three chlorine atoms = $3 \times (-1) = -3$
- ICl_3 has no charge, so the total ox. no. is zero (rule 4)
- ox. no. of I = +3

Hydrazine, N_2H_4
- nitrogen is more electronegative than hydrogen, so nitrogen is – and hydrogen is +
- ox. no. of each H atom = +1 (rule 2)
- for four hydrogen atoms = $4 \times (+1) = +4$
- N_2H_4 has no charge, so the total ox. no. is zero (rule 4)
- ox. no. of two N atoms = –4
- ox. no. of each N atom = –2

Compound ions

Compound ions are ions with two or more different atoms. Examples are the sulfate ion, SO_4^{2-}, and the nitrate ion, NO_3^-. We use rule 5 to work out the ox. no. which we do not know.

Nitrate ion, NO_3^-
- ox. no. of each O atom = –2
- for three oxygen atoms = $3 \times (-2) = -6$
- NO_3^- has a charge of 1–, so the total ox. no. of N and O atoms is –1 (rule 5)
- ox. no. of the nitrogen atom plus ox. no. of the three oxygen atoms (–6) = –1
- ox. no. of N = +5

3 State the ox. no. of the bold atoms in these compounds or ions:

a P_2O_5
b SO_4^{2-}
c H_2S
d Al_2Cl_6
e NH_3
f ClO_2^-
g $CaCO_3$

Redox and oxidation number

We can define oxidation and reduction in terms of the oxidation number changes of particular atoms during a reaction.

> Oxidation is an increase of oxidation number.
> Reduction is a decrease in oxidation number.

For example, when tin reacts with nitric acid, the oxidation numbers of each atom of tin and nitrogen change as shown below.

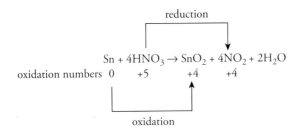

$$Sn + 4HNO_3 \rightarrow SnO_2 + 4NO_2 + 2H_2O$$

oxidation numbers 0   +5   +4   +4

Figure 7.3 Copper reacts with silver nitrate to form silver and copper(II) nitrate. The ox. no. of each copper atom has increased by two. The ox. no. of each silver ion decreases by one.

Each tin atom (Sn) has increased in ox. no. by +4: tin has been oxidised. Each nitrogen atom has decreased in ox. no. by −1: nitrogen has been reduced. The ox. no. of each oxygen atom is unchanged at −2. The ox. no. of each hydrogen atom is unchanged at +1. Oxygen and hydrogen are neither oxidised nor reduced.

In this reaction nitric acid is acting as an **oxidising agent**:

- oxidising agents increase the ox. no. of another atom
- an atom in the oxidising agent decreases in ox. no.
- the oxidising agent is the substance which gets reduced – it gains electrons.

In this reaction tin is acting as a **reducing agent**:

- reducing agents decrease the ox. no. of another atom
- an atom in the reducing agent increases in ox. no.
- the reducing agent is the substance which gets oxidised – it loses electrons.

4 a Deduce the change in ox. no. for the bold atoms or ions in each of the following equations. In each case, state whether oxidation or reduction has taken place.

  i $2\mathbf{I^-} + \mathbf{Br_2} \rightarrow I_2 + 2Br^-$
  ii $(\mathbf{NH_4})_2\mathbf{Cr_2O_7} \rightarrow N_2 + 4H_2O + Cr_2O_3$
  iii $\mathbf{As_2O_3} + 2\mathbf{I_2} + 2H_2O$
    $\rightarrow As_2O_5 + 2H^+ + 4I^-$
  iv $2K\mathbf{MnO_4} + 16H\mathbf{Cl}$
    $\rightarrow 2MnCl_2 + 2KCl + 5Cl_2 + 8H_2O$

  b Identify the reducing agent in each of the equations above.

Naming compounds

We sometimes use Roman numbers, in brackets, to name compounds. We use these systematic names to distinguish different compounds made of the same elements. For example, there are two types of iron chloride. We show the difference by naming them iron(II) chloride and iron(III) chloride. The numbers in brackets are the oxidation numbers of the iron.

- In iron(II) chloride, the ox. no. of the iron is +2. The compound contains Fe^{2+} ions. The formula is $FeCl_2$.
- In iron(III) chloride, the ox. no. of the iron is +3. The compound contains Fe^{3+} ions. The formula is $FeCl_3$.

We can also use oxidation numbers to distinguish between non-metal atoms in molecules and ions.

Oxides of nitrogen

There are several oxides of nitrogen, including N_2O, NO and NO_2. We distinguish between these according to the ox. no. of the nitrogen atom. (The ox. no. of oxygen is generally –2.)

- The ox. no. of N in N_2O is +1. So this compound is nitrogen(I) oxide.
- The ox. no. of N in NO is +2. So this compound is nitrogen(II) oxide.
- The ox. no. of N in NO_2 is +4. So this compound is nitrogen(IV) oxide.

Nitrate ions

Sodium, nitrogen and oxygen can form two different compounds $Na^+NO_2^-$ and $Na^+NO_3^-$ (Figure 7.4). The ox. no. of sodium is +1 and the ox. no. of oxygen is –2. So it is the ox. no. of nitrogen which varies.

- The ox. no. of N in the NO_2^- ion is +3. So $NaNO_2$ is sodium nitrate(III).
- The ox. no. of N in the NO_3^- ion is +5. So $NaNO_3$ is sodium nitrate(V).

Note that the ox. no. comes after the ion it refers to.

Ions containing oxygen and one other element have the ending -ate (but hydroxide ions, OH^-, are an exception to this rule). For example, ions containing chlorine and oxygen are chlorates and ions containing sulfur and oxygen are sulfates.

The names of inorganic acids containing oxygen end in –ic. The Roman number goes directly after the ion which contains the oxygen and another element.

- H_3PO_3 is phosphoric(III) acid because the ox. no. of phosphorus is +3.
- $HClO_4$ is chloric(VII) acid because the ox. no. of chlorine is +7.

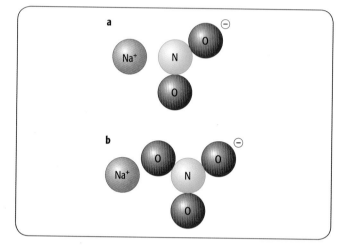

Figure 7.4 a One formula unit of 'sodium nitrate(III)' and **b** one formula unit of 'sodium nitrate(V)'.

Check-up

5 Give the full systematic names of the following:

  a Na_2SO_3 e $FeSO_4$
  b Na_2SO_4 f Cu_2O
  c $Fe(NO_3)_2$ g H_2SO_3
  d $Fe(NO_3)_3$ h Mn_2O_7

From name to formula

You can work out the formula of a compound from its name.

Worked example

3 Each formula unit of sodium chlorate(V) contains one sodium ion. What is the formula of sodium chlorate(V)?

We know that:
- sodium has an ox. no. of +1
- oxygen has an ox. no. of –2
- the ox. no. of chlorine is +5
- the chlorate(V) ion has a charge of 1– (to balance the 1+ charge of the sodium).

We can work out the formula of the chlorate(V) ion from the oxidation numbers of oxygen and chlorine (let n be the number of oxygen atoms):

$$ox.\ no.(Cl) + ox.\ no.(O) = -1$$
$$+5 \qquad n \times (-2) \qquad -1$$

$$n = 3$$

So the chlorate(V) ion is ClO_3^- and sodium chlorate(V) is $NaClO_3$.

Check-up

6 What are the formulae of:
  a sodium chlorate(I)
  b iron(III) oxide
  c potassium nitrate(III)
  d phosphorus(III) chloride

Balancing chemical equations using oxidation numbers

We can use oxidation numbers to balance equations involving redox reactions. This method is especially useful where compound ions such as nitrate(V) or manganate(VII) are involved.

Worked examples

4 Copper(II) oxide (CuO) reacts with ammonia (NH_3) to form copper, nitrogen (N_2) and water.

Step 1 Write the unbalanced equation and identify the atoms which change in ox. no. (shown here in red).

$$CuO + NH_3 \rightarrow Cu + N_2 + H_2O$$
$$+2\ -2 \quad -3\ +1 \qquad 0 \qquad 0 \quad +1\ -2$$

Step 2 Deduce the ox. no. changes.

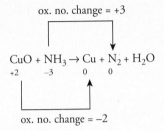

Step 3 Balance the ox. no. changes.

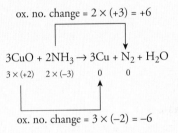

The change in ox. nos. are –2 for the copper and +3 for the nitrogen. To balance the ox. no. changes, we need to multiply the copper by 3 and the nitrogen in the ammonia by 2. The total ox. no. changes are then balanced (–6 and +6). Notice that we do not multiply the N_2 by 2 because there are already two atoms of nitrogen present. Once these ratios have been fixed you must not change them.

Step 4 Balance the atoms.
There are six hydrogen atoms in the $2NH_3$ on the left. These are balanced with six on the right (as $3H_2O$). This also balances the number of oxygen atoms. The final equation is

$$3CuO + 2NH_3 \rightarrow 3Cu + N_2 + 3H_2O$$

continued ⋯⟶

5 Manganate(VII) ions (MnO_4^-) react with Fe^{2+} ions in the presence of acid (H^+) to form Mn^{2+} ions, Fe^{3+} ions and water.

Step 1 Write the unbalanced equation and identify the atoms which change in ox. no.

$$\underset{+7\ -2}{MnO_4^-} + \underset{+2}{Fe^{2+}} + \underset{+1}{H^+} \rightarrow \underset{+2}{Mn^{2+}} + \underset{+3}{Fe^{3+}} + \underset{+1\ -2}{H_2O}$$

Step 2 Deduce the ox. no. changes.

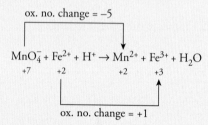

$$\underset{+7}{MnO_4^-} + \underset{+2}{Fe^{2+}} + H^+ \rightarrow \underset{+2}{Mn^{2+}} + \underset{+3}{Fe^{3+}} + H_2O$$

ox. no. change = +1

Step 3 Balance the ox. no. changes.

ox. no. change = 1 × (–5) = –5

$$\underset{+7}{MnO_4^-} + 5\underset{+2}{Fe^{2+}} + H^+ \rightarrow \underset{+2}{Mn^{2+}} + 5\underset{+3}{Fe^{3+}} + H_2O$$

ox. no. change = 5 × (+1) = +5

Step 4 Balance the charges.
Initially ignore the hydrogen ions, as these will be used to balance the charges.
- The total charge on the other reactants is:

  $(1-)$ (from MnO_4^-) + $(5 \times 2+)$ (from $5Fe^{2+}$) = 9+

- The total charge on the products is:

  $(2+)$ (from Mn^{2+}) + $(5 \times 3+)$ (from $5Fe^{3+}$) = 17+

- To balance the charges we need 8 H^+ ions on the left.

$$MnO_4^- + 5Fe^{2+} + 8H^+ \rightarrow Mn^{2+} + 5Fe^{3+} + H_2O$$

Step 5 Balance the hydrogen atoms in the water.

$$MnO_4^- + 5Fe^{2+} + 8H^+ \rightarrow Mn^{2+} + 5Fe^{3+} + 4H_2O$$

Check-up

7 Use the oxidation number method to balance these equations.
  a $H_2SO_4 + HI \rightarrow S + I_2 + H_2O$
  b $HBr + H_2SO_4 \rightarrow Br_2 + SO_2 + H_2O$
  c $V^{3+} + I_2 + H_2O \rightarrow VO^{2+} + I^- + H^+$

7.4 Electrolysis
Electrolytic cells

Electrolysis is the decomposition of a compound into its elements by an electric current. It is often used to extract metals which are high in the reactivity series. These metals cannot be extracted by heating their ores with carbon. Electrolysis is also used to produce non-metals such as chlorine and to purify some metals. Electrolysis is generally carried out in an electrolysis cell (Figure 7.5).

In the electrolysis cell:
- the **electrolyte** is the compound which is decomposed; it is either a molten ionic compound or a concentrated aqueous solution of ions
- the **electrodes** are rods, made from either carbon (graphite) or metal, which conduct electricity to and from the electrolyte
  - the **anode** is the positive electrode
  - the **cathode** is the negative electrode
- the power supply must be direct current.

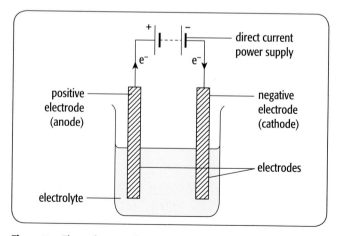

Figure 7.5 The main parts of an electrolysis cell. The actual structure of the cell will vary according to the element extracted. The e^- shows the direction of travel of the electrons around the external circuit.

Check-up

8 a Why does an ionic compound have to be molten to undergo electrolysis?

b Give **two** properties of graphite which make it a suitable material for use as an electrode. Explain your answers.

Redox reactions in electrolysis

During electrolysis, the positive ions (**cations**) move to the cathode. When they reach the cathode they gain electrons from the cathode. For example:

$$Cu^{2+} + 2e^- \rightarrow Cu$$

$$2H^+ + 2e^- \rightarrow H_2$$

Gain of electrons is reduction. Reduction always occurs at the cathode. If metal atoms are formed, they may be deposited as a layer of metal on the cathode. Alternatively they may form a molten layer in the cell. If hydrogen gas is formed, it bubbles off.

The negative ions (**anions**) move to the anode. When they reach the anode they lose electrons to the anode. For example:

$$2Cl^- \rightarrow Cl_2 + 2e^-$$

$$4OH^- \rightarrow O_2 + 2H_2O + 4e^-$$

Loss of electrons is oxidation. Oxidation always occurs at the anode.

Electrolysis is a redox reaction. For example, when molten zinc chloride is electrolysed the electrode reactions are:

cathode: $Zn^{2+} + 2e^- \rightarrow Zn$ (reduction)

anode: $2Cl^- \rightarrow Cl_2 + 2e^-$ (oxidation)

The electron loss at the anode balances the electron gain at the cathode. Overall, the reaction is:

$$ZnCl_2 \rightarrow Zn + Cl_2$$

Check-up

9 a Explain why cations move towards to the cathode during electrolysis.

b When lead iodide, PbI_2, is electrolysed the following reactions occur:

$$Pb^{2+} + 2e^- \rightarrow Pb \text{ and } 2I^- \rightarrow I_2 + 2e^-$$

i Which of these equations describes the reaction at the cathode? Explain your answer.

ii What is the ox. no. change of each iodide ion in the reaction

$$2I^- \rightarrow I_2 + 2e^-?$$

Extracting aluminium

Aluminium is extracted from bauxite ore. The first step is to purify the bauxite to get pure aluminium oxide, Al_2O_3, for electrolysis. The electrolysis of aluminium oxide is carried out in long narrow cells using carbon electrodes (see Figure 7.6).

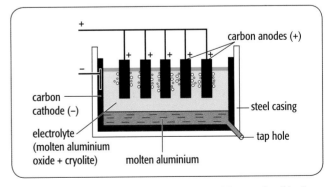

Figure 7.6 An electrolysis cell for extracting aluminium. Each cell is about 8 m long and 1 m deep and contains several graphite electrodes. The molten aluminium is removed by suction through a tube or via a tap hole at the bottom of the cell.

In order to carry out electrolysis, the aluminium oxide must be molten. The energy for melting the electrolyte is provided by the very high electric current (40 000 A) passed through the electrolyte. But there is a problem: the melting point of aluminium oxide is very high (2040 °C). A lot of energy would be required – and energy is expensive! The energy requirement is lowered by dissolving the aluminium oxide in a large amount of molten cryolite, Na_3AlF_6. The cryolite, which melts at about 1000 °C, has two main functions:

• it dissolves the aluminium oxide so that the melting point of the electrolyte is lowered to about 970 °C
• it improves the electrical conductivity of the electrolyte.

During electrolysis, aluminium ions move to the cathode and oxide ions move to the anode.

At the cathode

Aluminium ions gain electrons at the cathode. They are reduced to aluminium atoms.

$$Al^{3+} + 3e^- \rightarrow Al$$

Aluminium is denser than the electrolyte. It drops to the bottom of the electrolysis cell and is removed using a suction tube or through a tap hole at the bottom of the cell.

At the anode

Oxide ions lose electrons at the anode. They are oxidised to atoms of oxygen gas which then form O_2 molecules.

$$2O^{2-} \rightarrow O_2 + 4e^-$$

The oxygen reacts with the hot carbon electrodes. It oxidises them to carbon dioxide gas, which escapes from the electrolysis cell. So, the electrodes have to be replaced periodically as they get 'burnt away'.

Overall

The overall equation for the reaction is found by balancing the electrons gained at the cathode and lost at the anode.

$$4Al^{3+} + 12e^- \rightarrow 4Al$$

$$6O^{2-} \rightarrow 3O_2 + 12e^-$$

Fact file

A typical aluminium smelting plant will use as much electricity as a small town.

Overall equation:

$$4Al^{3+} + 6O^{2-} \rightarrow 4Al + 3O_2$$

or

$$2Al_2O_3 \rightarrow 4Al + 3O_2$$

Check-up

10 a The anodes can be lowered and raised in the cells used for the extraction of aluminium. Suggest why this is necessary.
   b What are the most essential points to consider when a company wants to build a new factory to extract aluminium from bauxite?
   c Give **two** reasons why it is cheaper to recycle aluminium than to extract it from its ore.

The electrolysis of brine

Brine is a concentrated aqueous solution of sodium chloride. It is obtained from sea water or by dissolving rock salt in water. The electrolysis of brine is used to produce chlorine, hydrogen and sodium hydroxide, all of which have important uses.

Figure 7.7 An industrial chlorine electrolysis cell.

Fact file

The electrolysis of brine produces the starting materials for many products.
- Sodium hydroxide is used to make soap and is also used in the extraction of aluminium.
- Chlorine is used in water purification and in making solvents, plastics and bleaches.
- Hydrogen is used for making margarine and ammonia.

The ions present in an aqueous solution of sodium chloride (the electrolyte) are:
- Na^+
- Cl^-
- H^+ (from water)
- OH^- (from water).

The hydrogen ions and hydroxide ions are formed because water is very slightly ionised.

$$H_2O \rightleftharpoons H^+ + OH^-$$

A diaphragm cell can be used to electrolyse brine (Figure 7.8):
- the electrolyte is aqueous sodium chloride (brine)
- the anodes are titanium
- the cathodes are steel
- the porous diaphragm separating the cathode and anode compartments is made from a mixture of asbestos and polymers; water and ions can pass through the diaphragm.

During electrolysis, sodium and hydrogen ions move to the cathode and chloride and hydroxide ions move to the anode.

At the cathode

Both sodium ions and hydrogen ions move to the cathode, but only hydrogen ions undergo reduction.

$$2H^+ + 2e^- \rightarrow H_2$$

Only H^+ ions are reduced because ions from elements lower in the electrochemical series are more likely to be reduced at the electrodes. Hydrogen is much lower than sodium in the electrochemical series. The sodium ions remain in the cathode compartment and the hydrogen gas is pumped off from the top of the cathode compartment.

As the hydrogen ions are removed from the electrolyte, more are formed from the water to replace them. This is because the equilibrium

$$H_2O \rightleftharpoons H^+ + OH^-$$

shifts to the right as H^+ ions are removed (see Chapter 8).

As more and more hydrogen ions are removed in this reaction, hydroxide ions accumulate in the cathode compartment. Both sodium and hydroxide ions are now present in this compartment. This solution is removed and concentrated to make sodium hydroxide.

The electrolyte level in the anode compartment is kept higher than in the cathode compartment. This makes sure that the flow of liquid is always towards the cathode compartment. This reduces the possibility of the sodium hydroxide solution moving back to the anode compartment.

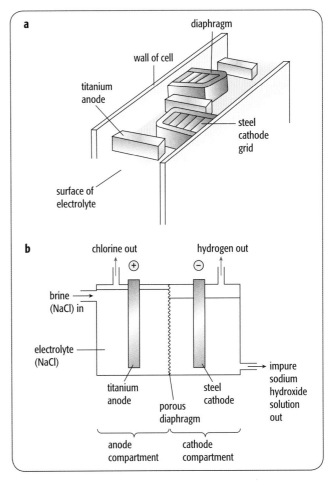

Figure 7.8 A diaphragm cell, used to electrolyse brine. **a** The arrangement of the electrodes and the diaphragms looking from the top with the cover removed. **b** A simplified diagram of part of the cell. The positions of the various parts shown are not accurate.

At the anode

Both chloride ions and hydroxide ions move to the anode, but only chloride ions undergo oxidation.

$$2Cl^- \rightarrow Cl_2 + 2e^-$$

Cl^- ions are oxidised at the anode because chloride ions are in far greater concentration than the hydroxide ions. The chlorine gas is pumped off from the top of the anode compartment.

Check-up

11 a Is the reaction at the steel electrode reduction or oxidation? Explain your answer.
  b The chlorine produced at the anode is contaminated with oxygen. Write a balanced half-equation to show how oxygen and water are formed from hydroxide ions.
  c Chlorine can react with sodium hydroxide solution to form a mixture of sodium chloride, NaCl, and sodium chlorate(I), NaClO. State the oxidation numbers of:
    i a chloride ion
    ii the chlorine atom in NaClO.

The electrolytic purification of copper

Although the copper produced by smelting in a furnace is pure enough to make water pipes, it is not pure enough to be used for electrical wiring. For this we need copper of 99.99% purity. Even small amounts of impurities reduce the conductivity of copper greatly. Electrolysis is the only way to make pure copper on a large scale (Figure 7.9). The electrolytic purification of copper is carried out in cells using
- an electrolyte of copper(II) sulfate, acidified with sulfuric acid
- an anode of impure copper
- a cathode of pure copper.

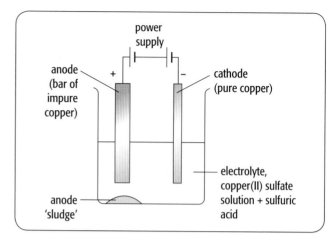

Figure 7.9 A simplified diagram of the electrolytic cell used to purify copper.

At the anode

Copper atoms lose electrons at the anode and are oxidised to copper(II) ions:

$$Cu \rightarrow Cu^{2+} + 2e^-$$

The copper(II) ions go into solution and are then attracted towards the cathode.

The copper anode decreases in thickness. Impurities from the anode are deposited on the bottom of the cell as anode 'sludge'.

At the cathode

Copper(II) ions gain electrons at the cathode and are reduced to copper atoms.

$$Cu^{2+} + 2e^- \rightarrow Cu$$

The copper atoms are deposited on the cathode. The copper cathode increases in thickness. When enough pure copper has been deposited on the cathode, the cathode is removed and replaced by a new one.

Fact file

The 'sludge' which drops from the anode during the refining of copper contains insoluble salts of gold, silver and platinum. The anode 'sludge' is treated to extract these valuable metals.

12 a During the electrolytic purification of copper, some impurities in the copper anode form soluble salts which dissolve in the electrolyte.
   i Why is this a problem?
   ii Suggest how this problem may be overcome.

continued ···⯈

b The copper(II) ions in the electrolyte give it a deep-blue colour. Explain why the colour of the electrolyte does not change during this electrolysis, even though copper(II) ions are removed at the cathode.

Summary

☐ Redox reactions can be explained in terms of
  – increase in oxidation number (oxidation state) which is oxidation or
  – decrease in oxidation number which is reduction.
☐ Oxidation numbers can be used to balance equations.
☐ Redox reactions can be explained in terms of electron loss (oxidation) or electron gain (reduction).
☐ The electrolysis of brine using a diaphragm cell produces chlorine at the anode and hydrogen at the cathode.
☐ Sodium hydroxide is produced in the diaphragm cell because sodium and hydroxide ions remain in solution after the electrolysis of concentrated sodium chloride solution.
☐ Aluminium is extracted from a mixture of molten aluminium oxide and cryolite using an electrolysis cell with carbon anodes.
☐ Cryolite is added to the aluminium oxide to lower the melting point of the electrolyte and help the aluminium oxide dissolve.
☐ Copper is purified by electrolysis using an impure copper anode, a cathode of pure copper and an electrolyte of aqueous copper(II) sulfate.

End-of-chapter questions

1 In the industrial production of nitric acid the following changes take place to the nitrogen.

$$\underset{\text{stage 1}}{N_2 \longrightarrow} \underset{\text{stage 2}}{NH_3 \longrightarrow} \underset{\text{stage 3}}{NO \longrightarrow} \underset{\text{stage 4}}{NO_2 \longrightarrow} HNO_3$$

    a Give the oxidation number of the nitrogen atom in each molecule.   [5]
    b For each stage, state whether oxidation or reduction has taken place. In each case explain your answer.   [2]
    c Give the full systematic name for NO_2.   [1]
    d Nitric acid, HNO_3, reacts with red phosphorus.

      $P + 5HNO_3 \rightarrow H_3PO_4 + 5NO_2 + H_2O$

      By referring to oxidation number changes, explain why this is a redox reaction.   [5]
    e Explain why nitric acid can be described as an oxidising agent in this reaction.   [1]

                                                   Total = 14

2 Calcium reacts with cold water to form calcium hydroxide, $Ca(OH)_2$, and hydrogen, H_2.

   a State the oxidation number of calcium in
      i calcium metal   [1]
      ii calcium hydroxide.   [1]
   b State the oxidation number of hydrogen in
      i water   [1]
      ii hydrogen gas.   [1]
   c Write two half-equations for the reaction between water and calcium hydroxide to show
      i the change from calcium to calcium ions   [1]
      ii the change from water to hydroxide ions and hydrogen.   [1]
   d In which one of the half-equations in part **c** is a reduction occurring? Give a reason for your answer.   [1]
   e Write a balanced equation for the reaction of calcium with water.   [1]
   f Explain the role played by water in this reaction.   [1]

                                                                Total = 9

3 The diagram shows a cell used in the electrolytic extraction of aluminium. The electrolyte is a mixture of aluminium oxide and cryolite.

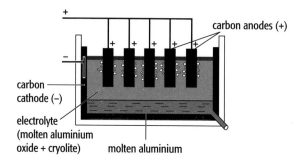

   a Explain why the electrolyte has to be molten for electrolysis to occur.   [1]
   b Explain why cryolite is added to the aluminium oxide.   [3]
   c Write a half-equation for the reaction occurring at
      i the anode (positive electrode)   [1]
      ii the cathode (negative electrode).   [1]
   d Explain why the reaction at the cathode is classed as reduction.   [1]
   e Explain why the anodes have to be replaced at regular intervals.   [4]

                                                                Total = 11

4   The unbalanced equation for the reaction of sulfur dioxide with bromine is shown below.

$$SO_2 + Br_2 + H_2O \rightarrow SO_4^{2-} + Br^- + H^+$$

a State the oxidation number of sulfur in
   i SO_2 [1]
   ii SO_4^{2-} [1]
b State the oxidation number of bromine in
   i Br_2 [1]
   ii Br^- [1]
c Identify the reducing agent in this reaction. Give a reason for your answer.   [1]
d State the change in oxidation number for
   i   each S atom   [1]
   ii each bromine atom.   [1]
e Construct a balanced equation for this reaction.   [2]
                                                                    Total = 9

5   Aluminium reacts with hydrochloric acid to form aluminium chloride, $AlCl_3$, and hydrogen.
    This is a redox reaction.
a Explain in term of electrons, what is meant by a **redox reaction**.   [3]
b i   Write a half-equation to show aluminium changing to aluminium ions. [1]
   ii Write a second half-equation to show what happens to the hydrogen ions from the acid.   [1]
   iii What is the change in oxidation number when a hydrogen ion turns into a hydrogen atom?   [1]
c Construct a balanced ionic equation for the reaction between aluminium atoms and hydrogen ions.   [1]
                                                                    Total = 7

6   Concentrated aqueous sodium chloride can be electrolysed in the laboratory using graphite
    electrodes, see diagram.

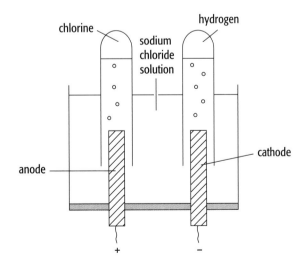

a Write the formulae for all the ions present in an aqueous solution of sodium chloride. [2]

b Write half-equations to show the reactions at
   i the anode (positive electrode) [1]
   ii the cathode (negative electrode). [1]

c Explain why the reaction at the anode is classed as oxidation. [1]

d After a while, the solution near the cathode becomes very alkaline. Explain why. [3]

e The chlorine produced at the anode can react with warm concentrated sodium hydroxide:

$$3Cl_2 + 6NaOH \rightarrow 5NaCl + NaClO_3 + 3H_2O$$

What are the oxidation number changes per atom of chlorine when
   i Cl_2 is converted to NaCl [1]
   ii Cl_2 is converted to $NaClO_3$? [1]

f Give the systematic name for the compound $NaClO_3$. [1]

Total = 11

7 Iodine, I_2, reacts with thiosulfate ions, $S_2O_3^{2-}$ to form iodide ions, I^-, and tetrathionate ions, $S_4O_6^{2-}$.

$$I_2 + 2S_2O_3^{2-} \rightarrow 2I^- + S_4O_6^{2-}$$

a State the oxidation number of each sulfur atom in:
   i a $S_2O_3^{2-}$ ion [1]
   ii a $S_4O_6^{2-}$ ion. [1]

b Explain in terms of electron transfer why the conversion of iodine to iodide ions is a reduction reaction. [1]

c When a salt containing iodide ions is warmed with concentrated sulfuric acid and MnO_2, iodine is evolved.

$$2I^- + MnO_2 + 6H^+ + 2SO_4^{2-} \rightarrow I_2 + Mn^{2+} + 2HSO_4^- + 2H_2O$$

   i State the systematic name for MnO_2. [1]
   ii What is the oxidation number of S in the SO_4^{2-} ion? [1]
   iii Which reactant gets oxidised in this reaction? Explain your answer by using oxidation numbers. [1]
   iv Which substance is the oxidising agent? Explain your answer. [1]

Total = 7

8   The compound $KBrO_3$ decomposes when heated.

$$2KBrO_3 \rightarrow 2KBr + 3O_2$$

a   State the oxidation numbers of bromine in
    i $KBrO_3$ [1]
    ii KBr [1]
b   Explain using oxidation numbers why this reaction is a redox reaction.   [3]
c   State the systematic name of $KBrO_3$.   [1]
d   When $KBrO_3$ reacts with hydrazine, N_2H_4, nitrogen gas is evolved.

$$2KBrO_3 + 3N_2H_4 \rightarrow 2KBr + 3N_2 + 6H_2O$$

    i   What is the oxidation number change of the bromine atom when $KBrO_3$ is converted to KBr? [1]
    ii What is the oxidation number change for each nitrogen atom when N_2H_4 is converted to N_2? [2]
    iii Use your answers to i and ii to explain why 2 moles of $KBrO_3$ react with 3 moles of N_2H_4. [3]

                                                                                            Total = 12

8 Equilibrium

8.1 Reversible reactions and equilibrium

Reversible reactions

Many chemical reactions go to completion. For example, when magnesium reacts with excess hydrochloric acid, the reaction stops when all the magnesium has been

Figure 8.1 The water in this reservoir is used to generate hydroelectric power. The water level in the reservoir does not change if the flow of water into the reservoir equals the flow of water out of the reservoir. It is in equilibrium.

used up. The products cannot be converted back to the reactants. This reaction is irreversible.

Some reactions, however, can be reversed. For example, when blue, hydrated copper(II) sulfate is heated, it loses its water of crystallisation and changes to white, anhydrous copper(II) sulfate.

$$CuSO_4.5H_2O(s) \quad \rightarrow \quad CuSO_4(s) \quad + \quad 5H_2O(l)$$
hydrated copper(II) sulfate $\qquad$ anhydrous copper(II) sulfate

This is called the **forward reaction**.

When water is added to anhydrous copper(II) sulfate, the reaction is reversed.

$$CuSO_4(s) + 5H_2O(l) \rightarrow CuSO_4.5H_2O(s)$$

This is called the **backward (or reverse) reaction**.

We can show these two reactions in the same equation by using two arrows.

$$CuSO_4.5H_2O(s) \rightleftharpoons CuSO_4(s) + 5H_2O(l)$$

A reaction in which the products can react together to re-form the original reactants is called a **reversible reaction**. In this case heating and adding water are not being carried out at the same time. However, there is a type of

Figure 8.2 Hydrated copper(II) sulfate (left) and anhydrous copper(II) sulfate (right).

chemical reaction in which the forward reaction and the backward reaction take place **at the same time**.

In many chemical reactions the reactants are not used up completely. Some products are formed but the maximum theoretical yield is not obtained. A mixture of products and reactants is formed. The products react together to re-form reactants at the same time as the reactants are forming products. This type of reversible reaction is called an **equilibrium** reaction. We show that equilibrium reactions are reversible by the sign $\rightleftharpoons$.

For example, consider the reaction between hydrogen and iodine carried out in a sealed glass tube at 400 °C:

$$H_2(g) + I_2(g) \rightleftharpoons 2HI(g)$$

Molecules of hydrogen iodide are breaking down to hydrogen and iodine at the same rate as hydrogen and iodine molecules are reacting together to form hydrogen iodide.

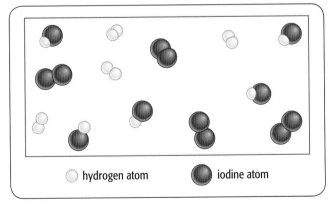

hydrogen atom   iodine atom

Figure 8.3 A snapshot of the dynamic equilibrium between hydrogen gas, iodine gas and hydrogen iodide gas.

Characteristics of equilibrium

An equilibrium reaction has four particular features under constant conditions:
- it is dynamic
- the forward and reverse reactions occur at the same rate
- the concentrations of reactants and products remain constant at equilibrium
- it requires a closed system.

1 It is dynamic

The phrase **dynamic equilibrium** means that the molecules or ions of reactants and products are continuously reacting. Reactants are continuously being changed to products and products are continuously being changed back to reactants.

2 The forward and backward reactions occur at the same rate

At equilibrium the rate of the forward reaction equals the rate of the backward reaction. Molecules or ions of reactants are becoming products, and those in the products are becoming reactants, at the same rate.

3 The concentrations of reactants and products remain constant at equilibrium

The concentrations remain constant because, at equilibrium, the rates of the forward and backward reactions are equal. The equilibrium can be approached from two directions. For example, in the reaction

$$H_2(g) + I_2(g) \rightleftharpoons 2HI(g)$$

We can start by:
- using a mixture of colourless hydrogen gas and purple iodine vapour, or
- using only colourless hydrogen iodide gas.

Figure **8.4** shows what happens when 5.00 mol of hydrogen molecules and 5.00 mol of iodine molecules react at 500 K in a vessel of volume 1 dm³. As time passes, the purple colour of the iodine vapour fades until equilibrium is reached. At equilibrium the mixture contains 0.68 mol of iodine, 0.68 mol of hydrogen and 8.64 mol of hydrogen iodide.

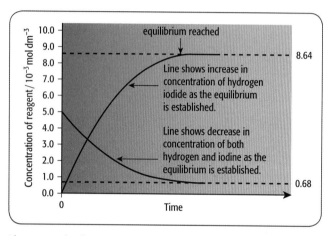

Figure 8.4 The changes in the concentrations of reagents as 5.00 mol of each of hydrogen and iodine react to form an equilibrium mixture with hydrogen iodide in a vessel of volume 1 dm³.

Figure **8.5** shows that the same equilibrium can be achieved when 10.00 mol of hydrogen iodide molecules decompose to iodine and hydrogen iodide. You can see that the same equilibrium concentrations of all three molecules are achieved.

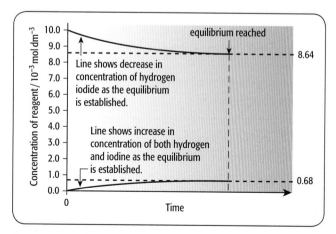

Figure 8.5 The changes in the concentrations of reagents as 10.00 mol of hydrogen iodide react to form an equilibrium mixture with hydrogen and iodine gases in a vessel of 1 m³.

4 Equilibrium requires a closed system

A **closed system** is one in which none of the reactants or products escapes from the reaction mixture. In an open system some matter is lost to the surroundings. Figure **8.6** shows the difference between a closed system and an **open system** when calcium carbonate is heated at a high temperature in a strong container.

Many chemical reactions can be studied without placing them in closed containers. They can reach equilibrium in open flasks if the reaction takes place entirely in solution and no gas is lost.

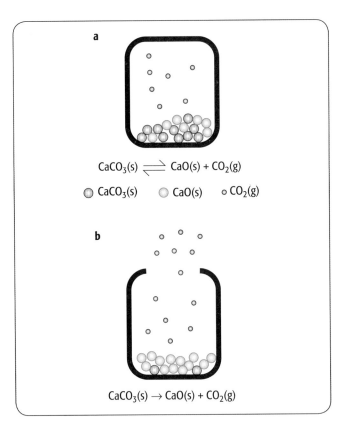

In the figure:

$CaCO_3(s) \rightleftharpoons CaO(s) + CO_2(g)$

○ $CaCO_3(s)$ ○ $CaO(s)$ ○ $CO_2(g)$

$CaCO_3(s) \rightarrow CaO(s) + CO_2(g)$

Check-up

2 A beaker contains saturated aqueous sodium chloride solution in contact with undissolved solid sodium chloride. Sodium ions and chloride ions are constantly moving from solid to solution and from solution to solid.
   a i Explain why this is a closed system.
      ii Explain why the concentration of the saturated sodium chloride solution does not change, even though ions are still moving into the solution from the solid.
   b Bromine is a reddish-brown liquid which vaporises at room temperature. Some liquid bromine is put in a closed jar. The colour of the bromine vapour above the liquid gets darker and darker until the depth of colour remains constant. Bromine liquid still remains in the jar. Explain what is happening in terms of changes in concentration of the bromine molecules in the vapour.

8.2 Changing the position of equilibrium

Position of equilibrium

The position of equilibrium refers to the relative amounts of products and reactants present in an equilibrium mixture.
- If a system in equilibrium is disturbed (e.g. by a change in temperature) and the concentration of products is increased relative to the reactants we say that the position of equilibrium has shifted to the right.
- If the concentration of products is decreased relative to the reactants we say that the position of equilibrium has shifted to the left.

Le Chatelier's principle

Changes in both concentration and temperature affect the position of equilibrium. When any of the reactants or products are gases, changes in pressure may also affect the position of equilibrium. The French chemist Henri Le Chatelier (1850–1936) observed how these factors affect the position of equilibrium. He put forward a general rule, known as **Le Chatelier's principle**:

> If one or more factors that affect an equilibrium is changed, the position of equilibrium shifts in the direction which reduces (opposes) the change.

We can predict the effect of changing concentration and pressure by referring to the stoichiometric equation for the reaction. We can predict the effect of changing the temperature by referring to the enthalpy change of the reaction.

How does change in concentration affect the position of equilibrium?

When the concentration of one or more of the reactants is increased:
- the system is no longer in equilibrium
- the position of equilibrium moves to the right to reduce the effect of the increase in concentration of reactant
- more products are formed until equilibrium is restored.

When the concentration of one or more of the products is increased:
- the system is no longer in equilibrium
- the position of equilibrium moves to the left to reduce the effect of the increase in concentration of product
- more reactants are formed until equilibrium is restored.

For example, look at the reaction:

$$CH_3COOH(l) + C_2H_5OH(l) \rightleftharpoons CH_3COOC_2H_5(l) + H_2O(l)$$
ethanoic acid   ethanol   ethyl ethanoate   water

What happens when we add more ethanol?
- The concentration of ethanol is increased.
- According to Le Chatelier's principle, some of the ethanol must be removed to reduce the concentration of the added ethanol.
- The position of equilibrium shifts to the right.
- More ethanol reacts with ethanoic acid and more ethyl ethanoate and water are formed.

What happens when we add more water?
- The concentration of water is increased.
- According to Le Chatelier's principle, some of the water must be removed to reduce the concentration of the added water.
- The position of equilibrium shifts to the left.
- So more water reacts with ethyl ethanoate and more ethanoic acid and ethanol are formed.

What happens when we remove some water?
- The concentration of water is decreased.
- According to Le Chatelier's principle, some water must be added to increase its concentration.
- The position of equilibrium shifts to the right.
- So more ethanoic acid reacts with ethanol and more water and ethyl ethanoate are formed.

Figure 8.7 Stalactites and stalagmites are formed as a result of water passing through rocks containing calcium carbonate. The solution running through these rocks contains water, dissolved carbon dioxide and calcium hydrogencarbonate:

$$CaCO_3(s) + H_2O(l) + CO_2(aq) \rightleftharpoons Ca(HCO_3)_2(aq)$$

When droplets of this mixture are formed on the roof of the cave, some of the carbon dioxide in the droplet escapes into the air. The position of equilibrium shifts to the left and calcium carbonate is deposited.

The effect of pressure on the position of equilibrium

Change in pressure only affects reactions where gases are reactants or products. The molecules or ions in solids and liquids are packed closely together and cannot be compressed very easily. In gases, the molecules are far apart (Figure 8.8).

3 a Use this reaction:

$$CH_3COOH(l) + C_2H_5OH(l) \rightleftharpoons CH_3COOC_2H_5(l) + H_2O(l)$$

Explain what happens to the position of equilibrium when:
  i more $CH_3COOC_2H_5(l)$ is added
  ii some $C_2H_5OH(l)$ is removed.
b Use this reaction:

$$Ce^{4+}(aq) + Fe^{2+}(aq) \rightleftharpoons Ce^{3+}(aq) + Fe^{3+}(aq)$$

Explain what happens to the position of equilibrium when:
  i the concentration of $Fe^{2+}(aq)$ ions is increased
  ii water is added to the equilibrium mixture.

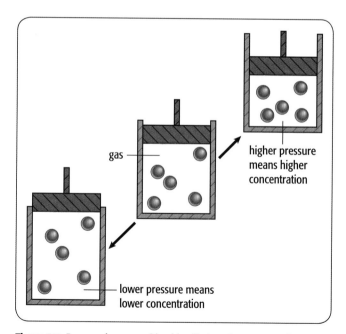

Figure 8.8 Pressure has a considerable effect on the concentration of gases.

gas

higher pressure means higher concentration

lower pressure means lower concentration

The pressure of a gas is caused by the molecules hitting the walls of the container. Each molecule in a mixture of gases contributes towards the total pressure. So, at constant temperature, the more gas molecules there are in a given volume, the higher the pressure.

Figure 8.9 shows what happens when we increase the pressure on the reaction represented by:

$$X(g) + Y(g) \rightleftharpoons Z(g)$$
$$\text{1 mol} \quad\quad \text{1 mol} \quad\quad \text{1 mol}$$

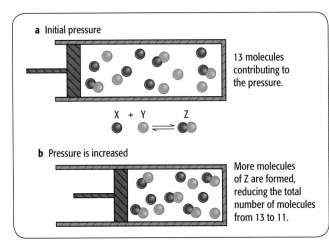

a Initial pressure

13 molecules contributing to the pressure.

X + Y ⇌ Z

b Pressure is increased

More molecules of Z are formed, reducing the total number of molecules from 13 to 11.

Figure 8.9 An increase in pressure in this case causes the equilibrium to shift to the right, to produce more molecules of Z than before, but fewer molecules in the reaction vessel overall.

In this reaction there are two moles of gas on the left and one on the right. When the pressure is increased at constant temperature:
• the molecules are closer together, because the pressure has increased
• the position of equilibrium shifts to minimise this increase
• it shifts in the direction of fewer gas molecules (in the direction which opposes the increase in pressure)
• more product, Z, is formed from X and Y until equilibrium is re-established.
   For example, consider the reaction:

$$2SO_2(g) + O_2(g) \rightleftharpoons 2SO_3(g)$$

There are three moles of gas molecules on the left of the equation and two on the right.
   What happens when we increase the pressure?
• The molecules are closer together, because the pressure is higher.
• According to Le Chatelier's principle, the reaction must shift in the direction which reduces the number of molecules of gas.

• The position of equilibrium shifts to the right.
• So more SO_2 reacts with O_2 to form SO_3.
What happens when we decrease the pressure?
• The molecules are further apart, because the pressure is lower.
• According to Le Chatelier's principle, the reaction must shift in the direction which increases the number of molecules of gas.
• The position of equilibrium shifts to the left.
• So more SO_2 and O_2 molecules are formed by the decomposition of SO_3 molecules.
Table 8.1 summarises the effect of changes in pressure on two other gas reactions.

Change in pressure	Fewer molecules of gas on right $N_2(g) + 3H_2(g) \rightleftharpoons 2NH_3(g)$	More molecules of gas on right $N_2O_4(g) \rightleftharpoons 2NO_2$
Pressure increase	equilibrium position shifts towards products: more NH_3 forms	equilibrium position shifts towards reactants: more N_2O_4 forms
Pressure decrease	equilibrium position shifts towards reactants: more N_2 and H_2 form	equilibrium position shifts towards products: more NO_2 forms

Table 8.1 The effect of changes in pressure on gas reactions.

Note that:
• if there are equal numbers of molecules of gas on each side of the equation, the position of equilibrium is not affected by a change in pressure
• in a reaction involving gases and solids (or liquids), it is only the molecules of gases which count when determining how pressure affects the position of equilibrium.

Check-up

4 **a** Predict the effect of increasing the pressure on the following reactions:
   i $N_2O_4(g) \rightleftharpoons 2NO_2(g)$
   ii $CaCO_3(s) \rightleftharpoons CaO(s) + CO_2(g)$
   b Predict the effect of decreasing the pressure on the reaction:

$$2NO_2(g) \rightleftharpoons 2NO(g) + O_2(g)$$

The effect of temperature on the position of equilibrium

The decomposition of hydrogen iodide is an endothermic reaction.

$$2HI \rightleftharpoons H_2 + I_2 \qquad\qquad \Delta H_r = +9.6\,kJ\,mol^{-1}$$

The effect of temperature on the equilibrium concentration of hydrogen iodide and hydrogen at equilibrium for the forward reaction is shown in Table 8.2.

Temperature / °C	Equilibrium concentration of HI / $mol\,dm^{-3}$	Equilibrium concentration of H_2 (or I_2) / $mol\,dm^{-3}$
25	0.934	0.033
230	0.864	0.068
430	0.786	0.107
490	0.773	0.114

Table 8.2 Effect of temperature on the decomposition of hydrogen iodide.

You can see from Table 8.2 that, as the temperature increases, the concentration of product increases. The position of equilibrium shifts to the right. We can explain this using Le Chatelier's principle:
- an increase in temperature increases the energy of the surroundings
- according to Le Chatelier's principle, the reaction will go in the direction that opposes the increase in energy
- so the reaction will go in the direction in which energy is absorbed, which is the endothermic reaction
- the position of equilibrium shifts to the right, producing more H_2 and I_2.

If an endothermic reaction is favoured by an increase in temperature, an exothermic reaction must be favoured by a decrease in temperature:
- a decrease in temperature decreases the energy of the surroundings
- according to Le Chatelier's principle, the reaction will go in the direction that opposes the decrease in energy
- so the reaction will go in the direction in which energy is released, which is the exothermic reaction.

Table 8.3 summarises the effect of temperature changes on the position of equilibrium for endothermic and exothermic reactions.

Temperature change	Endothermic reaction $2HI \rightleftharpoons H_2 + I_2$	Exothermic reaction $2SO_2(g) + O_2(g) \rightleftharpoons 2SO_3(g)$
Temperature increase	position of equilibrium shifts towards products: more H_2 and I_2 formed	position of equilibrium shifts towards reactants: more SO_2 and O_2 formed
Temperature decrease	position of equilibrium shifts towards reactant: more HI formed	position of equilibrium shifts towards product: more SO_3 formed

Table 8.3 Effect of temperature on endothermic and exothermic reactions.

Check-up

5 a Predict the effect of increasing the temperature on the reaction:

$$H_2(g) + CO_2(g) \rightleftharpoons H_2O(g) + CO(g)$$
$$\Delta H_r = +41.2\,kJ\,mol^{-1}$$

b In the reaction

$$Ag_2CO_3(s) \rightleftharpoons Ag_2O(s) + CO_2(g)$$

increasing the temperature increases the amount of carbon dioxide formed at constant pressure. Is this reaction exothermic or endothermic? Explain your answer.

Do catalysts have any effect on the position of equilibrium?

A catalyst is a substance which increases the rate of a chemical reaction. Catalysts speed up the time taken to reach equilibrium, but they have no effect on the position of equilibrium once this is reached. This is because they increase the rate of the forward and reverse reactions equally.

8.3 Equilibrium expressions and the equilibrium constant, K_c

Equilibrium expressions

When hydrogen reacts with iodine in a closed tube at 500 K, the following equilibrium is set up:

$$H_2 + I_2 \rightleftharpoons 2HI$$

Table 8.4 shows the relationship between the equilibrium concentrations of H_2, I_2 and HI. The square brackets in the last column refer to the concentration, in $mol\,dm^{-3}$, of the substance inside the brackets. The results are obtained as follows:

• several tubes are set up with different starting concentrations of hydrogen and iodine
• the contents of the tubes are allowed to reach equilibrium at 500 K
• the concentrations of hydrogen, iodine and hydrogen iodide at equilibrium are determined.

The last column in Table 8.4 shows the number we get by arranging the concentrations of H_2, I_2 and HI in a particular way. We get this expression by taking the square of the concentration of hydrogen iodide and dividing it by the concentrations of hydrogen and iodine at equilibrium. So for the first line of data in Table 8.4:

$$\frac{[HI]^2}{[H_2][I_2]} = \frac{(8.64 \times 10^{-3})^2}{(0.68 \times 10^{-3})(0.68 \times 10^{-3})}$$
$$= 161$$

You can see that this expression gives an approximately constant value close to about 160 whatever the starting concentrations of H_2, I_2 and HI.

We call this constant the **equilibrium constant**, K_c. The subscript 'c' refers to the fact that concentrations have been used in the calculations.

There is a simple relationship which links K_c to the equilibrium concentrations of reactants and products and the stoichiometry of the equation. This is called an **equilibrium expression**.

For a general reaction:

$$mA + nB \rightleftharpoons pC + qD$$

(where m, n, p and q are the number of moles in the equation)

concentration of product D
↓

$$K_c = \frac{[C]^p\,[D]^q}{[A]^m\,[B]^n}$$

← number of moles of product D
← number of moles of reactant B

↑
concentration of reactant B

Worked examples

1   Write an expression for K_c:

$$N_2(g) + 3H_2(g) \rightleftharpoons 2NH_3(g)$$

$$K_c = \frac{[NH_3]^2}{[N_2][H_2]^3}$$

2   Write an expression for K_c:

$$2SO_2(g) + O_2(g) \rightleftharpoons 2SO_3(g)$$

$$K_c = \frac{[SO_3]^2}{[SO_2]^2[O_2]}$$

Concentration of H_2 at equilibrium / $mol\,dm^{-3}$	Concentration of I_2 at equilibrium / $mol\,dm^{-3}$	Concentration of HI at equilibrium / $mol\,dm^{-3}$	$\dfrac{[HI]^2}{[H_2][I_2]}$
0.68×10^{-3}	0.68×10^{-3}	8.64×10^{-3}	161
0.50×10^{-3}	0.50×10^{-3}	6.30×10^{-3}	159
1.10×10^{-3}	2.00×10^{-3}	18.8×10^{-3}	161
2.50×10^{-3}	0.65×10^{-3}	16.1×10^{-3}	160

Table 8.4 The relationship between the equilibrium concentrations of H_2, I_2 and HI in the reaction $H_2 + I_2 \rightleftharpoons 2HI$.

In equilibrium expressions involving a solid, we ignore the solid. This is because its concentration remains constant, however much solid is present. For example:

$$Ag^+(aq) + Fe^{2+}(aq) \rightleftharpoons Ag(s) + Fe^{3+}(aq)$$

The equilibrium expression for this reaction is:

$$K_c = \frac{[Fe^{3+}(aq)]}{[Ag^+(aq)][Fe^{2+}(aq)]}$$

What are the units of K_c?

In the equilibrium expression each figure within a square bracket represents the concentration in $mol\,dm^{-3}$. The units of K_c therefore depend on the form of the equilibrium expression.

Worked examples

3 State the units of K_c for the reaction:

$$H_2 + I_2 \rightleftharpoons 2HI$$

$$K_c = \frac{[HI]^2}{[H_2][I_2]}$$

$$\text{Units of } K_c = \frac{(\cancel{mol\,dm^{-3}}) \times (\cancel{mol\,dm^{-3}})}{(\cancel{mol\,dm^{-3}}) \times (\cancel{mol\,dm^{-3}})}$$

The units of $mol\,dm^{-3}$ cancel, so K_c has no units.

4 State the units of K_c for the reaction:

$$2SO_2(g) + O_2(g) \rightleftharpoons 2SO_3(g)$$

$$K_c = \frac{[SO_3]^2}{[SO_2]^2[O_2]}$$

Units of K_c

$$= \frac{(\cancel{mol\,dm^{-3}}) \times (\cancel{mol\,dm^{-3}})}{(\cancel{mol\,dm^{-3}}) \times (\cancel{mol\,dm^{-3}}) \times (mol\,dm^{-3})}$$

$$= \frac{1}{mol\,dm^{-3}} = dm^3\,mol^{-1}$$

Check-up

6 Write equilibrium expressions for the following reactions and state the units of K_c.
  a $CO(g) + 2H_2(g) \rightleftharpoons CH_3OH(g)$
  b $4HCl(g) + O_2(g) \rightleftharpoons 2H_2O(g) + 2Cl_2(g)$

Some examples of equilibrium calculations

Worked examples

5 In this calculation we are given the number of moles of each of the reactants and products at equilibrium together with the volume of the reaction mixture.

Ethanol reacts with ethanoic acid to form ethyl ethanoate and water.

$$\underset{\text{ethanoic acid}}{CH_3COOH(l)} + \underset{\text{ethanol}}{C_2H_5OH(l)}$$
$$\rightleftharpoons \underset{\text{ethyl ethanoate}}{CH_3COOC_2H_5(l)} + \underset{\text{water}}{H_2O(l)}$$

$500\,cm^3$ of the reaction mixture at equilibrium contained 0.235 mol of ethanoic acid and 0.0350 mol of ethanol together with 0.182 mol of ethyl ethanoate and 0.182 mol of water. Use this data to calculate a value of K_c for this reaction.

Step 1 Write out the balanced chemical equation with the concentrations beneath each substance.

$$CH_3COOH(l) + C_2H_5OH(l)$$

$0.235 \times \frac{1000}{500}$ $\qquad$ $0.0350 \times \frac{1000}{500}$

$0.470\,mol\,dm^{-3}$ $\qquad$ $0.070\,mol\,dm^{-3}$

$$\rightleftharpoons CH_3COOC_2H_5(l) + H_2O(l)$$

$0.182 \times \frac{1000}{500}$ $\qquad$ $0.182 \times \frac{1000}{500}$

$0.364\,mol\,dm^{-3}$ $\qquad$ $0.364\,mol\,dm^{-3}$

Step 2 Write the equilibrium constant for this reaction in terms of concentrations

$$K_c = \frac{[CH_3COOC_2H_5][H_2O]}{[CH_3COOH][C_2H_5OH]}$$

continued ⋯⟶

Step 3 Substitute the equilibrium concentrations into the expression

$$K_c = \frac{(0.364) \times (0.364)}{(0.470) \times (0.070)} = 4.03$$

(to 3 significant figures)

Step 4 Add the correct units by referring back to the equilibrium expression:

$$\frac{(\cancel{mol\,dm^{-3}}) \times (\cancel{mol\,dm^{-3}})}{(\cancel{mol\,dm^{-3}}) \times (\cancel{mol\,dm^{-3}})}$$

The units of $mol\,dm^{-3}$ cancel, so K_c has no units. Therefore $K_c = 4.03$.

Note: if there are equal numbers of moles on the top and bottom of the equilibrium expression, you can use moles rather than concentration in $mol\,dm^{-3}$ in the calculation. In all other cases, if volumes are given, the concentrations must be calculated before they are substituted into the equilibrium expression.

6 In this example we are only given the initial concentrations of the reactants and the equilibrium concentration of the product.

Propanone reacts with hydrogen cyanide as follows:

$$CH_3COCH_3 + HCN \rightleftharpoons CH_3C(OH)(CN)CH_3$$
$$\text{propanone} \quad \text{hydrogen} \quad \text{product}$$
$$\text{cyanide}$$

A mixture of $0.0500\,mol\,dm^{-3}$ propanone and $0.0500\,mol\,dm^{-3}$ hydrogen cyanide is left to reach equilibrium at room temperature. At equilibrium the concentration of the product is $0.0233\,mol\,dm^{-3}$. Calculate K_c for this reaction.

Step 1 Write out the balanced chemical equation with all the data underneath:

	CH_3COCH_3	+	HCN	$\rightleftharpoons$	$CH_3C(OH)(CN)CH_3$
initial conc.	0.0500 $mol\,dm^{-3}$		0.0500 $mol\,dm^{-3}$		0
conc. at equilibrium	to be calculated		to be calculated		$0.0233\,mol\,dm^{-3}$

continued ⋯➤

Step 2 Calculate the equilibrium concentrations of the reactants

The chemical equation shows that for every mole of product formed, 1 mole of CH_3COCH_3 and 1 mole of HCN are consumed. So the equilibrium concentrations are as follows:
- CH_3COCH_3; $0.0500 - 0.0233 = 0.0267\,mol\,dm^{-3}$
- HCN; $0.0500 - 0.0233 = 0.0267\,mol\,dm^{-3}$

Step 3 Write the equilibrium constant for this reaction in terms of concentrations:

$$K_c = \frac{[CH_3C(OH)(CN)CH_3]}{[CH_3COCH_3]\,[HCN]}$$

Step 4 Substitute the equilibrium concentrations into the expression

$$K_c = \frac{(0.0233)}{(0.0267) \times (0.0267)} = 32.7$$

(to 3 significant figures)

Step 5 Add the correct units by referring back to the equilibrium expression.

$$\frac{(\cancel{mol\,dm^{-3}})}{(\cancel{mol\,dm^{-3}})(mol\,dm^{-3})} = \frac{1}{(mol\,dm^{-3})}$$
$$= dm^3\,mol^{-1}$$

So $K_c = 32.7\,dm^3\,mol^{-1}$

7 In this example we are given the initial and equilibrium concentration of the reactants but no information about the products.

Ethyl ethanoate is hydrolysed by water:

$$CH_3COOC_2H_5 + H_2O \rightleftharpoons CH_3COOH + C_2H_5OH$$
$$\text{ethyl ethanoate} \quad \text{water} \quad \text{ethanoic acid} \quad \text{ethanol}$$

0.1000 mol of ethyl ethanoate are added to 0.1000 mol of water. A little acid catalyst is added and the mixture made up to $1\,dm^3$ with an inert solvent. At equilibrium 0.0654 mol of water are present. Calculate K_c for this reaction.

continued ⋯➤

Step 1 Write out the balanced chemical equation with all the data underneath

$$CH_3COOC_2H_5 + H_2O$$
$$\rightleftharpoons CH_3COOH + C_2H_5OH$$

initial conc.	0.1000 $mol\,dm^{-3}$	0.1000 $mol\,dm^{-3}$	0	0
conc. at equilibrium		0.0654 $mol\,dm^{-3}$		

Step 2 Calculate the unknown equilibrium concentrations:
- the chemical equation shows that 1 mole of $CH_3COOC_2H_5$ reacts with 1 mole water, so the equilibrium concentration of $CH_3COOC_2H_5$ is also $0.0654\,mol\,dm^{-3}$ (since we started with the same initial concentrations of ethyl ethanoate and water)
- the amount of water used in forming the products is $(0.1000 - 0.0654) = 0.0346\,mol\,dm^{-3}$. The chemical equation shows that 1 mole of water formed 1 mole of ethanoic acid and 1 mole of ethanol. So the concentrations of both the products at equilibrium is $0.0346\,mol\,dm^{-3}$

$$CH_3COOC_2H_5 + H_2O$$
$$\rightleftharpoons CH_3COOH + C_2H_5OH$$

conc. at equilibrium / $mol\,dm^{-3}$	0.0654	0.0654	0.0346	0.0346

Step 3 Write the equilibrium constant for this reaction in terms of concentrations:

$$K_c = \frac{[CH_3COOH]\,[C_2H_5OH]}{[CH_3COOC_2H_5]\,[H_2O]}$$

Step 4 Substitute the equilibrium concentrations into the expression:

$$K_c = \frac{(0.0346) \times (0.0346)}{(0.0654) \times (0.0654)} = 0.280$$

(to 3 significant figures)

Step 5 Add the correct units by referring back to the equilibrium expression.

$$\frac{(\cancel{mol\,dm^{-3}}) \times (\cancel{mol\,dm^{-3}})}{(\cancel{mol\,dm^{-3}}) \times (\cancel{mol\,dm^{-3}})}$$

The units of $mol\,dm^{-3}$ cancel, so K_c has no units. Therefore $K_c = 0.280$.

Check-up

7 Calculate the value of K_c for the following reaction using the information below:

$$H_2(g) + CO_2(g) \rightleftharpoons H_2O(g) + CO(g)$$

initial concentration of $H_2(g) = 10.00\,mol\,dm^{-3}$
initial concentration of $CO_2(g) = 10.00\,mol\,dm^{-3}$
equilibrium concentration of $CO(g) = 9.47\,mol\,dm^{-3}$

Fact file

Some of the first calculations on chemical equilibrium were carried out by the Norwegian chemists Cato Guldberg and Peter Waage. They first published their ideas in 1864. Their law, relating the equilibrium constant to the concentrations of the substances present at equilibrium and to the stoichiometric equation, is sometimes called the law of mass action.

Fact file

Our red blood cells contain the pigment haemoglobin. Oxygen bonds to haemoglobin in an equilibrium reaction. The position of equilibrium in this reaction depends on the concentration of oxygen in the blood.

K_c and concentration changes

If all other conditions remain constant, the value of K_c does not change when the concentration of reactants or products is altered.

Take the example of the decomposition of hydrogen iodide.

$$2HI \rightleftharpoons H_2 + I_2$$

The equilibrium constant at $500\,K$ for this reaction is 6.25×10^{-3}.

$$K_c = \frac{[H_2]\,[I_2]}{[HI]^2} = 6.25 \times 10^{-3}$$

When more hydrogen iodide is added to the equilibrium mixture, the equilibrium is disturbed.
- The ratio of concentrations of products to reactants in the equilibrium expression decreases.
- To restore equilibrium, both $[H_2]$ and $[I_2]$ increase and $[HI]$ decreases.
- Equilibrium is restored when the values of the concentrations in the equilibrium expression are such that the value of K_c is once again 6.25×10^{-3}.

K_c and pressure changes

Where there are different numbers of gas molecules on each side of a chemical equation, a change in pressure alters the position of equilibrium. It is shifted in the direction which results in fewer gas molecules being formed. However, if all other conditions remain constant, the value of K_c does not change when the pressure is altered.

K_c and temperature changes

We have seen on page **134** that for an endothermic reaction, an increase in temperature shifts the reaction in the direction of more products.

So for the endothermic reaction $2HI \rightleftharpoons H_2 + I_2$:
- the concentrations of H_2 and I_2 increase as the temperature increases
- the concentration of HI falls as the temperature increases.

Look at how these changes affect the equilibrium expression:

$$K_c = \frac{[H_2]\,[I_2]}{[HI]^2}$$

We see that the equilibrium constant must increase with increasing temperature. This is because $[H_2]$ and $[I_2]$ are increasing and $[HI]$ is decreasing. Table 8.5 shows how the value of K_c for this reaction changes with temperature.

For an exothermic reaction, an increase in temperature shifts the reaction in favour of more reactants.

Now look at the exothermic reaction:

$$2SO_2 + O_2 \rightleftharpoons 2SO_3$$

Temperature / K	K_c (no units)
300	1.26×10^{-3}
500	6.25×10^{-3}
1000	18.5×10^{-3}

Table 8.5 Variation of K_c for the reaction $2HI \rightleftharpoons H_2 + I_2$ with temperature.

- The concentrations of SO_2 and O_2 increase as the temperature increases.
- The concentration of SO_3 falls as the temperature increases.

How do these changes affect the equilibrium expression?

$$K_c = \frac{[SO_3]^2}{[SO_2]^2\,[O_2]}$$

We see that the equilibrium constant must decrease with increasing temperature. This is because $[SO_2]$ and $[O_2]$ are increasing and $[SO_3]$ is decreasing.

Check-up

8 a Deduce the effect of increase in temperature on the value of K_c for the reaction:

$$2NO(g) + O_2(g) \rightleftharpoons 2NO_2(g)$$
$$\Delta H_r = -115\,kJ\,mol^{-1}$$

b Explain why increasing the concentration of oxygen in this reaction does not affect the value of K_c.

8.4 Equilibria in gas reactions: the equilibrium constant, K_p

Partial pressure

For reactions involving mixtures of gases, it is easier to measure the pressure than to measure concentrations. The total pressure in a mixture of gases is due to each molecule bombarding the walls of the container. At constant temperature, each gas in the mixture contributes to the total pressure in proportion to the number of moles present (Figure **8.10**). The pressure exerted by any one gas in the mixture is called its **partial pressure**.

Fact file

The concentration of a gas is related to its pressure by the ideal gas equation $pV = nRT$.

Rearranging this we get $\dfrac{n}{V} = \dfrac{p}{RT}$.

$\dfrac{n}{V}$ is the concentration. Since R is a constant, and if the temperature is constant, we see that the concentration of gas is proportional to the pressure of the gas.

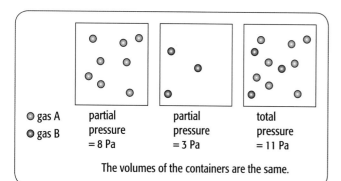

| gas A
gas B | partial
pressure
= 8 Pa | partial
pressure
= 3 Pa | total
pressure
= 11 Pa |

The volumes of the containers are the same.

Figure 8.10 Each gas in this mixture contributes to the pressure in proportion to the number of moles present.

The total pressure of a gas equals the sum of the partial pressures of the individual gases.

$$p_{total} = p_A + p_B + p_C \dots$$

where p_A, p_B, p_C are the partial pressures of the individual gases in the mixture.

Equilibrium expressions involving partial pressures

We write equilibrium expressions in terms of partial pressures in a similar way to equilibrium expressions in terms of concentrations. But there are some differences:

- we use p for partial pressure
- the reactants and products are written as subscripts after the p
- the number of moles of particular reactants or products is written as a power after the p
- square brackets are not used
- we give the equilibrium constant the symbol K_p (the equilibrium constant in terms of partial pressures).

For example, the equilibrium expression for the reaction:

$$N_2(g) + 3H_2(g) \rightleftharpoons 2NH_3(g)$$

is written as $K_p = \dfrac{p_{NH_3}^2}{p_{N_2} \times p_{H_2}^3}$

What are the units of K_p?

The units of pressure are pascals, Pa. The units of K_p depend on the form of the equilibrium expression.

Worked examples

8 For the reaction:

$$N_2O_4(g) \rightleftharpoons 2NO_2(g)$$

The equilibrium expression is:

$$K_p = \dfrac{p_{NO_2}^2}{p_{N_2O_4}}$$

The units are $\dfrac{\cancel{Pa} \times Pa}{\cancel{Pa}} = Pa$

9 For the reaction:

$$2SO_2(g) + O_2(g) \rightleftharpoons 2SO_3(g)$$

The equilibrium expression is:

$$K_p = \dfrac{p_{SO_3}^2}{p_{SO_2}^2 \times p_{O_2}}$$

The units are $\dfrac{\cancel{Pa} \times \cancel{Pa}}{\cancel{Pa} \times \cancel{Pa} \times Pa} = \dfrac{1}{Pa} = Pa^{-1}$

Check-up

10 Deduce the units of K_p for the following reactions:

  a $PCl_5(g) \rightleftharpoons PCl_3(g) + Cl_2(g)$

  b $N_2(g) + 3H_2(g) \rightleftharpoons 2NH_3(g)$

  c $3Fe(s) + 4H_2O(g) \rightleftharpoons Fe_3O_4(s) + 4H_2(g)$

Calculations using partial pressures

Worked examples

10 In this example we are given the partial pressure of each gas in the mixture.

  In the reaction

$$2SO_2(g) + O_2(g) \rightleftharpoons 2SO_3(g)$$

the equilibrium partial pressures at constant temperature are $SO_2 = 1.0 \times 10^6$ Pa, $O_2 = 7.0 \times 10^6$ Pa, $SO_3 = 8.0 \times 10^6$ Pa. Calculate the value of K_p for this reaction.

Step 1   Write the equilibrium expression for the reaction in terms of partial pressures.

$$K_p = \frac{p^2_{SO_3}}{p^2_{SO_2} \times p_{O_2}}$$

Step 2   Substitute the equilibrium concentrations into the expression.

$$K_p = \frac{(8.0 \times 10^6)^2}{(1.0 \times 10^6)^2 \times 7.0 \times 10^6} = 9.1 \times 10^{-6}$$

continued ⋯⟩

Step 3   Add the correct units.

The units are $\dfrac{\cancel{Pa} \times \cancel{Pa}}{\cancel{Pa} \times \cancel{Pa} \times Pa} = \dfrac{1}{Pa} = Pa^{-1}$

$$K_p = 9.1 \times 10^{-6}\,Pa^{-1}$$

11 In this calculation we are given the partial pressure of two of the three gases in the mixture as well as the total pressure.

  Nitrogen reacts with hydrogen to form ammonia.

$$N_2(g) + 3H_2(g) \rightleftharpoons 2NH_3(g)$$

The pressure exerted by this mixture of hydrogen, nitrogen and ammonia at constant temperature is 2.000×10^7 Pa. Under these conditions, the partial pressure of nitrogen is 1.490×10^7 Pa and the partial pressure of hydrogen is 0.400×10^7 Pa. Calculate the value of K_p for this reaction.

Step 1   Calculate the partial pressure of ammonia. We know that the total pressure is the sum of the partial pressures.

$$p_{total} = p_{N_2} + p_{H_2} + p_{NH_3}$$

$$2.000 \times 10^7 = (1.490 \times 10^7) + (0.400 \times 10^7) + p_{NH_3}$$

So partial pressure of $NH_3 = 0.110 \times 10^7$ Pa

Step 2   Write the equilibrium expression for the reaction in terms of partial pressures.

$$K_p = \frac{p^2_{NH_3}}{p_{N_2} \times p^3_{H_2}}$$

Step 3   Substitute the equilibrium concentrations into the expression.

$$K_p = \frac{(0.110 \times 10^7)^2}{(1.490 \times 10^7) \times (0.400 \times 10^7)^3}$$

Step 4   Add the correct units.

$$\dfrac{\cancel{Pa} \times \cancel{Pa}}{\cancel{Pa} \times \cancel{Pa} \times Pa \times Pa} = \dfrac{1}{Pa^2} = Pa^{-2}$$

$$K_p = 1.27 \times 10^{-15}\,Pa^{-2}$$

Fact file

We can work out partial pressures from the number of moles of each gas present in a mixture and the total pressure. The proportion which each gas contributes to mixture is called its mole fraction.

mole fraction

$$= \frac{\text{number of moles of a particular gas}}{\text{total number of moles of gas in the mixture}}$$

For example, in a mixture of 0.8 moles of gas A and 1.2 moles of gas B, the mole fraction of A is $\dfrac{0.8}{0.8 + 1.2} = 0.4$.

We find the partial pressure by using the relationship:

partial pressure = total pressure × mole fraction

Fact file

Doctors sometimes analyse the partial pressures of the gases in the lungs and the concentrations of gases dissolved in the blood in order to help diagnose patients with respiratory diseases.

Check-up

11 The information below gives the data for the reaction of hydrogen with iodine at 500 °C.

$$H_2(g) + I_2(g) \rightleftharpoons 2HI(g)$$

The table shows the initial partial pressures and the partial pressures at equilibrium of hydrogen, iodine and hydrogen iodide. The total pressure was constant throughout the experiment.

	Partial pressures / Pa		
	Hydrogen	Iodine	Hydrogen iodide
Initially	7.27×10^6	4.22×10^6	0
At equilibrium	3.41×10^6		7.72×10^6

a Deduce the partial pressure of the iodine at equilibrium.

b Calculate the value of K_p for this reaction, including the units.

8.5 Equilibria and the chemical industry

An understanding of equilibrium is important in the chemical industry. Equilibrium reactions are involved in some of the stages in the large-scale production of ammonia, sulfuric acid and many other chemicals.

Equilibrium and ammonia production

The synthesis of ammonia is carried out by the Haber process (for further details see page **193**). The equilibrium reaction involved is:

$$N_2(g) + 3H_2(g) \rightleftharpoons 2NH_3(g) \qquad \Delta H_r = -92\,\text{kJ}\,\text{mol}^{-1}$$

We can use Le Chatelier's principle to show how to get the best yield of ammonia. At high temperatures, when the reaction is faster, the position of equilibrium is to the left because the reaction is exothermic (ΔH is negative).

- What happens if we increase the pressure?
  - When we increase the pressure, the reaction goes in the direction which results in fewer molecules of gas being formed.
  - The equilibrium shifts in the direction which reduces the pressure.
  - In this case there are four molecules of gas on the left-hand side and two on the right-hand side. So the equilibrium shifts towards the right.
  - The yield of ammonia increases.
- What happens if we decrease the temperature?
  - A decrease in temperature decreases the energy of the surroundings.
  - The reaction will go in the direction in which energy is released.
  - Energy is released in the exothermic reaction, in which the position of equilibrium favours ammonia production.
  - This shifts the position of equilibrium to the right. The value of K_p increases.
- What happens if we remove ammonia by condensing it to a liquid? We can do this because ammonia has a much higher boiling point than hydrogen and nitrogen.
  - The position of equilibrium shifts to the right to replace the ammonia that has been removed.
  - More ammonia is formed from hydrogen and nitrogen to keep the value of K_p constant.

Equilibrium and the production of sulfuric acid

The synthesis of sulfuric acid is carried out by the Contact process (for further details see page **198**). The main equilibrium reaction involved is:

$$2SO_2(g) + O_2(g) \rightleftharpoons 2SO_3(g) \qquad \Delta H_r = -197\,kJ\,mol^{-1}$$

We can use Le Chatelier's principle to show how to get the best yield of sulfur trioxide.
- What happens when we increase the pressure?
  - When we increase the pressure, the reaction goes in the direction which results in fewer molecules of gas being formed, to reduce the pressure.
  - There are three molecules of gas on the left-hand side and two on the right-hand side, so the equilibrium shifts towards the right.

However, in practice, the reaction is carried out at just above atmospheric pressure. This is because the value of K_p is very high. The position of equilibrium is far over to the right even at atmospheric pressure. Very high pressure is unnecessary, and is not used as it is expensive.
- What happens if we decrease the temperature?
  - Decreasing the temperature shifts the position of equilibrium to the right.
  - A decrease in temperature decreases the energy of the surroundings so the reaction will go in the direction in which energy is released.
  - This is the exothermic reaction, in which the position of equilibrium favours SO_3 production. The value of K_p increases.

SO_3 is removed by absorbing it in 98% sulfuric acid. Although the SO_3 is absorbed in a continuous process, this does not affect the equilibrium significantly because the position of equilibrium is already far over to the right.

Check-up

12 The Haber process for the synthesis of ammonia may operate at a temperature of 450 °C and pressure of 1.50×10^7 Pa using an iron catalyst.

$$N_2(g) + 3H_2(g) \rightleftharpoons 2NH_3(g)$$

$$\Delta H_r = -92\,kJ\,mol^{-1}$$

continued ···⟶

a Suggest why the temperature of more than 450 °C is not used even though the rate of reaction would be faster.
b Suggest why the reaction is carried out at a high pressure rather than at normal atmospheric pressure. Explain your answer.
c Explain why the removal of ammonia as soon as it is formed is an important part of this industrial process.
d When the ammonia has been removed, why doesn't it decompose back to nitrogen and hydrogen?

8.6 Acid–base equilibria

Some simple definitions of acids and bases

A very simple definition of an **acid** is that it is a substance which neutralises a base. A salt and water are formed.

$$\underset{\text{acid}}{2HCl(aq)} + \underset{\text{base}}{CaO(s)} \rightarrow CaCl_2(aq) + H_2O(l)$$

The equation above also shows us a very simple definition of a base. A **base** is a substance which neutralises an acid. If we look at the formula for a number of acids in Table 8.6, we see that they all contain hydrogen atoms. When the acid dissolves in water, it ionises and forms hydrogen ions. Note that in organic acids such as carboxylic acids (see page **388**) only some of the hydrogen atoms are capable of forming ions.

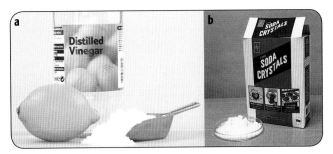

Figure 8.11 a The sour taste of lemons is due to citric acid and that of vinegar is due to ethanoic acid. **b** Washing soda is a base used to soften water prior to washing clothes. A solution of washing soda feels soapy.

Name of acid	Formula	Ions formed in water
hydrochloric acid	HCl	$H^+ + Cl^-$
nitric acid	HNO_3	$H^+ + NO_3^-$
sulfuric acid	H_2SO_4	$2H^+ + SO_4^{2-}$
ethanoic acid	CH_3COOH	$CH_3COO^- + H^+$
benzoic acid	C_6H_5COOH	$C_6H_5COO^- + H^+$

Table 8.6 Formulae and ions of some common acids.

A better definition of an acid is a substance which releases hydrogen ions when it dissolves in water. For example:

$$HCl(g) + aq \rightarrow H^+(aq) + Cl^-(aq)$$

The formulae for a number of bases are given in Table 8.7. Many metal oxides or hydroxides are bases. Some bases dissolve in water to form hydroxide ions in solution. A base which is soluble in water is called an **alkali**. For example:

$$NaOH(s) + aq \rightarrow Na^+(aq) + OH^-(aq)$$

Some alkalis are formed by the reaction of a base with water. When ammonia gas dissolves in water, some of the ammonia molecules react with water molecules. Hydroxide ions are released in this reaction.

$$NH_3(g) + H_2O(l) \rightarrow NH_4^+(aq) + OH^-(aq)$$

Aqueous ammonia is therefore an alkali. We can also see from the equation above that the ammonia has accepted a hydrogen ion to become NH_4^+. So a wider definition of a base is a substance which accepts hydrogen ions.

Name of base	Formula
calcium oxide	CaO
copper(II) oxide	CuO
sodium hydroxide	NaOH
calcium hydroxide	$Ca(OH)_2$
ammonia	NH_3

Table 8.7 The formulae of some common bases.

Check-up

13 a Write an equation to show potassium hydroxide dissolving in water.

 b Write an equation for liquid nitric acid dissolving in water.

 c Write ionic equations for:

  i the reaction in aqueous solution between sodium hydroxide and nitric acid

  ii the reaction in aqueous solution between potassium hydroxide and hydrochloric acid.

The Brønsted–Lowry theory of acids and bases

The definitions of acids and bases given above are limited to reactions taking place in water. In 1923 the Danish chemist J. Brønsted and the English chemist T. Lowry suggested a more general definition of acids and bases. This definition is based on the idea that in an acid–base reaction, a proton is transferred from an acid to a base (a proton is a hydrogen ion, H^+).

A Brønsted–Lowry acid is a proton donor.
A Brønsted–Lowry base is a proton acceptor.

When hydrochloric acid is formed, hydrogen chloride gas dissolves in water and reacts to form hydroxonium ions, H_3O^+, and chloride ions (Figure 8.12). You can see that the water is involved in the reaction.

$$HCl(g) + H_2O(l) \rightarrow H_3O^+(aq) + Cl^-(aq)$$

Hydrochloric acid is an acid because it donates a proton to water. This means that water is acting as a Brønsted–Lowry base. The water is accepting a proton.

H^+ donated

$$HCl(g) + H_2O(l) \rightarrow H_3O^+(aq) + Cl^-(aq)$$
acid   base

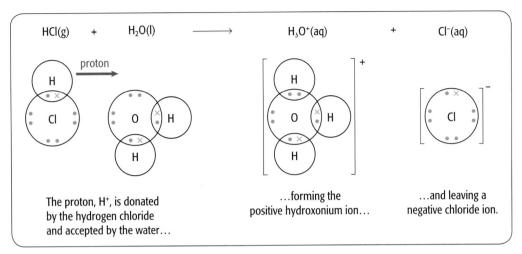

Figure 8.12 An acid is a proton donor. Hydrogen chloride is the acid in this reaction. A base is a proton acceptor. Water is the base in this reaction. Remember that a proton is a hydrogen ion, H^+.

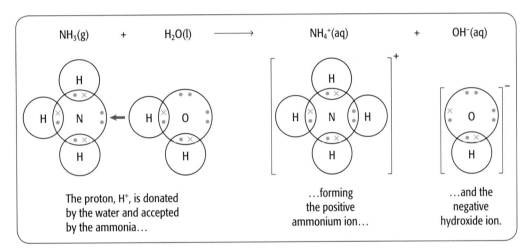

Figure 8.13 Water is the proton donor (it is the acid); ammonia is the proton acceptor (it is the base).

Water can also act as an acid. When ammonia reacts with water, it accepts a proton from the water and becomes an NH_4^+ ion (Figure **8.13**).

H⁺ donated

$$NH_3(g) + H_2O(l) \rightleftharpoons NH_4^+(aq) + OH^-(aq)$$
base   acid

Substances like water, which can act as either acids or bases are described as **amphoteric**.

Brønsted–Lowry acids and bases do not have to involve aqueous solutions. For example, when chloric(VII) acid

($HClO_4$) reacts with ethanoic acid (CH_3COOH) in an inert solvent, the following equilibrium is set up:

H⁺ donated

$$HClO_4 + CH_3COOH \rightleftharpoons ClO_4^- + CH_3COOH_2^+$$
acid   base

In this reaction $HClO_4$ is the acid because it is donating a proton to CH_3COOH. CH_3COOH is the base because it is a proton acceptor.

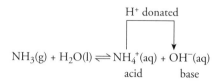

Fact file

Even corrosive acids such as nitric acid can act as bases!
When sulfuric acid and nitric acid react in an inert solvent, the
following equilibrium is set up:

$$H_2SO_4 + HNO_3 \rightleftharpoons HSO_4^- + H_2NO_3^+$$

Nitric acid is acting as a proton acceptor, so it is a base.

When an acid or base reacts with water, an equilibrium
mixture is formed. For acids such as hydrochloric acid,
the position of equilibrium is almost entirely in favour
of the products. But for ammonia the position of
equilibrium favours the reactants. The equations can be
written to show this. For example:

$$HCl(g) + aq \rightarrow H^+(aq) + Cl^-(aq)$$

A forward arrow is used as this reaction goes to completion.

$$NH_3(g) + H_2O(l) \rightleftharpoons NH_4^+(aq) + OH^-(aq)$$

An equilibrium arrow is used as this reaction does not go
to completion.

Check-up

14 Identify which reactants are acids and which
   are bases in the following reactions:
   a $NH_4^+ + H_2O \rightleftharpoons NH_3 + H_3O^+$
   b $HCOOH + HClO_2 \rightleftharpoons HCOOH_2^+ + ClO_2^-$

Conjugate acids and conjugate bases

In a reaction at equilibrium, products are being converted
to reactants at the same rate as reactants are being
converted to products. The reverse reaction can also be
considered in terms of the **Brønsted–Lowry theory** of
acids and bases.
   Consider the reaction:

$$NH_3(g) + H_2O(l) \rightleftharpoons NH_4^+(aq) + OH^-(aq)$$

In the reverse reaction, the NH_4^+ ion donates a proton
to the OH^- ion. So NH_4^+ is acting as an acid and OH^- is
acting as a base.

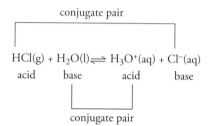

If a reactant is linked to a product by the transfer of a
proton we call this pair a **conjugate pair**. Consider the
following reaction:

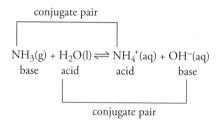

Looking at the forward reaction:
• Cl^- is the conjugate base of the acid HCl
• H_3O^+ is the conjugate acid of the base H_2O.
Looking at the reverse reaction:
• HCl is the conjugate acid of the base Cl^-
• H_2O is the conjugate base of the acid H_3O^+.
In a conjugate pair, the acid has one proton more.
   The conjugate pairs for the equilibrium between
ammonia and water to form ammonium ions and
hydroxide ions are:

conjugate pair

$$NH_3(g) + H_2O(l) \rightleftharpoons NH_4^+(aq) + OH^-(aq)$$

base · · · acid · · · acid · · · base

conjugate pair

Check-up

15 a Identify the acid and the base on the
     right-hand side of these equilibria.
     i $HClO_2 + HCOOH$
        $\rightleftharpoons ClO_2^- + HCOOH_2^+$
     ii $H_2S + H_2O \rightleftharpoons HS^- + H_3O^+$
   b Identify the acid on the right-hand side of
     this equation which is conjugate with the
     base on the left-hand side.

$$CH_3NH_2 + H_2O \rightleftharpoons CH_3NH_3^+ + OH^-$$

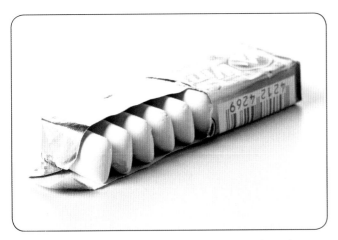

Figure 8.14 Many foods have high quantities of sugar in them. The sugar is converted to acid by bacteria in your mouth. This acid can attack the enamel on your teeth. By chewing sugar-free gum, more saliva is produced. Saliva is slightly alkaline. It neutralises the acid.

Strong and weak acids and bases

Strong acids

When hydrogen chloride dissolves in water to form a solution of concentration $0.1\,mol\,dm^{-3}$, it ionises almost completely. We say that the acid is almost completely **dissociated**.

$$HCl(g) + H_2O(l) \rightarrow H_3O^+(aq) + Cl^-(aq)$$

The position of equilibrium is so far over to the right that we can show this as an irreversible reaction. The pH of this solution is pH 1. The pH of a solution depends on the concentration of hydroxonium ions, H_3O^+. The higher the concentration of hydroxonium ions, the lower is the pH. The low pH shows that there is a high concentration of hydroxonium ions in solution.

> Acids which dissociate almost completely in solution are called **strong acids**.

The mineral acids, hydrochloric acid, sulfuric acid and nitric acid, are all strong acids.

Weak acids

When ethanoic acid dissolves in water to form a solution of concentration $0.1\,mol\,dm^{-3}$, it is only slightly ionised. There are many more molecules of ethanoic acid in solution than ethanoate ions and hydroxonium ions. We say that the acid is partially dissociated.

$$\underset{\text{ethanoic acid}}{CH_3COOH(l)} + H_2O(l) \rightleftharpoons \underset{\text{ethanoate ion}}{CH_3COO^-(aq)} + \underset{\substack{\text{hydroxonium}\\\text{ion}}}{H_3O^+(aq)}$$

The position of equilibrium is well over to the left. The pH of this solution is pH 2.9. The pH is much higher compared with a solution of hydrochloric acid of the same concentration. This is because the concentration of hydroxonium ions in solution is far lower.

> Acids which are only partially dissociated in solution are called **weak acids**.

Weak acids include most organic acids, hydrocyanic acid (HCN), hydrogen sulfide and 'carbonic acid'.

Fact file

Although we sometimes talk about the weak acid, carbonic acid, you will never see a bottle of it. The acid is really an equilibrium mixture of carbon dioxide dissolved in water. The following equilibrium is set up:

$$CO_2(g) + H_2O(l) \rightleftharpoons HCO_3^-(aq) + H^+(aq)$$

The amount of CO_2 which forms undissociated carbonic acid, H_2CO_3, is very small since H_2CO_3 ionises readily.

Strong bases

When sodium hydroxide dissolves in water to form a solution of concentration $0.1\,mol\,dm^{-3}$, it ionises completely.

$$NaOH(s) + aq \rightarrow Na^+(aq) + OH^-(aq)$$

The position of equilibrium is far over to the right. The solution formed is highly alkaline due to the high concentration of hydroxide ions present. The pH of this solution is pH 13.

> Bases which dissociate almost completely in solution are called **strong bases**.

The Group I metal hydroxides are strong bases.

Weak bases

When ammonia dissolves and reacts in water to form a solution of concentration $0.1\,mol\,dm^{-3}$, it is only slightly ionised. There are many more molecules of ammonia in solution than ammonium ions and hydroxide ions.

$$NH_3(g) + H_2O(l) \rightleftharpoons NH_4^+(aq) + OH^-(aq)$$

The position of equilibrium is well over to the left. The pH of this solution is pH 11.1. The pH is much lower compared with a solution of sodium hydroxide of the same concentration. This is because the concentration of hydroxide ions in solution is far lower.

> Bases which dissociate to only a small extent in solution are called **weak bases**.

Ammonia, amines (see page 390) and some hydroxides of transition metals are weak bases.

Table 8.8 compares the pH values of some typical strong and weak acids and bases.

Acid or base	pH of $1.0\,mol\,dm^{-3}$ solution	pH of $0.1\,mol\,dm^{-3}$ solution	pH of $0.01\,mol\,dm^{-3}$ solution
hydrochloric acid (strong acid)	0	1	2
ethanoic acid (weak acid)	2.4	2.9	3.4
sodium hydroxide (strong base)	14	13	12
ammonia (weak base)	11.6	11.1	10.6

Table 8.8 pH values of some typical strong and weak acids.

Summary

☐ A reversible reaction is one where the products can be changed back to reactants.
☐ Chemical equilibrium is dynamic because the backward and forward reactions are both occurring at the same time.
☐ A chemical equilibrium is reached when the rate of the forward and reverse reactions are equal.
☐ Le Chatelier's principle states that when the conditions in a chemical equilibrium change, the position of equilibrium shifts to oppose the change.
☐ Changes in temperature, pressure and concentration of reactants and products affect the position of equilibrium.
☐ For an equilibrium reaction, there is a relationship between the concentrations of the reactants and products which is given by the equilibrium constant K.
☐ Equilibrium constants in terms of concentrations, K_c, and partial pressure, K_p, can be deduced from appropriate data.
☐ The quantities of reactants and products present at equilibrium can be calculated from the equilibrium expression and a value of K_c (or K_p), given appropriate data.
☐ A change in temperature affects the value of the equilibrium constant for a reaction but changes in concentration, pressure or the presence of a catalyst do not affect the value of the equilibrium constant.
☐ The conditions used in the Haber process and the Contact process are chosen so that a good yield of product is made.
☐ The Brønsted–Lowry theory of acids and bases states that acids are proton donors and bases are proton acceptors.
☐ Strong acids and bases are completely ionised in aqueous solution whereas weak acids and bases are only slightly ionised.
☐ Strong and weak acids and bases can be distinguished by the pH values of their aqueous solutions.

End-of-chapter questions

1   The reaction

$$2SO_2(g) + O_2(g) \rightleftharpoons 2SO_3(g)$$

reaches dynamic equilibrium in a closed vessel. The forward reaction is exothermic. The reaction is catalysed by V_2O_5.

  a Explain the term **dynamic equilibrium**. [2]

  b What will happen to the position of equilibrium when:

    i   some sulfur trioxide, SO_3, is removed from the vessel? [1]

    ii the pressure in the vessel is lowered? [1]

    iii more V_2O_5 is added? [1]

    iv the temperature of the vessel is increased? [1]

  c State Le Chatelier's principle. [2]

  d Use Le Chatelier's principle to explain what will happen to the position of equilibrium
    in the reaction

$$H_2(g) + CO_2(g) \rightleftharpoons H_2O(g) + CO(g)$$

  when the concentration of hydrogen is increased. [5]

              Total = 13

2 Hydrogen, iodine and hydrogen iodide are in equilibrium in a sealed tube at constant temperature. The equation for the reaction is:

$$H_2 + I_2 \rightleftharpoons 2HI(g)$$ $\Delta H_r = -9.6\,kJ\,mol^{-1}$

The partial pressures of each gas are shown in the table below.

Gas	Partial pressure / Pa
H_2	2.330×10^6
I_2	0.925×10^6
HI	10.200×10^6

a Explain the meaning of the term **partial pressure**.   [2]
b Calculate the total pressure of the three gases in this mixture.   [1]
c Write an equilibrium expression for this reaction in terms of partial pressures.   [1]
d Calculate a value for K_p for this reaction, including the units.   [1]
e Use Le Chatelier's principle to explain what happens to the position of equilibrium in this
   reaction when:
   i   the temperature is increased   [5]
   ii some iodine is removed.   [5]

Total = 16

3 The equilibrium between three substances, **A**, **B** and **C** is shown below.

$$A(g) + B(g) \rightleftharpoons 2C(g)$$

Initially there were 0.1 mol of **A** and 0.2 mol of **B** in the reaction mixture. **A** and **B** reacted together to produce an equilibrium mixture containing 0.04 mol of **C**. The total volume of the mixture was $2.00\,dm^3$.

a Calculate the number of moles of **A** and **B** at equilibrium.   [2]
b Calculate the concentrations of **A**, **B** and **C** at equilibrium.   [3]
c i   Write the equilibrium expression for K_c.   [1]
   ii Calculate the value of K_c and give the units.   [2]

Total = 8

4   Gaseous hydrogen and gaseous iodine react together to form hydrogen iodide.

$$H_2 + I_2 \rightleftharpoons 2HI$$

a The graph shows how the amount of hydrogen iodide varies with time in a $1.00\,dm^3$ container. The initial amounts of hydrogen and iodine were $1.00\,mol\ H_2$ and $1.00\,mol\ I_2$.

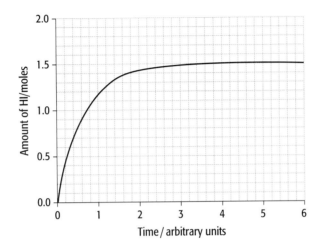

Time / arbitrary units

Draw a similar graph to show how the number of moles of hydrogen varies with time.   [5]
   b Calculate the number of moles of iodine present at equilibrium.   [1]
   c i Write the equilibrium expression for K_c for the reaction between gaseous hydrogen
         and iodine.   [1]
      ii Calculate the value of K_c and give the units.   [2]

Total = 9

5   a Describe **three** characteristic features of chemical equilibrium.   [3]
    b When 1 mol of N_2O_4 gas is allowed to come to equilibrium with NO_2 gas under standard
       conditions, only 20% of the N_2O_4 is converted to NO_2.

   $$N_2O_4 \rightleftharpoons 2NO_2 \qquad\qquad \Delta H_r = +58\,kJ\,mol^{-1}$$

      i   Give the equilibrium expression for this reaction.   [1]
      ii Calculate the value of K_c for the reaction. Assume that the volume of the reaction
          mixture is $1\,dm^3$.   [4]
    c Explain the effect on K_c of an increase in:
       i   pressure   [2]
       ii temperature.   [2]

Total = 12

6   This question is about the following reaction:

$$CH_3COOH(l) + C_2H_5OH(l) \rightleftharpoons CH_3COOC_2H_5(l) + H_2O(l)$$
    ethanoic acid   ethanol   ethyl ethanoate   water

9.20 g of ethanol are mixed with 12.00 g of ethanoic acid in an inert solvent. The total volume of solution is 250 cm^3. The mixture is left to equilibrate for several days. At equilibrium 70% of the reactants are converted to products.

a   What is the concentration of each reactant at the start?   [2]
b   What is the concentration of each reactant at equilibrium?   [2]
c   What is the concentration of each product at equilibrium?   [2]
d   i   Write the equilibrium expression for this reaction.   [1]
    ii   Calculate the value of K_c for the reaction.   [1]
    iii Explain why there are no units for K_c for this reaction.   [1]
e   What will happen to the numerical value of K_c if 100 cm^3 of water is added to the
    equilibrium mixture?   [1]
f   What will happen to the yield of ethyl ethanoate if 100 cm^3 of water is added to
    the equilibrium mixture? Explain your answer.   [2]

                                                                              Total = 12

7   a   Hydrogen chloride and ammonia both ionise in water:

$$HCl + H_2O \rightleftharpoons H_3O^+ + Cl^-$$ equation i

$$NH_3 + H_2O \rightleftharpoons NH_4^+ + OH^-$$ equation ii

    i   State the name of the ion H_3O^+.   [1]
    ii   Identify the acid and the base on the left-hand side of each equation.   [2]
    iii By referring to equation i and equation ii, explain why water is described as being **amphoteric**. [5]
    b   When dissolved in an organic solvent, hydrogen chloride reacts with hydrogen iodide as follows:

$$HCl + HI \rightleftharpoons H_2Cl^+ + I^-$$

    i   Use the Brønsted–Lowry theory of acids and bases to explain which reactant is the acid
         and which reactant is the base.   [2]
    ii   Identify which of the products is the conjugate acid and which is the conjugate base of the
         substances you have identified in part **b i**.   [1]
    c   Hydrochloric acid is a strong acid but ethanoic acid, CH_3COOH, is a weak acid.
    i   Explain the difference between a strong acid and a weak acid.   [2]
    ii   Suggest a value of the pH for a 0.1 mol dm^{-3} solution of ethanoic acid in water. [1]
    iii Write a chemical equation to show the reaction when ethanoic acid donates a
         proton to water.   [2]

                                                                              Total = 16

8 This question is about the reaction:

$$N_2(g) + 3H_2(g) \rightleftharpoons 2NH_3(g) \qquad\qquad \Delta H_r = -92\,kJ\,mol^{-1}$$

120.0 mol of hydrogen gas are mixed with 40.0 mol of nitrogen gas then pressurised. The mixture of gases is passed at constant pressure over an iron catalyst at 450 °C until the mixture reaches equilibrium. The total volume of the mixture is 1.0 dm³. 20% of the reactants are converted to ammonia.

  a How many moles of nitrogen and hydrogen remain at equilibrium? [2]
  b How many moles of ammonia are formed? [1]
  c Write an equilibrium expression for K_c. [1]
  d Calculate a value for K_c, including units. [2]
  e What will happen to the numerical value of K_c when the pressure is raised? [1]
  f What will happen to the numerical value of K_c when the temperature is raised? [1]

Total = 8

9 Ethanol can be manufactured by reacting ethene, C_2H_4, with steam.

$$C_2H_4(g) + H_2O(g) \rightleftharpoons C_2H_5OH(g)$$

  a Write the equilibrium expression in terms of partial pressures, K_p, for this reaction. [1]
  b State the units of K_p for this reaction. [1]
  c The reaction is at equilibrium at 290 °C and 7.00×10^6 Pa pressure. Under these conditions the partial pressure of ethene is 1.50×10^6 Pa and the partial pressure of steam is 4.20×10^6 Pa.
    i Calculate the partial pressure of ethanol. [1]
    ii Calculate the value of the equilibrium constant, K_p, under these conditions. [1]
  d The reaction is carried out in a closed system. Explain the meaning of the term **closed system**. [1]
  e Use Le Chatelier's principle to explain what will happen to position of equilibrium in this reaction when the pressure is increased. [3]
  f The results in the table below show the effect of temperature on the percentage of ethene converted to ethanol at constant pressure. Use this information to deduce the sign of the enthalpy change for this reaction. Explain your answer.

Temperature / °C	% of ethene converted
260	40
290	38
320	36

[4]

Total = 12

9.1 Introduction to reaction kinetics

Reaction kinetics is the study of the rates of chemical reactions. The data gathered from rate experiments can give us an insight into how reactions take place. We can then make deductions about the mechanism of a reaction.

Figure 9.1 Some chemical reactions are very fast (have a high rate of reaction) and others are much slower.

The **rate of a reaction** can be defined as follows:

$$\text{rate} = \frac{\text{change in amount of reactants or products}}{\text{time}}$$

The balanced chemical equation gives us no information about the rate of a reaction. Experiments are needed to measure the rate at which reactants are used up or products are formed. For example, if a reaction gives off a gas we can measure the volume of gas at regular time intervals (Figure 9.2).

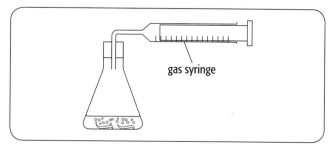

gas syringe

Figure 9.2 Measuring the volume of gas given off over time enables us to calculate the rate of reaction in cm^3 of gas per second.

Collision theory

When we explain the effects of concentration, temperature, surface area and catalysts on rates of reaction we use the **collision theory**. Collision theory states that in order to react with each other, particles must collide in the correct orientation and with sufficient energy. The particles might be atoms, ions or molecules.

When reactant particles collide they may simply bounce apart, without changing. This is called an **unsuccessful** collision. An unsuccessful collision will take place if the colliding particles do not have enough energy to react. If the reactant particles do have enough energy to react, they may change into product particles when they collide. This is called a **successful** (or effective) **collision** (Figure 9.3).

The minimum energy that colliding particles must possess for a successful collision to take place is called the **activation energy** of that particular reaction.

The activation energy for an exothermic reaction and an endothermic reaction can be shown on enthalpy profile diagrams (Figures 9.4 and 9.5).

According to the collision theory a reaction will speed up if
- the frequency of collisions increases
- the proportion of particles with energy greater than the activation energy increases.

A **catalyst** is a substance that increases the rate of a reaction but remains chemically unchanged itself at the end of the reaction. A catalyst does this by making it possible for the particles to react by an alternative mechanism. This alternative mechanism has a lower activation energy (Figure 9.6). You can read more about catalysts on page 157.

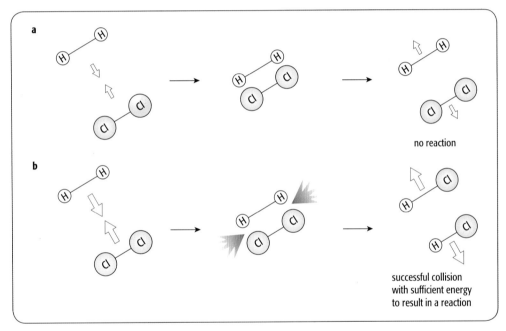

Figure 9.3 a Unsuccessful and **b** successful (or effective) collisions.

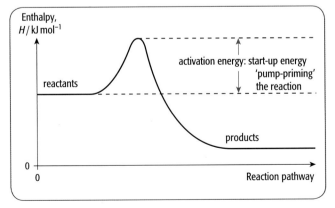

Figure 9.4 The activation energy in an exothermic reaction.

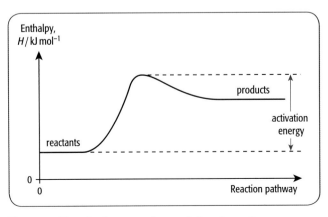

Figure 9.5 The activation energy in an endothermic reaction.

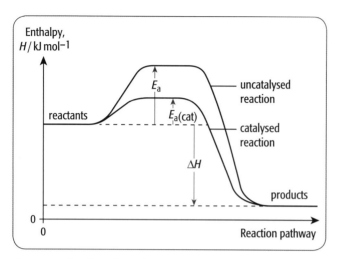

Figure 9.6 The effect of a catalyst on the activation energy in an exothermic reaction.

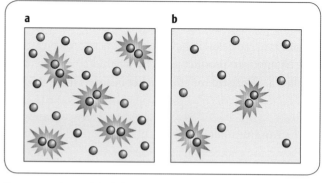

Figure 9.7 The particles in box **a** are closer together than those in box **b**. There are more particles in the same volume so the chances and frequency of collisions between reacting particles is increased. Therefore the rate of reaction is greater in box **a** than in box **b**.

The effect of pressure in reactions involving gases is similar to the effect of concentration in solutions. As we increase the pressure of reacting gases, there are more gas molecules in a given volume. This results in more collisions in any given time, and a faster rate of reaction.

Check-up

1 a Draw a different set of apparatus that could be used to monitor the reaction shown in Figure **9.2**.
  b What do we mean by:
   i the activation energy of a reaction
   ii a catalyst?
  c Does a catalyst work by increasing the frequency of collisions; by increasing the proportion of particles with energy greater than the activation energy; or by increasing the activation energy?
  d Use the collision theory to explain how increasing the surface area of a solid reactant increases the rate of reaction.

Check-up

2 a Dilute hydrochloric acid reacts with marble chips (calcium carbonate), giving off carbon dioxide gas. Which solution of acid will have the fastest initial rate of reaction: $50\,cm^3$ of $0.5\,mol\,dm^{-3}$, $10\,cm^3$ of $1.0\,mol\,dm^{-3}$ or $25\,cm^3$ of $0.5\,mol\,dm^{-3}$?
  b Explain your answer to part **a**.

9.2 The effect of concentration on rate of reaction

In chemistry we usually measure the concentration of solutions in moles per decimetre cubed, $mol\,dm^{-3}$. The more concentrated a solution the greater the number of particles of solute dissolved in a given volume of solvent. In reactions involving solutions, more concentrated reactants have a faster rate of reaction. This is because the random motion of the particles in solution results in more frequent collisions between reacting particles. This is shown in Figure **9.7**.

9.3 The effect of temperature on rate of reaction

To fully understand rates of reaction we need to look more closely at the energy possessed by the reactant particles. In a sample of any substance, at a given temperature, the particles will **not** all possess the same amount of energy as each other. A few particles will have a relatively small amount of energy. A few particles will have a relatively large amount of energy. Most particles will have an amount of energy somewhere in between. The distribution of energies at a given temperature can be shown on a graph (Figure **9.8**). This is called the **Boltzmann distribution**.

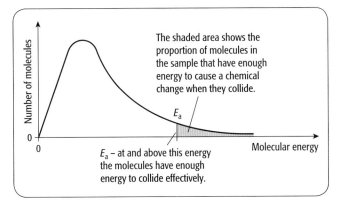

Figure 9.8 The Boltzmann distribution of molecular energies, showing the activation energy.

In Figure **9.8**, the activation energy is labelled. Remember that the activation energy is the minimum energy required for particles to react. When we raise the temperature of a reaction mixture, the average kinetic (movement) energy of the particles increases. Particles in solution and in gases will move around more quickly at a higher temperature, resulting in more frequent collisions. However, experiments show us that the effect of temperature on rate of reaction cannot be totally explained by more frequent collisions. The key factor is that the proportion of successful collisions increases greatly as we increase the temperature. The distribution of molecular energies changes as we raise the temperature, as shown in Figure **9.9**. The curve flattens and the peak shifts to the right.

The area under the curve represents the number of particles. The shaded area shows the number of particles with energy greater than the activation energy. For a

10 °C rise in temperature this area approximately doubles, as does the rate of many reactions.

Therefore increasing the temperature increases the rate of reaction because:

• the increased energy results in particles moving around more quickly which increases the frequency of collisions
• the proportion of successful collisions (i.e. those that result in a reaction) increases because the proportion of particles exceeding the activation energy increases. This is the more important factor.

Check-up

3 a What is the Boltzmann distribution?
  b Explain why a 10 °C rise in temperature can approximately double the rate of a reaction.

Fact file

Ludwig Boltzmann's ideas were not accepted by many of his peers in his lifetime. The frequent attacks on his work led him to feel disillusioned. Depressed and in bad health, he hanged himself. Soon after his death his theories were finally accepted by the scientific community.

9.4 Catalysis

In Figure **9.6** we saw how a catalyst works by providing an alternative mechanism (or route) with a lower activation energy. We can show this on a Boltzmann distribution (Figure **9.10**).

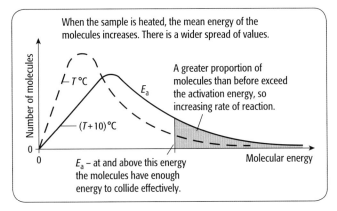

Figure 9.9 The Boltzmann distribution of molecular energies at temperatures *T*°C and (*T*+10)°C, showing the activation energy.

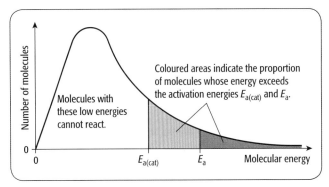

Figure 9.10 The Boltzmann distribution of molecular energies, showing the activation energy with and without a catalyst.

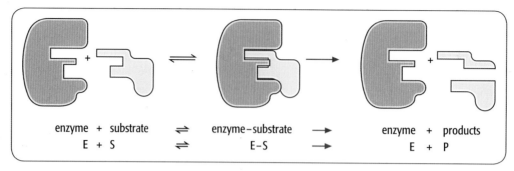

Figure 9.11 The 'lock and key' model of enzyme action. The substrate fits precisely into the active site of the enzyme. The enzyme then catalyses the breakdown of the substrate into the products, which can then leave the active site of the enzyme.

Notice that a catalyst does not affect the shape of the Boltzmann distribution. However, by providing a lower activation energy a greater proportion of molecules in the reaction mixture have sufficient energy to react. The shaded areas under the curve represent the numbers of molecules which have more energy than the activation energy.

Enzymes

Enzymes are biological catalysts. They are large protein molecules which enable the biochemical reactions that happen in living things to take place quickly at relatively low temperatures. Enzyme molecules are folded into special shapes that can accommodate reactant molecules at their 'active sites'. A simplified explanation of how they operate is given by a 'lock and key' mechanism (Figures **9.11** and **9.12**).

Enzymes are incredibly efficient. Most enzymes will only catalyse one reaction involving one particular molecule or pair of molecules. We say that enzymes are **specific**. The molecule that fits into the active site of an enzyme and reacts is called the **substrate** of that enzyme. However, most enzymes lose their effectiveness if temperatures rise above about 45 °C. At temperatures higher than this the increased molecular vibrations cause the protein molecules to lose their special shape. The substrate will no longer fit into the enzyme's active site. The enzymes become denatured. Large changes in pH also denature enzymes.

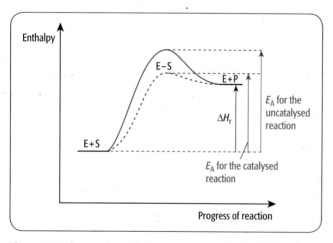

Figure 9.12 The energy profile for an enzyme-catalysed endothermic reaction, compared to the same reaction without a catalyst. As for inorganic catalysts, the enzyme provides a different reaction pathway with a lower activation energy (E_A) but the overall enthalpy change (ΔH_r) is unaffected.

Fact file

Human enzymes start to denature quickly at temperatures above 40 °C. However, enzymes in bacteria found in hot springs have optimum temperatures of about 70 °C.

Check-up

4 Enzymes are used in the biotechnology industry. They are far more efficient than traditional catalysts used in industrial processes.
   a Name the catalyst used in:
      i the Haber process
      ii the Contact process.
   b What would be the benefits of using enzymes instead of traditional catalysts in the industrial production of a chemical?

Summary

☐ Chemical kinetics is the study of rates of chemical reactions.
☐ Factors that affect the rate of a chemical reaction are:
  – surface area
  – concentration (or pressure of gases)
  – temperature
  – catalysts.
☐ The activation energy of a reaction is the minimum energy required by colliding particles for reaction to occur. Enthalpy profile diagrams show how the activation energy provides a barrier to reaction.
☐ At higher concentration (or pressure), more frequent collisions occur between reactant molecules. This increases reaction rate.
☐ At higher temperature, molecules have more kinetic energy, so a higher percentage of successful collisions occur between reactant molecules.
☐ The Boltzmann distribution represents the numbers of molecules in a sample with particular energies. The change in the Boltzmann distribution as temperature is increased shows how more molecules have energy greater than the activation energy. This, in turn leads to an increase in reaction rate.
☐ A catalyst increases the rate of a reaction by providing an alternative reaction pathway with a lower activation energy. More molecules have sufficient energy to react, so the rate of reaction is increased.
☐ Enzymes are protein molecules which act as very efficient catalysts in living things. They are specific in the reactions they catalyse.

End-of-chapter questions

1   a   Explain why gases react together faster at higher pressure.   [2]
    b   Explain why reactants in solution react faster at higher concentration.   [1]
    c   Explain why finely divided solids react more quickly than solid lumps.   [2]
    d   Explain why raising the temperature increases the rate of reaction.   [4]
                                                                                                    Total = 9

2   a   Sketch a graph to show the Boltzmann distribution of molecular energies. Label the axes.   [4]
    b   What is meant by **activation energy**?   [2]
    c   Shade an area on the graph to show the number of molecules capable of reacting.   [2]
    d   Mark on your graph a possible activation energy for the same reaction in the presence of a catalyst. [1]
    e   Shade an area on the graph to show the additional number of molecules capable of reacting due
        to the presence of a catalyst.   [1]
    f   Draw a second curve on your graph to show the Boltzmann distribution of molecular energies
        at a slightly higher temperature.   [2]
                                                                                                   Total = 12

3   The Haber process is exothermic (see page 142):
    a Sketch the enthalpy profile for the Haber process in the absence of a catalyst.   [1]
    b On the same diagram, sketch the enthalpy profile for the Haber process in the presence of a catalyst.   [1]
    c Label the activation energy on one of the profiles.   [1]

                                                                                              Total = 3

4   The activation energy for the uncatalysed decomposition of ammonia to its elements is $+335\,kJ\,mol^{-1}$.
    a Write the equation for this reaction, including state symbols.   [3]
    b The enthalpy of reaction for this decomposition is $+92\,kJ\,mol^{-1}$. Calculate the activation energy
       for the uncatalysed formation of ammonia from nitrogen and hydrogen.   [3]
    c If tungsten is used as a catalyst the activation energy changes. Explain how it will change.   [1]

                                                                                              Total = 7

10 Periodicity

Objectives

Candidates should, for the third period (sodium to argon), be able to:

- [ ] describe qualitatively (and indicate the periodicity in) the variations in atomic radius, ionic radius, melting point and electrical conductivity of the elements (see the Data Booklet)
- [ ] explain qualitatively the variation in atomic radius and ionic radius
- [ ] interpret the variation in melting point and in electrical conductivity in terms of the presence of simple molecular, giant molecular or metallic bonding in the elements
- [ ] explain the variation in first ionisation energy
- [ ] describe the reactions, if any, of the elements with oxygen (to give Na_2O, MgO, Al_2O_3, P_4O_{10}, SO_2, SO_3), chlorine (to give $NaCl$, $MgCl_2$, Al_2Cl_6, $SiCl_4$, PCl_5) and water (Na and Mg only)
- [ ] state and explain the variation in oxidation number of the oxides and chlorides in terms of their valence shell electrons
- [ ] describe the reactions of the oxides with water [treatment of peroxides and superoxides is **not** required]
- [ ] describe and explain the acid/base behaviour of oxides and hydroxides including, where relevant, amphoteric behaviour in reaction with sodium hydroxide (only) and acids
- [ ] describe and explain the reactions of the chlorides with water
- [ ] interpret the variations and trends in the four points above in terms of bonding and electronegativity
- [ ] suggest the types of chemical bonding present in chlorides and oxides from observations of their chemical and physical properties
- [ ] predict the characteristic properties of an element in a given group by using knowledge of chemical periodicity
- [ ] deduce the nature, possible position in the Periodic Table, and identity of unknown elements from given information about physical and chemical properties.

10.1 Introduction – structure of the Periodic Table

The Periodic Table was devised in 1869 by the Russian chemist Dmitri Mendeleev (Figure **10.1**). He organised the elements known at that time in order of their atomic mass, arranging elements with similar properties into vertical columns (Figure **10.2**). He left gaps where the pattern broke down, arguing that these spaces would eventually be filled by as-yet-undiscovered elements. For example, he left a space below silicon, and he made predictions of how the 'new' element would behave when it was discovered. He also changed the atomic mass order

Figure 10.1 Dmitri Mendeleev (1834–1907).

Figure 10.2 This version of Mendeleev's Periodic Table is on the building in St Petersburg where he worked.

in places where similar elements did not quite line up in columns. Some chemists doubted the relevance of his table, but they were convinced by the discovery of germanium in 1876. Germanium closely matched the properties that Mendeleev had predicted for the 'new' element below silicon, using his Periodic Table.

We now know that the chemical elements are arranged in order of atomic number, not atomic masses, in the Periodic Table. This explains why Mendeleev had to re-order some elements in his table (which was developed before scientists knew about the structure of the atom). The modern Periodic Table is shown in Figure 10.3. There are eight major groups (vertical columns), usually numbered by Roman numerals. The rows across the Periodic Table are called periods. In this chapter we will be looking for patterns going across the third period, from sodium (Na) to argon (Ar). The patterns seen across Period 3 are seen across other periods too. This recurrence of the same pattern is called **periodicity**.

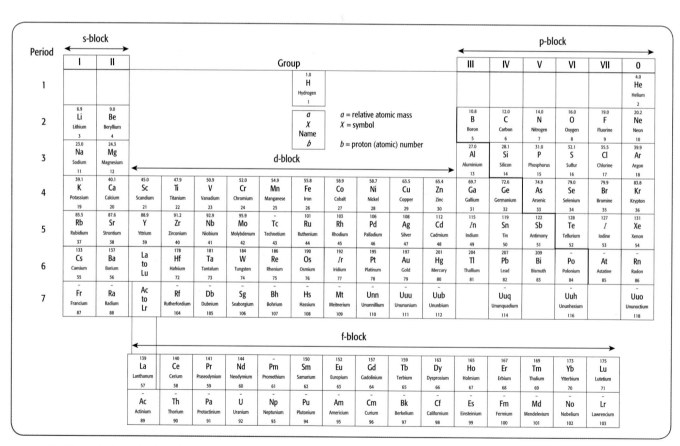

Figure 10.3 The Periodic Table of the elements.

10.2 Periodicity of physical properties

1 Periodic patterns of atomic radii

We can compare the size of different atoms using their atomic radii. The data for these measurements can come from an element's single covalent radius (Figure **10.4**). There are other measures of atomic radii, such as metallic radii and van der Waals' radii. However, covalent radii can be obtained for most elements so this provides the best data for comparison purposes across a period.

The values of the atomic radii of the elements in Period 3 are given in Table **10.1**. We can see the pattern across the period more clearly on a graph (Figure **10.5**).

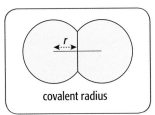

Figure 10.4 The distance between the two nuclei of the same type of atom can be determined, then divided by two to arrive at the atomic (single covalent) radii.

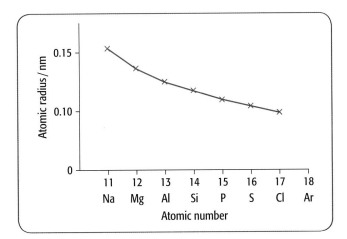

Figure 10.5 Plotting the atomic radii (single covalent radii) against atomic number for the elements in Period 3 (argon not included).

As shown in Figure **10.5**, the atomic radius decreases across Period 3. The same pattern is also found in other periods. Across a period, the number of protons (and hence the nuclear charge), and the number of electrons, increases by one with each successive element. The extra electron added to the atoms of each successive element occupies the same principal quantum shell (energy level). This means that the shielding effect remains roughly constant (see page **36**). So the greater attractive force exerted by the increasing positive nuclear charge on the outer (valence) shell electrons pulls them closer to the nucleus. Hence the atomic radius decreases across the period.

2 Periodic patterns of ionic radii

From your work in Chapter 4, you will know that the atoms of metallic elements produce positively charged ions (called cations), such as Na^+. On the other hand, the atoms of a non-metal form negatively charged ions (called anions), such as Cl^-. What pattern in ionic radii do we see going across Period 3? The data is shown in Table **10.2**. Figure **10.6** displays the ionic radii data from Table **10.2**.

The positively charged ions have effectively lost their outer shell of electrons (the third principal quantum shell or energy level) from their original atoms. Hence the cations are much smaller than their atoms. To add to this effect, there is also less shielding of the outer electrons in these cations compared with their original atoms.

Period 3 element	sodium (Na)	magnesium (Mg)	aluminium (Al)	silicon (Si)	phosphorus (P)	sulfur (S)	chlorine (Cl)	argon (Ar)
Atomic radius / nm	0.157	0.136	0.125	0.117	0.110	0.104	0.099	–

Table 10.1 The atomic (single covalent) radii of Period 3 elements (no data is available for argon). The units are nanometres, where $1\,nm = 10^{-9}\,m$.

Ions of Period 3 elements	Na$^+$	Mg^{2+}	Al^{3+}	Si^{4+}	P^{3-}	S^{2-}	Cl$^-$	Ar
Ionic radius / nm	0.095	0.065	0.050	0.041	0.212	0.184	0.181	–

Table 10.2 The ionic radii of Period 3 elements (no data is available for argon).

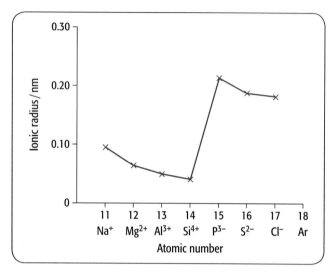

Figure 10.6 Plotting the ionic radii against atomic number for the elements in Period 3 (argon not included).

Going across the period, from Na$^+$ to Si^{4+}, the ions get smaller for reasons similar to the explanation given for the decreasing atomic radii across a period. The increasing nuclear charge attracts the outermost (valence-shell) electrons in the second principal quantum shell (energy level) closer to the nucleus with increasing atomic number.

The negatively charged ions are larger than their original atoms. They have gained extra electrons into their third principal quantum shell, increasing the repulsion between electrons, whilst keeping the same nuclear charge. This increases the size of the anion compared with its atom.

The anions decrease in size going from P^{3-} to Cl$^-$ as the nuclear charge increases across the period.

3 Periodic patterns of melting points and electrical conductivity

Physical properties, such as the melting point and electrical conductivity of the elements, also show trends across a period. Again using Period 3 as an example, we can show the data in tables and on graphs (see Tables 10.3 and 10.4 and Figure 10.7).

The electrical conductivity increases across the metals of Period 3 from sodium to aluminium. The electrical conductivity then drops dramatically to silicon, which is termed a semi-conductor, and falls even further to the insulators phosphorus and sulfur.

To explain the trend in melting points and electrical conductivity across a period, we have to consider the bonding and structure of the elements (Table 10.5).

Period 3 element	sodium (Na)	magnesium (Mg)	aluminium (Al)	silicon (Si)	phosphorus (P)	sulfur (S)	chlorine (Cl)	argon (Ar)
Melting point / K	371	923	932	1683	317	392	172	84

Table 10.3 The melting points of Period 3 elements (measured in kelvin, K, where 0 °C = 273 K).

Period 3 element	sodium (Na)	magnesium (Mg)	aluminium (Al)	silicon (Si)	phosphorus (P)	sulfur (S)	chlorine (Cl)	argon (Ar)
Electrical conductivity / 10^8 siemens per metre	0.218	0.224	0.382	2×10^{-10}	10^{-17}	10^{-23}	–	–

Table 10.4 The electrical conductivity of Period 3 elements (measured in siemens per metre, $S\,m^{-1}$, where a siemen is proportional to the ease with which electrons can pass through a material).

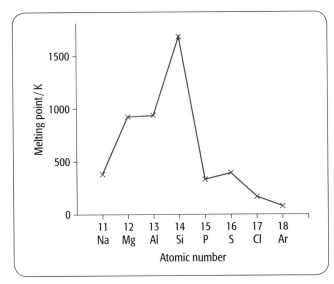

Figure 10.7 Plotting the melting point against atomic number for the elements in Period 3.

Sodium, magnesium and aluminium, at the start of Period 3, are all metallic elements. As you saw on page **60**, their metallic bonding can be described as positive ions arranged in a giant lattice held together by a 'sea' of delocalised electrons. The delocalised electrons are those from the outermost (valence) shell and they are free to move around within the structure of the metal. When a potential difference is applied these electrons drift through the metal towards the positive terminal. Both the melting point and the electrical conductivity increase going from sodium to magnesium to aluminium.

This can be explained by the number of electrons each metal donates into the 'sea' of delocalised electrons and the increasing charge on the metal ions in the giant metallic lattice. Each sodium atom donates one electron, forming Na^+ ions in the lattice, whereas each aluminium atom donates three electrons, forming Al^{3+} ions. This makes the metallic bonding in aluminium stronger as the electrostatic forces of attraction between its 3+ ions and the larger number of delocalised electrons holding the giant structure together are stronger. There are also more delocalised electrons available to drift through the structure when the metal conducts a current, making aluminium a better electrical conductor than sodium.

The element in the centre of Period 3, silicon, has the highest melting point because of its giant molecular structure (also called a giant covalent structure). Every silicon atom is held to its neighbouring silicon atoms by strong covalent bonds. However, its electrical conductivity is much lower than the metals at the start of the period because there are no delocalised electrons free to move around within its structure. Silicon is classed as a semi-metal or metalloid.

The elements to the right of silicon are all non-metallic elements. They exist as relatively small molecules. Sulfur exists as S_8 molecules, phosphorus as P_4 molecules and chlorine as Cl_2 molecules. Although the covalent bonds within each molecule are strong, there are only relatively weak van der Waals' forces between their molecules (see page **63**). Therefore it does not take much energy to break these weak intermolecular forces and melt the

Period 3 element	sodium (Na)	magnesium (Mg)	aluminium (Al)	silicon (Si)	phosphorus (P)	sulfur (S)	chlorine (Cl)	argon (Ar)
Bonding	metallic	metallic	metallic	covalent	covalent	covalent	covalent	–
Structure	giant metallic	giant metallic	giant metallic	giant molecular	simple molecular	simple molecular	simple molecular	simple molecular

Table 10.5 The bonding and structures of Period 3 elements.

elements. At room temperature, phosphorus and sulfur are solids with low melting points and chlorine is a gas.

Argon gas exists as single atoms with very weak van der Waals' forces between these atoms.

4 Periodic patterns of first ionisation energies

You have looked at the pattern in first ionisation energies for the first two periods on page 42. As stated, the pattern is the same in Period 3. This is shown in Table 10.6 and Figure 10.8.

In general, the first ionisation energy increases going across Period 3 as the positive nuclear charge increases and electrons successively fill the third quantum shell. As electrons are in the same shell the shielding effect is similar in atoms of each element. There are small 'dips' in the general trend across the period between Mg and Al, and between P and S. The same pattern appears in Period 2 for Be and B, and N and O. The explanation given on pages 42–3 also applies here in Period 3.

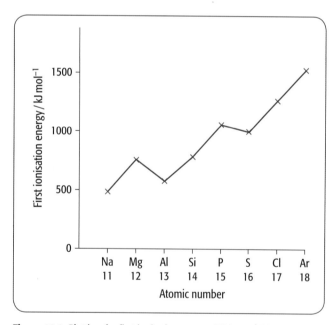

Figure 10.8 Plotting the first ionisation energy (X(g) → X$^+$(g) + e$^-$) against atomic number for the elements in Period 3.

Period 3 element	sodium (Na)	magnesium (Mg)	aluminium (Al)	silicon (Si)	phosphorus (P)	sulfur (S)	chlorine (Cl)	argon (Ar)
First ionisation energy / kJ mol^{-1}	494	736	577	786	1060	1000	1260	1520

Table 10.6 The first ionisation energy (X(g) → X$^+$(g) + e$^-$) of Period 3 elements in kilojoules per mole (kJ mol^{-1}).

10.3 Periodicity of chemical properties

We will now look at the chemistry of some of the elements of Period 3, focussing on their oxides and chlorides.

Reactions of Period 3 elements with oxygen

Sodium reacts vigorously when heated and placed in a gas jar of oxygen. The sodium burns with a yellow flame (Figure **10.9**). The main product when sodium burns in a limited amount of oxygen is a white solid, sodium oxide:

$$4Na(s) + O_2(g) \rightarrow 2Na_2O(s)$$

Magnesium also reacts vigorously when heated in oxygen, forming magnesium oxide. Aluminium metal is protected by a tough layer of aluminium oxide but powdered aluminium reacts well with oxygen. Both metals burn with bright white flames.

$$2Mg(s) + O_2(g) \rightarrow 2MgO(s)$$

$$4Al(s) + 3O_2(g) \rightarrow 2Al_2O_3(s)$$

Silicon reacts slowly with oxygen to form silicon(IV) oxide (silicon dioxide):

$$Si(s) + O_2(g) \rightarrow SiO_2(s)$$

Figure 10.9 Sodium reacts vigorously with oxygen gas.

Phosphorus reacts vigorously with oxygen. A yellow or white flame is seen, and clouds of white phosphorus(V) oxide are produced:

$$4P(s) + 5O_2(g) \rightarrow P_4O_{10}(s)$$

Sulfur powder burns gently with a blue flame in a gas jar of oxygen gas. Toxic fumes of sulfur dioxide gas are produced (Figure **10.10**):

$$S(s) + O_2(g) \rightarrow SO_2(g)$$

Figure 10.10 Sulfur burns gently in oxygen gas.

Further oxidation of sulfur dioxide gives sulfur trioxide. Their systematic names are sulfur(IV) oxide and sulfur(VI) oxide, respectively.

$$2SO_2(g) + O_2(g) \underset{}{\overset{V_2O_5 \text{ catalyst}}{\rightleftharpoons}} 2SO_3(g)$$

Chlorine and argon do not react with oxygen.

Reactions of Period 3 elements with chlorine

When sodium metal is heated then plunged into a gas jar of chlorine there is a vigorous reaction, forming sodium chloride:

$$2Na(s) + Cl_2(g) \rightarrow 2NaCl(s)$$

Magnesium and aluminium also react vigorously with chlorine gas:

$$Mg(s) + Cl_2(g) \rightarrow MgCl_2(s)$$

$$2Al(s) + 3Cl_2(g) \rightarrow Al_2Cl_6(s)$$

Silicon reacts slowly with chlorine, as it does with oxygen, giving silicon(IV) chloride:

$$Si(s) + 2Cl_2(g) \rightarrow SiCl_4(l)$$

Phosphorus also reacts slowly with excess chlorine gas:

$$2P(s) + 5Cl_2(g) \rightarrow 2PCl_5(l)$$

Sulfur does form chlorides, such as SCl_2 and S_2Cl_2, but you do not need to cover these for your AS examination.

Argon does not form a chloride.

Reaction of sodium and magnesium with water

Sodium reacts vigorously with cold water, melting into a ball of molten metal (Figure 10.11). It moves across the surface of the water, giving off hydrogen gas. It quickly gets smaller and smaller until it disappears, leaving a strongly alkaline solution (e.g. pH 14) of sodium hydroxide behind:

$$2Na(s) + 2H_2O(l) \rightarrow 2NaOH(aq) + H_2(g)$$

On the other hand, magnesium only reacts very slowly with cold water, taking several days to produce a test tube of hydrogen gas. The solution formed is very weakly alkaline (e.g. pH 11), as any magnesium hydroxide formed is only slightly soluble. Therefore

Figure 10.11 Sodium reacts vigorously with water.

fewer $OH^-(aq)$ ions enter the solution compared with the result when sodium is added to water. This is because sodium hydroxide is much more soluble in water than magnesium hydroxide.

$$Mg(s) + 2H_2O(l) \xrightarrow{\text{slow reaction}} Mg(OH)_2(aq) + H_2(g)$$

Hot magnesium does react vigorously with water in the form of steam to make magnesium oxide and hydrogen gas:

$$Mg(s) + H_2O(g) \rightarrow MgO(s) + H_2(g)$$

Check-up

5 **a i** The Group I metal lithium reacts in a similar way to sodium. It reacts with oxygen, producing lithium oxide. Write the balanced symbol equation, including state symbols, for this reaction.

   ii Lithium also reacts with chlorine. Write the balanced symbol equation, including state symbols, for this reaction.

 b i The Group II metal calcium reacts more vigorously with cold water than magnesium does, forming an alkaline solution. Write the balanced symbol equation, including state symbols, for this reaction.

   ii The solution formed when 0.01 mol of calcium react completely with $1\,dm^3$ of water is more alkaline than the solution formed when 0.01 mol of magnesium react completely with $1\,dm^3$ of water. Explain why.

10.4 Oxides of Period 3 elements
Oxidation numbers of oxides

Table 10.8 shows the formulae of some of the common oxides of the Period 3 elements.

The maximum oxidation number for each element rises as we cross the period. This happens because the Period 3 element in each oxide can use all the electrons in its outermost shell in bonding to oxygen (ox. no. = –2). They all exist in positive oxidation states because oxygen

Period 3 element	sodium (Na)	magnesium (Mg)	aluminium (Al)	silicon (Si)	phosphorus (P)	sulfur (S)	chlorine (Cl)	argon (Ar)
Formula of oxide	Na_2O	MgO	Al_2O_3	SiO_2	P_4O_{10}	SO_2, SO_3	Cl_2O_7	–
Oxidation number of Period 3 element	+1	+2	+3	+4	+5	+4, +6	+7	–

Table 10.8 Oxidation numbers of the Period 3 elements in some common oxides. Chlorine has other oxides, such as Cl_2O, in which its oxidation number is +1, and Cl_2O_5, in which its oxidation number is +5.

has a higher electronegativity than any of the Period 3 elements.

See page **62** for more about electronegativity.

Effect of water on oxides and hydroxides of Period 3 elements

The oxides of sodium and magnesium react with water to form hydroxides. The presence of excess aqueous hydroxide ions makes these solutions alkaline:

$$Na_2O(s) + H_2O(l) \rightarrow 2NaOH(aq)$$
strongly alkaline
solution

$$MgO(s) + H_2O(l) \rightarrow Mg(OH)_2(aq)$$
weakly alkaline
solution

Fact file

Magnesium oxide and magnesium hydroxide are commonly used in indigestion remedies (Figure **10.12**). These basic compounds neutralise excess acid in the stomach, relieving the pain:

$$MgO(s) + 2HCl(aq) \rightarrow MgCl_2(aq) + H_2O(l)$$

$$Mg(OH)_2(s) + 2HCl \rightarrow MgCl_2(aq) + 2H_2O(l)$$

Figure 10.12 The basic magnesium oxide or hydroxide reacts with acid in the stomach to form a salt plus water.

Aluminium oxide does not react or dissolve in water. However, it does react and dissolve when added to acidic or alkaline solutions.

- With acid:

$$Al_2O_3(s) + 3H_2SO_4(aq) \rightarrow Al_2(SO_4)_3(aq) + 3H_2O(l)$$

- With hot, concentrated alkali:

$$Al_2O_3(s) + 2NaOH(aq) + 3H_2O(l) \rightarrow 2NaAl(OH)_4(aq)$$

When aluminium oxide reacts with an acid it behaves like a base – it forms a salt plus water – and when it reacts with an alkali it behaves like an acid – reacting to form a salt. Compounds which can act as both acids and bases, such as aluminium oxide, are called **amphoteric**.

Silicon dioxide is also insoluble in water. Water cannot break down its giant molecular structure. However, it will react with and dissolve in hot concentrated alkali:

$$SiO_2(s) + 2NaOH(aq) \rightarrow Na_2SiO_3(aq) + H_2O(l)$$

Silicon dioxide acts as an acid, forming a salt plus water with an alkali. It does not react with acids, so it is classed as an acidic oxide.

Phosphorus(V) oxide reacts vigorously and dissolves in water to form an acidic solution of phosphoric(V) acid (pH 2):

$$P_4O_{10}(s) + 6H_2O(l) \rightarrow 4H_3PO_4(aq)$$
phosphoric(V) acid

The oxides of sulfur, SO_2 and SO_3, both react and dissolve in water forming acidic solutions (pH 1):

$$SO_2(g) + H_2O(l) \rightarrow H_2SO_3(aq)$$
sulfuric(IV) acid

$$SO_3(g) + H_2O(l) \rightarrow H_2SO_4(aq)$$
sulfuric(VI) acid

Summary of the acidic/basic nature of the Period 3 oxides

Table **10.9** shows a summary of the acidic or basic nature of the Period 3 oxides. You need to know this summary for your examination. We can explain the behaviour of the oxides by looking at their structure and bonding (Table **10.10** and Figure **10.13**).

Going across a period the elements get more electronegative as electrons are more strongly attracted by the increasing positive nuclear charge (see page **62**). The electronegativity values, which indicate the attraction of an atom for the electrons in a bond, are shown in Table **10.11**.

The electronegativity of oxygen is 3.5. The greater the difference in electronegativity between the Period 3 element and oxygen, the more likely it is that the oxide will have ionic bonding. Electrons will be transferred from sodium, magnesium and aluminium to the oxygen when their oxides are formed. The other Period 3 elements will form covalently bonded oxides in which bonding electrons are shared.

The oxides of the metals sodium and magnesium, with purely ionic bonding, produce alkaline solutions with water as their oxide ions, O^{2-}(aq), become hydroxide ions, OH^-(aq). The oxide ions behave as bases by accepting H^+ ions from water molecules:

$$O^{2-}(aq) + H_2O(l) \rightarrow 2OH^-(aq)$$

On the other hand, the covalently bonded non-metal oxides of phosphorus and sulfur dissolve and react in water to form acidic solutions. The acid molecules formed donate H^+ ions to water molecules, behaving as typical acids. For example, sulfuric(VI) acid:

$$H_2SO_4(aq) + H_2O(l) \rightarrow H_3O^+(aq) + HSO_4^-(aq)$$

The insoluble oxides of aluminium and silicon show their acidic nature by reacting and dissolving in an alkaline solution, such as sodium hydroxide, forming a soluble salt. This behaviour is typical of a covalently bonded oxide. However, aluminium oxide also reacts and dissolves in acidic solutions, forming a soluble salt – behaviour typical of a basic metal oxide with ionic

Period 3 oxide	Na_2O	MgO	Al_2O_3	SiO_2	P_4O_{10}	SO_2, SO_3
Acid/base nature	basic	basic	amphoteric	acidic	acidic	acidic

Table 10.9 The acid/base nature of the Period 3 oxides.

Period 3 oxide	Na_2O	MgO	Al_2O_3	SiO_2	P_4O_{10}	SO_2, SO_3
Relative melting point	high	very high	very high	very high	low	low
Electrical conductivity when in liquid state	good	good	good	none	none	none
Bonding	ionic	ionic	ionic (with a degree of covalent character)	covalent	covalent	covalent
Structure	giant ionic	giant ionic	giant ionic	giant covalent	simple molecular	simple molecular

Table 10.10 Some properties, bonding and structure of some Period 3 oxides.

Period 3 element	sodium (Na)	magnesium (Mg)	aluminium (Al)	silicon (Si)	phosphorus (P)	sulfur (S)	chlorine (Cl)	argon (Ar)
Electronegativity	0.9	1.2	1.5	1.8	2.1	2.5	3.0	–

Table 10.11 Electronegativity values for Period 3 oxides (no data is available for argon).

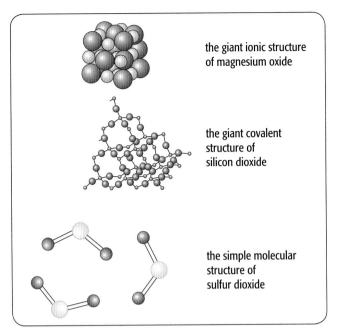

Figure 10.13 The structures of some Period 3 oxides.

bonding. This dual nature provides evidence that the bonding in aluminium oxide is not purely ionic nor is it purely covalent, hence its amphoteric nature.

Check-up

6 a The element germanium is in Group IV in Period 4. It is classed as a semi-metal or metalloid, as is silicon in the Period 3.
  i Predict the bonding and structure of the element germanium.
  ii Germanium(IV) oxide has properties similar to silicon dioxide. It is an acidic oxide. Write a balanced symbol equation, including state symbols, to

continued ···▸

show the reaction of germanium(IV) oxide with hot concentrated sodium hydroxide solution.
  iii What would you expect to happen if germanium(IV) oxide was added to $2.0 \, mol \, dm^{-3}$ hydrochloric acid?
 b Potassium oxide (K_2O) is a basic oxide. It reacts and dissolves in water, forming an alkaline solution.
  i Write a balanced symbol equation, including state symbols, to show the reaction of potassium oxide with water.
  ii Write a balanced symbol equation, including state symbols, to show the reaction of potassium oxide with dilute nitric acid.
  iii Predict the bonding and structure of potassium oxide.

10.5 Chlorides of Period 3 elements

Oxidation numbers of the Period 3 elements in chlorides

Table 10.12 shows the formulae of the common chlorides of the Period 3 elements.

The oxidation numbers rise as we cross Period 3, until we reach sulfur. This happens because Period 3 elements from sodium to phosphorus use all the electrons in their outermost shell in bonding to chlorine (ox. no. = –1). They all exist in positive oxidation states because chlorine has a higher electronegativity than any of the other Period 3 elements (see Table 10.11).

Period 3 element	sodium (Na)	magnesium (Mg)	aluminium (Al)	silicon (Si)	phosphorus (P)	sulfur (S)	chlorine (Cl)	argon (Ar)
Formula of chloride	NaCl	$MgCl_2$	Al_2Cl_6	$SiCl_4$	PCl_5	SCl_2	–	–
Oxidation number of Period 3 element	+1	+2	+3	+4	+5	+2	–	–

Table 10.12 Oxidation numbers of the Period 3 elements in their chlorides. Phosphorus also has a chloride with the formula PCl_3, in which its oxidation number is +3. Sulfur also has a chloride S_2Cl_2, in which its oxidation number is +1.

Effect of water on chlorides of Period 3 elements

As with the oxides of Period 3 elements, the chlorides also show characteristic behaviour when we add them to water. Once again, this is linked to their structure and bonding (Table 10.13).

At the start of Period 3, the ionic chlorides of sodium and magnesium do not react with water. The polar water molecules are attracted to the ions and break down the giant ionic structures. The solutions contain the metal ions and the chloride ions surrounded by water molecules. The metal ions and the chloride ions are called hydrated ions.

$$NaCl(s) \xrightarrow{\text{water}} Na^+(aq) + Cl^-(aq)$$

Aluminium chloride is sometimes represented as $AlCl_3$, which suggests that its bonding is likely to be ionic – with Al^{3+} ions and Cl^- ions in a giant lattice. In solid **hydrated** aluminium chloride crystals this is the case. However, **without water** it exists as Al_2Cl_6. This can be thought of as a dimer of $AlCl_3$ (two molecules joined together). This is a covalently bonded molecule (see Figure 10.14). Once we add water, the dimers are broken down and aluminium ions and chloride ions enter the solution. Each relatively small and highly charged Al^{3+} ion is hydrated and causes the water molecules bonded to it to lose a total of one H^+ ion, thus turning the solution acidic. We can show this in an equation as follows:

$$[Al(H_2O)_6]^{3+}(aq) \rightarrow [Al(H_2O)_5OH]^{2+}(aq) + H^+(aq)$$

The liquid chlorides, $SiCl_4$ and PCl_5, are hydrolysed in water, releasing white fumes of hydrogen chloride gas in a rapid reaction (Figure 10.15).

$$SiCl_4(l) + 2H_2O(l) \rightarrow SiO_2(s) + 4HCl(g)$$

The SiO_2 is seen as an off-white precipitate. Some of the hydrogen chloride produced dissolves in the water, leaving an acidic solution.

$$PCl_5(l) + 4H_2O(l) \rightarrow H_3PO_4(aq) + 5HCl(g)$$

Both products are soluble in water and are highly acidic.

Formula of chloride	NaCl	MgCl$_2$	Al$_2$Cl$_6$	SiCl$_4$	PCl$_5$	SCl$_2$
Bonding	ionic	ionic	covalent	covalent	covalent	covalent
Structure	giant ionic	giant ionic	simple molecular	simple molecular	simple molecular	simple molecular
Observations when added to water	white solids dissolve to form colourless solutions		chlorides react with water, giving off fumes of hydrogen chloride gas			
pH of solution formed with water	7	6.5	3	2	2	2

Table 10.13 The structure and bonding of the chlorides of Period 3 elements and the effect of water on these chlorides.

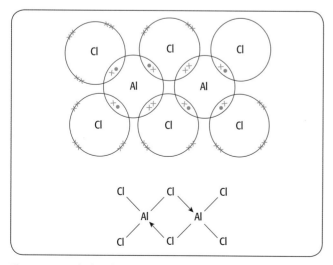

Figure 10.14 The bonding in Al$_2$Cl$_6$.

Figure 10.15 Silicon(IV) phosphorus(V) chloride is hydrolysed in water, releasing white fumes of hydrogen chloride gas.

Check-up

7 a The chloride of an unknown element, X, is a liquid at 20 °C. This chloride reacts with water, giving white fumes and leaving an acidic solution.

   i Does element X belong to Group I, Group II or Group V of the Periodic Table?

continued ⋯⟩

   ii What type of reaction takes place between X and water?

   iii Identify the white fumes given off when X reacts with water.

 b The chloride of an unknown element Y is a solid at 20 °C. This chloride does not react with water but dissolves to give a neutral solution. Does element Y belong to Group I, Group IV or Group VI of the Periodic Table?

Summary

☐ Periods in the Periodic Table are rows of elements whose outermost electrons are in the same principal quantum shell. The atoms of neighbouring members differ by one proton and one electron (and usually by one or more neutrons).

☐ Periodic variations may be observed across periods in physical properties such as ionisation energies, atomic radii, ionic radii, melting points and electrical conductivities.

☐ The main influences on ionisation energies, atomic radii and ionic radii are:
   – the size of the positive nuclear charge
   – the distance of the outermost (valence) electrons from the nucleus
   – the shielding effect on outer electrons by electrons in filled inner shells.

☐ Ionisation energies tend to increase across a period.

☐ Atomic radii decrease across a period due to increasing nuclear charge.

☐ Positive ions are much smaller than their atoms. Negative ions are slightly larger than their atoms.

☐ Across a period, the structures of the elements change from giant metallic, through giant molecular to simple molecular. Group 0 elements consist of individual atoms.

☐ Across a period, the oxides of Period 3 elements change from basic compounds with ionic bonding through to giant molecular in the centre of the period (Group 4) with silicon, going on to acidic covalently bonded simple molecules of the non-metal oxides. Aluminium oxide (in Group 3) is amphoteric, exhibiting both basic and acidic behaviour.

☐ Across a period, the chlorides of Period 3 elements change from ionic compounds that dissolve in water to covalent compounds that are hydrolysed, releasing fumes of hydrogen chloride and leaving an acidic solution.

End-of-chapter questions

1   **a** Explain what is meant by the term **periodic property**.   [2]
    b The graph shows how a periodic property varies when plotted against atomic number for
        Period 3 (sodium to argon).

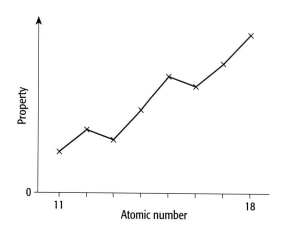

    i Identify the property.   [1]
    ii Explain the overall trend across the period.   [4]

                                                                                              Total = 7

2   The variation of melting point with atomic number for Periods 2 and 3 is shown in the graph below.

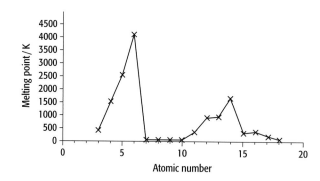

    a Explain what we mean when we say **melting point is a periodic property**.   [1]
    b Explain the following.
        i The melting point of silicon is much greater than that of phosphorus.   [4]
        ii The melting point of aluminium is greater than that of sodium.   [5]

                                                                                             Total = 10

3 a i Describe how the atomic radius varies across Periods 2 and 3.   [1]
   ii Explain this trend.   [4]
   b i Describe how the atomic radius varies down each group of the Periodic Table.   [1]
   ii Explain this trend.   [1]

   Total = 7

4 a Describe the acid–base nature of the solutions obtained when the following compounds
   are added to water. Use equations to illustrate your answers.
   i sodium chloride   [2]
   ii sulfur trioxide   [2]
   iii sodium oxide   [2]
   iv phosphorus(V) chloride.   [2]
   b i Write an equation for the reaction of magnesium with cold water.   [1]
   ii Predict and explain the pH of the resulting solution.   [2]
   c When magnesium is added to water, the reaction is very slow. In contrast, phosphorus(III)
   chloride (PCl_3) is a liquid that reacts vigorously with water. One of the products of this reaction
   is H_3PO_3, which forms in solution.
   i Write an equation, including state symbols, showing the reaction of phosphorus trichloride
   with water.   [1]
   ii Predict the pH of the solution obtained.   [1]
   iii State one observation a student watching the reaction would make.   [1]

   Total = 14

Learning outcomes

For Group II, students should be able to:

☐ describe the reactions of the elements with oxygen and water
☐ describe the behaviour of the oxides with water
☐ describe the thermal decomposition of the nitrates and carbonates
☐ interpret, and make predictions from, the trends in physical and chemical properties of the elements and their compounds
☐ explain the use of magnesium oxide as a refractory lining material and calcium carbonate as a building material
☐ describe the use of lime in agriculture.

For Group VII, students should be able to:

☐ describe the trends in volatility and colour of chlorine, bromine and iodine
☐ interpret the volatility of the elements in terms of van der Waals' forces
☐ describe the relative reactivity of the elements as oxidising agents

☐ describe and explain the reactions of the elements with hydrogen
  – describe and explain the relative thermal stabilities of the hydrides
  – interpret these relative stabilities in terms of bond energies
☐ describe and explain the reactions of halide ions with:
  – aqueous silver ions followed by aqueous ammonia
  – concentrated sulfuric acid
☐ outline a method for the manufacture of chlorine from brine by a diaphragm cell (see page **121**)
☐ describe and interpret in terms of changes of oxidation number the reaction of chlorine with cold, and with hot, aqueous sodium hydroxide
☐ explain the use of chlorine in water purification
☐ recognise the industrial importance and environmental significance of the halogens and their compounds (e.g. for bleaches, PVC and halogenated hydrocarbons as solvents, refrigerants and in aerosols) (see also page **235**).

11.1 Physical properties of Group II elements

The elements in Group II of the Periodic Table are sometimes referred to as the **alkaline earth metals**. As they are in Group II, the elements have atoms whose electronic configurations end with two electrons in their outermost principal quantum shell. These two outer electrons occupy an s sub-shell. Here are the electronic configurations of the first five elements in Group II:

Beryllium (Be) $1s^2 2s^2$
Magnesium (Mg) $1s^2 2s^2 2p^6 3s^2$
Calcium (Ca) $1s^2 2s^2 2p^6 3s^2 3p^6 4s^2$
Strontium (Sr) $1s^2 2s^2 2p^6 3s^2 3p^6 3d^{10} 4s^2 4p^6 5s^2$
Barium (Ba) $1s^2 2s^2 2p^6 3s^2 3p^6 3d^{10} 4s^2 4p^6 4d^{10} 5s^2 5p^6 6s^2$

One way of describing the size of an atom is its metallic radius. The metallic radius is half the distance between the nuclei in a giant metallic lattice (Figure **11.2**). See page **163** for other measures that describe the size of atoms.

Figure 11.1 Some of the colours in fireworks come from Group II metal compounds, e.g. strontium compounds will give red flames when heated and barium compounds produce apple-green flames.

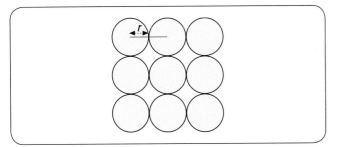

Figure 11.2 The metallic radius gives us a measure of the size of the atoms of metallic elements.

Group II element	Atomic number	Melting point / °C	Density / g cm^{-3}
beryllium (Be)	4	1280	1.85
magnesium (Mg)	12	650	1.74
calcium (Ca)	20	838	1.55
strontium (Sr)	38	768	2.6
barium (Ba)	56	714	3.5

Table 11.2 The melting points and densities of the Group II elements.

Look at the metallic radii of the Group II elements, shown in Table 11.1. The atoms of Group II elements get larger going down the group as the outer two electrons occupy a new principal quantum shell further from the nucleus.

Group II element	Metallic radius / nm
beryllium (Be)	0.122
magnesium (Mg)	0.160
calcium (Ca)	0.197
strontium (Sr)	0.215
barium (Ba)	0.217

Table 11.1 The metallic radii of the Group II elements.

There are also general trends in other physical properties, such as melting point and density, shown in Table 11.2 and Figures 11.3 and 11.4.

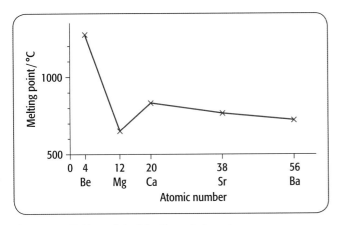

Figure 11.3 Melting points of the Group II elements.

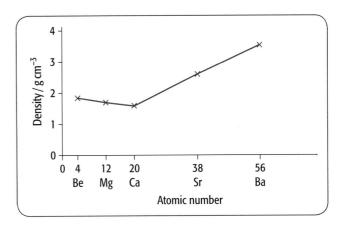

Figure 11.4 Density of the Group II elements.

11.2 Reactions of Group II elements

The Group II metals form ionic compounds. When they react, their atoms lose the two electrons from their outermost sub-shell (shown in blue on page 176) and form an ion with a complete outer shell. This creates a 2+ ion. For example, for magnesium:

$$\underset{\substack{\text{oxidation number} \quad 0}}{Mg} \rightarrow \underset{+2}{Mg^{2+}} + 2e^-$$

The metals act as reducing agents. They give away electrons and so they are oxidised when they react. The ionisation energies shown in Table 11.3 show how easily the two outer electrons are removed from the atoms.

Group II element	First ionisation energy / $kJ\,mol^{-1}$	Second ionisation energy / $kJ\,mol^{-1}$
beryllium (Be)	900	1760
magnesium (Mg)	736	1450
calcium (Ca)	590	1150
strontium (Sr)	548	1060
barium (Ba)	502	966

Table 11.3 The first and second ionisation energies of the Group II elements.

The metals in Group II get more reactive as we go down the group. As you can see from Table 11.3, it gets easier to remove the outer electrons going down Group II. So, although the positive charge on the nucleus increases down the group, the greater shielding effect and distance of the outermost electrons from the nucleus outweigh the attraction of the higher nuclear charge. This helps to explain the increase in reactivity going down the group. It gets easier for the atoms to form their 2+ ions.

> The Group II metals get more reactive going down the group.

Reaction with oxygen

The Group II metals burn in air, and more rapidly in oxygen, forming white solid oxides. For example, magnesium ribbon burns with a bright white flame once ignited in a Bunsen flame (Figure 11.5):

$$2Mg(s) + O_2(g) \rightarrow 2MgO(s)$$

Figure 11.5 Magnesium ribbon reacting with oxygen in the air.

The magnesium oxide formed is basic in character, as shown on page 169. Calcium oxide, CaO, reacts with water to form calcium hydroxide. If water is dripped onto the surface of a lump of calcium oxide it causes a vigorous reaction. It gives off so much heat that some of the water boils off as the solid lump appears to expand and crack open:

$$CaO(s) + H_2O(l) \rightarrow Ca(OH)_2(s)$$

In excess water, some of the sparingly soluble calcium hydroxide dissolves to form a weakly alkaline solution. The excess aqueous hydroxide ions in the solution result in its pH of 11:

$$Ca(OH)_2(s) \xrightarrow{\text{water}} Ca^{2+}(aq) + 2OH^-(aq)$$

In general, the reaction and dissolving of the Group II metal oxides in water is described by the following ionic equation:

$$O^{2-}(aq) + H_2O(l) \rightarrow 2OH^-(aq)$$

The metals get more reactive with oxygen going down the group. The larger atoms lose their outer two electrons more readily than the smaller atoms in the group. The reasons for this are given beneath Table 11.3.

The greater reactivity of barium metal is illustrated by the fact that it must be stored under oil to keep it out of contact with air.

Some of the Group II metals burn with characteristic flame colours. It is the 2+ ions formed in the reaction that cause the colours. We can test for calcium, strontium and barium in compounds using flame tests. A small amount of a salt is put on a nichrome wire and heated in a non-luminous Bunsen flame:
• calcium compounds give a brick red colour,
• strontium compounds give a scarlet/red colour,
• barium compounds give an apple-green colour.

Fact file

Magnesium powder is used in flares. The large surface area in a fine powder increases the rate of reaction with oxygen. In military aircraft the heat given off from decoy magnesium flares confuses the infrared detection systems in missiles so enemy fire cannot focus in and target the aircraft (Figure 11.6).

Figure 11.6 A military plane releasing its decoy flares to protect it from missile attack.

Reaction with water

We have seen on page **168** how magnesium reacts very slowly with cold water but will eventually form a weakly alkaline solution:

$$Mg(s) + 2H_2O(l) \rightarrow Mg(OH)_2(aq) + H_2(g)$$

Hot magnesium does react vigorously with water in the form of steam to make magnesium oxide and hydrogen gas (Figure **11.7**):

$$Mg(s) + H_2O(g) \rightarrow MgO(s) + H_2(g)$$

Calcium reacts more readily than magnesium with water:

$$Ca(s) + 2H_2O(l) \rightarrow Ca(OH)_2(aq) + H_2(g)$$

This reaction forms a cloudy white suspension of sparingly soluble calcium hydroxide. The calcium hydroxide that does dissolve makes the solution weakly alkaline. The hydrogen gas is given off at a steady rate. Going down the group, hydrogen is released more rapidly by the reaction of the element with water (Figure **11.8**). The resulting solutions also get more alkaline as the solubility of the hydroxides produced increases down the group.

Figure 11.8 Barium reacting vigorously with water.

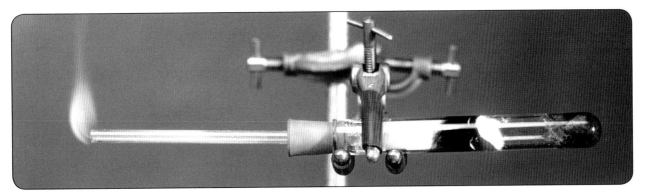

Figure 11.7 An experiment showing magnesium reacting with steam. The steam is given off from mineral wool soaked in water at the left-hand end of the test tube. The white magnesium oxide formed is visible inside the test tube and the hydrogen gas produced in the reaction has been ignited at the end of the straight tube.

11.3 Thermal decomposition of Group II carbonates and nitrates

The carbonates and nitrates of the Group II elements decompose when heated. The carbonates break down to form the metal oxide and give off carbon dioxide gas. For example:

$$MgCO_3(s) \xrightarrow{\text{heat}} MgO(s) + CO_2(g)$$

The temperature at which thermal decomposition takes place increases going down Group II.

The Group II nitrates also undergo thermal decomposition. For example:

$$2Ca(NO_3)_2(s) \xrightarrow{\text{heat}} 2CaO(s) + 4NO_2(g) + O_2(g)$$

A brown gas is observed when a Group II nitrate is heated. This is toxic nitrogen dioxide, NO_2 (nitrogen(IV) oxide).

As with the carbonates, a higher temperature is needed to thermally decompose the nitrates as Group II is descended.

11.4 Some uses of Group II compounds

We have just seen how the Group II carbonates decompose on heating. Limestone is made up mainly of calcium carbonate. There are many types of limestone, which provide useful rocks for building. They can be shaped into blocks that can be stuck to each other using mortar. Previously this mortar was made using lime and sand. Now it is more usual to use cement and sand, although the cement is made from lime – see below. Marble is another form of calcium carbonate used as a building material, for example to make expensive tiles.

However, most calcium carbonate is used to make cement. The first stage in the manufacture of cement is the roasting of limestone in a lime kiln (Figure **11.9**). At the high temperatures in the kiln, calcium carbonate

Figure 11.9 In a lime kiln calcium carbonate undergoes thermal decomposition to form calcium oxide and carbon dioxide. The calcium oxide goes on to be roasted with clay to make cement.

decomposes to form calcium oxide (also called lime or quicklime):

$$CaCO_3(s) \xrightarrow[\text{heat}]{} \underset{\text{lime}}{CaO(s)} + CO_2(g)$$

The cement made in a lime kiln is mixed with sand and small pieces of rock to make concrete, the most widely used building material in the world. Its tensile strength can be improved by letting the concrete set with iron rods running through it.

Slaked lime (calcium hydroxide) is also used by farmers to raise the pH of acidic soil. Calcium hydroxide is basic, so it will neutralise acid.

You have seen how magnesium oxide can be used to neutralise excess acid in the stomach. Magnesium oxide is also used to line kilns and furnaces, such as those used to fire ceramics. This is because of its very high melting point (see Figure 11.10). The Mg^{2+} ions and the O^{2-} ions are similar in size and both have a high charge density because of their relatively small size and high charge. This means the ions can be packed closely together and the electrostatic forces of attraction are very strong. (You can see its structure on page 171.) Its melting point of over 2800 °C is higher than the vast majority of other giant ionic compounds.

Figure 11.10 Kilns are lined with magnesium oxide because of its high melting point.

Check-up

4 a How is limestone turned into lime in industry?

b Which major construction materials are made from cement?

c Both calcium carbonate and magnesium oxide have giant ionic structures. Why is magnesium oxide used to line furnaces but calcium carbonate is not?

d When lightning strikes during a thunderstorm, the rain that falls is a dilute solution of nitric acid (HNO_3). Use a balanced chemical equation, including state symbols, to show how slaked lime (calcium hydroxide) added to soil can neutralise nitric acid.

11.5 Physical properties of Group VII elements

We will now look at the elements of Group VII, called the **halogens**. Their atoms all have seven electrons in the outer principal quantum shell. Here are the electronic configurations of the first four elements in Group VII:

Fluorine (F) $1s^2 2s^2 2p^5$
Chlorine (Cl) $1s^2 2s^2 2p^6 3s^2 3p^5$
Bromine (Br) $1s^2 2s^2 2p^6 3s^2 3p^6 3d^{10} 4s^2 4p^5$
Iodine (I) $1s^2 2s^2 2p^6 3s^2 3p^6 3d^{10} 4s^2 4p^6 4d^{10} 5s^2 5p^5$

The Group VII elements are all non-metals. At room temperature, they exist as diatomic molecules, i.e. molecules made up of two atoms, F_2, Cl_2, Br_2 and I_2 (Figure 11.11). There is a single covalent bond between

Figure 11.11 The Group VII elements are known as the halogens.

Group VII element	Atomic radius/ nm	Melting point/°C	Boiling point/°C	Colour
fluorine (F_2)	0.072	–220	–188	pale yellow
chlorine (Cl_2)	0.099	–101	–35	green/ yellow
bromine (Br_2)	0.114	–7	59	orange/ brown
iodine (I_2)	0.133	114	184	grey/black solid, purple vapour

Table 11.4 Some physical properties of the Group VII elements. The atomic radius value is taken from single covalent data (see page **163**).

the two atoms in each molecule. Table 11.4 shows some of their physical properties.

The melting points and boiling points of the halogens increase going down the group. The boiling point data gives us an idea of the volatility of the halogens, i.e. the ease with which they evaporate. All the values are relatively low because they have simple molecular structures. There are weak van der Waals' forces between their diatomic molecules. These forces increase as the number of electrons in the molecules increase with increasing atomic number. The greater the number of electrons, the greater the opportunities for instantaneous dipoles arising within molecules, and for induced dipoles to be produced on neighbouring molecules. So the larger the molecules, the stronger the van der Waals' forces between molecules, making iodine the least volatile and fluorine the most volatile of the halogens we are considering.

The colours of the halogens get darker going down the group.

Check-up

5 a What trend in volatility is seen going down Group VII?
  b What is the state of each halogen at 20 °C?
  c What is the trend in the atomic radii of the halogens? Explain this trend.
  d Astatine (At) lies below iodine at the bottom of Group VII. Predict its:
    i state at 20 °C
    ii colour
    iii atomic radius.

11.6 Reactions of Group VII elements

The halogen atoms require just one more electron to achieve a complete outer shell. Therefore they react with metallic elements, with each of their atoms gaining an electron from a metal atom to become ions with a 1– charge. For example:

$$Ca(s) + Cl_2(g) \rightarrow Ca^{2+}Cl^-_2(s)$$

When a halogen reacts with a metal, each halogen atom tends to gain one electron. Because of this, the halogens are oxidising agents. In the process of oxidising another substance they themselves are reduced. Their oxidation number is reduced from 0 in the element usually to –1 in the compound formed.

$$Cl_2 \rightarrow 2Cl^- + 2e^-$$
oxidation number   0   –1

The halogens also react with many non-metals, forming covalent bonds, e.g. in hydrogen chloride, HCl.

$$H_2(g) + Cl_2(g) \rightarrow 2HCl(g)$$

The reactions of chlorine with calcium and with hydrogen shown here can be repeated with the other halogens. In these experiments we find that the reactions of fluorine are more vigorous than those of chlorine. Bromine reacts less vigorously than chlorine and iodine is less reactive than bromine.

> The halogens get less reactive going down Group VII.

This pattern in reactivity corresponds to the trend in electronegativity going down the group, shown in Table 11.5.

Halogen	Electronegativity
fluorine (F)	4.0
chlorine (Cl)	3.0
bromine (Br)	2.8
iodine (I)	2.5

Table 11.5 Electronegativity values of the halogens.

A fluorine atom has the strongest pull on the pair of electrons in a covalent bond, while an iodine has the weakest attraction for electrons. We can explain this by looking at the atomic radii data in Table 11.4. The fluorine atom is the smallest in the group. Its outer shell is nearer to the attractive force of the nucleus and an electron entering its outer shell will also experience the least shielding from the positive nuclear charge. These factors outweigh the fact that fluorine's nuclear charge is only 9+ compared with iodine's 53+. Therefore fluorine is a much stronger oxidising agent (acceptor of electrons) than iodine.

> The halogens get less powerful as oxidising agents going down Group VII.

Fact file

Fluorine is the most electronegative of all the elements. It is the most reactive of all the non-metals in the Periodic Table. Fluorine gas is so reactive that glass, metals and water 'burn' in a stream of the gas – even when cold. Fluorine even forms compounds with the noble gases krypton, xenon and radon. The gas can be stored in containers made of a copper/nickel alloy as the alloy forms a fluoride layer that protects the metal beneath from further attack.

Displacement reactions

We can also judge the reactivity (or the oxidising power) of the halogens by looking at their displacement reactions with other halide ions in solution.

> A more reactive halogen can displace a less reactive halogen from a halide solution of the less reactive halogen.

Let's look at an example. When chlorine water, $Cl_2(aq)$, is added to a solution of sodium bromide, containing Br^- ions, the solution changes to a yellowish brown colour. The colour is caused by the presence of dissolved bromine molecules, $Br_2(aq)$, as in bromine water. The displacement reaction that takes place is:

$$Cl_2(aq) + 2NaBr(aq) \rightarrow 2NaCl(aq) + Br_2(aq)$$

We say that chlorine has displaced bromine from solution.

This is summarised in the ionic equation for this displacement reaction:

$$Cl_2(aq) + 2Br^-(aq) \rightarrow 2Cl^-(aq) + Br_2(aq)$$

The chlorine atoms are more electronegative than bromine atoms so have a stronger tendency to form negatively charged ions.

Likewise, bromine will displace iodine from an iodide solution:

$$Br_2(aq) + 2NaI(aq) \rightarrow 2NaBr(aq) + I_2(aq)$$

or

$$Br_2(aq) + 2I^-(aq) \rightarrow 2Br^-(aq) + I_2(aq)$$

The colours of the halogen molecules in solution are difficult to identify positively in these displacement reactions. However, the halogens dissolve well in cyclohexane (which forms a separate layer with water). The solutions in cyclohexane are distinctly different colours. Therefore adding some of this organic solvent after mixing the halogen/halide solutions, shaking the mixture and then allowing it to settle into layers shows clearly which halogen is present as its diatomic molecules (Figure 11.12).

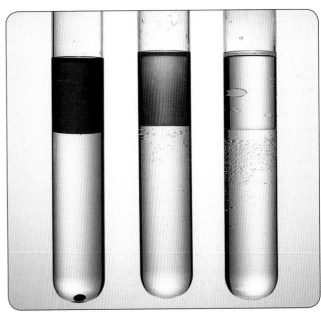

Figure 11.12 Cyclohexane forms a layer on top of water. Dissolved iodine is purple in this upper organic layer, bromine is orange and chlorine is very pale green.

Reactions with hydrogen

The halogens form hydrogen halides with hydrogen gas. One example of this is the reaction of hydrogen with chlorine to give hydrogen chloride (see page 182). The trend in reactivity is illustrated by their reactions (Table 11.6).

Equation for reaction	Description of reaction
$H_2(g) + F_2(g) \rightarrow 2HF(g)$	reacts explosively even in cool, dark conditions
$H_2(g) + Cl_2(g) \rightarrow 2HCl(g)$	reacts explosively in sunlight
$H_2(g) + Br_2(g) \rightarrow 2HBr(g)$	reacts slowly on heating
$H_2(g) + I_2(g) \rightleftharpoons 2HI(g)$	forms an equilibrium mixture on heating

Table 11.6 The reactions of hydrogen and the halogens, showing decreasing reactivity going down Group VII.

The hydrogen halides formed differ in their thermal stability. Hydrogen iodide can be decomposed by inserting a red hot wire into a sample of hydrogen iodide gas. The purple fumes seen are iodine vapour:

$$2HI(g) \rightarrow H_2(g) + I_2(g)$$

On the other hand, hydrogen fluoride and hydrogen chloride are not decomposed in temperatures up to $1500\,°C$. Hydrogen bromide is not as stable as HF and HCl, but is more resistant to decomposition than hydrogen iodide. At $430\,°C$, 10% of a sample of HBr

will decompose, whereas around 20% of HI decomposes at that temperature. We can explain this by looking at the bond energies of the hydrogen–halogen bonds (Table 11.7).

The hydrogen halides get less thermally stable going down Group VII.

most thermally stable	HF
↓	HCl
	HBr
least thermally stable	HI

Hydrogen–halogen bond	Bond energy / $kJ\,mol^{-1}$
H–F	562
H–Cl	431
H–Br	366
H–I	299

Table 11.7 Hydrogen–halogen bond energies.

As you can see in Table 11.7, the bond energies decrease down Group VII, making it easier to break the hydrogen–halogen bond. This is because the iodine atom is the largest atom, so the overlap of its outer shell with a hydrogen atom gives a much longer bond length than with the other smaller halogen atoms. The longer the bond, the weaker it is, and the less energy required to break it. Hence HI is less thermally stable than HF.

11.7 Reactions of the halide ions

Testing for halide ions

We can tell the halide ions, $Cl^-(aq)$, $Br^-(aq)$ and $I^-(aq)$, apart by using simple chemical tests. If an unknown compound is dissolved in dilute nitric acid and silver nitrate solution is added, a precipitate will be formed if the unknown solution contains halide ions. The precipitate will be silver chloride (AgCl), silver bromide (AgBr) or silver iodide (AgI). Because these precipitates are similar in colour (Figure 11.13) we can then add ammonia solution – dilute followed by concentrated – to verify the result. The results of the tests are shown in Table 11.8.

Figure 11.13 Colours of the silver halide precipitates: silver chloride (on the left), silver bromide and silver iodide (on the right).

The equation for the precipitation with silver nitrate solution, where X represents the halide ion, is:

$$AgNO_3(aq) + X^-(aq) \rightarrow AgX(s) + NO_3^-(aq)$$

The aqueous nitrate ions can be left out to produce the ionic equation; they are spectator ions that do not get involved in the reaction:

$$Ag^+(aq) + X^-(aq) \rightarrow AgX(s)$$

The added ammonia can form complex ions which are soluble:
- silver chloride forms complex ions with dilute ammonia
- silver bromide forms complex ions with concentrated ammonia.

Reactions of halide ions with concentrated sulfuric acid

Compounds that contain Cl^-, Br^- or I^- ions will react with concentrated sulfuric acid. All of these reactions produce one or more poisonous gases, so they must be performed with great care in a fume cupboard.

We can prepare hydrogen chloride gas by dropping concentrated sulfuric acid slowly onto the appropriate sodium salt (Figure 11.14):

$$NaCl(s) + H_2SO_4(l) \rightarrow NaHSO_4(s) + HCl(g)$$

The HCl produced is visible as white fumes.

However, we can't use the same reaction to prepare samples of pure hydrogen bromide or hydrogen iodide.

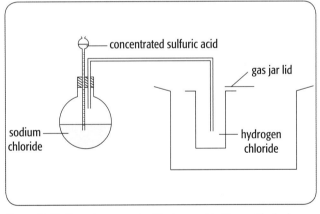

Figure 11.14 Preparing a sample of hydrogen chloride gas. The hydrogen chloride gas is more dense than air so displaces the air from the gas jar as it collects.

Halide ion	Colour of silver halide precipitate on addition of silver nitrate solution	Effect on precipitate of adding dilute ammonia solution	Effect on precipitate of adding concentrated ammonia solution
chloride, $Cl^-(aq)$	white	dissolves	dissolves
bromide, $Br^-(aq)$	cream	remains insoluble	dissolves
iodide, $I^-(aq)$	pale yellow	remains insoluble	remains insoluble

Table 11.8 Testing silver halide precipitates.

We saw on page **184** how increasingly easy it gets to decompose the hydrogen halides going down the group. When they decompose into their elements, the halide in HBr and HI is being oxidised. Concentrated sulfuric acid is a relatively strong oxidising agent. It is not strong enough to oxidise HCl but it will oxidise and decompose HBr and HI. So any HBr or HI formed in the reaction between sodium bromide, or sodium iodide, and concentrated sulfuric acid undergoes further reaction.

With sodium bromide, the sulfuric acid is reduced to sulfur dioxide gas by hydrogen bromide:

$$NaBr(s) + H_2SO_4(l) \rightarrow NaHSO_4(s) + HBr(g)$$

followed by oxidation of HBr(g):

$$2HBr(g) + H_2SO_4(l) \rightarrow Br_2(g) + SO_2(g) + 2H_2O(l)$$

A reddish brown gas is seen; this is bromine.

With sodium iodide, the sulfuric acid is reduced to sulfur dioxide, sulfur and hydrogen sulfide:

$$NaI(s) + H_2SO_4(l) \rightarrow NaHSO_4(s) + HI(g)$$

followed by oxidation of HI(g):

$$2HI(g) + H_2SO_4(l) \rightarrow I_2(g) + SO_2(g) + 2H_2O(l)$$

and:

$$6HI(g) + H_2SO_4(l) \rightarrow 3I_2(g) + S(s) + 4H_2O(l)$$

and:

$$8HI(g) + H_2SO_4(l) \rightarrow 4I_2(g) + H_2S(g) + 4H_2O(l)$$

Several observations can be made here:
• sulfur is seen as a yellow solid
• hydrogen sulfide has a strong smell of bad eggs
• iodine is produced as a violet/purple vapour.
Therefore, a mixture of gases is produced when NaBr or NaI react with concentrated sulfuric acid.

> It gets easier to oxidise the hydrogen halides going down Group VII.

Check-up

8 a You suspect that a solid compound might be potassium bromide. Describe how you would test your idea and the positive results you would get if you were correct.

 b i What would you **see** in a test tube in which concentrated sulfuric acid is added dropwise to solid potassium iodide that you would **not** see if the acid was added to potassium chloride?

 ii Give equations to describe the reactions taking place in the test tube between concentrated sulfuric acid and potassium iodide.

11.8 Disproportionation

The element chlorine (Cl_2, oxidation number = 0) undergoes a type of redox reaction called **disproportionation** when it reacts with alkali. Disproportionation can be thought of as a 'self reduction/oxidation' reaction. When chlorine reacts with dilute alkali some chlorine atoms are reduced and some are oxidised in the same reaction. The actual reaction that takes place depends on the temperature.

Chlorine in cold alkali (15 °C)

$$Cl_2(aq) + 2NaOH(aq) \rightarrow NaCl(aq) + \underset{\text{sodium chlorate(I)}}{NaClO(aq)} + H_2O(l)$$

The ionic equation for the reaction is:

$$\underset{\substack{\text{oxidation} \\ \text{number of Cl}}}{} \underset{0}{Cl_2(aq)} + 2OH^-(aq) \rightarrow \underset{-1}{Cl^-(aq)} + \underset{+1}{ClO^-(aq)} + H_2O(l)$$

The ionic equation for this redox reaction can be split into two half-equations, showing the reduction and oxidation.

• The **reduction** reaction (in which chlorine's oxidation number is reduced):

$$\underset{\text{oxidation number of Cl}}{} \underset{0}{\tfrac{1}{2}Cl_2} + e^- \rightarrow \underset{-1}{Cl^-}$$

• The **oxidation** reaction is:

$$\underset{\text{oxidation number of Cl}}{} \underset{0}{\tfrac{1}{2}Cl_2} + 2OH^- \rightarrow \underset{+1}{ClO^-} + H_2O + e^-$$

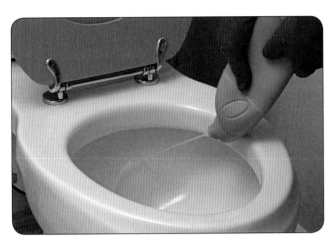

Figure 11.15 The reaction: $Cl_2(aq) + 2NaOH(aq) \rightarrow NaCl(aq) + NaClO(aq) + H_2O(l)$ is used in industry to produce bleach. The bleaching agent is the chlorate(I) ion (see opposite).

Chlorine in hot alkali (70 °C)

When we add chlorine and hot concentrated aqueous sodium hydroxide a different disproportionation reaction takes place:

$$3Cl_2(aq) + 6NaOH(aq) \rightarrow 5NaCl(aq) + NaClO_3(aq) + 3H_2O(l)$$

oxidation number of Cl: 0, −1, +5

reduction / oxidation

Check-up

9 a What type of reaction takes place between chlorine and hot aqueous sodium hydroxide?

b Write an ionic equation for the reaction of chlorine with hot aqueous sodium hydroxide.

c Write a half-equation to show the reduction reaction taking place in part **b**.

d Write a half-equation to show the oxidation reaction taking place in part **b**.

e Explain what happens in the reaction between chlorine and hot aqueous sodium hydroxide.

f Name the compound $NaClO_3$.

11.9 Uses of the halogens and their compounds

Chlorination of water

Adding a small amount of chlorine to a water supply will kill bacteria and make the water safer to drink. The chlorine undergoes disproportionation in water:

$$Cl_2(aq) + H_2O(l) \rightarrow HCl + HClO(aq)$$

oxidation number of Cl: 0, −1, +1

HClO is called chloric(I) acid. It decomposes slowly in solution, producing reactive oxygen atoms that kill bacteria in water:

$$HClO \rightarrow HCl + O$$

Bleach

Bleach is an equal mixture of sodium chloride (NaCl) and sodium chlorate(I) (NaClO), made from chlorine and cold alkali. It 'bleaches' colours and stains because oxygen atoms from the chlorate(I) ions oxidise dye and other coloured molecules. They also kill bacteria when toilets are cleaned with bleach (see Figure **11.15**).

Other uses

The halogens are found in many organic compounds such as the plastic PVC (poly(choroethene) or polyvinyl chloride) and halogenated hydrocarbons used as solvents, refrigerants and in aerosols. For more details see 'The uses of halogenoalkanes' on pages **235–6**

Summary

Group II

☐ The Group II elements magnesium to barium are typical metals with high melting points and they are good conductors of heat and electricity.

☐ Progressing down Group II from magnesium to barium, the atomic radius increases. This is due to the addition of an extra shell of electrons for each element as the group is descended.

☐ The Group II elements magnesium to barium react with water to produce hydrogen gas and the metal hydroxide, which may be sparingly soluble.

☐ The Group II elements magnesium to barium burn in air to form white solid oxides. These oxides form hydroxides with water. The hydroxides get more soluble in water going down the group so their solutions become more alkaline.

☐ Reactivity of the elements with oxygen or water increases down Group II as the first and second ionisation energies decrease.

☐ The Group II carbonates and nitrates get more resistant to thermal decomposition descending the group.

☐ Many of the compounds of Group II elements have important uses. Limestone, which contains mainly calcium carbonate, is used as a building material and is used to make cement. Slaked lime (calcium hydroxide) is used to neutralise acidic soil. Magnesium oxide is used to line furnaces because of its very high melting point.

Group VII

☐ The halogens chlorine, bromine and iodine exists as covalent diatomic molecules. They become increasingly less volatile and more deeply coloured on descending Group VII. The volatility decreases as van der Waals' forces between molecules increase.

☐ All the halogens are oxidising agents. Fluorine is the strongest oxidising agent and iodine is the weakest.

☐ Their reactivity decreases on descending the group.

☐ It gets easier to oxidise the hydrogen halides going down Group VII as the strength of the hydrogen–halogen bond decreases.

☐ Chlorine reacts with cold hydroxide ions in a disproportionation reaction. This reaction produces commercial bleach.

☐ The halogens all have important industrial uses, especially chlorine, which is used in the manufacture of many other useful products. Possibly the most important use of chlorine is in the prevention of disease by chlorination of water supplies.

End-of-chapter questions

Group II

You will need a copy of the Periodic Table (see page 497) to answer some of these questions.

1   Beryllium and radium are both in Group II.
   a Write the electron configuration of beryllium.   [2]
   b Give the equations for the reactions of beryllium and radium with oxygen.   [4]
   c Using dot-and-cross diagrams, and showing the outer electrons only, draw the electron
       configurations of beryllium and oxygen before and after bonding.   [5]
   d Draw a diagram to show the metallic bonding in both beryllium and radium.   [3]
   e Using your diagram, explain why beryllium has a higher melting point than radium.   [4]

                                                                                                Total = 18

2 a Limewater is calcium hydroxide.
   i Give the formula of calcium hydroxide. [1]
   ii Explain why calcium hydroxide is used in agriculture. [2]
  b Explain the use of magnesium oxide as a refractory lining. [6]

   Total = 9

3 For the following reactions, state which element is oxidised and which one is reduced, and give the changes in oxidation number.
  a $Sr + Cl_2 \rightarrow SrCl_2$ [3]
  b $Sr + 2H_2O \rightarrow Sr(OH)_2 + H_2$ [3]
  c $2Mg + CO_2 \rightarrow 2MgO + C$ [3]

   Total = 9

Group VII

4 a What is the molecular formula of bromine? [1]
  b Put the elements bromine, chlorine and iodine in order of boiling point, starting with the lowest. [2]
  c Explain the reasons for the trend described in part **b**. [2]

   Total = 5

5 a Which of these mixtures will result in a chemical reaction?
   i   bromine solution and sodium chloride solution [1]
   ii iodine solution and sodium bromide solution [1]
   iii chlorine solution and potassium bromide solution [1]
   iv bromine solution and sodium iodide solution [1]
  b Write a balanced chemical equation for each reaction that occurs in part **a**. [6]
  c What type of reaction occurs in part **a**? [1]
  d What trend do the reactions in part **a** show us? [1]
  e For one of the reactions that occurs in part **a**, identify the substance oxidised and the substance reduced. [2]
  f For one of the reactions that occurs in part **a**, rewrite the equation as an ionic equation. [1]
  g Chlorine is a stronger oxidising agent than bromine. Explain why this is true. [2]

   Total = 17

6 a Complete the equations below, including state symbols.
   i $AgNO_3(aq) + NaCl(aq) \rightarrow \ldots$ [2]
   ii $AgNO_3(aq) + NaBr(aq) \rightarrow \ldots$ [2]
   iii $AgNO_3(aq) + NaI(aq) \rightarrow \ldots$ [2]
  b What would you observe in each reaction in part **a**? [4]
  c What would you observe in each case if dilute ammonia solution were subsequently added? [1]
  d What would you observe in each case if concentrated ammonia solution were subsequently added? [1]

   Total = 12

7 **a** For the reaction of chlorine with water:
  i write a balanced chemical equation [2]
  ii give the oxidation numbers of chlorine before and after the reaction [3]
  iii give one use for the process. [1]
 b For the reaction of chlorine with cold dilute aqueous sodium hydroxide:
  i write a balanced chemical equation [2]
  ii give the oxidation numbers of chlorine before and after the reaction [3]
  iii give one use for the process. [1]
 c What name is given to the type of reaction in parts **a** and **b**? [1]

Total = 13

12 Nitrogen and sulfur

Learning outcomes

Candidates should be able to:

- explain the lack of reactivity of nitrogen
- describe:
  - the formation and structure of the ammonium ion
  - the displacement of ammonia from its salts
- describe the Haber process for the manufacture of ammonia from its elements, giving essential operating conditions, and interpret these conditions (qualitatively) in terms of the principles of kinetics and equilibria (see also Chapters **8** and **9**)
- understand the industrial importance of ammonia and nitrogen compounds derived from ammonia
- understand the environmental consequences of the uncontrolled use of nitrate fertilisers
- understand and explain the occurrence, and catalytic removal, of oxides of nitrogen

- explain why atmospheric oxides of nitrogen are pollutants, including their catalytic role in the oxidation of atmospheric sulfur dioxide
- describe the formation of atmospheric sulfur dioxide from the combustion of sulfur-contaminated carbonaceous fuels
- state the role of sulfur dioxide in the formation of acid rain and describe the main environmental consequences of acid rain
- state the main details of the Contact process for sulfuric acid production
- understand the industrial importance of sulfuric acid
- describe the use of sulfur dioxide in food preservation.

12.1 Nitrogen gas

Nitrogen is in Group V of the Periodic Table. It is a non-metallic element that makes up about 78% of the Earth's atmosphere. It exists as diatomic molecules, N_2. Nitrogen gas is the unreactive gas in air that dilutes the effects of the reactive gas, oxygen. To understand the lack of reactivity of nitrogen gas, we have to look at the bonding in its molecules.

The electronic configuration of a nitrogen atom is $1s^2 2s^2 2p^3$. Its atoms need to gain three electrons to achieve the noble gas configuration of neon with a complete outer shell. Nitrogen atoms do this by forming a triple covalent bond between two atoms (Figure **12.2**).

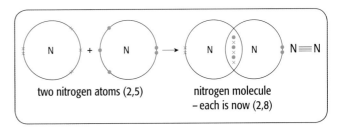

Figure 12.2 The bonding in a nitrogen molecule, N_2.

The triple covalent bond is very strong; its bond energy is almost $1000\,kJ\,mol^{-1}$. It is difficult to break and so nitrogen gas will only react under harsh conditions. For example, the nitrogen and oxygen in the air react together during thunderstorms. Lightning provides the activation energy needed for this reaction to occur (Figure **12.3**):

$$N_2(g) + O_2(g) \rightarrow \underset{\text{nitrogen(II) oxide}}{2NO(g)}$$

Figure 12.1 Nitrogen gas is used in the hold of oil tankers above the crude oil as it is pumped ashore. The unreactive gas helps to prevent the chance of an explosive mixture of crude oil vapour and air forming inside the tanker.

Figure 12.3 Nitrogen oxides are formed when lightning strikes.

The nitrogen(II) oxide formed is further oxidised by oxygen in the air to give nitrogen(IV) oxide, NO_2.

$$2NO(g) + O_2(g) \rightarrow \underset{\text{nitrogen(IV) oxide}}{2NO_2(g)}$$

Nitrogen(IV) oxide dissolves in water droplets and forms nitric acid which falls to earth in rain. This is a vital part of the natural nitrogen cycle:

$$2NO_2(g) + H_2O(l) + \tfrac{1}{2}O_2 \rightarrow \underset{\text{nitric acid}}{2HNO_3(aq)}$$

In this way, nitrogen gets into the soil in a soluble form that plants can absorb. They use the nitrate ions, NO_3^-, to make the proteins essential for growth.

Fact file

Plants also use nitrogen to make chlorophyll and nucleic acids – DNA and RNA. You can recognise a plant suffering from nitrogen deficiency by its stunted growth and its yellow leaves.

12.2 Ammonia and ammonium compounds

Ammonia is a very important compound of nitrogen. It is an alkaline gas whose formula is NH_3. In industry it is made on a large scale in the Haber process. The bonding in ammonia is shown in Figure 12.4. You learned why the presence of a lone pair of electrons on the nitrogen atom causes ammonia molecules to have a pyramidal shape on page 57.

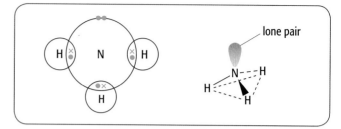

Figure 12.4 A dot-and-cross diagram showing the covalent bonding in an ammonia molecule and its pyramidal shape.

You have also learned that nitrogen's lone pair can be donated to an H^+ ion from an acid, forming a co-ordinate (or dative) covalent bond (see page 54). Ammonia is acting as a base in this reaction (because it is accepting an H^+ ion):

$$NH_3(aq) + H^+(aq) \rightarrow \underset{\text{ammonium ion}}{NH_4^+(aq)}$$

Ammonium compounds are very important fertilisers. Nitrogen is removed from the soil when crops are harvested. Ammonium compounds replace this nitrogen. Common ammonium salts include ammonium chloride, NH_4Cl, ammonium nitrate, NH_4NO_3, and ammonium sulfate, $(NH_4)_2SO_4$.

If we heat an ammonium salt with a base, the ammonium ion produces ammonia gas. We use this reaction to prepare ammonia gas in the laboratory (Figure 12.5). Ammonium chloride and calcium hydroxide, both in the solid state, are usually mixed then heated (Figure 12.5).

$$2NH_4Cl(s) + Ca(OH)_2(s)$$
$$\xrightarrow{\text{heat}} CaCl_2(s) + 2H_2O(l) + 2NH_3(g)$$

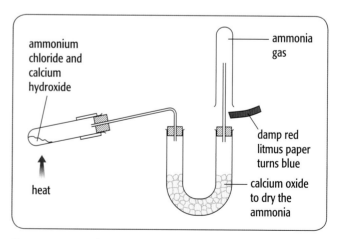

Figure 12.5 Preparing ammonia gas from an ammonium salt, NH_4Cl, and a base, $Ca(OH)_2$.

This reaction is used as the basis of the test for ammonium ions. If an unknown compound contains NH_4^+ ions it will give off ammonia when heated with a base. The ammonia given off is the only common alkaline gas. It turns red litmus blue.

Check-up

1. a Explain the lack of reactivity of nitrogen gas.
   b Write a balanced chemical equation, including state symbols, for the reaction of ammonia solution with dilute nitric acid.
   c Write a balanced chemical equation, including state symbols, for the reaction of solid ammonium sulfate with solid sodium hydroxide.

Figure 12.6 A modern ammonia plant.

The Haber process

You have met the Haber process before on page 142. It is used in industry to make ammonia (Figure 12.6). You looked at the conditions needed to improve the percentage of ammonia in the equilibrium mixture below.

$$\underset{\text{nitrogen}}{N_2(g)} + \underset{\text{hydrogen}}{3H_2(g)} \overset{Fe}{\rightleftharpoons} \underset{\text{ammonia}}{2NH_3(g)} \qquad \Delta H = -92\,kJ\,mol^{-1}$$

The nitrogen gas is obtained from air. The hydrogen is made from the reaction between natural gas (methane) and steam or is available as a by-product of the cracking of heavy fractions from crude oil (see page 221).

The effect of pressure

The production of a higher yield of ammonia is favoured by high pressure (as the position of equilibrium shifts to the right which has 2 moles of gas compared to the 4 moles of gas on the left-hand side of the equation). In industry a pressure of between 2500 kPa and 30 000 kPa (25–300 atmospheres) is used. Higher pressures would give a higher yield of ammonia, but are not used as there are safety and economic issues to consider. Higher pressures increase the risk of gases exploding out of the reaction vessel. The costs of making pipework and vessels to withstand such huge pressures is extremely high.

It also requires expensive compressors and a lot of energy to generate very high pressures. This again increases costs. So pressures around 20 000 kPa are used to increase the yield of ammonia as economically as possible. Look at Figure 12.7, which shows the effect of pressure on the yield of ammonia.

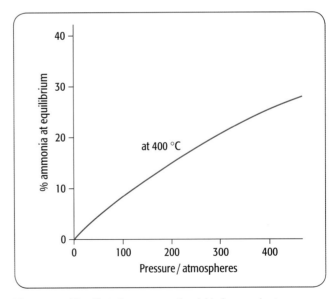

Figure 12.7 The effect of pressure on the yield of ammonia at equilibrium.

The effect of temperature

$$N_2(g) + 3H_2(g) \rightleftharpoons 2NH_3(g) \qquad \Delta H = -92\,kJ\,mol^{-1}$$

As you can see from the chemical equation for the Haber process, the production of ammonia is an exothermic reaction. The production of a higher yield of ammonia is therefore favoured by low temperatures (see page 142). You can see in Figure 12.8 how the yield of ammonia in the equilibrium mixture decreases as the temperature gets higher.

However, we know that increasing the temperature increases the rate of a reaction. Using low temperatures gives better yields of ammonia but the ammonia would be formed much too slowly. Therefore chemists choose

higher temperatures, usually between 400 °C and 450 °C. This temperature gives an acceptable yield of ammonia at an acceptable rate. At this temperature the equilibrium yield is only about 15%. In fact the reaction never reaches its position of equilibrium. As the mixture of gases leaves the reaction vessel, it is cooled down and the ammonia is condensed and collected as a liquid. The unreacted nitrogen and hydrogen are recycled to the reaction vessel.

Use of a catalyst

The catalyst used for the Haber process was found after thousands of 'trial and error' experiments. Iron worked best, and is still used with traces of other metal oxides added to enhance its effect further. The iron catalyst speeds up both the forward and reverse reactions to the same extent. Therefore it does not affect the yield of ammonia but it increases the rate at which the ammonia is formed. The iron is porous or finely divided to increase its surface area for the gases to react on.

Figure 12.9 shows a summary of the Haber process.

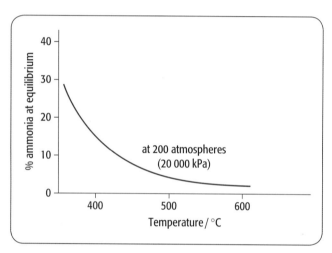

Figure 12.8 The effect of temperature on the yield of ammonia at equilibrium.

Conditions in the Haber process reaction vessel:
- temperature: 400–450 °C
- pressure: 25–300 atm, often about 200 atm (20 000 kPa)
- catalyst: iron

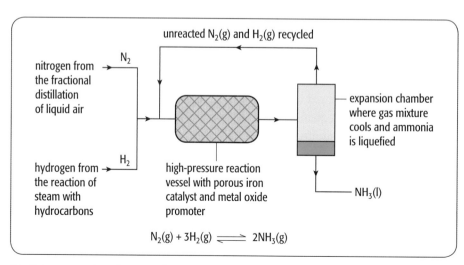

Figure 12.9 Summary of the Haber process to make ammonia.

Uses of ammonia and ammonium compounds

Farmers harvest crops to provide us with food. So each year millions of tonnes of fertilisers are spread onto fields to replace the nitrogen and other plant nutrients lost from the soil. About 85% of the millions of tonnes of ammonia produced each year are used to make fertilisers. A relatively small amount of ammonia itself is used as fertiliser, mainly in the USA. This is injected into the soil. However, the vast majority of ammonia is reacted with acids to make solid ammonium salts. The major nitrogen-based fertiliser is ammonium nitrate, NH_4NO_3. This is manufactured from ammonia and nitric acid.

$$NH_3(aq) + HNO_3(aq) \rightarrow NH_4NO_3(aq)$$

The ammonium nitrate solution is heated to evaporate off the water and melt the solid. The molten solid is sprayed into a tower with air blown into it. This solidifies the ammonium nitrate into pellets which are convenient for farmers to spread from tractors (Figure 12.10). Ammonium sulfate, $(NH_4)_2SO_4$, and ammonium phosphate, $(NH_4)_3PO_4$, are other ammonium salts used in fertilisers.

Figure 12.10 Ammonium nitrate is spread as pellets onto the soil.

The nitric acid used to make ammonium nitrate is itself made from ammonia. Fertiliser factories making ammonium nitrate often have three plants side by side, making:
- ammonia in the Haber process
- nitric acid from ammonia
- ammonium nitrate from nitric acid and ammonia.

Concentrated nitric acid has other important uses. It is used to make many types of explosive, such as trinitrotoluene (TNT). About 10% of ammonium nitrate is used to make explosives. Nitric acid is also needed in the manufacture of detergents, paints, pigments, dyes and nylon.

Check-up

2 **a** Why is the temperature chosen for the Haber process often described as a 'compromise' temperature?

 b Write a balanced equation, including state symbols, for the formation of ammonium sulfate fertiliser from ammonia solution.

 c Work out the percentage of nitrogen in ammonium nitrate fertiliser.
 (A_r values: N = 14.0, H = 1.0, O = 16.0)

Environmental problems caused by nitrogen compounds

Nitrate fertilisers

In order to work, nitrogen-based fertilisers, mainly ammonium nitrate and potassium nitrate (KNO_3) must be soluble in water. This has created an environmental problem. The nitrates can be washed, or leached, out of the soil by rain into groundwater. These can then find their way into rivers and lakes. Once in the rivers and lakes, the nitrates promote the growth of the water plants which can 'strangle' a river. But the biggest problem is the growth of algae (a simple water plant) on the surface, causing **eutrophication** (Figure 12.11).

Figure 12.11 Fertilisers leached from farmland have caused eutrophication in this river.

- A bloom of algae can spread across the surface, blocking out the light for other plant life in the water.
- When the plants and algae die, bacteria in the water feed on them, decomposing the plant material.
- The bacteria multiply rapidly with so much food available, using up the dissolved oxygen in the water.
- Fish extract dissolved oxygen from water taken in through their gills. Without oxygen they die, affecting the whole ecosystem.

This isn't the only problem with fertilisers being leached from the soil. Nitrates have also been detected in our drinking water, especially in agricultural areas. People are worried that nitrates in drinking water cause 'blue baby' syndrome (when a newborn baby's blood is starved of oxygen) as well as stomach cancer. But others argue that links between nitrates and disease have not been proven and that recommended nitrate levels are set unrealistically low.

Farmers can help limit the amount of nitrates in water by adding the most economical amounts of fertilisers at the right time of year. This will minimise the leaching of excess fertiliser from the soil.

Nitrogen oxides in the atmosphere

At the start of this chapter we saw how unreactive nitrogen gas is. However, in the extreme conditions in a thunderstorm nitrogen can react with oxygen to form nitrogen oxides – nitrogen(II) oxide, NO, and nitrogen(IV) oxide, NO_2. A similar oxidation of nitrogen takes place inside a car engine. In the engine's cylinders a mixture of air (mainly nitrogen plus oxygen) and fuel is compressed and ignited by a spark. Under these conditions (high pressure and high temperature) nitrogen forms nitrogen oxides. These are released into the atmosphere in the car's exhaust fumes.

Nitrogen oxides are pollutants. They cause acid rain and photochemical smog. Nitrogen oxides also catalyse the oxidation of sulfur dioxide, SO_2, in the atmosphere. The SO_3 that is produced by this oxidation reacts with rainwater, forming sulfuric acid. The reactions below show the catalytic activity of the nitrogen oxides:

$$SO_2(g) + NO_2(g) \rightarrow SO_3(g) + NO(g)$$

Then NO_2 is regenerated as NO reacts with oxygen in the air:

$$NO(g) + \tfrac{1}{2}O_2(g) \rightarrow NO_2(g)$$

This NO_2 molecule can then go on to oxidise another sulfur dioxide molecule, producing an NO molecule to make another NO_2 molecule. This will oxidise another sulfur dioxide molecule, and so on. Therefore NO_2 catalyses the oxidation of SO_2.

Nowadays, car exhaust systems are fitted with catalytic converters to help reduce the pollutants from motor vehicles (see page **219**). The reaction on the surface of the catalyst (e.g. platinum) reduces the nitrogen oxides to harmless nitrogen gas, which is released from the exhaust.

$$2CO(g) + 2NO(g) \rightarrow 2CO_2(g) + N_2(g)$$

Check-up

3 a Why is ammonia so important in providing enough food to feed the world?
   b Give one environmental problem and one health problem associated with nitrate fertilisers.
   c Explain how nitrogen oxides are involved in the formation of atmospheric sulfur(VI) oxide (SO_3).
   d The following reaction takes place in a car's catalytic converter once it is warmed up:

   $$2CO(g) + 2NO(g) \rightarrow 2CO_2(g) + N_2(g)$$

   Use oxidation numbers to explain which species is reduced and which is oxidised in the reaction.

12.3 Sulfur and its oxides

We have just seen how sulfur dioxide in the atmosphere can be oxidised by nitrogen(IV) oxide to form sulfur(VI) oxide (also known as sulfur trioxide). This reacts with water to form sulfuric acid, which is the main cause of acid rain.

$$SO_3(g) + H_2O(l) \rightarrow H_2SO_4(aq)$$

The sulfur dioxide is formed when we burn fossil fuels, especially coal. Crude oil, natural gas and coal have sulfur compounds present in them as impurities. When the fossil fuels (or fuels extracted from them, such as petrol or diesel) are burned, the sulfur impurities get oxidised to sulfur dioxide.

Acid rain has harmful effects on:
- plants (especially trees)
- rivers, streams and lakes (and the fish and other animals in these habitats)
- buildings, statues (Figure 12.12) and metal structures.

Figure 12.12 This limestone carving has been chemically weathered by acid rain.

The acid rain leaches (washes out) nutrients from the soil, and so prevents the healthy growth of plants. Not only that, the acid rain can attack the waxy layer on leaves. This increases water loss and makes the plant more susceptible to disease and pests. Trees that grow at high altitudes are especially vulnerable, as they are often in contact with the tiny droplets of water (sulfuric acid solution) in clouds.

Acid rain falling into streams, rivers and lakes will lower the pH of the water. Many aquatic animals are very sensitive to changes in pH. Many insect larvae cannot survive even slight increases in acidity. Other animals higher up the food chain may be more resistant, but their numbers will decrease as their food source dies off.

In our cities, the acid rain attacks buildings and statues, especially those made from carbonate rock. The most common of these is limestone, containing calcium carbonate. The main metal used in construction, iron in the form of steel, is also corroded by acid rain.

Chemists have found ways to reduce sulfur dioxide emissions from fossil fuels. They now produce 'low sulfur' versions of petrol and diesel. In power stations that burn fossil fuels, the sulfur is removed from the fuel before burning. Alternatively sulfur dioxide can be removed from the waste gases before they are released to the atmosphere.

Check-up

4 a Write a balanced equation, including state symbols, showing the formation of sulfuric acid from atmospheric sulfur(VI) oxide, SO_3.
b List three consequences of acid rain.

SO_2 in the food industry

Sulfur dioxide dissolves well in water, forming sulfuric(IV) acid (H_2SO_3, also known as sulfurous acid). Sulfuric(IV) acid is in equilibrium with hydrogensulfite ions, HSO_3^-, and sulfite ions, SO_3^{2-}:

$$H_2SO_3 \rightleftharpoons H^+ + HSO_3^- \rightleftharpoons 2H^+ + SO_3^{2-}$$

Sulfur dioxide solution is used to preserve many food products, especially acidic foods. It does so by inhibiting the growth of bacteria and fungi. Its ability to inhibit the growth of microbes is at its best at pH values less than 4.0. These products include wines, dried or semi-processed fruits and vegetables, fruit juices, pickles and syrups. It can also be found in some sausages (Figure 12.13).

As well as inhibiting the growth of yeast, bacteria and moulds, sulfur dioxide is also added to foods to stop the oxidation of fats and to prevent over-ripening of fruits after they have been picked.

Figure 12.13 Sulfur dioxide and its related sulfite compounds are used to preserve many foods.

12.4 Sulfuric acid

Sulfuric(VI) acid, H_2SO_4, is one of the most important manufactured chemicals. It has been said that the amount of sulfuric acid used by a country is one of the best indicators of how well developed it is.

The many uses of sulfuric acid are listed in the next section.

The chemical industry makes sulfuric acid in the Contact process. The raw materials needed are sulfur, air and water. Sulfur can be mined from underground. Poland and the USA export sulfur around the world. The sulfur extracted from the impurities in fossil fuels can also be used in the Contact process (Figure 12.14).

The Contact process
Stage 1
Sulfur is burned to form sulfur dioxide gas.

$$S(l) + O_2(g) \rightarrow SO_2(g)$$

Stage 2
This is the most important stage in the process. It takes place in a reaction vessel where sulfur dioxide is oxidised to sulfur trioxide (sulfur(VI) oxide). The conditions in the vessel have to be chosen carefully as this is a reversible reaction. For example, excess air is used to shift the position of equilibrium to the right, favouring the formation of SO_3:

$$2SO_2(g) + O_2(g) \rightleftharpoons 2SO_3(g) \qquad \Delta H = -197\,\text{kJ}\,\text{mol}^{-1}$$

Notice that the forward reaction is exothermic. Therefore the formation of SO_3 is favoured by low temperatures (see page 143). However, if the temperature is too low, the rate of reaction will be too slow. Therefore a

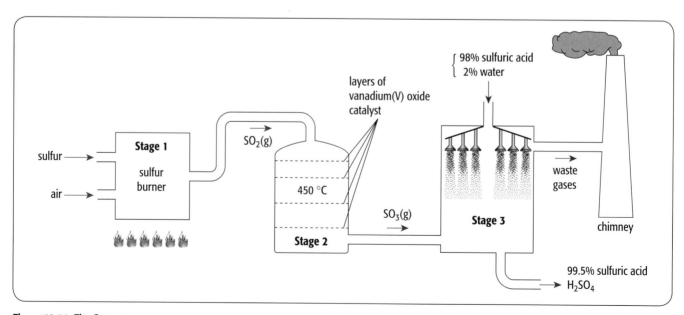

Figure 12.14 The Contact process.

compromise temperature of about 450 °C is chosen to achieve a reasonable rate. At a temperature of 450° C, the equilibrium yield of SO_3 is 97%. This is an excellent yield compared with the 15% yield of ammonia in the Haber process.

If you count the number of moles of gas molecules on either side of the equation, you will see that increasing the pressure favours the forward reaction. However, as the yield is 97% at 450 °C and atmospheric pressure, the pressure is only increased slightly. This saves the energy which would be needed to compress the gases to high pressures (and therefore saves money). A pressure just above 100 kPa is used. The main purpose of this slightly raised pressure is to push the gases through the pipes and reaction vessels.

The catalyst chosen is vanadium(V) oxide, which is arranged across the reaction vessel in layers to increase its surface area. The catalyst increases the rate of reaction by providing an alternative route of lower activation energy. The catalyst does not affect the yield of SO_3. The reaction on its surface is exothermic, so the gases heat up. They are cooled to 450 °C again before passing through the next layer of vanadium(V) oxide, as too high a temperature would decrease the yield of SO_3.

Stage 3

In the final stage, SO_3 must be converted into sulfuric acid. However, simply adding water to SO_3 results in a vigorous reaction in which the sulfuric acid forms as a fine mist which is difficult to condense. Therefore the SO_3 is added to a concentrated solution of sulfuric acid (98% acid and 2% water). The SO_3 effectively reacts with the water present forming an even more concentrated solution containing 99.5% sulfuric acid (see Figure 12.14).

$$SO_3(g) + H_2O(l) \rightarrow H_2SO_4(l)$$

In stage 2 we get 99.5% conversion of SO_2 to SO_3. Any SO_2 left at the end of the process must not be allowed to escape into the atmosphere as it is toxic and causes acid rain. Therefore the chimneys that emit the waste gases are fitted with 'scrubbers'. These scrubbers contain a base such as calcium carbonate or calcium hydroxide. The base neutralises most of the unconverted SO_2.

The uses of sulfuric acid

Like nitric acid, sulfuric acid is used to manufacture fertilisers, detergents, paints, pigments, dyes and synthetic fibres. It is also used to make various chemicals and plastics, as well as being used in car batteries, tanning leather and cleaning metal surfaces ('pickling').

Check-up

5 a Explain why a temperature of 450 °C is used in the Contact process.
   b Explain why a high pressure is not used in the Contact process.
   c What catalyst is used in the Contact process?
   d How does the use of a catalyst affect the equilibrium yield of SO_3 in the Contact process?

Summary

☐ Nitrogen, N_2, is a very unreactive gas because of the high bond energy of the $N\equiv N$ triple bond.

☐ Ammonia, NH_3, is a common compound of nitrogen. An ammonia molecule can act as a base, accepting an H^+ ion to form an ammonium ion, NH_4^+.

☐ Ammonia is manufactured in the Haber process:

$$N_2(g) + 3H_2(g) \xrightarrow{Fe} 2NH_3(g)$$

nitrogen hydrogen   ammonia

☐ Typical conditions for the Haber process are temperature of 450 °C, pressure of 200 atm and an iron catalyst.

☐ Most ammonia is used to make ammonium salts, which are used as fertilisers.

☐ Excess fertiliser can be leached out of soils into rivers and lakes where it causes eutrophication, killing aquatic life.

☐ Sulfur can be mined as the element and is used as a raw material for manufacturing sulfuric acid in the Contact process.

☐ Sulfur burns to form sulfur dioxide, SO_2 (a toxic gas which is the main cause of acid rain; it is used in solution as a food preservative).

☐ The Contact process operates at about 450 °C:

$$2SO_2(g) + O_2(g) \xrightarrow{V_2O_5} 2SO_3(g)$$

☐ The SO_3 is used to make concentrated sulfuric acid, H_2SO_4.

End-of-chapter questions

1 Ammonia is made in the Haber process.
  a What is the formula of ammonia? [1]
  b Write an equation for the formation of ammonia in the Haber process. [1]
  c What temperature, pressure and catalyst are used in the Haber process? [3]
  d Explain the temperature used in the Haber process. [2]
  e Explain the pressure used in the Haber process. [2]
  f Give **three** uses of ammonia. [3]
  g Give the formulae of the following ammonium salts:
    i ammonium chloride [1]
    ii ammonium nitrate [1]
    iii ammonium sulfate [1]
  h Ammonium chloride reacts with calcium hydroxide when heated to produce ammonia gas.
    i Is this reaction carried out using solids or solutions? [1]
    ii Write the balanced equation for this reaction. [1]

Total = 17

2 The reaction

$$2SO_2(g) + O_2(g) \rightleftharpoons 2SO_3(g)$$

reaches dynamic equilibrium. The forward reaction is exothermic. The reaction is catalysed by vanadium(V) oxide, V_2O_5. You are given a vessel containing all three gases at equilibrium.

a What will happen to the position of equilibrium if:

    i you add more oxygen to the vessel? [1]

    ii you remove some sulfur trioxide from the vessel? [1]

    iii the pressure in the vessel is lowcrcd? [1]

    iv more V_2O_5 is added? [1]

    v the temperature in the vessel is increased? [1]

b i State the temperature used in the Contact process. [1]

    ii Explain why the pressure chosen for the Contact process is just higher than atmospheric pressure. [1]

    iii Give **three** uses of sulfuric acid. [3]

    iv Why is it important that as little sulfur dioxide as possible is released into the atmosphere in the Contact process? [1]

    v Explain, including a balanced equation, how sulfur dioxide enters the atmosphere from a coal-fired power station. [3]

Total = 14

Learning outcomes

Candidates should be able to:

☐ interpret, and use the nomenclature, general formulae and displayed formulae of the following classes of compound:
- alkanes, alkenes
- halogenoalkanes
- alcohols (including primary, secondary and tertiary)
- aldehydes and ketones
- carboxylic acids, esters
- amines (primary only), nitriles

(Students will be expected to recognise the shape of the benzene ring when it is present in organic compounds. However, knowledge of benzene or its compounds is not required for AS.)

☐ interpret, and use the following terminology associated with organic reactions:
- functional group
- homolytic and heterolytic fission
- free radical, initiation, propagation, termination
- nucleophile, electrophile
- addition, substitution, elimination, hydrolysis
- oxidation and reduction

(In equations for organic redox reactions, the symbols [O] and [H] are acceptable.)

☐ – describe the shapes of the ethane and ethene molecules
- predict the shapes of other related molecules

☐ explain the shapes of the ethane and ethene molecules in terms of σ and π carbon–carbon bonds

☐ describe structural isomerism

☐ describe *cis–trans* isomerism in alkenes, and explain its origin in terms of restricted rotation due to the presence of π bonds

☐ explain what is meant by a **chiral centre** and that such a centre gives rise to optical isomerism

☐ deduce the possible isomers for an organic molecule of known molecular formula

☐ identify chiral centres and/or *cis–trans* isomerism in a molecule of given structural formula.

13.1 Introduction

The substances that form the basis of all living things are organic compounds (Figure **13.1**). All organic molecules contain carbon atoms. They tend to form the 'backbone' of organic molecules – from the proteins in muscles and enzymes to the DNA that determines our characteristics.

Not all carbon compounds are classified as organic compounds. The oxides of carbon and compounds containing carbonate and hydrogencarbonate ions are classed as inorganic compounds.

Figure **13.2** shows two types of three-dimensional (3D) diagrams representing a selection of organic molecules. The compounds shown are called **hydrocarbons**. Hydrocarbons are compounds of carbon and hydrogen only.

Figure 13.1 Living things are made of atoms covalently bonded to form molecules of organic compounds. All these molecules are based on carbon compounds. The complexity of life requires a great variety of different compounds. A great variety of organic compounds is possible because every carbon atom can bond with other carbon atoms to form chains and rings. These chains and rings are often found bonded to atoms of other elements, such as hydrogen, oxygen and nitrogen. This explains the millions of organic compounds that exist.

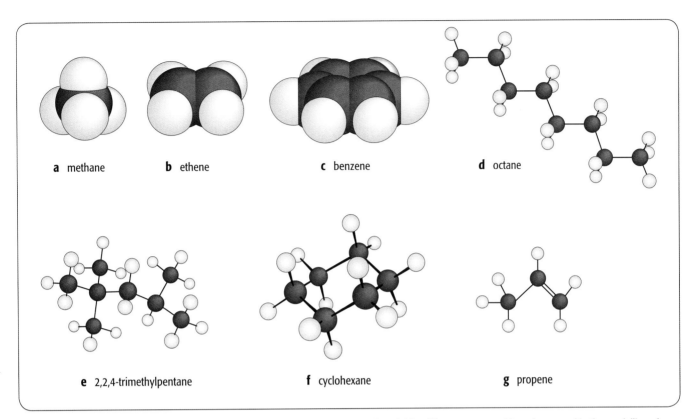

Figure 13.2 Examples of the variety of hydrocarbons. Chemists use various types of model for different purposes. The colours used in the modelling of molecules are shown in Table **13.1**. **a–c** These hydrocarbons are shown as space-filling models. Such models show the region of space occupied by the atoms and the surrounding electrons. **d–g** These hydrocarbons are shown as ball-and-stick models, which enable bonds between atoms to be clearly seen.

Colour	Atom/electron cloud
white	hydrogen
dark grey	carbon
red	oxygen
blue	nitrogen
yellow-green	fluorine
green	chlorine
orange-brown	bromine
brown	phosphorus
violet	iodine
pale yellow	sulfur
yellow ochre	boron
pink	lone pair electron clouds
green	π-bond electron clouds

Table 13.1 Colours used in molecular modelling in this text.

Fact file

There are over 4 million organic compounds known today, with more than 100 000 new compounds being produced each year by research chemists.

13.2 Representing organic molecules

We can represent organic molecules by a variety of different types of formula.

The **empirical formula** gives us the least detail. It tells us the simplest ratio of the different types of atoms present in the molecule. For example, an organic molecule called propene has the empirical formula CH_2. This tells us that it has twice as many hydrogen atoms as carbon atoms. We can calculate this from experimental data on the mass of each element, and hence the number of moles of each element, in a sample of the compound.

The **molecular formula** shows us the actual numbers of each type of atom in a molecule. To find this we need to know the relative molecular mass of the compound. The relative molecular mass of propene is 42. We know that its empirical formula is CH_2; this group of atoms has a relative mass of 14, as the relative atomic mass of C = 12 and H = 1. By dividing the relative molecular mass by the relative mass of the empirical formula ($42/14 = 3$), we see that there must be ($3 \times CH_2$) atoms in a propene molecule. So its molecular formula is C_3H_6.

Check-up

1 A compound contains the elements carbon, hydrogen and oxygen. Its empirical formula is CH_2O and its relative molecular mass is 60. What is the molecular formula of the compound?

Chemists can give more detail about a molecule by giving its **structural formula**. This tells us about the atoms bonded to each carbon atom in the molecule. The structural formula of propene is $CH_3CH=CH_2$. This tells us how many hydrogen atoms are bonded to each carbon atom, and that two of the carbon atoms in the molecule are joined by a double bond. Carbon-carbon double bonds are shown in a structural formula. However, **all** the bonds within a molecule are shown in its **displayed formula**. We can think of this representation as a 2D or flattened version of the 'ball and stick' models shown in Figure **13.2**. The displayed formula of propene is shown in Figure **13.3**.

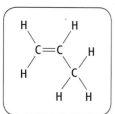

Figure 13.3 The displayed formula of propene, showing all the bonds in the molecule.

Check-up

2 Draw the displayed formula of:
   a ethene (molecular formula C_2H_4)
   b propane (molecular formula C_3H_8).

A simplified version of the displayed formula is called the **skeletal formula**. It has all the symbols for carbon and hydrogen atoms removed, as well as the carbon to hydrogen bonds. The carbon to carbon bonds are left in place. Figure **13.4** shows the skeletal formula of propene.

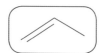

Figure 13.4 The skeletal formula of propene.

All other atoms that are not carbon or hydrogen, and their bonds, are included in the skeletal formula of an organic molecule. The displayed and skeletal formulae of an alcohol called butan-2-ol are shown in Figure **13.5**. Notice that the H atom in an OH group is included in a skeletal formula.

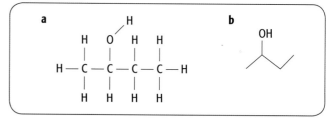

Figure 13.5 a The displayed formula of butan-2-ol; **b** the skeletal formula of butan-2-ol.

The 'zig-zag' in the carbon chain shown in a skeletal formula can be seen in the 3D representations of hydrocarbons in Figure **13.2**. You will see more detailed 3D displayed formulae later in this chapter when we look at optical isomers (see page **210**). Figure **13.6** shows the 3D displayed formula of butan-2-ol.

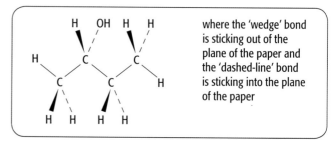

Figure 13.6 The 3D displayed formula of butan-2-ol.

Fact file

With complex molecules, chemists sometimes find it useful to combine structural and skeletal formulae when representing a molecule. The molecule of cholesterol shown in Figure 13.7 is an example.

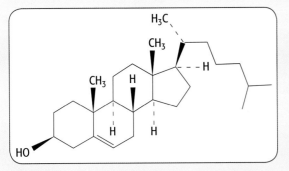

Figure 13.7 A useful way of combining structural and skeletal formulae.

Check-up

3 **a** Draw the skeletal formula of pentane, a straight-chain hydrocarbon whose molecular formula is C_5H_{12}.

   b Draw the structural formulae of the molecules shown in Figure 13.2, parts **d**, **e** and **f**.

13.3 Functional groups

There are many classes of organic compounds, some of which are shown in Table 13.2. Within a class of compounds all the compounds consist of molecules with a particular atom, or grouping of atoms, called a **functional group**. Different classes of compounds have different functional groups. The functional group

Structure of functional group	General formula	Name of an example	Structural formula of the example
alkenes, $\ce{C=C}$	C_nH_{2n}	ethene	$CH_2{=}CH_2$
arenes, ⬡	C_6H_5-	benzene	⬡
halogenoalkanes, $-X$, where $X = F, Cl, Br, I$	$C_nH_{2n+1}X$	chloromethane	CH_3Cl
alcohols, $-OH$	$C_nH_{2n+1}OH$	methanol	CH_3OH
aldehydes, $-C\!\!\begin{smallmatrix}O\\H\end{smallmatrix}$	$C_nH_{2n+1}CHO$	ethanal	CH_3CHO
ketones, $\ce{C-C(=O)-C}$	$C_nH_{2n+1}COC_mH_{2m+1}$	propanone	CH_3COCH_3
carboxylic acids, $-C\!\!\begin{smallmatrix}O\\OH\end{smallmatrix}$	$C_nH_{2n+1}COOH$	ethanoic acid	CH_3COOH
esters, $-C\!\!\begin{smallmatrix}O\\O-C\end{smallmatrix}$	$C_nH_{2n+1}COOC_mH_{2m+1}$	ethyl ethanoate	$CH_3COOC_2H_5$
amines, $-NH_2$	$C_nH_{2n+1}NH_2$	methylamine	CH_3NH_2
nitriles, $-C{\equiv}N$	$C_nH_{2n+1}CN$	ethanenitrile	CH_3CN

Table 13.2 Some common functional groups.

determines the characteristic chemical properties of the compounds which contain that specific functional group. The functional group in an alkene is the C=C double bond. The functional group in a carboxylic acid is the —COOH group.

The **general formula** of the class of compounds is given in Table 13.2. By substituting a number for n in the general formula you get the molecular formula of a particular compound containing that functional group. Note that this formula assumes there is just one functional group present in the molecule.

13.4 Naming organic compounds

Chemists have a system of naming organic compounds that can be applied consistently. This means that they can communicate with each other clearly when referring to organic compounds.

The class of hydrocarbons called alkanes provide the basis of the naming system. The stem of each name indicates how many carbon atoms are in the longest chain in one molecule of the compound. Table 13.3 shows the names of the first ten alkanes and the stems used in naming other molecules.

The position of side-chains or functional groups is indicated by numbering the carbon atoms in the longest chain. The numbering starts at the end that produces the lowest possible numbers in the name (Figure 13.8).

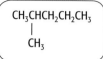

Figure 13.8 This is called 2-methylpentane, **not** 4-methylpentane.

Notice that the hydrocarbon side-chain is named by adding –yl to the normal alkane stem, in this case a methyl group. This type of group is called an alkyl group. If there is more than one of the same alkyl side-chain or functional group we indicate how many by inserting di (for two), tri (for three) or tetra (for four) in front of its name. Figure 13.9 shows an example.

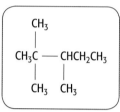

Figure 13.9 This is 2,2,3-trimethylpentane.

Notice that the numbers are separated from each other by commas whereas numbers and words are separated by hyphens.

If there is more than one type of alkyl side-chain, they are listed in the name in alphabetical order (Figure 13.10). The alkyl groups appear in its name in alphabetical order.

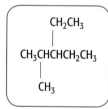

Figure 13.10 This is 3-ethyl-2-methylpentane.

Number of carbon atoms	Molecular formula of straight-chain alkane	Name of alkane	Stem used in naming
1	CH_4	methane	meth-
2	C_2H_6	ethane	eth-
3	C_3H_8	propane	prop-
4	C_4H_{10}	butane	but-
5	C_5H_{12}	pentane	pent-
6	C_6H_{14}	hexane	hex-
7	C_7H_{16}	heptane	hept-
8	C_8H_{18}	octane	oct-
9	C_9H_{20}	nonane	non-
10	$C_{10}H_{22}$	decane	dec-

Table 13.3 The stems used in naming simple organic compounds that contain a hydrocarbon chain.

Check-up

4 a Draw the displayed formula of:
   i   2-methylbutane
   ii 3,5-diethylheptane
   iii 2,4,6-trimethyloctane.
  b What is the name of the following hydrocarbon?

$$CH_3CH_2CCH_2CH_2CH_2CH_3$$

with CH_3 above and CH_2CH_3 below the third carbon.

In Table **13.2** we saw the names of compounds with common functional groups. We also use the numbering system where necessary to indicate the position of the functional group in a molecule. For some functional groups no number is needed because the group can only be positioned at the end of a chain. Examples of this include carboxylic acids, such as butanoic acid, and aldehydes, such as pentanal.

As well as alkyl groups, you also have to recognise aryl groups. Aryl compounds contain at least one benzene ring. A benzene molecule has six carbon atoms arranged in a hexagon, with each carbon atom bonded to one hydrogen atom. Figure **13.11** shows the displayed and skeletal formulae of benzene.

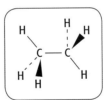

displayed formula   skeletal formula

Figure 13.11 Ways of representing benzene.

If only one alkyl group is bonded to a benzene ring, we do not have to include a number in the name as all six carbon atoms in the ring are equivalent. However, with two or more alkyl groups we need to indicate their positions, as shown in Figure **13.12**.

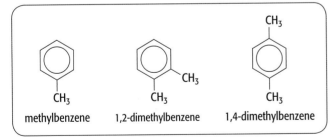

methylbenzene   1,2-dimethylbenzene   1,4-dimethylbenzene

Figure 13.12 Naming aryl compounds.

Check-up

5 Draw the structural formula of:
a propylbenzene
b 1-ethyl-4-methylbenzene
c 1,3,5-triethylbenzene.

13.5 Bonding in organic molecules

The ability of a carbon atom to bond to other carbon atoms, and the shapes of the molecules formed, can be explained by looking closely at the bonding involved.

Sigma (σ) bonds

Each carbon atom has six electrons, with an electronic configuration of $1s^2 2s^2 2p^2$. This means that carbon has four electrons in its outermost shell. By forming **single covalent bonds** with four other atoms, a carbon atom can gain the electronic configuration of the noble gas, neon (see page **53**). These single covalent bonds are known as **sigma (σ) bonds**.

The pair of electrons in a σ bond is found in a region of space (described as a lobe) between the nuclei of the two atoms sharing the electrons. The attraction between the negatively charged electrons and the positively charged nuclei bonds the atoms to each other (see page **58**).

In many organic compounds each carbon atom forms four σ bonds. The four bonding pairs of electrons around each carbon atom repel each other. They position themselves in a tetrahedral arrangement to get as far apart from each other as possible. The tetrahedral bond angle is 109.5° (see page **57**). Figure **13.13** shows the shape of an ethane molecule.

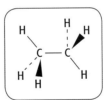

Figure 13.13 The bond angles are all close to 109.5° in an ethane molecule.

Pi (π) bonds

Carbon can also form double bonds between its atoms in organic molecules, as well as forming single bonds. A C=C double bond, as found in alkenes such as ethene, is made up of a σ bond and a **pi (π) bond**. The carbon atoms involved in the double bond will each form three σ bonds. This leaves each carbon atom with one spare outer electron in a 2p orbital. When these two p orbitals overlap they form a π bond. Figure **13.14** shows how the π bond is formed in ethene.

The two lobes that make up the π bond lie above and below the plane of the atoms in an ethene molecule.

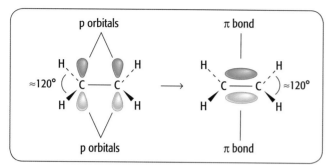

Figure 13.14 The overlap of p orbitals results in a π bond. Ethene is described as a **planar** molecule. All the carbon and hydrogen atoms in the ethene molecule lie in the same plane.

This maximises overlap of the p orbitals. The carbon atoms involved in the double bond are each surrounded by three pairs of electrons in the σ bonds. These are all in the plane of the molecule and repel each other to give bond angles of about 120°.

You can read about the special case of π bonding in a benzene molecule on page 374.

You can read about the special case of π bonding in a benzene molecule on page 374.

Check-up

6 Draw a 3D formula for:
   a propane
   b propene.

13.6 Structural isomerism

We have seen how a compound's molecular formula tells us the number and type of each atom in one molecule of the compound. However, for a given molecular formula there may be different ways of arranging these atoms. This means different molecules can be formed, with different structures, resulting in different compounds. Such compounds with the same molecular formula but different structural formulae are called **structural isomers**.

Structural isomers have the same molecular formula but different structural formulae.

There are three types of structural isomerism:
1 position isomerism
2 functional group isomerism
3 chain isomerism.

Position isomerism

In position isomerism, it is the position of the functional group that varies in each isomer. An example is provided by the compound with the molecular formula $C_3H_6Br_2$. Its four possible isomers are shown in Figure 13.15.

Br Br H
| | |
H — C — C — C — H
| | |
H H H

Br H Br
| | |
H — C — C — C — H
| | |
H H H

Br H H
| | |
H — C — C — C — H
| | |
Br H H

H Br H
| | |
H — C — C — C — H
| | |
H Br H

Figure 13.15 Position isomerism.

You need to take care when drawing the structural or displayed formula of different isomers not to repeat the same structure. Remember that there is free rotation about C—C single bonds. The three molecules shown in Figure 13.16 are all 1,2-dibromopropane; they are **not** three different isomers of $C_3H_6Br_2$.

H H H
| | |
Br — C — C — C — H   is the same as
| | |
H Br H

Br H H
| | |
H — C — C — C — H   is the same as
| | |
H Br H

Br   H
| |
H — C ——— C — Br
| |
H   H — C — H
          |
          H

Figure 13.16 These are different ways of representing the same molecule because of free rotation about C—C single bonds.

Check-up

7 **a** Name the four isomers in Figure 13.15.
b Draw displayed formulae and name the structural isomers of C_3H_7Cl.

Functional group isomerism

In functional group isomerism there are different functional groups present. For example, given the molecular formula C_3H_8O we can draw both an alcohol and an ether (Figure 13.17).

Figure 13.17 Functional group isomerism.

These two isomers have different functional groups and so have very different chemical properties.

Check-up

8 **a** Draw the displayed formulae and name the functional group isomers of C_3H_6O that are:
i an aldehyde
ii a ketone.
b Draw the displayed formula and name an isomer of C_3H_8O which could be used as an example of positional isomerism of one of the isomers in Figure 13.17.

Chain isomerism

Chain isomers differ in the structure of their carbon 'skeleton'. For example, butane and methylpropane are chain isomers, both with the molecular formula of C_4H_{10} (Figure 13.18).

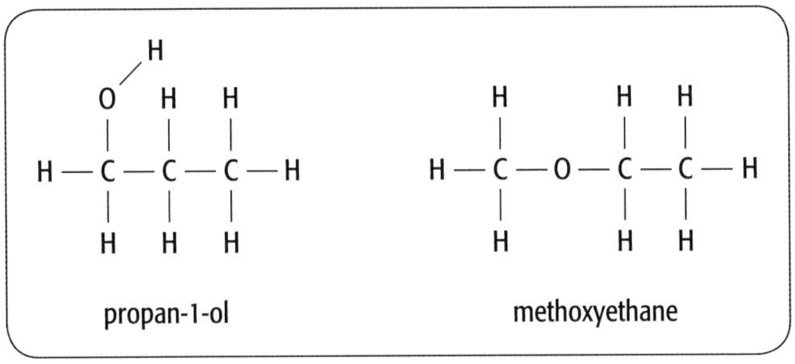

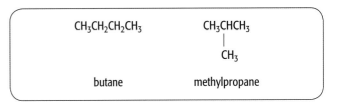

Figure 13.18 Chain isomerism.

Check-up

9 Draw the displayed formulae and give the names of the isomers of C_5H_{12}.

13.7 Stereoisomerism

In **stereoisomerism** we have compounds whose molecules have the same atoms bonded to each other but with different arrangements of the atoms in space.

There are two types of stereoisomerism:

1 *cis–trans* isomerism
2 optical isomerism.

Cis–trans isomerism

Unlike a C–C single bond, there is no free rotation about a C=C double bond. This results in the possibility of a different type of isomerism in unsaturated organic compounds. Figure 13.19 gives an example.

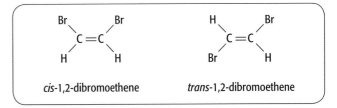

Figure 13.19 *Cis–trans* isomerism.

In *cis*-1,2-dibromoethene both the Br atoms remain fixed on the same side of the C=C double bond. On the other hand, in *trans*-1,2-dibromoethene the Br atoms are positioned across the C=C double bond. These two stereoisomers have different arrangements of the atoms in space so they are different compounds with different physical properties and different chemical properties. Whenever we have unsaturated compounds with the structures shown in Figure 13.20 we can have this *cis–trans* type of isomerism.

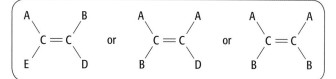

Figure 13.20 These three arrangements can result in *cis–trans* isomerism because there is restricted rotation about the C=C double bond.

Check-up

10 Draw the displayed formulae and name the *cis–trans* isomers of but-2-ene.

Optical isomerism

If a molecule contains a carbon atom that is bonded to four different atoms or groups of atoms, then it can form two optical isomers. The two different molecules are mirror images of each other and cannot be superimposed (Figure 13.21). The carbon atom with the four different groups attached is called the **chiral centre** of the molecule.

$$
\begin{array}{ccc}
& CH_3 & \\
& | & \\
& C & \\
HO & \diagup \quad \diagdown & H \\
& CO_2H &
\end{array}
\qquad
\begin{array}{ccc}
& CH_3 & \\
& | & \\
& C & \\
H & \diagup \quad \diagdown & OH \\
& CO_2H &
\end{array}
$$

mirror plane

Figure 13.21 These two molecules are optical isomers, sometimes referred to as enantiomers. Trying to superimpose the two isomers is like trying to superimpose your left hand on your right hand – it can't be done.

Fact file

The human body is very specific about which optical isomers it uses. Our body can only use one particular optical isomer of amino acids to make proteins. Fortunately for us, this is the optical isomer generally found in meat and vegetables.

Optical isomers differ in their effect on polarised light. Normal light is unpolarised. It can be thought of as fluctuating electric and magnetic fields, vibrating at right angles to each other in every possible direction. Passing this unpolarised light through a polariser results in polarised light, which vibrates in only one plane. A pair of optical isomers will rotate the plane of polarised light by equal amounts but in opposite directions. One will rotate polarised light clockwise and the other anticlockwise.

Check-up

11 The molecule CHBrClF exhibits optical isomerism. Draw the 3D displayed formulae of both optical isomers.

13.8 Organic reactions – mechanisms

Chemists find it useful to explain organic reactions by summarising the overall reaction in a series of steps called a reaction mechanism. Like all chemical reactions, organic reactions involve the breaking and making of chemical bonds. There are two ways in which covalent bonds can break:

• homolytic fission
• heterolytic fission.

Homolytic fission

In this type of bond breaking, both the atoms at each end of the bond leave with one electron from the pair that formed the covalent bond. This is shown in Figure 13.22, using the simple example of a hydrogen chloride molecule.

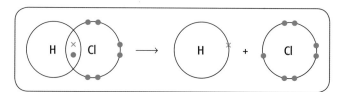

Figure 13.22 Homolytic fission of a covalent bond.

The species produced when a bond breaks homolytically are called **free radicals**. We can show the formation of free radicals by using an equation:

$$HCl \rightarrow H\bullet + Cl\bullet$$

H• and Cl• are free radicals. All free radicals have an unpaired electron (represented by the dot) and they are very reactive.

You can read more about a free-radical reaction on pages **219–20**.

- This type of reaction involves the formation of the free radicals in an **initiation step**. This requires an input of energy to break a covalent bond, resulting in two free radicals.
- The radicals formed can then attack reactant molecules, generating more free radicals. These reactions are called **propagation steps**. They can be thought of as a chain reaction, which only stops when free radicals react with each other.
- Two free radicals reacting together will form a molecule, with no free radicals generated. Therefore this is called a **termination step**.

Fact file

The filler used to repair small holes in car body work is hardened by adding benzoyl peroxide. This compound readily breaks down to form free radicals, which then promote the reaction that hardens the filler.

Check-up

12 Write an equation to show the homolytic fission of the Cl–Cl bond in a chlorine molecule, Cl_2.

Heterolytic fission

The second type of bond breaking involves the 'uneven' breaking of a covalent bond. In heterolytic fission the more electronegative atom takes both the electrons in the covalent bond. Again we can use hydrogen chloride to illustrate this (Figure **13.23**).

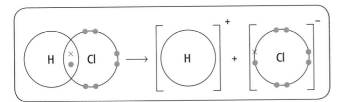

Figure 13.23 Heterolytic fission of a covalent bond.

We can show this type of bond breaking in an equation. A small curly arrow shows the movement of a pair of electrons:

$$H \overset{\frown}{-} Cl \longrightarrow H^+ + Cl^-$$

The heterolytic fission of a bond can involve a C–X bond, where X is an atom more electronegative than carbon. For example:

$$H_3C \overset{\frown}{-} Br \longrightarrow CH_3^+ + Br^-$$

In this case, as the bond breaks, the Br atom takes both the shared electrons, forming a bromide anion (a negatively charged ion). This leaves the methyl group one electron short, resulting in the formation of a positively charged ion. This type of alkyl ion is called a **carbocation**. These electron-deficient carbocations often appear in reaction mechanisms. They are an example of a species called an **electrophile**.

> An electrophile is an **acceptor** of a pair of electrons.

When an electrophile accepts a pair of electrons this results in the formation of a new covalent bond (see page **223**).

You will also meet **nucleophiles** when studying organic reactions. These are electron-rich species, i.e. they carry a negative, or partial negative, charge.

> A nucleophile is a **donator** of a pair of electrons.

When a nucleophile donates a pair of electrons this leads to the formation of a new covalent bond with the electron-deficient atom under attack (see pages **233–4**).

Check-up

13 a Write an equation to show the heterolytic fission of the C–Cl bond in chloromethane. Include a curly arrow in your answer.

b Which one of the following species is likely to act as a nucleophile: H_2; H^+; OH^-?

continued ⋯⟶

c Explain your answer to part **b**.
d Which one of the following species is likely to act as an electrophile: H_2; H^+; OH^-?
e Explain your answer to part **d**.

13.9 Types of organic reactions

Addition reactions involve the formation of a single product from two reactant molecules. An example is the addition reaction between an alkene and bromine (see page **223**):

$$C_2H_4 + Br_2 \rightarrow C_2H_4Br_2$$

Elimination reactions result in the removal of a small molecule from a larger one. An example is the dehydration of an alcohol by concentrated sulfuric acid (see page **243**):

$$C_2H_5OH \xrightarrow{\text{conc. } H_2SO_4} C_2H_4 + H_2O$$

Substitution reactions involve the replacement of one atom, or a group of atoms, by another. For example, the free radical substitution of alkanes by chlorine in sunlight (see page **220**):

$$CH_4 + Cl_2 \xrightarrow{\text{UV light}} CH_3Cl + HCl$$

Here an H atom in CH_4 has been replaced by a Cl atom.
Hydrolysis is the breakdown of a molecule by water. This type of reaction is often speeded up by acid or alkali. For example, the hydrolysis of a halogenoalkane by water to give an alcohol (see page **232**):

$$C_2H_5Br + H_2O \rightarrow C_2H_5OH + HBr$$

Hydrolysis with alkali is faster, and gives slightly different products:

$$C_2H_5Br + NaOH \rightarrow C_2H_5OH + NaBr$$

Oxidation is defined as the loss of electrons from a species. However, in organic reactions it is often simpler to think of oxidation reactions in terms of the number of oxygen and/or hydrogen atoms before and after a reaction.

> Oxidation is the addition of oxygen atoms to a molecule and/or the removal of hydrogen atoms from a molecule.

An example is the partial oxidation of ethanol to ethanal using acidified potassium dichromate(VI) solution (see page **243**):

$$C_2H_5OH + [O] \rightarrow CH_3CHO + H_2O$$

- before the reaction ethanol contains one O atom and six H atoms
- after the reaction ethanal contains one O atom and four H atoms.

In effect, the ethanol loses two H atoms, so we can say it has been oxidised.

Notice the use of [O] to simplify the chemical equation used to describe oxidation reactions. This is commonly used, but the equation must still be balanced – just like a normal equation. For example, in the complete oxidation of ethanol to ethanoic acid, using the reagents above but under harsher conditions (see page **243**):

$$C_2H_5OH + 2[O] \rightarrow CH_3COOH + H_2O$$

[O] represents an oxygen atom from the oxidising agent. The 2 in front of the [O] is needed to balance the equation for oxygen atoms.
Reduction is the chemical opposite of oxidation.

> In organic reactions reduction is the removal of oxygen atoms from a molecule and/or the addition of hydrogen atoms to a molecule.

For example, the reduction of a ketone, using sodium tetrahydridoborate, $NaBH_4$ (see page **248**):

$$CH_3COCH_3 + 2[H] \rightarrow CH_3CHOHCH_3$$

Notice the use of [H] to simplify the chemical equation used to describe reduction reactions. [H] represents a hydrogen atom from the reducing agent. The 2 in front of the [H] is necessary to balance the equation for hydrogen atoms.

Check-up

14 Classify these reactions, choosing from the types of reaction described above:
a $C_3H_7I + H_2O \rightarrow C_3H_7OH + HI$
b $CH_3CHO + 2[H] \rightarrow CH_3CH_2OH$
c $C_2H_5Br \rightarrow C_2H_4 + HBr$
d $C_2H_4 + H_2O \rightarrow C_2H_5OH$
e $C_2H_6 + Cl_2 \xrightarrow{\text{UV}} C_2H_5Cl + HCl$

Summary

☐ We can represent an organic molecule, with increasing detail, by using its:
- empirical formula
- molecular formula
- structural formula
- displayed formula
- 3D displayed formula.

☐ The presence of functional groups give organic compounds their characteristic reactions.

☐ Important functional groups include alcohols, halogenoalkanes, aldehydes, ketones, carboxylic acids, amines and nitriles.

☐ The shapes of organic molecules can be explained by the σ and π bonds between carbon atoms.

☐ There are two types of isomer – structural isomers and stereoisomers.

☐ Structural isomers have the same molecular formula but different structural formulae. We can group these into position, functional group or chain isomers.

☐ Stereoisomers have the same molecular formula but different arrangement of their atoms in space.
- *Cis–trans* isomers arise because of the restricted rotation around a C=C double bond.
- Optical isomers contain a chiral centre (a carbon atom bonded to four different atoms or groups of atoms), resulting in mirror images of the molecule that cannot be superimposed.

End-of-chapter questions

1 A carbon compound **P** has the percentage composition 85.7% carbon and 14.3% hydrogen.
Its relative molecular mass was found to be 56.
  a i Calculate its empirical formula. [4]
  ii Calculate its molecular formula. [1]
  b Write down the **names** and **displayed formulae** of all the non-cyclic isomers of compound
  P which have the following characteristics:
  i straight chain [6]
  ii branched chain. [2]

  Total = 13

2 A chemist was investigating the best way to produce 1,2-dichloroethane. He devised two
methods, **I** and **II**, of doing this.
  I He reacted ethane with chlorine in the presence of UV light by the following reaction:

$$C_2H_6(g) + 2Cl_2(g) \rightarrow C_2H_4Cl_2(l) + 2HCl(g)$$

  After doing this he found that 600 g of ethane gave 148.5 g of $C_2H_4Cl_2$.
  a i How many moles of ethane are there in 600 g? [1]
  ii How many moles of 1,2-dichloroethane would have been formed if the yield had been 100%? [1]
  iii How many moles of 1,2-dichloroethane are there in 148.5 g? [1]
  iv Calculate the percentage yield of 1,2-dichloroethane. [1]

II He reacted ethene with chlorine in the dark by the following reaction:

$$C_2H_4(g) + Cl_2(g) \rightarrow C_2H_4Cl_2(l)$$

In this reaction 140 g of ethene gave 396 g of $C_2H_4Cl_2$.

b Calculate the percentage yield for this reaction. Show your working. [3]

c There are isomers of the compound $C_2H_4Cl_2$. Draw the displayed formulae of the isomers and name them. [4]

d Choose from redox, substitution, elimination, addition and hydrolysis to give the type of reaction for:

   i reaction **I** [1]

   ii reaction **II**. [1]

Total = 13

14 Hydrocarbons

Learning outcomes

Candidates should be able to:

- be aware of the general unreactivity of alkanes, including their unreactivity towards polar reagents
- describe the chemistry of alkanes as exemplified by the following reactions of ethane:
  - combustion
  - substitution by chlorine and by bromine
- describe the mechanism of free-radical substitution at methyl groups with particular reference to the initiation, propagation and termination reactions
- describe the chemistry of alkenes as exemplified, where relevant, by the following reactions of ethene:
  - addition of hydrogen, steam, hydrogen halides and halogens
  - oxidation by cold, dilute, acidified manganate(VII) ions to form the diol
  - oxidation by hot, concentrated, acidified manganate(VII) ions leading to the rupture of the carbon-to-carbon double bond in order to determine the position of alkene linkages in larger molecules
  - polymerisation

- describe the mechanism of electrophilic addition in alkenes, using the reaction of bromine with ethene as an example
- explain the use of crude oil as a source of both aliphatic and aromatic hydrocarbons
- suggest how 'cracking' can be used to obtain more useful alkanes and alkenes of lower M_r from larger hydrocarbon molecules
- describe and explain how the combustion reactions of alkanes lead to their use as fuels in industry, in the home and in transport
- recognise the environmental consequences of:
  - carbon monoxide, oxides of nitrogen and unburnt hydrocarbons arising from the internal combustion engine, and of their catalytic removal
  - gases that contribute to the enhanced greenhouse effect
- describe the characteristics of addition polymerisation as exemplified by poly(ethene) and PVC
- recognise the difficulty of the disposal of poly(alkene)s, i.e. non-biodegradability and harmful combustion products.

14.1 Introduction – the alkanes

The majority of compounds found in the mixture of hydrocarbons we call crude oil are **alkanes**. We have met the first ten members of this homologous series in Table 13.3 (page 206). The general formula for the alkanes is C_nH_{2n+2}. For example, the molecular formula of pentane, in which $n = 5$, is C_5H_{12}. Figure 14.2 shows some different ways of representing pentane molecules.

Notice that all the carbon–carbon bonds are single covalent bonds. This means that alkanes have the maximum number of hydrogen atoms in their molecules and are known as **saturated hydrocarbons**.

Figure 14.1 Crude oil is our main source of hydrocarbons. Hydrocarbons are compounds containing carbon and hydrogen only. They provide us with fuels such as petrol, diesel and kerosene. Hydrocarbons are also the starting compounds we use to make many new compounds, such as most of the plastics we meet in everyday life.

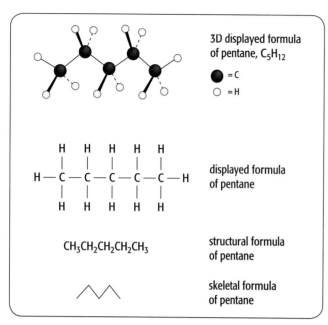

Figure 14.2 The 3D displayed formula shows the tetrahedral arrangement of atoms around each carbon atom (approximate bond angles of 109.5°).

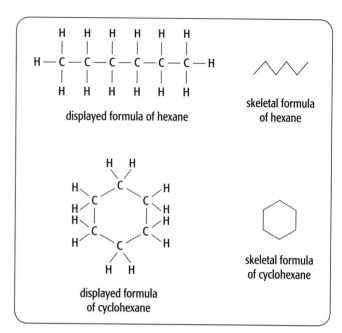

Figure 14.3 Hexane, C_6H_{14}, and cyclohexane, C_6H_{12}.

Check-up

1 Eicosane is a straight-chain alkane whose molecules contain 20 carbon atoms.
   a What is the molecular formula of eicosane?
   b Draw the skeletal formula of eicosane.

14.2 Sources of the alkanes

Crude oil is found trapped in layers of rock beneath the surface of the Earth. The actual composition of crude oil varies in different oilfields around the world. Crude oil is a complex mixture of hydrocarbons – alkanes, cycloalkanes and aromatic compounds.

• Cycloalkanes are saturated hydrocarbons in which there is a 'ring' consisting of three or more carbon atoms. Imagine the two carbon atoms at each end of a straight-chain alkane bonding to each other. These two carbon atoms could then only bond to two hydrogen atoms each, not three as in the straight-chain alkane. Cyclohexane, C_6H_{12}, is an example (Figure 14.3).

Notice that cyclohexane does **not** follow the general alkane formula, C_nH_{2n+2}.

• Aromatic hydrocarbons, which are also called arenes, are based on benzene rings (see Chapter 24).

The crude oil is brought to the surface at oil wells and transported to an oil refinery. At the refinery the crude oil is processed into useful fuels. The first step is fractional distillation of the oil. This separates the wide range of different hydrocarbons into fractions. The hydrocarbons in each fraction will have similar boiling points. This is carried out in tall fractionating columns (Figure 14.4).

The lower the molar mass of the hydrocarbons, the more volatile they are. They have lower boiling points and are collected nearer the top of the fractionating columns. These compounds are in high demand, especially the gasoline fraction (providing petrol) and the naphtha fraction (providing starting compounds for making many other chemicals in industry).

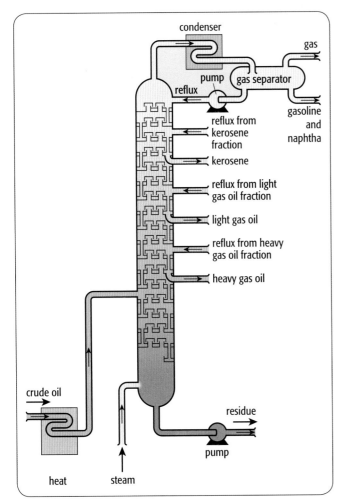

Figure 14.4 The fractional distillation of crude oil takes place in a fractionating column. The top of the column is at a lower temperature than the bottom of the column. The crude oil enters as vapour and liquid. The liquids are drawn off at the bottom of the column whilst more volatile hydrocarbons rise up the column. They condense at different levels as the temperature gradually falls and are collected as liquids. The most volatile hydrocarbons, which are short-chain alkanes (methane to butane), leave the top of the column as gases.

Check-up

2 a Draw the displayed formula and the skeletal formula of cyclopentane.
  b What is the general formula of cycloalkanes?
  c Give **two** differences between a molecule of cyclopentane and a molecule of pentane.
  d Which alkane would be collected at a higher temperature from a fractionating column in an oil refinery, ethane or decane?

14.3 Reactions of alkanes

The alkanes are generally unreactive compounds. This can be explained by the very small difference in electronegativity between carbon and hydrogen. The alkane molecules are non-polar, so they are not attacked by nucleophiles or electrophiles. They have no partial positive charges on any of their carbon atoms to attract nucleophiles, neither do they have areas of high electron density to attract electrophiles (see page **211**).

However, the alkanes do react with oxygen in combustion reactions and also undergo substitution by halogens in sunlight. These reactions are covered in the next sections.

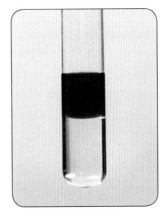

Figure 14.5 Non-polar alkanes do not react with polar compounds such as water. The hexane (dyed with iodine) and water shown here are immiscible – they do not mix and they do not react.

Check-up

3 a What would happen if octane was added to a solution of sodium hydroxide?
  b Explain your answer to part **a**.

Combustion of alkanes

Alkanes are often used as fuels (Figure **14.6**). We burn them for many reasons:
• to generate electricity in power stations
• to heat our homes and cook our food
• to provide energy needed in industrial processes
• to provide power for ships, aeroplanes, trains, lorries, buses, cars and motorbikes.

Figure 14.6 Alkanes are useful fuels.

If an alkane is burnt in plenty of oxygen, it will undergo complete combustion. The carbon will be oxidised fully to form carbon dioxide and the hydrogen will be oxidised to form water:

$$\text{alkane} + \text{oxygen} \xrightarrow{\text{complete combustion}} \text{carbon dioxide} + \text{water}$$

For example, octane can be found in petrol. Some of it will undergo complete combustion in a car engine:

$$\text{octane} + \text{oxygen} \rightarrow \text{carbon dioxide} + \text{water}$$

$$2C_8H_{18} + 25O_2 \rightarrow 16CO_2 + 18H_2O$$

The equation can also be written as:

$$C_8H_{18} + 12\tfrac{1}{2}O_2 \rightarrow 8CO_2 + 9H_2O$$

Pollution from burning hydrocarbon fuels

When the petrol or diesel is mixed with air inside a car engine, there is a limited supply of oxygen. In these conditions, not all the carbon in the hydrocarbon fuel is fully oxidised to carbon dioxide. Some of the carbon is only partially oxidised to form carbon monoxide gas. This is called incomplete combustion. For example:

$$\text{octane} + \text{oxygen} \xrightarrow{\text{incomplete combustion}} \text{carbon monoxide} + \text{water}$$

$$2C_8H_{18} + 17O_2 \longrightarrow 16CO + 18H_2O$$

or

$$C_8H_{18} + 8\tfrac{1}{2}O_2 \longrightarrow 8CO + 9H_2O$$

Carbon monoxide is a toxic gas that bonds with the haemoglobin in your blood. The haemoglobin molecules can then no longer bond to oxygen and so cannot transport oxygen around your body. Victims of carbon monoxide poisoning will feel dizzy, then lose consciousness. If not removed from the toxic gas, the victim will die. Carbon monoxide is odourless, so this adds to the danger. This is why faulty gas heaters in which incomplete combustion occurs can kill unsuspecting people in rooms with poor ventilation.

Check-up

4 Give the balanced symbol equations for:
a the complete combustion of heptane, C_7H_{16}, giving carbon dioxide and water
b the incomplete combustion of nonane, C_9H_{20}, giving carbon monoxide and water
c the incomplete combustion of methane, CH_4.

As well as carbon monoxide, road traffic also releases acidic nitrogen oxides. These contribute to the problem of acid rain. Acid rain can kill trees and aquatic animals in lakes (Figure 14.7). Acid raid also corrodes metals, such as iron.

Figure 14.7 These trees have been damaged by acid rain.

In normal combustion, nitrogen gas in the air does not get oxidised. However, in the very high temperatures in car engines oxidation of nitrogen does take place. A variety of nitrogen oxides can be formed and released in the car's exhaust fumes (Figure 14.8).

Figure 14.8 The vast numbers of cars on the roads pollute our atmosphere.

As well as toxic carbon monoxide and acidic nitrogen oxides, cars also release unburnt hydrocarbons into the air. Some of these are carcinogens (cause cancers).

Cars can now be fitted with a catalytic converter in their exhaust system (Figure 14.9). Once warmed up, a catalytic converter can cause the following reactions to take place:
- the oxidation of carbon monoxide to form carbon dioxide
- the reduction of nitrogen oxides to form harmless nitrogen gas
- the oxidation of unburnt hydrocarbons to form carbon dioxide and water.

Unfortunately, catalytic converters can do nothing to reduce the amount of carbon dioxide (a greenhouse gas) given off in the exhaust gases of cars.

Figure 14.9 Catalytic converters reduce the pollutants from car exhausts. Precious metals, such as platinum, are coated on a honeycomb structure to provide a large surface area for the reactions to occur on.

The following equation describes the reaction between carbon monoxide and nitrogen monoxide. It takes place on the surface of the catalytic converter:

$$2CO + 2NO \rightarrow 2CO_2 + N_2$$

Notice that more carbon dioxide is released in place of carbon monoxide. Carbon dioxide is not a toxic gas but it is still considered a pollutant because of its contribution to enhanced global warming.

Carbon dioxide occurs naturally in the air. The gas absorbs infrared radiation given off by the Earth as it cools down at night. This helps to keep the Earth at the right temperature to support life. Without it all the water on our planet would be constantly frozen. The problem of **enhanced global warming** has arisen because of the huge increase in the amount of CO_2 produced by human activity in the last 200 years. This extra CO_2 traps more heat and is causing the average temperature of the Earth to rise. This increase in temperature could cause rising sea levels, resulting in the flooding of low-lying areas of land. The climate will also change around the world, with more extreme weather predicted.

Check-up

5 a Name two pollutants from a car engine that are oxidised in a catalytic converter.
   b Name a pollutant that is reduced in a catalytic converter.
   c Which pollutant from a car engine is not diminished by the use of a catalytic converter? What environmental problem does this pollutant contribute to?

Substitution reactions of alkanes

The alkanes will undergo substitution reactions with halogens in sunlight. For example:

$$\underset{\text{methane}}{CH_4} + Cl_2 \xrightarrow{\text{sunlight}} \underset{\text{chloromethane}}{CH_3Cl} + HCl$$

In this reaction a hydrogen atom in the methane molecule has been replaced by a chlorine atom. However, the reaction does not take place in darkness (Figure 14.10). So what role does the sunlight play in the mechanism of the substitution reaction?

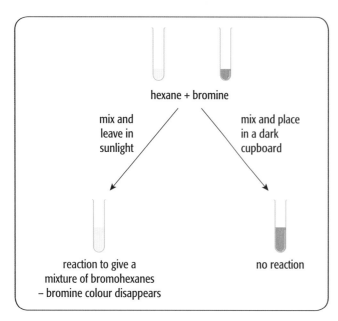

Figure 14.10 A substitution reaction takes place between alkanes and bromine in sunlight but not in darkness.

Initiation step

The first step in the mechanism is the breaking of the Cl—Cl bond by ultraviolet light from the Sun. This is an example of homolytic fission of a covalent bond (see page 210). This is called the initiation step in the mechanism:

$$Cl_2 \xrightarrow{\text{UV light}} 2Cl\bullet$$

As the Cl—Cl bond breaks, each chlorine atom takes one electron from the pair of electrons in the Cl—Cl bond. Two Cl• atoms are formed. These Cl• atoms, each with an unpaired electron, are called free radicals.

Propagation steps

Free radicals are very reactive. They will attack the normally unreactive alkanes. A chlorine free radical will attack the methane molecule:

$$CH_4 + Cl\bullet \rightarrow CH_3\bullet + HCl$$

In this propagation step, a C—H bond in CH_4 breaks homolytically. A methyl free radical, $CH_3\bullet$, is produced. This can then attack a chlorine molecule, forming chloromethane and regenerating a chlorine free radical:

$$CH_3\bullet + Cl_2 \rightarrow CH_3Cl + Cl\bullet$$

Then the first propagation step can be repeated as the chlorine free radical can attack another methane molecule. This forms the methyl free radical which regenerates another chlorine free radical, and so on …

The word 'propagation' usually refers to growing new plants. In this mechanism the substitution reaction progresses (grows) in a kind of chain reaction.

This reaction is not really suitable for preparing specific halogenoalkanes because we get a mixture of substitution products. In the reaction between methane and chlorine, the products can include dichloromethane, trichloromethane and tetrachloromethane as well as chloromethane. These other products result from propagation steps in which a chlorine free radical attacks a halogenoalkane already formed. For example:

$$CH_3Cl + Cl\bullet \rightarrow CH_2Cl\bullet + HCl$$

This can then be followed by:

$$CH_2Cl\bullet + Cl_2 \rightarrow CH_2Cl_2 + Cl\bullet$$
$$\text{dichloromethane}$$

The more chlorine gas in the reaction mixture to start with, the greater the proportions of CH_2Cl_2, $CHCl_3$ and CCl_4 formed as products.

Termination steps

Whenever two free radicals meet they will react with each other. A single molecule is the only product. As no free radicals are made that can carry on the reaction sequence, the chain reaction stops. Examples of termination steps include:

$$CH_3\bullet + Cl\bullet \rightarrow CH_3Cl$$
$$CH_3\bullet + CH_3\bullet \rightarrow C_2H_6$$

- In the initiation step we start with a molecule and get two free radicals formed.
- In the propagation steps we start with a molecule plus a free radical and get a different molecule and a different free radical formed.
- In termination steps we start with two free radicals and end up with a molecule and no free radicals.

Overall, the reaction between alkanes and halogens, involving initiation, propagation and termination steps, is called **free-radical substitution**.

Check-up

6 Bromine can react with ethane to form bromoethane.
  a What conditions are needed for the reaction between ethane and bromine to take place?
  b What do we call this type of reaction?

continued ⟶

c Write an equation to show the reaction of ethane and bromine to form bromoethane.

d Why is this reaction not a good way to prepare a pure sample of bromoethane?

e i Name the three steps in the mechanism of this reaction.

ii Write an equation to show the first step in the mechanism.

iii What type of bond breaking does this first step involve?

14.4 The alkenes

We have looked at the nature of the double bond found in the hydrocarbons called **alkenes** on pages 207–8. Alkenes with one double bond per molecule have the general formula C_nH_{2n}. One example is ethene, C_2H_4. Alkanes are described as saturated hydrocarbons; however, alkenes are described as **unsaturated hydrocarbons**.

Oil refineries provide useful alkenes for the chemical industry. On page **216** we saw how crude oil is separated into fractions at a refinery. Oil companies find that the demand for the each fraction differs. The lighter fractions, such as the gasoline fraction, are in high demand. So, some of the excess heavier fractions are converted to lighter hydrocarbons. The large, less useful hydrocarbon molecules are broken down into smaller, more useful molecules. The process is called **cracking**.

The larger hydrocarbon molecules are fed into a steel chamber which contains no oxygen, so combustion does not take place. The larger hydrocarbon molecules are heated to a high temperature and are passed over a catalyst (Figure **14.11**).

When large alkane molecules are cracked they form smaller alkane molecules and alkene molecules. One possible example of a cracking reaction is:

$$CH_3(CH_2)_8CH_3 \rightarrow CH_3(CH_2)_4CH_3 + CH_2{=}CHCH_2CH_3$$

$$C_{10}H_{22} \quad \rightarrow \quad C_6H_{14} \quad + \quad C_4H_8$$

The low-molecular mass alkanes formed (C_6H_{14} in this example) make very useful fuels and are in high demand. However, the alkenes produced (C_4H_8 in this example) are also very useful. They are more reactive than the alkanes because of their double bonds. This makes them useful for the chemical industry as the starting compounds (feedstock) for making many new products. These include most plastics (see page **224**).

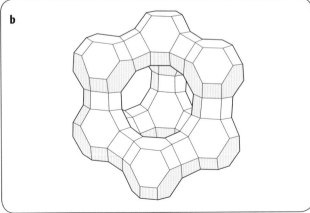

Figure 14.11 a A catalytic cracker occupies the bulk of the central part of this view of an oil refinery. **b** A computer graphic showing a zeolite catalyst used to crack hydrocarbons.

14.5 Addition reactions of the alkenes

Most reactions of the alkenes are examples of **addition** reactions. In these reactions one of the two bonds in the carbon–carbon double bond is broken and a new single bond is formed from each of the two carbon atoms. The general addition reactions are shown in Figure 14.12.

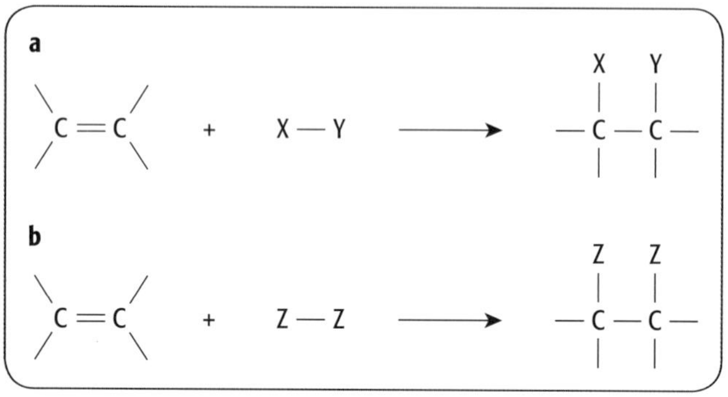

Figure 14.12 General equations for addition reactions of the alkenes: **a** with a hydrogen halide such as hydrogen bromide, and **b** with a halogen such as chlorine. In an addition reaction a single product is always formed.

Addition of hydrogen, $H_2(g)$

When hydrogen and an alkene are passed over a finely divided nickel catalyst at 140 °C, the addition reaction produces an alkane:

$$CH_2{=}CH_2 + H_2 \xrightarrow{\text{Ni catalyst}} CH_3CH_3$$
ethene   ethane

The addition reaction with hydrogen is used in the manufacture of margarine (Figure 14.13).

Figure 14.13 Unsaturated oils, such as sunflower oil, contain hydrocarbon chains with several C=C double bonds. These become partially saturated by reacting them with hydrogen. This raises the melting points of the oils, changing them from liquids to soft solids that can be spread easily.

Addition of steam, $H_2O(g)$

The addition of steam to alkenes is used in industry to make alcohols. Steam and the gaseous alkene, in the presence of concentrated phosphoric acid catalyst, are reacted at a temperature of 330 °C and a pressure of 6 MPa. When the alkene is ethene, the product is ethanol (Figure 14.14). However, the ethanol found in alcoholic drinks is always produced by the fermentation of glucose.

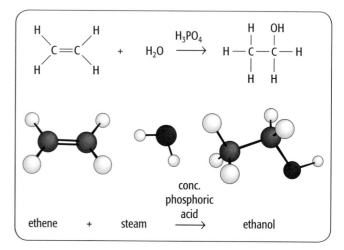

Figure 14.14 The reaction between ethene and steam.

Addition of hydrogen halides, HX(aq)

When an alkene is bubbled through a concentrated solution of a hydrogen halide (HF, HCl, HBr, HI) at room temperature, the product is a halogenoalkane. For example:

$$CH_2{=}CH_2 + HBr \rightarrow CH_3CH_2Br$$
ethene   bromoethane

With longer alkenes there are always two possible products that could be formed. For example, with propene:

$$CH_3CH{=}CH_2 + HBr \rightarrow CH_3CH_2CH_2Br$$
propene   1-bromopropane

and

$$CH_3CH{=}CH_2 + HBr \rightarrow CH_3CHBrCH_3$$
propene   2-bromopropane

Where two products are formed, the major product is the one which has the halogen atom bonded to the carbon with the least number of hydrogen atoms (in this case $CH_3CHBrCH_3$).

Addition of halogens, X_2(aq)

If we bubble an alkene through a solution of chlorine or bromine at room temperature, we again get an addition reaction. The colour of the halogen molecules in solution, which is pale green for chlorine water and orange/yellow for bromine water, is removed. In fact, bromine water is used to test for the presence of the C=C bond in compounds. The compound to be tested is shaken with bromine water. If it is unsaturated the bromine water will be decolorised (Figure 14.15).

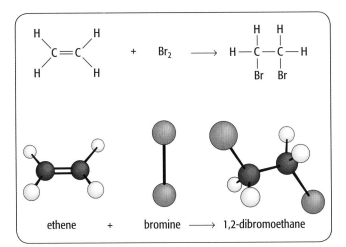

ethene + bromine → 1,2-dibromoethane

Figure 14.15 The reaction between ethene and bromine.

Check-up

8 a What conditions are used in the reaction between an alkene and hydrogen?
  b Name the product formed when propene reacts with chlorine.
  c Ethanol can be used as a solvent. How is this ethanol made in industry?
  d What will be formed when ethene gas is bubbled through a concentrated solution of hydrochloric acid?

The mechanism of electrophilic addition to alkenes

On pages 207–8 we saw how the double bond in ethene is formed from a σ bond and a π bond. There are four electrons in total in these two bonds. So although ethene is a non-polar molecule, there is an area of high electron density around the C=C bond. This makes the alkenes open to attack by electrophiles (see page 211).

Remember that an electrophile is an **acceptor** of a pair of electrons. In a molecule such as HBr the H atom carries a partial positive charge and the Br atom carries a partial negative charge. HBr is a polar molecule because of the difference in electronegativity between the H atom and the Br atom. In the mechanism of addition, the H atom acts as the electrophile, accepting a pair of electrons from the C=C bond in the alkene.

But how can a non-polar molecule such as Br_2 act as an electrophile? As the bromine molecule and ethene molecules approach each other, the area of high electron density around the C=C bond repels the pair of electrons in the Br—Br bond away from the nearer Br atom. This makes the nearer Br atom slightly positive and the further Br atom slightly negative. Figure 14.16 shows the mechanism of electrophilic addition.

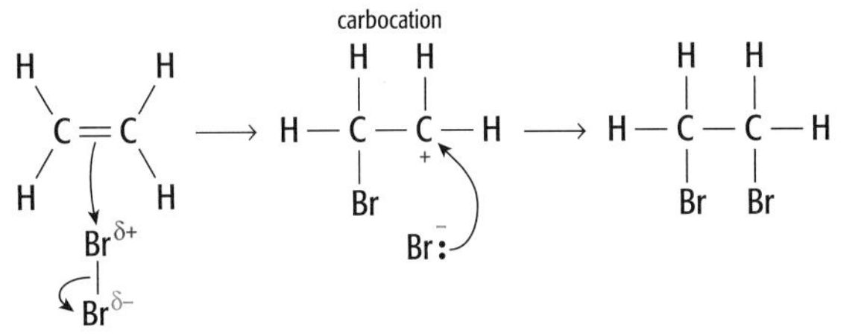

Figure 14.16 The mechanism of electrophilic addition of bromine to ethene.

As the new bond between the C and Br atom forms, the Br—Br bond breaks heterolytically. The Br^- ion formed then attacks the highly reactive carbocation intermediate. So one Br atom bonds to each carbon atom, producing 1,2-dibromoethane.

Check-up

9 a Define the term **electrophile**.
  b Explain how a chlorine molecule can act as an electrophile in its reaction with an alkene.
  c Draw the mechanism for the reaction between ethene and chlorine.

Addition polymerisation

Ethene molecules can react with each other under the right conditions to form **polymer** molecules. A polymer is a long-chain molecule made up of many repeating units. The small, reactive molecules that react together to make the polymer are called **monomers**. Up to 10 000 ethene monomers can bond together to form the polymer chains of poly(ethene). Poly(ethene) is commonly used to make carrier bags.

We can show the reaction as:

$$n\text{C}_2\text{H}_4 \rightarrow -\!\!\left[\text{C}_2\text{H}_4\right]\!\!-_n$$

ethene   poly(ethene)

where n = a very large number

or using the displayed formulae:

n is very large, e.g. up to 10 000

The section of the polymer shown in the brackets is the repeat unit of the polymer.

The reaction is called **addition polymerisation**. As in other addition reactions, it involves the breaking of the π bond in each C=C bond, then the monomers link together. Other alkenes also polymerise to make polymers with different properties. Examples of other poly(alkenes) include poly(propene) and poly(phenylethene).

Figure 14.17 Some useful everyday containers made from poly(alkene)s.

We can also use substituted alkenes, such as chloroethene, as monomers:

$$n\text{H}_2\text{C}=\text{CHCl} \rightarrow -\!\!\left[\text{H}_2\text{C}-\text{CHCl}\right]\!\!-_n$$

chloroethene   poly(chloroethene)

where n = a very large number

The $-\!\!\left[\text{H}_2\text{C}-\text{CHCl}\right]\!\!-$ section of the polymer chain is the repeat unit of poly(chloroethene) (Figure **14.18**). In poly(alkenes) made of one type of monomer, the repeat unit is the same as the monomer but the C=C double bond has changed to a C—C single bond. Notice that, as in any other addition reaction of the alkenes, addition polymerisation yields only one product.

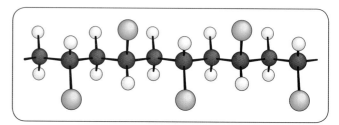

Figure 14.18 A 3D displayed formula of part of the poly(chloroethene) molecule. Its common name is PVC, as the old name for chloroethene was vinyl chloride.

Check-up

10 Tetrafluoroethene, C_2F_4, is the monomer for the polymer PTFE which is used in the non-stick coating on pans.

   a What does PTFE stand for?

   b What do we call the type of reaction used to form PTFE?

   c Write a chemical equation to show the formation of PTFE from C_2F_4.

   d Draw the repeat unit in PTFE.

Disposal of poly(alkene) plastics

Plastics are widely used in many aspect of everyday life. However, the large-scale use of poly(alkene)s has created a problem when we come to dispose of them. During their useful life, one of the poly(alkene)s' useful properties is their lack of reactivity. As they are effectively huge alkane molecules they resist chemical attack. So they can take hundreds of years to decompose when dumped in landfill sites, taking up valuable space. They are non-biodegradable. Therefore throwing away poly(alkenes) creates rubbish that will pollute the environment for centuries (Figure 14.19).

One way to solve this problem would be to burn the poly(alkene)s and use the energy released to generate

Figure 14.19 A beach littered with poly(alkene) plastic waste.

electricity. As we have seen on page **218**, if hydrocarbons burn in excess oxygen the products are carbon dioxide and water. So this solution would not help combat global warming, but would help to conserve our supplies of fossil fuels which currently generate most of our electricity. However, we have also seen that toxic carbon monoxide is also produced from incomplete combustion of hydrocarbons. It is also difficult to separate other plastic waste from the poly(alkene)s. If poly(chloroethene) is burnt acidic hydrogen chloride gas will be given off. This would have to be neutralised before releasing the waste gas into the atmosphere.

Scientists are now developing biodegradable plastics. The use of biodegradable plastics is becoming more common as people become more aware of the issues related to the disposal of poly(alkene)s.

Check-up

11 a How could poly(alkene) waste be used to conserve fossil fuels?

  b Why would your answer to part **a** add to the problem of enhanced global warming?

  c A waste batch of poly(ethene) pellets was burned in an inefficient industrial incinerator. Name a toxic gas that would be released.

Oxidation of the alkenes

Alkenes can be oxidised by acidified potassium manganate(VII) solution, which is a powerful oxidising agent. The products formed will depend on the conditions chosen for the reaction.

Cold dilute acidified manganate(VII) solution

If an alkene is shaken with a dilute solution of acidified manganate(VII) ions at room temperature, the pale purple solution turns colourless. The alkene is converted into a diol, i.e. a compound with two alcohol (—OH) groups:

$$ \underset{\text{ethene}}{\begin{array}{c} H \\ \backslash \\ H \end{array} C=C \begin{array}{c} H \\ / \\ H \end{array}} + \begin{array}{c} O \\ / \ \backslash \\ H \quad H \end{array} + [O] \longrightarrow \underset{\text{ethane-1,2-diol}}{H - \overset{\overset{\displaystyle OH}{|}}{\underset{\underset{\displaystyle H}{|}}{C}} - \overset{\overset{\displaystyle OH}{|}}{\underset{\underset{\displaystyle H}{|}}{C}} - H} $$

This reaction can be used as a test to find out whether a compound is unsaturated. However, the decolorisation of bromine water is a more commonly used test (see page **223**).

Check-up

12 a Name and draw the displayed formula of the organic product formed when propene is oxidised by a cold solution of acidified potassium manganate(VII).

  b Name and draw the displayed formula of the organic product formed when but-2-ene is oxidised by a cold solution of acidified potassium manganate(VII).

Hot, concentrated manganate(VII) solution

Under these harsher conditions, the C=C bond in the alkene is broken completely. The —OH groups in the diol formed initially are further oxidised to ketones, aldehydes, carboxylic acids or carbon dioxide gas. The actual products depend on what is bonded to the carbon atoms involved in the C=C bond. Figure **14.20** shows the oxidation products from each type of group bonded to a carbon atom in the C=C bond.

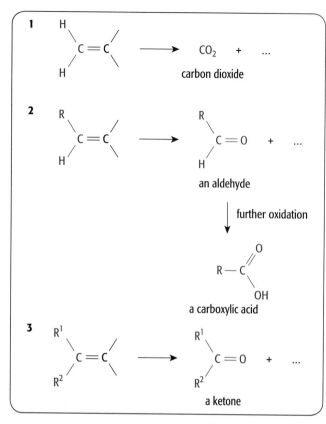

Figure 14.20 Oxidation with hot, concentrated manganate(VII) solution.

To see what is formed when 2-methylprop-1-ene is heated with concentrated potassium manganate(VII) look at equations **1** and **3** in Figure **14.20**. The actual oxidation can be represented as:

$$(CH_3)_2C{=}CH_2 + 4[O] \rightarrow (CH_3)_2C{=}O + CO_2 + H_2O$$

2-methylprop-1-ene   propanone, a ketone

We can use this reaction to determine the position of the double bond in larger alkenes. To do this we would need to identify the products of the oxidation reaction and work backwards to deduce the original alkene. If, for example, carbon dioxide is given off in the oxidation, this tells us that the double bond was between the end two carbon atoms in the alkene.

We can summarise the oxidations under harsh conditions in three reactions.

1 $H_2C{=}CH_2 \rightarrow CO_2 + CO_2$

If a carbon atom is bonded to two hydrogen atoms we get oxidation to a CO_2 molecule.

2 $RHC{=}CHR \rightarrow RCHO + RCHO$
$$\rightarrow RCOOH + RCOOH$$

If a carbon atom is bonded to one hydrogen atom and one alkyl group we get oxidation to a —COOH (carboxylic acid) group.

3 $R^1R^2C{=}CR^3R^4 \rightarrow R^1R^2C{=}O + R^3R^4C{=}O$

If a carbon atom is bonded to two alkyl groups we get oxidation to a C=O (ketone) group.

Check-up

13 a i What effect does a hot, concentrated solution of acidified potassium manganate(VII) have on an alkene?
  ii Why is this reaction useful to chemists?
  b An alkene is known to be either but-1-ene or but-2-ene. When heated with concentrated acidified potassium manganate(VII) solution, bubbles of carbon dioxide gas were given off. Name the alkene.
  c Pent-2-ene is heated with concentrated acidified potassium manganate(VII) solution.
  i Draw the displayed formulae of the products and name them.
  ii Write a balanced chemical equation for this reaction, using [O] to show oxygen atoms involved.
  d 2-Methylbut-2-ene is heated with concentrated acidified potassium manganate(VII) solution.
  i Draw the displayed formulae of the products and name them.
  ii Write a balanced chemical equation for this reaction, using [O] to show oxygen atoms involved.

Summary

- [ ] Alkanes are saturated hydrocarbons with the general formula C_nH_{2n+2}.
- [ ] Alkanes are relatively unreactive as they are non-polar. Most reagents are polar and do not usually react with non-polar molecules.
- [ ] Alkanes are widely used as fuels. When they burn completely they produce carbon dioxide and water. However, they produce toxic carbon monoxide gas when they burn in a limited supply of oxygen, e.g. in a car engine.
- [ ] Cracking of the less useful fractions from the fractional distillation of crude oil produces a range of more useful alkanes with lower molecular masses, as well as alkenes.
- [ ] Chlorine atoms or bromine atoms can substitute for hydrogen atoms in alkanes in the presence of ultraviolet light, producing halogenoalkanes. This is called a free radical substitution reaction. The Cl—Cl or Br—Br bond undergoes homolytic fission in ultraviolet light, producing reactive Cl• or Br• free radicals. This initiation step of free-radical substitution is followed by propagation steps involving a chain reaction which regenerates the halogen free radicals. Termination steps occur, when two free radicals combine.
- [ ] Alkenes are unsaturated hydrocarbons with one carbon–carbon double bond consisting of a σ bond and a π bond. Their general formula is C_nH_{2n}.
- [ ] Alkenes are more reactive than alkanes because they contain a π bond. The characteristic reaction of the alkenes is addition, which occurs across the π bond:
    - ethene produces ethane when reacted with hydrogen over a nickel catalyst
    - ethene produces 1,2-dibromoethane when reacted with bromine at room temperature
    - ethene produces chloroethane when reacted with hydrogen chloride at room temperature
    - ethene produces ethanol when reacted with steam in the presence of concentrated H_3PO_4 catalyst.
- [ ] The mechanism of the reaction of bromine with ethene is electrophilic addition. Electrophiles accept a pair of electrons from an electron-rich atom or centre, in this case the π bond. A carbocation intermediate is formed after the addition of the first bromine atom. This rapidly reacts with a bromide ion to form 1,2-dibromoethane.
- [ ] Alkenes produce many useful polymers by addition polymerisation. For example, poly(ethene) is made from $CH_2{=}CH_2$ and poly(chloroethene) is made from $CH_2{=}CHCl$.
- [ ] The disposal of poly(alkene) plastic waste is difficult as much of it is chemically inert and non-biodegradable.
- [ ] When burnt, waste plastics may produce toxic products such as hydrogen chloride from PVC (poly(chloroethene)).
- [ ] Mild oxidation of alkenes by cold, dilute acidified manganate(VII) solution gives a diol. However, a hot, concentrated acidified manganate(VII) solution will break the C=C bond and give two oxidation products. Identifying the two products formed will indicate the position of the C=C bond in the original alkene.

End-of-chapter questions

1 2-Methylpentane, 3-ethylpentane and 2,3-dimethylbutane are alkanes.
   a For each one give:
      i its molecular formula [3]
      ii its structural formula [3]
      iii its displayed formula [3]
      iv its skeletal formula. [3]
   b Give the general formula that is used to represent alkanes. [1]
   c Two of the alkanes in this question are isomers of each other. Identify which two and identify
     the type of isomerism they show. [2]
   d Using terms from part **a** of this question, define **isomers**. [2]
   e Name the alkane whose structural formula is $CH_3CH(CH_3)CH_2CH(CH_3)_2$. [1]

                                            Total = 18

2 a Alkanes are **saturated hydrocarbons**. Explain the words **saturated** and **hydrocarbons**. [2]
   b Alkanes are generally unreactive. Explain why this is so. [2]
   c Write balanced symbol equations for the complete combustion of:
      i methane [2]
      ii ethane. [2]

                                            Total = 8

3 Use the passage below and your own knowledge to answer the questions that follow.

Methane reacts with bromine to give bromomethane and hydrogen bromide. The mechanism for
the reaction is called free-radical substitution and involves homolytic fission of chemical bonds.
The reaction proceeds via initiation, propagation and termination steps.

   a By what mechanism does bromine react with methane? [1]
   b Write a balanced symbol equation for this reaction. [2]
   c Bonds break in this reaction. What type of bond breaking is involved? [1]
   d What essential conditions are required for this reaction? Why? [2]
   e For this reaction, write down an equation for:
      i an initiation step [2]
      ii a propagation step [2]
      iii a termination step. [2]

                                            Total = 12

4 In a similar reaction to the one in question **3**, 1.50 g of ethane reacts with chlorine. 1.29 g
of chloroethane is formed.
(A_r values: H = 1.0, C = 12.0, Cl = 35.5)
Calculate:
   a the number of moles of ethane that were used [2]
   b the number of moles of chloroethane that were formed [2]
   c the percentage yield [2]
   d the number of grams of chloroethane that would have formed if the percentage yield
     had been 60.0%. [2]

                                            Total = 8

5   Propene, *cis*-pent-2-ene and *trans*-pent-2-ene are alkenes.
   a For each one give:
       i   its molecular formula   [3]
       ii its structural formula   [3]
       iii its displayed formula   [3]
       iv its skeletal formula.   [3]
   b Give the general formula that is used to represent alkenes.   [1]
   c **Two** of these alkenes are isomers of each other. Identify which two.   [1]
   d Why is it not possible to change one of these two isomers into the other at room temperature? [2]
   e Give displayed formulae and the names of the four alkenes with molecular formula C_4H_8.   [8]
   f 3-Methylpent-2-ene has two *cis–trans* isomers. Draw and name the **two** isomers.   [3]
                                                                                          Total = 27

6   Using structural formulae throughout, give balanced symbol equations for the following reactions.
   a Propene with bromine.   [1]
   b Propene with hydrogen. Name the catalyst used. Which industrial process uses a similar reaction? [3]
   c Propene with hydrogen bromide. Give structural formulae for both possible products.   [2]
   d Propene with steam. Give structural formulae for both possible products. Give the formula
      of the catalyst used.   [3]
                                                                                          Total = 9

7 a Alkenes are **unsaturated hydrocarbons**. Explain the word **unsaturated**.   [1]
   b Describe the bonding between the two carbon atoms in ethene.   [2]
   c Describe and draw the shape of an ethene molecule, labelling all bond angles.   [2]
   d Explain the meaning of the term **functional group**. Which functional group is present
      in all alkenes?   [2]
   e Describe a simple chemical test to determine whether an unknown hydrocarbon is unsaturated.
      Describe the result if the test is positive.   [2]
                                                                                          Total = 9

8   Use the passage below and your own knowledge to answer the questions that follow.

     Ethene reacts with bromine to give 1,2-dibromoethane as the only product. The mechanism
     for the reaction is electrophilic addition and involves heterolytic fission of chemical bonds.
     The bromine molecules behave as electrophiles in this reaction.

   a By what mechanism does bromine react with ethene?   [1]
   b Write a balanced symbol equation for this reaction.   [2]
   c Bonds break in this reaction. What type of bond breaking is involved?   [1]
   d Show the mechanism of the reaction as fully as you can, using curly arrows.   [5]
   e Which substance behaves here as an electrophile? Explain what is meant by the term **electrophile**. [2]
                                                                                          Total = 11

9 In a similar reaction to the reaction described in question **8**, 2.80 g of ethene react with chlorine. 8.91 g of dichloroethane are formed.

(A_r values: H = 1.0, C = 12.0, Cl = 35.5)

Calculate:

  a the number of moles of ethene that were used   [2]

  b the number of moles of dichloroethane that were formed   [2]

  c the percentage yield   [2]

  d the number of grams of dichloroethane that would have formed if the percentage yield had been 80.0%.   [2]

Total = 8

10 Alkenes are important industrial chemicals, particularly as raw materials for the manufacture of polymers. Ethene can be used to make poly(ethene). Ethene is used to make chloroethene, which is then used to make poly(chloroethene), and ethene is also used to make tetrafluoroethene, which is used to make poly(tetrafluoroethene).

  a Use displayed formulae to write an equation for the formation of poly(chloroethene) from chloroethene.   [3]

  b Why do waste (used) poly(alkene)s cause problems in a landfill site?   [2]

  c Burning halogenated polymers such as PVC can release toxic waste products such as HCl into the environment. Explain how this can be minimised.   [2]

Total = 7

15 Halogenoalkanes

Learning outcomes

Candidates should be able to:

☐ recall the chemistry of halogenoalkanes as exemplified by:
- the following nucleophilic substitution reactions of bromoethane: hydrolysis, formation of nitriles, formation of primary amines by reaction with ammonia
- the elimination of hydrogen bromide from 2-bromopropane

☐ describe the mechanism of nucleophilic substitution (by both S_N1 and S_N2 mechanisms) in halogenoalkanes

☐ interpret the different reactivities of halogenoalkanes (with particular reference to hydrolysis and to the relative strengths of the C—Hal bonds)

☐ explain the uses of fluoroalkanes and fluorohalogenoalkanes e.g. CFCs, anaesthetics, flame retardants, plastics, in terms of their relative chemical inertness

☐ recognise the concern about the effect of chlorofluoroalkanes on the ozone layer.

15.1 Introduction

We can think of the halogenoalkanes as alkanes which have one or more hydrogen atoms replaced by halogen atoms.

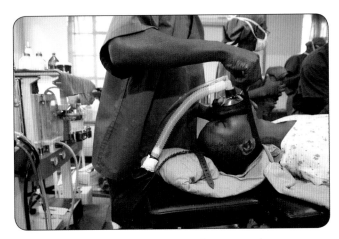

Figure 15.1 If you have ever had an operation, you may have a halogenoalkane to thank for putting you to sleep. You might have heard of an early anaesthetic called chloroform. Its systematic name is trichloromethane. Nowadays you may receive a gas known as 'halothane':

The halogens are the elements in Group VII of the Periodic Table: fluorine (F), chlorine (Cl), bromine (Br) and iodine (I).

The simplest halogenoalkanes, whose molecules contain just one halogen atom, will have the general formula $C_nH_{2n+1}X$, where X is F, Cl, Br or I.

15.2 Nucleophilic substitution reactions

1 Substitution reactions with alkali, OH⁻(aq)

When an aqueous solution of sodium hydroxide is added to a halogenoalkane, a nucleophilic substitution reaction takes place. The organic product formed is an alcohol:

$$\underset{\text{bromoethane}}{CH_3CH_2Br} + NaOH \rightarrow \underset{\text{ethanol}}{CH_3CH_2OH} + NaBr$$

We can also show this equation as:

$$CH_3CH_2Br + OH^- \rightarrow CH_3CH_2OH + Br^-$$

The hydroxide ion behaves as a nucleophile here, because it is donating a pair of electrons. This is why this reaction is called a **nucleophilic** substitution.

The reaction is carried out under reflux in the laboratory. This enables us to heat the reaction mixture

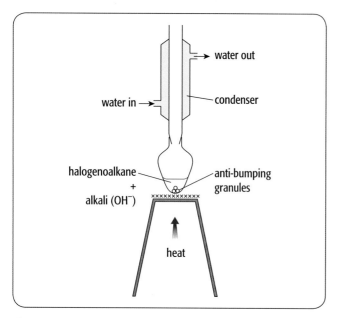

Figure 15.2 Reflux apparatus for hydrolysis of halogenoalkane.

without evaporating off the volatile organic compounds in the reaction flask. The apparatus is shown in Figure 15.2.

Similar reactions occur with other halogenoalkanes, but the reaction rates differ. We can investigate the rate of hydrolysis using silver nitrate solution. The water in the silver nitrate solution acts as the nucleophile, again forming the alcohol. The reaction is called **hydrolysis** (breakdown by water). It is a very similar reaction to the reaction that happens with alkali:

$$CH_3CH_2Br + H_2O \rightarrow CH_3CH_2OH + H^+ + Br^-$$

However, the hydrolysis with water occurs more slowly than with $OH^-(aq)$. This is because the negatively charged hydroxide ion is a more effective nucleophile than a water molecule.

From the equation above you can see that a halide ion, in this case Br^-, is produced in the reaction. On page 185 we used silver nitrate solution to test for halide ions. Remember that chlorides give a white precipitate (of silver chloride), bromides give a cream precipitate (silver bromide) and iodides produce a pale yellow precipitate (silver iodide). We can time how long it takes for test tubes containing the halogenoalkanes and silver nitrate solution to become opaque.

We find that:
- the fastest nucleophilic substitution reactions take place with the iodoalkanes
- the slowest nucleophilic substitution reactions take place with the fluoroalkanes.

Fluoroalkanes	least reactive
Chloroalkanes	
Bromoalkanes	↓
Iodoalkanes	most reactive

The substitution involves the breaking of the carbon–halogen bond. Looking at the bond energies (Table 15.1) helps us to explain the rates of reaction. Notice that the C—I bond is the weakest so it is broken most easily. It forms an I^- ion during the substitution reaction. This is shown clearly in an ionic equation:

$$\underset{\text{iodoethane}}{CH_3CH_2I} + OH^- \rightarrow \underset{\text{ethanol}}{CH_3CH_2OH} + I^-$$

There is more about the mechanism of nucleophilic substitution on pages **233–4**.

Bond	Bond energy / kJ mol^{-1}
C—F	467 (strongest bond)
C—Cl	346
C—Br	290
C—I	228 (weakest bond)

Table 15.1 Bond energy values of the carbon–halogen bonds.

Check-up

1 **a** Why does the hydrolysis of a halogenoalkane happen more quickly with $OH^-(aq)$ ions than with water molecules?

   b Explain why silver nitrate solution can be used to investigate the rate of hydrolysis of the halogenoalkanes. Include ionic equations for the formation of the precipitates.

2 Substitution with cyanide ions, CN⁻ (in ethanol)

In this reaction the nucleophile is the CN^- ion. To carry out the reaction, a solution of potassium cyanide, KCN, in ethanol (known as an ethanolic or alcoholic solution of potassium cyanide) is heated under reflux with the halogenoalkane. An ionic equation for this reaction is:

$$CH_3CH_2Br + CN^- \rightarrow CH_3CH_2CN + Br^-$$
$$\text{bromoethane} \qquad \text{propanenitrile}$$

Notice that in the reaction with the cyanide ion, an extra carbon atom is added to the original halogenoalkane chain.

Sometimes a new compound is needed with one more carbon atom than the best available organic raw material (the starting compound). Therefore, if we can convert the starting compound to a halogenoalkane, we can then reflux with ethanolic KCN to make a nitrile. We now have an intermediate with the correct number of carbon atoms.

3 Substitution with ammonia, NH₃ (in ethanol)

If a halogenoalkane is heated with an excess of ammonia dissolved in ethanol under pressure, an amine is formed.

$$CH_3CH_2Br + NH_3 \rightarrow CH_3CH_2NH_2 + HBr$$
$$\text{bromoethane} \qquad \text{ethylamine}$$

Here the nucleophile is the ammonia molecule. Ethylamine is a **primary** amine, as the nitrogen atom is attached to only one alkyl group. If the ammonia is not in excess, we get a mixture of amine products. This is because the primary amine itself acts as a nucleophile and will attack halogenoalkane molecules, forming secondary amines and so on.

Check-up

2 Why can ammonia and amine molecules act as nucleophiles?

15.3 Mechanism of nucleophilic substitution in halogenoalkanes

Many of the reactions of halogenoalkanes are nucleophilic substitutions. In these reactions, the nucleophile attacks the carbon atom bonded to the halogen. Remember from Chapter 13 that nucleophiles are donors of an electron pair and are attracted to electron-deficient atoms.

The carbon–halogen bond is polarised because the halogen is more electronegative than carbon. Therefore the carbon atom carries a partial positive charge as the electron pair in the carbon–halogen bond is drawn nearer to the halogen atom (Figure 15.3). The halogen atom is replaced by the nucleophile in the substitution reaction.

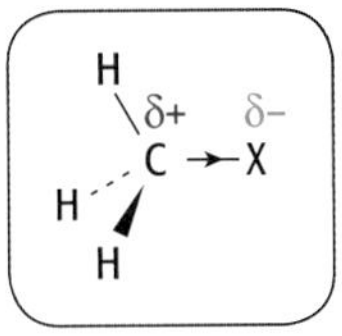

Figure 15.3 The carbon–halogen bond is polarised.

There are two possible mechanisms that can operate in nucleophilic substitution reactions of halogenoalkanes. The mechanism is determined by the structure of the halogenoalkane involved in the reaction.

Mechanism for primary halogenoalkanes (S_N2)

In primary halogenoalkanes the halogen is bonded to a carbon atom which is itself bonded to one other carbon atom and two hydrogen atoms. This means that the carbon atom bonded to the halogen is attached to one alkyl group. For example, 1-chloropropane, $CH_3CH_2CH_2Cl$, is a primary halogenoalkane. On pages 231–2 we looked at the hydrolysis of bromoethane, another primary halogenoalkane. Figure 15.4 shows the mechanism for that reaction.

The OH⁻ ion donates a pair of electrons to the δ+ carbon atom, forming a new covalent bond. At the same time, the C—Br bond is breaking. The Br atom takes both the electrons in the bond and leaves as a Br⁻ ion.

This mechanism is called an **S_N2 mechanism**. The 'S' stands for substitution and the 'N' stands for nucleophilic. The '2' tells us that the rate of the reaction (which is determined by the slow step in the mechanism) involves two reacting species. Experiments show us that the rate depends on both the concentration of the halogenoalkane and the concentration of the hydroxide ions present.

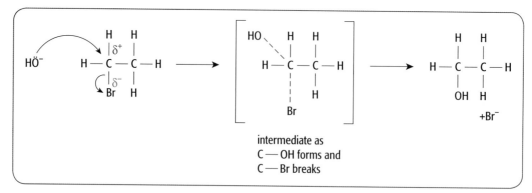

Figure 15.4 The mechanism of nucleophilic substitution in a primary halogenoalkane.

intermediate as
C—OH forms and
C—Br breaks

Check-up

3 Show the mechanism, using appropriate curly arrows, for the hydrolysis of 1-chloropropane, $CH_3CH_2CH_2Cl$, by alkali.

Mechanism for tertiary halogenoalkanes (S_N1)

In a **tertiary** halogenoalkane the carbon atom bonded to the halogen atom is also bonded to three other carbon atoms (alkyl groups). For example, 2-bromo-2-methylpropane is a tertiary halogenoalkane. Its structure is shown in Figure 15.5.

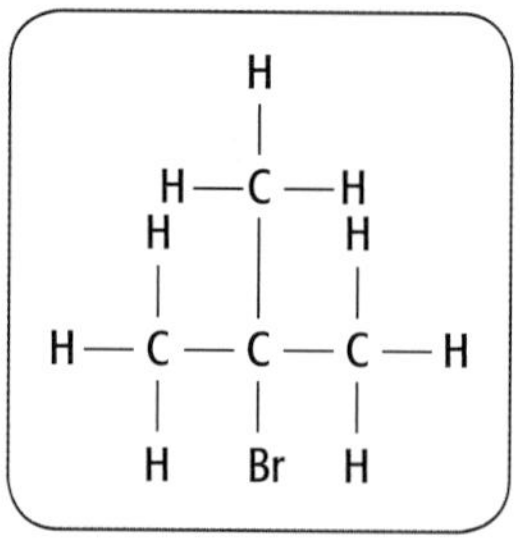

Figure 15.5 A tertiary halogenoalkane.

A tertiary halogenoalkane reacts with a hydroxide ion by a two-step mechanism. The first step in the mechanism is the breaking of the carbon–halogen bond. This forms a tertiary carbocation, which is attacked immediately by the hydroxide ion (Figure 15.6).

This mechanism is known as an **S_N1 mechanism**. The '1' tells us that the rate of the reaction only depends on

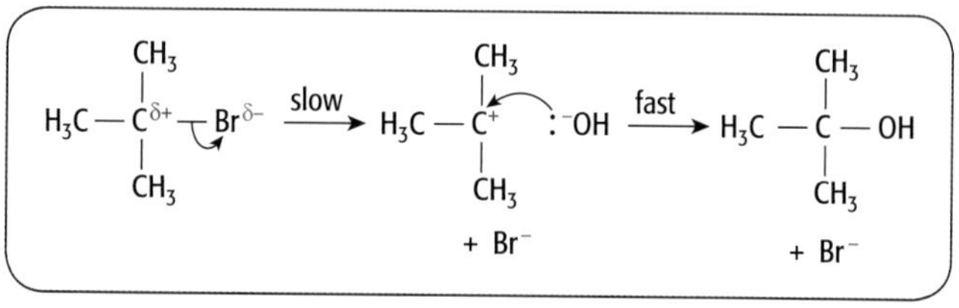

Figure 15.6 The mechanism of nucleophilic substitution in a tertiary halogenoalkane.

one reagent, in this case the concentration of the halogenoalkane.

The breaking of the C—Br bond is an example of heterolytic fission of a covalent bond (see page 211).

The Br^- ion forms again, as in the S_N2 mechanism, but in this case a carbocation ion forms. This does not happen with primary halogenoalkanes. This is because tertiary carbocations are more stable than primary carbocations. Alkyl groups tend to release electrons to atoms attached to them. Therefore a tertiary carbocation has three alkyl groups donating electrons towards the positively charged carbon atom, reducing its charge density. This makes it more stable than a primary carbocation, which just has one alkyl group releasing electrons (Figure 15.7).

The S_N1 mechanism and the S_N2 mechanism are both likely to play a part in the nucleophilic substitution of **secondary** halogenoalkanes.

Check-up

4 a Draw the structure (displayed formula) of 2-chloro-2-methylbutane.
b Show the mechanism for the hydrolysis of 2-chloro-2-methylbutane by alkali.

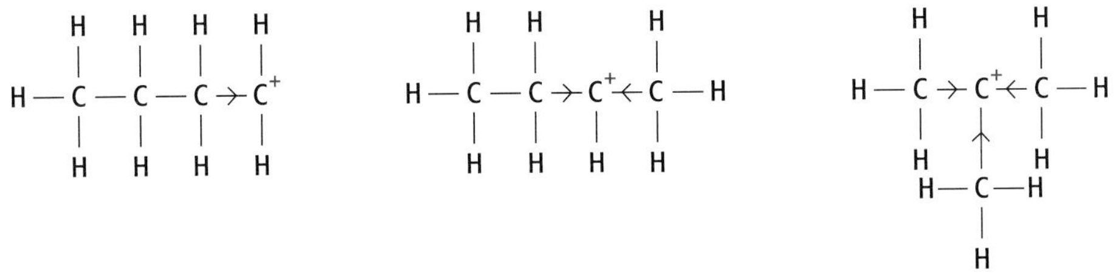

primary carbocation (least stable)

secondary carbocation

tertiary carbocation (most stable)

Figure 15.7 The trend in the stability of primary, secondary and tertiary carbocations.

15.4 Elimination reactions

Halogenoalkanes also undergo elimination reactions. An elimination reaction involves the loss of a small molecule from the original organic molecule. In the case of halogenoalkanes this small molecule is effectively a hydrogen halide, such as HCl or HBr.

The reagent used in elimination reactions is ethanolic sodium hydroxide:

$CH_3CHBrCH_3 + NaOH(\text{ethanol})$
2-bromopropane

$\rightarrow CH_2{=}CHCH_3 + H_2O + NaBr$
propene

The original 2-bromopropane molecule has lost an H atom and a Br atom. We can think of it as HBr being eliminated from the halogenoalkane. The ethanolic OH^- ion acts as a base, accepting an H^+ from the halogenoalkane to form water. The C—Br bond breaks heterolytically, forming a Br^- ion and leaving an alkene as the organic product.

Notice the importance of the conditions used in organic reactions. If we use NaOH(aq), a nucleophilic substitution reaction occurs and an alcohol is produced. If we use NaOH(ethanol), an elimination reaction occurs and an alkene is produced.

Check-up

5 Write a balanced equation for the reaction of bromoethane with ethanolic sodium hydroxide.

15.5 Uses of halogenoalkanes

Halogenoalkanes are rarely found naturally but they are important in the chemical industry. They are frequently made as intermediates for making other useful substances but have also found some uses themselves. We have already seen at the start of this chapter how some halogenoalkanes are important anaesthetics, for example 2-bromo-2-chloro-1,1,1-trifluoroethane (halothane).

Halogenoalkanes are also used as flame retardants. Introducing a halogen atom into an alkane greatly reduces its flammability. If a flammable material is treated with a flame retardant it becomes much safer to use. The foam inside cushions is an example of a flammable material which can be treated like this (Figure 15.8).

Another use of halogenoalkanes is in the manufacture of plastics. One of the most common plastics is PVC (polyvinylchloride). Its systematic name is poly(chloroethene). The monomer used to make PVC, called chloroethene, is itself made from 1,2-dichloroethane. The non-stick lining of pans is also a

Figure 15.8 Some halogenoalkanes have found uses as flame retardants.

'halogeno-polymer'. Its name is poly(tetrafluoroethene). The strength of the C—F bond means that it can be used at high temperatures during cooking without breaking down.

CFCs

CFCs are chlorofluorocarbons. Chemists refer to them as chlorofluoroalkanes. These organic compounds are all chemically inert (very unreactive). They are not flammable and are not toxic. These properties made volatile CFCs useful as aerosol propellants, solvents, and as the refrigerants inside fridges. They were also used as blowing agents for polymers such as expanded polystyrene. Dichlorodifluoromethane is an example of a CFC used for these purposes.

When the compounds were discovered in the 1930s, people could see no drawbacks to using the new 'wonder compounds'. However, CFCs have caused a serious environmental issue – the depletion of the ozone layer in the upper atmosphere. The ozone layer protects the Earth by absorbing harmful UV radiation arriving from the Sun.

It turns out that CFCs are unreactive in normal conditions, but high up in the atmosphere they become totally different. The CFCs can persist in the atmosphere for about a hundred years. They diffuse up to the stratosphere – and that's where the problem starts. The UV light from the Sun breaks the C—Cl bonds in the CFC molecules. This releases highly reactive chlorine atoms, called chlorine free radicals. These chlorine free radicals react with ozone molecules. In a sequence of chain reactions, it has been estimated that each chlorine free radical can destroy a million ozone molecules (Figure **15.9**).

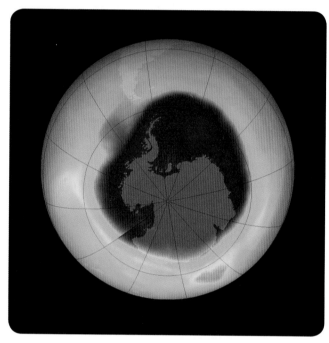

Figure 15.9 Banning the use of CFCs has meant that the hole in the ozone layer over Antarctica is now getting smaller.

Governments have tackled the problem and most industrialised countries have banned the use of CFCs. Chemists developed new compounds for fridges and aerosols, such as HFCs, hydrofluorocarbons. These break down more quickly once released into the air because of the presence of hydrogen in their molecules so they never even reach the ozone layer. There are now signs that the ozone layer is recovering from the effects of chlorofluoroalkanes. The hole in the ozone layer is very slowly closing up.

Check-up

6 How can such unreactive compounds as CFCs cause so much damage to the ozone layer?

Summary

- [ ] If one or more of the hydrogen atoms in an alkane are replaced by halogen atoms, the compound is called a halogenoalkane.
- [ ] Iodoalkanes are the most reactive halogenoalkanes, while fluoroalkanes are the least reactive. This is explained by the trend in the bond strength of the carbon–halogen bonds. The C—F bond is the strongest bond, while the C—I bond is the weakest bond – so it is most easily broken in its reactions.
- [ ] Halogenoalkanes are attacked by nucleophiles. This happens because the carbon bonded to the halogen carries a partial positive charge due to the higher electronegativity of the halogen. Halogenoalkanes undergo nucleophilic substitution.
- [ ] Suitable nucleophiles include aqueous alkali, OH^-(aq), cyanide, CN^-, and ammonia, NH_3.
- [ ] The reaction with OH^- ions (or with water) is known as hydrolysis, and an alcohol is formed.
- [ ] Halogenoalkanes will also undergo elimination reactions when heated with ethanolic sodium hydroxide, forming alkenes.
- [ ] The halogenoalkanes have many uses including anaesthetics, flame retardants, solvents and making plastics.
- [ ] Chlorofluoroalkanes have been responsible for damaging the Earth's ozone layer but alternative inert compounds, such as fluoroalkanes, are now replacing the use of CFCs.

End-of-chapter questions

1   1-bromobutane will undergo reactions when heated, as shown by reactions **A** and **B**.

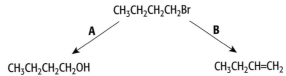

   a For reactions **A** and **B** give the reagents used in each case.   [2]
   b Reaction **A** was repeated using 1-iodobutane instead of 1-bromobutane. Explain any difference
      in the rate of reaction observed.   [2]
   c What type of organic reaction is **A**?   [1]
   d Show the mechanism for reaction **A**.   [3]
   e Reaction **A** was repeated with 2-bromo-2-methylpropane instead of 1-bromobutane.
      i   Name the organic compound formed.   [1]
      ii The mechanism of the reaction with 2-bromo-2-methylpropane differs from the mechanism
          of reaction **A**. Describe how the mechanisms differ.   [2]
   f What type of reaction is **B**?   [1]
   g If reaction **B** was repeated with 2-bromobutane, name the other organic products that can form
      as well as the product shown above.   [1]

                                                                                                   Total = 13

2   Bromochlorodifluoromethane has been used in fire extinguishers. However, its breakdown products
    were found to be toxic.
    a Draw the displayed formula of bromochlorodifluoromethane.   [1]
    b CF_3CH_2F is being introduced as a replacement for various CFCs in refrigerants and aerosols.
       Name this compound.   [1]
    c What is the main environmental problem caused by the use of CFCs?   [1]

                                                                                                    Total = 3

16 Alcohols and esters

Learning outcomes

Candidates should be able to:

- [ ] recall the chemistry of alcohols, exemplified by ethanol:
  - combustion
  - substitution to give halogenoalkanes
  - reaction with sodium
  - oxidation to carbonyl compounds and carboxylic acids
  - dehydration to alkenes
  - ester formation
- [ ] classify hydroxy compounds (alcohols) into primary, secondary and tertiary alcohols

- [ ] suggest characteristic distinguishing reactions, e.g. mild oxidation
- [ ] describe the formation of esters from carboxylic acids, using ethyl ethanoate as an example
- [ ] describe the acid and base hydrolysis of esters
- [ ] state the major commercial uses of esters, e.g. solvents, perfumes, flavourings.

16.1 Introduction – the alcohols

Alcohols are organic molecules containing the hydroxyl group, —OH. With one hydroxyl group substituted into an alkane molecule, the general formula is $C_nH_{2n+1}OH$. The alcohols are named by taking the '-e' off the alkane stem and adding '-ol'. For example, CH_3OH is called methanol. For alcohol molecules with three or more carbon atoms the position of the hydroxyl group is shown by inserting a number to indicate which carbon atom is bonded to the —OH group. Figure 16.1 gives some examples.

Propan-1-ol is classified as a **primary alcohol**. The carbon atom bonded to the OH— group is attached to **one** other carbon atom (or alkyl group). Propan-2-ol is a **secondary alcohol** as the carbon atom bonded to the —OH group is attached to **two** other carbon atoms (or alkyl groups). With **three** alkyl groups attached, 2-methylpropan-2-ol is an example of a **tertiary alcohol**.

The alcohols have higher boiling points than expected when compared with other organic molecules with similar relative molecular masses. Even methanol, the

alcohol with the lowest molar mass, is a liquid at room temperature. This occurs because of hydrogen bonding between alcohol molecules (see page **66**). Hydrogen bonding also explains why the smaller alcohol molecules mix so well with water.

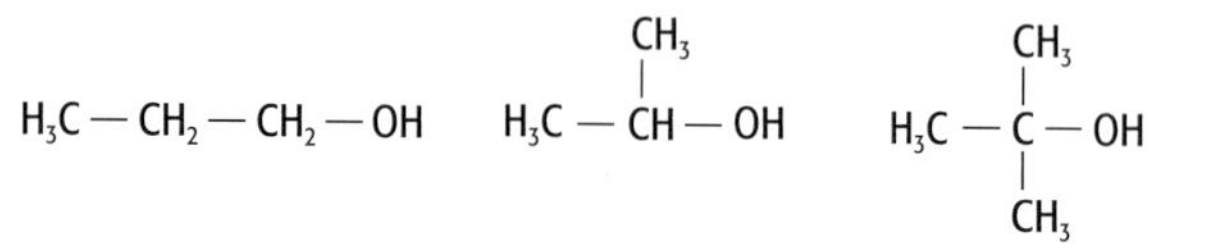

Check-up

1 a Explain how hydrogen bonds arise:
      i   between ethanol molecules
      ii between ethanol and water molecules.
   b Ethanol mixes with water in all proportions but hexan-1-ol is less miscible with water. Why is this?

16.2 Reactions of the alcohols

1 Combustion

When ignited, the alcohols react with oxygen in the air. The products of complete combustion are carbon dioxide and water. For example, ethanol burns with a clean blue flame in a good supply of air:

alcohol + oxygen → carbon dioxide + water

$$C_2H_5OH + 3O_2 \rightarrow 2CO_2 + 3H_2O$$
ethanol

Ethanol is sometimes used in Brazil as a car fuel. This reduces their use of petrol.

$$H_3C-CH_2-CH_2-OH \qquad H_3C-\overset{\displaystyle CH_3}{\underset{\displaystyle |}{CH}}-OH \qquad H_3C-\overset{\displaystyle CH_3}{\underset{\displaystyle \underset{\displaystyle CH_3}{|}}{\overset{\displaystyle |}{C}}}-OH$$

propan-1-ol   propan-2-ol   2-methylpropan-2-ol
primary alcohol   secondary alcohol   tertiary alcohol

Figure 16.1 Notice that the numbering to show the position of the —OH group in an alcohol starts from the end of the molecule which gives the smaller number.

A country like Brazil has few oil reserves but can grow plenty of sugar cane, which can be fermented to make ethanol (Figure 16.3). As well as conserving the world's diminishing supplies of crude oil, sugar cane has the advantage of absorbing CO_2 as it grows. Although the CO_2 is effectively returned to the atmosphere during fermentation and when the ethanol burns, **biofuels** such as ethanol are said to be 'carbon neutral'. Overall, they do not increase the greenhouse gases in the air (in theory). Even if we take into account the CO_2 produced in growing, harvesting, transporting and processing the sugar cane, it is still much better for the environment to use 'bio-ethanol' as a fuel than petrol or diesel from crude oil.

Figure 16.2 The fuel called 'gasohol' is a mixture of ethanol and petrol.

Figure 16.3 Sugar cane is the raw material for making ethanol. The sugar from the plants is fermented with yeast to make the ethanol.

Check-up

2 **a** Write a balanced equation for the complete combustion of:
  i propan-1-ol
  ii butan-1-ol.
 b Glucose can be fermented with yeast in anaerobic conditions. Name the products of the reaction.

Fact file

Ethanol is used as a solvent as well as a fuel. We often use it as 'methylated spirits', which contains about 90% ethanol. For example, we can clean oil-based paints from brushes with this solvent. The name 'methylated' comes from the traditional additive, methanol, which is added to make the ethanol undrinkable. This means that methylated spirits is not taxed like alcoholic drinks, so it is much cheaper. Unfortunately, some alcoholics who cannot afford alcoholic drinks do drink 'meths', which can result in blindness and eventually death. Nowadays manufacturers of methylated spirits tend to add less-toxic but foul-tasting additives and emetics (vomit-inducing substances) to the ethanol.

2 Substitution to form a halogenoalkane

In this substitution reaction, the —OH group in the alcohol is replaced by a halogen atom to produce a halogenoalkane. The carbon atom bonded to the hydroxyl group will carry a partial positive charge (as oxygen is more electronegative than carbon). This makes it open to nucleophilic attack. The initial attack on the alcohol is by the partially negative halogen atom in the hydrogen halide:

alcohol + hydrogen halide → halogenoalkane + water

For example:

$$CH_3CH_2OH + HCl \rightarrow CH_3CH_2Cl + H_2O$$
ethanol   chloroethane

The dry hydrogen chloride gas for this reaction can be made *in situ* (in the reaction vessel). Sodium chloride and concentrated sulfuric acid are used for this.

$$NaCl + H_2SO_4 \rightarrow NaHSO_4 + HCl$$

The alcohol is heated under reflux (see apparatus on page 232) with the reactants to make the halogenoalkane. The halogenoalkane made can then be distilled off from the reaction mixture and collected as oily droplets under water (Figure 16.4).

Sulfur dichloride oxide, $SOCl_2$, is also used to substitute a chlorine atom into an alcohol molecule:

$$C_2H_5OH + SOCl_2 \rightarrow C_2H_5Cl + HCl + SO_2$$

Notice that in this reaction the two by-products of the reaction (HCl and SO_2) are both gases. These escape from the reaction mixture, leaving the halogenoalkane.

We can also use phosphorus halides to provide the halogen atoms for this substitution reaction.

For chloroalkanes we can use solid phosphorus(V) chloride, PCl_5:

$$C_2H_5OH + PCl_5 \xrightarrow{\text{room temperature}} C_2H_5Cl + HCl + POCl_3$$

Figure 16.4 Bromoethane being distilled off following the reaction between ethanol and hydrogen bromide. The white solid visible in the pear-shaped flask is sodium bromide (as crystals). The sodium bromide reacts with concentrated sulfuric acid to make the hydrogen bromide needed for the reaction.

The release of acidic hydrogen chloride gas from this reaction can be used as a test for the hydroxyl group. The HCl gas causes 'steamy fumes' to be observed.

Phosphorus(III) chloride can also be used to halogenate an alcohol, but this reaction does require heating.

For bromoalkanes and iodoalkanes we can make the phosphorus(III) halide, PBr_3 or PI_3, *in situ* using red phosphorus and bromine or iodine. These are warmed with the alcohol. For example:

$$3C_2H_5OH + PI_3 \rightarrow \underset{\text{iodoethane}}{3C_2H_5I} + H_3PO_3$$

Check-up

3 a Write a balanced equation to show the reaction between ethanol and hydrogen bromide.
  b What are the reagents and conditions used for this reaction?
  c What do we call this type of reaction?

3 Reaction with sodium metal

In the reaction with hydrogen halides, the C—O bond in the alcohol breaks. However, in some other reactions the O—H bond in the alcohol breaks. The reaction with sodium metal is an example:

$$\underset{\text{ethanol}}{C_2H_5OH} + \underset{\text{sodium}}{Na} \rightarrow \underset{\text{sodium ethoxide}}{C_2H_5O^-Na^+} + \underset{\text{hydrogen}}{H_2}$$

The reaction is similar to sodium's reaction with water, but less vigorous. In both cases hydrogen gas is given off and a basic ionic compound is formed. With ethanol, if the excess ethanol is evaporated off after the reaction, a white crystalline solid is left. This is the sodium ethoxide. Other alcohols react in a similar way with sodium. For example, propan-1-ol would produce sodium propoxide plus hydrogen gas. In general:

alcohol + sodium $\rightarrow$ sodium alkoxide + hydrogen

We find that the longer the hydrocarbon chain, the less vigorous the reaction.

Figure 16.5 Sodium reacting with ethanol. The pink colour is from some phenolphthalein indicator that has been added to the ethanol, showing the basic nature of the sodium ethoxide formed.

Check-up

4 Lithium reacts with alcohols in a similar way to sodium. A small piece of lithium metal is dropped onto a watch-glass containing propan-1-ol.
   a What would you observe?
   b Name the products of the reaction.
   c What difference would you expect to see if you used sodium instead of lithium in this reaction?

4 Esterification

Another reaction that involves the breaking of the O—H bond in alcohols is **esterification**, i.e. the making of esters. An esterification reaction is usually between an alcohol and a carboxylic acid. The general equation is:

$$\text{carboxylic acid} + \text{alcohol} \underset{}{\overset{\text{acid catalyst}}{\rightleftharpoons}} \text{ester} + \text{water}$$

For this reaction to take place, the carboxylic acid and alcohol are heated under reflux with a strong acid catalyst (usually concentrated sulfuric acid). The reaction is

Figure 16.6 Esters contribute to the complex mixture of substances blended in a perfume.

reversible, so an equilibrium can be established with all the reactants and products shown in the general equation present.

The esters formed usually have sweet, fruity smells. They are present naturally in fruits and we use them in artificial flavourings and perfumes (Figure 16.6). They are also used as solvents, e.g. in nail varnish remover.

Here is an example of an esterification reaction:

$$C_2H_5OH + CH_3C\overset{O}{\underset{OH}{\diagup}} \underset{}{\overset{H_2SO_4}{\rightleftharpoons}} CH_3C\overset{O}{\underset{OC_2H_5}{\diagup}} + H_2O$$

ethanol   ethanoic acid   ethyl ethanoate   water

The ester formed is called ethyl ethanoate. What would be the ester formed if ethanol was reacted with propanoic acid? Would it be propyl ethanoate or ethyl propanoate? The answer is ethyl propanoate. That's because the first part of an ester's name comes from the alcohol, in this case ethanol, giving 'ethyl …'. The second part comes from the carboxylic acid, in this case propanoic acid, giving '… propanoate', and making the ester ethyl propanoate:

$$\underset{\text{propanoic acid}}{CH_3CH_2COOH} + \underset{\text{ethanol}}{C_2H_5OH}$$

$$\overset{H_2SO_4}{\rightleftharpoons} \underset{\text{ethyl propanoate}}{CH_3CH_2COOC_2H_5} + \underset{\text{water}}{H_2O}$$

Esters can be **hydrolysed** by heating under reflux with either an acid or a base.

Refluxing with an acid simply reverses the preparation of the ester from an alcohol and a carboxylic acid. The acid catalyses the reaction. The reaction is reversible and forms an equilibrium mixture. In acid hydrolysis, there are always both reactants and products present after the reaction. The equation for the acid hydrolysis of ethyl ethanoate is:

$$H_3C-C\overset{O}{\underset{O-CH_2CH_3}{\big<}} + H_2O \overset{H^+(aq)}{\rightleftharpoons} H_3C-C\overset{O}{\underset{O-H}{\big<}} + CH_3CH_2OH$$

However, when an ester is refluxed with an alkali (a soluble base), such as aqueous sodium hydroxide, it is fully hydrolysed. Unlike acid hydrolysis, this is not a reversible reaction. An alcohol and the sodium salt of the acid are formed. The equation for the base hydrolysis of ethyl ethanoate is:

$$H_3C-C\overset{O}{\underset{O-CH_2CH_3}{\big<}} + NaOH \longrightarrow H_3C-C\overset{O}{\underset{O^-Na^+}{\big<}} + CH_3CH_2OH$$

sodium
ethanoate

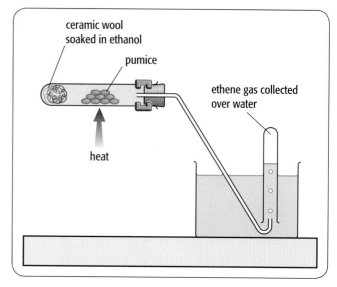

Figure 16.7 The dehydration of ethanol to give ethene.

porous pot or pumice also catalyse the reaction. For example:

$$C_2H_5OH \xrightarrow{Al_2O_3 \text{ catalyst}} CH_2{=}CH_2 + H_2O$$
ethanol   ethene   water

Figure 16.7 shows how the ethene gas formed can be collected.

Check-up

5 a Name the ester formed in each of the following reactions:
   i   butan-1-ol + ethanoic acid
   ii ethanol + hexanoic acid
   iii pentan-1-ol and methanoic acid.
 b Write the structural formula of each ester formed in part **a**.

5 Dehydration

Alcohols can also undergo elimination reactions in which water is lost and alkenes are formed. As the small molecule removed from the alcohol molecule is H_2O, this reaction is also known as **dehydration**.

$$\text{alcohol} \xrightarrow{\text{catalyst}} \text{alkene} + \text{water}$$

The reaction takes place when alcohol vapour is passed over a hot catalyst of aluminium oxide powder. Pieces of

Check-up

6 Concentrated sulfuric acid or phosphoric acid can also be used to catalyse the dehydration of an alcohol. The alcohol and concentrated acid are heated to about 170 °C. The concentrated acid does not change chemically during the reaction.
 a Write an equation showing the dehydration of ethanol using concentrated sulfuric acid.
 b If propan-1-ol was used instead of ethanol, name the organic product formed.

6 Oxidation

On page **238** we saw how alcohols can be classified as primary, secondary or tertiary. For many reactions the class of alcohol makes no difference to the type of products formed. In organic chemistry, we can usually generalise for the whole homologous series. However, when alcohols are oxidised, different products are obtained from primary, secondary and tertiary alcohols.

Alcohols can be oxidised by potassium dichromate(VI) solution, $K_2Cr_2O_7$, acidified with dilute sulfuric acid. The solution's orange colour is caused by the dichromate(VI) ions. When the dichromate(VI) ions react as an oxidising agent, they turn into chromium(III) ions, which form a green solution. The reaction mixture needs to be warmed before the oxidation takes place.

The product formed when an alcohol is oxidised can be used to distinguish between primary, secondary and tertiary alcohols. You can learn about the chemical tests for the products on page **250**.

- With tertiary alcohols, no reaction takes place under these relatively mild conditions. A mixture of a tertiary alcohol, dilute sulfuric acid and potassium dichromate(VI) solution remains orange when warmed.
- A secondary alcohol, such as propan-2-ol, will be oxidised to form a ketone. In this case propanone is formed and the reaction mixture turns green:

$$H_3C - \underset{\underset{H}{|}}{\overset{\overset{OH}{|}}{C}} - CH_3 + [O] \longrightarrow H_3C - \overset{\overset{O}{||}}{C} - CH_3 + H_2O$$

propanone

These oxidation equations use [O] to show oxygen from the oxidising agent. You have met this type of simplified equation for oxidation reactions before on page **212**.

- With a primary alcohol, such as ethanol, the alcohol is oxidised to an aldehyde. Ethanol is oxidised to ethanal:

$$CH_3CH_2OH + [O] \longrightarrow H_3C - \overset{\overset{O}{||}}{C} - H + H_2O$$

ethanal

The ethanal formed can be further oxidised to form ethanoic acid. This is achieved by refluxing with excess acidified potassium dichromate(VI):

$$H_3C - \overset{\overset{O}{||}}{C} - H + [O] \longrightarrow H_3C - \overset{\overset{O}{||}}{C} - OH$$

ethanoic acid

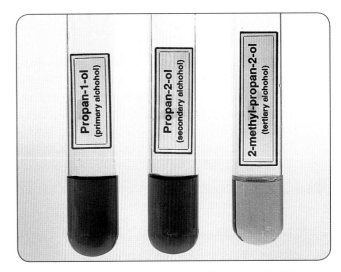

Figure 16.8 Before warming with the labelled alcohol, each of these tubes contained orange acidified potassium dichromate(VI) solution. After warming, the orange dichromate(VI) ions have been reduced to green chromium(III) ions by the primary and secondary alcohols. This shows that both the primary and secondary alcohols have been oxidised but the tertiary alcohol, 2-methylpropan-2-ol, has not.

Given three unknown alcohols, one primary, one secondary and one tertiary, it would be easy to distinguish the tertiary alcohol. Figure **16.8** shows the results of warming each class of alcohol with acidified potassium dichromate(VI).

Check-up

7 Propan-1-ol can be oxidised to propanal, CH_3CH_2CHO, and then to propanoic acid, CH_3CH_2COOH.
   a What reagents and conditions should be used to oxidise propan-1-ol to propanal?
   b Write a balanced chemical equation for this oxidation. Oxygen from the oxidising agent should be shown as [O].
   c What reagents and conditions should be used to oxidise propan-1-ol to propanoic acid?
   d Write a balanced chemical equation for this oxidation. Again, show oxygen from the oxidising agent as [O].

Summary

☐ The complete combustion of alcohols forms carbon dioxide and water.
☐ A nucleophilic substitution reaction takes place between alcohols and hydrogen halides to form halogenoalkanes.
☐ Alcohols react with sodium metal to give sodium alkoxides and hydrogen gas.
☐ An alcohol will react with a carboxylic acid, in the presence of a strong acid catalyst, to form an ester and water.
☐ Esters can be hydrolysed by acid or by a base. Acid hydrolysis is a reversible reaction but base hydrolysis is not reversible.
☐ Elimination of water from an alcohol produces an alkene; the reaction is a dehydration. Dehydration may be carried out by passing alcohol vapour over heated pumice, porous pot or aluminium oxide catalysts.
☐ A primary alcohol can be oxidised to an aldehyde by heating the alcohol gently with acidified potassium dichromate(VI) (and distilling out the aldehyde as it forms – see page **247**).
☐ A primary alcohol can be further oxidised to a carboxylic acid by refluxing the alcohol with excess acidified potassium dichromate(VI).
☐ A secondary alcohol can be oxidised to a ketone by heating the alcohol with acidified potassium dichromate(VI).
☐ Acidified potassium dichromate(VI) changes colour from orange to green when a primary or secondary alcohol is oxidised by it.
☐ Tertiary alcohols cannot be oxidised by refluxing with acidified potassium dichromate(VI).

End-of-chapter questions

1   Pentan-2-ol, butan-1-ol and 2-methylpropan-2-ol are alcohols.
   a For each one give:
      i   molecular formula   [3]
      ii structural formula   [3]
      iii displayed formula   [3]
      iv skeletal formula   [3]
      v   is it a primary, secondary or tertiary alcohol?   [3]
   b Give the general formula that is used to represent alcohols.   [1]
   c Two of the alcohols in this question are isomers of each other. Identify which two and identify
         the type of isomerism they show.   [2]
   d Name the alcohol whose structural formula is $CH_3CH_2COH(CH_3)_2$.   [1]
                                                                              Total = 19

2   Write a balanced chemical equation for each of the following processes. Structural or
   displayed formulae should be used for all organic substances.
   a Making ethanol using ethene as feedstock. Include the formula of the catalyst used. [2]
   b The complete combustion of ethanol in oxygen.   [2]
   c The dehydration of butan-2-ol when passed over hot Al_2O_3. Give three equations, one for each
         of the **three** possible products.   [3]
   d The reaction of ethanoic acid with ethanol. Name the catalyst used, the type of reaction
         and the products.   [4]
                                                                              Total = 11

3   Primary and secondary alcohols can be oxidised by heating with a mixture of potassium dichromate(VI) and dilute sulfuric(VI) acid.
    • A primary alcohol can be oxidised to two different products, depending on the conditions used.
    • A secondary alcohol forms one product when oxidised.
    • Tertiary alcohols cannot be oxidised.
    a What is the formula of potassium dichromate(VI)?   [1]
    b Using a primary alcohol of your choice as example:
        i   give the displayed formulae of the **two** products it could be oxidised to   [2]
        ii   state the conditions needed to give each product   [2]
        iii state which homologous series each product belongs to   [2]
        iv   write a balanced chemical equation for each reaction. The convention [O] may be used for
             the oxidising agent.   [2]
    c Using a secondary alcohol of your choice as example:
        i   give the displayed formula of the product it could be oxidised to   [2]
        ii   state which homologous series the product belongs to   [1]
        iii write a balanced chemical equation for the reaction. The convention [O] may be used for
             the oxidising agent.   [1]
    d Why are tertiary alcohols resistant to oxidation?   [1]
                                                                                    Total = 14

Learning outcomes

Candidates should be able to:

☐ describe
  – the formation of aldehydes and ketones from primary and secondary alcohols respectively using acidified dichromate solution, $Cr_2O_7^{2-}/H^+$
  – the reduction of aldehydes and ketones, e.g. using $NaBH_4$
☐ describe the mechanism of the nucleophilic addition reactions of hydrogen cyanide with aldehydes and ketones
☐ describe the use of 2,4-dinitrophenylhydrazine (2,4-DNPH) reagent to detect the presence of carbonyl compounds

☐ deduce the nature (aldehyde or ketone) of an unknown carbonyl compound from the results of simple tests (i.e. Fehling's and Tollens' reagents; ease of oxidation)
☐ describe the formation of carboxylic acids from alcohols, aldehydes and nitriles
☐ describe the reactions of carboxylic acids in the formation of:
  – salts
  – esters (see Chapter 16).

17.1 Introduction – aldehydes and ketones

You have met aldehydes and ketones, the main classes of carbonyl compounds, in Chapter 16. Remember:

• aldehydes can be formed from the oxidation of primary alcohols
• ketones can be formed from the oxidation of secondary alcohols (see page 243).

In aldehydes the carbon atom in the carbonyl group, C=O, is bonded to a carbon atom and a hydrogen atom. In other words, the carbonyl group is positioned at the end of a carbon chain. In ketones the carbonyl group is attached to two other carbon atoms. Tables 17.1 and 17.2 give examples from the start of these homologous series.

Fact file

Aromatic carbonyl compounds have very distinctive, almond-like odours. Benzaldehyde is used to make almond essence, the flavouring used in some cakes and puddings. Benzaldehyde is also a component of the mixtures that make up the smells and flavours of many fruits such as mangoes, cherries, apricots, plums and peaches.

Figure 17.1 Heptan-2-one, a ketone, is responsible for the smell of blue cheese. Benzaldehyde, an aldehyde, contributes to the flavours of many fruits.

heptan–2–one

benzaldehyde

Name	Structural formula
methanal	HCHO
ethanal	CH_3CHO
propanal	CH_3CH_2CHO
butanal	$CH_3CH_2CH_2CHO$
pentanal	$CH_3CH_2CH_2CH_2CHO$

Table 17.1 The names of aldehydes are derived from the name of the equivalent alkane, with the '-e' at the end of the name replaced by '-al'. Notice that numbers are not needed when naming aldehydes as the carbonyl group is always at the end of the carbon chain.

Name	Structural formula
propanone	CH_3COCH_3
butanone	$CH_3COCH_2CH_3$
pentan-2-one	$CH_3COCH_2CH_2CH_3$
pentan-3-one	$CH_3CH_2COCH_2CH_3$

Table 17.2 Ketones are named by replacing the '-e' with '-one'. However, in ketone molecules larger than butanone we need to indicate the position of the carbonyl group.

Check-up

1 a Name the following compounds:
   i $CH_3CH_2CH_2CH_2CH_2CHO$
   ii $CH_3CH_2CH_2CH_2CH_2CH_2COCH_3$
  b Draw the displayed formula of:
   i methanal
   ii propanal
   iii pentan-3-one.
  c Draw the skeletal formula of the compounds listed in part **a**.

17.2 Preparation of aldehydes and ketones

1 Oxidation of a primary alcohol

The general equation for the reaction in which an aldehyde is made from a primary alcohol is:

primary alcohol + oxygen atom from oxidising agent
$\rightarrow$ aldehyde + water

For example:

$$CH_3CH_2CH_2OH + [O] \rightarrow CH_3CH_2CHO + H_2O$$
propan-1-ol   propanal

The oxidising agent used is a solution of potassium dichromate(VI), which is orange, acidified with dilute sulfuric acid. To make the aldehyde, the primary alcohol is heated **gently** with acidified dichromate solution. The reaction mixture turns green as the orange dichromate ions, $Cr_2O_7^{2-}$(aq) ions are reduced to Cr^{3+}(aq) ions.

The oxidising agent is added one drop at a time to the warm alcohol. The aldehyde product has a lower boiling point than the alcohol. The aldehyde must be distilled off as it forms. The formation of ethanal is shown in Figure 17.2.

If the ethanal formed is not distilled off as soon as it is formed, further heating with acidified dichromate solution will oxidise it to ethanoic acid.

2 Oxidation of a secondary alcohol

The general equation for making a ketone is:

secondary alcohol + oxygen atom from oxidising agent
$\rightarrow$ ketone + water

For example:

$$CH_3CH(OH)CH_3 + [O] \rightarrow CH_3COCH_3 + H_2O$$
propan-2-ol   propanone

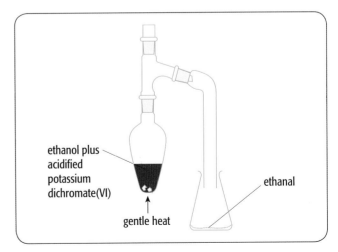

ethanol plus acidified potassium dichromate(VI)

ethanal

gentle heat

Figure 17.2 Distilling off and collecting the aldehyde, ethanal, formed in the mild oxidation of a primary alcohol, ethanol. The aqueous ethanal formed smells like rotting apples.

Once again the oxidising agent used is a solution of potassium dichromate(VI), acidified with dilute sulfuric acid. To produce a ketone this oxidising agent must be heated with a secondary alcohol. The ketone formed **cannot** be further oxidised, even if we reflux the reaction mixture and add excess oxidising agent. Therefore we do not need to distil out the ketone product immediately.

Check-up

2 a i Write a balanced equation for the oxidation of ethanol to ethanal, using [O] to represent an oxygen atom from the oxidising agent.

    ii Give practical details to explain how you would use the reaction described in part **a i** to prepare and collect a sample of ethanal.

b i Write a balanced equation for the oxidation of butan-2-ol to butanone, using [O] to represent an oxygen atom from the oxidising agent.

    ii What do you observe in the reaction vessel if the oxidising agent used in part **b i** is potassium dichromate(VI) solution, acidified with dilute sulfuric acid, and the reaction mixture is heated?

17.3 Reduction of aldehydes and ketones

Chemical reduction of an aldehyde or ketone produces an alcohol.

    aldehyde + reducing agent → primary alcohol

    ketone + reducing agent → secondary alcohol

The reducing agent used is usually sodium tetrahydridoborate, $NaBH_4$. The aldehyde or ketone is warmed with an aqueous solution of sodium tetrahydridoborate in the reduction reaction. In the same way that we have used the symbol [O] in organic oxidation equations, we use the symbol [H] in reduction equations. [H] represents a hydrogen atom from the reducing agent. Look at the examples below:

$$CH_3CHO + 2[H] \rightarrow CH_3CH_2OH$$
$$\text{ethanal} \qquad\qquad\qquad \text{ethanol}$$

$$CH_3COCH_3 + 2[H] \rightarrow CH_3CH(OH)CH_3$$
$$\text{propanone} \qquad\qquad\qquad \text{propan-2-ol}$$

The reduction reaction can be thought of as a **nucleophilic addition** reaction, where the nucleophile is the H^- ion.

Check-up

3 a Write a balanced equation for the reaction that takes place when propanal is warmed with a solution of sodium tetrahydridoborate, using the symbol [H] to represent a hydrogen atom from the reducing agent.

b Name the product formed in the reduction reaction if pentan-3-one is warmed with a solution of sodium tetrahydridoborate.

17.4 Nucleophilic addition with HCN

The addition reactions we have met so far have involved electrophilic addition across the C=C bond in alkene molecules (see page 222). Aldehydes and ketones both undergo addition reactions with hydrogen cyanide, HCN. In this case, addition of HCN takes place across the C=O bond. However, the attack is by a nucleophile, not an electrophile. We can show this using the addition reaction of propanal with HCN. The HCN is generated in the reaction vessel by the reaction of potassium cyanide, KCN, and dilute sulfuric acid.

CH₃CH₂
    \\
     C=O + HCN ⟶ CH₃CH₂ — C — C≡N
    / |
   H   H

propanal   2-hydroxybutanenitrile

Notice that a carbon atom has been added to the propanal molecule. This is a useful reaction in synthetic chemistry as it increases the length of the hydrocarbon chain by one carbon atom. The nitrile group (—C≡N) added can then be easily hydrolysed to a carboxylic acid or reduced to an amine. The hydrolysis can be carried out by refluxing with dilute hydrochloric acid:

$$-CN + H^+ + 2H_2O \rightarrow -COOH + NH_4^+$$

The reduction of the nitrile group to an amine can be carried out using sodium and ethanol:

$$-CN + 4[H] \rightarrow -CH_2NH_2$$

Mechanism of nucleophilic addition

The carbonyl group, C=O, in aldehydes and ketones is polarised due to the high electronegativity of the oxygen atom. The electrons in the C=O bond are drawn nearer to the O atom, giving it a partial negative charge and leaving the C atom with a partial positive charge. This makes the C atom open to attack by a nucleophile such as the cyanide ion, CN⁻.

The negatively charged intermediate formed in the first step in the mechanism is highly reactive and quickly reacts with an H⁺ ion (from HCN, from dilute acid or from water present in the reaction mixture). This forms the **hydroxynitrile** product. For example:

Fact file

Hydrogen cyanide is a highly toxic, colourless gas which smells of almonds. It contributes to the flavour of some fruits but is not a danger as it is only present in very low concentrations.

Check-up

4 a Name the organic product that would be formed in the nucleophilic addition of HCN to:
  i ethanal
  ii propanone.
 b Use diagrams and curly arrows to describe the mechanism of the reaction in part **a i**.

17.5 Testing for aldehydes and ketones

Testing for the carbonyl group

The presence of a carbonyl group in an aldehyde or ketone can be easily tested for by adding a solution of 2,4-dinitrophenylhydrazine (often abbreviated to 2,4-DNPH). If an aldehyde or ketone is present, a deep-orange precipitate is formed (Figure 17.3).

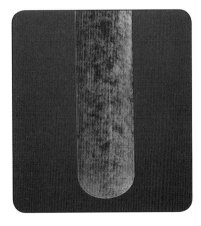

Figure 17.3 The orange precipitate formed from 2,4-DNPH in a test with propanone, a ketone.

The structure of 2,4-dinitrophenylhydrazine is:

The precipitate formed can be purified by recrystallisation and its melting point can be measured experimentally. The identity of the compound that precipitated out can then be found by referring to melting point data. From this, the specific aldehyde or ketone used in the test can be identified.

The reaction of an aldehyde or ketone with 2,4-dinitrophenylhydrazine is an example of a **condensation reaction**. In a condensation reaction two molecules join together and in the process eliminate a small molecule, in this case water. The equation for the reaction of ethanal with 2,4-DNPH is:

atoms lost in condensation reaction to form water

2,4-dinitrophenylhydrazine   2,4-dinitrophenylhydrazone

Other classes of organic compound that also contain the carbonyl group (such as carboxylic acids and esters) do not form precipitates.

Distinguishing between aldehydes and ketones

As we saw on pages 247–8, aldehydes can be further oxidised to form carboxylic acids but ketones cannot be oxidised easily. We can use this difference to distinguish between an aldehyde and a ketone in simple chemical tests. The two tests most commonly used involve Tollens' reagent and Fehling's solution.

Testing with Tollens' reagent
Tollens' reagent is an aqueous solution of silver nitrate in excess ammonia solution, sometimes called ammoniacal silver nitrate solution. The silver ions, Ag^+, in the solution act as a mild oxidising agent. When warmed, the Ag^+ ions will oxidise an aldehyde to form a carboxylate ion.

Under alkaline conditions any carboxylic acid formed is immediately neutralised to the carboxylate ion, $-COO^-$; H^+ is removed from $-COOH$ and a salt is formed.

In the redox reaction with an aldehyde, the Ag^+ ions themselves are reduced to silver atoms. The silver atoms form a 'mirror' on the inside of the tube, giving a positive test for an aldehyde (Figure 17.4).

There will be no change observed when a ketone is warmed with Tollens' reagent. It remains a colourless mixture in the test tube.

Figure 17.4 The 'before' and 'after' observations when Tollens' reagent is warmed with an aldehyde, such as ethanal.

Testing with Fehling's solution
Fehling's solution is an alkaline solution containing copper(II) ions. When warmed with an aldehyde the Cu^{2+} ions act as an oxidising agent. The aldehyde is oxidised to a carboxylate ion whilst the Cu^{2+} ions are reduced to Cu^+ ions. The clear blue Fehling's solution turns an opaque red/orange colour as a precipitate of copper(I) oxide forms throughout the solution (Figure 17.5).

Once again, ketones are not oxidised so the Fehling's solution remains blue when warmed.

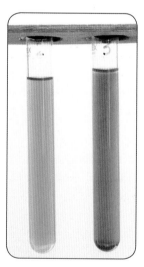

Figure 17.5 The 'before' (left) and 'after' (right) observations when Fehling's solution is warmed with an aldehyde, such as ethanal.

5 The melting points of the derivatives of the reaction between 2,4-DNPH and various aldehydes and ketones are shown in the table.

Product of reaction between 2,4-DNPH with …	Melting point / °C
ethanal	168
propanal	155
butanal	126
propanone	126
butanone	116

a What would be observed when each of the carbonyl compounds in the table is mixed with 2,4-DNPH?

continued ⋯⟶

b A derivative was formed between 2,4-DNPH and an unknown carbonyl compound.
  i The melting point of the derivative was 126 °C. What does this result tell you?
  ii The unknown carbonyl compound formed an orange precipitate when warmed with Fehling's solution. Name the unknown compound.
  iii Describe and explain the different results obtained when the compound named in part **b ii** is warmed with Tollens' reagent in a test tube and then the same test is performed on butanone.
c Write a half-equation to show silver ions acting as an oxidising agent in a positive test for an aldehyde.
d Write a half-equation to show copper(II) ions acting as an oxidising agent in a positive test for an aldehyde.

Summary

☐ Aldehydes and ketones contain the carbonyl group, $C=O$:
  – in aldehydes, the carbonyl group is joined to just one other carbon atom
  – in ketones, the carbonyl group is joined to two other carbon atoms.
☐ The names of aldehydes are derived from the name of the alkane with the '-e' at the end replaced by '-al'. Similarly, ketones are named with the '-e' replaced by '-one'.
☐ Carbonyl compounds are readily reduced by $NaBH_4$:
  – reduction of an aldehyde forms a primary alcohol
  – reduction of a ketone produces a secondary alcohol.
☐ Aldehydes are readily oxidised under mild conditions to carboxylic acids. Ketones are not oxidised under mild conditions.
☐ The polar nature of the carbonyl group in aldehydes and ketones enables them to undergo nucleophilic addition by reacting with the cyanide ions (CN^-) from HCN. The product is a hydroxynitrile.
☐ The reagent 2,4-dinitrophenylhydrazine (2,4-DNPH) can be used to identify the presence of a carbonyl group in an aldehyde or ketone. It produces an orange precipitate. The melting point of the product is used to identify particular aldehydes and ketones.
☐ As aldehydes are readily oxidised, they may be distinguished from ketones on warming with suitable oxidising reagents:
  – with aldehydes, Tollens' reagent produces a silver mirror inside a warmed test tube and Fehling's solution turns from a blue solution to a red/orange precipitate when warmed
  – with ketones, there is no oxidation reaction so no changes are observed when ketones are warmed with Tollens' reagent or Fehling's solution.

End-of-chapter questions

1 a Name the following compounds:
   i CH_3COCH_3 [1]
   ii $CH_3CH_2CH_2OH$ [1]
   iii CH_3CHO [1]
   iv $CH_3CH(OH)CH_3$ [1]
   v $CH_3COCH_2CH_3$ [1]
   vi CH_3CH_2CHO [1]
   b Which of the compounds in part **a** are alcohols and which are carbonyl compounds? [1]
   c Which of the carbonyl compounds in part **a** are aldehydes and which are ketones? [1]
   d Two of the compounds in part **a** could be made by oxidising two of the others.
   i Identify these four compounds, stating which could be made from which. [4]
   ii State the reagents and conditions you would use to carry out each oxidation and write a
      balanced chemical equation for each oxidation. [O] can be used in oxidation equations. [4]
   e Ethanol could be made by the reduction of one of the compounds in part **a**.
   i Identify which compound this is. [1]
   ii State the reagent you would use to carry out the reduction. [1]
   iii Write a balanced chemical equation for the reduction. [H] can be used in reduction equations. [1]

Total = 19

2 a What reagent would you add to an unknown compound to see if it contains a carbonyl group? [1]
   b What result would you get if the unknown compound does contain a carbonyl group? [1]
   c Why would it be useful to find the melting point of the product of this test? [1]

Total = 3

3 a Draw the skeletal formulae of:
   i pentan-2-one [1]
   ii pentan-3-one [1]
   iii pentanal. [1]
   b Describe the results you would expect to see if pentan-3-one and pentanal are separately
   treated with Tollens' reagent. Where a reaction takes place, name the organic product and
   name the type of reaction that takes place. [4]

Total = 7

4 Ethanol can be made from ethanal using sodium tetrahydridoborate(III) as a reducing agent.
   a Give the formula of sodium tetrahydridoborate(III). [1]
   b What other reagent is necessary for the reaction to take place? [1]
   c The reaction mechanism proceeds in a similar way to the steps in the reaction of ethanal
   with HCN, but the initial attack is by the H^- ion instead of the CN^- ion. The intermediate
   then gains an H^+ ion from a water molecule to form the product, ethanol. Name the mechanism
   and describe it as fully as you can, using curly arrows to show the movement of electron pairs. [7]

Total = 9

5   A compound, X, has the following percentage composition: 66.7% carbon, 11.1% hydrogen
    and 22.2% oxygen.
    a Calculate the empirical formula of X.   [3]
    b The relative molecular mass of X is 72. Calculate the molecular formula.   [1]
    c Give the structural formulae and names of the three isomers of X that are carbonyl compounds. [3]
    d Explain how you could identify X using chemical means.   [5]
                                                                          Total = 12

Learning outcomes

Candidates should be able to:

☐ explain and use the term **lattice energy**

☐ explain and use the terms **ionisation energy, enthalpy change of atomisation** and **electron affinity**

☐ construct Born–Haber cycles

☐ use Born–Haber cycles to calculate lattice energies

☐ explain, in qualitative terms, the effect of ionic charge and ionic radius on the numerical magnitude of a lattice energy

☐ interpret and explain qualitatively the trend in the thermal stability of the nitrates and carbonates of Group II

elements in terms of the charge density of the cation and the polarisability of the large anion

☐ apply Hess's law to construct energy cycles to determine enthalpy changes of solution and enthalpy changes of hydration

☐ interpret and explain qualitatively the variation in solubility of Group II sulfates in terms of the relative values of the enthalpy change of hydration and the corresponding lattice energy.

18.1 Introducing lattice energy

In Chapters **4** and **5** you studied ionic bonding and the lattice structure of sodium chloride. When ions combine to form a crystalline lattice there is a huge release of energy. The reaction is highly exothermic. The energy given out when ions of opposite charges come together to form a crystalline lattice is called the **lattice energy**, $\Delta H^{\ominus}_{\text{latt}}$.

> Lattice energy is the enthalpy change when 1 mole of an ionic compound is formed from its gaseous ions under standard conditions.

Figure 18.1 A model of the sodium chloride lattice. The energy released when gaseous ions combine to form a lattice is called the lattice energy.

Equations describing the lattice energy of sodium chloride and magnesium chloride are shown here.

$$\text{Na}^+(g) + \text{Cl}^-(g) \rightarrow \text{NaCl}(s) \qquad \Delta H^{\ominus}_{\text{latt}} = -787 \, \text{kJ} \, \text{mol}^{-1}$$

$$\text{Mg}^{2+}(g) + 2\text{Cl}^-(g) \rightarrow \text{MgCl}_2(s) \quad \Delta H^{\ominus}_{\text{latt}} = -2526 \, \text{kJ} \, \text{mol}^{-1}$$

Note that:

- it is the **gaseous** ions that combine
- the lattice energy is always exothermic: the value of $\Delta H^{\ominus}_{\text{latt}}$ is always negative, because the definition specifies the bonding together of ions, not the separation of ions.

The large exothermic value of the lattice energy shows that the ionic lattice is very stable with respect to its gaseous ions. The more exothermic the lattice energy, the stronger the ionic bonding in the lattice.

It is impossible to determine the lattice energy of a compound by a single direct experiment. We can, however, calculate a value for $\Delta H^{\ominus}_{\text{latt}}$ using several experimental values and an energy cycle called a Born–Haber cycle. In order to do this, we first need to introduce two more types of enthalpy change.

Check-up

1 **a** Give values for the standard conditions of temperature and pressure.

   b Write equations describing the lattice energy of:

   i magnesium oxide

   ii potassium bromide

   iii sodium sulfide.

Fact file

The quantity that we have defined as lattice energy is more accurately called the lattice enthalpy. However, the term lattice energy is commonly applied to lattice enthalpy as well. Lattice energy is the internal energy change when 1 mole of an ionic compound is formed from its gaseous ions at 0 K. Lattice enthalpy values are very close to the corresponding lattice energy values. You can find out more about internal energy change by using a search engine on the Internet.

b Write equations, including state symbols, that represent the enthalpy change of atomisation of:
  i oxygen
  ii barium
  iii bromine.
c What is the numerical value of the enthalpy change of atomisation of helium? Explain your answer.

18.2 Enthalpy change of atomisation and electron affinity

Enthalpy change of atomisation

The standard **enthalpy change of atomisation**, $\Delta H^{\ominus}_{at}$, is the enthalpy change when 1 mole of gaseous atoms is formed from its element under standard conditions.

The standard enthalpy change of atomisation of lithium relates to the equation:

$$Li(s) \rightarrow Li(g) \qquad \Delta H^{\ominus}_{at} = +161\,kJ\,mol^{-1}$$

and the standard enthalpy change of atomisation of chlorine relates to the equation:

$$\tfrac{1}{2}Cl_2(g) \rightarrow Cl(g) \qquad \Delta H^{\ominus}_{at} = +122\,kJ\,mol^{-1}$$

Values of $\Delta H^{\ominus}_{at}$ are always positive (endothermic) because energy must be supplied to break the bonds holding the atoms in the element together.

Check-up

2 a The bond energy of the chlorine molecule is $+244\,kJ\,mol^{-1}$. Why is the enthalpy change of atomisation half this value?

continued ⋯⟶

Electron affinity

The energy change occurring when a gaseous non-metal atom accepts one electron is called the **electron affinity**. The symbol for electron affinity is $\Delta H^{\ominus}_{ea}$.

The first electron affinity, $\Delta H^{\ominus}_{ea1}$, is the enthalpy change when 1 mole of electrons is added to 1 mole of gaseous atoms to form 1 mole of gaseous 1– ions under standard conditions.

Equations representing the first electron affinity of chlorine and sulfur are;

$$Cl(g) + e^- \rightarrow Cl^-(g) \qquad \Delta H^{\ominus}_{ea1} = -348\,kJ\,mol^{-1}$$

$$S(g) + e^- \rightarrow S^-(g) \qquad \Delta H^{\ominus}_{ea1} = -200\,kJ\,mol^{-1}$$

Note that:
• the change is from gaseous atoms to gaseous 1– ions
• the enthalpy change for the first electron affinity, $\Delta H^{\ominus}_{ea1}$ is generally exothermic: $\Delta H^{\ominus}_{ea}$ is negative.

When an element forms an ion with more than one negative charge, we must use successive electron affinities; (this is rather like the successive ionisation energies we used on page **36**). The 1st, 2nd and 3rd electron affinities have symbols $\Delta H^{\ominus}_{ea1}$, $\Delta H^{\ominus}_{ea2}$ and $\Delta H^{\ominus}_{ea3}$.

The **second electron affinity**, $\Delta H^{\ominus}_{ea2}$, is the enthalpy change when 1 mole of electrons is added to 1 mole of gaseous 1– ions to form 1 mole of gaseous 2– ions under standard conditions.

The equations representing the 1st and 2nd electron affinities of oxygen are:

1st electron affinity:
$$O(g) + e^- \rightarrow O^-(g) \quad \Delta H^{\ominus}_{ea1} = -141\,kJ\,mol^{-1}$$

2nd electron affinity:
$$O^-(g) + e^- \rightarrow O^{2-}(g) \quad \Delta H^{\ominus}_{ea2} = +798\,kJ\,mol^{-1}$$

Note that 2nd electron affinities are always endothermic ($\Delta H^{\ominus}_{ea2}$ is positive), and so are 3rd electron affinities.

The overall enthalpy change in forming an oxide ion, O^{2-}, from an oxygen atom is found by adding together the 1st and 2nd electron affinities:

$$O(g) + 2e^- \rightarrow O^{2-}(g)$$

$$\Delta H^{\ominus}_{ea1} + \Delta H^{\ominus}_{ea2} = (-141) + (+798) = +657\,kJ\,mol^{-1}$$

Check-up

3 a Suggest why the 2nd and 3rd electron affinities are always endothermic.

b The 1st electron affinity of sulfur is $-200\,kJ\,mol^{-1}$. The second electron affinity of sulfur is $+640\,kJ\,mol^{-1}$. Calculate a value for the enthalpy change $S(g) + 2e^- \rightarrow S^{2-}(g)$

c Write equations representing:
  i the 1st electron affinity of iodine
  ii the 2nd electron affinity of sulfur.

18.3 Born–Haber cycles

Components of the Born–Haber cycle

We have seen how we can apply Hess's law in energy cycles to work out enthalpy changes (page 101). A **Born–Haber cycle** is a particular type of enthalpy cycle used to calculate lattice energy. In simple terms it can be represented by Figure 18.2.

We can determine the lattice energy of a compound if we know:

• its enthalpy change of formation, $\Delta H^{\ominus}_f$
• the enthalpy changes involved in changing the elements from their standard states to their gaseous ions, $\Delta H^{\ominus}_1$.

According to Hess's law, Figure 18.2 shows that

$$\Delta H^{\ominus}_1 + \Delta H^{\ominus}_{latt} = \Delta H^{\ominus}_f$$

Rearranging this equation we get:

$$\Delta H^{\ominus}_{latt} = \Delta H^{\ominus}_f - \Delta H^{\ominus}_1$$

The enthalpy change $\Delta H^{\ominus}_1$ involves several steps.

Taking lithium fluoride as an example, the relevant enthalpy cycle can be written to show these steps (Figure 18.3).

The enthalpy changes need to calculate $\Delta H^{\ominus}_1$ are as follows.

Step 1 Convert solid lithium to gaseous lithium atoms: the enthalpy change required is the enthalpy change of atomisation of lithium, $\Delta H^{\ominus}_{at}$.

$$Li(s) \rightarrow Li(g) \qquad \Delta H^{\ominus}_{at} = +161\,kJ\,mol^{-1}$$

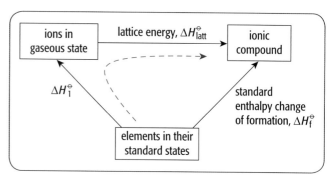

Figure 18.2 A simple enthalpy cycle that can be used to calculate lattice energy. The dashed line shows the two-step route: using Hess's law, $\Delta H^{\ominus}_1 + \Delta H^{\ominus}_{latt} = \Delta H^{\ominus}_f$.

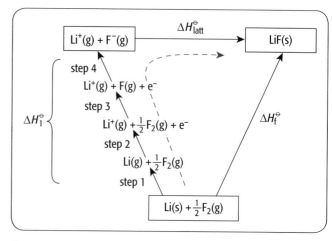

Figure 18.3 An enthalpy cycle that can be used to calculate the lattice energy of lithium fluoride. The dashed line shows the two-step route.

Step 2 Convert gaseous lithium atoms to gaseous lithium ions: the enthalpy change required is the 1st ionisation energy of lithium, $\Delta H_{i1}^{\ominus}$ (see page **34**).

$$Li(g) \rightarrow Li^{+}(g) + e^{-} \qquad \Delta H_{i1}^{\ominus} = +520 \, kJ \, mol^{-1}$$

Step 3 Convert fluorine molecules to fluorine atoms: the enthalpy change required is the enthalpy change of atomisation of fluorine, $\Delta H_{at}^{\ominus}$.

$$\tfrac{1}{2}F_2(g) \rightarrow F(g) \qquad \Delta H_{at}^{\ominus} = +79 \, kJ \, mol^{-1}$$

Step 4 Convert gaseous fluorine atoms to gaseous fluoride ions: the enthalpy change required is the 1st electron affinity of fluorine, $\Delta H_{ea1}^{\ominus}$.

$$F(g) + e^{-} \rightarrow F^{-}(g) \qquad \Delta H_{ea1}^{\ominus} = -328 \, kJ \, mol^{-1}$$

Step 5 By adding all these values together, we get a value for $\Delta H_1^{\ominus}$.

The enthalpy change of formation of lithium fluoride is $-617 \, kJ \, mol^{-1}$. We now have all the information we need to calculate the lattice energy.

Calculating lattice energies

Applying Hess's law to find the lattice energy of lithium fluoride:

$$\Delta H_{latt}^{\ominus} = \Delta H_f^{\ominus} - \Delta H_1^{\ominus}.$$

We know that:

$$\Delta H_1^{\ominus} = \Delta H_{at}^{\ominus}[Li] + \Delta H_{i1}^{\ominus}[Li] + \Delta H_{at}^{\ominus}[F] + \Delta H_{ea1}^{\ominus}[F]$$

So

$$\Delta H_{latt}^{\ominus}$$
$$= \Delta H_f^{\ominus} - \{\Delta H_{at}^{\ominus}[Li] + \Delta H_{i1}^{\ominus}[Li] + \Delta H_{at}^{\ominus}[F] + \Delta H_{ea1}^{\ominus}[F]\}$$

Putting in the figures:

$$\Delta H_{latt}^{\ominus} = (-617) - \{(+161) + (+520) + (+79) + (-328)\}$$
$$= +432$$

$$\Delta H_{latt}^{\ominus} = (-617) - (+432) = -1049 \, kJ \, mol^{-1}$$

Note: take care to account for the signs of the enthalpy changes. The values of the enthalpy changes of formation and the electron affinity may be negative or positive.

Check-up

4 a Write equations to represent:
   i the 1st ionisation energy of caesium
   ii the 3rd ionisation energy of aluminium
   iii the enthalpy change of formation of calcium oxide
   iv the enthalpy change of formation of iron(III) chloride
  b Calculate the lattice energy for sodium chloride, given that:

$$\Delta H_f^{\ominus}[NaCl] = -411 \, kJ \, mol^{-1}$$

$$\Delta H_{at}^{\ominus}[Na] = +107 \, kJ \, mol^{-1}$$

$$\Delta H_{at}^{\ominus}[Cl] = +122 \, kJ \, mol^{-1}$$

$$\Delta H_{i1}^{\ominus}[Na] = +496 \, kJ \, mol^{-1}$$

$$\Delta H_{ea1}^{\ominus}[Cl] = -348 \, kJ \, mol^{-1}$$

Fact file

Lattice energies can be calculated theoretically using a complex equation. The lattice energy is inversely proportional to the sum of the radii of the cation and the anion. The number of charges on each ion as well as the way the ions are arranged in the crystal are also taken into account.

The Born–Haber cycle as an energy level diagram

We can show the Born–Haber cycle as an energy level diagram (Figure **18.4**). This is the best, and clearest, type of diagram for a Born–Haber cycle. You should therefore choose to draw this type of diagram in an examination if you are asked to construct a Born–Haber cycle.

To draw the cycle you:
- start by putting down the elements in their standard state on the left-hand side
- add the other enthalpy changes in the order of steps 1 to 4 shown in Figure **18.4**
- complete the cycle by adding the enthalpy change of formation and lattice energy.

Note that the arrows going upwards represent an increase in energy ($\Delta H^{\ominus}$ is positive) and the arrows going downwards represent a decrease in energy ($\Delta H^{\ominus}$ is negative).

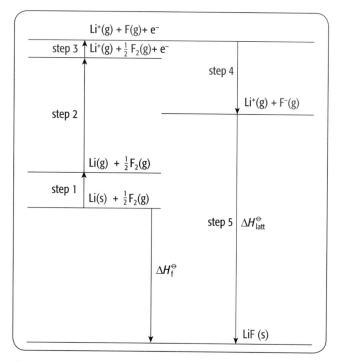

Figure 18.4 Born–Haber cycle for lithium fluoride.

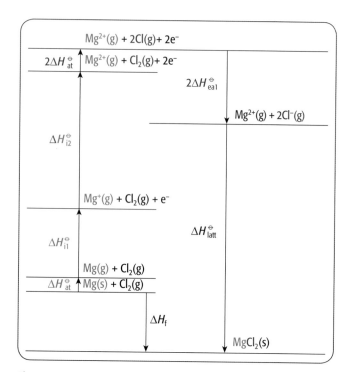

Figure 18.5 Born–Haber cycle for magnesium chloride.

Check-up

5 a Draw a fully labelled Born–Haber cycle for potassium bromide, naming each step.
b State the name of the enthalpy changes represented by the following equations:
  i $\frac{1}{2}I_2(s) \rightarrow I(g)$
  ii $N(g) + e^- \rightarrow N^-(g)$
  iii $Sr(s) + Cl_2(g) \rightarrow SrCl_2(s)$
  iv $Cd^{2+}(g) + 2Cl^-(g) \rightarrow CdCl_2(s)$

The Born–Haber cycle for magnesium chloride

The Born–Haber cycle for magnesium chloride is shown in Figure 18.5.

There are a few minor differences between this cycle and the one for lithium fluoride.

1 The magnesium ion is Mg^{2+}, so the 1st and the 2nd ionisation energies need to be taken into account:

$$Mg(g) \rightarrow Mg^+(g) + e^- \qquad \Delta H^\ominus_{i1} = +736 \, kJ \, mol^{-1}$$

$$Mg^+(g) \rightarrow Mg^{2+}(g) + e^- \qquad \Delta H^\ominus_{i2} = +1450 \, kJ \, mol^{-1}$$

2 There are two chloride ions in $MgCl_2$, so the values of the enthalpy change of atomisation and the first electron affinity of chlorine must be multiplied by 2.

$$Cl_2(g) \rightarrow 2Cl(g) \qquad 2\Delta H^\ominus_{at} = 2 \times (+122) = +244 \, kJ \, mol^{-1}$$

$$2Cl(g) + 2e^- \rightarrow 2Cl^-(g)$$
$$2\Delta H^\ominus_{ea1} = 2 \times (-348) = -696 \, kJ \, mol^{-1}$$

In order to calculate the lattice energy we need some additional information:

$$\Delta H^\ominus_f \, [MgCl_2] = -641 \, kJ \, mol^{-1}$$

$$\Delta H^\ominus_{at} \, [Mg] = +148 \, kJ \, mol^{-1}$$

According to Hess's law:

$$\Delta H^\ominus_{latt} = \Delta H^\ominus_f - \{\Delta H^\ominus_{at} [Mg] + \Delta H^\ominus_{i1} [Mg] + \Delta H^\ominus_{i2} [Mg] + 2\Delta H^\ominus_{at} [Cl] + 2\Delta H^\ominus_{ea1} [Cl]\}$$

$$\Delta H^\ominus_{latt} = (-641) - \underbrace{\{(+148) + (+736) + (+1450) + 2 \times (122) + 2 \times (-348)\}}_{= +1882}$$

$$\Delta H^\ominus_{latt} = (-641) - (+1882) = -2523 \, kJ \, mol^{-1}$$

Constructing a Born–Haber cycle for aluminium oxide

Aluminium oxide, Al$_2$O$_3$, contains two aluminium ions (Al^{3+}) and three oxide ions (O^{2-}).

• In order to form 1 mole of gaseous Al^{3+} ions from 1 mole of Al(s), we apply the following sequence of enthalpy changes:

$$Al(s) \xrightarrow[+326\,kJ\,mol^{-1}]{\Delta H^{\ominus}_{at}} Al(g) \xrightarrow[+577\,kJ\,mol^{-1}]{\Delta H^{\ominus}_{i1}} Al^{+}(g) \xrightarrow[+1820\,kJ\,mol^{-1}]{\Delta H^{\ominus}_{i2}} Al^{2+}(g) \xrightarrow[+2740\,kJ\,mol^{-1}]{\Delta H^{\ominus}_{i3}} Al^{3+}(g)$$

• In order to form 1 mole of gaseous O^{2-} ions from oxygen molecules, we apply the following sequence of enthalpy changes:

$$\tfrac{1}{2}O_2(g) \xrightarrow[+249\,kJ\,mol^{-1}]{\Delta H^{\ominus}_{at}} O(g) \xrightarrow[-141\,kJ\,mol^{-1}]{\Delta H^{\ominus}_{ea1}} O^{-}(g) \xrightarrow[+798\,kJ\,mol^{-1}]{\Delta H^{\ominus}_{ea2}} O^{2-}(g)$$

18.4 Factors affecting the value of lattice energy

Lattice energy arises from the electrostatic force of attraction of oppositely charged ions when the crystalline lattice is formed. The size and charge of these ions can affect the value of the lattice energy.

Lattice energy and ion size

As the size of the ion increases, the lattice energy becomes less exothermic. This applies to both anions and cations. Figure 18.6 shows that:

• for any given anion, e.g. F^{-}, the lattice energy gets less exothermic as the size of the cation increases from Li^{+} to Cs^{+}

• for any given cation, e.g. Li^{+}, the lattice energy gets less exothermic as the size of the anion increases from F^{-} to I^{-}.

Ions with the same charge have a lower charge density if their radius is larger. This is because the same charge is spread out over a larger volume. A lower charge density results in weaker electrostatic forces of attraction in the ionic lattice. Sodium fluoride has a less exothermic lattice energy than lithium fluoride. This reflects the lower charge density on sodium ions compared with lithium ions.

Lattice energy and charge on the ions

The lattice energy becomes more exothermic as the charge on the ion increases.

We can see this by comparing lithium fluoride, LiF, with magnesium oxide, MgO. These compounds have the same arrangement of ions in their lattice structure. The cations, Li^{+} and Mg^{2+} have similar sizes. The anions

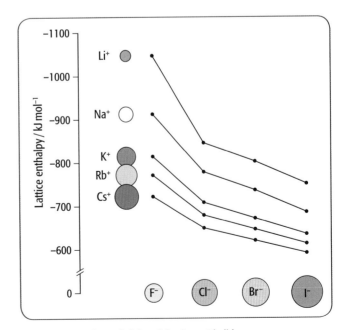

Figure 18.6 Lattice enthalpies of the Group I halides.

F^- and O^{2-} are fairly similar in size (although they are much larger than the cations). The major physical difference between LiF and MgO is the charge on the ions. This affects the lattice energy:

$$\Delta H^\ominus_{latt}[LiF] = -1049\,kJ\,mol^{-1}$$

$$\Delta H^\ominus_{latt}[MgO] = -3923\,kJ\,mol^{-1}$$

Magnesium oxide has a greater lattice energy than lithium fluoride. The doubly charged Mg^{2+} and O^{2-} ions in magnesium oxide attract each other more strongly than the singly charged ions of the same size in LiF. For ions of similar size, the greater the charge on the ion, the higher the charge density. This results in stronger ionic bonds being formed.

Check-up

8 **a** For each pair of compounds, suggest which will have the most exothermic lattice energy.
   i KCl and BaO (ionic radii are similar)
   ii MgI_2 and SrI_2
   iii CaO and NaCl (ionic radii are similar).
 b Place the following compounds in order of increasingly exothermic lattice energy. Explain your answer.
   LiF   MgO   RbCl

9 Students taking physics A-level learn that the electrostatic force between two charged particles is proportional to $\dfrac{Q_1 \times Q_2}{r^2}$, where Q_1 and Q_2 are the charges on the particles and r is the distance between the centres of the particles. Use this relationship to explain why:
 a magnesium oxide has a greater lattice energy than lithium fluoride
 b lithium fluoride has a greater lattice energy than potassium bromide.

18.5 Ion polarisation

In our model of an ionic lattice, we have thought of the ions as being spherical in shape. This is not always the case. In some cases, the positive charge on the cation in an ionic lattice may attract the electrons in the anion towards it. This results in a distortion of the electron cloud of the anion and the anion is no longer spherical (Figure 18.7). We call this distortion, **ion polarisation**. The ability of a cation to attract electrons and distort an anion is called the **polarising power** of the cation.

Figure 18.7 Ion polarisation. A small highly charged cation can distort the shape of the anion.

Factors affecting ion polarisation

The degree of polarisation of an anion depends on:
• the charge density of the cation and
• the ease with which the anion can be polarised – its polarisability.

An anion is more likely to be polarised if:
• the cation is small
• the cation has a charge of 2+ or 3+
• the anion is large
• the anion has a charge of 2– or 3–

Fact file
Kazimierz Fajans was born in Poland but worked mainly in Germany and the USA. He drew up a set of rules about the polarisation of a negative ion by a positive ion.

Fact file
A small highly charged cation such as Fe^{3+} can attract electrons and distort a larger anion to such an extent that the bond formed has a considerable amount of covalent character. Pure ionic bonding and pure covalent bonding are extremes. Many ionic compounds have some covalent character due to ion polarisation. Many covalent compounds have some degree of charge separation, i.e. they are polar, due to bond polarisation (see Chapter **4**, page **62**).

Check-up

10 a Explain why a cation with a smaller ionic radius has a higher charge density.

b Which one of the following ions will be the best polariser of the large nitrate ion? Explain your answer.

Cs⁺   Li⁺   Na⁺   K⁺

c Which one of these ions will be most polarised by a Mg²⁺ ion? Explain your answer.

Br⁻   Cl⁻   F⁻   I⁻

The thermal stability of Group II carbonates and nitrates

The Group II carbonates decompose to their oxides and carbon dioxide on heating. For example:

$$CaCO_3(s) \xrightarrow{heat} CaO(s) + CO_2(g)$$

Table **18.1** shows the decomposition temperature and enthalpy change of reaction, $\Delta H_r^\ominus$, for some Group II carbonates.

The relative ease of thermal decomposition is shown by the values of the enthalpy changes of reaction. The more positive the enthalpy change, the more stable is the carbonate relative to its oxide and carbon dioxide. This is also reflected by the decomposition temperatures:

Group II carbonate	Decomposition temperature / °C	Enthalpy change of reaction / kJ mol⁻¹
magnesium carbonate	540	+117
calcium carbonate	900	+176
strontium carbonate	1280	+238
barium carbonate	1360	+268

Table 18.1 Enthalpy change of reaction values for the decomposition of some Group II carbonates

the further down the group, the higher the temperature required to decompose the carbonate (see page **180**).

So the relative stabilities of these carbonates increases down the group in the order:

$$BaCO_3 > SrCO_3 > CaCO_3 > MgCO_3.$$

We can explain this trend using ideas about ion polarisation:
- the carbonate ion has a relatively large ionic radius so it is easily polarised by a small highly charged cation
- the Group II cations increase in ionic radius down the Group:

$$Mg^{2+} < Ca^{2+} < Sr^{2+} < Ba^{2+}$$

- the smaller the ionic radius of the cation, the better it is at polarising the carbonate ion (Figure **18.8**)
- so the degree of polarisation of the carbonate ion by the Group II cation follows the order

$$Mg^{2+} > Ca^{2+} > Sr^{2+} > Ba^{2+}$$

- the greater the polarisation of the carbonate ion, the easier it is to weaken a carbon–oxygen bond in the carbonate and form carbon dioxide and the oxide on heating.

A similar pattern is observed with the thermal decomposition of Group II nitrates: these decompose to form the oxide, nitrogen dioxide and oxygen. For example:

$$2Mg(NO_3)_2(s) \rightarrow 2MgO(s) + 4NO_2(g) + O_2(g)$$

The order of stability with respect to the products is in the order:

$$Ba(NO_3)_2 > Sr(NO_3)_2 > Ca(NO_3)_2 > Mg(NO_3)_2.$$

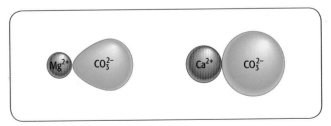

Figure 18.8 Magnesium ions are better polarisers of carbonate ions than calcium ions.

Fact file

The difference in thermal stability of Group II carbonates can be analysed by comparing Born–Haber cycles involving the lattice energies of calcium carbonate and calcium oxide. The unequal changes in the lattice energies of calcium carbonate and calcium oxide as the cation size increases can be related to the increasing thermal stability down the group.

Check-up

11 Use ideas about ion polarisation to explain why magnesium nitrate undergoes thermal decomposition at a much lower temperature than barium nitrate.

18.6 Enthalpy changes in solution

When an ionic solid dissolves in water, the crystal lattice breaks up and the ions separate. It requires a large amount of energy to overcome the attractive forces between the ions. How does this happen, even when the water is not heated? We will answer this question in this section.

Enthalpy change of solution

The **enthalpy change of solution**, $\Delta H^{\ominus}_{sol}$, is the energy absorbed or released when 1 mole of an ionic solid dissolves in sufficient water to form a very dilute solution.

The enthalpy changes of solution for magnesium chloride and sodium chloride are described by the equations below:

$$MgCl_2(s) + aq \rightarrow MgCl_2(aq) \qquad \Delta H^{\ominus}_{sol} = -55 \, \text{kJ mol}^{-1}$$

or

$$MgCl_2(s) + aq \rightarrow Mg^{2+}(aq) + 2Cl^-(aq)$$
$$\Delta H^{\ominus}_{sol} = -55 \, \text{kJ mol}^{-1}$$

NaCl(s) + aq → NaCl(aq) $\qquad \Delta H^{\ominus}_{sol} = +3.9 \, \text{kJ mol}^{-1}$

or

NaCl(s) + aq → Na$^+$(aq) + Cl$^-$(aq) $\quad \Delta H^{\ominus}_{sol} = +3.9 \, \text{kJ mol}^{-1}$

Note that:
- the symbol for enthalpy change of solution is $\Delta H^{\ominus}_{sol}$
- the symbol 'aq' represents the very large amount of water used
- enthalpy changes of solution can be positive (endothermic) or negative (exothermic)
- a compound is likely to be soluble in water only if $\Delta H^{\ominus}_{sol}$ is negative or has a small positive value; substances with large positive values of $\Delta H^{\ominus}_{sol}$ are relatively insoluble.

Check-up

12 a Write equations to represent the enthalpy change of solution of:
   i   potassium sulfate
   ii zinc chloride.
   b The enthalpies of solution of some metal halides are given below. What do these values tell you about the relative solubilities of these four compounds?

   sodium chloride, $\Delta H^{\ominus}_{sol} = +3.9 \, \text{kJ mol}^{-1}$

   silver chloride, $\Delta H^{\ominus}_{sol} = +65.7 \, \text{kJ mol}^{-1}$

   sodium bromide, $\Delta H^{\ominus}_{sol} = -0.6 \, \text{kJ mol}^{-1}$

   silver bromide, $\Delta H^{\ominus}_{sol} = +84.5 \, \text{kJ mol}^{-1}$

Fact file

'Soluble' and 'insoluble' are only relative terms. Magnesium carbonate is regarded as being insoluble because only 0.6 g of the salt dissolves in every dm^3 of water. No metallic salts are absolutely insoluble in water. Even lead carbonate, which is regarded as insoluble, dissolves to a very small extent: 0.000 17 g dissolves in every dm^3 of water. If salts were completely insoluble they could not have a value for $\Delta H^{\ominus}_{sol}$.

Enthalpy change of hydration

The lattice energy for sodium chloride is $-788 \, \text{kJ mol}^{-1}$. This means that we need to supply (at least) $+788 \, \text{kJ mol}^{-1}$ to overcome the forces of attraction between the ions. But $\Delta H^{\ominus}_{sol}$ [NaCl] is only $+3.9 \, \text{kJ mol}^{-1}$. Where does the energy needed to separate the ions come from? The answer is that it comes from the strong attraction between the ions and the water molecules.

When an ionic solid dissolves in water, bonds are formed between water molecules and the ions. These bonds are called ion–dipole bonds. Water is a polar molecule. The $\delta-$ oxygen atoms in water molecules are attracted to the positive ions in the ionic compound. The $\delta+$ hydrogen atoms in water molecules are attracted to the negative ions in the ionic compound (Figure **18.9**).

The energy released in forming ion–dipole bonds is sufficient to compensate for the energy that must be put in to separate the anions and cations that are bonded together in the crystal lattice.

The energy released when gaseous ions dissolve in water is called the **enthalpy change of hydration**.

> The enthalpy change of hydration, $\Delta H^{\ominus}_{hyd}$, is the enthalpy change when 1 mole of a specified gaseous ion dissolves in sufficient water to form a very dilute solution.

The enthalpy changes of hydration for calcium ions and chloride ions are described by the equations below:

$$Ca^{2+}(g) + aq \rightarrow Ca^{2+}(aq) \qquad \Delta H^{\ominus}_{hyd} = -1650 \, \text{kJ mol}^{-1}$$

$$Cl^{-}(g) + aq \rightarrow Cl^{-}(aq) \qquad \Delta H^{\ominus}_{hyd} = -364 \, \text{kJ mol}^{-1}$$

Note that:
- the symbol for enthalpy change of hydration is $\Delta H^{\ominus}_{hyd}$
- the enthalpy change of hydration is always exothermic
- the value of $\Delta H^{\ominus}_{hyd}$ is more exothermic for ions with the same charge but smaller ionic radii, e.g. $\Delta H^{\ominus}_{hyd}$ is more exothermic for Li^{+} than for Na^{+}
- the value of $\Delta H^{\ominus}_{hyd}$ is more exothermic for ions with the same radii but a larger charge e.g. $\Delta H^{\ominus}_{hyd}$ is more exothermic for Mg^{2+} than for Li^{+}.

Check-up

13 a Why is the enthalpy change of hydration always exothermic?
  b Write equations to represent:
   i the hydration of a sodium ion
   ii the hydration of a chloride ion.
  c Draw diagrams to show:
   i 4 water molecules hydrating a magnesium ion
   ii 2 water molecules hydrating a bromide ion.
   Show the dipole on each water molecule.
  d Explain why the value of $\Delta H^{\ominus}_{hyd}$ for magnesium ions is much more exothermic than $\Delta H^{\ominus}_{hyd}$ for potassium ions.

14 Name the changes associated with the equations below:
  a $KBr(s) + aq \rightarrow KBr(aq)$
   (for 1 mole of KBr)
  b $K^{+}(g) + aq \rightarrow K^{+}(aq)$
   (for 1 mole of K^{+} ions)
  c $K^{+}(g) + Br^{-}(g) \rightarrow KBr(s)$
   (for 1 mole of KBr)
  d $Br^{-}(g) + aq \rightarrow Br^{-}(aq)$
   (for 1 mole of Br^{-} ions)

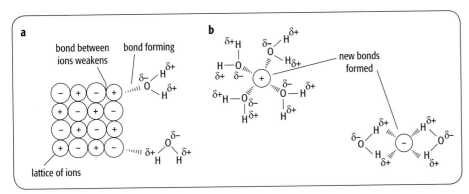

Figure 18.9 a Water molecules forming ion–dipole bonds with an ionic compound. **b** Hydrated ions in solution.

Calculating enthalpy changes in solution

We can calculate the enthalpy change of solution or the enthalpy change of hydration by constructing an enthalpy cycle and using Hess's law (Figure **18.10**).

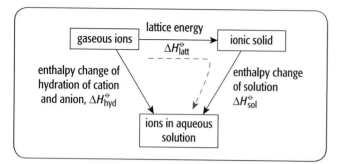

Figure 18.10 An enthalpy cycle involving lattice energy, enthalpy change of hydration and enthalpy change of solution.

We can see from this enthalpy cycle that

$$\Delta H^{\ominus}_{latt} + \Delta H^{\ominus}_{sol} = \Delta H^{\ominus}_{hyd}$$

Note that the $\Delta H^{\ominus}_{hyd}$ values for both anions and cations are added together to get the total value of $\Delta H^{\ominus}_{hyd}$.
    We can use this energy cycle to calculate:
• the value of $\Delta H^{\ominus}_{sol}$
• the value of $\Delta H^{\ominus}_{hyd}$.

Worked example

1   Determine the enthalpy change of solution of sodium fluoride using the following data:
• lattice energy = $-902\,kJ\,mol^{-1}$
• enthalpy change of hydration of sodium ions = $-406\,kJ\,mol^{-1}$
• enthalpy change of hydration of fluoride ions = $-506\,kJ\,mol^{-1}$

Step 1:   draw the enthalpy cycle (Figure **18.11**)

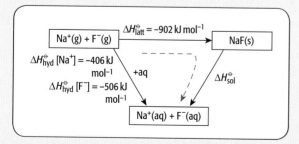

Figure 18.11 An enthalpy cycle to determine $\Delta H^{\ominus}_{sol}$ of NaF.

continued ⋯➔

Step 2:   rearrange the equation and substitute the figures to find $\Delta H^{\ominus}_{sol}$

$$\Delta H^{\ominus}_{latt} + \Delta H^{\ominus}_{sol} = \Delta H^{\ominus}_{hyd}$$

so

$$\Delta H^{\ominus}_{sol} = \Delta H^{\ominus}_{hyd} - \Delta H^{\ominus}_{latt}$$

$$\Delta H^{\ominus}_{sol} = (-406) + (-506) - (-902)$$

$$= -912 + 902$$

$$\Delta H^{\ominus}_{sol}\,[NaF] = -10\,kJ\,mol^{-1}$$

An energy level diagram for this enthalpy cycle is shown in Figure **18.12**.

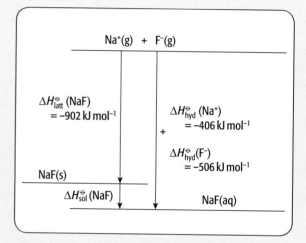

Figure 18.12 An energy level diagram to determine $\Delta H^{\ominus}_{sol}$ of NaF.

2   Determine the enthalpy change of hydration of the chloride ion using the following data.
• lattice energy of lithium chloride = $-846\,kJ\,mol^{-1}$
• enthalpy change of solution of lithium chloride = $-37\,kJ\,mol^{-1}$
• enthalpy change of hydration of lithium ion = $-519\,kJ\,mol^{-1}$

Step 1:   draw the enthalpy cycle (Figure **18.13**).

continued ⋯➔

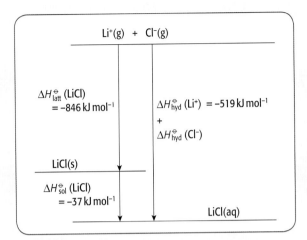

Figure 18.13 An enthalpy cycle to determine $\Delta H^{\ominus}_{hyd}[Cl^-]$.

Step 2 rearrange the equation and substitute the figures to find $\Delta H^{\ominus}_{hyd}[Cl^-]$.

$$\Delta H^{\ominus}_{latt} + \Delta H^{\ominus}_{sol} = \Delta H^{\ominus}_{hyd}[Li^+] + \Delta H^{\ominus}_{hyd}[Cl^-]$$

so

$$\Delta H^{\ominus}_{hyd}[Cl^-] = \Delta H^{\ominus}_{latt} + \Delta H^{\ominus}_{sol} - \Delta H^{\ominus}_{hyd}[Li^+]$$

$$\Delta H^{\ominus}_{hyd}[Cl^-] = (-846) + (-37) - (-519)$$

$$= -883 + 519$$

$$\Delta H^{\ominus}_{hyd}[Cl^-] = -364 \, kJ \, mol^{-1}$$

Check-up

15 a Draw an enthalpy cycle to calculate the enthalpy of hydration of magnesium ions when magnesium chloride dissolves in water.

b Calculate the enthalpy of hydration of magnesium ions given that:

$$\Delta H^{\ominus}_{latt}[MgCl_2] = -2592 \, kJ \, mol^{-1}$$

$$\Delta H^{\ominus}_{sol}[MgCl_2] = -55 \, kJ \, mol^{-1}$$

$$\Delta H^{\ominus}_{hyd}[Cl^-] = -364 \, kJ \, mol^{-1}$$

The solubility of Group II sulfates

Table 18.2 shows the solubility in water of some Group II sulfates. The solubility decreases as the radius of the metal ion increases. We can explain this variation in solubility in terms of the relative values of enthalpy change of hydration and the corresponding lattice energy.

Compound	Solubility in $mol \, dm^{-3}$
magnesium sulfate	1.83
calcium sulfate	4.66×10^{-2}
strontium sulfate	7.11×10^{-4}
barium sulfate	9.43×10^{-6}

Table 18.2 Solubilities in water of some Group II sulfates.

Change in hydration enthalpy down the group
- Smaller ions (with the same charge) have greater enthalpy changes of hydration
- so the enthalpy change of hydration decreases (gets less exothermic) in the order $Mg^{2+} > Ca^{2+} > Sr^{2+} > Ba^{2+}$
- this decrease is relatively large down the group and it depends entirely on the increase in the size of the cation since the anion is unchanged (it is the sulfate ion in every case).

Change in lattice energy down the group
- Lattice energy is greater if the ions (with the same charge) forming the lattice are small
- so the lattice energy decreases in the order $Mg^{2+} > Ca^{2+} > Sr^{2+} > Ba^{2+}$
- the lattice energy is also inversely proportional to the sum of the radii of the anion and cation
- the sulfate ion is much larger than the group II cations
- so the sulfate ion contributes a relatively greater part to the change in the lattice energy down the group
- so the decrease in lattice energy is relatively smaller down the group and it is determined more by the size of the large sulfate ion than the size of the cations.

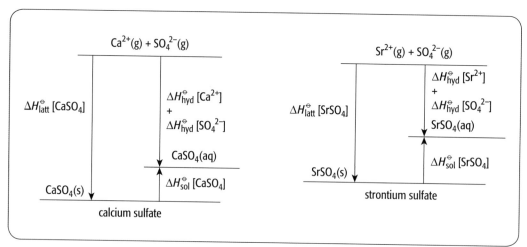

Figure 18.14 Enthalpy cycles comparing the enthalpy change of solution of calcium sulfate and strontium sulfate.

Difference in enthalpy change of solution of Group II sulfates

On page 262 we saw that substances which have a very low solubility in water are likely to have $\Delta H^{\ominus}_{sol}$ with a high positive (endothermic) value. As a rough guide, the higher the positive value of $\Delta H^{\ominus}_{sol}$ the less soluble the salt.

We have seen that:

- the lattice energy of the sulfates decreases (gets less exothermic) by relatively smaller values down the group
- the enthalpy change of hydration decreases (gets less exothermic) by relatively larger values down the group
- so applying Hess's law, the value of $\Delta H^{\ominus}_{sol}$ gets more endothermic down the group (Figure 18.14)
- so the solubility of the Group II sulfates decreases down the group.

Check-up

16 a Draw an enthalpy cycle as an energy level diagram showing the relationship between lattice energy, enthalpy change of solution and enthalpy change of hydration for barium sulfate. $\Delta H^{\ominus}_{sol}$ [BaSO$_4$] is very endothermic.

  b Explain why magnesium sulfate is more soluble than barium sulfate by referring to the relative values of the lattice energies and enthalpy changes of hydration.

Summary

- ☐ The lattice energy ($\Delta H^{\ominus}_{latt}$) is the energy change when gaseous ions come together to form 1 mole of a solid lattice (under standard conditions).
- ☐ The standard enthalpy change of atomisation ($\Delta H^{\ominus}_{at}$) is the enthalpy change when 1 mole of gaseous atoms is formed from the element in its standard state under standard conditions.
- ☐ The 1st ionisation energy of an element ($\Delta H^{\ominus}_{i1}$) is the energy needed to remove one electron from each atom in 1 mole of atoms of the element in the gaseous state to form gaseous 1+ ions.
- ☐ The 1st electron affinity ($\Delta H^{\ominus}_{ea1}$) is the enthalpy change when 1 mole of electrons is added to 1 mole of gaseous atoms to form 1 mole of gaseous 1− ions under standard conditions.
- ☐ A Born–Haber cycle is a type of enthalpy cycle (Hess cycle) which includes lattice energy, enthalpy change of formation and relevant electron affinities, enthalpy changes of atomisation and enthalpy changes of ionisation.
- ☐ Lattice energies can be calculated from a Born–Haber cycle.
- ☐ Lattice energies are exothermic. The greater the value of the lattice energy, the stronger the ionic bonding holding the lattice together.

- The value of the lattice energy depends on:
  - the size of the ions (the smaller the ion, the more exothermic the lattice energy)
  - the charge on the ions (the greater the charge on the ions, the more exothermic the lattice energy).
- The thermal stability of the carbonates and nitrates of Group II elements depends on the degree to which the Group II cation is able to polarise the larger anion:
  - smaller cations have a higher charge density and are better polarisers of a given anion
  - larger anions are more polarised by a given cation.
- The standard enthalpy change of solution ($\Delta H^{\ominus}_{sol}$) is the enthalpy change when 1 mole of an ionic solid dissolves in sufficient water to form a very dilute solution. $\Delta H^{\ominus}_{sol}$ may be exothermic or endothermic.
- The enthalpy change of hydration ($\Delta H^{\ominus}_{hyd}$) is the enthalpy change when 1 mole of gaseous ions dissolves in sufficient water to form a very dilute solution. $\Delta H^{\ominus}_{hyd}$ is always exothermic.
- The value of $\Delta H^{\ominus}_{hyd}$ depends on:
  - the size of the ion ($\Delta H^{\ominus}_{hyd}$ is more exothermic, the smaller the ion)
  - the charge on the ion ($\Delta H^{\ominus}_{hyd}$ is more exothermic, the greater the charge).
- Hess's law can be applied to construct energy cycles to determine enthalpy changes of solution and enthalpy changes of hydration.
- The decrease in solubility of Group II sulfates down the group can be explained in terms of the relative values of the enthalpy change of hydration and the corresponding lattice energy.

End-of-chapter questions

Examiner's tip

Learn a mental check list to help you construct Born–Haber cycles:
- have I included the enthalpy of formation?
- have I included both enthalpies of atomisation?
- have I converted all atoms into ions of the **correct charge**?
- have I considered **how many moles of each ion** are in 1 mole of the compound?

The last two points get forgotten most often, especially the final one – which is important in question **1**, parts **a** and **b**, question **3**, part **b ii**, and question **4**, part **c**.

1   The table shows the enthalpy changes needed to calculate the lattice energy of potassium oxide, K_2O.

Type of enthalpy change	Value of enthalpy change / $kJ\,mol^{-1}$
1st ionisation energy of potassium	+418
1st electron affinity of oxygen	−141
2nd electron affinity of oxygen	+798
enthalpy change of formation of K_2O	−361
enthalpy change of atomisation of potassium	+89
enthalpy change of atomisation of oxygen	+249

a Copy the incomplete Born–Haber cycle shown below. On the lines **A** to **E** of your copy of the Born–Haber cycle, write the correct symbols relating to potassium and oxygen. [5]

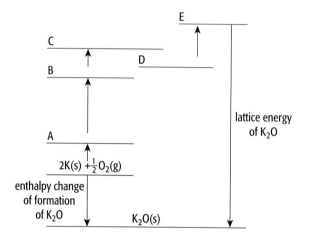

b Use the data in the table above to calculate the lattice energy of potassium oxide. [2]

c Describe how, and explain why, the lattice energy of sodium oxide differs from that of potassium sulfide, K_2S. [4]

d Explain why the 2nd electron affinity of oxygen has a positive value. [1]

Total = 12

2 The lattice energy of sodium chloride can be calculated using the following enthalpy changes:
- enthalpy change of formation of sodium chloride
- enthalpy changes of atomisation of sodium and chlorine
- 1st ionisation energy of sodium
- 1st electron affinity of chlorine

a State the meaning of the terms:
   i first ionisation energy [3]
   ii enthalpy change of atomisation [2]

b Draw and label a Born–Haber cycle to calculate the lattice energy of sodium chloride. [4]

c Explain why the lattice energy of sodium chloride has a value which is lower than the lattice energy of lithium chloride. [2]

Total = 11

3 **a** Draw an enthalpy (Hess's law) cycle to show the dissolving of magnesium iodide in water. [5]

b The table shows the values for all but one of the enthalpy changes relevant to this cycle.

Enthalpy change	Value / kJ mol^{-1}
lattice energy	−2327
enthalpy change of hydration of Mg^{2+} ion	−1920
enthalpy change of hydration of I^- ion	−314

      i Define enthalpy change of hydration. [2]
      ii Use the values in the table to calculate the value for the enthalpy change of solution
         of magnesium iodide. [3]
   c Draw a diagram to show how water molecules are arranged around a magnesium ion. [2]
   d Explain why the enthalpy change of hydration of a magnesium ion is more exothermic
     than the enthalpy change of hydration of a sodium ion. [3]

                                                                   Total = 15

4 The lattice energy of magnesium bromide, $MgBr_2$, can be calculated using the enthalpy changes
   shown in the table.

Type of enthalpy change	Value of enthalpy change / $kJ\,mol^{-1}$
1st ionisation energy of magnesium	+736
2nd ionisation energy of magnesium	+1450
1st electron affinity of bromine	−325
enthalpy change of formation of $MgBr_2$	−524
enthalpy change of atomisation of magnesium	+150
enthalpy change of atomisation of bromine	+112

   a State the meaning of the terms:
      i lattice energy [2]
      ii 2nd ionisation energy. [3]
   b Draw and label a Born–Haber cycle to calculate the lattice energy of magnesium bromide. [4]
   c Calculate the lattice energy of magnesium bromide. [2]

                                                                   Total = 11

5 **a** For each of the following pairs of compounds, state with reasons which one you would expect
     to have the higher lattice energy.
      i NaCl and KBr [2]
      ii KCl and SrS [2]
   b In some crystal lattices, some of the ions are polarised.
      i State the meaning of the term **ion polarisation**. [2]
      ii Explain why a magnesium ion is a better polariser of an iodide ion than a sodium ion. [2]
      iii Use ideas about ion polarisation to explain why barium carbonate is more stable to thermal
         decomposition than magnesium carbonate. [3]

                                                                   Total = 11

6 The diagram shows the enthalpy changes when sodium chloride is dissolved in water.

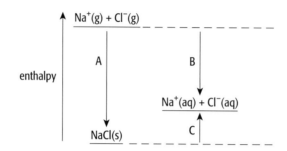

a Define the following terms:
   i enthalpy change of solution [2]
   ii enthalpy change of hydration. [2]
b Write symbol equations that describe the following:
   i enthalpy change of solution of sodium chloride [2]
   ii enthalpy change of hydration of the chloride ion. [2]
c Name the enthalpy changes labelled **A**, **B** and **C**. [3]
d Draw the water molecules around magnesium ions and sulfate ions in a solution of magnesium sulfate. [3]
e Explain, in terms of differences of lattice energies and enthalpy changes of hydration, why magnesium sulfate is more soluble in water than calcium sulfate. [5]

Total = 19

Learning outcomes

Candidates should be able to:

- define the terms:
  - **standard electrode (redox) potential**
  - **standard cell potential**
- describe the standard hydrogen electrode
- describe methods used to measure the standard electrode potentials of:
  - metals or non-metals in contact with their ions in aqueous solution
  - ions of the same element in different oxidation states
- calculate a standard cell potential by combining two standard electrode potentials
- use standard cell potential to:
  - deduce and explain the direction of electron flow in a simple cell
  - predict the feasibility of a reaction.
- construct redox equations using the relevant half-equations
- describe and deduce from electrode potential values, the relative reactivity of the Group VII elements as oxidising agents
- predict qualitatively how the value of an electrode potential varies with the concentration of the aqueous ion

- state the possible advantages of developing other types of cell, e.g. the H_2/O_2 fuel cell, and improved batteries (as in electric vehicles) in terms of smaller size, lower mass and higher voltage
- state the relationship, $F = Le$, between the Faraday constant, the Avogadro constant and the charge on the electron
- predict the identity of the substance liberated during electrolysis from:
  - the state of electrolyte (molten or aqueous)
  - the position of the ions (in the electrolyte) in the redox series (electrode potential)
  - the concentration of the ions in the electrolyte
- calculate:
  - the quantity of charge passed during electrolysis
  - the mass and/or volume of substance liberated during electrolysis, including those in the electrolysis of H_2SO_4(aq) and Na_2SO_4(aq)
- describe the determination of a value of the Avogadro constant by an electrolytic method.

19.1 Redox reactions revisited

In Chapter 7 (page 111) you learnt to construct equations for redox reactions from relevant half-equations. You also used the concept of oxidation numbers to show whether a particular reactant has been oxidised or reduced during a chemical reaction.

Electrons may be gained or lost in redox reactions.

- The species (atom, ion or molecule) losing electrons is being oxidised. It acts a reducing agent.
- The species gaining electrons is being reduced. It acts an oxidising agent.

Make sure that you can do check-up questions 1 and 2 before continuing with this chapter. Refer back to Chapter 7 (page 117) if you need some help.

Check-up

1. In each of the chemical reactions **a** to **c**:
   - **i** Which species gains electrons?
   - **ii** Which species loses electrons?
   - **iii** Which species is the oxidising agent?
   - **iv** Which species is the reducing agent?
   - **a** $CuCl_2 + Fe \rightarrow FeCl_2 + Cu$
   - **b** $Cu + Br_2 \rightarrow Cu^{2+} + 2Br^-$
   - **c** $PbO_2 + SO_2 \rightarrow PbSO_4$

2. Construct full redox equations from the following pairs of half-equations.
   - **a** The reaction of iodide ions with hydrogen peroxide:
     $$I^- \rightarrow \tfrac{1}{2}I_2 + e^-$$
     $$H_2O_2 + 2H^+ + 2e^- \rightarrow 2H_2O$$

continued ⋯⟩

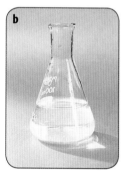

Figure 19.1 Manganese can exist in various oxidation states: **a** manganese(0), the metal; **b** manganese(II) as Mn^{2+}(aq) ions; **c** manganese(III) as Mn^{3+}(aq) ions; **d** manganese(IV) as MnO_2; **e** Mn(VI) as MnO_4^{2-} ions; **f** Mn(VII) as MnO_4^- ions. Manganese metal is a good reductant whilst MnO_4^-(aq) in acidic solution is a good oxidant.

b The reaction of chloride ions with acidified manganese(IV) oxide:
$$Cl^- \rightarrow \tfrac{1}{2}Cl_2 + e^-$$
$$MnO_2 + 4H^+ + 2e^- \rightarrow Mn^{2+} + 2H_2O$$

c The reaction of acidified MnO_4^- ions with Fe^{2+} ions:
$$Fe^{2+} \rightarrow Fe^{3+} + e^-$$
$$MnO_4^- + 8H^+ + 5e^- \rightarrow Mn^{2+} + 4H_2O$$

19.2 Electrode potentials

Introducing electrode potentials

A redox equilibrium exists between two chemically related species which are in different oxidation states. For example, when a copper rod is placed in contact with an aqueous solution of its ions the following equilibrium exists:

$$Cu^{2+}(aq) + 2e^- \rightleftharpoons Cu(s)$$

There are two opposing reactions in this equilibrium.

- Metal atoms from the rod entering the solution as metal ions. This leaves electrons behind on the surface of the rod. For example:

$$Cu(s) \rightarrow Cu^{2+}(aq) + 2e^-$$

- Ions in solution accepting electrons from the metal rod and being deposited as metal atoms on the surface of the rod. For example:

$$Cu^{2+}(aq) + 2e^- \rightarrow Cu(s)$$

The redox equilibrium is established when the rate of electron gain equals the rate of electron loss.

For unreactive metals such as copper, if this equilibrium is compared to the equilibrium set up by other metals, the equilibrium set up by copper lies further over to the right.

$$Cu^{2+}(aq) + 2e^- \rightleftharpoons Cu(s)$$

Cu^{2+}(aq) ions are therefore relatively easy to reduce. They gain electrons readily to form copper metal.

For reactive metals such as vanadium, the equilibrium lies further over to the left.

$$V^{2+}(aq) + 2e^- \rightleftharpoons V(s)$$

V^{2+}(aq) ions are therefore relatively difficult to reduce. They gain electrons much less readily by comparison.

The position of equilibrium differs for different combinations of metals placed in solutions of their ions.

When a metal is put into a solution of its ions an electric potential (voltage) is established between the metal and the metal ions in solution. We cannot measure this potential directly. But we can measure the **difference** in potential between the metal/metal ion system and another system. We call this value the **electrode potential**, E. Electrode potential is measured in volts. The system we use for comparison is the standard hydrogen electrode.

Fact file

It is thought that the absolute electrical potentials that we cannot measure are caused by the formation of an electrical double layer when an element is placed in a solution of its ions. For example, when zinc is placed in a solution containing zinc ions, a tiny number of zinc atoms on the surface of the metal are converted to zinc ions which go into solution. This leaves an excess of electrons on the surface of the zinc. The solution around the metal now has excess Zn^{2+} ions. Some of these cations near the surface of the zinc are attracted to its surface. So an electrical double layer is formed. This build up of charge causes an electric potential (voltage) between the metal and the metal ions in solution (Figure **19.2**).

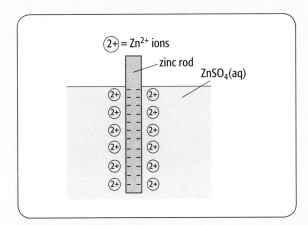

Figure 19.2 The separation of charge when a zinc rod is placed in a solution of Zn^{2+} ions results in an electrical double layer.

The standard hydrogen electrode

The **standard hydrogen electrode** is one of several types of half-cell which can be used as reference electrodes. Figure **19.3** shows a standard hydrogen electrode. This electrode consists of:

• hydrogen gas at 101 kPa pressure, in equilibrium with
• H^+ ions of concentration $1.00\,mol\,dm^{-3}$
• a platinum electrode covered with platinum black in contact with the hydrogen gas and the H^+ ions.

The platinum black is finely divided platinum which allows close contact of hydrogen gas and H^+ ions in

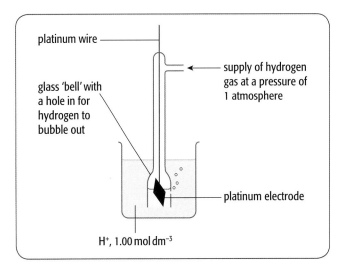

Figure 19.3 The standard hydrogen electrode.

solution so that equilibrium between H_2 gas and H^+ ions is established quickly. The platinum electrode is inert so it does not take part in the reaction.

The E° values for all half-cells are measured relative to this electrode. When connected to another half-cell, the value read on the voltmeter gives the standard electrode potential for that half-cell.

The half-equation for the hydrogen electrode can be written:

$$2H^+(aq) + 2e^- \rightleftharpoons H_2(g)$$

or

$$H^+(aq) + e^- \rightleftharpoons \tfrac{1}{2}H_2(g)$$

The way that the half-equation is balanced makes no difference to the value of E°. The equation does not affect the tendency for the element to gain electrons.

Electrode potential and redox reactions

Electrode potential values give us an indication of how easy it is to reduce a substance.
Note that:

• By convention, the electrode potential refers to the reduction reaction. So the electrons appear on the left-hand side of the half-equation. For example:

$$Al^{3+}(aq) + 3e^- \rightleftharpoons Al(s)$$

• The more positive (or less negative) the electrode potential, the easier it is to reduce the ions on the left.

So the metal on the right is relatively unreactive and is a relatively poor reducing agent. For example:

$$Ag^+(aq) + e^- \rightleftharpoons Ag(s) \qquad \text{voltage} = +0.80\,V$$

- The more negative (or less positive) the electrode potential, the more difficult it is to reduce the ions on the left. So the metal on the right is relatively reactive and is a relatively good reducing agent. For example:

$$Zn^{2+}(aq) + 2e^- \rightleftharpoons Zn(s) \qquad \text{voltage} = -0.76\,V$$

Check-up

3 Refer to the list of electrode potentials below to answer parts **a** to **d**.

$$Ag^+(aq) + e^- \rightleftharpoons Ag(s) \qquad \text{voltage} = +0.80\,V$$

$$Co^{2+}(aq) + 2e^- \rightleftharpoons Co(s) \quad \text{voltage} = -0.28\,V$$

$$Cu^{2+}(aq) + 2e^- \rightleftharpoons Cu(s) \quad \text{voltage} = +0.34\,V$$

$$Pb^{2+}(aq) + 2e^- \rightleftharpoons Pb(s) \quad \text{voltage} = -0.13\,V$$

$$Zn^{2+}(aq) + 2e^- \rightleftharpoons Zn(s) \quad \text{voltage} = -0.76\,V$$

a Which metal in the list is the best reducing agent?
b Which metal ion in the list is most difficult to reduce?
c Which metal in the list is most reactive?
d Which metal ion in the list is the easiest to reduce?

Combining half-cells

In order to measure the electrode potential relating to the half-equation

$$Cu^{2+}(aq) + 2e^- \rightarrow Cu(s)$$

we place a pure copper rod in a solution of $Cu^{2+}(aq)$ ions (for example copper(II) sulfate solution). This Cu^{2+}/Cu system is called a **half-cell** (Figure 19.4).

Figure 19.4 The Cu^{2+}/Cu half-cell.

We use the following standard conditions to make the half-cell:
- the $Cu^{2+}(aq)$ ions have a concentration of $1.00\,mol\,dm^{-3}$.
- the temperature is 25 °C (298 K)
- the copper rod must be pure.

If we connect two half-cells together we have made an **electrochemical cell**. We can measure the voltage between these two half-cells. Figure **19.5** shows a Cu^{2+}/Cu half-cell connected to a Zn^{2+}/Zn half-cell to make a complete electrochemical cell.

Half-cells are connected together using:
- wires connecting the metal rods in each half-cell to a high-resistance voltmeter; the electrons flow round this external circuit from the metal with the more negative (or less positive) electrode potential to the metal with the less negative (or more positive) electrode potential
- a **salt bridge** to complete the electrical circuit allowing the movement of ions between the two half-cells so that ionic balance is maintained; a salt bridge does not allow the movement of electrons.

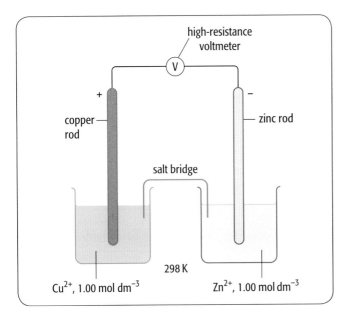

Figure 19.5 One type of electrochemical cell is made by connecting a Cu^{2+}/Cu half-cell to a Zn^{2+}/Zn half-cell. The voltage generated by this cell is +1.10 V.

A salt bridge can be made from a strip of filter paper (or other inert porous material) soaked in a saturated solution of potassium nitrate.

The voltages for the half-cells in Figure 19.5 can be represented by the following half-equations:

$$Cu^{2+}(aq) + 2e^- \rightleftharpoons Cu(s) \qquad \text{voltage} = +0.34\,V$$

$$Zn^{2+}(aq) + 2e^- \rightleftharpoons Zn(s) \qquad \text{voltage} = -0.76\,V$$

The relative values of these voltages tell us that Zn^{2+} ions are more difficult to reduce than Cu^{2+} ions. So Cu^{2+} ions will accept electrons from the Zn^{2+}/Zn half-cell and zinc will lose electrons to the Cu^{2+}/Cu half-cell.

Half-equations can be used to show us the contents of half-cells. A half-cell does not have to be a metal/metal ion system. We can construct half-cells for any half-equation written. For example:

$$Fe^{3+}(aq) + e^- \rightleftharpoons Fe^{2+}(aq)$$

$$Cl_2(g) + 2e^- \rightleftharpoons 2Cl^-(aq)$$

$$MnO_4^-(aq) + 8H^+(aq) + 5e^- \rightleftharpoons Mn^{2+}(aq) + 4H_2O(l)$$

Note that the oxidised species (having the higher oxidation number) is always written on the left-hand side and the reduced form on the right-hand side.

Standard electrode potential

The position of equilibrium of a reaction may be affected by changes in the concentration of reagents, temperature and pressure of gases. So the voltage of an electrochemical cell will also depend on these factors. We therefore need to use standard conditions when comparing electrode potentials. These are:

- concentration of ions at $1.00\,mol\,dm^{-3}$
- a temperature of 25 °C (298 K)
- if gases are involved, they should be at a pressure of 1 atmosphere (101 kPa)
- the value of the electrode potential of the half-cell is measured relative to the standard hydrogen electrode.

Under these conditions, the electrode potential we measure is called the **standard electrode potential**. This has the symbol, $E^\ominus$. It is spoken of as 'E standard'.

> The standard electrode potential for a half-cell is the voltage measured under standard conditions with a standard hydrogen electrode as the other half-cell.

19.3 Measuring standard electrode potentials

There are three main types of half-cell whose $E^{\ominus}$ value can be obtained when connected to a standard hydrogen electrode:

- metal/metal ion half-cell
- non-metal/non-metal ion half-cell
- ion/ion half-cell.

Half-cells containing metals and metal ions

Figure 19.6 shows how to measure the $E^{\ominus}$ value for a Cu^{2+}/Cu half-cell. The Cu^{2+}/Cu half-cell is connected to a standard hydrogen electrode and the voltage measured. The voltage is +0.34 V. The copper is the positive terminal (positive pole) of the cell and the hydrogen electrode is the negative terminal. The two half-equations are:

$$Cu^{2+}(aq) + 2e^- \rightleftharpoons Cu(s) \qquad E^{\ominus} = +0.34\,V$$

$$H^+(aq) + e^- \rightleftharpoons \tfrac{1}{2}H_2(g) \qquad E^{\ominus} = 0.00\,V$$

- The $E^{\ominus}$ values show us that Cu^{2+} ions are easier to reduce than H^+ ions (they have a more positive $E^{\ominus}$ value).
- Cu^{2+} ions are more likely to gain electrons than H^+ ions.
- So Cu^{2+} ions will accept electrons from the $H^+/\tfrac{1}{2}H_2$ half-cell and $\tfrac{1}{2}H_2$ will lose electrons to the Cu^{2+}/Cu half-cell.

Figure 19.7 shows how to measure the $E^{\ominus}$ value for a Zn^{2+}/Zn half-cell. The voltage of the Zn^{2+}/Zn half-cell

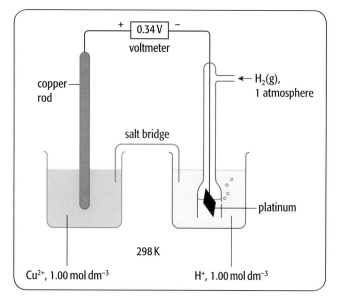

Figure 19.6 Measuring the standard electrode potential of a Cu^{2+}/Cu half-cell.

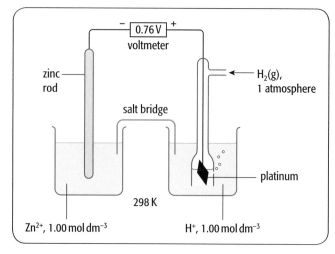

Figure 19.7 Measuring the standard electrode potential of a Zn^{2+}/Zn half-cell.

is –0.76 V. The zinc is the negative terminal (negative pole) of the cell and the hydrogen electrode is the positive terminal. The two half-equations are:

$$H^+(aq) + e^- \rightleftharpoons \tfrac{1}{2}H_2(g) \qquad E^{\ominus} = 0.00\,V$$

$$Zn^{2+}(aq) + 2e^- \rightleftharpoons Zn(s) \qquad E^{\ominus} = -0.76\,V$$

- The $E^{\ominus}$ values show us that Zn^{2+} ions are more difficult to reduce than H^+ ions (they have a more negative $E^{\ominus}$ value).
- Zn^{2+} ions are less likely to gain electrons than H^+ ions.
- So Zn^{2+} ions will lose electrons to the $H^+/\tfrac{1}{2}H_2$ half-cell and $\tfrac{1}{2}H_2$ will gain electrons from the Zn^{2+}/Zn half-cell.

From these two examples, we can see that:

- Reduction takes place at the positive terminal of the cell. For example, in the Zn^{2+}/Zn; $H^+/\tfrac{1}{2}H_2$ cell:

$$H^+(aq) + e^- \rightleftharpoons \tfrac{1}{2}H_2(g)$$

- Oxidation takes place at the negative terminal of the cell. For example, in the Zn^{2+}/Zn: $H^+/\tfrac{1}{2}H_2$ cell:

$$Zn(s) \rightarrow Zn^{2+}(aq) + 2e^-$$

Check-up

5 a Write half-equations for the three reactions taking place in the half-cells shown **on the left** in Figure 19.8. Write

continued ⋯⟶

each equation as a reduction (electrons on the left-hand side of the equation).

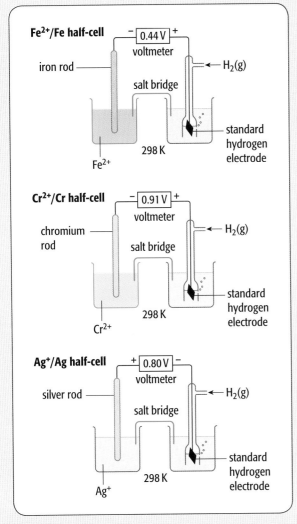

Figure 19.8 Measuring standard electrode potentials.

b What are the standard electrode potentials for these half-cell reactions?
c List all the necessary conditions in each cell.

Half-cells containing non-metals and non-metal ions

In half-cells which do not contain a metal, electrical contact with the solution is made by using platinum wire or platinum foil as an electrode. The redox equilibrium is established at the surface of the platinum. The platinum electrode is inert so plays no part in the reaction.

The platinum must be in contact with both the element and the aqueous solution of its ions.

Figure 19.9 shows a $\frac{1}{2}Cl_2/Cl^-$ half-cell connected to a standard hydrogen electrode. The voltage of the $\frac{1}{2}Cl_2/Cl^-$ half-cell is +1.36 V. So the $\frac{1}{2}Cl_2/Cl^-$ half-cell forms the positive terminal of the cell and the hydrogen electrode is the negative terminal. The two half-equations are:

$$\frac{1}{2}Cl_2(g) + e^- \rightleftharpoons Cl^-(aq) \qquad E^\ominus = +1.36\,V$$

$$H^+(aq) + e^- \rightleftharpoons \frac{1}{2}H_2(g) \qquad E^\ominus = 0.00\,V$$

- The $E^\ominus$ values show us that Cl_2 molecules are easier to reduce than H^+ ions (they have a more positive $E^\ominus$ value).
- Cl_2 molecules are more likely to gain electrons than H^+ ions.
- So Cl_2 molecules will gain electrons from the $H^+/\frac{1}{2}H_2$ half-cell and H_2 molecules will lose electrons to the $\frac{1}{2}Cl_2/Cl^-$ half-cell.

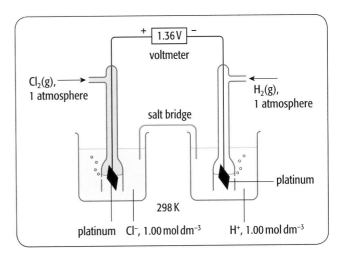

Figure 19.9 Measuring the standard electrode potential of a Cl_2/Cl^- half-cell.

Check-up

6 a Look at Figure 19.10. Write a half-equation for the half-cell on the left-hand side.
b What is the $E^\ominus$ value for this half-cell?

continued ⋯⇨

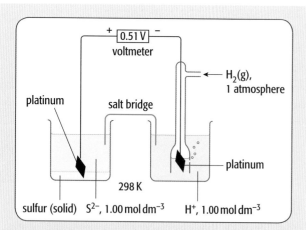

Figure 19.10 Measuring the standard electrode potential of an S/S²⁻ half-cell.

7 Draw a diagram to show how you would measure the standard electrode potential for the half-cell:

$$\tfrac{1}{2}I_2 + e^- \rightleftharpoons I^-(aq)$$

Include the actual $E^\ominus$ value of +0.54 V on your diagram.

Half-cells containing ions of the same element in different oxidation states

Half-cells can contain two ions of different oxidation states derived from the same element. For example a mixture of Fe^{3+} and Fe^{2+} ions can form a half-cell using a platinum electrode. In this type of half-cell, the concentration of each ion present is $1.00\,\text{mol}\,\text{dm}^{-3}$. Figure 19.11 shows the set-up for a cell used to measure the standard electrode potential of the Fe^{3+}/Fe^{2+} half-cell.

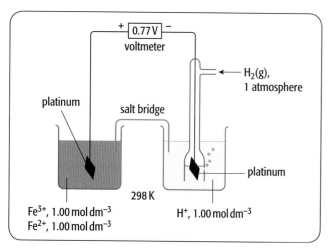

Figure 19.11 Measuring the standard electrode potential of the Fe^{3+}/Fe^{2+} half-cell.

The voltage of this half-cell is +0.77 V.

$$Fe^{3+}(aq) + e^- \rightleftharpoons Fe^{2+}(aq) \qquad\qquad E^\ominus = +0.77\,V$$

Some reactions involve several ionic species. For example:

$$MnO_4^-(aq) + 8H^+(aq) + 5e^- \rightleftharpoons Mn^{2+}(aq) + 4H_2O(l)$$

The H^+ ions are included because they are essential for the conversion of MnO_4^- (manganate(VII) ions) to Mn^{2+} ions. So the half-cell contains:
- $1.00\,\text{mol}\,\text{dm}^{-3}$ $MnO_4^-(aq)$ ions
- $1.00\,\text{mol}\,\text{dm}^{-3}$ $Mn^{2+}(aq)$ ions
- $1.00\,\text{mol}\,\text{dm}^{-3}$ $H^+(aq)$ ions

Figure 19.12 shows the set-up of a cell used to measure the standard electrode potential of the MnO_4^-/Mn^{2+} half-cell.

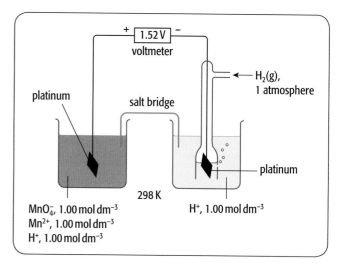

Figure 19.12 Measuring the standard electrode potential of the MnO_4^-/Mn^{2+} half-cell.

Check-up

8 What is the $E^\ominus$ value for the half-cell on the **left-hand side** of Figure 19.12?

9 Why is platinum used in preference to other metals in half-cells where the reaction does not involve a metallic element?

10 Show, with the aid of a diagram, how you would measure the $E^\ominus$ value for the half-cell shown by the equation:

$$VO^{2+} + 2H^+ + e^- \rightleftharpoons V^{3+} + H_2O$$

19.4 Using $E^\ominus$ values

Using $E^\ominus$ values to predict cell voltages

We can use $E^\ominus$ values to calculate the voltage of an electrochemical cell made up of two half-cells, even when neither of them is a standard hydrogen electrode. The voltage measured is the difference between the $E^\ominus$ values of the two half-cells. We call this value the **standard cell potential**.

For the electrochemical cell shown in Figure **19.13**, the two relevant half-equations are:

$$Ag^+(aq) + e^- \rightleftharpoons Ag(s) \qquad\qquad E^\ominus = +0.80\,V$$
$$Zn^{2+}(aq) + 2e^- \rightleftharpoons Zn(s) \qquad\qquad E^\ominus = -0.76\,V$$

The voltage of this cell is $+0.80 - (-0.76) = +1.56\,V$ (Figure **19.14**).

Notice that in order to calculate the cell voltage, we always subtract the less positive $E^\ominus$ value from the more positive $E^\ominus$ value.

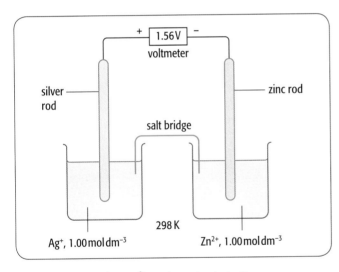

Figure 19.13 An Ag^+/Ag, Zn^{2+}/Zn electrochemical cell.

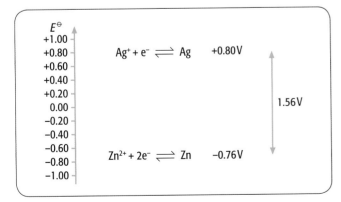

Figure 19.14 The difference between $+0.80\,V$ and $-0.76\,V$ is $+1.56\,V$.

The $E^\ominus$ value for the Ag^+/Ag half-cell is more positive than for the Zn^{2+}/Zn half-cell. So the Ag^+/Ag half-cell is the positive pole and the Zn^{2+}/Zn half-cell is the negative pole of the cell.

For the electrochemical cell shown in Figure **19.15**, the relevant half-equations are:

$$Fe^{3+}(aq) + e^- \rightleftharpoons Fe^{2+}(aq) \qquad\qquad E^\ominus = +0.77\,V$$
$$Cu^{2+}(aq) + 2e^- \rightleftharpoons Cu(s) \qquad\qquad E^\ominus = +0.34\,V$$

The voltage of this cell is $+0.77 - (+0.34) = +0.43\,V$.

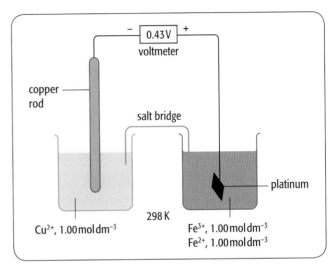

Figure 19.15 A Cu^{2+}/Cu, Fe^{3+}/Fe^{2+} electrochemical cell.

The $E^\ominus$ value for the Fe^{3+}/Fe^{2+} half-cell is more positive than for the Cu^{2+}/Cu half-cell. So the Fe^{3+}/Fe^{2+} half-cell is the positive pole and the Cu^{2+}/Cu half-cell is the negative pole of the cell.

Check-up

11 a Draw a diagram of an electrochemical cell consisting of a Cr^{3+}/Cr half-cell and a Cl_2/Cl^- half-cell.

   b Use the data in Appendix 2 (page **498**) to calculate the cell voltage.

   c Which half-cell is the positive pole?

12 a Draw a diagram of an electrochemical cell consisting of a Mn^{2+}/Mn half-cell and a Pb^{2+}/Pb half-cell.

   b Use the data in Appendix 2 (page **498**) to calculate the cell voltage.

   c Which half-cell is the positive pole?

$E^\ominus$ values and the direction of electron flow

We can deduce the direction of electron flow in the wires in the external circuit by comparing the $E^\ominus$ values for the two half-cells which make up the electrochemical cell. For example in Figure 19.13 these voltages are:

$$Ag^+(aq) + e^- \rightleftharpoons Ag(s) \qquad\qquad E^\ominus = +0.80\,V$$
$$Zn^{2+}(aq) + 2e^- \rightleftharpoons Zn(s) \qquad\qquad E^\ominus = -0.76\,V$$

The relative values of these voltages tell us that Zn^{2+} ions are more difficult to reduce than Ag^+ ions. So
• Zn metal will lose electrons to the Ag^+/Ag half-cell
• Ag^+ ions will accept electrons from the Zn^{2+}/Zn half-cell
The electrons move through the wires in the external circuit. They do not travel through the electrolyte solution.

So the electron flow is from the Zn^{2+}/Zn half-cell to the Ag^+/Ag half-cell. In other words, the flow is from the negative pole to the positive pole. It may help you to remember that the more **positive** pole attracts the **negative** electrons.

In the electrochemical cell in Figure 19.15, the electrons move in the external circuit from the Cu^{2+}/Cu half-cell to the Fe^{3+}/Fe^{2+} half-cell.

$$Fe^{3+}(aq) + e^- \rightleftharpoons Fe^{2+}(aq) \qquad\qquad E^\ominus = +0.77\,V$$
$$Cu^{2+}(aq) + 2e^- \rightleftharpoons Cu(s) \qquad\qquad E^\ominus = +0.34\,V$$

The negative pole of this cell is provided by the Cu^{2+}/Cu half-cell. This because the Cu^{2+}/Cu half-cell is better at losing electrons than the Fe^{3+}/Fe^{2+} half-cell.

Check-up

13 State the direction of the electron flow in the electrochemical cells represented by the following pairs of half-equations. Use the data in Appendix 2 (page 498) to help you.

a $F_2 + 2e^- \rightleftharpoons 2F^-$ and $Mn^{2+} + 2e^- \rightleftharpoons Mn$

b $Sn^{4+} + 2e^- \rightleftharpoons Sn^{2+}$ and $I_2 + 2e^- \rightleftharpoons 2I^-$

c $Cr_2O_7^{2-} + 14H^+ + 6e^- \rightleftharpoons 2Cr^{3+} + 7H_2O$ and $Cu^{2+} + 2e^- \rightleftharpoons Cu$

d $Ni^{2+} + 2e^- \rightleftharpoons Ni$ and $Fe^{3+} + 3e^- \rightleftharpoons Fe$

Using $E^\ominus$ values to predict if a reaction will occur

Standard electrode potential values, $E^\ominus$, give us a measure of how easy or difficult it is to oxidise or reduce a species. We can compare the oxidising and reducing powers of elements and ions by comparing the $E^\ominus$ values for their half reactions.

Figure 19.16 compares the oxidising and reducing powers of selected elements and ions. The $E^\ominus$ values are listed in order of increasingly negative values. For each half-equation, the more oxidised form is on the left and the more reduced form is on the right.

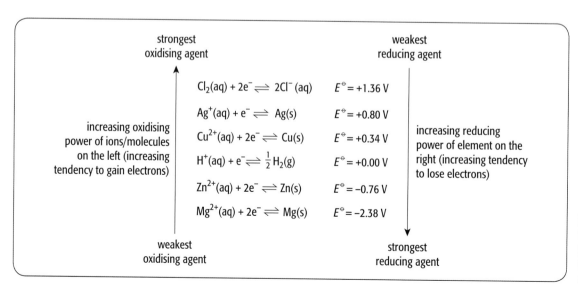

Figure 19.16 Standard electrode potentials for some oxidising and reducing agents.

- The more positive the value of $E^\ominus$, the greater is the tendency for the half-equation to proceed in the forward direction.
- The less positive the value of $E^\ominus$, the greater is the tendency for the half-equation to proceed in the reverse direction.
- The more positive the value of $E^\ominus$, the easier it is to reduce the species on the left of the half-equation.
- The less positive the value of $E^\ominus$, the easier it is to oxidise the species on the right of the half-equation.

We can make an electrochemical cell from the two half-cells:

$$Cu^{2+}(aq) + 2e^- \rightleftharpoons Cu(s) \qquad E^\ominus = +0.34\,V$$

$$Zn^{2+}(aq) + 2e^- \rightleftharpoons Zn(s) \qquad E^\ominus = -0.76\,V$$

When these two half-cells are connected together, a reaction takes place in each of the half-cells. The $E^\ominus$ values can be used to predict whether the reaction happening in each half-cell is a reduction (i.e. forward direction) reaction, or an oxidation (i.e. backwards direction) reaction. If the reactions happening in each half-cell are combined, we can produce an ionic equation for the reaction that takes place in the electrochemical cell as a whole.

Cu^{2+} has a greater tendency to gain electrons than Zn^{2+}, so the chemical reaction that proceeds in this half-cell is in the forward direction:

$$Cu^{2+}(aq) + 2e^- \rightarrow Cu(s)$$

Zn has a greater tendency to lose electrons than Cu, so the chemical reaction that proceeds in this half-cell is in the reverse direction:

$$Zn(s) \rightarrow Zn^{2+}(aq) + 2e^-$$

We can combine these two half-equations to show the direction of the reaction in the electrochemical cell as a whole.

$$Zn(s) + Cu^{2+}(aq) \rightarrow Zn^{2+}(aq) + Cu(s)$$

This is the reaction taking place in the electrochemical cell. But it is also the reaction that takes place if a piece of zinc metal is placed directly into a $1.00\,mol\,dm^{-3}$ solution of Cu^{2+} ions. A reaction is said to be **feasible** if it is likely to occur. The reaction between zinc metal and copper ions is feasible.

If the forward reaction is feasible, the reverse reaction (between Cu metal and zinc ions) is not feasible. If a piece of copper metal is placed directly into a $1.00\,mol\,dm^{-3}$ solution of Zn^{2+} ions no reaction takes place.

Figure 19.17 As predicted by the $E^\ominus$ values, zinc reacts with Cu^{2+} ions but copper does not react with Zn^{2+} ions.

We can predict whether a reaction is likely to occur by referring to a list of half reactions with their $E^\ominus$ values listed in descending order from most positive to most negative (see Figure **19.16**). When we select two half-equations, the direction of the reaction is given by a clockwise pattern (reactant, product, reactant, product) starting from the top left as shown in Figure **19.18** for the cell made from the two half-cells Cu^{2+}/Cu and Zn^{2+}/Zn.

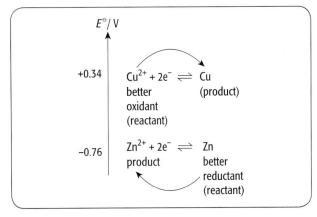

Figure 19.18 A reaction occurs in a direction so that the stronger oxidising agent reacts with the stronger reducing agent.

Here are some examples of using $E^\ominus$ values to predict whether a reaction occurs or not.

Worked examples

1 Will chlorine oxidise Fe^{2+} ions to Fe^{3+} ions?
- Write down the two half-equations with the more positive $E^{\ominus}$ value first.

$$\tfrac{1}{2}Cl_2(g) + e^- \rightleftharpoons Cl^-(aq) \qquad E^{\ominus} = +1.36\,V$$
$$Fe^{3+}(aq) + e^- \rightleftharpoons Fe^{2+}(aq) \qquad E^{\ominus} = +0.77\,V$$

- Identify the stronger oxidising agent and the stronger reducing agent.
  Cl_2 is the better oxidising agent. This is because the more positive value of $E^{\ominus}$ indicates that Cl_2 molecules are more likely to accept electrons than are Fe^{3+} ions.
  Fe^{2+} is the better reducing agent. This is because the more negative value of $E^{\ominus}$ indicates that Fe^{2+} ions are more likely to release electrons than are Cl^- ions.
- The stronger oxidising agent reacts with the stronger reducing agent, meaning that the reaction is feasible.
- The top reaction goes in the forward direction and the bottom reaction goes in the reverse direction:

$$\tfrac{1}{2}Cl_2(g) + e^- \rightleftharpoons Cl^-(aq)$$
$$Fe^{2+}(aq) \rightleftharpoons Fe^{3+}(aq) + e^-$$

- Combine the two half-equations:

$$\tfrac{1}{2}Cl_2(g) + Fe^{2+}(aq) \rightarrow Cl^-(aq) + Fe^{3+}(aq)$$

This reaction is feasible. The prediction made using $E^{\ominus}$ values is correct, this reaction takes place in a suitable electrochemical cell, or when Cl_2 gas is bubbled into a $1.00\,mol\,dm^{-3}$ solution of Fe^{2+} ions.
This means that this reaction

$$Cl^-(aq) + Fe^{3+}(aq) \rightarrow \tfrac{1}{2}Cl_2(g) + Fe^{2+}(aq)$$

is not feasible. If a $1.00\,mol\,dm^{-3}$ solution of Fe^{3+} ions is added to a $1.00\,mol\,dm^{-3}$ solution of Cl^- ions, no reaction takes place. This prediction has been made using $E^{\ominus}$ values, and it is correct. $E^{\ominus}$ values are a very powerful tool for predicting which redox reactions are feasible, and which ones are not feasible.

2 Will iodine, I_2, oxidise Fe^{2+} ions to Fe^{3+} ions?
- Give the two half-equations, with most positive $E^{\ominus}$ value first.

$$Fe^{3+}(aq) + e^- \rightleftharpoons Fe^{2+}(aq) \qquad E^{\ominus} = +0.77\,V$$
$$\tfrac{1}{2}I_2(aq) + e^- \rightleftharpoons I^-(aq) \qquad E^{\ominus} = +0.54\,V$$

- Identify the stronger oxidising agent and the stronger reducing agent.
  Fe^{3+} is the better oxidising agent. It is more likely to accept electrons than I_2 molecules.
  I^- is the better reducing agent. It is more likely to release electrons than Fe^{2+} ions.
- I_2 is a relatively weaker oxidising agent and Fe^{2+} is a relatively weaker reducing agent. So the reaction is NOT feasible. (The reaction that is feasible is the reaction between Fe^{3+} ions and I^- ions.)

3 Will hydrogen peroxide, H_2O_2, reduce acidified manganate(VII) ions, MnO_4^-, to Mn^{2+} ions?
- Write down the two half-equations with the more positive $E^{\ominus}$ value first.

$$MnO_4^-(aq) + 8H^+(aq) + 5e^- \rightleftharpoons Mn^{2+}(aq) + 4H_2O(l)$$
$$E^{\ominus} = +1.52\,V$$

$$O_2(g) + 2H^+(aq) + 2e^- \rightleftharpoons H_2O_2(aq)$$
$$E^{\ominus} = +0.68\,V$$

- Identify the stronger oxidising agent and the stronger reducing agent.
  The system $MnO_4^- + H^+$ is the better oxidising agent. It more likely to accept electrons than the system $O_2 + 2H^+$.
  H_2O_2 is the better reducing agent. It is more likely to release electrons than Mn^{2+} ions.
- The stronger oxidising agent reacts with the stronger reducing agent, so the reaction is feasible.
- The top reaction goes in the forward direction and the bottom reaction goes in the reverse direction:

$$MnO_4^-(aq) + 8H^+(aq) + 5e^- \rightleftharpoons Mn^{2+}(aq) + 4H_2O(l)$$

$$H_2O_2(aq) \rightleftharpoons O_2(g) + 2H^+(aq) + 2e^-$$

continued ⋯▸

continued ⋯▸

- Balance the electrons, so that 10 electrons are involved in each half-equation:

$$2MnO_4^-(aq) + 16H^+(aq) + 10e^- \rightleftharpoons 2Mn^{2+}(aq) + 8H_2O(l)$$

$$5H_2O_2(aq) \rightleftharpoons 5O_2(g) + 10H^+(aq) + 10e^-$$

- Combine the two half-equations:

$$2MnO_4^-(aq) + 6H^+(aq) + 5H_2O_2(aq) \rightleftharpoons 2Mn^{2+}(aq) + 8H_2O(l) + 5O_2(g)$$

Note that 10 H^+ ions have been cancelled from each side.

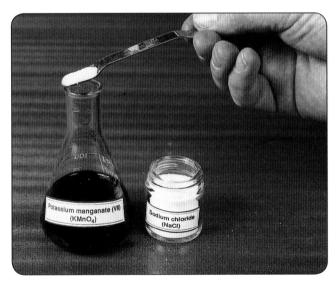

Figure 19.19 If the $KMnO_4$(aq) is acidified, would it be safe to do this in an open lab or would chlorine gas be produced? You will answer this question in Check-up question **14**, part **a**.

Check-up

14 Use the data in Appendix 2 (page 498) to predict whether or not the following reactions are feasible. If a reaction does occur, write a balanced equation for it.
   a Can MnO_4^- ions oxidise Cl^- ions to Cl_2 in acidic conditions?
   b Can MnO_4^- ions oxidise F^- ions to F_2 in acidic conditions?
   c Can H^+ ions oxidise V^{2+} ions to V^{3+} ions?
   d Can H^+ ions oxidise Fe^{2+} ions to Fe^{3+} ions?

continued ⋯⟶

15 Suggest a suitable reagent which can carry out each of the following oxidations or reductions. Use the data in Appendix 2 (page 498) to help you.
   a The reduction of Zn^{2+} ions to Zn.
   b The oxidation of Br^- ions to Br_2.
   c The reduction of acidified SO_4^{2-} ions to SO_2.
   d The oxidation of Cl^- ions to Cl_2.

We can use the relative voltage of the half-cells to predict whether a reaction takes place without considering which species is the best oxidant or reductant. The procedure is given in the examples below.

Worked examples

4 Will bromine oxidise silver to silver ions?

   Step 1 Write the equation for the suggested reaction.

   $$\tfrac{1}{2}Br_2 + Ag \rightarrow Br^- + Ag^+$$

   Step 2 Write the two half-equations:

   $$\tfrac{1}{2}Br_2 + e^- \rightleftharpoons Br^-$$

   $$Ag \rightleftharpoons Ag^+ + e^-$$

   Step 3 Include the value of $E^\ominus$ for each half reaction but reverse the sign of the half-equation showing oxidation (loss of electrons). This is because the data book values are always for the reduction reaction.

   $$\tfrac{1}{2}Br_2 + e^- \rightleftharpoons Br^- \qquad E^\ominus = +1.07\,V$$

   $$Ag \rightleftharpoons Ag^+ + e^- \qquad E^\ominus = -0.80\,V$$

   Step 4 Add the two voltages. This is because we are combining the two half-equations.

   $$= +1.07 + (-0.80) = +0.27\,V$$

   Step 5 If the value of the sum of the two voltages is positive the reaction will occur as written. If the value of the sum of the two voltages is negative the reaction will not occur.

continued ⋯⟶

In this case the sum of the two voltages is positive so bromine will oxidise silver to silver ions.

5 Will iodine oxidise silver to silver ions?

Step 1 Write the equation for the suggested reaction.

$$\tfrac{1}{2}I_2 + Ag \rightarrow I^- + Ag^+$$

Step 2 The two half-equations are

$$\tfrac{1}{2}I_2 + e^- \rightleftharpoons I^-$$

$$Ag \rightleftharpoons Ag^+ + e^-$$

Step 3 Write the $E^\ominus$ values, with sign reversed for the oxidation reaction.

$$\tfrac{1}{2}I_2 + e^- \rightleftharpoons I^- \qquad\qquad E^\ominus = +0.54\,V$$

$$Ag \rightleftharpoons Ag^+ + e^- \qquad\qquad E^\ominus = -0.80\,V$$

Step 4 Add the two voltages.

$$= +0.54 + (-0.80) = -0.26\,V$$

Step 5 The sum of the two voltages is negative, so iodine will not oxidise silver to silver ions.

Check-up

16 Use the cell voltage method described in Worked examples 4 and 5 above to answer Check-up question 14, parts **a** to **d**.

$E^\ominus$ values and oxidising and reducing agents

Look back at Figure **19.16** (page 280). Note the following as the values of $E^\ominus$ for each of these reduction reactions gets more negative.

- The species on the left of the equation become weaker oxidising agents. They accept electrons less readily.
- The species on the right of the equation become stronger reducing agents. They release electrons more readily.

Cu will not reduce Zn^{2+} ions to Zn. So how can we reduce Zn^{2+} ions? The answer is to react the Zn^{2+} ions with a stronger reducing agent, which should have an

$E^\ominus$ value more negative than the $E^\ominus$ value for Zn^{2+}/Zn. In Figure **19.16** we see that the half-equation Mg^{2+}/Mg has a more negative $E^\ominus$ value. So Mg is a suitable reducing agent.

$$Zn^{2+}(aq) + e^- \rightleftharpoons Zn(s) \qquad\qquad E^\ominus = -0.76\,V$$

$$Mg^{2+}(aq) + 2e^- \rightleftharpoons Mg(s) \qquad\qquad E^\ominus = -2.38\,V$$

Zn^{2+} is the better oxidising agent. It is more likely to accept electrons than Mg^{2+} ions. Mg is the better reducing agent. It is more likely to release electrons than Zn.

Nitric acid is a good oxidising agent, but it will not oxidise chloride ions to chlorine. So how can we oxidise Cl^- ions? The answer is to react the Cl^- ions with a stronger oxidising agent, which should have an $E^\ominus$ value more positive than the $E^\ominus$ value for Cl_2/Cl^-. The half-equation

$$MnO_4^-(aq) + 8H^+(aq) + 5e^- \rightleftharpoons Mn^{2+}(aq) + 4H_2O(l)$$

provides a suitable oxidising agent.

This half-equation has a more positive $E^\ominus$ value than that for the Cl_2/Cl^- half-equation. So acidified MnO_4^- ions are a suitable oxidising agent to oxidise chloride ions to chlorine (see Figure **19.19**).

$$MnO_4^-(aq) + 8H^+(aq) + 5e^- \rightleftharpoons Mn^{2+}(aq) + 4H_2O(l)$$
$$E^\ominus = +1.52\,V$$

$$\tfrac{1}{2}Cl_2(g) + e^- \rightleftharpoons Cl^-(aq) \qquad\qquad E^\ominus = +1.36\,V$$

Acidified MnO_4^- is the better oxidising agent. It is more likely to accept electrons than Cl_2 molecules. Cl^- is the better reducing agent. It is more likely to release electrons than Mn^{2+}.

We can explain the relative oxidising abilities of the halogens in a similar way. The standard electrode potentials for the halogens are:

$$\tfrac{1}{2}F_2 + e^- \rightleftharpoons F^- \qquad\qquad E^\ominus = +2.87\,V$$

$$\tfrac{1}{2}Cl_2 + e^- \rightleftharpoons Cl^- \qquad\qquad E^\ominus = +1.36\,V$$

$$\tfrac{1}{2}Br_2 + e^- \rightleftharpoons Br^- \qquad\qquad E^\ominus = +1.07\,V$$

$$\tfrac{1}{2}I_2 + e^- \rightleftharpoons I^- \qquad\qquad E^\ominus = +0.54\,V$$

Based on these $E^{\ominus}$ values, as we go down Group VII from F_2 to I_2, the oxidising ability of the halogen decreases and the ability of halide ions to act as reducing agents increases.

Figure 19.20 Aqueous chlorine displaces bromine from a solution of potassium bromide. We can use $E^{\ominus}$ values to explain why a halogen higher in Group VII displaces a halogen lower in the Group from a solution of its halide ions.

Check-up

17 Use the $E^{\ominus}$ values for the halogens (see page **498**) to explain the following:
   a Why bromine can oxidise an aqueous solution of iodide ions.
   b Why bromine does not react with chloride ions.

18 Use the data in Appendix 2 (page **498**) to answer these questions.
   a Of the ions Ag^+, Cr^{2+} and Fe^{2+}, which one needs the strongest reducing agent to reduce it to metal atoms?
   b Of the atoms Ag, Cr and Fe, which one needs the strongest oxidising agent to oxidise it to an ion?

How does the value of *E* vary with ion concentration?

In Chapter **8** (page **131**) we saw that the position of an equilibrium reaction is affected by changes in concentration, temperature and pressure. Redox equilibria

are no different. When we compare the voltage of a standard half-cell, X, with a standard hydrogen electrode, we are measuring $E^{\ominus}$ for the half-cell X. If we change the concentration or temperature of half-cell X, the electrode potential also changes. Under these non-standard conditions we use the symbol E for the electrode potential.

What happens to the electrode potential when we change the concentration of ions in a half-cell? Let us take an example of a metal/metal ion equilibrium:

$$Zn^{2+}(aq) + e^- \rightleftharpoons Zn(s) \qquad\qquad E^{\ominus} = -0.76\,V$$

- If $[Zn^{2+}]$ is greater than $1.00\,mol\,dm^{-3}$, the value of E becomes less negative / more positive (for example $-0.61\,V$).
- If $[Zn^{2+}]$ is less than $1.00\,mol\,dm^{-3}$, the value of E becomes more negative / less positive (for example $-0.80\,V$).

We can apply Le Chatelier's principle to redox equilibria. If we increase the concentration of the species on the left of the equation, the position of equilibrium will shift to the right. So the value of E becomes more positive / less negative.

If two different ions are present in the half-cell, we have to consider both ions.

Let us take the equilibrium between Fe^{3+} ions and Fe^{2+} ions as an example.

$$Fe^{3+} + e^- \rightleftharpoons Fe^{2+} \qquad\qquad E^{\ominus} = +0.77\,V$$
$$1.00\,mol\,dm^{-3} \quad 1.00\,mol\,dm^{-3}$$

- If $[Fe^{3+}]$ is greater than $1.00\,mol\,dm^{-3}$ (keeping $[Fe^{2+}]$ = $1.00\,mol\,dm^{-3}$) the value of E becomes more positive (for example $+0.85\,V$).
- If $[Fe^{3+}]$ is less than $1.00\,mol\,dm^{-3}$ (keeping $[Fe^{2+}]$ = $1.00\,mol\,dm^{-3}$) the value of E becomes less positive (for example $0.70\,V$).
- If $[Fe^{2+}]$ is greater than $1.00\,mol\,dm^{-3}$ (keeping $[Fe^{3+}]$ = $1.00\,mol\,dm^{-3}$) the value of E becomes less positive (for example $+0.70\,V$).
- If $[Fe^{2+}]$ is less than $1.00\,mol\,dm^{-3}$ (keeping $[Fe^{3+}]$ = $1.00\,mol\,dm^{-3}$) the value of E becomes more positive (for example $0.85\,V$).

You can see from the above that if we increase the concentration of both the Fe^{3+} and Fe^{2+} ions, these effects may cancel each other out.

How can we predict whether or not a given reaction will occur under non-standard conditions? The answer is that if the $E^{\ominus}$ values of the two half reactions involved differ by more than 0.30 V, then the reaction predicted by the $E^\ominus$ values is highly likely to occur. So chlorine is likely to oxidise Fe^{2+} ions even if the conditions are not standard. This is because the difference in their $E^\ominus$ values is 0.59 V which is considerably greater than 0.30 V.

$$\tfrac{1}{2}Cl_2(g) + e^- \rightleftharpoons Cl^-(aq) \qquad\qquad E^\ominus = +1.36\,V$$

$$Fe^{3+}(aq) + e^- \rightleftharpoons Fe^{2+}(aq) \qquad\qquad E^\ominus = +0.77\,V$$

We cannot, however, predict with confidence whether the reaction between MnO_4^- ions and Cl_2 will take place if the conditions are too far from standard.

$$MnO_4^-(aq) + 8H^+(aq) + 5e^- \rightleftharpoons Mn^{2+}(aq) + 4H_2O(l)$$
$$E^\ominus = +1.52\,V$$

$$\tfrac{1}{2}Cl_2(g) + e^- \rightleftharpoons Cl^-(aq) \qquad\qquad E^\ominus = +1.36\,V$$

This is because the difference in $E^\ominus$ values is 0.16 V which is considerably smaller than 0.30 V.

Fact file

The figure 0.30 V given here to enable us to tell if a reaction will still occur under non-standard conditions is a rough guide only. If $E^\ominus$ values differ by less than 0.30 V, non-standard conditions may result in an unexpected outcome. If you want a bit more precision about this, try finding out about the Nernst equation!

Check-up

19 The half-cell

$$Cr_2O_7^{2-} + 14H^+ + 6e^- \rightleftharpoons 2Cr^{3+} + 7H_2O$$

has an $E^\ominus$ value of +1.33 V.
   a Suggest how the value of E changes if the other species are kept at $1.00\,mol\,dm^{-3}$ but:
   i $[Cr_2O_7^{2-}]$ is increased
   ii $[H^+]$ is decreased
   iii $[Cr^{3+}]$ is increased.
   b What effect would each of these concentration changes have on the

continued ⋯⋗

strength of the acidified $Cr_2O_7^{2-}$ solution as an oxidising agent?
   c What conditions would you use to make a solution of $Cr_2O_7^{2-}$ as strong an oxidising agent as possible?
   d Use Le Chatelier's principle to explain your answer to part **c**.

Feasibility predictions based on $E^\ominus$ don't always work!

The feasibility of a reaction based on $E^\ominus$ values is no guarantee that a reaction will proceed quickly. It only tells us that a reaction is possible, and that the reverse reaction does not occur. Some reactions are feasible, but they proceed so slowly that they do not **seem** to be taking place. Take, for example, the lack of reactivity of zinc with cold water. Remember that water contains H^+ ions. The relevant half-equations are:

$$H^+ + e^- \rightleftharpoons \tfrac{1}{2}H_2(g) \qquad\qquad E^\ominus = 0.00\,V$$

$$Zn^{2+}(aq) + 2e^- \rightleftharpoons Zn(s) \qquad\qquad E^\ominus = -0.76\,V$$

Even when the low concentration of H^+ ions is taken into account, $E^\ominus$ values predict that a reaction should occur. The rate of reaction between zinc and water, however, is extremely slow. It is the rate of reaction rather than the value of $E^\ominus$ which is determining the lack of reactivity.

Check-up

20 An industrial process relies on a reaction that is impractically slow under normal conditions. How might you try to solve this problem? Use your knowledge of reaction rates to suggest several different approaches.

21 Describe two limitations to using $E^\ominus$ values to predict the feasibility of a reaction.

19.5 Cells and batteries

The variety of cells

The ordinary dry cells used in torches, toys and radios have voltages ranging from 1.5 V to 2.0 V. Several of these cells are often needed to produce enough power and the voltage of these 'batteries' drops gradually during their lifetime.

A wide variety of electrochemical cells have been developed for specific functions in recent years. Many cells are small but they do not necessarily produce a high voltage for a long time. Batteries of several cells joined together give a higher voltage but take up more space. When selecting a cell for a particular job we need to consider:
- whether or not the cell can be recharged
- the size and mass of the cell
- the voltage of the cell
- the nature of the electrolyte
- how long the cell can deliver its maximum voltage
- the cost of the cell.

Fact file
The first use of the word 'battery' in connection with electricity was in 1748, when Benjamin Franklin used the term to describe a set of charged glass plates placed on top of each other. The first electrochemical battery was developed by Alessandro Volta in 1791. It consisted of alternating discs of zinc and copper separated by strips of cloth soaked in brine.

Rechargeable cells

The electrochemical cells that you have studied so far are called primary cells. In these cells the redox reactions continue until the reactants reach a low concentration and the voltage of the cell declines. The cell is then of no use any more. Some electrochemical cells can be recharged by passing an electric current through them. The products are then changed back to reactants so the cell can function again. These cells are called secondary cells or storage cells.

A car battery is a secondary cell which consists of plates of lead and lead(IV) oxide immersed in sulfuric acid (Figure 19.21). The voltage of each cell is 2 V. In order to operate the car's starter motor, a higher voltage is required. So a car battery consists of six of these cells

in series to provide 12 V. The battery is recharged by the car's alternator while the car engine is running. Lead–acid batteries are very heavy but are cheap to manufacture.

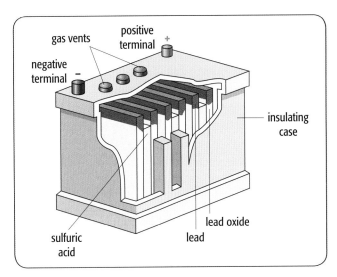

Figure 19.21 The storage cell used in a car.

Fact file
The half-equations in a lead–acid car battery are:

$$Pb^{2+}(aq) + 2e^- \rightleftharpoons Pb(s) \qquad E^\circ = -0.13\,V$$

$$PbO_2(s) + 4H^+(aq) + 2e^- \rightleftharpoons Pb^{2+}(aq) + 2H_2O(l)$$
$$E^\circ = +1.47\,V$$

Can you explain why the overall reaction is:

$$Pb(s) + PbO_2(s) + 4H^+(aq) \rightarrow 2Pb^{2+}(aq) + 2H_2O(l)$$

When the battery is recharged both the half-reactions are reversed. So the overall reaction during charging is:

$$2Pb^{2+}(aq) + 2H_2O(l) \rightarrow Pb(s) + PbO_2(s) + 4H^+(aq)$$

The cell voltage is approx. 2 V, not 1.60 V, due to non-standard conditions.

Improved batteries for electric vehicles have been developed.
- Nickel–cadmium cells are smaller and have a lower mass than lead–acid cells but they give a lower voltage. They do not 'run down' as quickly.
- Aluminium–air batteries are lightweight and produce a higher voltage than a lead–acid battery. They are expensive and are not true secondary cells because the aluminium anode has to be replaced from time to time.

Solid state cells

In recent years, primary cells have been developed with improved voltage and reduced size. Cells the size of a large button are used in heart pacemakers, hearing aids and other medical uses as well as in watches and calculators. They have several advantages:

• they are lightweight and small
• they give a high voltage, for example 3.0 V
• they give a constant voltage over time
• they do not contain liquids or paste, so they do not leak.

Commonly used 'button' cells use lithium or zinc as the negative pole and iodine, manganese(IV) oxide or silver oxide as the positive pole.

Figure 19.22 Button cells like these are used to power watches and hearing aids.

Check-up

22 The nickel–cadmium cell is rechargeable. The half-equations for the electrode reactions are:

$$Cd(OH)_2 + 2e^- \rightarrow Cd + 2OH^-\quad E^\ominus = -0.81\,V$$
$$NiO_2 + 2H_2O + 2e^- \rightarrow Ni(OH)_2 + 2OH^-$$
$$E^\ominus = +0.49\,V$$

a Which of these reactions proceeds in a forward direction when electrical energy is being taken from the cell?

continued ⋯⋗

b Predict the cell voltage, assuming that all conditions are standard.

c Write an equation for the cell reaction that occurs when electrical energy is being taken from the cell.

d Write an equation for the cell reaction that occurs when the cell is being recharged.

23 Lithium is often used as the negative pole in 'button' cells used to power watches.

a Explain why lithium is often used to make electrochemical cells.

b The half-equations for a lithium/iodine button cell are:

$$Li^+ + e^- \rightarrow Li \qquad\qquad E^\ominus = -3.04\,V$$
$$\tfrac{1}{2}I_2(s) + e^- \rightleftharpoons I^-(aq) \qquad E^\ominus = +0.54\,V$$

  i Predict the cell voltage of this cell using the $E^\ominus$ values for the two half-equations above.

  ii The actual voltage of a lithium/iodine button cell is 2.8 V. Suggest why this is different from the value you calculated in part **a**.

c Give **two** advantages of a lithium/iodine cell compared with an ordinary dry cell.

Hydrogen–oxygen fuel cells

A **fuel cell** is an electrochemical cell in which a fuel gives up electrons at one electrode and oxygen gains electrons at the other electrode. Fuel cells are increasingly used instead of petrol to power buses and cars. The fuel is stored in tanks in the vehicle and oxygen comes from the air. The energy released in a fuel cell produces a voltage which can be used to power the electric motor of the vehicle.

One type of fuel cell is the hydrogen–oxygen fuel cell. Hydrogen gas and oxygen gas are bubbled through two porous platinum-coated electrodes where the half reactions take place. Electrons flow through the external circuit from the negative to the positive pole. As they do so, their energy is used to drive an electric motor or other device. The overall reaction is:

$$2H_2 + O_2 \rightarrow 2H_2O$$

Figure 19.23 Fuel cells may eventually replace petrol and diesel engines in cars.

Fact file

A hydrogen–oxygen fuel cell with an acidic electrolyte is shown in Figure **19.24**.

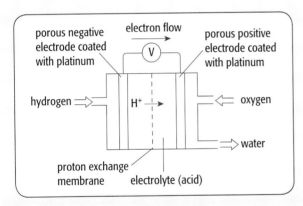

Figure 19.24 A hydrogen–oxygen fuel cell.

At the negative electrode, hydrogen gas loses electrons:

$$H_2(g) \rightarrow 2H^+(aq) + 2e^-$$

The electrons move round the external circuit where they can do a useful job of work, e.g. drive an electric motor. The H^+ ions diffuse through the membrane to the positive electrode. The reaction at the positive electrode is:

$$4H^+(aq) + O_2(g) + 4e^- \rightarrow 2H_2O$$

The electrons travel through the external circuit from the negative electrode to the positive electrode.

Fuel cells have several advantages over petrol and diesel engines.

- Water is the only product made – no carbon dioxide or harmful nitrogen oxides are released.
- They produce more energy per gram of fuel burnt than petrol engines do.
- They are very efficient – the transmission of energy from the fuel cell to the motor is direct. There are no moving parts where energy is wasted as heat.

There are several limitations to hydrogen–oxygen fuel cells.

- High cost: the materials used to make the electrodes and membrane are expensive.
- Manufacturing of fuel cells involves the production of toxic by-products.
- Storage of hydrogen: high-pressure tanks are needed in order to store a sufficient amount of fuel. At present refuelling has to be done more often compared with a petrol engine.
- Manufacturing hydrogen: the hydrogen needed for fuel cells can only be produced cheaply by using fossil fuels.
- Fuel cells do not work well at low temperatures: if the temperature falls much below 0 °C, the fuel cell 'freezes'.

Check-up

24 A car's fuel tank holds 40 kg of petrol.
- 1 kg of petrol releases 5×10^7 J of energy when it burns.
- Only 40% of the energy released when the petrol burns is converted into useful work.
- 1×10^6 J of work is needed to drive the car 1 km.
   a How many joules of energy are released when 40 kg of petrol burns?
   b How many of these joules of energy are available to move the car forward?
   c How far can the car travel on 40 kg of petrol?

25 A fuel cell vehicle with a similar volume fuel tank can store 400 g of hydrogen at high pressure.
- 2 g of hydrogen release 286 000 J of energy when used in the vehicle's fuel cells.

continued ⋯⁙

- 60% of the energy released from the fuel cell is converted into useful work.
- 1×10^6 J of work is needed to drive the car 1 km.

a How many joules of energy are released when 400 g of hydrogen is used in the vehicle's fuel cells?

b How many of these joules of energy are available to move the car forward?

c How far can the car travel on 400 g of hydrogen?

26 Compare and comment on your answers to questions 24 and 25.

19.6 More about electrolysis

Introduction

In Chapter 7 (page **119**) we studied the electrolysis of aluminium oxide and aqueous sodium chloride. During electrolysis:

- cations (positive ions) move towards the cathode where they gain electrons; gain of electrons is reduction
- anions (negative ions) move towards the anode where they lose electrons; loss of electrons is oxidation.

In this section we shall find out how the nature of the electrolyte and the concentration of aqueous electrolytes affects the products of electrolysis.

Electrolysis of molten electrolytes

When pure molten ionic compounds containing two simple ions are electrolysed, a metal is formed at the cathode and a non-metal at the anode. Some examples are shown in Table **19.1**.

Compound electrolysed	Cathode product	Anode product
aluminium oxide	aluminium	oxygen
magnesium bromide	magnesium	bromine
sodium chloride	sodium	chlorine
zinc iodide	zinc	iodine

Table 19.1 The products formed at the cathode and anode when some molten salts are electrolysed.

Let us take the electrolysis of molten zinc chloride as an example.

At the cathode, the metal ions gain electrons and are reduced to the metal.

$$Zn^{2+} + 2e^- \rightarrow Zn$$

At the anode, the non-metal ions lose electrons and are oxidised to a non-metal.

$$2Cl^- \rightarrow Cl_2 + 2e^-$$

Electrolysis of aqueous solutions

Aqueous solutions of electrolytes contain more than one cation and more than one anion. For example, an aqueous solution of sodium chloride contains Na^+, Cl^-, H^+ and OH^- ions. The H^+ and OH^- ions arise from the ionisation of water:

$$H_2O \rightleftharpoons H^+ + OH^-$$

So – we have to ask, which ions are **discharged** (changed into atoms or molecules) during the electrolysis of aqueous solutions?

Amongst other things this depends on:

- the relative electrode potential of the ions
- the concentration of the ions.

Electrolysis products and electrode potentials

When an aqueous ionic solution is electrolysed using inert electrodes, there is usually only one product obtained at each electrode. The ease of discharge of cations at the cathode is related to their electrode potentials. Figure **19.25** shows some half reactions and their electrode potentials.

$E^\ominus$/ V

+0.80	$Ag^+(aq) + e^- \rightleftharpoons Ag(s)$
+0.34	$Cu^{2+}(aq) + 2e^- \rightleftharpoons Cu(s)$
0.00	$H^+(aq) + e^- \rightleftharpoons \frac{1}{2} H_2(g)$
−0.13	$Pb^{2+}(aq) + 2e^- \rightleftharpoons Pb(s)$
−0.76	$Zn^{2+}(aq) + 2e^- \rightleftharpoons Zn(s)$
−2.38	$Mg^{2+}(aq) + 2e^- \rightleftharpoons Mg(s)$
−2.71	$Na^+(aq) + e^- \rightleftharpoons Na(s)$

increasing ease of discharge of cation at cathode

Figure 19.25 The ease of discharge of ions at a cathode in electrolysis is related to the electrode potential of the ions.

The cation which is most easily reduced is discharged at the cathode. So the cation in the half-equation with the most positive $E^{\ominus}$ value will be discharged.

When a concentrated aqueous solution of sodium chloride ($1.00\,mol\,dm^{-3}$) is electrolysed, H^+ ions and Na^+ ions are present in the solution. Hydrogen rather than sodium is formed at the cathode because H^+ ions are more easily reduced than Na^+ ions.

$$H^+ + e^- \rightleftharpoons \tfrac{1}{2}H_2 \qquad\qquad E^{\ominus} = 0.00\,V$$

$$Na^+(aq) + e^- \rightleftharpoons Na(s) \qquad E^{\ominus} = -2.71\,V$$

When a concentrated aqueous solution of copper(II) sulfate ($1.00\,mol\,dm^{-3}$) is electrolysed, H^+ ions and Cu^{2+} ions are present in the solution. Copper rather than hydrogen is formed at the cathode because Cu^{2+} ions are more easily reduced than H^+ ions.

$$Cu^{2+}(aq) + 2e^- \rightleftharpoons Cu(s) \qquad E^{\ominus} = +0.34\,V$$

$$H^+ + e^- \rightleftharpoons \tfrac{1}{2}H_2 \qquad\qquad E^{\ominus} = 0.00\,V$$

At the anode, using graphite electrodes, the ease of discharge of anions follows the order:

$$SO_4^{2-}(aq)\ \ NO_3^-(aq)\ \ Cl^-(aq)\ \ OH^-(aq)\ \ Br^-(aq)\ \ I^-(aq)$$

increasing ease of discharge
increasing ease of oxidation

When a concentrated aqueous solution of sodium sulfate ($1.00\,mol\,dm^{-3}$) is electrolysed, OH^- ions and SO_4^{2-} ions are present in the solution. Hydroxide ions are discharged

Fact file

We usually carry out electrolysis using graphite electrodes both in the laboratory and in industry. Based on $E^{\ominus}$ values, OH^- ions should be discharged more readily (forming water and oxygen gas) than Cl^- ions. So why are Cl^- ions discharged in preference? Oxygen **is** given off as predicted if shiny platinum electrodes are used. But these are expensive. Oxygen is less readily discharged if other electrodes are used. This can result in an anion just below OH^- (such as Cl^-) being discharged instead. This is called the over-voltage effect because a higher voltage is needed to discharge the OH^- ion.

at the anode because OH^- ions are more easily oxidised than SO_4^{2-} ions. The OH^- ions are oxidised to oxygen, which bubbles off at the anode.

$$4OH^-(aq) \rightarrow O_2(g) + 2H_2O(l) + 4e^-$$

When a concentrated aqueous solution of sodium iodide ($1.00\,mol\,dm^{-3}$) is electrolysed, I^- ions and OH^- ions are present in the solution. Iodide ions are discharged at the anode because I^- ions are more easily oxidised than OH^- ions.

$$I^-(aq) \rightarrow \tfrac{1}{2}I_2(aq) + e^-$$

Note that in the discussion above, we have used standard electrode potentials. If conditions are standard, the concentration of the aqueous solution is $1.00\,mol\,dm^{-3}$ with respect to the ionic compound dissolved in water. But the concentration of hydrogen and hydroxide ions in solution is very low. We saw on page 283 that we can use electrode potential values to predict whether or not a reaction will occur under non-standard conditions. As long as the difference in electrode potentials is greater than $0.30\,V$, we can be fairly sure that the predictions will be correct.

Check-up

27 An aqueous solution of sodium sulfate is electrolysed using carbon electrodes.
   a Explain why hydrogen is formed at the cathode and not sodium.
   b Write a half-equation for the reaction occurring at the anode.

28 Predict the electrolysis products at the anode and cathode when the following are electrolysed:
   a molten aluminium iodide
   b a concentrated aqueous solution of magnesium chloride
   c a concentrated aqueous solution of sodium bromide
   d molten zinc oxide.

Electrolysis products and solution concentration

When aqueous solutions are electrolysed, the ions are rarely present at concentrations of $1.00 \, mol \, dm^{-3}$. On page **285** we saw that the value of E changes with the concentration of the ion. An ion, Z, higher in the discharge series may be discharged in preference to one below it if Z is present at a relatively higher concentration than normal. For this to be possible, the E values of the competing ions are usually less than 0.30 V different from each other.

When a concentrated solution of sodium chloride is electrolysed, chloride ions are discharged at the anode in preference to hydroxide ions. This is because chloride ions are present in a much higher concentration than hydroxide ions. The chloride ions fall below the hydroxide ions in the discharge series.

But what happens when we electrolyse an extremely dilute solution of sodium chloride?

We find that oxygen, rather than chlorine, is formed at the anode. This is because the relatively lower concentration of Cl^- ions allows OH^- ions to fall below Cl^- ions in the discharge series. In reality, the electrolysis of a dilute aqueous solution of sodium chloride gives a mixture of chlorine and oxygen at the anode. The proportion of oxygen increases the more dilute the solution.

Check-up

29 A concentrated aqueous solution of hydrochloric acid is electrolysed.
  a Write half-equations to show the reactions at:
    i   the cathode
    ii the anode.
  b A very dilute solution of hydrochloric acid is electrolysed. What substance or substances are formed at the anode? Explain your answer.

19.7 Quantitative electrolysis

The mass of substance deposited during electrolysis

The mass of a substance produced at an electrode during electrolysis is proportional to:
• the time over which a constant electric current passes
• the strength of the electric current.

Combining current and time, we get the relationship:

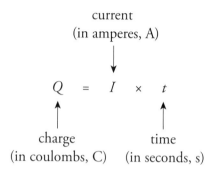

The mass of a substance produced at an electrode (anode or cathode) during electrolysis is proportional to the quantity of electricity (in coulombs) which passes through the electrolyte.

Fact file

The Faraday unit is named after Michael Faraday, an English scientist (1791–1867). Although he had very little proper education, Faraday became one of the great experimental scientists of his age. He proposed two laws of electrolysis (**Faraday's laws**). These (in modified form) are:
• Faraday's first law: the mass of substance produced at an electrode is proportional to the quantity of electricity passed
• Faraday's second law: the number of Faradays required to discharge 1 mole of an ion at an electrode is equal to the charge on the ion.

Faraday was famous for his lectures but had to give up work after 1855 because he lost his memory.

The quantity of electricity is often expressed in terms of a unit called the **Faraday** (symbol F). 1 Faraday is the quantity of electric charge carried by 1 mole of electrons or 1 mole of singly charged ions. Its value is $96\,500 \, C \, mol^{-1}$ (to 3 significant figures).

During the electrolysis of silver nitrate solution, silver is deposited at the cathode:

$$\underset{1 \, mol}{Ag^+} + \underset{1 \, mol}{e^-} \rightarrow \underset{1 \, mol}{Ag}$$

1 Faraday of electricity (96 500 C) is required to deposit 1 mole of silver.

During the electrolysis of copper(II) sulfate solution, copper is deposited at the cathode:

$$\underset{1 \, mol}{Cu^{2+}} + \underset{2 \, mol}{2e^-} \rightarrow \underset{1 \, mol}{Cu}$$

The equation shows that 2 moles of electrons are needed to produce 1 mole of copper from Cu^{2+} ions. So it requires 2 Faradays of electricity ($2 \times 96\,500\,C$) to deposit 1 mole of copper.

During the electrolysis of molten sodium chloride, chlorine is produced at the anode:

$$\underset{2\,mol}{2Cl^-} \rightarrow \underset{1\,mol}{Cl_2} + \underset{2\,mol}{2e^-}$$

The equation shows that 2 moles of electrons are released when 1 mole of chlorine gas is formed from 2 moles of Cl^- ions. So it requires 2 Faradays of electricity ($2 \times 96\,500\,C$) to produce 1 mole of Cl_2.

During the electrolysis of an aqueous solution of sulfuric acid or aqueous sodium sulfate, oxygen is produced at the anode:

$$4OH^-(aq) \rightarrow O_2(g) + 2H_2O(l) + 4e^-$$

The equation shows that 4 moles of electrons are released when 1 mole of oxygen gas is formed from 4 moles of OH^- ions. So it requires 4 Faradays of electricity ($4 \times 96\,500\,C$) to produce 1 mole of O_2.

Calculating amount of substance produced during electrolysis

We can use the value of F to calculate:
- the mass of substance deposited at an electrode
- the volume of gas produced at an electrode.

Worked examples

6 Calculate the mass of lead deposited at the cathode during electrolysis when a current of 1.50 A flows through molten lead(II) bromide for 20.0 min.
(A_r value: [Pb] = 207; $F = 96\,500\,C\,mol^{-1}$)

Step 1 Write the half-equation for the reaction.

$$Pb^{2+} + 2e^- \rightarrow Pb$$

Step 2 Find the number of coulombs required to deposit 1 mole of product at the electrode.

2 moles of electrons are required per mole of Pb formed

$= 2F$
$= 2 \times 96\,500$
$= 193\,000\,C\,mol^{-1}$

continued ⋯⇢

Step 3 Calculate the charge transferred during the electrolysis.

$Q = I \times t$
$\quad = 1.50 \times 20 \times 60$
$\quad = 1800\,C$

Step 4 Calculate the mass by simple proportion using the relative atomic mass.

$193\,000\,C$ deposits 1 mole Pb, which is 207 g Pb

so $1800\,C$ deposits $\dfrac{1800}{193\,000} \times 207 = 1.93\,g$ Pb

7 Calculate the volume of oxygen produced at r.t.p. when a concentrated aqueous solution of sulfuric acid is electrolysed for 30.0 min using a current of 0.50 A.
($F = 96\,500\,C\,mol^{-1}$; 1 mole of gas occupies $24.0\,dm^3$ at r.t.p.)

Step 1 Write the half-equation for the reaction.

$$4OH^-(aq) \rightarrow O_2(g) + 2H_2O(l) + 4e^-$$

Step 2 Find the number of coulombs required to produce 1 mole of gas.

4 moles of electrons are released per mole of O_2 formed

$= 4F$
$= 4 \times 96\,500$
$= 386\,000\,C\,mol^{-1}$

Step 3 Calculate the charge transferred during the electrolysis.

$Q = I \times t$
$\quad = 0.50 \times 30 \times 60$
$\quad = 900\,C$

Step 4 Calculate the volume by simple proportion using the relationship 1 mole of gas occupies $24.0\,dm^3$ at r.t.p.

$386\,000\,C$ produces 1 mole O_2, which is $24\,dm^3$ O_2

so $900\,C$ produces $\dfrac{900}{386\,000} \times 24.0$

$= 0.0560\,dm^3$ O_2 at r.t.p.

30 Calculate the mass of silver deposited at the cathode during electrolysis when a current of 1.80 A flows through an aqueous solution of silver nitrate for 45.0 min.
(A_r value: [Ag] = 108; F = 96 500 C mol^{-1})

31 Calculate the volume of hydrogen produced at r.t.p. when a concentrated aqueous solution of sulfuric acid is electrolysed for 15.0 min using a current of 1.40 A.
(F = 96 500 C mol^{-1}; 1 mole of gas occupies 24.0 dm^3 at r.t.p.)

32 Calculate the volume of oxygen produced at r.t.p. when a concentrated aqueous solution of sodium sulfate is electrolysed for 55.0 min using a current of 0.70 A.
(F = 96 500 C mol^{-1}; 1 mole of gas occupies 24.0 dm^3 at r.t.p.)

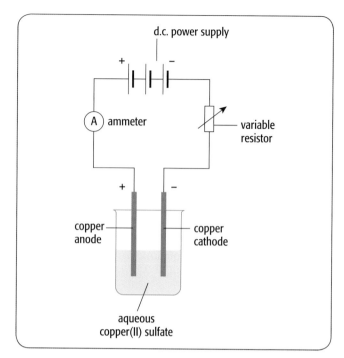

Figure 19.26 Apparatus for calculating the mass of copper deposited during the electrolysis of aqueous copper(II) sulfate.

The Faraday constant and the Avogadro constant

The Avogadro constant, L, is the number of specified particles in 1 mole (see page 4).

We can use an electrolytic method to find a value for the Avogadro constant by calculating the charge associated with 1 mole of electrons.

$$L = \frac{\text{charge on 1 mole of electrons}}{\text{charge on 1 electron}}$$

We can calculate the charge on the electron by experiment. You do not have to know how this is done. The results show us that the charge on the electron is approximately 1.60×10^{-19} C.

The charge on 1 mole of electrons can be found from a simple electrolytic experiment. The apparatus for this is shown in Figure 19.26.

The procedure is:
• weigh the pure copper anode and pure copper cathode separately
• arrange the apparatus as shown in Figure 19.26; the variable resistor is used to keep the current constant
• pass a constant electric current for a measured time interval
• remove the cathode and anode and wash and dry them with distilled water and then with propanone
• reweigh the cathode and anode.

The cathode increases in mass because copper is deposited. The anode decreases in mass because the copper goes into solution as copper ions. The decrease in mass of the anode is measured. This is preferred because the copper does not always 'stick' to the cathode very well.

A sample calculation is shown below, using a current of 0.20 A for 34 min.
• mass of anode at start of the experiment = 56.53 g
• mass of anode at end of experiment = 56.40 g
• mass of copper removed from anode = 0.13 g
• quantity of charge passed $Q = I \times t$
$$= 0.20 \times 34 \times 60$$
$$= 408 \text{ C}$$

To deposit 0.13 g of copper requires 408 C, so to deposit 1 mole of copper (63.5 g) requires $\dfrac{63.5}{0.13} \times 408\,\text{C}$

But the equation for the electrolysis shows that 2 moles of electrons are needed to produce 1 mole of copper:

$$Cu^{2+} + 2e^- \rightarrow Cu$$

The charge on 1 mole of electrons $= \dfrac{63.5}{0.13} \times 408 \times \dfrac{1}{2}$

$$= 99\,600\,\text{C}$$

If the charge on one electron is $1.60 \times 10^{-19}\,\text{C}$,

$$L = \dfrac{99600}{1.60 \times 10^{-19}} = 6.2 \times 10^{23}\,\text{mol}^{-1} \text{ (to 2 significant figures)}$$

This is in good agreement with the accurate value of $6.02 \times 10^{23}\,\text{mol}^{-1}$.

Check-up

33 A student passed a constant electric current of 0.15 A through a solution of silver nitrate, using pure silver electrodes, for 45 min exactly. The mass of the anode decreased by 0.45 g. Use this data to calculate the charge on a mole of electrons.
(A_r value: [Ag] = 108)

34 An accurate value of the Faraday constant is $96\,485\,\text{C}\,\text{mol}^{-1}$. An accurate value for the charge on one electron is $1.6022 \times 10^{-19}\,\text{C}$. Use these values to calculate a value of the Avogadro constant to 5 significant figures.

Summary

- [ ] A half-cell can consist of an element in contact with its aqueous ions or two different aqueous ions of the same element in different oxidation states in contact with a platinum electrode.
- [ ] Two half-cells joined together form an electrochemical cell.
- [ ] A standard hydrogen electrode is a half-cell in which hydrogen gas at a pressure of 101 kPa bubbles through a solution of $1.00\,\text{mol}\,\text{dm}^{-3}\ H^+(aq)$ ions.
- [ ] The standard electrode potential of a half-cell ($E^\ominus$) is the voltage of the half-cell under standard conditions compared with a standard hydrogen electrode.
- [ ] The standard cell potential ($E^\ominus_{cell}$) is the voltage developed under standard conditions when two half-cells are joined.
- [ ] The standard cell potential is calculated from the difference between the standard electrode potentials of two half-cells.
- [ ] The direction of electron flow in a simple cell is from the half-cell which has the more negative (or less positive) electrode potential to the half-cell which has the less negative (or more positive) electrode potential.
- [ ] The value of $E^\ominus_{cell}$ can be used to predict whether a reaction is likely to take place (whether the reaction is feasible).
- [ ] A particular redox reaction will occur if the $E^\ominus$ of the half-equation involving the species being reduced is more positive than the $E^\ominus$ of the half-equation of the species being oxidised.
- [ ] The ability of the halogens to act as oxidising agents depends on the $E^\ominus$ of the half-equation involving $X_2 + 2e^- \rightleftharpoons 2X^-$ (where X is a halogen atom). The more positive the value of $E^\ominus$ for this half reaction, the better the halogen is as an oxidising agent.
- [ ] Redox equations can be constructed by combining the relevant half-equations.
- [ ] The value of the $E^\ominus$ of a half-cell containing a metal in contact with its aqueous ions becomes more negative as the concentration of the aqueous ion decreases.
- [ ] A fuel cell uses the energy from reaction of a fuel (such as hydrogen) with oxygen to generate a voltage.
- [ ] Improved batteries (as in electric vehicles) have advantages in terms of smaller size, lower mass and higher voltage.
- [ ] The Faraday constant (F) is the electric charge, in coulombs, on 1 mole of electrons.
- [ ] The relationship between the Faraday constant, the Avogadro constant (L) and the charge on an electron (e) is given by $F = Le$.
- [ ] A value for the Avogadro constant can be determined by an electrolytic method using the relationship $F = Le$.

☐ The nature of the substances liberated during electrolysis depends on:
  – the state of the electrolyte (molten or aqueous); a metal is formed at the cathode when molten metal salts are electrolysed; hydrogen may be formed at the cathode when dilute aqueous solutions of metal salts are electrolysed
  – the position of the ions (in the electrolyte) in the redox series; ions lower in the redox series are more likely to be discharged than those higher in the series
  – the concentration of the ions in the electrolyte; when different ions are not very far apart in the redox series, the ion present in greater concentration is more likely to be discharged.
☐ The quantity of charge, in coulombs, passed during electrolysis is found by multiplying the current, in amps, by time, in seconds, $Q = It$.
☐ The mass and/or volume of substance liberated during electrolysis can be calculated from the quantity of charge and the number of Faradays required to discharge 1 mole of ions.

End-of-chapter questions

1   The diagram shows an electrochemical cell designed to find the standard electrode potential for zinc.

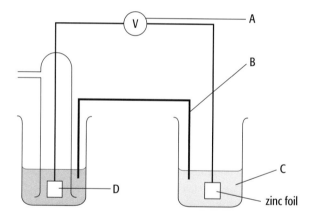

a	Name the apparatus labelled **A** and give a characteristic it should have.	[2]
b i	Name part **B** and give its two functions.	[3]
ii	Describe how part **B** can be prepared.	[2]
c	What is **C**?	[2]
d	Name part **D** and give its two functions.	[3]
e	Give the **three** standard conditions for the measurement of a standard electrode potential.	[3]

Total = 15

Examiner's tip

Question **2**, part **c**, involves three questions in which you have two choices of answer.
To be sure of getting your answers the right way round, apply the rules carefully. To start with, the half-cell with the more positive $E^\ominus$ value will attract and accept electrons, so reduction takes place here. Remember OIL RIG – Oxidation Is Loss, Reduction Is Gain (of electrons).

2 The diagram shows an electrochemical cell involving two metal/metal-ion systems.

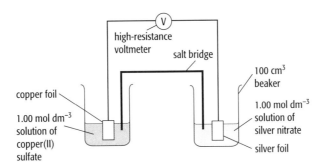

The standard electrode potential for the half-cells are:

$Ag^+ + e^- \rightleftharpoons Ag$ $\quad E^\ominus = +0.80\,V$

$Cu^{2+} + 2e^- \rightleftharpoons Cu$ $\quad E^\ominus = +0.34\,V$

a Calculate a value for the cell voltage. Show your working. [2]
b Write the balanced ionic equation for the overall cell reaction. [2]
c In this reaction:
 i Which substance is oxidised? Explain your answer. [1]
 ii Which substance is reduced? Explain your answer. [1]
 iii In which direction do the electrons flow? Explain your answer. [2]
d The contents of the Cu^{2+}/Cu half-cell are diluted with water. The contents of the Ag^+/Ag half-cell are kept the same. Suggest what effect this will have on the value of the cell voltage, *E*. Explain your answer. [3]

Total = 11

Examiner's tip

Question **3**, part **a**, is another definition! Make sure you learn them – definitions are easy marks.
Question **3**, part **b**, includes the word 'standard', so don't forget standard conditions when you are labelling. This is also relevant for several of the other questions that follow.

3 **a** Define the term **standard electrode potential.** [3]
b Draw a labelled diagram to show how the standard electrode potential of a half-cell containing chlorine gas and chloride ions can be measured. [5]
c Write a half-equation for this half-cell. [1]

d The standard electrode potential of a Cl_2/Cl^- half-cell is +1.36 V. This Cl_2/Cl^- half-cell was connected to a standard half-cell containing solid iodine in equilibrium with iodide ions. The standard electrode potential of an I_2/I^- half-cell is +0.54 V.

  i Calculate the standard cell voltage for this cell. [1]

  ii Write the balanced ionic equation for the overall cell reaction. [2]

  Total = 12

4 **a** In the presence of acid, the manganate(VII) ion is a powerful oxidising agent. The half-equation for its reduction in acid solution is:

$$MnO_4^-(aq) + 8H^+(aq) + 5e^- \rightleftharpoons Mn^{2+}(aq) + 4H_2O(l) \qquad E^\ominus = +1.51\,V$$

  a **i** Explain why the presence of an acid is necessary for the $MnO_4^-(aq)$ to function as an oxidising agent. [1]

  ii Give **two** reasons for the $MnO_4^-(aq)$ acting as an oxidising agent in acidic solution. [2]

  b Iodide ions are oxidised to iodine according to the half-cell equation:

$$\tfrac{1}{2}I_2(aq) + e^- \rightleftharpoons I^-(aq) \qquad E^\ominus = +0.54\,V$$

  i Explain why an acidified solution of mangante(VII) ions can be used to oxidise iodide ions to iodine. [5]

  ii Write the balanced equation for this reaction. [2]

  Total = 10

5 Liquid bromine is added to an aqueous solution of potassium iodide. The following reaction takes place.

$$Br_2(l) + 2I^-(aq) \rightarrow 2Br^-(aq) + I_2(aq) \qquad E^\ominus_{cell} = +0.53\,V$$

  a Write two half-equations for this reaction. [2]

  b Draw a labelled diagram to show two linked half-cells which could be used to measure the standard cell potential for this reaction. [7]

  c The standard cell potential for this reaction is +0.53 V. Does the position of equilibrium favour the reactants or the products? Explain your answer. [4]

  d The standard electrode potentials for a number of half-equations are shown below:

$$Fe^{3+}(aq) + e^- \rightarrow Fe^{2+}(aq) \qquad\qquad E^\ominus = +0.77\,V$$

$$I_2(aq) + 2e^- \rightarrow 2I^-(aq) \qquad\qquad E^\ominus = +0.54\,V$$

$$Ni^{2+}(aq) + 2e^- \rightarrow Ni(s) \qquad\qquad E^\ominus = -0.25\,V$$

$$Pb^{4+}(aq) + 2e^- \rightarrow Pb^{2+}(aq) \qquad\qquad E^\ominus = +1.69\,V$$

  Which atom or ion in this list will reduce iodine to iodide ions? Explain your answer. [4]

  Total = 17

6 The list below gives the standard electrode potentials for five half reactions.

$$Cu^{2+}(aq) + e^- \rightarrow Cu(s) \qquad\qquad E^\ominus = +0.34\,V$$

$$Fe^{2+}(aq) + 2e^- \rightarrow Fe(s) \qquad\qquad E^\ominus = -0.44\,V$$

$$Fe^{3+}(aq) + e^- \rightarrow Fe^{2+}(aq) \qquad E^\ominus = +0.77\,V$$

$$I_2(aq) + 2e^- \rightarrow 2I^-(aq) \qquad\qquad E^\ominus = +0.54\,V$$

$$Zn^{2+}(aq) + 2e^- \rightarrow Zn(s) \qquad\quad E^\ominus = -0.76\,V$$

a What is the meaning of **standard electrode potential**? [3]

b Which species in the list is:

   i the strongest oxidising agent? [1]

   ii the strongest reducing agent? [1]

c A cell was set up as shown below.

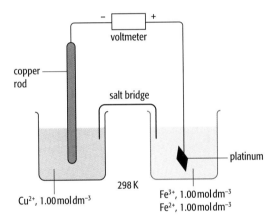

   i Calculate the standard cell potential of this cell. [1]

   ii In which direction do the electrons flow in the external circuit? Explain your answer. [2]

   iii Write an equation for the complete cell reaction. [2]

d The concentration of copper(II) ions in the left-hand electrode was increased from $1.00\,mol\,dm^{-3}$ to $1.30\,mol\,dm^{-3}$. The concentration of ions in the right-hand cell was not changed.

   i What effect does this change have on the E value of the Cu^{2+}/Cu half-cell? [1]

   ii What effect does this change have on the E value for the complete electrochemical cell? [1]

   iii Why is the direction of the cell reaction unlikely to be altered by this change in concentration? [1]

e Lithium–iodine button cells are often used to power watches. Suggest **two** reasons, other than size, why button cells are used to power watches rather than ordinary 'dry cells'. [2]

Total = 15

7   An electric current of 1.04 A was passed through a solution of dilute sulfuric acid for 6.00 min.
    The volume of hydrogen produced at r.t.p. was $43.5\,cm^3$.
    a   How many coulombs of charge were passed during the experiment?   [1]
    b   How many coulombs of charge are required to liberate 1 mole of hydrogen gas? $F = 96\,500\,C\,mol^{-1}$ [2]
    c   In another experiment, copper(II) sulfate was electrolysed using copper electrodes. Copper was
        deposited at the cathode.
        i   Write a half-equation for this reaction.   [1]
        ii A student conducted an experiment to calculate a value for the Faraday constant, F. An electric
            current of 0.300 A was passed through the solution of copper(II) sulfate for exactly 40 min.
            0.240 g of copper was deposited at the cathode. Use this information to calculate a value for F.
            Express your answer to 3 significant figures.
            (A_r value: [Cu] = 63.5)   [3]
        iii The charge on one electron is approximately $1.60 \times 10^{-19}\,C$. Use this information and your
            answer to part ii to calculate a value for the Avogadro constant.   [2]
                                                                                                   Total = 9

8   An aqueous solution of silver nitrate is electrolysed.
    a   i   Explain why silver rather than hydrogen is produced at the cathode.   [2]
        ii Write an equation for the reaction occurring at the cathode.   [1]
    b   i   Write an equation for the reaction occurring at the anode.   [1]
        ii Is the anode reaction an oxidation or reduction reaction? Explain your answer.   [1]
    c   Explain why the silver nitrate solution becomes acidic during this electrolysis.   [3]
    d   Calculate the mass of silver deposited at the cathode when the electrolysis is carried out for
        exactly 35 min using a current of 0.18 A. A_r [Ag] = 108; $F = 96\,500\,C\,mol^{-1}$ [3]
                                                                                                  Total = 11

20 Ionic equilibria

Learning outcomes

Candidates should be able to:

- explain the terms **pH**, **pK_a** and **K_w** and use them in calculations
- calculate $[H^+(aq)]$ and pH values for strong and weak acids and strong bases
- explain the choice of suitable indicators for acid–base titrations, given appropriate data
- describe the changes in pH during acid-base titrations and explain these changes in terms of the strengths of the acids and bases
- explain how buffer solutions control pH

- describe and explain the uses of buffer solutions, including the role of HCO_3^- in controlling pH in the blood
- calculate the pH of buffer solutions, given appropriate data
- show understanding of and use the concept of solubility product, K_{sp}
- calculate K_{sp} from concentrations and vice versa
- show understanding of the common ion effect.

20.1 Introduction

In Chapter 8 (page 147) we learned that acids and bases can be classed as strong or weak.

- Strong acids ionise completely in water. For example, hydrochloric acid solution consists entirely of $H_3O^+(aq)$ and $Cl^-(aq)$:

$$HCl(g) + H_2O(l) \rightarrow H_3O^+(aq) + Cl^-(aq)$$

- Weak acids only ionise to a small extent in water. For example, ethanoic acid solution consists mostly of un-ionised $CH_3COOH(aq)$:

$$CH_3COOH(aq) + H_2O(l) \rightleftharpoons CH_3COO^-(aq) + H_3O^+(aq)$$

The pH of the resulting solutions can be related to the concentration of H_3O^+ ions formed.

In this chapter:

- we shall use hydrogen ion concentrations to calculate pH values for solutions of strong acids
- we will use equilibrium expressions to calculate hydrogen ion concentrations for solutions of weak acids, in order to calculate their pH values
- we shall also learn about ionic equilibria related to the solubility of salts.

The ionic product of water, K_w

Water is able to act as either an acid (by donating protons, H^+) or a base (by accepting protons). In pure water, the following equilibrium exists.

$$\text{H}^+ \text{ donated}$$

$$H_2O(l) + H_2O(l) \rightleftharpoons H_3O^+(aq) + OH^-(aq)$$
$$\text{acid} \qquad\qquad \text{base}$$

We can simplify this equation by writing hydroxonium ions, H_3O^+, as simple hydrogen ions, H^+:

$$H_2O(l) \rightleftharpoons H^+(aq) + OH^-(aq)$$

Figure 20.1 Compost in a compost bin. The pH of compost changes as the plant material is broken down by bacterial action. The chemical reactions in compost involve weak acids and weak bases.

The equilibrium expression for this reaction is:

$$K_c = \frac{[H^+(aq)][OH^-(aq)]}{[H_2O(l)]}$$

The extent of ionisation of water is very low. The concentration of hydrogen ions and hydroxide ions in pure water (and hence the value of K_c) is extremely small. Because of this, we can regard the concentration of water as being constant. We can therefore incorporate this into the value of K_c. The equilibrium expression then becomes:

$$K_w = [H^+][OH^-]$$

K_w is called the **ionic product of water**. Its value at 298 K is $1.00 \times 10^{-14} \, mol^2 \, dm^{-6}$.

We can use this equation to find the hydrogen ion concentration in pure water; for simplicity we will now omit the state symbol (aq). For each molecule of water that ionises, one H^+ ion and one OH^- ion are produced.

$$[H^+] = [OH^-]$$

We can rewrite the equilibrium expression

$$K_w = [H^+][OH^-]$$

as:

$$K_w = [H^+]^2$$

Rearranging this equation to find the hydrogen ion concentration $[H^+]$ in pure water:

$$[H^+] = \sqrt{K_w} = \sqrt{1.00 \times 10^{-14}} = 1.00 \times 10^{-7} \, mol \, dm^{-3}$$

20.2 pH calculations

We know that the lower the hydrogen ion concentration, the higher the pH. The pH values of some familiar aqueous solutions are shown in Table 20.1.

Defining pH

The range of possible hydrogen ion concentrations in different solutions is very large. It can range from $10^{-15} \, mol \, dm^{-3}$ to $10 \, mol \, dm^{-3}$. In order to overcome the problem of dealing with a wide range of numbers, the Danish chemist Søren Sørensen introduced the **pH** scale.

Solution	pH
hydrochloric acid ($1.00 \, mol \, dm^{-3}$)	0.0
stomach 'juices' (contains HCl(aq))	1.0–2.0
lemon juice	2.3
vinegar	3
coffee	around 5
rainwater (normal)	5.7
saliva	6.3–6.8
fresh milk	around 6.5
pure water	7.0
sea water	around 8.5
milk of magnesia	10
soapy water (cheap soap!)	11
bench sodium hydroxide ($1.00 \, mol \, dm^{-3}$)	14

Table 20.1 pH values of some familiar aqueous solutions.

Fact file

The term 'pH' was introduced by the Danish Scientist Søren Sørensen while he was working out how to improve the quality of beer. The term pH is short for the power of the H^+ ion concentration. Sørensen used the word 'potenz' (meaning power) when he first devised the term – it's lucky for us that both terms begin with the letter 'p'!

pH is defined as the negative logarithm to the base 10 of the hydrogen ion concentration. In symbols this is written:

$$pH = -\log_{10}[H^+]$$

Note that:
- the negative sign is introduced to make the pH values positive in most cases
- the logarithms used are to the base 10 (not to the base e) so make sure that when doing calculations, you press the log or lg button on your calculator (not the ln button)
- we can use this equation to convert $[H^+]$ to pH or pH to $[H^+]$.

Calculating pH values from [H⁺]

Here is an example of the use of logarithms to calculate pH from hydrogen ion concentrations.

Worked example

1 Calculate the pH of a solution whose H^+ ion concentration is $5.32 \times 10^{-4}\,mol\,dm^{-3}$.

$$pH = -\log_{10}[H^+]$$
$$= -\log_{10}(5.32 \times 10^{-4})$$
$$= 3.27$$

Use your own calculator to check that you can get the correct answer. Try it several times. If you cannot get this answer (3.27) check with your calculator's instruction booklet, or find your teacher or a member of your teaching group to work with to solve this problem.

Check-up

1 Calculate the pH of the following solutions:
   a $[H^+] = 3.00 \times 10^{-4}\,mol\,dm^{-3}$
   b $[H^+] = 1.00 \times 10^{-2}\,mol\,dm^{-3}$
   c $[H^+] = 4.00 \times 10^{-8}\,mol\,dm^{-3}$
   d $[H^+] = 5.40 \times 10^{-12}\,mol\,dm^{-3}$
   e $[H^+] = 7.80 \times 10^{-10}\,mol\,dm^{-3}$

You should notice that the solutions in Check-up **1**, parts **c**, **d** and **e**, are alkalis; they all have pH values greater than 7. Even though they are alkalis they each still have a small concentration of H^+ ions, and this concentration is used to calculate the pH. They each have a small concentration of H^+ ions because $H_2O \rightleftharpoons H^+ + OH^-$ is an equilibrium. Even when there is an excess of OH^- ions there is still a small concentration of H^+ ions. In the same way, the solutions in Check-up 1, parts **a** and **b**, have a small concentration of OH^- ions, even though the solutions are acids.

Calculating [H⁺] from pH

Here is an example of the use of logarithms to calculate hydrogen ion concentration from pH. Use your own calculator to check that you get the correct answer.

Worked example

2 Calculate the hydrogen ion concentration of a solution whose pH is 10.5.

$$pH = -\log_{10}[H^+]$$
$$[H^+] = 10^{-pH}$$
$$= 10^{-10.5}$$
$$= 3.16 \times 10^{-11}\,mol\,dm^{-3}$$

Use your own calculator to check that you can get the correct answer. Try it several times. If you cannot get this answer (3.16×10^{-11}) check with your calculator's instruction booklet, or find your teacher or a member of your teaching group to work with to solve this problem.

Check-up

2 Calculate the concentration of hydrogen ions in solutions having the following pH values:
   a pH 2.90
   b pH 3.70
   c pH 11.2
   d pH 5.40
   e pH 12.9

The pH of strong acids

Monobasic acids contain only one replaceable hydrogen atom per molecule. Strong monobasic acids such as hydrochloric acid are completely ionised in

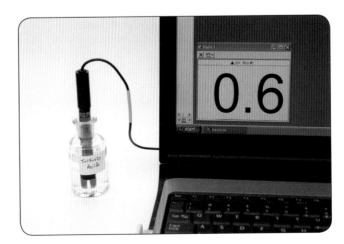

Figure 20.2 A pH electrode allows us to determine pH accurately.

solution. It follows from this, that the concentration of hydrogen ions in solution is approximately the same as the concentration of the acid. (We are making the assumption that the concentration of H^+ ions arising from the ionisation of water molecules is very small compared with those arising from the acid.)

- pH of $0.1\,mol\,dm^{-3}$ HCl is $-log(1\times10^{-1}\,mol\,dm^{-3}) = pH\ 1$
- pH of $0.01\,mol\,dm^{-3}$ HCl is $-log(1\times10^{-2}\,mol\,dm^{-3}) = pH\ 2$
- pH of $0.001\,mol\,dm^{-3}$ HCl is $-log(1\times10^{-3}\,mol\,dm^{-3}) = pH\ 3$

Diluting the acid 10 times reduces the value of the H^+ ion concentration by one-tenth and increases the pH by a value of one.

Calculating the pH of strong bases

Strong bases, such as sodium hydroxide, ionise completely in solution. The concentration of hydroxide ions in a solution of sodium hydroxide is therefore approximately the same as the concentration of the sodium hydroxide.

To calculate the pH of a solution of strong base we need to know:

- the concentration of OH^- ions in solution
- the equilibrium expression for the ionisation of water:
$$K_w = [H^+][OH^-]$$
- the value of K_w for water.

Since $K_w = [H^+][OH^-]$

$$[H^+] = \frac{K_w}{[OH^-]}$$

We can calculate the $[H^+]$ and then calculate pH.

Worked example

3   Calculate the pH of a solution of sodium hydroxide of concentration $0.0500\,mol\,dm^{-3}$.

$K_w = 1.00\times10^{-14}\,mol^2\,dm^{-6}$ (at 298 K).

Step 1   Write the expression relating $[H^+]$ to K_w and $[OH^-]$

$$[H^+] = \frac{K_w}{[OH^-]}$$

Step 2   Substitute the values into the expression to calculate $[H^+]$.

$$[H^+] = \frac{1.00\times10^{-14}}{0.0500} = 2.00\times10^{-13}\,mol\,dm^{-3}$$

Step 3   Calculate the pH.

$$\begin{aligned} pH &= -log_{10}[H^+] \\ &= -log(2.00\times10^{-13}) \\ &= 12.7 \end{aligned}$$

A quick way to get the same answer is to:

- find $-log_{10}[OH^-]$ (in this example $-log_{10}[OH^-] = -log_{10}(0.0500) = 1.3$)
- subtract this value from 14 (in this example $14 - 1.3 = 12.7$).

This works because $-log_{10}[H^+] - log_{10}[OH^-] = 14$

Check-up

3   Find the pH of the following strong acids and strong bases:
  a $1.00\,mol\,dm^{-3}$ HNO_3
  b $0.500\,mol\,dm^{-3}$ HNO_3
  c   an aqueous solution containing $3.00\,g$ HCl per dm^3
  d $0.001\,00\,mol\,dm^{-3}$ KOH ($K_w = 1.00\times10^{-14}\,mol^2\,dm^{-6}$)
  e   an aqueous solution containing $0.200\,g$ of NaOH per dm^3 ($K_w = 1.00\times10^{-14}\,mol^2\,dm^{-6}$)

20.3 Weak acids – using the acid dissociation constant, K_a

K_a and pK_a

The equilibrium law (see page 135) can be applied to aqueous solutions of weak acids and weak bases. For example, when ethanoic acid dissolves in water the following equilibrium results:

$$CH_3COOH(aq) + H_2O(l) \rightleftharpoons H_3O^+(aq) + CH_3COO^-(aq)$$

We can simplify this equation to:

$$\underset{\text{ethanoic acid}}{CH_3COOH(aq)} \rightleftharpoons H^+(aq) + \underset{\text{ethanoate ion}}{CH_3COO^-(aq)}$$

Figure 20.3
Friedrich Ostwald (1853–1932) was a German chemist who developed the idea of 'degree of dissociation' of weak acids and bases. He was one of the most famous physical chemists of his day. But strangely enough, he didn't accept the atomic theory until 1906.

We can write the general formula for a monobasic acid as HA. The balanced equation for the partial ionisation of this weak acid is:

$$HA(aq) \rightleftharpoons H^+(aq) + A^-(aq)$$

The general equilibrium expression applying to a monobasic acid then becomes:

$$K_a = \frac{[H^+][A^-]}{[HA]}$$

The value of K_a indicates the extent of dissociation of the acid.

- A high value for K_a (for example, $40 \, mol \, dm^{-3}$) indicates that the position of equilibrium lies to the right. The acid is almost completely ionised.
- A low value for K_a (for example, $1.0 \times 10^{-4} \, mol \, dm^{-3}$) indicates that the position of equilibrium lies to the left. The acid is only slightly ionised and exists mainly as HA molecules and comparatively few H^+ and A^- ions.

Since K_a values for many acids are very low, we can use **pK_a values** to compare their strengths.

$$pK_a = -\log_{10} K_a$$

Table **20.2** shows the range of values of K_a and pK_a for various acids. Note that the less positive the value of pK_a, the more acidic is the acid.

The equilibrium expression for this reaction is:

$$K_a = \frac{[H^+][CH_3COO^-]}{[CH_3COOH]}$$

K_a is called the **acid dissociation constant**. At 298 K the value of K_a for the dissociation of ethanoic acid is $1.74 \times 10^{-5} \, mol \, dm^{-3}$.

The units of K_a are determined in the same way as for K_c (see page 136). For the dissociation of a monobasic acid the units are $mol \, dm^{-3}$.

Acid or ion	Equilibrium in aqueous solution	K_a / $mol \, dm^{-3}$	pK_a
nitric	$HNO_3 \rightleftharpoons H^+ + NO_3^-$	about 40	−1.4
sulfuric(IV)	$H_2SO_3 \rightleftharpoons H^+ + HSO_3^-$	1.5×10^{-2}	1.82
hydrated Fe^{3+} ion	$[Fe(H_2O)_6]^{3+} \rightleftharpoons H^+ + [Fe(H_2O)_5(OH)]^{2+}$	6.0×10^{-3}	2.22
hydrofluoric	$HF \rightleftharpoons H^+ + F^-$	5.6×10^{-4}	3.25
nitric(III)	$HNO_2 \rightleftharpoons H^+ + NO_2^-$	4.7×10^{-4}	3.33
methanoic	$HCOOH \rightleftharpoons H^+ + HCOO^-$	1.6×10^{-4}	3.80
benzoic	$C_6H_5COOH \rightleftharpoons H^+ + C_6H_5COO^-$	6.3×10^{-5}	4.20
ethanoic	$CH_3COOH \rightleftharpoons H^+ + CH_3COO^-$	1.7×10^{-5}	4.77
propanoic	$CH_3CH_2COOH \rightleftharpoons H^+ + CH_3CH_2COO^-$	1.3×10^{-5}	4.89
hydrated Al^{3+} ion	$[Al(H_2O)_6]^{3+} \rightleftharpoons H^+ + [Al(H_2O)_5(OH)]^{2+}$	1.0×10^{-5}	5.00
carbonic	$CO_2 + H_2O \rightleftharpoons H^+ + HCO_3^-$	4.5×10^{-7}	6.35
silicic	$SiO_2 + H_2O \rightleftharpoons H^+ + HSiO_3^-$	1.3×10^{-10}	9.89
hydrogencarbonate ion	$HCO_3^- \rightleftharpoons H^+ + CO_3^{2-}$	4.8×10^{-11}	10.3
hydrogensilicate ion	$HSiO_3^- \rightleftharpoons H^+ + SiO_3^{2-}$	1.3×10^{-12}	11.9
water	$H_2O \rightleftharpoons H^+ + OH^-$	1.0×10^{-14}	14.0

Table 20.2 Acid dissociation constants, K_a, for a range of acids, for aqueous solutions in the region of 0.0–0.01 $mol \, dm^{-3}$.

Calculating K_a for a weak acid

We can calculate the value of K_a for a weak acid if we know:
- the concentration of the acid
- the pH of the solution.

From the general equation:

$$HA(aq) \rightleftharpoons H^+ + A^-$$

we can see that for each molecule of HA that ionises, one H^+ ion and one A^- ion are produced. (This assumes that we ignore the H^+ ions arising from the ionisation of water.)

$$[H^+] = [A^-]$$

We can rewrite the equilibrium expression

$$K_a = \frac{[H^+][A^-]}{[HA]}$$

as

$$K_a = \frac{[H^+]^2}{[HA]}$$

In order to calculate the value of K_a we make two assumptions.
- We ignore the concentration of hydrogen ions produced by the ionisation of the water molecules present in the solution. This is reasonable because the ionic product of water ($1.00 \times 10^{-14}\,mol^2\,dm^{-6}$) is negligible compared with the values for most weak acids (see Table 20.2).

- We assume that the ionisation of the weak acid is so small that the concentration of undissociated HA molecules present at equilibrium is approximately the same as that of the original acid.

Worked example 4 shows how to calculate the value of K_a using the pH and the concentration of the weak acid.

Worked example

4 Calculate the value of K_a for methanoic acid. A solution of $0.010\,mol\,dm^{-3}$ methanoic acid, HCOOH, has a pH of 2.90.

Step 1 Convert pH to $[H^+]$.

$$[H^+] = 10^{-2.90}$$
$$= 1.26 \times 10^{-3}\,mol\,dm^{-3}$$

Step 2 Write the equilibrium expression.

$$K_a = \frac{[H^+]^2}{[HA]} \text{ or } K_a = \frac{[H^+]^2}{[HCOOH]}$$

Step 3 Enter the values into the expression and calculate the answer.

$$K_a = \frac{(1.26 \times 10^{-3})^2}{(0.010)}$$
$$= 1.59 \times 10^{-4}\,mol\,dm^{-3}$$

Calculating the pH of a weak acid

We can calculate the pH value (or $[H^+]$) of a weak acid if we know:
- the concentration of the acid
- the value of K_a for the acid.

Again, we make the same assumptions about the concentration of hydrogen ions produced by the ionisation of water and the equilibrium concentration of the weak acid. The value of the pH calculated will not be significantly affected by these factors unless we require great accuracy (for example calculating pH to the 3rd decimal place).

Worked example 5 shows how to calculate pH from the value of K_a and concentration of the weak acid.

Worked example

5 Calculate the pH of $0.100 \, mol \, dm^{-3}$ ethanoic acid, CH_3COOH. ($K_a = 1.74 \times 10^{-5} \, mol \, dm^{-3}$)

Step 1 Write the equilibrium expression for the reaction.

$$CH_3COOH(aq) \rightleftharpoons H^+(aq) + CH_3COO^-(aq)$$

$$K_a = \frac{[H^+]^2}{[HA]} \text{ or } K_a = \frac{[H^+]^2}{[CH_3COOH]}$$

Step 2 Enter the values into the expression.

$$1.74 \times 10^{-5} = \frac{[H^+]^2}{(0.100)}$$

Step 3 Rearrange the equation.

$$[H^+]^2 = 1.74 \times 10^{-5} \times 0.100 = 1.74 \times 10^{-6}$$

Step 4 Take the square root.

$$[H^+] = \sqrt{1.74 \times 10^{-6}} = 1.32 \times 10^{-3} \, mol \, dm^{-3}$$

Step 5 Calculate pH.

$$
\begin{aligned}
pH &= -\log_{10}[H^+] \\
&= -\log_{10}(1.32 \times 10^{-3}) \\
&= 2.88 \text{ (to 3 significant figures)}
\end{aligned}
$$

Check-up

6 Use the data from Table **20.2** to work out the pH values of the following solutions:
   a $0.0200 \, mol \, dm^{-3}$ aqueous benzoic acid
   b $0.0100 \, mol \, dm^{-3}$ hydrated aluminium ions
   c $0.100 \, mol \, dm^{-3}$ aqueous methanoic acid

20.4 Indicators and acid–base titrations

In Chapter 1 (page 16) we learned that indicators are used to detect the end-point in acid–alkali titrations. You may also have used indicators such as litmus to test whether a substance is acidic or alkaline. In this section we shall look more closely at how specific indicators are used in titrations involving strong and weak acids and bases.

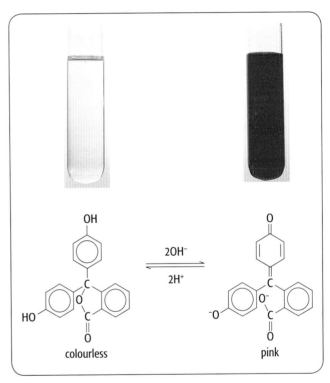

colourless   pink

Figure 20.4 The colour change in phenolphthalein is due to small differences in the structure of its molecule when hydrogen ions or hydroxide ions are added.

Introducing indicators

An **acid–base indicator** is a dye or mixture of dyes which changes colour over a specific pH range. In simple terms, many indicators can be considered as weak acids in which the acid (HIn) and its conjugate base (In⁻) have different colours.

$$HIn \rightleftharpoons H^+ + In^-$$

un-ionised   conjugate base
indicator   colour B
colour A

• Adding an acid to this indicator solution shifts the position of equilibrium to the left. There are now more molecules of colour A.

- Adding an alkali shifts the position of equilibrium to the right. There are now more ions of colour B.
- The colour of the indicator depends on the relative concentrations of HIn and In⁻. The colour of

the indicator during a titration depends on the concentration of H^+ ions present.

Indicators usually change colour over a pH range of between 1 and 2 pH units. In the middle of the range there is a recognisable end-point where the indicator has a colour in between the two extremes of colour. For example, bromothymol blue is yellow in acidic solution and blue in alkaline solution. The colour change takes place between pH 6.0 and pH 7.6. The end-point, which is a greyish-green colour, occurs when the pH is 7.0.

The pH at which indicators begin to change colour varies considerably. Table **20.3** shows the colours, ranges and end-points of some indicators.

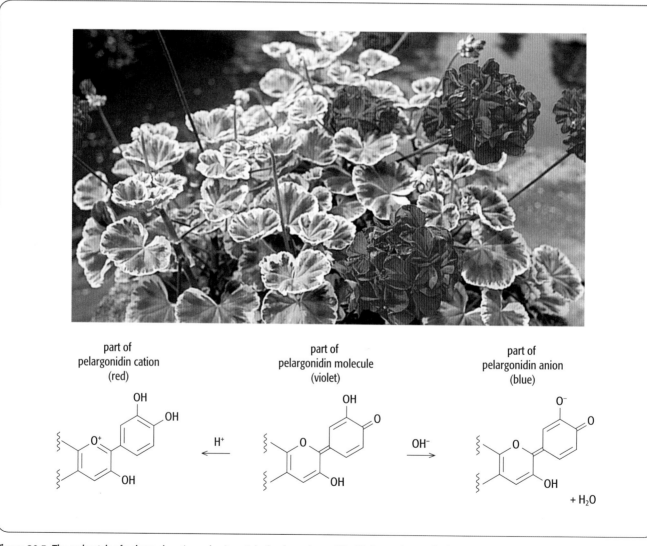

part of pelargonidin cation (red) part of pelargonidin molecule (violet) part of pelargonidin anion (blue)

Figure 20.5 The red petals of pelargonium (geranium) contain the dye pelargonidin. Hydrogen ions or hydroxide ions can make small changes in its molecular structure to produce different colours.

Name of dye	Colour at lower pH	pH range	End-point	Colour at higher pH
methyl violet	yellow	0.0–1.6	0.8	blue
methyl yellow	red	2.9–4.0	3.5	yellow
methyl orange	red	3.2–4.4	3.7	yellow
bromophenol blue	yellow	2.8–4.6	4.0	blue
bromocresol green	yellow	3.8–5.4	4.7	blue
methyl red	red	4.2–6.3	5.1	yellow
bromothymol blue	yellow	6.0–7.6	7.0	blue
phenolphthalein	colourless	8.2–10.0	9.3	pink/violet
alizarin yellow	yellow	10.1–13.0	12.5	orange/red

Table 20.3 Some of the chemical indicators used to monitor pH, with their pH ranges of use and pH of end-point.

Monitoring pH change

In Chapter 1 (page 16) we described the titration procedure for determining the amount of acid required to neutralise an alkali. Figure 20.6 shows the apparatus used to follow the changes in pH when a base is titrated with an acid.

The procedure is:
- set up the apparatus with the pH electrode connected to the computer via a data logger
- switch on the magnetic stirrer

- deliver the acid at a constant slow rate from the burette into the alkali in the flask
- stop when the pH has reached a nearly constant low value.

The pH of the reaction mixture can also be monitored manually. You record the pH after fixed volumes of acid have been added to the flask.

The graphs recorded on the computer or drawn by hand show how pH varies with the volume of acid added. The shapes of these graphs are characteristic and depend on whether the acid and base used in the titration are strong or weak.

Strong acids with strong bases

Figure 20.7 shows how the pH changes when $0.100 \, mol \, dm^{-3}$ sodium hydroxide (a strong base) is titrated with $0.100 \, mol \, dm^{-3}$ hydrochloric acid (a strong acid) in the presence of bromothymol blue indicator.

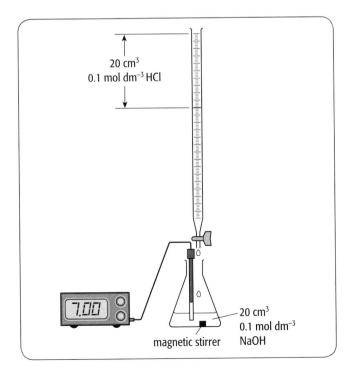

Figure 20.6 Measuring the pH change during the titration of sodium hydroxide with hydrochloric acid.

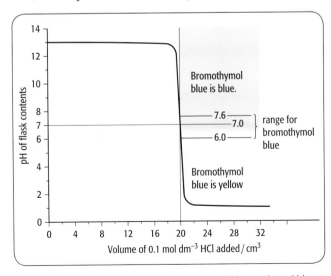

Figure 20.7 A strong acid–strong base titration with bromothymol blue as indicator.

These results show:
- a sharp fall in the graph line between pH 10.5 and pH3.5; in this region tiny additions of H⁺ ions result in a rapid change in pH
- a midpoint of the steep slope at pH 7
- the midpoint of the sharp fall corresponds to the point at which the H⁺ ions in the acid have exactly reacted with the OH⁻ ions in the alkali; this is the end-point of the titration
- that bromothymol blue indicator changed from blue to yellow over the range 7.6 to 6.0 where the slope is steepest.

Because there is a sharp change in pH over the region pH 3.5 to 10.5 we can use other indicators which change colour within this region. For example, phenolphthalein changes colour in the pH range 8.2 to 10.0 (Figure 20.8). Because the sharp pH change occurs over such a wide pH range, there are many indicators which can be used to determine the end-point of the reaction of a strong acid with a strong base.

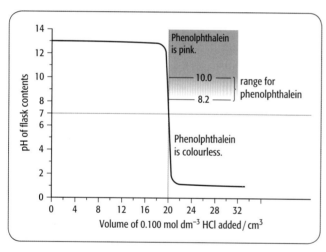

Figure 20.8 A strong acid–strong base titration with phenolphthalein as indicator.

Check-up

7 Use Table **20.3** to identify:
  a those indicators which could be used for a strong acid–strong base titration like the one in Figure **20.8**
  b those indicators which could not be used.

Strong acids with weak bases

Figure **20.9** shows how the pH changes when $0.100 \, mol \, dm^{-3}$ aqueous ammonia (a weak base) is titrated with $0.100 \, mol \, dm^{-3}$ nitric acid (a strong acid).

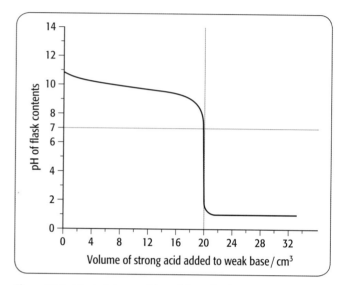

Figure 20.9 A typical strong acid–weak base titration.

These results show:
- a sharp fall in the graph line between pH 7.5 and pH 3.5
- that the midpoint of the steep slope is at about pH 5.

Because there is a sharp change in pH over the region 3.5 to 7.5 we can use methyl red as an indicator for this titration. This is because methyl red changes colour between pH 4.2 and pH 6.3, values which correspond with the region of sharpest pH change. Phenolphthalein would not be a suitable indicator to use because it only changes colour in alkaline regions (pH 8.2–10) which do not correspond to the sharp pH change. The phenolphthalein would change colour only gradually as more and more acid is added, instead of changing suddenly on the addition of a single drop at the end-point.

Weak acids with strong bases

Figure **20.10** shows how the pH changes when $0.100 \, mol \, dm^{-3}$ aqueous sodium hydroxide (a strong base) is titrated with $0.100 \, mol \, dm^{-3}$ benzoic acid (a weak acid).
These results show:
- a sharp fall in the graph line between pH 11 and pH 7.5
- that the midpoint of the steep slope is at about pH 9.

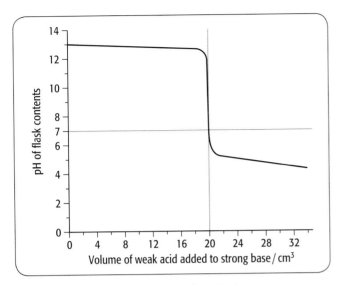

Figure 20.10 A typical weak acid–strong base titration.

Because there is a sharp change in pH over the region pH 7.5 to 11 we can use phenolphthalein as an indicator for this titration. This is because phenolphthalein changes colour between pH 8.2 and pH 10, values which correspond with the region of sharpest pH change. Methyl orange would not be a suitable indicator to use because it only changes colour in acidic regions which do not correspond to the sharp pH change.

Weak acids with weak bases

Figure **20.11** shows how the pH changes when $0.100 \, mol \, dm^{-3}$ aqueous ammonia (a weak base) is titrated with $0.100 \, mol \, dm^{-3}$ aqueous benzoic acid (a weak acid). These results show that there is no sharp fall in the graph line. No acid–base indicator is suitable to determine

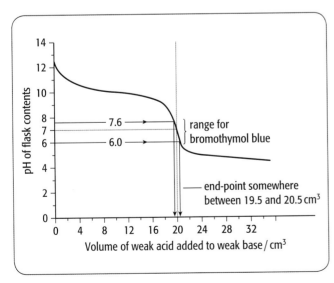

Figure 20.11 A typical weak acid–weak base titration.

the end-point of this reaction. In the example shown bromothymol blue:
- starts changing colour when $19.50 \, cm^3$ of acid have been added
- finishes changing colour when $20.50 \, cm^3$ of acid have been added.

Such a gradual colour change on addition of acid is not acceptable when accuracy of reading the end-point to the nearest $0.05 \, cm^3$ is required.

20.5 Buffer solutions
What is a buffer solution?

A **buffer solution** is a solution in which the pH does not change significantly when small amounts of acids or alkalis are added. A buffer solution is used to keep pH (almost) constant.

One type of buffer solution is a mixture of a weak acid and one of its salts. An example is an aqueous mixture of ethanoic acid and sodium ethanoate. Mixtures of ethanoic acid and sodium ethanoate in different proportions act as buffers between pH values of 4 and 7. We can understand how a buffer solution works by referring to the equilibria involved.

Ethanoic acid is a weak acid. So it stays mostly in the un-ionised form (CH_3COOH) and only gives rise to a low concentration of ethanoate ions in solution:

$$CH_3COOH(aq) \rightleftharpoons H^+(aq) + CH_3COO^-(aq)$$
ethanoic acid   ethanoate ion

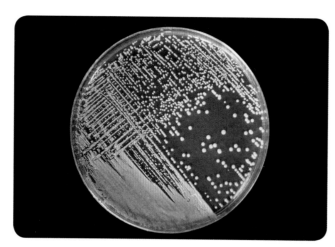

Figure 20.12 The pH of this agar plate for growing bacteria is kept constant by using a buffer solution. The buffer solution is incorporated in the agar jelly used to make the plate.

Sodium ethanoate is fully ionised in aqueous solution:

$$CH_3COONa(s) + aq \rightarrow Na^+(aq) + CH_3COO^-(aq)$$

sodium ethanoate   ethanoate ion

The buffer solution contains relatively high concentrations of both CH_3COOH and CH_3COO^-. We say that there are reserve supplies of the acid (CH_3COOH) and its conjugate base (CH_3COO^-). The pH of a buffer solution depends on the ratio of the concentration of the acid and the concentration of its conjugate base. If this does not change very much, the pH changes very little.

In the buffer solution ethanoic acid molecules are in equilibrium with hydrogen ions and ethanoate ions:

$$CH_3COOH(aq) \rightleftharpoons H^+(aq) + CH_3COO^-(aq)$$

relatively high   relatively high
concentration   concentration
of ethanoic acid   of ethanoate ions

We can use this equation to explain how buffer solutions work.

An increase in hydrogen ion concentration would greatly lower the pH of water, but when H^+ ions are added to the buffer solution:

- addition of H^+ ions shifts the position of equilibrium to the left because H^+ ions combine with CH_3COO^- ions to form more CH_3COOH until equilibrium is re-established
- the large reserve supply of CH_3COO^- ensures that the concentration of CH_3COO^- ions in solution does not change significantly

- the large reserve supply of CH_3COOH ensures that the concentration of CH_3COOH molecules in solution does not change significantly
- so the pH does not change significantly.

An increase in hydroxide ion concentration would greatly increase the pH of water, but when OH^- ions are added to the buffer solution:

- the added OH^- ions combine with H^+ ions to form water
- this reduces the H^+ ion concentration
- the position of equilibrium shifts to the right
- so CH_3COOH molecules ionise to form more H^+ and CH_3COO^- ions until equilibrium is re-established
- the large reserve supply of CH_3COOH ensures that the concentration of CH_3COOH molecules in solution does not change significantly
- the large reserve supply of CH_3COO^- ensures that the concentration of CH_3COO^- ions in solution does not change significantly
- so the pH does not change significantly.

Fact file

In unpolluted regions, rainwater has a pH of 5.7. This is because carbon dioxide dissolves in the rainwater to form a dilute solution of the weak acid carbonic acid, H_2CO_3. This acid and its conjugate base, HCO_3^-, act as a buffer solution. It minimises changes in pH if very small amounts of acid or alkali are added to the rainwater. But in regions where there is pollution caused by the emission of acidic oxides of nitrogen and sulfur, the pH of the rainwater falls to around 4. The rainwater can no longer act as a buffer because the concentrations of the H_2CO_3 and HCO_3^- are not high enough to cope with the large amounts of acidic pollution involved.

No buffer solution can cope with the excessive addition of acids or alkalis. If very large amounts of acid or alkali are added, the pH will change significantly.

Buffer solutions which resist changes in pH in alkaline regions are usually a mixture of a weak base and its conjugate acid. An example is a mixture of aqueous ammonia with ammonium chloride.

Aqueous ammonia is a weak base, so there is only a low concentration of ammonium ions in ammonia solution:

$$NH_3(aq) + H_2O(l) \rightleftharpoons NH_4^+(aq) + OH^-(aq)$$

Ammonium chloride is fully ionised in aqueous solution. This supplies the reserve supplies of the conjugate acid, NH_4^+.

$$NH_4Cl(aq) \rightarrow NH_4^+(aq) + Cl^-(aq)$$

Check-up

9 A mixture of 0.500 mol dm^{-3} aqueous ammonia and 0.500 mol dm^{-3} ammonium chloride acts as a buffer solution.
  a Explain how this buffer solution minimises changes in pH on addition of
    i dilute hydrochloric acid
    ii dilute sodium hydroxide.
  b Explain why dilute aqueous ammonia alone will not act as a buffer solution.

Calculating the pH of a buffer solution

We can calculate the pH of a buffer solution if we know:
- the K_a of the weak acid
- the equilibrium concentration of the weak acid and its conjugate base (salt).

To do the calculation we use the equilibrium expression for the particular reaction.

Worked example

6 Calculate the pH of a buffer solution containing 0.600 mol dm^{-3} propanoic acid and 0.800 mol dm^{-3} sodium propanoate. (K_a propanoic acid = 1.35×10^{-5} mol dm^{-3})

Step 1 Write the equilibrium expression.

$$K_a = \frac{[H^+][C_2H_5COO^-]}{[C_2H_5COOH]}$$

Step 2 Rearrange the equilibrium expression to make [H$^+$] the subject.

$$[H^+] = K_a \times \frac{[C_2H_5COOH]}{[C_2H_5COO^-]}$$

continued ⋯⇢

Note that in this expression, the ratio determining [H$^+$], and hence pH, is the ratio of the concentration of the acid to the salt (conjugate base).

Step 3 Substitute the data given.

$$[H^+] = 1.35 \times 10^{-5} \times \frac{(0.600)}{(0.800)}$$

$$= 1.01 \times 10^{-5} \text{ mol dm}^{-3}$$

Step 4 Calculate the pH.

$$\begin{aligned} pH &= -\log_{10}[H^+] \\ &= -\log_{10}(1.01 \times 10^{-5}) \\ &= -(-4.99) \\ &= 4.99 \end{aligned}$$

Fact file

We can make the numbers easier to deal with in calculations involving buffer solutions by using logarithms throughout. So instead of using the expression:

$$[H^+] = K_a \times \frac{[acid]}{[salt]}$$

we can use the expression:

$$pH = pK_a + \log_{10}\left(\frac{[salt]}{[acid]}\right)$$

Check-up

10 a Calculate the pH of the following buffer solutions:
    i 0.0500 mol dm^{-3} methanoic acid and 0.100 mol dm^{-3} sodium methanoate. (K_a of methanoic acid = 1.60×10^{-4} mol dm^{-3})
    ii 0.0100 mol dm^{-3} benzoic acid and 0.0400 mol dm^{-3} sodium benzoate. (K_a of benzoic acid = 6.3×10^{-5} mol dm^{-3})

continued ⋯⇢

b How many moles of sodium ethanoate must be added to $1.00\,dm^3$ of $0.100\,mol\,dm^{-3}$ ethanoic acid to produce a buffer solution of pH 4.90?
(K_a of ethanoic acid $= 1.74 \times 10^{-5}\,mol\,dm^{-3}$)
Hint: first find the hydrogen ion concentration, then rearrange the equilibrium expression to make [(sodium) ethanoate] the subject of the expression.

Uses of buffer solutions

Buffer solutions play an important part in many industrial processes including electroplating, the manufacture of dyes and in the treatment of leather. They are also used to make sure that pH meters record the correct pH.

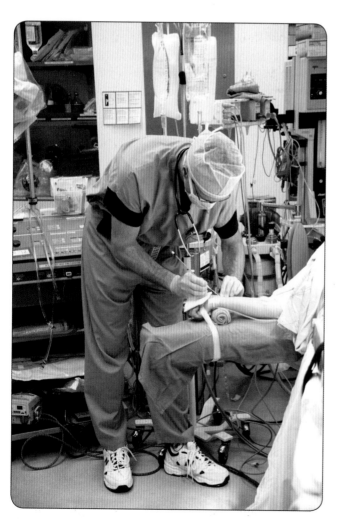

Figure 20.13 Anaesthetists monitor the pH of patients' blood.

Many animals depend on buffers to keep a constant pH in various parts of their bodies. In humans, the pH of the blood is kept between 7.35 and 7.45 by a number of different buffers in the blood:
- hydrogencarbonate ions, HCO_3^-
- haemoglobin and plasma proteins
- dihydrogenphosphate ($H_2PO_4^-$) and hydrogenphosphate (HPO_4^{2-}) ions.

The cells in our body produce carbon dioxide as a product of aerobic respiration (the oxidation of glucose to provide energy). Carbon dioxide combines with water in the blood to form a solution containing hydrogen ions.

$$CO_2(aq) + H_2O(aq) \rightleftharpoons H^+(aq) + \underset{\text{hydrogencarbonate ion}}{HCO_3^-(aq)}$$

This reaction is catalysed by the enzyme carbonic anhydrase. When the blood passes through the small blood vessels around our lungs hydrogencarbonate ions are rapidly converted to carbon dioxide and water. The carbon dioxide escapes into the lungs.

Fact file

The enzyme carbonic anhydrase is one of the best catalysts of a specific enzyme reaction known. It catalyses the reaction

$$CO_2(aq) + H_2O(aq) \rightleftharpoons H^+(aq) + HCO_3^-(aq)$$

It increases the rate of reaction by one million times! This is because the water and carbon dioxide molecules are precisely positioned near a zinc atom and nitrogen atoms on the enzyme surface. During the reaction, the water molecule is first deprotonated to form an OH^- ion.

The production of H^+ ions, if left unchecked, would lower the pH of the blood and cause 'acidosis'. This may disrupt some body functions and eventually lead to coma. The equilibrium between carbon dioxide and hydrogencarbonate is the most important buffering system in the blood.

If the H^+ ion concentration increases:
- the position of this equilibrium shifts to the left
- H^+ ions combine with HCO_3^- ions to form carbon dioxide and water until equilibrium is restored
- this reduces the concentration of hydrogen ions in the blood and helps keep the pH constant.

If the H^+ ion concentration decreases:
• the position of this equilibrium shifts to the right
• some carbon dioxide and water combine to form H^+ and HCO_3^- ions until equilibrium is restored
• this increases the concentration of hydrogen ions in the blood and helps keep the pH constant.

Check-up

11 a One of the buffers in blood plasma is a mixture of dihydrogenphosphate ions ($H_2PO_4^-$) and hydrogenphosphate (HPO_4^{2-}) ions.

   i Identify the conjugate acid and base in this buffer.

   ii Write a balanced equation for the equilibrium between these two ions.

  b Some proteins in the blood can act as buffers. The equation below shows a simplified equilibrium equation for this reaction. (Pr = protein)

$$HPr \rightleftharpoons H^+ + Pr^-$$

Explain how this system can act as a buffer to prevent the blood getting too acidic.

20.6 Equilibrium and solubility

In Chapter 5 (page 82) we learned that most ionic compounds dissolve in water and in Chapter 18 (page 264) we related solubility to enthalpy change of solution. Some ionic compounds, however, are insoluble or only slightly soluble in water. But even 'insoluble' ionic compounds may dissolve to a very small extent in water. Solubility is generally quoted as the number of grams or number of moles of compound needed to saturate 100 g or 1 kg of water at a given temperature. We say that a solution is saturated when no more solute dissolves in it.
• Sodium chloride is regarded as a soluble salt: a saturated solution contains 36 g per 100 g of water.
• Lead(II) chloride is regarded as an insoluble salt: a saturated solution contains 0.99 g per 100 g of water.

Solubility product

An equilibrium is established when an undissolved ionic compound is in contact with a saturated solution of

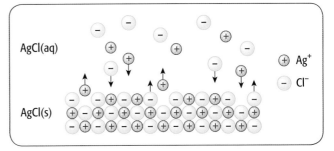

Figure 20.14 An equilibrium is established between solid silver chloride and its saturated solution. The water molecules are not shown.

its ions. The ions move from the solid to the saturated solution at the same rate as they move from the solution to the solid (Figure **20.14**).

When solid silver chloride dissolves it is in contact with saturated silver chloride solution and the following equilibrium is set up:

$$AgCl(s) \rightleftharpoons Ag^+(aq) + Cl^-(aq)$$

The equilibrium expression relating to this equation is:

$$K_c = \frac{[Ag^+(aq)][Cl^-(aq)]}{[AgCl(s)]}$$

For any solid, the concentration of the solid phase remains constant (see page **136**) and can be combined with the value of K_c.

So we can write this equilibrium expression as:

$$K_{sp} = [Ag^+(aq)][Cl^-(aq)]$$

K_{sp} is called the **solubility product**. Values are quoted at 298 K.

> Solubility product is the product of the concentrations of each ion in a saturated solution of a sparingly soluble salt at 298 K, raised to the power of their relative concentrations.

$$K_{sp} = [C^{y+}(aq)]^a[A^{x-}(aq)]^b$$

where a is the number of C^{y+} cations in one formula unit of the compound and b is the number of A^{x-} anions in one formula unit of the compound

So for Fe_2S_3 (which contains Fe^{3+} ions and S^{2-} ions) the equilibrium is:

$$Fe_2S_3(s) \rightleftharpoons 2Fe^{3+}(aq) + 3S^{2-}(aq)$$

and the equilibrium expression is:

$$K_{sp} = [Fe^{3+}(aq)]^2[S^{2-}(aq)]^3$$

The idea of solubility product only applies to ionic compounds which are only slightly soluble.

The units of solubility product depend on the number of each type of ion present in solution. You can work the units out in the same way as for general equilibrium expressions (see page 136), but you don't have to do any cancelling. For example, for the expression:

$$\begin{aligned} K_{sp} &= [Mg^{2+}(aq)] \times [OH^-(aq)]^2 \\ &= mol\,dm^{-3} \times (mol\,dm^{-3})^2 \\ &= mol^3\,dm^{-9} \end{aligned}$$

The idea of solubility product is only useful for sparingly soluble salts. The smaller the value of K_{sp} the lower is the solubility of the salt. Some values of K_{sp} are given in Table 20.4.

Compound	K_{sp} / $(mol\,dm^{-3})^{x+y}$
AgCl	1.8×10^{-10}
Al(OH)$_3$	1.0×10^{-32}
BaCO$_3$	5.5×10^{-10}
BaSO$_4$	1.0×10^{-10}
CaCO$_3$	5.0×10^{-9}
CoS	2.0×10^{-26}
CuS	6.3×10^{-36}
Fe(OH)$_2$	7.9×10^{-16}
Fe$_2$S$_3$	1.0×10^{-88}
HgI$_2$	2.5×10^{-26}
Mn(OH)$_2$	1.0×10^{-11}
PbCl$_2$	1.6×10^{-5}
Sb$_2$S$_3$	1.7×10^{-93}
SnCO$_3$	1.0×10^{-9}
Zn(OH)$_2$	2.0×10^{-17}
ZnS	1.6×10^{-23}

Table 20.4 Some values of solubility product at 298 K.

Check-up

12 a Write equilibrium expressions for the solubility products of the following:
  i $Fe(OH)_2$
  ii Fe_2S_3
  iii $Al(OH)_3$
b State the units of solubility product for each of the compounds in part **a**.

Solubility product calculations

You may be asked to calculate the solubility product of a compound from its solubility, or you may be asked to calculate the solubility of a compound from its solubility product. An example of each of these types of calculation is shown below.

Worked examples

7 Calculating solubility product from solubility.
A saturated solution of magnesium fluoride, MgF_2, has a solubility of $1.22 \times 10^{-3}\,mol\,dm^{-3}$. Calculate the solubility product of magnesium fluoride.

Step 1 Write down the equilibrium equation.

$$MgF_2(s) \rightleftharpoons Mg^{2+}(aq) + 2F^-(aq)$$

Step 2 Calculate the concentration of each ion in solution.
When 1.22×10^{-3} mol dissolves to form $1\,dm^3$ of solution the concentration of each ion is:

$$[Mg^{2+}] = 1.22 \times 10^{-3}\,mol\,dm^{-3}$$

$$\begin{aligned}[F^-] &= 2 \times 1.22 \times 10^{-3}\,mol\,dm^{-3} \\ &= 2.44 \times 10^{-3}\,mol\,dm^{-3}\end{aligned}$$

(The concentration of F^- is $2 \times 1.22 \times 10^{-3}\,mol\,dm^{-3}$ because each formula unit contains $2 \times F^-$ ions.)

Step 3 Write down the equilibrium expression.

$$K_{sp} = [Mg^{2+}][F^-]^2$$

continued ⋯▸

Step 4 Substitute the values.

$$K_{sp} = (1.22 \times 10^{-3}) \times (2.44 \times 10^{-3})^2$$
$$= 7.26 \times 10^{-9}$$

Step 5 Add the correct units.

$$(mol\,dm^{-3}) \times (mol\,dm^{-3})^2 = mol^3\,dm^{-9}$$

Answer $= 7.26 \times 10^{-9}\,mol^3\,dm^{-9}$

8 Calculating solubility from solubility product
Calculate the solubility of copper(II) sulfide
in $mol\,dm^{-3}$.
(K_{sp} for CuS $= 6.3 \times 10^{-36}\,mol^2\,dm^{-6}$)

Step 1 Write down the equilibrium equation.

$$CuS(s) \rightleftharpoons Cu^{2+}(aq) + S^{2-}(aq)$$

Step 2 Write the equilibrium expression in terms
of one ion only.
From the equilibrium equation $[Cu^{2+}] = [S^{2-}]$

So $K_{sp} = [Cu^{2+}][S^{2-}]$ becomes $K_{sp} = [Cu^{2+}]^2$

Step 3 Substitute the value of K_{sp}.

$$(6.3 \times 10^{-36}) = [Cu^{2+}]^2$$

Step 4 Calculate the concentration.
In this case we take the square root of K_{sp}

$$[Cu^{2+}] = \sqrt{K_{sp}}$$

$$[Cu^{2+}] = \sqrt{6.3 \times 10^{-36}} = 2.5 \times 10^{-18}\,mol\,dm^{-3}$$

b Calculate the solubility in $mol\,dm^{-3}$
of zinc sulfide, ZnS.
($K_{sp} = 1.6 \times 10^{-23}\,mol^2\,dm^{-6}$)

c Calculate the solubility of silver carbonate,
Ag_2CO_3. ($K_{sp} = 6.3 \times 10^{-12}\,mol^2\,dm^{-6}$)
Hint: you have to divide by 4 then take
the cube root – can you see why? You
should have a cube root button on your
calculator ($\sqrt[3]{\ }$).

Predicting precipitation

The solubility product can be used to predict whether
precipitation will occur when two solutions are mixed.
For example: will we get a precipitate when we mix a
solution of barium chloride, $BaCl_2$, with a very dilute
solution of sodium carbonate?

Both barium chloride and sodium carbonate are
soluble salts, but barium carbonate is relatively insoluble.
We must consider the equilibrium for the insoluble salt
dissolving in water:

$$BaCO_3(s) \rightleftharpoons Ba^{2+}(aq) + CO_3^{2-}(aq)$$

The solubility product is given by:

$$K_{sp} = [Ba^{2+}][CO_3^{2-}] = 5.5 \times 10^{-10}\,mol^2\,dm^{-6}$$

If $[Ba^{2+}][CO_3^{2-}]$ is greater than $5.5 \times 10^{-10}\,mol^2\,dm^{-6}$ a
precipitate will form.

If $[Ba^{2+}][CO_3^{2-}]$ is less than $5.5 \times 10^{-10}\,mol^2\,dm^{-6}$ no
precipitate will form.

Check-up

13 a Calculate the solubility product of the
following solutions:
  i a saturated aqueous solution of
cadmium sulfide, CdS (solubility =
$1.46 \times 10^{-11}\,mol\,dm^{-3}$)
  ii a saturated aqueous solution of
calcium fluoride, CaF_2, containing
$0.0168\,g\,dm^{-3}$ CaF_2

Worked example

9 Will a precipitate form if we mix equal volumes
of solutions of $1.00 \times 10^{-4}\,mol\,dm^{-3}$ Na_2CO_3 and
$5.00 \times 10^{-5}\,mol\,dm^{-3}$ $BaCl_2$?
  • $[Ba^{2+}] = 2.50 \times 10^{-5}\,mol\,dm^{-3}$
  • $[CO_3^{2-}] = 5.00 \times 10^{-5}\,mol\,dm^{-3}$

$$[Ba^{2+}][CO_3^{2-}] = (2.50 \times 10^{-5}) \times (5.00 \times 10^{-5})$$
$$= 1.25 \times 10^{-9}\,mol^2\,dm^{-6}$$

This value is greater than the solubility product,
so a precipitate of barium carbonate forms.

Figure 20.15 The shell of this nautilus is composed mainly of calcium carbonate. The nautilus adjusts conditions so shell material is formed when the concentration of calcium ions and carbonate ions in seawater are high enough to precipitate calcium carbonate.

The common ion effect

> The **common ion effect** is the reduction in the solubility of a dissolved salt achieved by adding a solution of a compound which has an ion in common with the dissolved salt. This often results in precipitation.

An example of the common ion effect can be seen when we add a solution of sodium chloride to a saturated solution of silver chloride and silver chloride precipitates. Why is this?

In a saturated solution of silver chloride in water, we have the following equilibrium:

$$AgCl(s) \rightleftharpoons Ag^+(aq) + Cl^-(aq)$$

We now add a solution of sodium chloride:
- the chloride ion is common to both sodium chloride and silver chloride
- the added chloride ions shift the position of equilibrium to the left
- silver chloride is precipitated.

The addition of the common ion, Cl^-, has reduced the solubility of the silver chloride because its solubility product has been exceeded: When $[Ag^+][Cl^-]$ is greater than the K_{sp} for silver chloride a precipitate will form.

> ### *Fact file*
> One of the last stages in the manufacture of soap involves 'salting out'. The main constituent of soap is sodium stearate, $C_{17}H_{35}COO^-Na^+$. It is 'salted out' by adding a concentrated solution of sodium chloride. The product of the stearate and sodium ion concentrations becomes greater than the solubility product for sodium stearate and so sodium stearate precipitates out. This is an example of the common ion effect, the common ion being Na^+.

The solubility of an ionic compound in aqueous solution containing a common ion is less than its solubility in water.

For example, the solubility of barium sulfate, $BaSO_4$, in water is $1.0 \times 10^{-5} \, mol \, dm^{-3}$ and the solubility of barium sulfate in $0.100 \, mol \, dm^{-3}$ sulfuric acid, H_2SO_4, is only $1.0 \times 10^{-9} \, mol \, dm^{-3}$.

We can explain the lower solubility in sulfuric acid by referring to the solubility product of barium sulfate:

$$K_{sp} = [Ba^{2+}][SO_4^{2-}] = 1.0 \times 10^{-10} \, mol^2 \, dm^{-6}$$

If we ignore the very small amount of $SO_4^{2-}(aq)$ from the barium sulfate then $[SO_4^{2-}]$ is $0.1 \, mol \, dm^{-3}$ (from the sulfuric acid). This gives:

$$1.0 \times 10^{-10} = [Ba^{2+}] \times [0.1]$$

$$[Ba^{2+}] = 1.0 \times 10^{-9} \, mol \, dm^{-3}$$

Check-up

14 a Thallium(I) chloride is a salt which is sparingly soluble in water. When hydrochloric acid is added to a saturated solution of thallium(I) chloride, a precipitate is formed. Explain why a precipitate is formed.

b Calcium sulfate is a sparingly soluble salt which can be made by mixing solutions containing calcium and sulfate ions. A $0.001\,00\,mol\,dm^{-3}$

solution of aqueous calcium chloride, $CaCl_2$, is mixed with an equal volume of $0.001\,00\,mol\,dm^{-3}$ solution of aqueous sodium sulfate, Na_2SO_4.

i Calculate the concentration of calcium and sulfate ions when these solutions of calcium chloride and sodium sulfate are mixed.

ii Will a precipitate of calcium sulfate form? (K_{sp} of calcium sulfate = $2.0 \times 10^{-5}\,mol^2\,dm^{-6}$)

continued ⋯→

Summary

- ☐ pH is a measure of the hydrogen ion concentration: $pH = -\log_{10}[H^+(aq)]$.
- ☐ K_a is the dissociation constant for an acid. It is the equilibrium constant for the dissociation of a weak acid, HA(aq):

$$HA \rightleftharpoons H^+(aq) + A^-(aq)$$

- ☐ Acid strengths can be compared using pK_a values: $pK_a = -\log_{10}K_a$.
- ☐ A lower value of pK_a means greater acid strength.
- ☐ K_w is the ionic product for water:

$$K_w = [H^+(aq)][OH^-aq] = 1.00 \times 10^{-14}\,mol^2\,dm^{-6}$$

- ☐ $pK_w = -\log_{10}K_w$.
- ☐ For weak acids hydrogen ion concentration (and therefore pH) can be calculated from the equilibrium concentrations in the equilibrium expression:

$$K_a = \frac{[H^+(aq)][A^-aq]}{[HA(aq)]}$$

when the value of K_a is known.

- ☐ The pH value of a strong base can be calculated by using the expression $K_w = [H^+(aq)][OH^-aq]$.
- ☐ pH titration curves enable end-points for acid–base titrations to be found.
- ☐ The exact shape of a pH titration curve depends on the strengths of the acid and base used.
- ☐ pH titration curves can be used to suggest appropriate indicators for particular acid–base titrations.
- ☐ A buffer solution minimises pH changes on addition of a small amount of acid or base.
- ☐ A buffer solution is a mixture of a weak acid and its conjugate base.
- ☐ Buffer solutions control pH by maintaining a fairly constant ratio of weak acid and its conjugate base.
- ☐ The pH of a buffer solution can be calculated by using the equilibrium concentrations of the weak acid and its conjugate base and the K_a value of the weak acid.
- ☐ Buffer solutions have many uses. In our bodies, the HCO_3^- ion acts as a buffer which prevents the blood from becoming too acidic.

- The solubility product, K_{sp}, is the equilibrium expression showing the equilibrium concentrations of the ions in a saturated solution of a sparingly soluble salt taking into account the relative number of each ion present.
- The addition of a common ion to a saturated solution of a sparingly soluble salt (e.g. adding a concentrated solution of (sodium) chloride to a saturated solution of silver chloride) causes precipitation of the sparingly soluble salt.

End-of-chapter questions

Examiner's tip
you have to know how to calculate the pH of four different types of solution:
- a strong acid
- a weak acid
- a strong base (an alkali)
- a buffer.

Each of these requires a different approach. Practise them until you always choose the correct method for each one.

1 a Write general expressions for the terms:
    i pH   [1]
    ii K_w [1]
    iii K_a [1]
  b What is the pH of $0.004\,00\,mol\,dm^{-3}$ HCl(aq)? Show your working. [2]
  c What is the pH of $0.004\,00\,mol\,dm^{-3}$ butanoic acid(aq)? ($K_a = 1.51 \times 10^{-5}\,mol\,dm^{-3}$) [3]
  d 0.25 mol of sodium hydroxide is dissolved in $2.00\,dm^3$ of water. Calculate the concentration and pH of the sodium hydroxide solution. ($K_w = 1.00 \times 10^{-14}\,mol^2\,dm^{-6}$) [3]

Total = 11

2 a Sketch the graph of pH that would be obtained when $10.0\,cm^3$ of $0.200\,mol\,dm^{-3}$ HCl is titrated against $0.200\,mol\,dm^{-3}$ aqueous ammonia. [3]
  b Explain why methyl orange is a suitable indicator for this titration but phenolphthalein is not. [2]
  c Sketch the graph that would be obtained if $25.0\,cm^3$ of $0.200\,mol\,dm^{-3}$ sodium hydroxide is titrated against $0.100\,mol\,dm^{-3}$ ethanoic acid solution. [3]
  d Explain why phenolphthalein is a suitable indicator for this titration but methyl orange is not. [2]
  e Bromocresol green and bromothymol blue are indicators. Their pK_a values are: bromocresol green = 4.7 and bromothymol blue = 7.0. Would either of these indicators be suitable for the titration in part **a** or the titration in part **c**? Explain your answer. [4]

Total = 14

3 a What is the pH of a solution containing $0.100\,mol\,dm^{-3}$ ethanoic acid and $0.100\,mol\,dm^{-3}$ sodium ethanoate?
    (K_a of $CH_3COOH = 1.74 \times 10^{-5}\,mol\,dm^{-3}$) [3]
  b How many moles of sodium ethanoate must be added to $2.00\,dm^3$ of $0.0100\,mol\,dm^{-3}$ ethanoic acid to produce a buffer solution of pH 5.40? [5]

c Explain why the pH of a solution containing $0.100 \, mol \, dm^{-3}$ ethanoic acid and $0.100 \, mol \, dm^{-3}$ sodium ethanoate does not change significantly when a small amount of hydrochloric acid is added. [3]

Total = 11

4 Copper(I) bromide, CuBr, is a sparingly soluble salt.
($K_{sp} = 3.2 \times 10^{-8} \, mol^2 \, dm^{-6}$)
  a What do you understand by the terms:
    i solubility product [2]
    ii common ion effect [2]
  b Calculate the solubility of CuBr in:
    i pure water [2]
    ii an aqueous solution of $0.0100 \, mol \, dm^{-3}$ sodium bromide. [1]
    iii Explain the difference in your answers to part **b**, **ii** and **iii**. [2]

Total = 9

5 A buffer solution consists of $6.00 \, g$ of ethanoic acid (CH_3COOH) and $12.3 \, g$ of sodium ethanoate (CH_3COONa) in $200 \, cm^3$ of aqueous solution.
(A_r values: H = 1.0, C = 12.0, O = 16.0, Na = 23.0; K_a for $CH_3COOH = 1.74 \times 10^{-5} \, mol \, dm^{-3}$)
  a What is the concentration of ethanoic acid in the buffer? [2]
  b What is the concentration of sodium ethanoate in the buffer? [2]
  c Calculate the pH of the buffer solution. [2]
  d Using this solution as an example, explain why the pH of a buffer solution changes very little when small amount of hydrogen ions or hydroxide ions are added to it. [3]
  e Explain how the carbon dioxide/hydrogencarbonate buffer helps control blood pH. [3]

Total = 12

6 A saturated solution of copper(I) sulfide, Cu_2S, contains $1.91 \times 10^{-12} \, g$ of Cu_2S dissolved in $1 \, dm^3$ of water.
(A_r values: Cu = 63.5, S = 32.1)
  a Write an equilibrium expression for the solubility product of copper(I) sulfide. [1]
  b Calculate the value of the solubility product of copper(I) sulfide, stating the units. [5]
  c Copper(II) chromate has a solubility of $1.9 \times 10^{-3} \, mol \, dm^{-3}$ in water. Copper(II) sulfate has a solubility of $1.4 \times 10^{-1} \, mol \, dm^{-3}$ in water. What will you observe when $10 \, cm^3$ of an aqueous solution of $0.0100 \, mol \, dm^{-3}$ copper(II) sulfate is added to an equal volume of a saturated solution of copper(II) chromate. Explain your answer. [3]

Total = 9

7   **a** What is the pH of $0.25\,mol\,dm^{-3}$ HCl(aq)?   [1]
    b What is the pH of $0.0500\,mol\,dm^{-3}$ sodium hydroxide? ($K_w = 1.00 \times 10^{-14}\,mol^2\,dm^{-6}$)   [2]
    c The graph shows how the pH changes when $0.100\,mol\,dm^{-3}$ ethanoic acid is titrated
           with $0.100\,mol\,dm^{-3}$ sodium hydroxide.

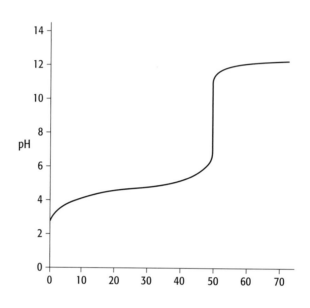

    i   Explain why methyl orange ($pK_a = 3.7$) is not a suitable indicator to use for this titration.   [1]
    ii Would phenolphthalein be a suitable indicator to use for this titration? Explain your answer.   [1]
    d Propanoic acid is a weak acid. A $0.0500\,mol\,dm^{-3}$ solution of propanoic acid has a pH of 3.1.
           Calculate the value of K_a for propanoic acid. Show all your working.   [4]

                                                                                                        Total = 9

21 Reaction kinetics

Learning outcomes

Candidates should be able to:

- explain and use the terms
  - **rate equation**
  - **order of reaction**
  - **rate constant**
  - **half-life of a reaction**
  - **rate-determining step**
- construct and use rate equations of the form rate = $k[A]^m[B]^n$ (limited to simple cases of single-step reactions and of multi-step processes with a rate-determining step for which m and n are 0, 1 or 2) including:
  - deducing the order of a reaction by the initial rates method
  - justifying, for zero- and first-order reactions, the order of reaction from concentration–time graphs
  - verifying that a suggested reaction mechanism is consistent with the observed kinetics
  - predicting the order that would result from a given reaction mechanism (and vice versa)
  - calculating an initial rate using concentration data (integrated forms of the rate equation are not required)
- show understanding that the half-life of a first-order reaction is independent of concentration
- use the half-life of a first-order reaction in calculations
- calculate a rate constant using the initial rates method
- devise a suitable experimental technique for studying the rate of a reaction, from given information
- outline the different modes of action of homogeneous and heterogeneous catalysts, including:
  - the Haber process
  - the catalytic removal of oxides of nitrogen in the exhaust gases from car engines
  - the catalytic role of atmospheric oxides of nitrogen in the oxidation of atmospheric sulfur dioxide
  - the catalytic role of Fe^{3+} in the $I^-/S_2O_3^{2-}$ reaction.

21.1 Introduction

In Chapter 9 you learned why reaction rate is increased when:

- the concentrations of the reactants are increased
- the temperature is increased
- a catalyst is added to the reaction mixture.
  In this chapter you will find out about:
- quantitative aspects of reaction rates
- how the data gathered from experiments on rates of reaction can be used to confirm possible reaction mechanisms
- more about how catalysts speed up reaction rates.

Figure 21.1 The Northern Lights (*aurora borealis*) are the result of many complex reactions taking place in the upper atmosphere. A knowledge of reaction rates is needed to understand the natural reactions involved and how these might be disturbed by artificial emissions.

21.2 Rate of reaction

Defining rate of reaction

We calculate **rate of reaction** by measuring a decrease in concentration of a particular reactant or an increase in concentration of a particular product over a period of time.

$$\text{rate of reaction} = \frac{\text{change in concentration}}{\text{time taken for this change}}$$

Units of concentration are usually expressed in $mol\,dm^{-3}$, units of time are usually expressed in seconds, so the units of rate of reaction are normally $mol\,dm^{-3}\,s^{-1}$. For very slow reactions, you may see the units of rates expressed as $mol\,dm^{-3}\,min^{-1}$ or $mol\,dm^{-3}\,h^{-1}$.

Methods for following the course of a reaction

In order to find out how the rate of reaction changes with time we need to select a suitable method to follow the progress of a reaction. This method will measure either the rate of disappearance of a reactant, or the rate of appearance of a product. There are two main types of method: sampling and continuous.

1 Sampling

This method involves taking small samples of the reaction mixture at various times and then carrying out a chemical analysis on each sample. An example is the alkaline hydrolysis of bromobutane:

$$C_4H_9Br + OH^- \rightarrow C_4H_9OH + Br^-$$

Samples are removed at various times and 'quenched' to stop or slow down the reaction e.g. by cooling the sample in ice. The hydroxide ion concentration can be found by titration with a standard solution of a strong acid.

2 Continuous

In this method a physical property of the reaction mixture is monitored over a period of time. Some examples are using colorimetry, a conductivity meter or measuring changes in gas volume or gas pressure.

Colorimetry can be used to monitor the change in colour of a particular reactant. For example, this method can be used to follow the reaction of iodine with propanone:

$$CH_3COCH_3 + I_2 \rightarrow CH_3COCH_2I + HI$$

As the reaction proceeds, the colour of the iodine fades. Changes in electrical conductivity of the solution can be measured. For example, this method can be used to follow the reaction:

$$(CH_3)_3CBr + H_2O \rightarrow (CH_3)_3COH + H^+ + Br^-$$

As the reaction proceeds, the electrical conductivity of the solution increases because ions are being formed in the reaction. This method can sometimes be used even if there are ions on both sides of the equation. This is due to the fact that ions vary in their conductivities. For example the small H^+ and OH^- ions have very high conductivities but Br^- ions have a low conductivity.

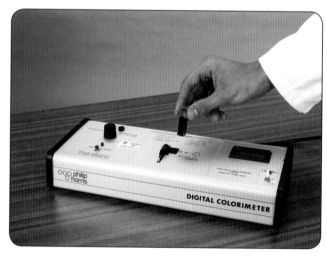

Figure 21.2 A colorimeter can be used to monitor the progress of a reaction. It measures the transmission of light through a 'cell' containing the reaction mixture. The less concentrated the colour of the reaction mixture, the more light is transmitted through the 'cell'.

Changes in gas volume or gas pressure can be measured. For example, this method can be used to follow the reaction of benzenediazonium chloride, $C_6H_5N\equiv N^+Cl^-$, with water.

$$C_6H_5N\equiv N^+Cl^-(aq) + H_2O(l)$$
$$\rightarrow C_6H_5OH(aq) + N_2(g) + HCl(aq)$$

The reaction can be monitored by measuring the change in volume of gas released with time. You may have used this method to follow the rate of the reaction between calcium carbonate and hydrochloric acid. If you did, you will have measured the change in volume of carbon dioxide gas released with time.

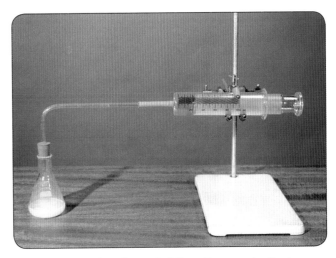

Figure 21.3 Rate of reaction can be followed by measuring the change in volume of a gas given off in a reaction. In this experiment CO_2 is being given off when $CaCO_3$ reacts with HCl.

Fact file

The progress of some reactions can be followed by measuring small changes in the volume of the reaction mixture. For example, during the hydration of methylpropene, the volume decreases.

$$(CH_3)_2C{=}CH_2 + H_2O \xrightarrow{H^+} (CH_3)_3COH$$

An instrument called a dilatometer (Figure **2.14**) is used to measure the small changes in volume. The temperature has to be controlled to an accuracy of $\pm0.001\,°C$. Can you think why?

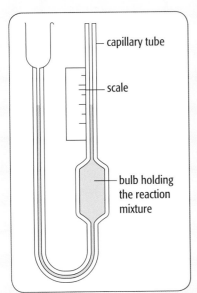

Figure 21.4
A dilatometer.

Check-up

2 a Suggest a suitable method for following the progress of each of these reactions:
   i $H_2O_2(aq) + 2I^-(aq) + 2H^+(aq)$
      $\rightarrow 2H_2O(l) + I_2(aq)$
   ii $HCOOCH_3(aq) + H_2O(l)$
      $\rightarrow HCOOH(aq) + CH_3OH(aq)$
   iii $2H_2O_2(aq) \rightarrow 2H_2O(l) + O_2(g)$
   iv $BrO_3^-(aq) + 5Br^-(aq) + 6H^+(aq)$
      $\rightarrow 3Br_2(aq) + 3H_2O(l)$
   b Why is it essential that the temperature is kept constant when measuring the progress of a reaction?

Calculating rate of reaction graphically

Rate of reaction usually changes as the reaction proceeds. This is because the concentration of reactants is decreasing. Taking the isomerisation of cyclopropane to propene as an example:

cyclopropane → propene

The progress of this reaction can be followed by measuring the decrease in concentration of cyclopropane or increase in concentration of propene. Table **21.1** shows these changes at 500 °C. The measurements were all made

Time / min	[cyclopropane] / $mol\,dm^{-3}$	[propene] / $mol\,dm^{-3}$
0	1.50	0.00
5	1.23	0.27
10	1.00	0.50
15	0.82	0.68
20	0.67	0.83
25	0.55	0.95
30	0.45	1.05
35	0.37	1.13
40	0.33	1.17

Table 21.1 Concentrations of reactant (cyclopropane) and product (propene) at 5-minute intervals (temperature = 500 °C (773 K)).

at the same temperature because reaction rate is affected markedly by temperature.

Note that we put square brackets, [ ], around the cyclopropane and propene to indicate concentration; [propene] means 'concentration of propene'.

Figure **21.5** shows how the concentration of propene changes with time.

We can see from Figure **21.5b** that the concentration of propene increases from 0.00 to 0.27 $mol\,dm^{-3}$ in the first 5 minutes. In Chapter **6** (page **94**) we used the symbol Δ (Greek capital 'delta') to represent a change in a particular quantity. So we can write:

$$\text{rate of reaction} = \frac{\Delta[\text{propene}]}{\Delta\ \text{time}} = \frac{0.27}{5}$$
$$= 0.054\,mol\,dm^{-3}\,min^{-1}$$

This gives the **average** rate of reaction over the first 5 minutes. You will notice, however, that the graph is a curve which becomes shallower with time. So the rate decreases with time. By measuring the change in concentration over shorter and shorter time intervals we get an increasingly accurate value of the reaction rate. If we make the time interval over which we measure the reaction almost zero, we obtain a reaction rate at a particular instant. We do this by drawing tangents at particular points on the curve. Line B in Figure **21.5b** shows a tangent drawn at the start of the curve. This gives a much more accurate value of the initial rate of reaction.

Figure **21.6** shows how to draw a tangent and calculate the rate at a particular point on a curve. In this case, we are using a graph of concentration of cyclopropane against time.

The procedure is:

- Select a point on the graph corresponding to a particular time (10 minutes in this example).
- Draw a straight line at this point so that it just touches the line. The two angles between the straight line and the curve should look very similar.
- Extend the tangent to meet the axes of the graph.
- Calculate the slope (gradient) of the tangent. This is a measure of the rate of reaction. In this example the slope is:

$$\text{slope} = \frac{0.00 - 1.40}{35 \times 60} = -6.67 \times 10^{-4}\,mol\,dm^{-3}\,s^{-1}$$

Note:

- we convert the minutes to seconds by multiplying by 60
- the sign of the slope is negative because the reactant concentration is decreasing

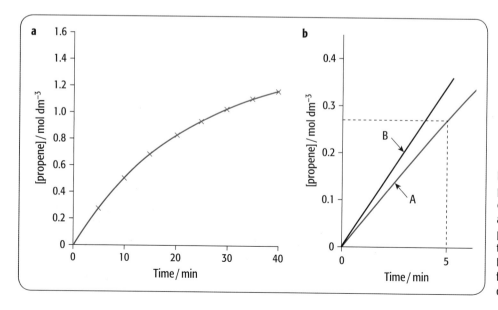

Figure 21.5 How the concentration of propene changes with time in the reaction cyclopropane → propene.
a shows the whole curve; **b** shows the first part of the curve magnified. Line A shows the average rate over the first 5 minutes. Line B shows the actual initial rate found by drawing a tangent at the start of the curve.

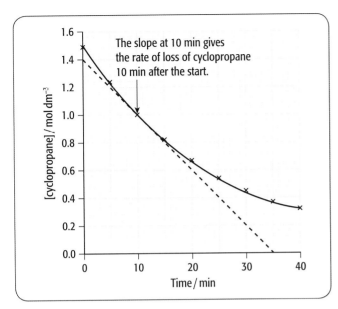

Figure 21.6 The rate of decrease of cyclopropane concentration over times as the reaction proceeds. The rate of reaction at a given time can be found by drawing a tangent and measuring the gradient.

- the value of $-6.67 \times 10^{-4} \, \text{mol dm}^{-3} \, \text{s}^{-1}$ refers to the rate of change of cyclopropane concentration
- this is the rate of reaction when the cyclopropane concentration is $1.00 \, \text{mol dm}^{-3}$.

Changes in rate as the reaction proceeds

As time passes, the concentration of cyclopropane falls. We can find the rate at different concentrations of cyclopropane by drawing tangents at several points on the graph. Figure **21.7** shows how this is done for

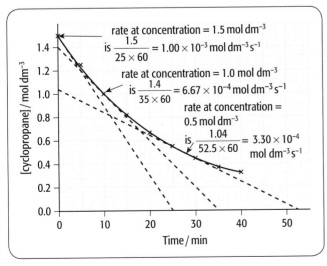

Figure 21.7 Calculation of the rate of decrease of cyclopropane concentration, made at regular intervals.

[cyclopropane] / mol dm^{-3}	Rate / mol dm^{-3} s^{-1}	$\dfrac{\text{rate}}{\text{[cyclopropane]}}$ / s^{-1}
1.50	1.00×10^{-3}	6.67×10^{-4}
1.00	6.67×10^{-4}	6.67×10^{-4}
0.50	3.30×10^{-4}	6.60×10^{-4}

Table 21.2 Rates of decrease for cyclopropane at different concentrations, calculated from Figure **21.7**.

cyclopropane concentrations of $1.50 \, \text{mol dm}^{-3}$ (the initial rate), $1.00 \, \text{mol dm}^{-3}$ and $0.05 \, \text{mol dm}^{-3}$. The data is summarised in Table **21.2**.

A graph of rate of reaction against concentration of cyclopropane (Figure **21.8**) shows us that the rate is directly proportional to the concentration of cyclopropane. So, if the concentration of cyclopropane is doubled the rate of reaction is doubled and if the concentration of cyclopropane falls by one-third, the rate of reaction falls by one-third.

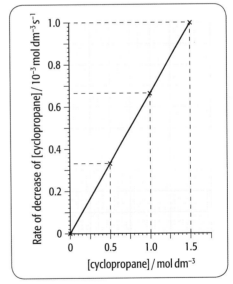

Figure 21.8
The rate of decrease of cyclopropane. Notice how the gradient (rate/concentration) is constant.

Fact file

The complete course of some very fast reactions can be monitored using stopped-flow spectrophotometry. In this technique, very small volumes of reactants are driven at high speed into a mixing chamber. From here they go to an observation cell where the progress of the reaction is monitored (usually by measuring the transmission of ultraviolet radiation through the sample). A graph of rate of reaction against time can be generated automatically.

3 a i Plot the data in Table **21.1** for increase in propene concentration with time.

ii Calculate the rate after 10 minutes (when the propene concentration is $0.50\,mol\,dm^{-3}$) by drawing a tangent.

b Use the same method to calculate the rate of reaction at propene concentrations of $0.00\,mol\,dm^{-3}$, $0.30\,mol\,dm^{-3}$ and $0.90\,mol\,dm^{-3}$

c i Calculate the concentration of cyclopropane when the concentration of propene is 0.00, 0.30, 0.50 and $0.90\,mol\,dm^{-3}$.

ii Plot a graph of rate of reaction against [cyclopropane]. Note that the graph is for cyclopropane concentration NOT [propene] since it is the concentration of the reactant which is affecting the rate not the product.

21.3 Rate equations

The rate constant and rate equations

The third column in Table **21.2** shows that the rate of the reaction is proportional to cyclopropane concentration (within the limits of experimental error). We can express this mathematically as:

rate of reaction = $k \times$ [cyclopropane]

The proportionality constant, k, is called the **rate constant**.

The overall expression (rate of reaction = $k\times$[cyclopropane]) is the **rate equation** for this particular reaction. Rate equations are generally written without the $\times$ sign. For example:

rate = k[cyclopropane]

Rate equations can only be determined from experimental data. They cannot be found from the stoichiometric equation.

Some experimentally determined rate equations are shown in Table **21.3**.

You can see from equation **1**, that the rate of reaction is proportional to the concentration of both H_2 and I_2; however, in equation **2**, CO and O_2 do not appear in the rate equation, even though they are present in the

Stoichiometric equation	rate equation
1 $H_2(g) + I_2(g) \rightarrow 2HI(g)$	rate = $k[H_2][I_2]$
2 $NO(g) + CO(g) + O_2(g)$ $\rightarrow NO_2(g) + CO_2(g)$	rate = $k[NO]^2$
3 $2H_2(g) + 2NO(g)$ $\rightarrow 2H_2O(g) + N_2(g)$	rate = $k[H_2][NO]^2$
4 $BrO_3^-(aq) + 5Br^-(aq) + 6H^+(aq)$ $\rightarrow 3Br_2(aq) + 3H_2O(l)$	rate $= k[BrO_3^-][Br^-][H^+]^2$

Table 21.3 Rate equations for some reactions.

stoichiometric equation. Similarly in reactions **3** and **4** there is no relationship between the rate equation and the stoichiometry of the chemical equation.

In order the find the rate equation we have to conduct a series of experiments. Using reaction **3** as an example:
- first find how the concentration of $H_2(g)$ affects the rate by varying the concentration of $H_2(g)$, while keeping the concentration of NO(g) constant
- the results show that the rate is proportional to the concentration of hydrogen (rate = $k_1[H_2]$)
- then find how the concentration of NO(g) affects the rate by varying the concentration of NO(g) while keeping the concentration of $H_2(g)$ constant
- the results show that the rate is proportional to the square of the concentration of NO (rate = $k_2[NO]^2$).

Combining the two rate equations we get the overall rate equation: rate = $k[H_2][NO]^2$.

The rate equations for some reactions may include compounds which are not present in the chemical equation.

4 Write rate equations for each of the following reactions:

a cyclopropane $\rightarrow$ propene
where rate is proportional to the concentration of cyclopropane

b $2HI(g) \rightarrow H_2(g) + I_2(g)$
where rate is proportional to the square of the hydrogen iodide concentration

c $C_{12}H_{22}O_{11}(aq) + H_2O(l) \xrightarrow{H^+} 2C_6H_{12}O_6(aq)$
where rate is proportional to the concentration of $C_{12}H_{22}O_{11}$ and to the concentration of H^+ ions

continued ⋯⋗

d $2HgCl_2(aq) + K_2C_2O_4(aq)$
$\rightarrow Hg_2Cl_2(s) + 2KCl(aq) + 2CO_2(g)$
where rate is proportional to the concentration of $HgCl_2$ and to the square of the concentration of $K_2C_2O_4$

e $CH_3COCH_3 + I_2 \xrightarrow{H^+} CH_3COCH_2I + HI$
where rate is proportional to the concentration of CH_3COCH_3 and to the concentration of H^+ ions, but the concentration of I_2 has no effect on the rate.

Order of reaction

The order of a reaction shows how the concentration of a reagent affects the rate of reaction.

> The **order of reaction** with respect to a particular reactant is the power to which the concentration of that reactant is raised in the rate equation.

For example, for a rate equation involving only one particular reactant, the order is the power of the concentration shown in the rate equation. For equation 2 in Table **21.3**, the rate equation is rate $= k[NO]^2$ and so the order is 2 with respect to [NO].

When you are writing about order of reaction, you must distinguish carefully between the order with respect to a particular reactant and the overall order of reaction. Taking equation 3 in Table **21.3** as an example:

rate $= k[H_2][NO]^2$

We say that this reaction is:
- first-order with respect to H_2 (since rate is proportional to $[H_2]^1$)
- second-order with respect to NO (since rate is proportional to $[NO]^2$)
- third-order overall (since the sum of the powers is $1+2=3$).

In general terms, for a reaction A + B $\rightarrow$ products, the rate equation can be written in the form:

rate of reaction $= k[A]^m[B]^n$

In this equation:
- [A] and [B] are the concentrations of the reactants
- m and n are the orders of the reaction
- the values of m and n can be 0, 1, 2, 3 or rarely higher

- when the value of m or n is 0 we can ignore the concentration term because any number to the power of zero = 1.

Fact file

Orders of reaction are not always whole numbers. A few reactions have fractional orders. For example, the reaction:

$CH_3CHO(g) \rightarrow CH_4(g) + CO(g)$

has an overall order of 1.5. The rate equation for this reaction is:

rate $= k[CH_3CHO]^{1.5}$

Many reactions involving free radicals have fractional orders of reaction.

Check-up

5   For each of the reactions **a** to **d** in Check-up 4, state:

   i   the order of reaction with respect to each reactant

   ii   the overall order of reaction.

Units of k

The units of k vary according to the form of the rate equation.

Worked examples

1   From equation 1 in Table **21.3**.

   Step 1   Write the rate equation

     rate $= k[H_2][I_2]$

   Step 2   Rearrange the equation in terms of k.

$$k = \frac{\text{rate}}{[H_2][I_2]}$$

   Step 3   Substitute the units.

$$k = \frac{\text{mol dm}^{-3}\ \text{s}^{-1}}{(\text{mol dm}^{-3}) \times (\text{mol dm}^{-3})}$$

continued ⋯⟩

Step 4 Cancel mol dm^{-3}.

$$k = \frac{\cancel{\text{mol dm}^{-3}}\ \text{s}^{-1}}{(\cancel{\text{mol dm}^{-3}}) \times (\text{mol dm}^{-3})}$$

Step 5 Units of k.

$$\text{s}^{-1}\,\text{mol}^{-1}\,\text{dm}^{3} = \text{dm}^{3}\,\text{mol}^{-1}\,\text{s}^{-1}$$

- when writing the units on one line, the indices on the bottom change sign
- we usually put the unit with the positive index first
- don't forget the s^{-1} arising from the units of rate.

2 From equation 3 in Table **21.3**.

Step 1 Write the rate equation.

$$\text{rate} = k[\text{H}_2][\text{NO}]^2$$

Step 2 Rearrange the equation in terms of k.

$$k = \frac{\text{rate}}{[\text{H}_2][\text{NO}]^2}$$

Step 3 Substitute the units.

$$k = \frac{\text{mol dm}^{-3}\ \text{s}^{-1}}{(\text{mol dm}^{-3}) \times (\text{mol dm}^{-3})^2}$$

Step 4 Cancel mol dm^{-3}.

$$k = \frac{\cancel{\text{mol dm}^{-3}}\ \text{s}^{-1}}{(\cancel{\text{mol dm}^{-3}}) \times (\text{mol dm}^{-3})^2}$$

Step 5 Units of k.

units of $k = \text{s}^{-1}\,\text{mol}^{-2}\,\text{dm}^{6} = \text{dm}^{6}\,\text{mol}^{-2}\,\text{s}^{-1}$

Check-up

6 State the units of k corresponding to each of the following rate equations:
  a rate = $k[\text{NO}]^2$
  b rate = $k[\text{NH}_3]^0$
  c rate = $k[\text{BrO}_3^-][\text{Br}^-][\text{H}^+]^2$
  d rate = $k[\text{cyclopropane}]$

21.4 Which order of reaction?

We can identify the order of a reaction in three ways:
- plot a graph of reaction rate against concentration of reactant
- plot a graph of concentration of reactant against time
- deduce successive half-lives from graphs of concentration against time.

Graphs of reaction rate against time

A graph of reaction rate against time tells us whether a reaction is zero, first, second or third order with respect to a particular reagent (or overall). It is very rare to obtain an order with respect to a particular reagent higher than second order. Figure **21.9** shows the shapes of the graphs expected for different orders of reaction.

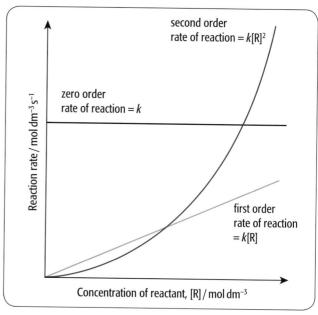

Figure 21.9 Zero-, first- and second-order reactions: how changes in the concentration of a reactant affect the reaction rate.

We shall now look at some examples of zero-, first- and second-order reactions.

Zero-order

$$2\text{NH}_3(g) \xrightarrow{\text{hot tungsten}} \text{N}_2(g) + 3\text{H}_2(g)$$

The rate equation derived from experiments is:

$$\text{rate} = k[\text{NH}_3]^0$$

The plot of reaction rate against concentration is a horizontal straight line (see Figure **21.9**). The reaction rate does not change with concentration. For a zero-order reaction, k is numerically equal to the reaction rate:

rate = k

This is because any number to the power of zero = 1.

First-order

$$2N_2O(g) \xrightarrow{\text{gold}} 2N_2(g) + O_2(g)$$

The rate equation derived from experiments is:

rate = $k[N_2O]^1$

This is usually written as:

rate = $k[N_2O]$

The plot of reaction rate against concentration is an inclined straight line going through the origin (see Figure 21.9). The rate is directly proportional to the concentration of N$_2$O. So doubling the concentration of N$_2$O doubles the rate of reaction.

Second-order

$$NO_2(g) + CO(g) \longrightarrow NO(g) + CO_2(g)$$

The rate equation derived from experiments is:

rate = $k[NO]^2$

The plot of reaction rate against concentration is an upwardly curved line (see Figure 21.9).

In this case, reaction rate is directly proportional to the square of the concentration of NO$_2$(g). When the concentration of NO$_2$(g) doubles, the rate of reaction increases four-fold. If we consider the second-order rate equation as written above, we can see that this is true by comparing the rates at two different concentrations, 1 mol dm^{-3} and 2 mol dm^{-3}.

rate at 1 mol dm^{-3} = $k(1)^2$ = $1k$
rate at 2 mol dm^{-3} = $k(2)^2$ = $4k$

Check-up

7   Draw sketch graphs of reaction rate against concentration of the reactant in bold for each of the following reactions:
   a   **NO**(g) + CO(g) + O$_2$(g) → NO$_2$(g) + CO$_2$(g)

continued ⋯▸

for which the rate equation is:

rate = $k[NO]^2$

b $2HI(g) \xrightarrow{\text{gold}} H_2(g) + I_2(g)$
   for which the rate equation is:

rate = k

Note: the catalyst influences the order here – the order is not the same as for the uncatalysed reaction.
c $(CH_3)_3CCl + OH^- \rightarrow (CH_3)_3COH + Cl^-$
   for which the rate equation is:

$k[(CH_3)_3CCl]$

Graphs of concentration of reactant against time

Figure 21.10 shows how we can distinguish between zero-, first- and second-order reactions by plotting a graph of concentration against time.

For a zero-order reaction, the graph is a descending straight line. The rate of reaction is the slope (gradient) of the graph. The reaction proceeds at the same rate whatever the concentration of the reactant.

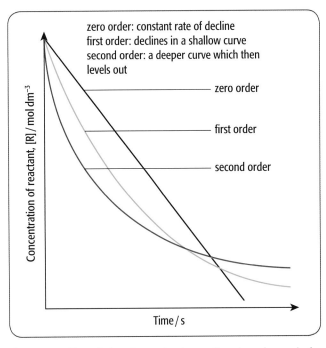

Figure 21.10 Zero-, first- and second-order reactions: how changes in the concentration of a reactant affect the time taken for a reaction to proceed.

For first- and second-order reactions, the graph is a curve. The curve for the second-order reaction is much deeper than for a first-order reaction. It also appears to have a relatively longer 'tail' as it levels off. We can also distinguish between these two curves by determining successive half-lives of the reaction.

Check-up

8 For each of the reactions **a** to **c** in Check-up 7, draw a sketch graph to show how the concentration of the bold reactant changes with time.

Half-life and reaction rates

Half-life, $t_{\frac{1}{2}}$, is the time taken for the concentration of a reactant to fall to half of its original value.

Figure **21.11** shows how half-life is measured for the cyclopropane to propene reaction that we studied earlier. Three successive half-lives are shown. Table **21.4** shows the values of the successive half-lives obtained from Figure **21.11**.

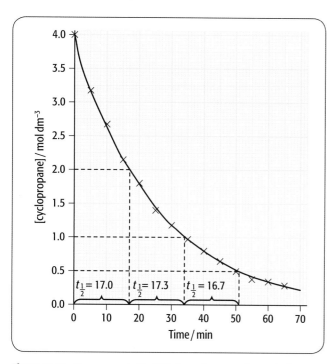

Figure 21.11 Measurement of half-life for cyclopropane isomerisation.

Δ[cyclopropane] / mol dm^{-3}	Half-life / min
4.00 to 2.00	17.0
2.00 to 1.00	34.3 – 17.0 = 17.3
1.00 to 0.50	51.0 – 34.3 = 16.7

Table 21.4 A constant half-life indicates a first-order reaction.

You can see that the successive half-lives have values which are fairly close to each other (17.0, 17.3, 16.7). The mean half-life is 17.0 minutes for this reaction. We can tell that this reaction is first order because the successive half-lives are more or less constant. In a first-order reaction like this the half-life is independent of the original concentration of reactant. This means that whatever the starting concentration of cyclopropane, the half-life will always be 17 minutes.

We can distinguish zero-, first- and second-order reactions from their successive half-lives (Figure **21.12**).

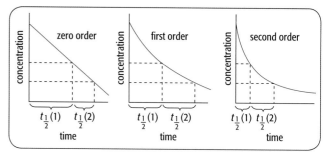

Figure 21.12 The half-life of zero-, first- and second-order reactions can be determined from graphs of concentration against time.

- A zero-order reaction has successive half-lives which decrease with time.
- A first-order reaction has a half-life which is constant.
- Second-order reactions have successive half-lives which increase with time. (This also applies to reactions with a higher order for a particular reagent but we will not be discussing these.)

Check-up

9 Benzenediazonium chloride, $C_6H_5N_2Cl$, decomposes at room temperature:

$$C_6H_5N_2Cl(aq) + H_2O(l)$$
$$\rightarrow C_6H_5OH(aq) + N_2(g) + HCl(aq)$$

continued ⋯⟶

a Describe how this reaction can be monitored.

b Using the data in the table, plot a graph of concentration of $C_6H_5N_2Cl$ against time.

Time / s	$[C_6H_5N_2Cl] / 10^{-4}\, mol\, dm^{-3}$
0	5.8
200	4.4
400	3.2
600	2.5
800	1.7
1000	1.2
1200	0.8
1400	0.5
1600	0.3

c From your graph, find the value of two successive half-lives.

d Use the values of these half-lives to deduce the order of the reaction.

21.5 Calculations involving the rate constant, k

Calculating k from initial concentrations and initial rate

In the presence of hydrogen ions, hydrogen peroxide, H_2O_2, reacts with iodide ions to form water and iodine:

$$H_2O_2(aq) + 2I^-(aq) + 2H^+(aq) \rightarrow 2H_2O(l) + I_2(aq)$$

The rate equation for this reaction is:

rate of reaction = $k[H_2O_2][I^-]$

The progress of the reaction can be followed by measuring the initial rate of formation of iodine. Table 21.5 shows the rates of reaction obtained using various initial concentrations of each reactant.

The procedure for calculating k is shown below, using the data for experiment 1.

Step 1 Write out the rate equation.

rate = $k[H_2O_2][I^-]$

Step 2 Rearrange the equation in terms of k

$$k = \frac{rate}{[H_2O_2][I^-]}$$

Step 3 Substitute the values

$$k = \frac{3.50 \times 10^{-6}}{(0.0200) \times (0.0100)}$$

$$k = 1.75 \times 10^{-2}\, dm^3\, mol^{-1}\, s^{-1}$$

Note: the concentration of hydrogen ions is ignored because $[H^+]$ does not appear in the rate equation. The reaction is zero order with respect to $[H^+]$.

Calculating k from half-life

For a first-order reaction, half-life is related to the rate constant by the expression:

$$t_{\frac{1}{2}} = \frac{0.693}{k}, \text{where } t_{\frac{1}{2}} \text{ is the half-life, measured in s}$$

We can rewrite this in the form:

$$k = \frac{0.693}{t_{\frac{1}{2}}}$$

Experiment	$[H_2O_2] / mol\, dm^{-3}$	$[I^-] / mol\, dm^{-3}$	$[H^+] / mol\, dm^{-3}$	Initial rate of reaction / $mol\, dm^{-3}\, s^{-1}$
1	0.0200	0.0100	0.0100	3.50×10^{-6}
2	0.0300	0.0100	0.0100	5.30×10^{-6}
3	0.0050	0.0200	0.0200	1.75×10^{-6}

Table 21.5 Rates of reaction obtained using different initial concentrations of H_2O_2, I^- ions and H^+ ions.

So, for the first-order reaction cyclopropane to propene, for which the half-life is 17.0 min, we:
- convert minutes to seconds
- then substitute the half-life into the expression:

$$k = \frac{0.693}{t_{\frac{1}{2}}} = \frac{0.693}{17.0 \times 60} = 6.79 \times 10^{-4} \, dm^3 \, mol^{-1} \, s^{-1}$$

This value is very close to the ones quoted in Table 21.2. Rate constants for zero- and second-order reactions can also be calculated from half-lives but the calculations are more complex.

We can also use the expression $t_{\frac{1}{2}} = \frac{0.693}{k}$ to calculate the half-life of a first-order reaction if we know the rate constant.

Fact file

We can write the rate equations in a form involving mathematical differentiation and integration.

In the equation $t_{\frac{1}{2}} = \frac{0.693}{k}$, the number 0.693 arises from the integrated form of the rate equation for a first-order reaction which is $kt_{\frac{1}{2}} = \ln 2$. If you type 'ln 2 =' into your calculator you get 0.693.

Check-up

10 a Use the data from experiments 2 and 3 in Table 21.5 to calculate the rate constant for the following reaction.
$H_2O_2(aq) + 2I^-(aq) + 2H^+(aq)$
$\rightarrow 2H_2O(l) + I_2(aq)$
The rate equation for this reaction is:
rate of reaction = $k[H_2O_2][I^-]$

b Use the formula $t_{\frac{1}{2}} = \frac{0.693}{k}$ to calculate a value for the rate constant of a reaction which is first order and has a half-life of 480 s.

c A first-order reaction has a rate constant of $9.63 \times 10^{-5} \, s^{-1}$. Calculate a value for the half-life of this reaction.

21.6 Deducing order of reaction from raw data

We can use any of the three methods mentioned in Section 21.4 (page 330) to determine the order of a reaction. In this section we shall look in detail at some more complex examples.

Using data from the course of a reaction

In this method we carry out one or more experiments with known initial concentrations of reactants and follow the course of the reaction until it is complete (or nearly complete).

The steps in analysing the data are as follows.

Step 1 Plot a graph to show how the concentration of a particular reactant (or product) changes with time.

Step 2 Take tangents at various points along the curve which correspond to particular concentrations of the reactant.

Step 3 Calculate the slope (gradient) at each concentration selected. The rate of reaction is calculated from the slope of the graph.

Step 4 Plot a graph of rate of reaction against concentration.

Worked example

3 Methanol reacts with hydrochloric acid at 25 °C. The products are chloromethane and water.

$$CH_3OH(aq) + HCl(aq) \rightarrow CH_3Cl(g) + H_2O(l)$$

Equimolar amounts of methanol and hydrochloric acid are mixed at 25 °C. The progress of the reaction is followed by
- taking a small sample of the reaction mixture from time to time, then
- titrating each sample with a standard solution of sodium hydroxide.

The data obtained is shown in Table 21.6

continued ⋯⟩

Time / min	[HCl] / mol dm^{-3}	[CH$_3$OH] / mol dm^{-3}
0	1.84	1.84
200	1.45	1.45
400	1.22	1.22
600	1.04	1.04
800	0.91	0.91
1000	0.81	0.81
1200	0.72	0.72
1400	0.66	0.66
1600	0.60	0.60
1800	0.56	0.56
2000	0.54	0.54

Table 21.6 Data for the reaction between methanol and hydrochloric acid.

Step 1 Draw a graph of concentration (of hydrochloric acid) against time (Figure **21.13**).

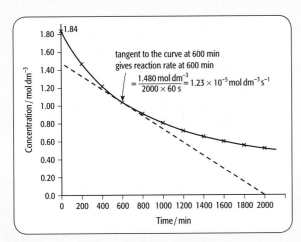

Figure 21.13 The concentration of hydrochloric acid and methanol fall at the same rate as time passes.

Step 2 Draw tangents to the curve at various places corresponding to a range of concentrations. In Figure **21.13** the tangent drawn corresponds to [HCl] = 1.04 mol dm^{-3}.

Step 3 For each tangent drawn, calculate the gradient and then the rate of reaction. In Figure **21.13**, the rate corresponding to [HCl] = 1.04 mol dm^{-3} is

continued ⋯⋗

$$\frac{1.480}{2000 \times 60} = 1.23 \times 10^{-5} \, mol \, dm^{-3} \, s^{-1}$$

(multiply by 60 to convert minutes to seconds) Table **21.7** shows the rates corresponding to five different concentrations of hydrochloric acid.

Time / min	Concen-tration / mol dm^{-3}	Rate from graph / mol dm^{-3} min^{-1}	Rate from graph / mol dm^{-3} s^{-1}
0	1.84	2.30×10^{-3}	3.83×10^{-5}
200	1.45	1.46×10^{-3}	2.43×10^{-5}
400	1.22	1.05×10^{-3}	1.75×10^{-5}
600	1.04	0.74×10^{-3}	1.23×10^{-5}
800	0.91	0.54×10^{-3}	0.90×10^{-5}

Table 21.7 Values calculated for the reaction between methanol and hydrochloric acid.

Step 4 Plot a graph of rate of reaction against concentration.

Figure **21.14** shows a plot of rate against the concentration of [HCl] or [CH$_3$OH]. We have included the [CH$_3$OH] because if you look at the data in Table **21.6**, you will see that the concentration of CH$_3$OH is decreasing at the same rate as the decrease in concentration of HCl.

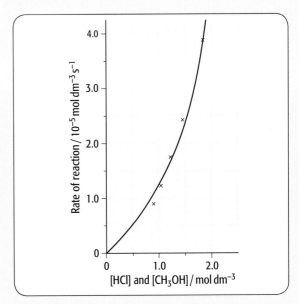

Figure 21.14 A graph showing how concentration changes of hydrochloric acid or methanol affect rate of reaction. The curve shows that the reaction is likely to be second order.

continued ⋯⋗

Figure **21.14** shows an upward curve. This indicates that the reaction is second order. But second order with respect to what? Since the concentrations of both HCl and CH₃OH are decreasing at the same rate, either of these may be second order. The possibilities are:

- rate = $k[CH_3OH][HCl]$
- rate = $k[CH_3OH]^2$
- rate = $k[HCl]^2$

Further experiments would have to be carried out to confirm one or other of these possibilities. The only thing we can be sure of is that the reaction is second order overall.

Check-up

11 Suggest how the experiment for the reaction between methanol and hydrochloric acid might be re-designed to obtain evidence for the effect of changing the HCl concentration whilst controlling the CH₃OH concentration.

Using initial rates

The initial rates method is often used when the rate of reaction is slow.

- Carry out several experiments with different known initial concentrations of each reactant.
- Measure the initial rates of reaction by either:
  - taking the tangent of the curve at the start of each experiment or
  - measuring the concentration of a reactant or product soon after the experiment has started.
- For each reactant, plot a graph of initial rate against concentration of that particular reactant.

Worked example

4 Nitrogen(V) oxide, N_2O_5, decomposes to nitrogen(IV) oxide and oxygen.

$$2N_2O_5(g) \rightarrow 4NO_2(g) + O_2(g)$$

continued ⋯⇢

Table **21.8** shows how the initial rate of reaction varies with the initial concentration of N_2O_5.

Initial concentration, $[N_2O_5]$ / mol dm⁻³	Initial rate / 10^{-5} mol dm⁻³ s⁻¹
3.00	3.15
1.50	1.55
0.75	0.80

Table 21.8 Data for the decomposition of nitrogen(V) oxide.

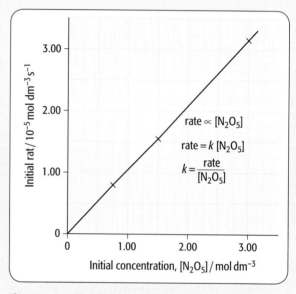

Figure 21.15 The initial rate of decomposition of nitrogen(V) oxide is directly proportional to the initial concentration.

A graph of the data (Figure **21.15**) shows that the initial rate of reaction is directly proportional to the initial concentration of N_2O_5.

$$\text{rate of reaction} \propto [N_2O_5]$$
$$= k[N_2O_5]$$

Check-up

12 a State the order of reaction for the decomposition of nitrogen(V) oxide.

b Use the data for 3.00 mol dm⁻³ N_2O_5 in Table **21.8** to calculate a value for the rate constant for this decomposition.

Worked example

5 The equation below describes the reaction of propanone with iodine. Hydrogen ions catalyse this reaction.

$$CH_3COCH_3 + I_2 \xrightarrow{H^+} CH_3COCH_2I + HI$$

The progress of the reaction can be followed by using a colorimeter. The brown colour of the iodine fades as the reaction proceeds. The experimental results are shown in Table 21.9.

Experiment	[HCl] / mol dm^{-3}	[propanone] / mol dm^{-3} 10^{-3}	[iodine] / mol dm^{-3} 10^{-3}	Initial rate / 10^{-6} mol dm^{-3} s^{-1}
1	1.25	0.50	1.25	10.9
2	0.625	0.50	1.25	5.4
3	1.25	0.25	1.25	5.1
4	1.25	0.50	0.625	10.7

Table 21.9 Experimental results for the reaction of propanone with iodine at varying aqueous concentrations.

Note that:
- the data is from real experiments, so experimental errors have to be taken into account
- the hydrogen ions have been provided by the hydrochloric acid.

In this method we see how changing the concentration of each reactant in turn affects the rate of reaction. In order to make a fair comparison, we must make sure that the concentrations of the other reactants are kept constant.

Compare experiments 1 and 2 (propanone and iodine concentrations are constant):
- doubling the concentration of H$^+$ ions from 0.625 to 1.25 mol dm^{-3} doubles the rate of reaction
- the reaction is first order with respect to H$^+$ ions.

Compare experiments 1 and 3 (hydrochloric acid and iodine concentrations are constant):
- doubling the concentration of propanone from 0.25×10^{-3} to 0.50×10^{-3} mol dm^{-3} doubles the rate of reaction
- the reaction is first order with respect to propanone.

continued ⋯⟶

Compare experiments 1 and 4 (hydrochloric acid and propanone concentrations are constant):
- doubling the concentration of iodine from 0.625×10^{-3} to 1.25×10^{-3} mol dm^{-3} has no effect on the rate of reaction
- the reaction is zero order with respect to iodine.

Figure 21.16 The rate of reaction between propanone and iodine can be followed by the loss of colour of the reaction mixture as the reaction proceeds.

Check-up

13 a Write the rate equation for the acid-catalysed reaction of iodine with propanone.

b Use your rate equation and the information in Table 21.9 (experiment 1) to calculate a value for the rate constant for this reaction.

21.7 Kinetics and reaction mechanisms

The rate-determining step

In Worked example 5 you saw that for the reaction:

$$CH_3COCH_3 + I_2 \xrightarrow{H^+} CH_3COCH_2I + HI$$

the iodine did not appear in the rate equation but the H$^+$ ions did.

- A reactant that appears in the chemical equation may have no affect on reaction rate.

- A substance which is not a reactant in the chemical equation can affect reaction rate.

In organic chemistry, you have met the idea that reactions occur in a number of steps. We call this the reaction mechanism. These steps do not take place at the same rate. The overall rate of reaction depends on the slowest step. We call this the **rate-determining step**. If the concentration of a reactant appears in the rate equation, then that reactant (or substances which react together to form it) appears in the rate-determining step. If a substance does not appear in the overall rate equation it does not take part in the rate-determining step. So, for the reaction between propanone and iodine, H^+ ions are involved in the rate-determining step but iodine is not.

Verifying possible reaction mechanisms

We can use kinetic data to confirm proposed reaction mechanisms. It is important to realise that the mechanism is not deduced from the kinetic data. The kinetic data simply shows us that a proposed reaction mechanism is possible.

Various mechanisms have been proposed for the reaction

$$CH_3COCH_3 + I_2 \xrightarrow{H^+} CH_3COCH_2I + HI$$

Figure 21.17 shows one proposed mechanism.

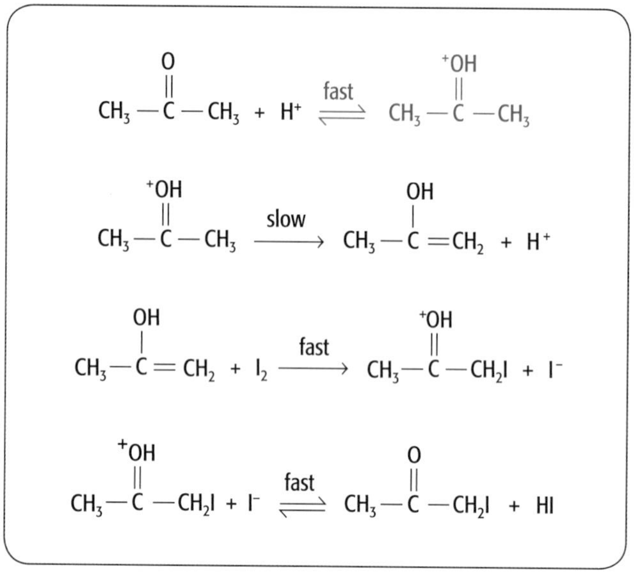

Figure 21.17 Propanone molecules rapidly accept hydrogen ions to form an intermediate that slowly forms propen-2-ol. This reacts rapidly with iodine to give the products.

The rate equation for this reaction is

$$rate = k[CH_3COCH_3][H^+]$$

We could not have deduced this reaction mechanism from the rate equation. But the mechanism is consistent with the rate equation.

The slow step (the rate-determining step) does not involve either propanone or hydrogen ions directly. However, the intermediate with the formula

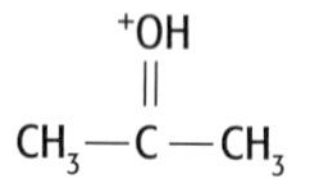

$$\overset{+OH}{\underset{||}{CH_3-C-CH_3}}$$

is derived from substances which react together to form it (propanone and hydrogen ions). So both $[CH_3COCH_3]$ and $[H^+]$ appear in the rate equation.

The reaction between iodine and the intermediate $CH_3C(OH)=CH_2$ is fast and iodine molecules are not involved in the mechanism until after the rate-determining step. So the rate of reaction does not depend on the concentration of iodine.

On page 336 we saw that the rate equation for the reaction

$$2N_2O_5(g) \rightarrow 4NO_2(g) + O_2(g)$$

is rate = $k[N_2O_5]$. Figure 21.18 shows a suggested mechanism for this reaction. The rate equation suggests that a single N_2O_5 molecule is involved in the rate-determining step. This fits in with the proposed mechanism which suggests that the decomposition of N_2O_5 to form NO_2 and NO_3 is the slow step. The steps which follow the slow step are relatively fast and so have no effect on reaction rate.

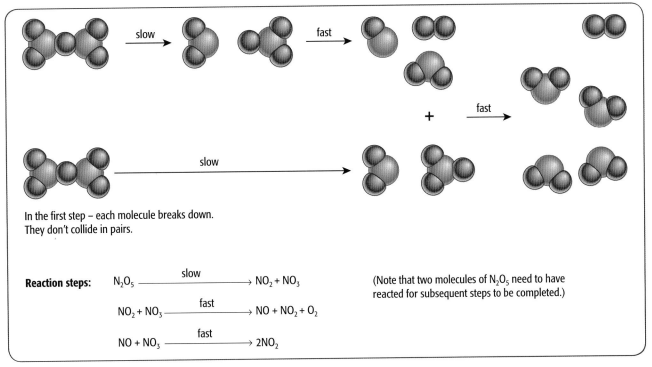

In the first step – each molecule breaks down. They don't collide in pairs.

Reaction steps:

$$N_2O_5 \xrightarrow{\text{slow}} NO_2 + NO_3$$

$$NO_2 + NO_3 \xrightarrow{\text{fast}} NO + NO_2 + O_2$$

$$NO + NO_3 \xrightarrow{\text{fast}} 2NO_2$$

(Note that two molecules of N_2O_5 need to have reacted for subsequent steps to be completed.)

Figure 21.18 The rate equation tells us that the decomposition of individual molecules of nitrogen(V) oxide is the rate-determining step. The subsequent reactions are very much faster by comparison, and do not influence the overall rate. Try to match the reaction steps with the illustrations to get a picture of what is happening.

Fact file

If there is only a single species (atom, ion or molecule) in the rate-determining step we call the reaction unimolecular. If two species (which can be the same or different) are involved in the rate-determining step, we say that the reaction is bimolecular. Mechanisms which involve a trimolecular step are rare. This is because it is unlikely that three species will collide at the same time.

Check-up

14 An acidified solution of hydrogen peroxide reacts with iodide ions.

$$H_2O_2(aq) + 2H^+(aq) + 2I^-(aq)$$
$$\rightarrow 2H_2O(l) + I_2(aq)$$

The rate equation for this reaction is

$$\text{rate} = [H_2O_2][I^-]$$

The mechanism below has been proposed for this reaction.

continued ⋯➔

$$H_2O_2 + I^- \xrightarrow{\text{slow}} H_2O + IO^-$$

$$H^+ + IO^- \xrightarrow{\text{fast}} HIO$$

$$HIO + H^+ + I^- \xrightarrow{\text{fast}} I_2 + H_2O$$

Explain why this mechanism is consistent with the rate equation.

Predicting the order of a reaction from reaction mechanisms

We can predict the order of reaction from a given reaction mechanism if we know the intermediates present in the rate-determining step (or substances which react together to form the intermediate). Take, for example, the reaction of propanone with bromine in alkaline solution.

$$CH_3COCH_3 + Br_2 + OH^-$$
$$\rightarrow CH_3COCH_2Br + H_2O + Br^-$$

The reaction mechanism is shown in Figure **21.19**.

Figure 21.19 The reaction mechanism for the bromination of propanone in alkaline conditions.

The rate-determining step in this reaction is the slow step. The slow step involves one molecule of propanone and one hydroxide ion, so only these two species appear in the rate equation. The reaction is second order overall, first order with respect to propanone and first order with respect to hydroxide ions.

$$\text{rate} = k[CH_3COCH_3][OH^-]$$

Bromine does not appear in the rate equation since it takes part in a fast step after the rate-determining step.

21.8 Catalysis

In Chapter 9 (page 155) you saw that catalysts increase the rate of a chemical reaction. They do this by providing an alternative pathway for the reaction with lower activation energy. We can divide catalysts into two main classes.

Figure 21.20 Addition polymers are produced using metallocene catalysts such as $[(C_5H_5)_2ZrCH_3]^+$. The strength and puncture resistance of this polymer film is being shown with a ball-point pen.

- **Homogeneous catalysis** occurs when the catalyst is in the same phase as the reaction mixture. For example: hydrogen ions catalyse the hydrolysis of esters.

$$CH_3COOC_2H_5(aq) + H_2O(l)$$
$$\underset{H^+(aq)}{\rightleftharpoons} CH_3COOH(aq) + C_2H_5OH(aq)$$

In this reaction the reactants, products and catalyst are all in the aqueous phase.
- **Heterogeneous catalysis** occurs when the catalyst is in a different phase to the reaction mixture. For example, the decomposition of aqueous hydrogen peroxide catalysed by manganese(IV) oxide.

$$2H_2O_2(aq) \xrightarrow{MnO_2(s)} 2H_2O(l) + O_2(g)$$

The manganese(IV) oxide is in the solid phase, whereas the hydrogen peroxide is in aqueous solution.

Homogeneous catalysis

Homogeneous catalysis often involves changes in oxidation number of the ions involved in catalysis. For example, small amounts of iodide ions catalyse the decomposition of hydrogen peroxide. In the catalysed reaction, iodide ions, I^-, are first oxidised to iodate(I) ions, IO^-. The IO^- ions then react with further molecules of hydrogen peroxide and are reduced back to iodide ions.

$$H_2O_2(aq) + I^-(aq) \rightarrow H_2O(l) + IO^-(aq)$$

$$H_2O_2(aq) + IO^-(aq) \rightarrow H_2O(l) + I^-(aq) + O_2(g)$$

The overall equation is:

$$2H_2O_2(aq) \xrightarrow{I^-} 2H_2O(l) + O_2(g)$$

Ions of transition elements are often good catalysts because of their ability to change oxidation number.

Examples of homogeneous catalysis
The iodine–peroxodisulfate reaction
Peroxodisulfate (persulfate) ions, $S_2O_8^{2-}$, oxidise iodide ions to iodine. This reaction is very slow.

$$S_2O_8^{2-}(aq) + 2I^-(aq) \rightarrow 2SO_4^{2-}(aq) + I_2(aq)$$

The peroxodisulfate and iodide ions both have a negative charge. In order to collide and react, these ions need considerable energy to overcome the repulsive forces when like charges approach each other.

Fe^{3+}(aq) ions catalyse this reaction. The catalysis involves two redox reactions.

- Reaction 1: reduction of Fe^{3+} ions to Fe^{2+} ions by I$^-$ ions:

$$2Fe^{3+}(aq) + 2I^- \rightarrow 2Fe^{2+}(aq) + I_2(aq)$$

- Reaction 2: oxidation of Fe^{2+} ions back to Fe^{3+} by S$_2$O$_8^{2-}$ ions:

$$2Fe^{2+}(aq) + S_2O_8^{2-} \rightarrow 2Fe^{3+}(aq) + 2SO_4^{2-}(aq)$$

In both reactions 1 and 2, positively charged iron ions react with negatively charged ions. Since ions with unlike charges are attracted to each other, these reactions are more likely to occur than direct reaction between S$_2$O$_8^{2-}$ and I$^-$ ions.

You should notice that it doesn't matter what the order is of the two reactions. The oxidation of Fe^{2+} ions to Fe^{3+} by S$_2$O$_8^{2-}$ ions could happen first:

$$2Fe^{2+}(aq) + S_2O_8^{2-} \rightarrow 2Fe^{3+}(aq) + 2SO_4^{2-}(aq)$$

followed by

$$2Fe^{3+}(aq) + 2I^- \rightarrow 2Fe^{2+}(aq) + I_2(aq)$$

This reaction is catalysed by Fe^{3+}(aq) and it is also catalysed by Fe^{2+}(aq).

Figure 21.21 shows an energy level profile for the catalysed and the uncatalysed reactions. Notice that the catalysed reaction has two energy 'humps' because it is a two-stage reaction.

In order for this catalysis to work, the standard electrode potentials for the reactions involving the catalyst must lie between the electrode potentials involving the two reactants (Figure 21.22). The use of electrode potentials in

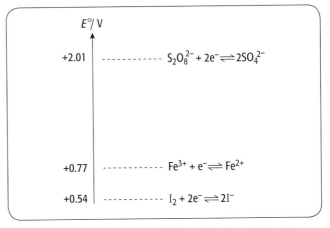

Figure 21.22 The electrode potential diagram for the catalysis of the reaction S$_2$O$_8^{2-}$ + 2I$^-$ → 2SO$_4^{2-}$ + I$_2$

this way only predicts that the catalysis is possible. It does not give any information about the rate of reaction.

Oxides of nitrogen and acid rain

Sulfur dioxide is produced when fossil fuels containing sulfur are burnt. When sulfur dioxide escapes into the atmosphere it contributes to acid rain. One of the steps in the formation of acid rain is the oxidation of sulfur dioxide to sulfur trioxide.

$$SO_2(g) + \tfrac{1}{2}O_2(g) \rightarrow SO_3(g)$$

This oxidation is catalysed by a wide variety of mechanisms. Nitrogen(IV) oxide present in the atmosphere from a variety of sources (see page 196) can catalyse the oxidation of sulfur dioxide. The nitrogen(IV) oxide is reformed by reaction with atmospheric oxygen.

$$SO_2(g) + NO_2(g) \rightarrow SO_3(g) + NO(g)$$

$$NO + \tfrac{1}{2}O_2 \rightarrow NO_2(g)$$

Check-up

15 a Which of the pairs of substances **i** to **iv** below might catalyse the reaction:

$$S_2O_8^{2-}(aq) + 2I^-(aq) \rightarrow 2SO_4^{2-}(aq) + I_2(aq)$$

Explain your answer.

i   Ni(s) / Ni^{2+}(aq) $E^\ominus = -0.25\,V$

ii Mn^{3+}(aq) / Mn^{2+}(aq) $E^\ominus = +1.49\,V$

continued ⋯⟩

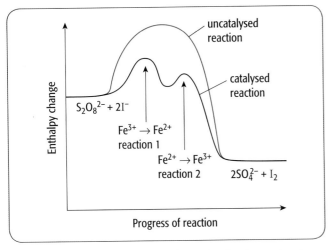

Figure 21.21 Energy level profiles for the catalysed and uncatalysed reactions of peroxodisulfate ions with iodide ions.

iii $Ce^{4+}(aq) / Ce^{3+}(aq)$ $E^{\ominus} = +1.70\,V$

iv $Cu^{2+}(aq) / Cu^{+}(aq)$ $E^{\ominus} = +0.15\,V$

b Describe in terms of oxidation number change, which species are being oxidised and which are being reduced in these equations:

i $SO_2(g) + NO_2(g) \rightarrow SO_3(g) + NO(g)$

ii $NO + \frac{1}{2}O_2 \rightarrow NO_2(g)$

Heterogeneous catalysis

Heterogeneous catalysis often involves gaseous molecules reacting at the surface of a solid catalyst. The mechanism of this catalysis can be explained using the theory of **adsorption**. Chemical adsorption (also called chemisorption) occurs when molecules become bonded to atoms on the surface of a solid. Transition elements such as nickel are particularly good at chemisorbing hydrogen gas. Figure **21.23** shows the process of adsorption of hydrogen onto a nickel surface.

Fact file

You must be careful to distinguish between the words adsorb and absorb. Adsorb means to bond to the surface of a substance. Absorb means to move right into the substance – rather like a sponge absorbs water.

The stages in adsorption of hydrogen onto nickel are:
- hydrogen gas diffuses to the surface of the nickel
- the hydrogen is physically adsorbed onto the surface – weak van der Waals' forces link the hydrogen molecules to the nickel
- the hydrogen becomes chemically adsorbed onto the surface – this causes stronger bonds to form between the hydrogen and the nickel
- this causes weakening of the hydrogen–hydrogen covalent bond.

Examples of heterogeneous catalysis

Iron in the Haber process

Particular conditions of temperature and pressure are required to form ammonia from nitrogen and hydrogen (see page **193**). The reaction is catalysed by iron. The catalyst works by allowing hydrogen and nitrogen molecules to come close together on the surface of the iron. They are then more likely to react. Figure **21.24** shows the five steps in this heterogeneous catalysis.

1 Diffusion: nitrogen gas and hydrogen gas diffuse to the surface of the iron.

2 Adsorption: the reactant molecules are chemically adsorbed onto the surface of the iron. The bonds formed between the reactant molecules and the iron are:
- strong enough to weaken the covalent bonds within the nitrogen and hydrogen molecules so the atoms can react with each other
- weak enough to break and allow the products to leave the surface.

3 Reaction: the adsorbed nitrogen and hydrogen atoms react on the surface of the iron to form ammonia.

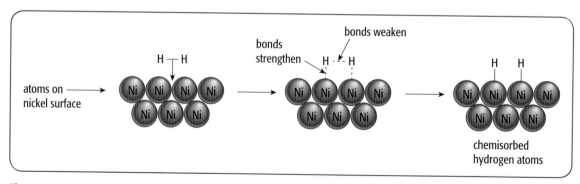

Figure 21.23 The adsorption of hydrogen onto a nickel surface.

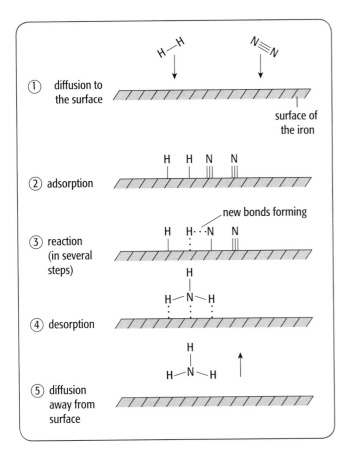

Figure 21.24 A possible mechanism for catalysis in the Haber process.

4 **Desorption**: the bonds between the ammonia and the surface of the iron weaken and are eventually broken.
5 **Diffusion**: ammonia diffuses away from the surface of the iron.

Fact file

The rate-determining step in ammonia synthesis is the chemical adsorption of nitrogen onto the catalyst surface:

$$N \equiv N \quad \longrightarrow \quad N \quad N$$

The best catalysts for ammonia synthesis are iron, ruthenium and osmium. These form fairly strong bonds with nitrogen but not too strong. Metals to the right of these three metals in the Periodic Table are poor adsorbers of nitrogen, whereas those to the left of them bond to nitrogen too strongly.

Transition elements in catalytic converters

In Chapter 14 (page 219) you learnt how catalytic converters convert harmful nitrogen oxides and carbon monoxide present in the exhaust gases from car engines to harmless gases. The 'honeycomb' structure inside the catalytic converter contains small beads coated with platinum, palladium or rhodium. These act as heterogeneous catalysts. Possible steps in the catalytic process include:
• adsorption of nitrogen oxides and carbon monoxide onto the catalyst surface
• weakening of the covalent bonds within the nitrogen oxides and carbon monoxide
• formation of new bonds between
  – adjacent nitrogen atoms (to form nitrogen molecules)
  – carbon monoxide and oxygen atoms to form carbon dioxide
• desorption of nitrogen molecules and carbon dioxide molecules from the surface of the catalyst.

Check-up

16 a Describe in general terms what is meant by **desorption**.
   b Nickel acts as a catalyst for the hydrogenation of alkenes. For example:

$$CH_2{=}CH_2 + H_2 \xrightarrow{Ni} CH_3{-}CH_3$$

   Suggest how nickel catalyses this reaction by referring to the processes of adsorption, reaction on the metal surface and desorption.
   c In catalytic converters, rhodium catalyses the reduction of nitrogen(II) oxide, NO, to nitrogen. Draw diagrams to suggest:
   i   how NO is adsorbed onto the surface of the rhodium metal
   ii how nitrogen is formed.

Summary

☐ Rate of reaction is a measure of the rate at which reactants are used up or the rate at which products are formed. The units of rate are $mol\,dm^{-3}\,s^{-1}$.

☐ Rate of reaction is related to concentrations of reactants by a rate equation which can only be determined by experiment.

☐ The general form of the rate equation is:

rate $= k[A]^m[B]^n$, where:

– k is the rate constant
– [A] and [B] are the concentrations of those reactants which affect the rate of reaction
– m is the order of the reaction with respect to A and n is the order of reaction with respect to B.

☐ The overall order of reaction is the sum of the orders in the rate equation. For example above:

overall order is $m + n$

☐ The order of reaction for a given reactant can be determined experimentally by either:
– measuring the initial rate of reaction using different concentrations of a given reactant whilst keeping the concentrations of all other reactants fixed or
– determining the change in concentration of a specific reactant as the experiment proceeds, the rate being calculated from tangents taken at several points on the graph.

☐ The order of reaction can be determined from graphs of reaction rate against concentration.

☐ The half-life of a reaction is the time taken for the concentration of a reactant to halve.

☐ In a first-order reaction the half-life is independent of the concentration(s) of the reactant(s).

☐ The half-life of a first-order reaction may be used in calculations to find the first-order rate constant using the relationship

$$t_{\frac{1}{2}} = \frac{0.693}{k}.$$

☐ The rate-determining step is the slowest step in a reaction mechanism. The rate-determining step determines the overall rate of reaction.

☐ The order of reaction with respect to a particular reactant shows how many molecules of that reactant are involved in the rate-determining step of a reaction.

☐ The rate equation provides evidence to support the suggestion of a reaction mechanism.

☐ The order of a reaction can be predicted from a given reaction mechanism knowing the rate-limiting step.

☐ Homogeneous catalysis occurs when a catalyst and the reactants are in the same phase.

☐ The mechanism of homogeneous catalysis usually involves redox reactions.

☐ Examples of homogeneous catalysis include:
– the catalytic role of atmospheric oxides of nitrogen in the atmospheric oxidation of sulfur dioxide
– Fe^{2+} or Fe^{3+} ions catalysing the reaction between iodide ions and peroxodisulfate ions.

☐ Heterogeneous catalysis occurs when a catalyst is in a different phase from the reactants.

☐ The mechanism of heterogeneous catalysis involves the processes of adsorption, reaction and desorption.

☐ Examples of heterogeneous catalysis include:
– the use of iron in the Haber process
– the catalytic removal of oxides of nitrogen in the exhaust gases from car engines.

End-of-chapter questions

1   The rate of reaction between butanone and iodine is studied. In this experiment, iodine is in excess. The
    concentration of butanone is measured at various time intervals. The results are shown in the table below.

Time / min	0	10	20	30	40	50	60	80	100	120
[butanone] / mol dm^{-3}	0.080	0.055	0.035	0.024	0.015	0.010	0.007	0.003	0.001	0.001

   a Plot this data on a suitable graph.   [3]
   b Show from your graph that this data is consistent with the reaction being first order with
          respect to butanone.   [2]
   c Find the gradient of your graph when the butanone concentration is:
          • 0.070 mol dm^{-3}
          • 0.040 mol dm^{-3}
          • 0.010 mol dm^{-3} [2]
   d Use your answers to part **c** to plot a suitable graph to show rate of reaction (on the vertical axis)
          against concentration (on the horizontal axis).   [3]
   e Explain how the graph you plotted in part **d** is consistent with the reaction being first order
          with respect to butanone.   [2]

                                                                                                    Total = 12

2 The reaction

$$A + B + C \rightarrow ABC$$

is zero order with respect to one reactant, first order with respect to another reactant and second order with respect to another reactant.

a i Explain what is meant by the term **order of reaction** with respect to a given reactant. [2]

ii Use the data in the table below to deduce the order with respect to each of the reactants, A, B and C.

Experiment	[A] / mol dm^{-3}	[B] / mol dm^{-3}	[C] / mol dm^{-3}	Rate / mol dm^{-3} s^{-1}
1	0.100	1.00	1.00	0.00783
2	0.200	1.00	1.00	0.00802
3	0.300	1.00	1.00	0.00796
4	1.00	0.100	1.00	0.00008
5	1.00	0.200	1.00	0.00031
6	1.00	0.300	1.00	0.00073
7	1.00	1.00	0.100	0.00078
8	1.00	1.00	0.200	0.00158
9	1.00	1.00	0.300	0.00236

[9]

b i Write the rate equation for this reaction. [1]

ii State the overall order of the reaction. [1]

iii Calculate the value of the rate constant using experiment 6. Include the units in your answer. [3]

c Suggest a possible mechanism consistent with the rate equation you have proposed and the chemical equation

$$A + B + C \rightarrow ABC$$

[3]

Total = 19

3 The rate equation for the reaction between iodine and propanone is:

$$\text{rate} = k[CH_3COCH_3][H^+][I_2]^0$$

a State the order of reaction with respect to iodine. [1]

b State the overall order of reaction. [1]

c i What is meant by the term **half-life**? [1]

ii In an experiment a large excess of iodine is reacted with a small concentration of propanone in the presence of H$^+$(aq). The concentration of propanone is measured at regular time intervals. What happens to the value of the half-life of the propanone concentration as the concentration of propanone decreases? [1]

d Copy the sketch graph. Plot additional points at 10-second intervals up to 50 s. Join all the points with a smooth curve. [4]

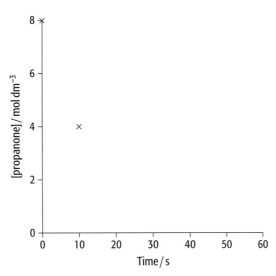

e Explain the term **rate-determining step**. [2]
f Suggest a possible mechanism for the rate-determining step for the reaction between iodine and propanone. [3]

Total = 13

4   The decomposition of hydrogen peroxide, H_2O_2, to oxygen and water is catalysed by manganese(IV) oxide.
   a Define the term **catalyst**. [2]
   b The results for the decomposition of a sample of hydrogen peroxide are shown in the table.

Time / min	0	1	2	3	4	5	6	7	8
$[H_2O_2]$ / mol dm^{-3}	1.60	1.04	0.61	0.40	0.25	0.16	0.10	0.06	0.04

   i Draw a graph of concentration of hydrogen peroxide (vertical axis) against time (horizontal axis). Draw a curve of best fit. [3]
   ii Use your graph to determine the half-life of the reaction. Show your working. [2]
   iii Use your graph to find the rate of reaction after 2 min. [4]
   c i Give the rate equation for the reaction. Explain your answer. [3]
   ii Use your answer to part **b, iii**, to calculate the value of the rate constant, k, and give the units. [3]
   iii Using your rate equation, find the rate of reaction when $[H_2O_2]$ = 2 mol dm^{-3}. [2]

Total = 19

5   Peroxodisulfate ions, $S_2O_8^{2-}$, react with iodide ions in aqueous solution to form iodine and sulfate ions.

$$S_2O_8^{2-}(aq) + 2I^-(aq) \rightarrow 2SO_4^{2-}(aq) + I_2(aq) \qquad \textbf{equation 1}$$

The initial rates of reaction are compared by timing how long it takes to produce a particular amount of iodine using four different initial concentrations of $S_2O_8^{2-}$. The results are shown in the table.

$[S_2O_8^{2-}]$ / mol dm^{-3}	Initial rate of reaction / s^{-1}
0.0200	4.16×10^{-3}
0.0150	3.12×10^{-3}
0.0120	2.50×10^{-3}
0.0080	1.70×10^{-3}

a Plot a suitable graph to calculate rate of reaction.   [3]
b Deduce the order of reaction with respect to peroxodisulfate ions. Explain your answer.   [2]
c The reaction is first order with respect to iodide ions. Use this information and your answer to
   part **b** to write the overall rate equation for the reaction.   [1]
d The reaction between peroxodisulfate ions and iodide ions is slow. The reaction can be speeded up
   by adding a few drops of $Fe^{3+}(aq)$ ions. The following reactions then take place:

$$2I^-(aq) + 2Fe^{3+}(aq) \rightarrow I_2(aq) + 2Fe^{2+}(aq) \qquad \textbf{equation 2}$$

$$2Fe^{2+}(aq) + S_2O_8^{2-}(aq) \rightarrow 2Fe^{3+}(aq) + 2SO_4^{2-}(aq) \qquad \textbf{equation 3}$$

i   What type of catalysis is occurring here? Explain your answer.   [2]
ii By referring to equations **1**, **2** and **3** above, suggest why $Fe^{3+}(aq)$ ions catalyse the reaction
    between peroxodisulfate ions and iodide ions.   [4]

Total = 12

6   The rate of reaction between butanone and iodine is studied. In this experiment, butanone is
    in excess. The concentration of iodine is measured every 10 minutes for 1 hour. The results are
    shown in the table.

Time / min	0	10	20	30	40	50	60
$[I_2]$ / mol dm^{-3}	0.060	0.051	0.041	0.032	0.022	0.012	0.003

a Plot this data on a suitable graph.   [3]
b Show from the graph that this data is consistent with the reaction being zero order with respect
   to iodine.   [1]

c The balanced chemical equation for the reaction is

$$CH_3CH_2COCH_3 + I_2 \rightarrow CH_3CH_2COCH_2I + HI$$

Could this reaction occur in a single step? Explain your answer. [2]

d The rate equation for the reaction is

$$\text{rate} = k[CH_3CH_2COCH_3]$$

Explain the different meanings of the balanced chemical equation and the rate equation. [4]

Total = 10

7 Nitrogen oxides can be removed from the exhaust gases of a car engine by using a catalytic converter. Many catalytic converters contain metals such as platinum and rhodium. These act as heterogeneous catalysts.

a i What is meant by the term **heterogeneous catalysis**? [2]

ii Explain in general terms how heterogeneous catalysts work. [4]

b Nitrogen(IV) oxide and carbon monoxide from car exhausts can react in a catalytic converter.

$$NO_2(g) + CO(g) \rightarrow NO(g) + CO_2(g)$$

The rate equation for this reaction is

$$\text{rate} = k[NO_2]^2$$

Suggest a two-step reaction mechanism for this reaction that is consistent with this rate equation. [2]

c Nitrogen(IV) oxide is formed when nitrogen(II) oxide reacts with oxygen.

$$2NO(g) + O_2(g) \rightarrow 2NO_2(g)$$

The table shows the data obtained from a series of experiments to investigate the kinetics of this reaction.

Experiment	[NO] / mol dm^{-3}	[O$_2$] / mol dm^{-3}	Initial rate / mol dm^{-3} s^{-1}
1	0.001 00	0.003 00	21.3
2	0.001 00	0.004 00	28.4
3	0.003 00	0.004 00	256

i Deduce the order of reaction with respect to each reactant. In each case, show your reasoning. [4]

ii Deduce the rate equation for this reaction. [1]

iii State the units of the rate constant, k, for this reaction. [1]

Total = 14

8 Bromate(V) ions react with bromide ions in acidic solution to form bromine.

$$BrO_3^-(aq) + 5Br^-(aq) + 6H^+(aq) \rightarrow 3Br_2(aq) + 3H_2O(l)$$

a Suggest **two** methods of following the progress of this reaction. For each method explain your answer. [4]

b The initial rates of reaction were compared using the initial concentrations of reactants shown in the table.

Experiment	$[BrO_3^-]$ / $mol\,dm^{-3}$	$[Br^-]$ / $mol\,dm^{-3}$	$[H^+]$ / $mol\,dm^{-3}$	Relative rate of formation of bromine
1	0.040	0.20	0.24	1
2	0.040	0.20	0.48	4
3	0.080	0.20	0.48	8
4	0.040	0.10	0.48	2

i Deduce the order of reaction with respect to each reactant. In each case, show your reasoning. [6]

ii Deduce the rate equation for this reaction. [1]

iii State the units of the rate constant, k, for this reaction. [1]

Total = 12

22 Group IV

22.1 Introduction

In Chapter 11 (page 176) you studied the elements of Groups II and VII. There are trends in the properties of the elements down each of these groups. But there are also similarities. For example, all Group II elements are metals and all Group VII elements are non-metals with diatomic molecules. The Group IV elements, however, show a far greater variation in properties with increase in proton number. The metallic character of the elements increases down the group (Table 22.1).

Metalloids or semi-metals differ from metals in two ways.

• **Metalloids** have very small electrical conductivities at room temperature; metals conduct electricity very well by comparison.

• The electrical conductivity of metalloids increases with increase in temperature; the conductivity of metals decreases with increase in temperature.

Although tin and lead are both metals, their reactivity is low compared with the metals from Groups I and II.

Element	Symbol	Metal or non- metal?
carbon	C	non-metal
silicon	Si	metalloid
germanium	Ge	metalloid
tin	Sn	metal
lead	Pb	metal

Table 22.1 Metallic character of Group IV elements.

22.2 Variation in properties

Table 22.2 shows the trends in melting point and relative electrical conductivity of the Group IV elements.

The melting point decreases markedly down the group (although the data for tin spoils the trend). The electrical conductivity increases down the group.

To explain the trend in melting points and electrical conductivity down the group, we have to consider the structure and bonding of the elements.

Figure 22.1 Some of the Group IV elements are very different in both their physical and chemical properties. (**a**) Carbon in the form of diamond is a very hard non-metal with a very high melting point. (**b**) Lead is a soft metal with a comparatively low melting point.

Element	Melting point / °C	Relative electrical conductivity
carbon (diamond)	3550	non-conductor (insulator)
silicon	1410	semi-conductor
germanium	937	semi-conductor
tin	232	conductor
lead	327	conductor

Table 22.2 Melting point and electrical conductivity of Group IV elements.

Bond	Bond energy / kJ mol^{-1}
C–C	350
Si–Si	222
Ge–Ge	188

Table 22.3 Bond energies for Group IV elements.

Melting points

Carbon (diamond), silicon and germanium have giant molecular structures with strong covalent bonds throughout. They all have a similar structure to diamond (see Chapter 5, page 85). The difference in melting points can be related to their bond energies (Table 22.3).

The decrease in melting point from carbon to germanium reflects the decreasing amount of energy required to break the bonds between the atoms as we descend the group from carbon to germanium.

At room temperature both tin and lead have a metallic structure. The ions in the metallic structure are held together by the electrostatic attraction between their positive charges and the negative charges of the delocalised electrons. The strength of metallic bonding decreases as the size of the ions increases.

Both tin and lead have relatively large ions. So the metallic bonding is relatively weak and the melting points are relatively low.

Fact file

Tin exists in several forms. The common metallic form of tin under standard conditions is called white tin. On cooling below 13.2 °C this changes to grey tin. This change is catalysed by aluminium and zinc. In countries where winters are very cold, articles made from white tin may suffer 'tin plague' and begin to change to the powdery grey form. After a time the surface of these articles may become damaged or even get holes in them.

Electrical conductivity

Carbon in the form of diamond does not conduct electricity because the four outer electrons on each carbon atom are used in forming the very strong covalent bonds. There are no delocalised electrons free to move around within its structure. Graphite does conduct electricity (see page **84**).

Silicon and germanium conduct to a very small but measurable extent. The weaker bonding in silicon and germanium allows some electrons to move out of position especially if there are traces of other 'contaminating' atoms in the lattice. The electrons are not delocalised though.

Tin and lead are electrical conductors because the delocalised electrons are free to move throughout the lattice.

Check-up

1. a Below 13 °C, tin has a molecular structure similar to diamond. Suggest a value for the Sn–Sn covalent bond energy for this structure. Use the bond energies in Table **22.3** to help you.

   b Use ideas about charge density of the ions in a metal structure to suggest why the melting points of tin and lead are much lower than that of iron, assuming that the charge on each ion is the same.

   c Use your knowledge of the structure and bonding in diamond to explain why it does not conduct electricity.

22.3 The tetrachlorides

Structure and bonding

All of the elements in Group IV form a compound with chlorine, in which each molecule consists of one atom of the Group IV element and four chlorine atoms. These compounds are called tetrachlorides. The tetrachlorides all have:

- the general formula XCl_4, where X is the symbol for a Group IV element
- simple covalent molecules
- a tetrahedral structure.

The Group IV tetrachlorides are all volatile liquids at room temperature. So they all have low boiling points (Table 22.4).

Tetrahalide	Boiling point / °C
CCl_4	76
$SiCl_4$	57
$GeCl_4$	87
$SnCl_4$	114
$PbCl_4$	105

Table 22.4 The boiling points of the Group IV tetrachlorides.

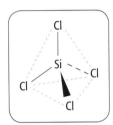

Figure 22.2 The tetrahedral structure of silicon(IV) chloride (silicon tetrachloride).

Thermal stability

The thermal stability of the tetrachlorides decreases towards the bottom of the group. As the X—Cl bonds become longer and weaker down Group IV, the tetrachlorides become less stable.

- CCl_4, $SiCl_4$ and $GeCl_4$ are stable at high temperatures. They do not decompose on heating.
- Tin(IV) chloride decomposes readily on heating to form tin(II) chloride and chlorine.

$$SnCl_4(l) \xrightarrow{heat} SnCl_2(s) + Cl_2(g)$$

- Lead(IV) chloride decomposes explosively in a similar way.

Reaction with water

All the tetrachlorides except CCl_4 are hydrolysed by water. For example:

$$SiCl_4(l) + 2H_2O(l) \rightarrow SiO_2(s) + 4HCl(g)$$

Similar equations can be written for the hydrolysis of the tetrachlorides of germanium and tin.

The ease of hydrolysis increases from silicon(IV) chloride to lead(IV) chloride as the metallic nature of the elements increases. Lead(IV) chloride is also hydrolysed to lead(IV) oxide but the heat released in the reaction is sufficient to decompose the tetrachloride as well. So lead(II) chloride is formed as a product as well as lead(IV) oxide.

Check-up

2 a Explain why the Group IV tetrachlorides have low boiling points.
   b Write a balanced equation for:
   i the reaction of germanium(IV) chloride with water
   ii the thermal decomposition of lead(IV) chloride.
   c Draw the displayed formula of tin(IV) chloride, showing the 3-dimensional shape of the molecule.

22.4 The oxides

The Group IV elements form oxides with oxidation states of +2 and +4 (Table 22.5).

Oxidation state +2	Oxidation state +4
carbon monoxide (CO)	carbon dioxide (CO_2)
silicon(II) oxide (SiO)	silicon(IV) oxide (SiO_2)
germanium(II) oxide (GeO)	germanium(IV) oxide (GeO_2)
tin(II) oxide (SnO)	tin(IV) oxide (SnO_2)
lead(II) oxide (PbO)	lead(IV) oxide (PbO_2)

Table 22.5 Oxides of Group IV elements.

Fact file

Many older chemistry books suggest that silicon(II) oxide (silicon monoxide) is unstable or does not exist. It is, however, a brownish-black solid which is stable at room temperature. It decomposes at about 400 °C to silicon dioxide and silicon. It has an increasing number of practical uses including applications in the field of electronics and protecting surfaces against corrosion and wear.

Bonding and thermal stability of the oxides

Most of the Group IV oxides do not decompose on heating; they are stable to heat. This reflects the strong bonding in their structures. It takes a lot of energy to break these bonds.

Oxidation state +2

- Carbon monoxide has a simple molecular structure. The strong triple covalent bond in carbon monoxide makes the molecules thermally stable.

- SiO and GeO have giant molecular structures. The covalent bonding in these two oxides is relatively weak and they decompose on heating in a disproportionation reaction (see page 186). For example:

$$2GeO(s) \rightarrow GeO_2(s) + Ge(s)$$

- SnO and PbO have a considerable degree of ionic character. They do not decompose on heating.

Oxidation state +4
- Carbon dioxide has a simple molecular structure. The strong bonds make it thermally stable.
- SiO_2 and GeO_2 have giant molecular (giant covalent) structures.
- SnO_2 and PbO_2 are giant covalent structures although they have a little ionic character as well.
- Lead(IV) oxide is the only one of the Group IV oxides in oxidation state +4 that decomposes readily on heating:

$$2PbO_2(s) \xrightarrow{heat} 2PbO(s) + O_2(g)$$

This reflects the decreasing stability of the +4 oxidation state towards the bottom of the group (see page 355).

Fact file
When lead(II) oxide, PbO, is heated, it does not form PbO_2. It forms a bright red solid called triplumbic tetroxide, Pb_3O_4, also known as red lead oxide. This compound behaves chemically as a mixture of lead(II) oxide and lead(IV) oxide, $PbO_2.2PbO$.

Check-up

3 a Use ideas about ionisation energies to suggest why oxides of the Group IV elements in the +4 oxidation states do not exist as simple 4+ ions.
b How does the degree of covalent character of the oxides of the Group IV elements in the +2 oxidation state change down the group?
c Write a balanced equation to describe the thermal decomposition of silicon(II) oxide.
d Name the type of redox reaction occurring in part **c** and justify your answer.

Acid–base properties of the oxides
Table 22.6 shows the acid–base character of the Group IV oxides. From the table you will notice that:
- many of the oxides are **amphoteric** – an amphoteric oxide is one which can act as an acid or a base
- the Group IV oxides in both the +2 and +4 oxidation states become more basic down the group
- the oxides with oxidation state +2 are often less acidic (more basic) than those of the corresponding oxide with oxidation state +4.

Oxidation state +2	Acid–base character	Oxidation state +4	Acid–base character
CO	very weakly acidic	CO_2	acidic
SiO	—	SiO_2	very weakly acidic
GeO	amphoteric	GeO_2	amphoteric (more acidic than basic character)
SnO	amphoteric	SnO_2	amphoteric
PbO	amphoteric (more basic than acidic character)	PbO_2	amphoteric

Table 22.6 Acid–base character of the Group IV oxides.

The +2 oxidation state
CO is very slightly soluble in water. It forms a neutral solution. It does, however, react with hot concentrated sodium hydroxide solution. So it is an acidic oxide.

GeO, SnO and PbO all react with concentrated hydrochloric acid in a similar way. For example:

$$SnO(s) + 2HCl(aq) \rightarrow SnCl_2(aq) + H_2O(l)$$

$$PbO(s) + 2HCl(aq) \rightarrow PbCl_2(s) + H_2O(l)$$

GeO, SnO and PbO all react with aqueous alkalis such as sodium hydroxide. For example:

$$PbO(s) + 2OH^-(aq) \rightarrow PbO_2^{2-}(aq) + H_2O(l)$$
plumbate(II) ion

GeO and SnO react in a similar manner to form germinate(II) and stannate(II) ions.

The +4 oxidation state

CO_2 is slightly soluble in water, forming a weakly acidic solution:

$$CO_2(aq) + H_2O(l) \rightleftharpoons HCO_3^-(aq) + H^+(aq)$$
$$\rightleftharpoons CO_3^{2-}(aq) + 2H^+(aq)$$

The positions of both of these equilibria lie well over to the left. Most of the dissolved carbon dioxide is in the form $CO_2(aq)$, so carbon dioxide solution is only weakly acidic.

CO_2 also reacts with alkalis:

$$CO_2(g) + 2OH^-(aq) \rightarrow CO_3^{2-}(aq) + H_2O(l)$$

SiO_2 does not react with acids (except hydrofluoric acid). It reacts with hot concentrated alkalis to form silicate(IV) ions and water, so it is an acidic oxide.

$$SiO_2 + 2OH^- \rightarrow SiO_3^{2-} + H_2O$$

GeO_2, SnO_2 and PbO_2 are all amphoteric. They react with concentrated hydrochloric acid to form the tetrachlorides. For example:

$$SnO_2(s) + 4HCl(aq) \rightarrow SnCl_4(l) + 2H_2O(l)$$

GeO_2, SnO_2 and PbO_2 all react with hot concentrated alkalis. For example:

$$SnO_2(s) + 2OH^-(aq) \rightarrow \underset{\text{stannate(IV) ion}}{SnO_3^{2-}(aq)} + H_2O(l)$$

GeO_2 and PbO_2 react in a similar manner to form germinate(IV) and plumbate(IV) ions.

The ease of reaction with alkali follows the order $GeO_2 > SnO_2 > PbO_2$. Molten sodium hydroxide is needed to form a plumbate, PbO_3^{2-}, from PbO_2.

Check-up

4 a Write equations for:
     i   the reaction of carbon dioxide with sodium hydroxide
     ii   the reaction of lead(IV) oxide with cold concentrated hydrochloric acid
     iii Why must lead(IV) oxide be reacted with **cold** concentrated hydrochloric acid for this reaction to take place?
   b   Both tin(II) oxide and tin(IV) oxide are amphoteric. What does the term **amphoteric oxide** mean?

continued ⋯⟩

---

   c   i   How do the acid–base characteristics of the Group IV oxides with oxidation state +2 change down the group?
       ii   Is silicon(II) oxide likely to be acidic, amphoteric or basic? Give a reason for your answer.

22.5 Relative stability of the +2 and +4 oxidation states

Introduction

The stability of the +4 oxidation state relative to the +2 oxidation state decreases down the group. We can see this by comparing the relative reactivities of the oxides.

For example, the +4 oxidation state of carbon compounds is more stable than the +2 state, so carbon monoxide is readily oxidised to the more stable carbon dioxide. This means that carbon monoxide is a good reducing agent; for example, it reduces iron(III) oxide to iron:

$$\underset{+3}{Fe_2O_3}(s) + 3\underset{+2}{CO}(g) \xrightarrow{heat} 2\underset{0}{Fe}(l) + 3\underset{+4}{CO_2}(g)$$

At the other end of Group IV, the +2 oxidation state in lead compounds is more stable than the +4 state. So lead(IV) oxide is readily reduced to the more stable lead(II) state. This means that lead(IV) oxide is a good oxidising agent; for example, it oxidises hydrochloric acid to chlorine:

$$\underset{+4}{PbO_2}(s) + 4\underset{-1}{HCl}(aq) \rightarrow \underset{+2}{PbCl_2}(aq) + \underset{0}{Cl_2}(g) + 2H_2O(l)$$

Between these extremes, there is a gradual change in stability of the +2 compared with the +4 state.
- The +4 state of germanium compounds is definitely more stable than the +2 state. Germanium(II) compounds are good reducing agents.
- The +4 state of tin is slightly more stable than the +2 state. So tin(II) compounds generally act as weak reducing agents.

Figure 22.3 Lead(II) oxide (left) and lead(IV) oxide(right).

Fact file

The reason why the +4 oxidation state is less stable at the bottom of the group can only be explained using complex Born–Haber cycles. These are the main ideas.

- Compounds low in the group having the +2 oxidation state have greater ionic character than those in the +4 oxidation state.
- Compounds with oxidation state +4 low in the group have more covalent character but the covalent bonding is weaker. The energy released on forming these bonds is low.
- It takes less energy to oxidise an element to a low oxidation state than to a high oxidation state. For example, the sum of the ionisation energies is much smaller to produce a 2+ ion than a 4+ ion.
- For elements at the bottom of the group, the energy released on forming covalent bonds or 'ions' in the +4 oxidation state is not enough to compensate for the extra energy required to form the +4 oxidation state.
- At the bottom of the group, the +4 oxidation state becomes less energetically stable with respect to the +2 oxidation state.

Redox reactions in Group IV

As we go down Group IV the +4 oxidation state becomes more highly oxidising and the +2 oxidation state becomes more stable and less reducing.

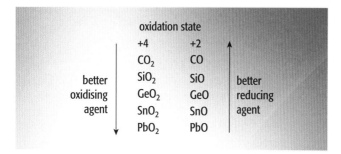

We can extend these ideas to apply to ions of the Group IV elements in aqueous solution. You saw on page **280** that standard electrode potential values, $E^\ominus$, can help to predict whether a redox reaction will occur or not:

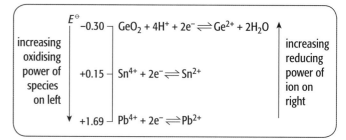

Figure 22.4 Comparing the oxidising power of some Group IV ions.

- the more positive the value of $E^\ominus$, the greater is the tendency for the half-equation to proceed in the forward direction
- the less positive the value of $E^\ominus$, the greater is the tendency for the half-equation to proceed in the reverse direction
- the more positive the value of $E^\ominus$, the easier it is to reduce the species on the left of the half-equation
- the less positive the value of $E^\ominus$, the easier it is to oxidise the species on the right of the half-equation.

Figure **22.4** shows an electrode potential diagram to show the oxidising power of some Group IV ions in aqueous solution.

From Figure **22.4**, we can see that as the values of $E^\ominus$ get more positive from Ge(IV) to Pb^{4+}, the oxidised form (Ge^{4+} or Pb^{4+}) is more readily reduced to the +2 state. The further down Group IV, the better the oxidising power of the 4+ ion. We can also see that as the value of $E^\ominus$ gets more positive from Ge(IV) to Pb^{4+} the reduced form (Ge^{2+} or Pb^{2+}) is harder to oxidise to the +4 state. The further up Group IV, the better the reducing power of the 2+ ion.

Worked examples

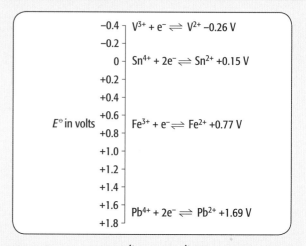

Figure 22.5 Comparing Pb^{4+}(aq) and Sn^{4+}(aq) as oxidising agents.

continued ⋯▸

1 Compare the ability of Pb^{4+} and Sn^{4+} ions to oxidise V^{2+} ions to V^{3+} ions.

We can deduce from Figure 22.5 that both Pb^{4+} and Sn^{4+} ions are able to oxidise V^{2+} ions to V^{3+}. This is because the half-equations relating to both Pb^{4+} and Sn^{4+} have more positive $E^{\ominus}$ values than the half-equation relating to V^{3+}:

$$V^{3+}(aq) + e^- \rightleftharpoons V^{2+}(aq) \qquad E^{\ominus} = -0.26\,V$$

$$Sn^{4+}(aq) + 2e^- \rightleftharpoons Sn^{2+}(aq) \qquad E^{\ominus} = +0.15\,V$$

$$Pb^{4+}(aq) + 2e^- \rightleftharpoons Pb^{2+}(aq) \qquad E^{\ominus} = +1.69\,V$$

The half-equation with the most positive value will go in the forward direction and the half-equation with the less positive value will go in the reverse direction (see page 281). So the overall reactions are:

$$2V^{2+}(aq) + Sn^{4+}(aq) \rightarrow 2V^{3+}(aq) + Sn^{2+}(aq)$$

$$2V^{2+}(aq) + Pb^{4+}(aq) \rightarrow 2V^{3+}(aq) + Pb^{2+}(aq)$$

Pb^{4+} is a stronger oxidising agent than Sn^{4+} because its half-equation has a more positive value of $E^{\ominus}$ compared with the half-equation involving V^{3+}.

2 Compare the ability of Pb^{4+} and Sn^{4+} ions to oxidise Fe^{2+} ions to Fe^{3+} ions.

Pb^{4+} can oxidise Fe^{2+} ions to Fe^{3+} ions because its half-equation has a more positive $E^{\ominus}$ value:

$$Fe^{3+}(aq) + e^- \rightleftharpoons Fe^{2+}(aq) \qquad E^{\ominus} = +0.77\,V$$

$$Pb^{4+}(aq) + 2e^- \rightleftharpoons Pb^{2+}(aq) \qquad E^{\ominus} = +1.69\,V$$

So the reaction is:

$$2Fe^{2+}(aq) + Pb^{4+}(aq) \rightarrow 2Fe^{3+}(aq) + Pb^{2+}(aq)$$

Sn^{4+} is not able to oxidise Fe^{2+} ions to Fe^{3+} ions because its half-equation has a less positive $E^{\ominus}$ value:

$$Fe^{3+}(aq) + e^- \rightleftharpoons Fe^{2+}(aq) \qquad E^{\ominus} = +0.77\,V$$

$$Sn^{4+}(aq) + 2e^- \rightleftharpoons Sn^{2+}(aq) \qquad E^{\ominus} = +0.15\,V$$

Sn^{2+} ions can, however, act as a reducing agent: the half-equation with the most positive value will go in the forward direction and the half-equation with the less positive value will go in the reverse direction:

$$2Fe^{3+}(aq) + Sn^{2+}(aq) \rightarrow 2Fe^{2+}(aq) + Sn^{4+}(aq)$$

Fact file

Tables of values of $E^{\ominus}$ often have tin and lead ions written in the form:

$$Sn^{4+} + 2e^- \rightleftharpoons Sn^{2+} \text{ or}$$

$$Pb^{4+} + 2e^- \rightleftharpoons Pb^{2+}$$

However, many compounds of the Group IV elements are insoluble in water, so the compounds are often dissolved in acids or alkalis. For example, the half-equation:

$$Pb^{4+} + 2e^- \rightleftharpoons Pb^{2+} \qquad\qquad E^{\ominus} = +1.69\,V$$

relates to the ions dissolved in $1.1\,mol\,dm^{-3}$ chloric(VII) acid, $HClO_4$.

Check-up

5 a Use the list of $E^{\ominus}$ values below to determine which of the following species can oxidise hydrogen sulfide to sulfur. Write balanced equations for any reactions.

   i Sn^{2+}
   ii Sn^{4+}
   iii PbO_2

$$Sn^{2+}(aq) + 2e^- \rightleftharpoons Sn(s) \qquad E^{\ominus} = -0.14\,V$$

$$PbO_2 + 4H^+ + 2e^- \rightleftharpoons Pb^{2+}(aq) + 2H_2O(l) \qquad E^{\ominus} = +1.47\,V$$

$$S(s) + 2H^+(aq) + 2e^- \rightleftharpoons H_2S(aq) \qquad E^{\ominus} = +0.14\,V$$

$$Sn^{4+}(aq) + 2e^- \rightleftharpoons Sn^{2+}(aq) \qquad E^{\ominus} = +0.15\,V$$

   b Use the list of $E^{\ominus}$ values below to determine:
   i which species is the strongest oxidising agent
   ii which species is the strongest reducing agent.

$$Pb^{4+}(aq) + 2e^- \rightleftharpoons Pb^{2+}(aq) \qquad E^{\ominus} = +1.69\,V$$

$$PbO_2(s) + 2H_2O(l) + 2e^- \rightleftharpoons Pb(OH)_2(aq) + 2OH^-(aq) \qquad E^{\ominus} = +0.28\,V$$

$$Sn^{2+}(aq) + 2e^- \rightleftharpoons Sn(s) \qquad E^{\ominus} = -0.14\,V$$

$$Sn^{4+}(aq) + 2e^- \rightleftharpoons Sn^{2+}(aq) \qquad E^{\ominus} = +0.15\,V$$

22.6 Ceramics from silicon(IV) oxide

In Chapter 5 (page 86) we defined a ceramic as 'an inorganic non-metallic solid prepared by heating a substance or mixture of substances to a high temperature'. Silicon(IV) oxide (commonly called silicon dioxide) is used to make a variety of ceramics. It is either used on its own or mixed with clay (which is largely a mixture of aluminium and silicon oxides).

Ceramics containing silicon(IV) oxide are used:
• for furnace linings
• as abrasives (for example in sandpaper)
• in the manufacture of glass and porcelain.

The properties of silicon(IV) oxide which make it an ideal ceramic include:
• its very high melting and boiling point: it needs a high temperature to break the strong covalent bonds in the giant molecular structure
• it is an electrical and thermal insulator: none of the electrons in its structure are free to move
• it is hard: it is difficult to break the 3-dimensional network of strong covalent bonds
• it is generally chemically unreactive (apart from reaction with concentrated alkali and hydrofluoric acid)
• it can be moulded at a very high temperature into a variety of shapes without affecting its strength.

Figure 22.6 The surface of this heat-resistant ceramic dish is coated with a layer containing silicon dioxide. The dish can withstand the high temperatures of a hot oven.

Check-up

6 a Dishes for baking food in the oven are made from ceramics containing silicon(IV) oxide. Explain in terms of the bonding and chemical properties why silicon(IV) oxide is used to make these dishes.

   b Ceramics containing silicon dioxide are used as electrical insulators in high-voltage electricity pylons. Explain why ceramics based on silicon dioxide are good electrical insulators.

Summary

☐ There is a general trend of decreasing melting point and increasing electrical conductivity down Group IV. This can be explained by differences in the structure and bonding of the elements.

☐ Carbon, silicon and germanium have giant covalent structures. Tin and lead have metallic structures. On descending the group, the bonding between the atoms gets weaker.

☐ Group IV elements form tetrachlorides which are covalent molecules with a tetrahedral structure. Their thermal stability decreases down the group.

☐ The reactivity of the Group IV tetrachlorides with water increases down the group as the metallic nature of the element increases.

☐ Group IV elements form oxides with oxidation states +2 and +4.

☐ The acidic character of the oxides with oxidation state +2 and +4 decreases down the group and the basic character increases.

☐ Group IV oxides with oxidation state +2 are more basic than the corresponding oxides with oxidation state +4.

☐ The thermal stability of the oxides with oxidation state +2 can be explained in terms of their bonding.

☐ The relative stability of the oxides with oxidation state +4 decreases down the group.

☐ The relative stability of higher and lower oxidation states of the Group IV oxides and aqueous cations of Group IV elements, can be explained with reference to $E^{\ominus}$ values.

☐ Ceramics based on silicon(IV) oxide are used for furnace linings and abrasives.

End-of-chapter questions

Examiner's tip
Questions **1a** and **1b** require you to 'explain', but before you do so, state clearly
what the structure and bonding is in each element or compound you are referring to.

1   The melting points of the Group IV elements are given in the table.

Element	Melting point / °C
carbon (diamond)	3550
silicon	1410
germanium	937
tin	232
lead	327

a   Describe and explain how the trend in melting point is related to the structure and bonding in
    these elements.   [7]
b   Carbon dioxide is a gas but tin(IV) oxide is a solid. Explain this difference in terms of structure
    and bonding.   [4]
c i   Write a balanced equation for the reaction of silicon(IV) oxide with sodium hydroxide.   [2]
   ii   Explain in terms of structure and bonding why silicon(IV) oxide is used as a lining in furnaces. [3]
d   Tin(IV) oxide reacts with both acids and bases.
    i   State the general name given to the type of oxide which can react both as an acid and a base. [1]
    ii   Write a balanced equation for the reaction of tin(IV) oxide with hydrochloric acid.   [2]
    iii Write a balanced equation for the reaction of tin(IV) oxide with sodium hydroxide to form
         sodium stannate(IV). Stannate(IV) compounds contain the SnO_3^{2-} ion.   [2]
                                                                                      Total = 21

Examiner's tip
Your A Level chemistry exam will contain some AS material. Questions **2a** and **2b** focus on areas of
AS chemistry that commonly come up on the A Level papers – molecular shapes and structure and
bonding/intermolecular forces. Make sure you know these subject areas well.

2   Germanium is an element in Group IV of the Periodic Table. It forms a number of compounds
     including $GeCl_4$, GeO and GeO_2.
     a i   Draw a diagram to show the 3-dimensional structure of germanium(IV) chloride.   [1]
        ii   State the value of the Cl—Ge—Cl bonds angle in germanium(IV) chloride.   [1]
     b   Explain why germanium(IV) chloride has a low boiling point.   [3]

c Germanium(IV) chloride is hydrolysed by water. Write a balanced equation for this reaction. [2]

d Germanium(II) oxide oxidises rapidly in air to form germanium(IV) oxide. This reaction is not reversible. What does this tell you about the relative stability of these oxides? [1]

e Germanium(II) oxide undergoes disproportionation on heating to form germanium(IV) oxide and germanium.

   i What is the meaning of the term **disproportionation**? [2]

   ii Write a balanced equation for this reaction. [1]

Total = 11

3 This question is about compounds of tin and lead.

  a Oxides of tin and lead exist in two different oxidation states, +2 and +4. Give the formula of:

   i the most stable oxide of tin [1]

   ii the most stable oxide of lead. [1]

  b Tin and lead form tetrahalides.

   i Describe and explain the difference in the thermal stability of tin(IV) chloride and lead(IV) chloride. [2]

   ii Write a balanced equation for the thermal decomposition of tin(IV) chloride. [1]

  c A list of standard electrode potentials is given below. Use this list to answer the questions which follow.

$$V^{3+}(aq) + e^- \rightleftharpoons V^{2+}(aq) \qquad E^\ominus = -0.26\,V$$

$$I_2(aq) + 2e^- \rightleftharpoons 2I^-(aq) \qquad E^\ominus = +0.54\,V$$

$$GeO_2(aq) + 4H^+(aq) + 2e^- \rightleftharpoons Ge^{2+}(aq) + 2H_2O(l) \qquad E^\ominus = -0.30\,V$$

$$Pb^{4+}(aq) + 2e^- \rightleftharpoons Pb^{2+}(aq) \qquad E^\ominus = +1.69\,V$$

$$PbO_2(s) + 4H^+(aq) + 2e^- \rightleftharpoons Pb^{2+}(aq) + 2H_2O(l) \qquad E^\ominus = +1.47\,V$$

$$Sn^{4+}(aq) + 2e^- \rightleftharpoons Sn^{2+}(aq) \qquad E^\ominus = +0.15\,V$$

   i Which species in the list is the strongest reducing agent? Explain your answer. [3]

   ii Which species in the list is the strongest oxidising agent? [1]

   iii Which species in the list will oxidise iodide ions to iodine? [1]

   iv Write a balanced equation for the oxidation of V^{2+} ions to V^{3+} ions by lead(IV) oxide in acidic solution. [2]

Total = 12

4 The Group IV elements and their compounds show marked differences descending the group.
   a Describe and explain how the electrical conductivity changes down the group (from carbon in the form of diamond to lead).   [6]
   b i Describe how the relative stabilities of the Group IV oxides in oxidation states +2 and +4 change down the group.   [2]
     ii Write a balanced equation for the thermal decomposition of lead(IV) oxide.   [2]
   c Describe the acid–base characteristics of the Group IV oxides of oxidation state +4.   [3]
   d Write a balanced equation for the reaction of lead(II) oxide with sodium hydroxide to form sodium plumbate(II). Plumbate(II) compounds contain the PbO_2^{2-} ion.   [2]

   Total = 15

Learning outcomes

Candidates should be able to:

☐ explain what is meant by a **transition element**, in terms of d-block elements forming one or more stable ions with incomplete d orbitals

☐ state the electronic configuration of a first-row transition element and of its ions

☐ state that the atomic radii, ionic radii and first ionisation energies of the transition elements are relatively invariant

☐ contrast, qualitatively, the melting point, density, atomic radius, ionic radius, first ionisation energy and conductivity of the transition elements with those of calcium as a typical s-block element

☐ describe the tendency of transition elements to have variable oxidation states

☐ predict from a given electronic configuration, the likely oxidation states of a transition element

☐ describe and explain the use of Fe^{3+}/Fe^{2+}, MnO_4^-/Mn^{2+} and $Cr_2O_7^{2-}/Cr^{3+}$ as examples of redox systems (see also Chapter **19**)

☐ predict, using $E^{\ominus}$ values, the likelihood of redox reactions

☐ explain the reactions of transition elements with ligands to form complexes, including the complexes of copper(II) ions with water, hydroxide and ammonia

☐ explain qualitatively that ligand exchange may occur, including the complexes of copper(II) ions with water, hydroxide and ammonia

☐ describe the shape and symmetry of the d orbitals, and the splitting of degenerate d orbitals into two energy levels in octahedral complexes using the complexes of copper(II) ions with water and ammonia as examples

☐ explain the origin of colour in transition element complexes resulting from the absorption of light energy as an electron moves between two non-degenerate d orbitals

☐ describe, in qualitative terms, the effects of different ligands on the absorption, and hence colour, using the complexes of copper(II) ions with water, hydroxide and ammonia as examples.

23.1 What is a transition element?

The transition elements are found in the d block of the Periodic Table, between Groups II and III. However, not all d-block elements are classified as transition elements.

> A transition element is a d-block element which forms one or more stable ions with an incomplete d sub-shell.

We do not define Sc and Zn as transition elements.

- Scandium forms only one ion (Sc^{3+}) and this has no electrons in its 3d sub-shell – the electronic configuration of Sc^{3+} is (Ar) $3d^0 4s^0$.
- Zinc forms only one ion (Zn^{2+}) and this has a complete 3d sub-shell – the electronic configuration of Zn^{2+} is (Ar) $3d^{10} 4s^0$.

In this chapter we will be looking at the transition elements in the first row of the d block. These are the metals titanium (Ti) through to copper (Cu), according to the definition above.

Electronic configurations

Atoms

Table **23.1** shows the electronic configurations of the atoms in the first row of the transition elements.

In atoms of the transition elements, the 4s sub-shell is normally filled and the rest of the electrons occupy orbitals in the 3d sub-shell. However, chromium and copper atoms are the exceptions. Chromium atoms have just one electron in the 4s sub-shell. The remaining five electrons are arranged in the 3d sub-shell so that each orbital is occupied by one electron. Copper atoms also

Element	Electronic configuration
titanium (Ti)	$1s^2 2s^2 2p^6 3s^2 3p^6 \mathbf{3d^2} \mathbf{4s^2}$
vanadium (V)	$1s^2 2s^2 2p^6 3s^2 3p^6 \mathbf{3d^3} \mathbf{4s^2}$
chromium (Cr)	$1s^2 2s^2 2p^6 3s^2 3p^6 \mathbf{3d^5} \mathbf{4s^1}$
manganese (Mn)	$1s^2 2s^2 2p^6 3s^2 3p^6 \mathbf{3d^5} \mathbf{4s^2}$
iron (Fe)	$1s^2 2s^2 2p^6 3s^2 3p^6 \mathbf{3d^6} \mathbf{4s^2}$
cobalt (Co)	$1s^2 2s^2 2p^6 3s^2 3p^6 \mathbf{3d^7} \mathbf{4s^2}$
nickel (Ni)	$1s^2 2s^2 2p^6 3s^2 3p^6 \mathbf{3d^8} \mathbf{4s^2}$
copper (Cu)	$1s^2 2s^2 2p^6 3s^2 3p^6 \mathbf{3d^{10}} \mathbf{4s^1}$

Table 23.1 Electronic configurations of the first row of transition elements.

have just one electron in the 4s sub-shell. The remaining ten electrons are arranged in the 3d sub-shell so that each orbital is filled by two electrons.

Ions

The transition elements are all metals. In common with all metals, their atoms tend to lose electrons so they form positively charged ions. However, each transition metal can form more than one ion. For example, the common ions of copper are Cu^+ and Cu^{2+}. We say that the transition metals have **variable oxidation states**. The resulting ions are often different colours (Figure **23.1**).

Table **23.2** shows the most common oxidation states of the first row of the transition elements.

The existence of variable oxidation states means that the names of compounds containing transition elements must have their oxidation number included, e.g. manganese(IV) oxide, cobalt(II) chloride.

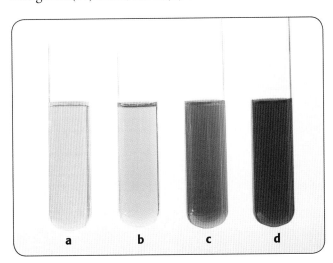

Figure 23.1 Vanadium and its oxidation states: **a** a solution containing VO_2^+ ions; **b** a solution containing VO^{2+} ions; **c** a solution containing V^{3+} ions; **d** a solution containing V^{2+} ions.

Element	Most common oxidation states
titanium (Ti)	+3, +4
vanadium (V)	+2, +3, +4, +5
chromium (Cr)	+3, +6
manganese (Mn)	+2, +4, +6, +7
iron (Fe)	+2, +3
cobalt (Co)	+2, +3
nickel (Ni)	+2
copper (Cu)	+1, +2

Table 23.2 Common oxidation states of the transition elements.

When transition elements form ions, their atoms lose electrons from the 4s sub-shell first, followed by 3d electrons.

Notice the partially filled d sub-shells (see definition of transition element on the previous page) in the following examples of ions:

$$V \text{ atom} = 1s^2 2s^2 2p^6 3s^2 3p^6 3d^3 4s^2$$
$$\rightarrow V^{3+} \text{ ion} = 1s^2 2s^2 2p^6 3s^2 3p^6 3d^2 4s^0$$

$$Fe \text{ atom} = 1s^2 2s^2 2p^6 3s^2 3p^6 3d^6 4s^2$$
$$\rightarrow Fe^{3+} \text{ ion} = 1s^2 2s^2 2p^6 3s^2 3p^6 3d^5 4s^0$$

$$Cu \text{ atom} = 1s^2 2s^2 2p^6 3s^2 3p^6 3d^{10} 4s^1$$
$$\rightarrow Cu^{2+} \text{ ion} = 1s^2 2s^2 2p^6 3s^2 3p^6 3d^9 4s^0$$

The most common oxidation state is +2, usually formed when the two 4s electrons are lost from the atoms. The maximum oxidation number of the transition elements at the start of the row involves all the 4s and 3d electrons in the atoms. For example, vanadium's maximum oxidation state is +5, involving its two 4s electrons and its three 3d electrons. At the end of the row, from iron onwards, the +2 oxidation state dominates as 3d electrons become increasingly harder to remove as the nuclear charge increases across the period.

The higher oxidation states of the transition elements are found in complex ions or in compounds formed with oxygen or fluorine. Common examples are the chromate(VI) ion, CrO_4^{2-}, and the manganate(VII) ion, MnO_4^-.

Check-up

1 **a** State the electronic configurations of the following atoms or ions:
   i   Ti   iv Fe^{3+}
   ii Cr   v Ni^{2+}
   iii Co   vi Cu^+

   b Explain why scandium (which forms only one ion, Sc^{3+}) and zinc (which forms only one ion, Zn^{2+}) are not called transition elements.

   c Why is the maximum oxidation state of manganese +7?

   d Look back at the different oxidation states of vanadium shown in Figure **23.1**. State the oxidation state of the vanadium in each photo **a–e**.

continued ⋯→

23.2 Physical properties of the transition elements

The transition elements commonly have physical properties which are typical of most metals:
- they have high melting points
- they have high densities
- they are hard and rigid, and so are useful as construction materials (Figure 23.2)
- they are good conductors of electricity and heat.

The first ionisation energy, the atomic radius and the ionic radius of transition elements do not vary much as we go across the first row. The data is given in Table 23.3.

From previous work looking at periodic properties in Chapter 10, we would expect the 1st ionisation energy, atomic radius and ionic radius of positively charged ions to vary across a period. In general, the 1st ionisation energy would increase as the increasing nuclear charge has a tighter hold on electrons filling the same main energy level or shell, and the shielding effect stays roughly the same. For similar reasons the atomic radius and ionic radius of a positively charged ion would be expected to decrease across a period. However, the transition elements show only a very small variation.

Comparing the transition elements with an s-block element

The s-block metal which lies immediately before the first row of d-block elements in the Periodic Table is calcium (Ca), in Group II. When we compare the properties of calcium with the first row of transition elements we find

Element	1st ionisation energy / kJ mol^{-1}	Atomic radius / nm	Ionic radius / nm
titanium (Ti)	661	0.132	Ti^{2+} 0.090
vanadium (V)	648	0.122	V^{3+} 0.074 or V^{2+} 0.090
chromium (Cr)	653	0.117	Cr^{3+} 0.069 or Cr^{2+} 0.085
manganese (Mn)	716	0.117	Mn^{2+} 0.080
iron (Fe)	762	0.116	Fe^{2+} 0.076
cobalt (Co)	757	0.116	Co^{2+} 0.078
nickel (Ni)	736	0.115	Ni^{2+} 0.078
copper (Cu)	745	0.117	Cu^{2+} 0.069

Table 23.3 There are comparatively small variations in 1st ionisation energy, atomic radius and ionic radius of the first-row transition elements.

Figure 23.2 The transition elements iron and copper are very important in the construction industry.

some differences despite the fact that they are all metals. You need to know the following comparisons:

- the melting point of calcium (839 °C) is **lower** than that of a transition element (e.g. titanium at 1660 °C)
- the density of calcium (1.55 g cm^{-3}) is **lower** than that of a transition element (e.g. nickel at 8.90 g cm^{-3})
- the atomic radius of calcium (0.197 nm) is **larger** than that of a transition element (e.g. iron at 0.116 nm)
- the ionic radius of the calcium ion, Ca^{2+}, (0.099 nm) is **larger** than that of a transition element (e.g. Mn^{2+} at 0.080 nm)
- the first ionisation energy of calcium (590 kJ mol^{-1}) is **lower** than that of a transition element (e.g. chromium at 653 kJ mol^{-1} or cobalt at 757 kJ mol^{-1})
- the electrical conductivity of calcium is **higher** than that of a transition element (with the exception of copper).

Check-up

2 **a** Explain why the 1st ionisation energy of calcium is lower than that of cobalt.
  b Explain why the density of calcium is lower than the density of nickel.

23.3 Redox reactions

We have seen how the transition elements can exist in various oxidation states. When a compound of a transition element is treated with a suitable reagent, the oxidation state of the transition element can change. Whenever a reaction involves reactants changing their oxidation states the reaction is a redox reaction, involving the transfer of electrons. Remember that a species is reduced when its oxidation state is reduced (gets lower in value). Its oxidation state is lowered when it gains electrons, and, as well as being reduced, it is acting as an oxidising agent. For example, in the half-equation:

$$Fe^{3+}(aq) + e^- \rightarrow Fe^{2+}(aq)$$
pale yellow   pale green

Fe^{3+} has been reduced to Fe^{2+} by gaining one electron. In the equation as shown Fe^{3+} is acting as an oxidising agent. For this reaction to happen another half-equation is needed in which the reactant loses one or more electrons, i.e. acts as a reducing agent. In Chapter **19** (page **280**) we saw how we can use standard electrode potential values, $E^{\ominus}$, to predict whether or not such reactions should take place.

Another half-equation we could consider would be:

$$MnO_4^-(aq) + 8H^+(aq) + 5e^- \rightarrow Mn^{2+}(aq) + 4H_2O(l)$$
purple   pale pink

Both half-equations are written below as they appear in tables of data showing standard electrode potentials:

$$Fe^{3+}(aq) + e^- \rightleftharpoons Fe^{2+}(aq) \qquad E^{\ominus} = +0.77\,V$$

$$MnO_4^-(aq) + 8H^+(aq) + 5e^- \rightleftharpoons Mn^{2+}(aq) + 4H_2O(l)$$
$$E^{\ominus} = +1.52\,V$$

Can Fe^{3+} ions oxidise Mn^{2+} to MnO$_4^-$ ions, or can MnO$_4^-$ ions in acid solution oxidise Fe^{2+} ions to Fe^{3+} ions?

The magnitude of the positive values provides a measure of the tendency of the half-equations to proceed to the right-hand side. The values show us that MnO$_4^-$(aq) is more likely to accept electrons and proceed in the forward direction, changing to Mn^{2+}(aq) than Fe^{3+}(aq) is to accept electrons and change to Fe^{2+}(aq). MnO$_4^-$(aq) is a more powerful oxidising agent than Fe^{3+}(aq). Therefore MnO$_4^-$(aq) ions are capable of oxidising Fe^{2+}(aq) ions to form Fe^{3+}(aq), and the top half-equation proceeds in the reverse direction.

We can now combine the two half-cells to get the overall reaction. Notice the sign of the Fe(III)/Fe(II) half-cell has changed by reversing its direction. The Fe^{2+}/Fe^{3+} equation also has to be multiplied by 5 so that the electrons on either side of the equation cancel out (this does not affect the value of $E^{\ominus}$).

$$5Fe^{2+}(aq) \rightarrow 5Fe^{3+}(aq) + 5e^- \qquad E^{\ominus} = -0.77\,V$$

$$MnO_4^-(aq) + 8H^+(aq) + 5e^- \rightarrow Mn^{2+}(aq) + 4H_2O(l)$$
$$E^{\ominus} = +1.52\,V$$

$$MnO_4^-(aq) + 5Fe^{2+}(aq) + 8H^+(aq)$$
$$\rightarrow Mn^{2+}(aq) + 5Fe^{3+}(aq) + 4H_2O(l)$$
$$E^{\ominus} = +0.75\,V$$

The relatively large positive value of $E^{\ominus}$ (+0.75 V) tells us that the reaction is likely to proceed in the forward direction as written. In fact we use this reaction to calculate the amount of iron (Fe^{2+} ions) in a sample, such as an iron tablet, by carrying out a titration.

- A known volume (e.g. 25 cm^3) of an unknown concentration of Fe^{2+}(aq) is placed in a conical flask.
- A solution of a known concentration of potassium manganate(VII) is put in a burette.

- The potassium manganate(VII) solution is titrated against the solution containing $Fe^{2+}(aq)$ in the conical flask.
- The purple colour of the manganate(VII) ions is removed in the reaction with $Fe^{2+}(aq)$. The end-point is reached when the $Fe^{2+}(aq)$ ions have all reacted, the first permanent purple colour appears in the conical flask.

Figure 23.3 Manganate(VII) ions can be used to determine the percentage of Fe^{2+} in an iron tablet.

Worked example

1 0.420 g of iron ore were dissolved in acid, so that all of the iron present in the original ore was then present as $Fe^{2+}(aq)$. The solution obtained was titrated against $0.0400\,mol\,dm^{-3}$ $KMnO_4$ (aq). The titre was $23.50\,cm^3$.

a Calculate the number of moles of MnO_4^- in the titre.
Use the equation:

$$n = V \times c$$

where n = number of moles, V = volume of solution in dm^3 and c = concentration

$$n = \frac{23.50}{1000} \times 0.0400 = 0.000\,940\,mol$$

continued ⋯→

b Calculate the number of moles of Fe^{2+} in the solution.
The equation for the reaction in the titration is:

$$5Fe^{2+} + MnO_4^- + 8H^+ \rightarrow 5Fe^{3+} + Mn^{2+} + 4H_2O$$

$$\text{number of moles of } Fe^{2+} = 5 \times 0.000\,940$$
$$= 0.004\,70\,mol$$

c Calculate the mass of iron in the solution (A_r of iron is 55.8).
moles of Fe = moles of Fe^{2+} = 0.004 70 mol

$$\text{mass of Fe} = n \times A_r$$
$$= 0.004\,70 \times 55.8$$
$$= 0.262\,g$$

d Calculate the percentage mass of iron in the 0.420 g of iron ore.

$$\text{percentage mass of iron} = \frac{0.262}{0.420} \times 100\%$$
$$= 62.4\%$$

You can achieve a more accurate result for the mass of Fe^{2+} in a solution by using dichromate(VI) ions, $Cr_2O_7^{2-}(aq)$, to oxidise it in a titration. This is because compounds such as potassium dichromate(VI) can be prepared to a higher degree of purity than potassium manganate(VII). In a titration with $Fe^{2+}(aq)$ and dichromate(VI) we need an indicator of the end-point that will be oxidised as soon as the $Fe^{2+}(aq)$ has all reacted.

The half-equation and value for $E^\ominus$ for the use of dichromate as an oxidising agent is:

$$Cr_2O_7^{2-}(aq) + 14H^+(aq) + 6e^- \rightleftharpoons 2Cr^{3+}(aq) + 7H_2O(l)$$
$$E^\ominus = +1.33\,V$$

Check-up

3 a Write two half-equations for the reactions that take place when $Fe^{2+}(aq)$ is oxidised by dichromate(VI) ions.
   b Combine the two half-equations and write the equation for the oxidation of $Fe^{2+}(aq)$ by dichromate(VI) ions.

continued ⋯→

c Work out the $E^{\ominus}$ value of the cell made when the two half-cells in part **a** are connected and the reaction in part **b** takes place. Explain what this value predicts about the likelihood of Fe^{2+}(aq) being oxidised by dichromate(VI) ions.

d How many moles of Fe^{2+}(aq) can 1 mole of dichromate(VI) oxidise?

e In a titration, 25.0 cm³ of an solution containing Fe^{2+}(aq) ions was completely oxidised by 15.30 cm³ of 0.00100 mol dm⁻³ potassium dichromate(VI) solution.

   i How many moles of potassium dichromate(VI) are there in 15.30 cm³ of 0.00100 mol dm⁻³ solution?

   ii How many moles of Fe^{2+} were present in the 25.0 cm³ of solution?

   iii What was the concentration of the Fe^{2+}(aq) in the flask at the start of the titration?

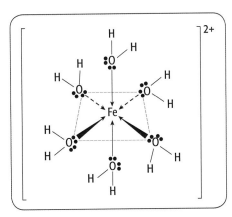

Figure 23.4 $[Fe(H_2O)_6]^{2+}$; the complex ion formed between an Fe^{2+} ion and six water molecules. It is called a hexaaquairon(II) ion.

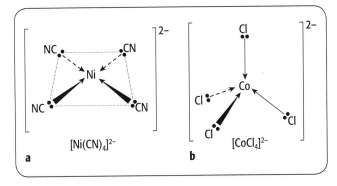

Figure 23.5 The complex ion formed between a transition metal ion and a larger ligand can only fit four ligands around the central ion. These are arranged in either a square planar shape (as in **a** $[Ni(CN)_4]^{2-}$) or a tetrahedral shape (as in **b** $[CoCl_4]^{2-}$).

23.4 Ligands and complex formation

In the previous section on redox reactions we have learned about the oxidation of Fe^{2+}(aq) ions. When these ions are in solution the Fe^{2+} ion is surrounded by six water molecules. Each water molecule bonds to the central Fe^{2+} ion by forming a co-ordinate (dative) bond from the oxygen atom into vacant orbitals on the Fe^{2+} ion (Figure 23.4). The water molecules are called **ligands** and the resulting ion is called a **complex ion**. Its formula is written as $[Fe(H_2O)_6]^{2+}$. The shape of a complex with six ligands is octahedral.

Figure 23.5 shows the shape of complexes with four ligands.

All ligands can donate an electron pair to a central transition metal ion. The **co-ordination number** of a complex is the number of co-ordinate (dative) bonds to the central metal ion. Some ligands can form two co-ordinate bonds from each ion or molecule to the transition metal ion. These are called **bidentate** ligands, as shown in Figure 23.6. Most ligands, such as water and ammonia, form just one co-ordinate bond and are called **monodentate** ligands.

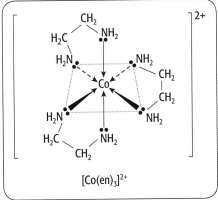

Figure 23.6 $[Co(en)_3]^{2+}$ is an example of a complex ion containing the bidentate ligand $NH_2CH_2CH_2NH_2$ (abbreviated to 'en').

Table 23.4 shows some common ligands.

Notice in Table 23.4 that the charge on a complex is simply the sum of the charges on the central metal ion and on each ligand in the complex. Some complexes will carry no charge, e.g. $Cu(OH)_2(H_2O)_4$.

Name of ligand	Formula	Example of complex	Co-ordination number	Shape of complex
water	H_2O	$[Fe(H_2O)_6]^{2+}$	6	octahedral (see Figure 23.4)
ammonia	NH_3	$[Co(NH_3)_6]^{3+}$	6	octahedral
chloride ion	Cl^-	$[CuCl_4]^{2-}$	4	tetrahedral (see Figure 23.5b)
cyanide ion	CN^-	$[Ni(CN)_4]^{2-}$	4	square planar (see Figure 23.5a)
hydroxide ion	OH^-	$[Cr(OH)_6]^{3-}$	6	octahedral
thiocyanate ion	SCN^-	$[FeSCN]^{2+}$ or $[Fe(SCN)(H_2O)_5]^{2+}$	6	octahedral
ethanedioate ion (abbreviated as 'ox' in the formulae of complexes)	$^-OOC\text{-}COO^-$	$[Mn(ox)_3]^{3-}$	6	octahedral
ethane-1,2-diamine (abbreviated as 'en' in the formulae of complexes)	$NH_2CH_2CH_2NH_2$	$[Co(en)_3]^{3+}$	6	octahedral (see Figure 23.6)

Table 23.4 Some common ligands and their complexes.

Check-up

4 a What is the oxidation number of the transition metal in each of the following complexes?
   i $[Co(NH_3)_6]^{3+}$
   ii $[Ni(CN)_4]^{2-}$
   iii $[Cr(OH)_6]^{3-}$
   iv $[Co(en)_3]^{3+}$
   v $Cu(OH)_2(H_2O)_4$

b $EDTA^{4-}$ ions can act as ligands. A single $EDTA^{4-}$ ion can form six co-ordinate bonds to a central transition metal ion to form an octahedral complex. It is called a hexadentate ligand. Give the formula of such a complex formed between Ni^{2+} and $EDTA^{4-}$.

c Which ligands in Table 23.4 are bidentate?

Substitution of ligands

The ligands in a complex can be exchanged, wholly or partially, for other ligands. This is a type of substitution reaction. It happens if the new complex formed is more stable than the original complex. The complexes of copper(II) ions can be used to show ligand substitution reactions.

Whenever we write Cu^{2+}(aq) we are really referring to the complex ion $[Cu(H_2O)_6]^{2+}$. This ion gives a solution of copper sulfate its blue colour. On adding sodium hydroxide solution, we see a light blue precipitate forming. Two water ligands are replaced by two hydroxide ligands in the reaction:

$$[Cu(H_2O)_6]^{2+}(aq) + 2OH^-(aq)$$
blue solution

$$\rightarrow Cu(OH)_2(H_2O)_4(s) + 2H_2O(l)$$
pale blue precipitate

If you now add concentrated ammonia solution, the pale blue precipitate dissolves and we get a deep blue solution:

$$Cu(OH)_2(H_2O)_4(s) + 4NH_3(aq)$$
$$\rightarrow [Cu(H_2O)_2(NH_3)_4]^{2+}(aq) + 2H_2O(l) + 2OH^-(aq)$$
deep blue solution

The first reaction can also be achieved by adding concentrated ammonia solution to copper sulfate solution drop by drop or by adding a dilute solution of ammonia. The pale blue precipitate formed will then dissolve and form the deep blue solution when excess ammonia is added. The structure of $[Cu(H_2O)_2(NH_3)_4]^{2+}$(aq) is shown in Figure 23.7.

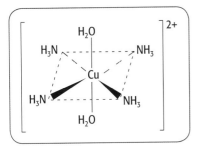

Figure 23.7 The structure of $[Cu(H_2O)_2(NH_3)_4]^{2+}$(aq).

Water ligands in $[Cu(H_2O)_6]^{2+}$ can also be exchanged for chloride ligands if we add concentrated hydrochloric acid drop by drop. A yellow solution forms, containing the complex ion $[CuCl_4]^{2-}$ (Figure 23.8):

$$[Cu(H_2O)_6]^{2+}(aq) + 4Cl^-(aq)$$
blue solution

$$\rightarrow [CuCl_4]^{2-}(aq) + 6H_2O(l)$$
yellow solution

Check-up

5 a Blue cobalt chloride paper gets its blue colour from $[CoCl_4]^{2-}$ ions. What is the oxidation number of the cobalt in this complex ion?

b Blue cobalt chloride paper is used to test for water. If water is present the

continued ···>

paper turns pink as a complex forms between the cobalt ion and six water ligands (Figure 23.9). Write an equation to show the ligand substitution reaction that takes place in a positive test for water.

Figure 23.9 A positive test for the presence of water using anhydrous cobalt chloride paper.

The colour of complexes

You cannot fail to notice the striking colours of complexes containing transition metal ions. But how do these colours arise? White light is made up of all the colours of the visible spectrum. When a solution containing a transition metal ion in a complex appears coloured, part of the visible spectrum is absorbed by the solution. However, that still doesn't explain why part of

$[CuCl_4]^{2-}$
This yellow complex forms on adding concentrated HCl.

Start here

$[Cu(H_2O)_6]^{2+}$
The well-known blue Cu^{2+} complex with water.

$[Cu(H_2O)_2(NH_3)_4]^{2+}$
This dark blue complex forms on adding concentrated NH_3.

Figure 23.8 The equations for the changes are: $[Cu(H_2O)_6]^{2+} + 4Cl^- \rightleftharpoons [CuCl_4]^{2-}(aq) + 6H_2O(l)$ and $[Cu(H_2O)_6]^{2+} + 4NH_3 \rightleftharpoons [Cu(H_2O)_2(NH_3)_4]^{2+} + 4H_2O$

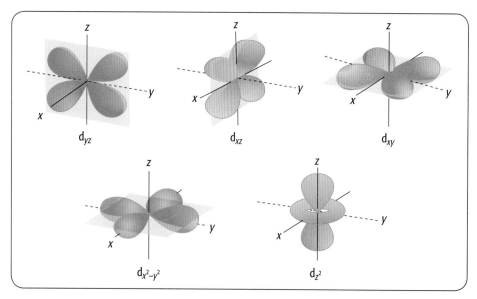

Figure 23.10 The degenerate d orbitals in a transition metal atom.

the spectrum is absorbed by transition metal ions. To answer this question we must look in more detail at the d orbitals in the ions.

The five d orbitals in an isolated transition metal atom or ion are described as **degenerate**, meaning they are all at the same energy level (Figure **23.10**).

In the presence of ligands a transition metal ion is not isolated. The co-ordinate bonding from the ligands causes the five d orbitals in the transition metal ion to split into two sets of **non-degenerate** orbitals at slightly different energy levels (Figure **23.11**). In a complex with six ligands, the ligands are arranged in an octahedral shape around the central metal ion. The lone pairs donated by the ligands into the transition metal ion repel electrons

in the two $d_{x^2-y^2}$ and d_{z^2} orbitals shown in Figure **23.10** more than those in the other three d orbitals. This is because these d orbitals line up with the co-ordinate bonds in the complex's octahedral shape and so they are closer to the bonding electrons in the octahedral arrangement, increasing repulsion between electrons. Therefore the orbitals are split, with these two d orbitals at a slightly higher energy level than the d_{yz}, d_{xz} and d_{xy} orbitals (Figure **23.11**).

A Cu^{2+} ion has an electronic configuration of $[Ar]\,3d^9$. Figure **23.11** shows how the nine d electrons are distributed between the non-degenerate orbitals formed in a complex with ligands. The difference in the energy between the non-degenerate d orbitals is

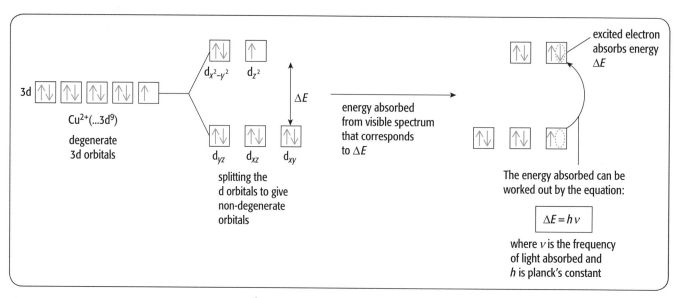

Figure 23.11 The splitting of the 3d orbitals in a $Cu(H_2O)_6^{2+}$ complex ion.

labelled ΔE. ΔE is part of the visible spectrum of light. So, when light shines on the solution containing the $Cu(H_2O)_6^{2+}$ complex, an electron absorbs this amount of energy. It uses this energy to jump into the higher of the two non-degenerate energy levels. In copper complexes, the rest of the visible spectrum that passes through the solution makes it appear blue in colour.

The exact energy difference (ΔE) between the non-degenerate d orbitals in a transition metal ion is affected by many factors. One of these factors is the identity of the ligands that surround the transition metal ion. As you have seen, a solution containing $Cu(H_2O)_6^{2+}$ is a light royal blue whereas a solution containing $Cu(NH_3)_2(H_2O)_2^{2+}$ is a very deep shade of blue. The colour change arises because the presence of the ammonia ligands causes the d orbitals to split by a different amount of energy. This means that the size of ΔE changes and this results in a slightly different amount of energy being absorbed by electrons jumping up to the higher orbitals. Therefore a different colour is absorbed from visible light, so a different colour is seen.

Check-up

6   a   What do we mean by 'degenerate atomic orbitals'?
    b   Explain why an octahedral complex of a transition element is coloured.
    c   Draw the non-degenerate 3d orbitals in a Ni^{2+} ion on a diagram similar to Figure 23.11. The electrons should be shown in the configuration that gives the lowest possible energy.

7   a   A solution of Sc^{3+} ions is colourless. Suggest a reason for this.
    b   A solution of Zn^{2+} ions is colourless. Suggest a reason for this.

Summary

- ☐ Each of the transition elements forms at least one ion with a partially filled d orbital. They are metals with similar physical and chemical properties.
- ☐ When a transition element is oxidised, it loses electrons from the 4s sub-shell first and then the 3d sub-shell to form a positively charged ion.
- ☐ Transition elements can exist in several oxidation states.
- ☐ Many reactions involving transition elements are redox reactions. Some redox reactions are used in titrations to determine concentrations.
- ☐ A ligand is a molecule or ion with one or more lone pairs of electrons available to donate to a transition metal ion. Transition elements form complexes by combining with ligands. Ligands bond to transition metal ions by one or more co-ordinate bonds.
- ☐ Ligands can be exchanged for other ligands in a complex. This can result in a change of colour.
- ☐ Transition metal compounds are often coloured because of d orbital splitting, caused by ligands. Different ligands will split the d orbitals by different amounts, resulting in differently coloured complexes.

End-of-chapter questions

1   Define the following terms:
    a   transition element [1]
    b   ligand [1]
    c   complex ion. [2]
                                                                          Total = 4

2   Use sub-shell notation ($1s^2 2s^2 2p^6$, etc.) to give the electronic configurations of the following:
    a   an Fe atom [1]
    b   a Co^{2+} ion [1]
    c   a Ti^{3+} ion. [1]
                                                                          Total = 3

3   a   Give the formulae of two iron compounds in which iron has different oxidation states.
        Give the oxidation states of the iron in each compound. [4]
    b   Explain why complexes of iron compounds are coloured. [3]
                                                                          Total = 7

4   Write balanced ionic equations and describe the observations for the reactions that occur when:
    a   sodium hydroxide solution is added to a solution containing $[Cu(H_2O)_6]^{2+}(aq)$ [2]
    b   excess concentrated ammonia solution is added to a solution containing $[Cu(H_2O)_6]^{2+}(aq)$. [3]
                                                                          Total = 5

5   The half-cell reactions given below are relevant to the questions that follow.

   $$Cl_2 + 2e^- \rightleftharpoons 2Cl^- \qquad\qquad\qquad E^\ominus = +1.36\,V$$

   $$Fe^{3+} + e^- \rightleftharpoons Fe^{2+} \qquad\qquad\qquad E^\ominus = +0.77\,V$$

   $$MnO_4^- + 8H^+ + 5e^- \rightleftharpoons Mn^{2+} + 4H_2O \qquad E^\ominus = +1.51\,V$$

   $$SO_4^{2-} + 4H^+ + 2e^- \rightleftharpoons SO_2 + 2H_2O \qquad E^\ominus = +0.17\,V$$

   In order to standardise a solution of $KMnO_4$, a student weighed out 5.56 g of $FeSO_4.7H_2O$, dissolved it in sulfuric acid and then made it up to a total volume of 250 cm^3 with distilled water. She then took 25.0 cm^3 portions of this solution, and added 10 cm^3 of 2.00 mol dm^{-3} sulfuric acid to each. She then titrated these solutions against the potassium manganate(VII) solution. The average titre was 21.2 cm^3.

a Using the electrode potentials, explain why she used sulfuric acid and not hydrochloric acid in her titrations. [4]

b What was the concentration of the iron(II) sulfate solution? [3]

c **i** Write the full ionic equation for the reaction between the manganate(VII) solution and the iron(II) sulfate. [2]

    ii How does the student know that she has reached the end-point for the reaction? [1]

d What is the concentration of the manganate(VII) solution? [2]

e If the student passed sulfur dioxide gas through $25.0\,cm^3$ of the manganate(VII) solution, what volume of gas would be required to completely decolorise the manganate(VII)? (1 mol of gas occupies $24.0\,dm^3$ at room temperature and pressure) [5]

Total = 17

24 Benzene and its compounds

Learning outcomes

Candidates should be able to:

- interpret, and use the nomenclature, general formulae and displayed formulae of the following classes of compound:
  - arenes
  - halogenoarenes
  - phenols
- describe the shape of the benzene molecule
- explain the shape of the benzene molecule in terms of σ and π carbon–carbon bonds
- describe the chemistry of arenes as exemplified by the following reactions of benzene and methylbenzene:
  - substitution reactions with chlorine and with bromine
  - nitration
  - oxidation of the side-chain to give a carboxylic acid
  - describe the mechanism of electrophilic substitution in arenes, using the mono-nitration of benzene as an example
  - describe the effect of the delocalisation of electrons in arenes in such reactions

- predict whether halogenation will occur in the side-chain or aromatic nucleus in arenes depending on reaction conditions
- apply the knowledge of positions of substitution in the electrophilic substitution of arenes
- interpret the different reactivities of halogenoalkanes, e.g. CFCs, anaesthetics, flame retardants, plastics and chlorobenzene (with particular reference to hydrolysis and to the relative strengths of the C—Hal bonds)
- recall the chemistry of phenol, as exemplified by the following reactions:
  - with bases
  - with sodium
  - nitration of, and bromination of, the aromatic ring
- explain the relative acidities of water, phenol and ethanol.

24.1 Introduction to benzene

The 'benzene ring' is a particularly important functional group which is found in many organic compounds. A benzene ring is a hexagon made of six carbon atoms bonded together in a particular way. Benzene rings are found in many compounds that are commercially important – for example as medicines, dyes and plastics.

Organic compounds containing one or more benzene rings are called **arenes**. In general, compounds of benzene are known as aryl compounds or aromatic compounds; an example is chlorobenzene, which is one of the halogenoarenes.

The simplest arene is benzene itself. Its formula is C_6H_6. The early organic chemists struggled to work out its structure. However, around 1865 Friedrich August Kekulé seemed to have solved the problem. He proposed a hexagonal ring of carbon atoms, each bonded to one hydrogen atom. In Kekulé's structure the hexagonal ring contained three double C=C bonds (Figure 24.2). This is reflected in benzene's name, which has the same ending as the alkenes.

As analytical techniques were developed, however, chemists found out that the benzene molecule was a planar, perfectly symmetrical molecule. Kekulé's structure would suggest three shorter double C=C bonds and three longer single C—C bonds in the ring. This would produce a distorted

Figure 24.1 This is a vanilla orchid. Its seed pods contain a substance called vanillin. Its molecules are based on a benzene ring. It is called an aromatic compound. Vanillin is used to flavour foods such as ice cream and chocolate. Its structure is:

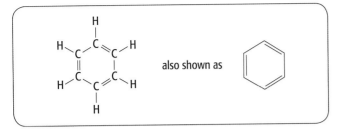

Figure 24.2 Kekulé's structure of benzene.

hexagonal shape, not the perfect hexagonal arrangement of carbon atoms in benzene's actual molecules. Figure 24.3 shows how we represent benzene's displayed formula.

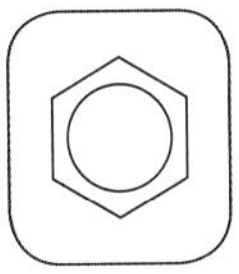

Figure 24.3 The displayed formula of benzene.

We can now measure actual bond lengths. This was impossible in the 19th century when Kekulé worked. Table 24.1 shows that the bond length of the carbon–carbon bonds in benzene lie between the values for C—C single bonds and C=C double bonds.

Bond	Bond length / nm
C—C	0.154
C=C	0.134
carbon to carbon bond in benzene	0.139

Table 24.1 Comparing bond lengths.

The chemistry of benzene also suggests that the Kekulé structure is incorrect. If there were three C=C bonds in benzene it would undergo addition reactions like the alkenes (see page 222). However, this is not the case. For example, ethene will decolorise bromine water on mixing but benzene needs much harsher conditions.

Fact file

Friedrich August Kekulé's proposal for the structure of a benzene molecule was inspired by a dream. He was pondering the problem when he fell asleep in front of a fire. He claimed he saw chains of 'snake-like' carbon atoms swirling around when one 'snake' suddenly bit its own tail. As he woke up, this gave him the idea of the hexagonal ring of carbon atoms.

The actual structure of benzene can be explained by considering the bonding in the molecule. Each carbon atom shares:
• one pair of electrons with one of its neighbouring carbon atoms
• one pair of electrons with its other neighbouring carbon atom
• one pair of electrons with a hydrogen atom.
These are σ (sigma) bonds; covalent bonds with the pair of electrons found mainly between the nuclei of the atoms bonded to each other. Each carbon atom forms three σ bonds. That leaves one electron spare on each of the six carbon atoms. Each carbon atoms contributes this one electron to a π (pi) bond (see page 59). However, the π bonds formed are not localised between pairs of carbon atoms as in an alkene (see page 208). Instead, the π bonds in benzene spread over all six carbon atoms in the hexagonal ring. The six electrons in the π bonds are said to be **delocalised**.

The π bonding in benzene is formed by the overlap of carbon p atomic orbitals, one from each of the six carbon atoms. To achieve maximum overlap, the benzene molecule must be planar. The lobes of the p orbitals overlap to form a ring of delocalised electrons above and below the plane of the carbon atoms in the benzene molecule. This is shown in Figure 24.4.

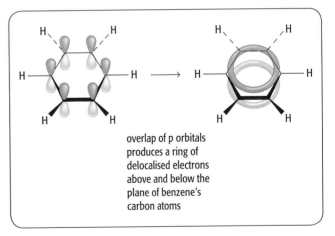

overlap of p orbitals produces a ring of delocalised electrons above and below the plane of benzene's carbon atoms

Figure 24.4 The π bonding in benzene.

Check-up

1 a How many electrons are involved in the π bonding system in a benzene molecule?
  b From which type of atomic orbital do the electrons in part **a** come from?
  c What do we mean by the term 'delocalised electrons' in benzene?
  d What is the difference between the π bonding in benzene and the π bonding in hex-3-ene?

Naming aryl compounds

You saw how to name aryl compounds with alkyl side-chains on page 207. Some aryl compounds have functional groups that are substituted directly into the benzene ring in place of a hydrogen atom. You need to know the names of the compounds in Table **24.2**.

Displayed formula of aryl compound	Name
Cl	chlorobenzene
NO$_2$	nitrobenzene
OH	phenol
OH, Br, Br, Br (2,4,6 positions)	2,4,6-tribromophenol: notice the numbering of the carbon atoms in the benzene ring to describe the position of each substituted group (see page 207)
NH$_2$	phenylamine

Table 24.2 The names of some aryl compounds. The phenyl group can be written as C_6H_5, e.g. phenylamine is $C_6H_5NH_2$.

Check-up

2 a Draw the displayed formula of:
  i 1,3,5-tribromobenzene
  ii 1,3-dichloro-5-nitrobenzene.
  b Name the molecules below:
  i OH, CH$_3$

  ii Br, Cl, Cl

24.2 Reactions of arenes

Most reactions of benzene maintain the highly stable delocalised ring of π bonding electrons intact. This occurs by substituting an atom, or group of atoms, for one or more hydrogen atoms attached to the benzene ring. The initial attack is usually by an electrophile, which is attracted to the high electron density around the benzene ring.

Electrophilic substitution with chlorine or bromine

Benzene will react with bromine in the presence of an anhydrous iron(III) bromide catalyst. The catalyst can be made in the reaction vessel by adding iron filings to the benzene and bromine. The substitution reaction is:

$$\text{benzene} + Br_2 \xrightarrow[\text{FeBr}_3\text{ catalyst}]{\text{anhydrous}} \text{bromobenzene} + HBr$$

At first sight the electrophile that starts the attack on benzene is not obvious. The electrophile is created when an iron(III) bromide molecule polarises a bromine molecule. The Br_2 molecule forms a dative (co-ordinate) bond with iron(III) bromide by donating a lone pair of electrons from one bromine atom into an empty 3d orbital in the iron. This draws electrons from the other bromine atom in the Br_2 molecule making it partially positive, creating the electrophile. We can think of the electrophile as a Br^+ cation:

$$\overset{\delta+}{Br} \longrightarrow \overset{\delta-}{Br} \longrightarrow FeBr_3 \longrightarrow Br^+ + [FeBr_4]^-$$

The Br^+ cation and the 'electron-rich' benzene ring are attracted to each other, as the mechanism shows. Remember that the curly arrows show the movement of a pair of electrons.

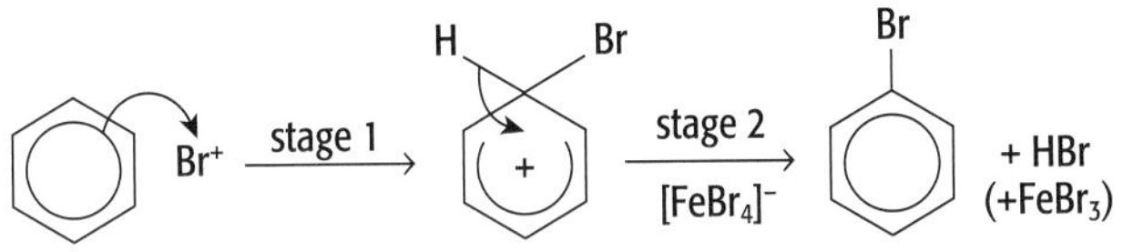

A similar reaction happens when chlorine gas is bubbled through benzene at room temperature in the presence of a catalyst such as iron(III) chloride or aluminium chloride. The products of this electrophilic substitution are chlorobenzene and hydrogen chloride. The catalysts in these reactions, i.e. $FeBr_3$, $AlCl_3$ and $FeCl_3$, are known as 'halogen carriers'.

When we halogenate methylbenzene or other alkylarenes, the halogen atom substitutes into the benzene ring at positions 2 or 4. These positions are 'activated' by any electron-donating groups bonded directly to the benzene ring. Other examples of arenes that are activated in these positions are phenol and phenylamine. So when we react methylbenzene with chlorine gas, using an anhydrous aluminium chloride catalyst, two products can be made:

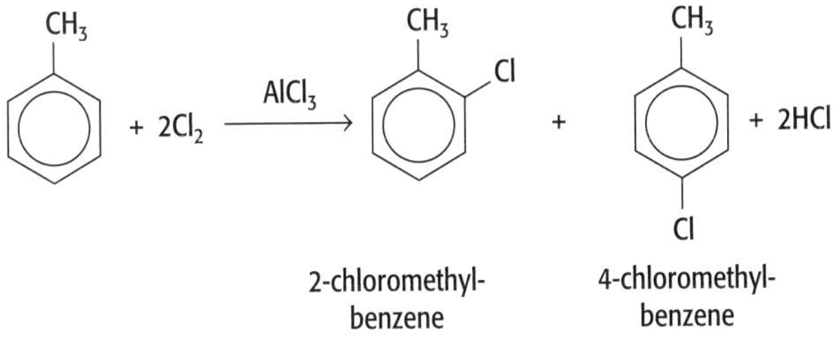

2-chloromethyl-benzene

4-chloromethyl-benzene

If excess chlorine gas is bubbled through, we can form 1-methyl-2,4-dichlorobenzene, 1-methyl-2,6-dichlorobenzene and 1-methyl-2,4,6-trichlorobenzene. (Remember that the 2 and 6 positions in substituted arenes are equivalent).

The carbon–halogen bond in halogenoarenes is stronger than the equivalent bond in a halogenoalkane because one of the lone pairs on the halogen atom overlaps slightly with the π bonding system in the benzene ring. This gives the carbon–halogen bond a partial double bond character.

Notice that the methyl side-chain is not affected under the conditions used in the reaction above. However, we learned on page **219** that chlorine will react with alkanes in the presence of UV light or strong sunlight. This is a free radical substitution reaction. So if the chlorine gas is passed into boiling methylbenzene, in the presence of UV light, the following reaction takes place:

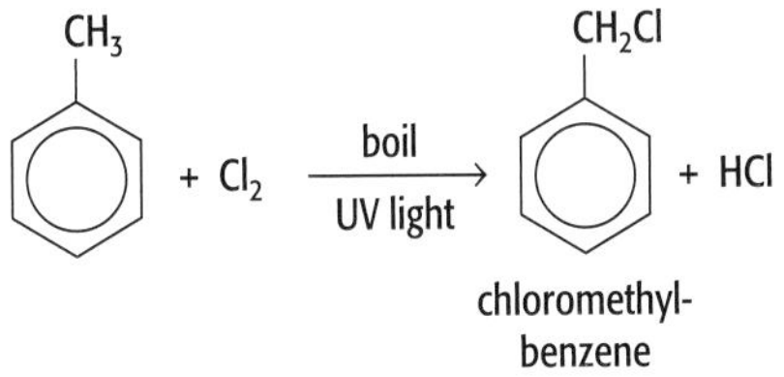

chloromethyl-benzene

Notice that there is no substitution into the benzene ring under these conditions. In excess chlorine, eventually all three of the hydrogen atoms on the methyl side-chain will be replaced by chlorine atoms.

Fact file

The compound shown below is used as a fire retardant. It is non-toxic and extremely unreactive. However, some people are becoming concerned that it will degrade in the environment to produce products that are toxic. Many other halogenoarenes have already been banned.

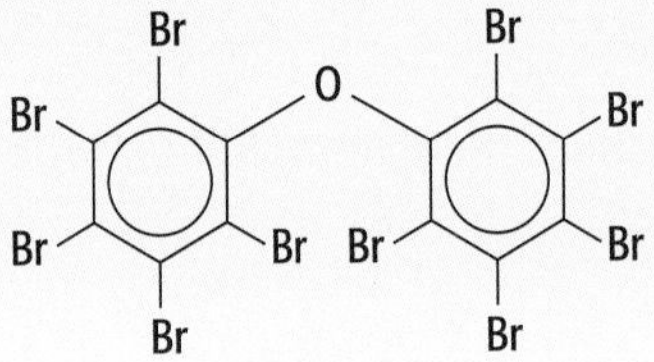

Check-up

3 **a** Write the equation for the reaction of chlorine with benzene in the presence of an iron(III) chloride catalyst.
   b What do we call the mechanism of the reaction in part **a**?
   c Draw the mechanism of the reaction in part **a**, with Cl^+ as the attacking species and using curly arrows to show the movement of electron pairs.
   d Draw the displayed formula of the 'tri-substituted' halogenoarene produced if methylbenzene is added to excess

continued ⋯➔

bromine at room temperature in the presence of iron(III) bromide.

e How would the reaction in part **d** differ if the methylbenzene and bromine were boiled in the presence of ultraviolet light?

f Name the mechanism of the reaction in part **e**.

Nitration of benzene

The nitration of benzene is another example of an electrophilic substitution. Nitration refers to the introduction of the $-NO_2$ group into a molecule. In this reaction the electrophile is the NO_2^+ ion, known as the nitronium ion (or nitryl cation). This is made from a mixture of concentrated nitric acid and concentrated sulfuric acid:

$$HNO_3 + 2H_2SO_4 \rightarrow NO_2^+ + 2HSO_4^- + H_3O^+$$

This 'nitrating mixture' is refluxed with benzene at about 55 °C to make nitrobenzene:

The mechanism of the electrophilic substitution is:

In stage 1 in the mechanism, the electrophile, NO_2^+, is attracted to the high electron density of the π bonding system in benzene. A pair of electrons from the benzene ring is donated to the nitrogen atom in NO_2^+, and forms a new covalent bond. At this point, benzene's delocalised ring of electrons is disrupted. There are now four π bonding electrons and a positive charge spread over five carbon atoms.

However, the full delocalised ring is restored in stage 2 when the C–H bond breaks heterolytically. Both electrons in the C–H covalent bond go into nitrobenzene's π bonding system, and hydrogen leaves as an H^+ ion. There are now six electrons spread over the six carbon atoms so the chemical stability of the benzene ring is retained in this substitution reaction.

Further nitration of the nitrobenzene produces 1,3-dinitrobenzene and 1,3,5-trinitrobenzene. Unlike the electron-donating methyl group in methylbenzene (which activates the 2 and 4 positions in the benzene ring), the $-NO_2$ group is electron-withdrawing. This type of group (which includes $-COOH$) deactivates the 2 and 4 positions in the benzene ring. Therefore, when there is a nitro group bonded to the benzene ring, further substitution takes place at the 3 and 5 positions.

Check-up

4 a Copy and complete the two equations below that can be used to show the nitration of methylbenzene:

   i $C_6H_5CH_3 + NO_2^+ \rightarrow$ _____ + _____

   ii $C_6H_5CH_3 + HNO_3$
    $\xrightarrow{H_2SO_4}$ _____ + _____

   iii Name the possible mono-substituted products in parts **i** and **ii**.

   iv 1-methyl-2,4-dinitrobenzene and 1-methyl-2,4,6-trinitrobenzene are formed on further nitration of methylbenzene. Draw the displayed formula of each compound.

b Benzene also undergoes electrophilic substitution when refluxed with fuming sulfuric acid for several hours. This is called sulfonation. The electrophile is the SO_3 molecule and the product formed is benzenesulfonic acid, $C_6H_5SO_3H$.

   i Which atom in the SO_3 molecule accepts an electron pair in the mechanism of sulfonation?

   ii Write an equation in the style of part **a i** for the sulfonation of benzene to form benzenesulfonic acid.

Oxidation of the side-chain in arenes

The presence of the benzene ring in an alkylarene, such as methylbenzene, can affect the characteristic reactions of its alkyl side-chain. For example, alkanes are not usually oxidised by a chemical oxidising agent such as potassium manganate(VII). However, in alkylarenes the alkane side-chain is oxidised to form a carboxylic acid. For example, methylbenzene produces benzoic acid when refluxed with alkaline potassium manganate(VII) or another strong oxidising agent such as acidified potassium dichromate(VI):

24.3 Phenol

Phenol, C_6H_5OH, is a crystalline solid which melts at 43 °C. It is used to manufacture a wide range of products (Figure 24.5). It's structure is:

Figure 24.5 Araldite adhesive, compact discs and TCP antiseptic are all manufactured using phenol as a starting material.

Fact file

In the 19th century phenol was the first antiseptic to be used in surgery by Joseph Lister. Many people used to die when their wounds became infected after an operation. However, when Lister sprayed the operating theatre and recovery wards with phenol death rates were dramatically reduced. Nowadays, derivatives of phenol are used because phenol itself is toxic and caustic. Compounds such as 2,4,6-trichlorophenol, found in TCP® and Dettol®, still kill bacteria without the nasty side-effects of phenol.

The melting point of phenol is relatively high for an aryl compound of its molecular mass because of hydrogen bonding between its molecules. However, the large non-polar benzene ring makes phenol only sparingly soluble in water as it disrupts hydrogen bonding with water molecules.

Phenol is weakly acidic, losing an H^+ ion from its hydroxyl group:

$$C_6H_5OH(aq) \rightleftharpoons \underset{\text{phenoxide ion}}{C_6H_5O^-(aq)} + H^+(aq)$$

The position of this equilibrium lies well over to the left-hand side. However, phenol is still a stronger acid than water or an alcohol. The values of pK_a are shown in Table 24.3. Remember: the higher the value of pK_a, the weaker the acid (see page 305).

Weak acid	Dissociation in water	pK_a at 25 °C
phenol	$C_6H_5OH(aq)$ $\rightleftharpoons C_6H_5O^-(aq) + H^+(aq)$	10.0
water	$H_2O(l)$ $\rightleftharpoons H^+(aq) + OH^-(aq)$	14.0
ethanol	$C_2H_5OH(aq)$ $\rightleftharpoons C_2H_5O^-(aq) + H^+(aq)$	16.0

Table 24.3 Comparing the acidity of phenol, water and ethanol.

Phenol is more acidic than water, with ethanol being the least acidic of the three compounds. We can explain this by looking at the conjugate bases formed on the right-hand side of the equations in Table 24.3. The phenoxide ion, $C_6H_5O^-(aq)$, has its negative charge spread over the whole ion as one of the lone pairs on the oxygen atom overlaps with the delocalised π bonding system in the benzene ring.

phenoxide ion, with negative charge spread over the whole ion

$CH_3CH_2 \rightarrow O^-$

ethoxide ion, with negative charge concentrated on the oxygen

This delocalisation reduces the charge density of the negative charge on the phenoxide ion compared with $OH^-(aq)$ or $C_2H_5O^-(aq)$. Therefore $H^+(aq)$ ions are not as strongly attracted to the phenoxide ion as they are to hydroxide or ethoxide ions, making phenoxide ions less likely to re-form the undissociated molecules.

Alternatively, we can explain the greater acidity of phenol by saying that phenol ionises to form a more stable negative ion, so the ionisation of phenol is more likely. This results in the position of equilibrium in the phenol equation in Table 24.3 lying further to the right-hand side (i.e. more molecules donating H^+ ion) than the other equations.

Ethanol is a weaker acid than water due to the electron-donating alkyl (ethyl) group attached to the oxygen atom in the ethoxide ion. This has the effect of concentrating more negative charge on this oxygen atom, which more readily accepts an H^+ ion. This explains why the position of equilibrium lies further to the left-hand side, favouring the undissociated ethanol molecules.

Check-up

5 a Place the following molecules in order of their acidity, starting with the most acidic:

CH_3COOH C_6H_5OH HCl
C_3H_7OH H_2O

b Would you expect methanol to be more or less acidic than phenol? Explain your answer.

24.4 Reactions of phenol

We can divide the reactions of phenol into those involving the hydroxyl group, —OH, and those involving substitution into the benzene ring.

Breaking of the O—H bond in phenol

Although phenol is sparingly soluble in water, it dissolves well in an alkaline solution. As you have just learned, phenol is a weak acid so it will react with an alkali to give a salt plus water:

$$\text{C}_6\text{H}_5{-}OH + NaOH \longrightarrow \text{C}_6\text{H}_5{-}O^-Na^+ + H_2O$$

The salt formed, sodium phenoxide, is soluble in water.

Phenol also reacts vigorously with sodium metal, giving off hydrogen gas and again forming sodium phenoxide:

$$2\,\text{C}_6\text{H}_5{-}OH + 2Na \longrightarrow 2\,\text{C}_6\text{H}_5{-}O^-Na^+ + H_2$$

Substitution into the benzene ring of phenol

Compared with benzene, phenol reacts more readily with electrophiles. The overlap of one of the lone pairs of electrons on the oxygen atom in the —OH group with the π bonding system increases the electron density of the benzene ring in phenol. This makes the benzene ring more open to attack from electron-deficient electrophiles. It 'activates' the benzene ring, especially at positions 2, 4 and 6.

Phenol therefore undergoes similar reactions to benzene, but phenol does so under milder conditions. For example, bromine water will not react with benzene at room temperature. To produce bromobenzene we need pure bromine (not a solution) and an iron(III) bromide catalyst. However, bromine water reacts readily with phenol, decolorising the orange solution and forming a white precipitate of 2,4,6-tribromophenol (Figure 24.6). Similar reactions happen between phenol and chlorine or iodine.

$$\text{C}_6\text{H}_5OH + 3Br_2 \longrightarrow \text{(2,4,6-tribromophenol)} + 3HBr$$

Figure 24.6 Bromine water is added to aqueous phenol.

This activation of the benzene ring is also shown in the nitration of phenol. With benzene, we need a mixture of concentrated nitric and sulfuric acids to reflux with benzene at about 55 °C for nitration to take place (see page 378). However, the activated ring in phenol readily undergoes nitration with dilute nitric acid at room temperature:

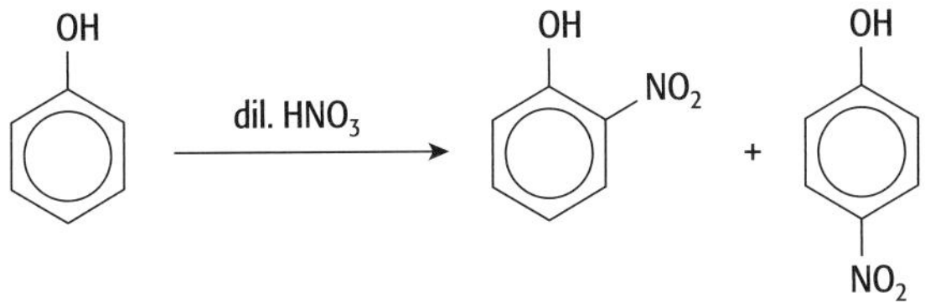

If we use concentrated nitric acid we get 2,4,6-trinitrophenol formed, shown below:

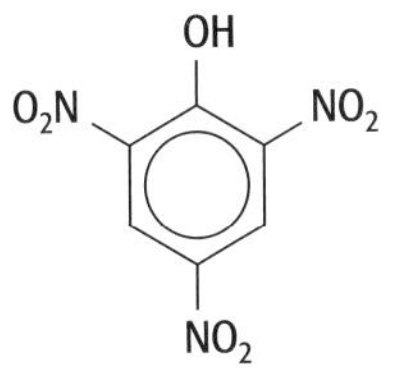

Check-up

6 **a** Place these molecules in order of ease of nitration, with the most reactive first:

C_6H_6 $C_6H_5CH_3$ C_6H_5COOH C_6H_5OH

b i Write a balanced equation to show the reaction when excess chlorine is bubbled through phenol at room temperature.

ii How would the reaction conditions differ from those in part **b i** if you wanted to make chlorobenzene from benzene and chlorine?

Summary

- ☐ The benzene molecule, C_6H_6, is symmetrical, with a planar hexagonal shape.
- ☐ Arenes have considerable energetic stability because of the delocalised π bonding electrons that lie above and below the plane of the benzene ring.
- ☐ The main mechanism for arene reactions is electrophilic substitution. This enables arenes to retain their delocalised π electrons. Hydrogen atoms on the benzene ring may be replaced by a variety of other atoms or groups including halogen atoms and nitro (—NO_2) groups.
- ☐ Despite the name ending in -ene, arenes do not behave like alkenes. Arenes undergo electrophilic substitution whereas alkenes undergo electrophilic addition.
- ☐ Sometimes the presence of the benzene ring affects the usual reactions of its side-chain, e.g. methylbenzene is oxidised by refluxing with alkaline potassium manganate(VII) to form benzoic acid.
- ☐ When the —OH group is joined directly to a benzene ring, the resulting compound is called a phenol.
- ☐ Phenols are weakly acidic, but are more acidic than water and alcohols. The acidity of phenol is due to delocalisation of the negative charge on the phenoxide ion into the π bonding electron system on the benzene ring.
- ☐ When reacted with sodium hydroxide, phenol forms a salt (sodium phenoxide) plus water. The reaction of sodium metal with phenol produces sodium phenoxide and hydrogen gas.
- ☐ The —OH group enhances the reactivity of the benzene ring towards electrophiles. The —OH group is said to activate the benzene ring. For example, bromine water is decolorised by phenol at room temperature, producing a white precipitate of 2,4,6-tribromophenol.

End-of-chapter questions

1 a What is the empirical formula of benzene?   [1]
   b What is the molecular formula of benzene?   [1]
   c i Draw the full structural formula of the Kekulé structure of benzene, showing all atoms and using
         double bonds and single bonds.   [1]
      ii Draw the skeletal formulae for the Kekulé and delocalised structures of benzene.   [2]
                                                                            Total = 5

2 Benzene reacts with bromine.
   a Write a balanced chemical equation for this reaction.   [1]
   b Name the catalyst used.   [1]
   c What visual observations could be made during the reaction?   [2]
                                                                            Total = 4

3 Phenol is an aryl compound.
   a i What is the molecular formula of phenol?   [1]
      ii What is the empirical formula of phenol?   [1]
   b Molten phenol reacts with sodium metal. Give **one** observation and write a balanced chemical
      equation for the reaction.   [2]
   c Phenol reacts with sodium hydroxide solution. Name the type of reaction and write a balanced
      chemical equation for the reaction.   [2]
   d The reactions in parts **b** and **c** both give the same organic product. Name it.   [1]
   e Phenol reacts with bromine water. Give the name of the product, **two** visual observations and a
      balanced chemical equation, and comment on how this shows that phenol is more reactive
      than benzene.   [7]
   f Explain why phenol is more reactive than benzene. Your answer must include reference to the
      model used for the arrangement of electrons.   [4]
                                                                            Total = 18

4 Benzene can be nitrated to give nitrobenzene.
   a Name the mechanism for this reaction.   [2]
   b The species attacking benzene in the reaction is NO_2^+. How is this generated in the reaction mixture?
      (Name the substances used and give chemical equations leading to the formation of NO_2^+.)   [4]
   c Suggest a suitable temperature for this reaction.   [1]
   d Use curly arrows to show the mechanism of how benzene reacts with NO_2^+ to produce nitrobenzene.   [3]

e The structure of a common household substance is given below:

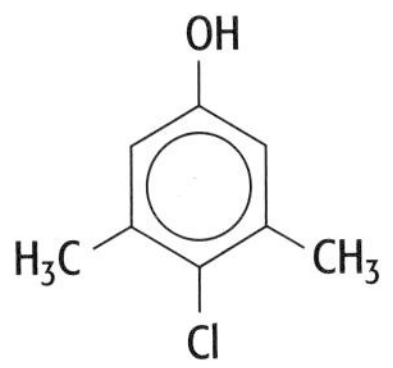

$$OH$$

$$H_3C \quad CH_3$$

$$Cl$$

    i Give the molecular formula of the compound. [1]

   ii Suggest a use for this compound in the home. Explain your suggestion. [2]

  iii When bromine water is added to a solution of the compound, it is decolorised. Suggest a structure for the product of the reaction. [2]

Total = 15

5 **a** Describe the bonding in benzene. Include a description of the model used for the arrangement of electrons in the molecule. [5]

   b Cyclohexene decolorises bromine water; benzene has no effect on bromine water. Explain the difference in reactivity towards bromine water. [5]

Total = 10

25 Carboxylic acids and acyl compounds

Learning outcomes

Candidates should be able to:

- [ ] describe the reactions of carboxylic acids in the formation of acyl chlorides
- [ ] explain the acidity of carboxylic acids and of chlorine substituted ethanoic acids in terms of their structures
- [ ] describe the hydrolysis of acyl chlorides
- [ ] describe the reactions of acyl chlorides with alcohols, phenols and primary amines
- [ ] explain the relative ease of hydrolysis of acyl chlorides, alkyl chlorides and aryl chlorides

- [ ] describe the formation of esters from acyl chlorides, using ethyl ethanoate and phenyl benzoate as examples
- [ ] describe the reaction of CH_3CO- compounds with alkaline aqueous iodine to give tri-iodomethane
- [ ] deduce the presence of a $CH_3CH(OH)-$ group in an alcohol from its reaction with alkaline aqueous iodine to form tri-iodomethane.

25.1 The acidity of carboxylic acids

Carboxylic acids display the typical reactions of all acids due to the presence of excess $H^+(aq)$ ions in their aqueous solutions. For example, they react with bases to form a salt plus water. Their salts are called carboxylates. The carboxylate salt formed by the reaction of ethanoic acid with sodium hydroxide is called sodium ethanoate, $CH_3COO^-Na^+$.

The carboxylic acids are weak acids. The majority of their molecules are undissociated in water. For example:

$$CH_3COOH(aq) \rightleftharpoons CH_3COO^-(aq) + H^+(aq)$$

ethanoic acid   ethanoate ion

The position of this equilibrium lies well over to the left-hand side. The dissociation constant, K_a, of ethanoic acid at $25\,°C$ is $1.7 \times 10^{-5}\,mol\,dm^{-3}$ (see page 307). Remember that the smaller the value of K_a, the weaker the acid.

The carboxylic acids are stronger acids than alcohols.

- The O—H bond in the carboxylic acid is weakened by the carbonyl group, C=O.

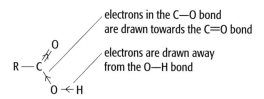

electrons in the C—O bond are drawn towards the C=O bond

electrons are drawn away from the O—H bond

- The carboxylate ion is stabilised by delocalisation of electrons around the —COO⁻ group. This delocalisation spreads out the negative charge on the carboxylate ion, making it less likely to bond with an $H^+(aq)$ ion to re-form the undissociated acid molecule.

negative charge is spread over the whole –COO⁻ group (the bond lengths of both carbon–oxygen bonds are equal)

Electron-withdrawing groups bonded to the carbon atom next to the —COOH group make the acid stronger. There are two reasons for this:

- electron-withdrawing groups further weaken the O—H bond in the undissociated acid molecule

Figure 25.1 Vinegar contains ethanoic acid – a carboxylic acid.

- electron-withdrawing groups further delocalise the negative charge on the $-COO^-$ group of the carboxylate ion, stabilising the $-COO^-$ group and making it less likely to bond with an H^+ ion.

Chlorine atoms are an example of an electron-withdrawing group. The dissociation constants of ethanoic acid and its three substituted chloro derivatives are shown in Table 25.1.

Acid	K_a at 25 °C / $mol\,dm^{-3}$
ethanoic acid, CH_3COOH	1.7×10^{-5}
chloroethanoic acid, $CH_2ClCOOH$	1.3×10^{-3}
dichloroethanoic acid, $CHCl_2COOH$	5.0×10^{-2}
trichloroethanoic acid, CCl_3COOH	2.3×10^{-1}

Table 25.1 The larger the value of K_a, the stronger the acid.

Trichloroethanoic acid, CCl_3COOH, has three strongly electronegative Cl atoms all withdrawing electrons from the $-COOH$ group, weakening the O—H bond more than the other acids in Table 25.1. Once the O—H bond is broken, the resulting anion is also stabilised more effectively by its three electron-withdrawing Cl atoms, making it less attractive to H^+ ions. This makes the CCl_3COOH the strongest of the acids listed in Table 25.1 as it has most Cl atoms (Figure 25.2).

Fact file

Trichloroethanoic acid is used for chemical facial peels in clinics. It is used as a 'medium' strength peel to remove deep wrinkles and imperfections on the skin. The immediate results make the face look like it has severe sunburn and patients are usually kept in hospital for a week.

Ethanoic acid is the weakest acid in Table 25.1, as the methyl group is electron donating. This has the opposite effect to electron-withdrawing groups:
- it strengthens the O—H bond in the acid's $-COOH$ group
- it donates negative charge towards the $-COO^-$ group of the carboxylate ion, making it more likely to accept an H^+ ion.

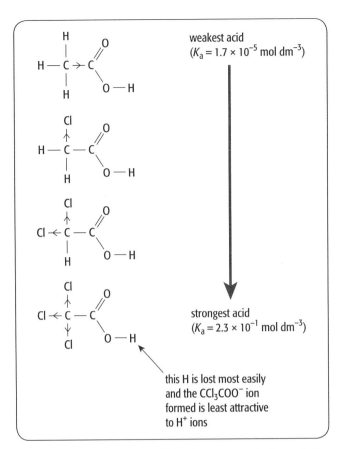

Figure 25.2 The more electron-withdrawing groups on the C atom in the $-COOH$ group, the stronger the acid.

Check-up

1 a Place the following acids in order of strength, starting with the strongest acid first.

CH_3CH_2COOH CH_3CCl_2COOH
$CH_3CHClCOOH$

  b Explain why ethanoic acid is a stronger acid than ethanol.

  c Predict which would be the stronger acid – methanoic acid or ethanoic acid – and explain your reasoning.

25.2 Acyl chlorides

Many useful compounds can be synthesised from carboxylic acids. However, the synthetic reactions that are needed can be difficult to do because carboxylic acids are quite unreactive. One way round this is to first convert the carboxylic acid into a compound called an **acyl chloride**. Acyl chlorides are much more reactive than carboxylic acids.

An acyl chloride is similar in structure to a carboxylic acid but the —OH group has been replaced by a Cl atom. The displayed formula of ethanoyl chloride is:

ethanoyl chloride

The structural formula of ethanoyl chloride can be written as CH_3COCl.

Making acyl chlorides

We can prepare acyl chlorides from their corresponding carboxylic acid using phosphorus(V) chloride, phosphorus(III) chloride or sulfur dichloride oxide ($SOCl_2$).

$$CH_3COOH + PCl_5 \rightarrow CH_3COCl + POCl_3 + HCl$$

No special conditions are required for this reaction.

$$3CH_3COOH + PCl_3 \rightarrow 3CH_3COCl + H_3PO_3$$

Heat is required for this reaction.

$$CH_3COOH + SOCl_2 \rightarrow CH_3COCl + SO_2 + HCl$$

No special conditions are required for this reaction.

The acyl chlorides are reactive compounds. The carbonyl carbon has electrons drawn away from it by the Cl atom as well as by its O atom. This gives the carbonyl carbon a relatively large partial positive charge and makes it particularly open to attack from nucleophiles.

Check-up

2 a Write a balanced equation to show the formation of:

   i propanoyl chloride from a suitable carboxylic acid and $SOCl_2$

   ii methanoyl chloride from a suitable carboxylic acid and PCl_3

   iii butanoyl chloride from a suitable carboxylic acid and PCl_5.

continued ···➔

b Which of these reactions only proceeds under certain conditions?

c In its reaction with a nucleophile, why does an acyl chloride react faster than an alcohol?

Reactions of acyl chlorides

The acyl chlorides are reactive liquids. When they react with nucleophiles the C—Cl bond breaks and white fumes of hydrogen chloride, HCl, are given off. In general we can say:

$$ROCl + HZ \rightarrow ROZ + HCl$$

where HZ can be water, an alcohol, ammonia or an amine. Notice that HZ contains either an oxygen or nitrogen atom with a lone pair of electrons that can be donated. HZ can therefore act as a nucleophile.

Hydrolysis of acyl chlorides

Water is a suitable nucleophile to attack an acyl chloride molecule. A lone pair on the oxygen atom in water initiates the attack on the δ+ carbonyl carbon atom. The reaction produces a carboxylic acid and hydrogen chloride. It is an example of a hydrolysis reaction, i.e. the breakdown of a compound by water. For example:

$$\underset{\text{propanoyl chloride}}{CH_3CH_2COCl} + H_2O \rightarrow \underset{\text{propanoic acid}}{CH_3CH_2COOH} + HCl$$

The acyl chloride can be added to water using a dropping pipette. The reaction is immediate and you see the white fumes of HCl rising from the liquid.

The reaction is far more vigorous than the hydrolysis of chloroalkanes (see page **232**). The hydrolysis of chloroalkanes needs a strong alkali, such as aqueous sodium hydroxide, to be refluxed with the chloroalkane to hydrolyse it. The nucleophile needed to hydrolyse a chloroalkane is the negatively charged hydroxide ion, OH⁻; however, a neutral water molecule is sufficient to hydrolyse an acyl chloride quickly at room temperature. This difference is because the carbon bonded to the chlorine atom in a chloroalkane is not as strongly δ+ as the carbon atom in an acyl chloride. Remember, in an acyl chloride the carbon bonded to the chlorine atom is also attached to an oxygen atom. It has two strongly electronegative atoms pulling electrons away from it.

Therefore the attack by the nucleophile is much more rapid.

Aryl chlorides, such as chlorobenzene, will not undergo hydrolysis. The carbon atom bonded to the chlorine atom is part of the delocalised π bonding system of the benzene ring. The p orbitals from the Cl atom tend to overlap with the delocalised π electrons in the benzene ring. This causes the C—Cl bond to have some double bond character, making it stronger and hydrolysis does not occur.

The ease of hydrolysis, starting with the compounds most readily broken down, is:

acyl chloride > chloroalkane > aryl chloride

Check-up

3 a Name the products of the hydrolysis of propanoyl chloride.

  b i Place the following compounds in order of ease of hydrolysis, starting with the most reactive first.

C_6H_5Cl CH_3CH_2COCl $CH_3CH_2CH_2Cl$

   ii Explain your answer to part **i**.
   iii If a reaction occurs with water, what will you **see** in part **i**?

Reaction with alcohols and phenol

When acyl chlorides react with alcohols and phenol, we get esters (and HCl) formed. The reactions happen more quickly than the reactions of alcohols or phenol with carboxylic acids. The acyl chloride reactions also go to completion and do not form an equilibrium mixture. Therefore they are useful in the synthesis of esters in the chemical industry.

Ethanoyl chloride will react vigorously with ethanol to form an ester:

ethanoyl   ethanol   ethyl
chloride   ethanoate

With phenol, the reaction with an acyl chloride proceeds if warmed. There is no reaction between phenol and carboxylic acids, so acyl chlorides must be used if you want to make phenyl esters. The reaction takes place in the presence of a base. The initial reaction between phenol and the base creates the phenoxide ion, $C_6H_5O^-$, which acts as a nucleophile to attack the acyl chloride.

phenyl ethanoate

benzoyl   sodium   phenyl
chloride   phenoxide   benzoate

Reaction with amines

Amines contain nitrogen atoms with a lone pair of electrons. This lone pair of electrons is available to attack the carbonyl carbon atom in acyl chlorides. The reaction is vigorous and the organic product is a substituted amide. For example:

N-methylethanamide

Check-up

4 a Using an acyl chloride as a starting compound in each case, name the reactants you would use to make:
   i ethyl ethanoate
   ii methyl butanoate
   iii phenyl benzoate.
  b Complete the following equation:

$$CH_3CH_2COCl + CH_3CH_2CH_2NH_2$$
$$\rightarrow \underline{\quad\quad} + \underline{\quad\quad}$$

25.3 Reactions to form tri-iodomethane

Tri-iodomethane (iodoform) forms as a yellow precipitate with methyl ketones, i.e. compounds containing the CH_3CO- group (Figure 25.3). Note that ethanal, CH_3CHO, an aldehyde, also contains the CH_3CO- group. Chemists use the appearance of the yellow precipitate as evidence of the CH_3CO- group in an unknown compound.

The reagent used is an alkaline solution of iodine, which is warmed with the substance being tested. The reaction involves two steps:

• the carbonyl compound is halogenated – the three hydrogen atoms in the CH_3 group are replaced by iodine atoms
• the intermediate is hydrolysed to form the yellow precipitate of tri-iodomethane, CHI_3 (Figure 25.3).

When separated from the reaction mixture, the yellow crystals of tri-iodomethane can be positively identified by their melting point of 119 °C.

Figure 25.3 The yellow precipitate of tri-iodomethane forming.

Here R is an alkyl group in a methyl ketone:

$$RCOCH_3 \xrightarrow[\text{halogenation}]{I_2, \text{ NaOH(aq)}} RCOCI_3$$
a methyl ketone

$$\xrightarrow[\text{hydrolysis}]{\text{NaOH(aq)}} RCOO^-Na^+ + CHI_3$$
tri-iodomethane

The tri-iodomethane test is also used for the $CH_3CH(OH)-$ group, as the secondary alcohol is oxidised first of all by the alkaline iodine solution. This oxidation forms a methyl ketone which then reacts as shown above to give the yellow tri-iodomethane precipitate. You should note that there are two organic products formed in this reaction: one is tri-iodomethane and the other is the sodium salt of a carboxylic acid.

Check-up

5 a i When propanone is warmed with alkaline iodine solution, a yellow precipitate is formed. Name and draw the displayed formula of the yellow precipitate.
   ii Give the structural formulae of the organic products formed in both steps of the reaction in part **i**.
  b Explain, naming any organic products formed, why ethanol gives a positive test when warmed with alkaline iodine solution.
  c Which of these compounds will give a yellow precipitate when treated with alkaline aqueous iodine?
    i butanone
    ii butanal
    iii pentan-3-one
    iv pentan-2-one
    v ethanal
    vi methanal

Fact file

The traditional name of tri-iodomethane is iodoform. It can be used as an antiseptic to aid the healing of wounds. It was first synthesised in 1822 but its molecular formula was not worked out until 1834 by the French chemist Jean-Baptiste Dumas.

Summary

☐ Carboxylic acids are weak acids. Their strength is increased if the carbon atom next to the —COOH group has electron-withdrawing atoms, such as chlorine, bonded to it.

☐ Acyl chlorides (RCOCl) are made by reacting carboxylic acids with PCl_5, PCl_3 or $SOCl_2$.

☐ Acyl chlorides are reactive liquids. They are easily hydrolysed by water, forming a carboxylic acid whilst giving off white fumes of hydrogen chloride.

☐ Acyl chlorides also react with alcohols and phenols to give esters and react with amines to give substituted amides. They are more reactive than their corresponding carboxylic acids.

☐ Chemists can use alkaline iodine solution to test for:
  – methyl ketones
  – ethanol or secondary alcohols with an adjacent methyl group.
  A yellow precipitate of tri-iodomethane is formed in a positive test.

End-of-chapter questions

1 Acyl chlorides and carboxylic acids can both be used to prepare esters.
  a i Give the reagents and conditions required to make ethyl ethanoate directly from a carboxylic acid. [3]
    ii Write an equation to show the formation of ethyl ethanoate in part **a i**. [1]
  b i Give the reagents and conditions required to make phenyl benzoate from an acyl chloride. [3]
    ii Write an equation to show the formation of phenyl benzoate in part **b i**. [1]
                                    Total = 8

2 **a** Draw the displayed formula of butanoyl chloride. [1]
  b i Give the name and formula of a reagent that can be used to prepare butanoyl chloride from butanoic acid. [2]
    ii Write a balanced equation for the reaction in part **b i**. [1]
    iii Butanoic acid is a weaker acid than 2-chlorobutanoic acid. Explain why. [2]
    iv Draw the skeletal formula of 2-chlorobutanoic acid. [1]
    v Name a chloro-substituted butanoic acid that is a stronger acid than 2-chlorobutanoic acid. [1]
                                      Total = 8

3 An alcohol has the molecular formula C_3H_8O. When warmed with an alkaline solution of iodine it forms a yellow precipitate.
  a Name the yellow precipitate. [1]
  b Draw the displayed formula of the alcohol. [1]
  c The first stage in the reaction of the alcohol with alkaline iodine solution is an oxidation reaction. Name the organic product of this first stage. [1]
  d There are four isomeric alcohols with the formula C_4H_9OH.
    i Name the four isomeric alcohols. [1]
    ii Classify each one as a primary, secondary, or tertiary alcohol [1]
    iii Which of the four isomeric alcohols will give a yellow precipitate when warmed with an alkaline solution of iodine? [1]
                                      Total = 6

Learning outcomes

Candidates should be able to:

- [ ] describe the formation of ethylamine (by nitrile reduction – see also Chapter **15**, page **233**) and of phenylamine (by the reduction of nitrobenzene)
- [ ] explain the basicity of amines
- [ ] explain the relative basicities of ammonia, ethylamine and phenylamine in terms of their structures
- [ ] describe the reaction of phenylamine with:
  - aqueous bromine
  - nitrous acid to give the diazonium salt and phenol
- [ ] describe the coupling of benzenediazonium chloride and phenol and the use of similar reactions in the formation of dyestuffs
- [ ] describe the formation of amides from the reaction between R^1NH_2 and R^2COCl
- [ ] describe amide hydrolysis on treatment with aqueous alkali or acid
- [ ] describe the acid–base properties of amino acids and the formation of zwitterions
- [ ] describe the formation of peptide bonds between amino acids and, hence, explain protein formation
- [ ] describe the hydrolysis of proteins
- [ ] describe the formation of polyamides (see also Chapter **27**, page **400**).

26.1 Amines

The basicity of amines

There are three classes of amine: primary, secondary and tertiary.

- Primary amines have an $-NH_2$ group bonded to an alkyl or aryl group, e.g. ethylamine, $C_2H_5NH_2$ (Figure **26.2**), or phenylamine, $C_6H_5NH_2$.
- Secondary amines have two alkyl or aryl groups attached to an $-NH-$ group, e.g. dimethylamine, $(CH_3)_2NH$ (Figure **26.3**).
- Tertiary amines have three alkyl or aryl groups attached to the same nitrogen atom, e.g. trimethylamine, $(CH_3)_3N$ (Figure **26.3**).

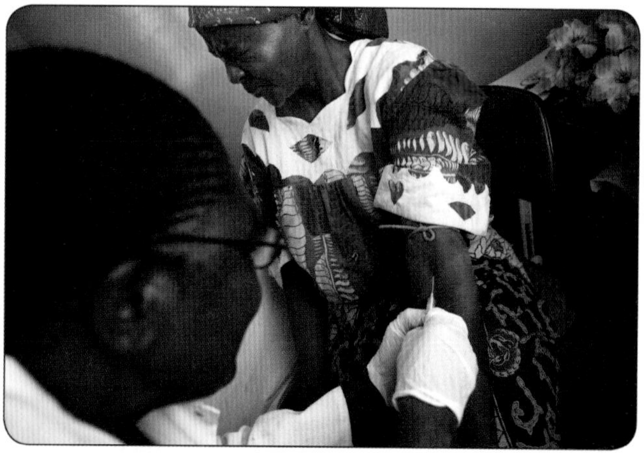

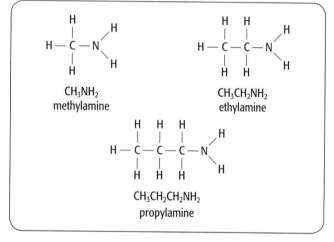

CH_3NH_2
methylamine

$CH_3CH_2NH_2$
ethylamine

$CH_3CH_2CH_2NH_2$
propylamine

Figure 26.2 Three primary amines.

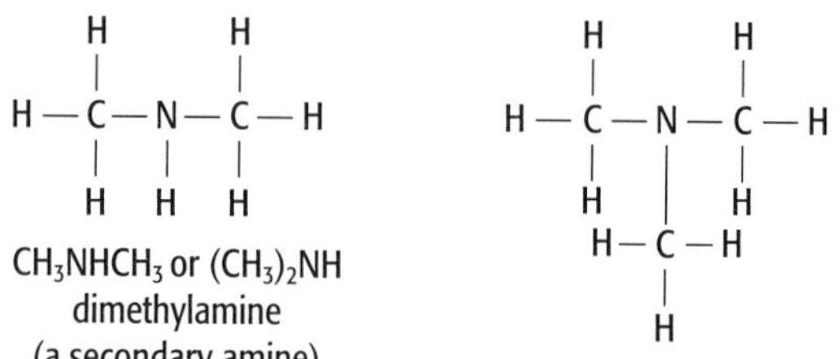

CH_3NHCH_3 or $(CH_3)_2NH$
dimethylamine
(a secondary amine)

$(CH_3)_3N$
trimethylamine
(a tertiary amine)

Figure 26.3 A secondary amine and a tertiary amine.

Figure 26.1 Amines and their derivatives are used in drugs to treat many diseases such as malaria and sleeping sickness.

Fact file

Some primary amines do not have the —NH_2 group at the end of an alkyl chain. We indicate the position of the —NH_2 group on the hydrocarbon chain by numbering from the nearest end of the molecule. In these cases we refer to the —NH_2 group as the 'amino' group, e.g. $CH_3CH_2CHNH_2CH_2CH_2CH_3$ is called 3-aminohexane.

We can think of the amines as substituted ammonia (NH_3) molecules. For example, a primary amine is an ammonia molecule with one of its H atoms replaced by an alkyl or aryl group. Ammonia and the amines act as bases because of the lone pair of electrons on the nitrogen atom. Remember that a base is a proton (H^+ ion) acceptor. The nitrogen atom donates its lone pair to an H^+ ion, forming a co-ordinate (dative) bond.

For ammonia:

$$NH_3 + H^+ \rightarrow NH_4^+$$

For a primary amine:

$$RNH_2 + H^+ \rightarrow RNH_3^+$$

Dilute hydrochloric acid reacts with ammonia and with amines to produce salts.

For ammonia:

$$NH_3 + HCl \rightarrow NH_4^+Cl^-$$
ammonium chloride

For a primary amine:

$$CH_3NH_2 + HCl \rightarrow CH_3NH_3^+Cl^-$$
methylammonium chloride

Ammonia and the amines have different strengths as bases. Their strength as bases depends on the availability of the lone pair of electrons on the N atom to bond with an H^+ ion.

Let us consider ammonia, ethylamine and phenylamine as examples. We find that the strongest base of the three is ethylamine, followed by ammonia and, finally, phenylamine.

Ethylamine is a stronger base than ammonia because the ethyl group is electron-donating in nature (Figure 26.4). By releasing electrons to the N atom, the ethyl group makes the lone pair more readily available to bond with an H^+ ion than it is in ammonia. Ammonia has three H atoms bonded to the N atom.

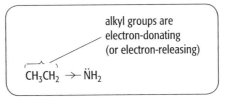

Figure 26.4
Ethylamine is a stronger base than ammonia.

Ammonia is a stronger base than phenylamine because one of the p orbitals on the nitrogen atom in phenylamine overlaps with the π bonding system in the benzene ring. This causes the lone pair of the N atom in phenylamine to be delocalised into the benzene ring. This then makes the lone pair less available to form a co-ordinate bond with an H^+ ion than it is in ammonia (Figure 26.5).

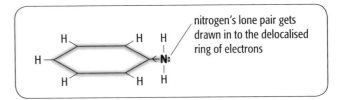

Figure 26.5 Phenylamine is a very weak base.

Check-up

1 **a** Name the following compounds:
    i $CH_3CH_2CH_2CH_2CH_2NH_2$
    ii $(CH_3CH_2CH_2)_2NH$
    iii $C_2H_5NH_3^+Cl^-$
  b Predict whether diethylamine is a stronger or weaker base than ethylamine. Explain your reasoning.

Making amines
Preparing ethylamine

1 In Chapter 15 (page 233) you learned how bromoethane undergoes nucleophilic substitution with ammonia to form a mixture of amines. In order to prepare ethylamine (whilst avoiding the formation of secondary and tertiary amines and ammonium salts) we use excess hot ethanolic ammonia:

$$CH_3CH_2Br + NH_3 \rightarrow CH_3CH_2NH_2 + HBr$$
ethylamine

HBr, which could react with the ethylamine, is removed by the excess ammonia, forming NH_4Br. The excess ammonia also reduces the chances of bromoethane being attacked by ethylamine; ethylamine is also a nucleophile.

2 We also learned in Chapter 15 (pages 232–3) about the formation of nitriles by reacting a halogenoalkane with the CN^- ion. To carry out the reaction, a solution of potassium cyanide, KCN, in ethanol is heated under reflux with the halogenoalkane:

$$CH_3Br + CN^- \rightarrow CH_3CN + Br^-$$
bromomethane ethanenitrile

Notice that we start with bromomethane, not bromoethane, as the cyanide group adds a carbon atom to the alkyl group. We can then reduce (add hydrogen to) the ethanenitrile to make ethylamine. The nitrile and hydrogen gas are passed over a nickel catalyst. Alternatively, sodium and ethanol are used for the reduction:

$$CH_3CN + 4[H] \rightarrow CH_3CH_2NH_2$$
ethylamine

Preparing phenylamine

Phenylamine is made by reducing nitrobenzene. This reduction is carried out by heating nitrobenzene with tin and concentrated hydrochloric acid.

The phenylamine is separated from the reaction mixture by steam distillation (Figure 26.6).

Figure 26.6 Steam generated in the round-bottomed flask is passed into the reaction mixture and phenylamine is distilled off and collected.

Check-up

2 a i Give the reagents and conditions needed to make butylamine from butanenitrile.
   ii Name the bromoalkane that can be used to make the butanenitrile in part **a i**.
  b i Give the name and structural formula of the aryl amine formed when 2-nitrophenol reacts with tin and concentrated hydrochloric acid.
   ii What type of reaction takes place in part **b i**?

Reactions of phenylamine

Phenylamine with aqueous bromine

The reaction of aqueous bromine with phenylamine is similar to the reaction of aqueous bromine with phenol (see page 380); a white precipitate is formed. The nitrogen in the $-NH_2$ group in phenylamine has a lone pair of electrons that can be delocalised into the benzene ring so that the π bonding system extends to include the C—N bond. The extra electron density in the benzene ring makes it more readily attacked by electrophiles. Remember that the 2, 4 and 6 positions around the benzene ring are activated when electron-donating groups, such as $-NH_2$ or $-OH$, are attached to the ring:

2,4,6-tribromophenylamine

Diazotisation and coupling reactions

Phenylamine is an important compound in the synthesis of dyes. The first step is the reaction between phenylamine and nitrous acid (nitric(III) acid), HNO_2, to give a diazonium salt. Nitrous acid is unstable, so it has to be made in the test tube, then the phenylamine is added. We can make the nitrous acid using sodium nitrite (sodium nitrate(III)) and dilute hydrochloric acid:

The first step is the production of benzenediazonium chloride:

$$\text{\textcircled{}}-NH_2 + HNO_2 + HCl \longrightarrow \text{\textcircled{}}-\overset{+}{N}\equiv N\ Cl^- + 2H_2O$$

benzenediazonium
chloride

This reaction is called **diazotisation**. Note that the positive charge on the diazonium ion is on the nitrogen atom with four bonds.

The reaction mixture must be kept below 10 °C by using ice. This is because the diazonium salt is unstable and will decompose easily, giving off nitrogen gas, N_2, at higher temperatures.

In the second step, the diazonium ion reacts with an alkaline solution of phenol in a **coupling** reaction:

$$\text{\textcircled{}}-N_2^+ + \text{\textcircled{}}-OH \longrightarrow \text{\textcircled{}}-N\overset{}{=}N-\text{\textcircled{}}-OH + H^+$$

The positively charged diazonium ion acts as an electrophile. It substitutes into the benzene ring of phenol at the 4 position. An orange dye is formed, called an **azo dye**. The delocalised π bonding system extends between the two benzene rings through the —N=N— group which acts like a 'bridge'. This makes the azo dye, called 4-hydroxyphenylazobenzene, very stable (an important characteristic of a good dye). The azo dye forms immediately on addition of the phenol to the solution containing the diazonium ion (Figure 26.7).

By using alternative aryl compounds to phenol, we can make a range of brightly coloured dyes. For example, Figure 26.8 shows a molecule of a compound used as a yellow dye.

Figure 26.7 The azo dye (also called a diazonium dye) forms in a coupling reaction between the diazonium ion and an alkaline solution of phenol.

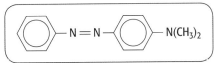

Figure 26.8
A molecule of a yellow azo dye.

Check-up

3 a i Which would be more readily attacked by an electrophile – benzene or phenylamine? Explain your answer.
  ii Write a general equation to show the equation for the reaction of phenylamine with excess of an electrophile, represented as X⁺.
 b i Why is the reaction of phenylamine to make the diazonium ion carried out below 10 °C?
  ii Write a balanced equation to show how nitrous acid is made for the reaction in part **b i** to take place.
  iii Show the two steps that would be used to make the yellow dye shown in Figure 26.8, starting from phenylamine.

26.2 Amides
Making an amide

An amide group is represented in structural formulae by —CONH₂. For example, ethanamide can be shown as CH₃CONH₂. Its displayed formula is:

$$H-\overset{\overset{\displaystyle H}{|}}{\underset{\underset{\displaystyle H}{|}}{C}}-C\overset{\nearrow O}{\searrow_{NH_2}}$$

ethanamide

Ethanamide can be made by reacting ethanoyl chloride with concentrated ammonia solution:

$$CH_3COCl + NH_3 \rightarrow CH_3CONH_2 + HCl$$

On page 387 we saw how a primary amine reacts with an acyl chloride to produce a substituted amide.

$$\underset{\text{butanoyl chloride}}{C_3H_7COCl} + \underset{\text{ethylamine}}{C_2H_5NH_2} \rightarrow \underset{\text{\textit{N}-ethylbutanamide}}{C_3H_7CONHC_2H_5} + HCl$$

Both these reactions occur at room temperature, releasing white fumes of hydrogen chloride immediately as the reactants are added together. If there is an excess of the amine, it will react with the HCl formed to make its salt. For example, in the previous reaction ethylamine will form ethylammonium chloride, $C_2H_5NH_3^+Cl^-$.

Hydrolysis of amides

The characteristic —CONH— group in substituted amides links the two hydrocarbon sections of their molecules together. This link can be broken by hydrolysis with an acid or an alkali. The amide is refluxed with, for example, hydrochloric acid or sodium hydroxide solution, to hydrolyse it:

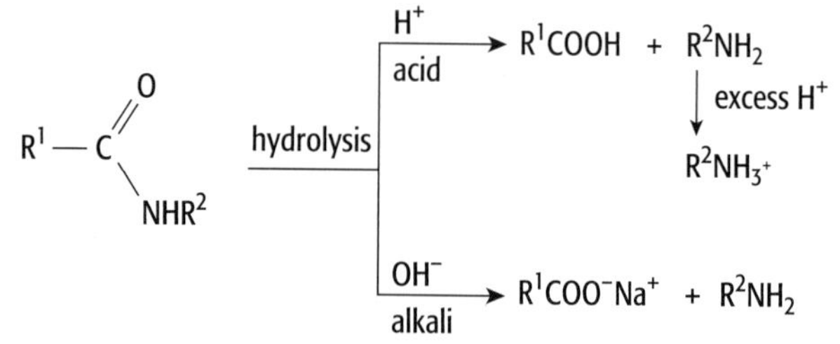

$$R^1-C\underset{NHR^2}{\overset{O}{=}} \xrightarrow{hydrolysis} \begin{cases} \underset{acid}{\overset{H^+}{\longrightarrow}} R^1COOH + R^2NH_2 \xrightarrow{excess\ H^+} R^2NH_3^+ \\ \underset{alkali}{\overset{OH^-}{\longrightarrow}} R^1COO^-Na^+ + R^2NH_2 \end{cases}$$

The products of hydrolysis of a substituted amide with acid are a carboxylic acid (R^1COOH) and a primary amine (R^2NH_2). The amine formed will react with excess acid in the reaction vessel to make its ammonium salt, e.g. $R^2NH_3^+Cl^-$ with excess hydrochloric acid.

With an alkali, such as aqueous sodium hydroxide, the products are the sodium salt of the carboxylic acid ($R^1COO^-Na^+$) and the primary amine (R^2NH_2).

If we reflux an unsubstituted amide ($RCONH_2$) with acid, the products are the corresponding carboxylic acid and ammonia. The ammonia in solution reacts with excess acid to make an ammonium salt.

With an alkali, the products are the salt of the carboxylic acid and ammonia.

26.3 Amino acids

Amino acids are an important group of compounds that all contain the amino group ($-NH_2$) and the carboxylic acid group ($-COOH$). One type of amino acid has the $-NH_2$ group bonded to the C atom next to the $-COOH$ group. These 2-amino-carboxylic acids are the 'building blocks' that make up proteins.

The general structure of a 2-amino-carboxylic acid molecule is shown in Figure 26.9.

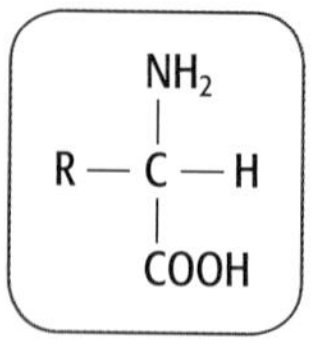

Figure 26.9 The general structure of an amino acid.

The general structural formula of a 2-amino-carboxylic acid is $RCH(NH_2)COOH$.

The R group is the part of the amino acid which can vary in different amino acids. The simplest amino acid is glycine, aminoethanoic acid, in which R is an H atom:

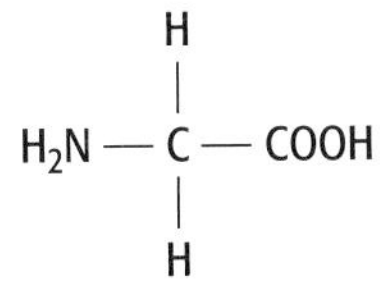

$$\begin{array}{c} H \\ | \\ H_2N - C - COOH \\ | \\ H \end{array}$$

glycine (aminoethanoic acid)

Alanine, 2-aminopropanoic acid, is an amino acid in which the R group is CH_3.

The R group can be acidic (e.g. it contains another —COOH group), basic (e.g. it contains another —NH_2 group) or neutral (e.g. when it is an alkyl group).

Amino acids will undergo most reactions of amines and carboxylic acids. However, each molecule can interact within itself due to its basic —NH_2 group and its acidic —COOH group:

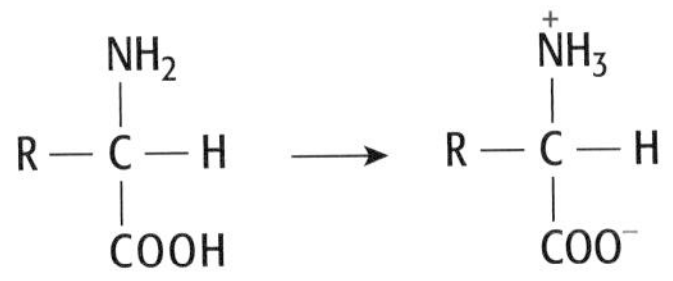

$$\begin{array}{c} NH_2 \\ | \\ R - C - H \\ | \\ COOH \end{array} \longrightarrow \begin{array}{c} \overset{+}{N}H_3 \\ | \\ R - C - H \\ | \\ COO^- \end{array}$$

The ion is called a zwitterion (from the German 'zwei' meaning 'two') as it carries two charges: one positive (—NH_3^+) and one negative (—COO^-). The ionic nature of the zwitterions gives amino acids relatively strong intermolecular forces of attraction. They are crystalline solids which are soluble in water.

A solution of amino acids contains zwitterions which have both acidic and basic properties (i.e. are amphoteric). They will resist changes in pH when small amounts of acid or alkali are added to them. Solutions that do this are called buffer solutions (see pages 311–15).

If acid is added, the —COO^- part of the zwitterion will accept an H^+ ion, re-forming the undissociated —COOH group. This leaves a positively charged ion:

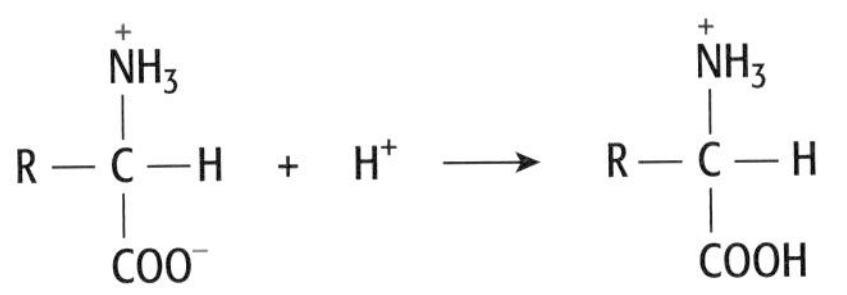

$$\begin{array}{c} \overset{+}{N}H_3 \\ | \\ R - C - H \\ | \\ COO^- \end{array} + H^+ \longrightarrow \begin{array}{c} \overset{+}{N}H_3 \\ | \\ R - C - H \\ | \\ COOH \end{array}$$

If alkali is added, the —NH_3^+ part of the zwitterion will donate an H^+ ion to the hydroxide ion ($H^+ + OH^- \rightarrow H_2O$), re-forming the amine —NH_2 group. This leaves a negatively charged ion:

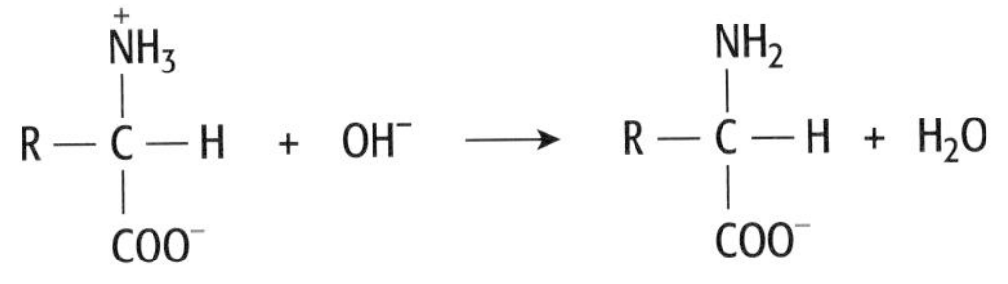

$$\begin{array}{c} \overset{+}{N}H_3 \\ | \\ R - C - H \\ | \\ COO^- \end{array} + OH^- \longrightarrow \begin{array}{c} NH_2 \\ | \\ R - C - H \\ | \\ COO^- \end{array} + H_2O$$

Check-up

5 a i What is the general structural formula of a 2-amino-carboxylic acid?
   ii Why are all amino acids solids at 20 °C?
   b i Draw the displayed formula of the 2-amino-carboxylic acid called serine, in which the R group is HO—CH_2—.
   ii Draw the displayed formula of the zwitterion of serine.
   iii Draw the displayed formula of the ion of serine present in acidic conditions.
   iv Draw the displayed formula of the ion of serine present in alkaline conditions.

26.4 Peptides and proteins

Amino acid molecules can also react with each other; the acidic —COOH group in one molecule reacts with the basic —NH_2 group in another molecule. When two amino acids react together, the resulting molecule is called a **dipeptide**:

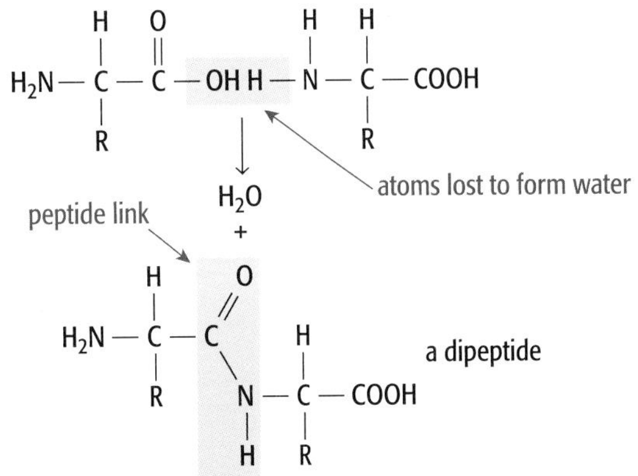

Notice the amide link between the two amino acids. An amide link between two amino acid molecules is also called a peptide link. The reaction is a **condensation reaction** as a small molecule, in this case water, is eliminated when the reactant molecules join together.

You can see that the dipeptide product still has an —NH_2 group at one end and a —COOH group at the other end. Therefore the reaction can continue, forming longer chains of amino acids. The longer molecules become known as polypeptides, and then proteins as they get even longer sequences of amino acids. **Proteins** are natural polymers. In animals and plants, enzymes catalyse these reactions. The proteins are formed by condensation polymerisation reactions. You can learn more about these reactions on page 399 (when we look at how we make synthetic polyamides such as nylon).

We find proteins in muscle (Figure 26.10), hair, skin, blood, nerves and tendons, as well as in enzymes, antibodies and many hormones.

Figure 26.10
Muscle tissue is largely protein, built up from amino acids in your food.

You will often see polypeptides represented by sequences of three-letter abbreviations of the common names of their constituent amino acids. For example, glycine is shown in the sequence as Gly-, alanine as Ala- etc. (Figure 26.11).

Figure 26.11 Here is part of the amino acid sequence of one of the hormones in a sheep:
Ser-Tyr-Ser-Met-Glu-His-Phe-Arg-Try-Gly-Lys-Pro-Val-Gly-Lys ... etc.

Hydrolysis of proteins

As you learned on page 394, the amide or peptide link can be broken down by hydrolysis. In the laboratory we can break down polypeptides and proteins by refluxing them with strong acid or alkali. We can show the hydrolysis of the peptide link as:

$$-\overset{\overset{\displaystyle O}{\|}}{C}-\overset{}{\underset{\overset{\displaystyle |}{H}}{N}}- \ + \ H_2O \ \xrightarrow{\text{hydrolysis}} \ -C\overset{\displaystyle O}{\underset{\displaystyle OH}{<}} \ + \ \overset{\overset{\displaystyle H}{|}}{\underset{\overset{\displaystyle |}{H}}{N}}-$$

With acid reflux, the products of hydrolysis of a peptide are its original 2-amino-carboxylic acids. The amine ($-NH_2$) groups will react with excess acid in the reaction vessel to make their ammonium salts.

With an excess of alkali, such as aqueous sodium hydroxide, refluxing produces the sodium salts of the original 2-amino-carboxylic acids.

Fact file

Human proteins are made from 20 different amino acids. Twelve of these can be made by enzymes in the human body, but eight cannot. These eight amino acids are called the 'essential amino acids', which we must get from our food.

Check-up

6 The R groups in the 2-amino-carboxylic acids alanine and valine are $-CH_3$ and $(CH_3)_2CH-$ respectively.
   a Draw the displayed formula of each of these amino acids.
   b Give an equation to show the formation of a dipeptide made from alanine and valine.
   c What would be the products of the reaction if you refluxed the dipeptide made in part **b** with an excess of aqueous sodium hydroxide?
   d What do we call the type of reaction described in part **c**?

Summary

- Primary amines contain the —NH$_2$ group.
- Ethylamine is prepared either by reducing ethanenitrile, e.g. with hydrogen gas using a nickel catalyst, or by treating bromoethane with an excess of hot, ethanolic ammonia.
- Phenylamine is prepared by reducing nitrobenzene using tin and concentrated hydrochloric acid.
- Like ammonia, amines behave as bases. Because of the lone pair of electrons on their nitrogen atom, they can readily accept protons (H$^+$ ions), reacting to form salts.
- Ethylamine is a stronger base than ammonia because of the electron-releasing ethyl group.
- Phenylamine is a weaker base than ammonia because the lone pair on the N atom of phenylamine is delocalised into the benzene ring.
- Phenylamine reacts with nitrous acid (nitric(III) acid) below 10 °C, to form benzenediazonium chloride and water; this reaction is called diazotisation.
- Diazonium salts react with other aromatic compounds (such as phenol) to form dyes; this is known as a coupling reaction. Diazonium dyes are commercially important.
- The stability of diazonium dyes arises from the extensively delocalised π bonding electron system.
- There are about 20 naturally occurring amino acids (2-amino-carboxylic acids) with the general formula RCH(NH$_2$)COOH, where R may be H, CH$_3$ or another organic group.
- The amino group of an amino acid interacts with the acid group to form a zwitterion.
- Amino acids react with both acids and bases to form salts.
- Two amino acids react together in a condensation reaction, bonding together by a peptide (amide) link to form a dipeptide and water. Repetition of this condensation reaction many times leads to the formation of polypeptides and proteins.
- Proteins or polypeptides are hydrolysed by refluxing in a strong acid, such as HCl(aq), forming 2-amino-carboxylic acids. In hydrolysis using excess alkali, such as NaOH(aq), the sodium salts of the 2-amino-carboxylic acids are formed.

End-of-chapter questions

1 Ethylamine and phenylamine are two organic nitrogen compounds. Both compounds are basic.
   a Draw the displayed formula of each compound, including lone pairs. [2]
   b Write a balanced symbol equation for the reaction between one of these compounds and an acid to form a salt. [2]
   c Which structural feature of each compound accounts for the basicity? [1]
                                  Total = 5

2 Phenylamine can be made using nitrobenzene as starting material.
   a Name this type of reaction. [1]
   b What reagents are used to bring about this change? [2]
   c Write a balanced symbol equation for this reaction. The conventions [O] or [H] may be used if necessary. [2]
                                    Total = 5

3 Phenylamine reacts with nitrous acid (nitric (III) acid) to form a diazonium salt.
  a Which two reagents would you use to prepare the nitrous acid? [2]
  b What are the essential conditions for the reaction? [1]
  c Give the displayed formula of the diazonium salt. [3]
  d Write a balanced symbol equation for this reaction. [2]

  Total = 8

4 The diazonium salt formed in question **3** reacts with phenol to form a useful substance, **X**.
  a What are the essential conditions for the reaction? [2]
  b Give the displayed formula of **X**. [2]
  c Write a balanced symbol equation for this change. [1]
  d Give a possible use for **X**. [1]

  Total = 6

5 The formulae of two amino acids, glycine (Gly) and alanine (Ala), are given here:
  glycine is H_2NCH_2COOH, alanine is $H_2NCH(CH_3)COOH$
  a i Give the systematic names of both amino acids. [2]
     ii Draw their skeletal formulae. [2]
  b Alanine can exist as two stereoisomers.
     i Draw these two stereoisomers, showing how they differ in their spatial arrangements. [2]
     ii Explain why glycine does not have stereoisomers. [2]

  Total = 8

6 Both glycine and alanine are amphoteric.
  a Explain the term **amphoteric**. [1]
  b What structural features of both glycine and alanine enable them to be amphoteric? [4]
  c i Amino acids form zwitterions. Using glycine as an example, explain the term **zwitterion**. [1]
     ii State and explain **two** physical properties of amino acids that can be explained by the existence of zwitterions. [4]
  d Draw the **two** different dipeptides that can be formed when alanine and glycine react together through a condensation reaction. [4]

  Total = 14

7 The structure of a certain tripeptide is shown here:

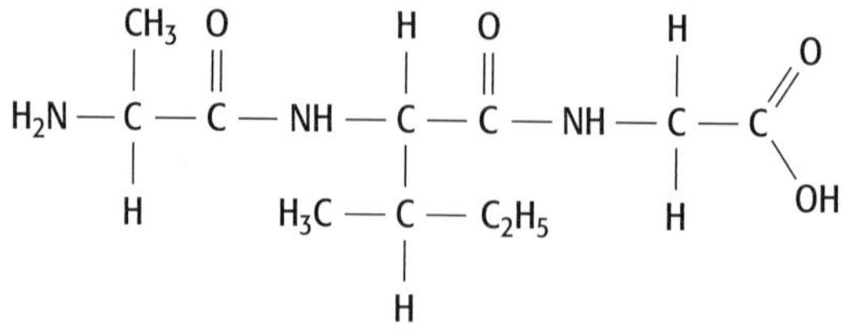

  a i Draw the displayed formulae of the three amino acids that make up the tripeptide. [3]
     ii Which of these amino acids has two chiral carbon atoms? [1]
  b This tripeptide can be split up into the three amino acids by refluxing with aqueous hydrochloric acid.
     i Which bond is broken in this reaction? [1]
     ii The reaction can be described as hydrolysis. Explain why, using a diagram. [3]

  Total = 8

Learning outcomes

Candidates should be able to:

☐ describe the characteristics of condensation polymerisation:
  - in polyesters as exemplified by Terylene
  - in polyamides as exemplified by peptides, proteins, nylon 6 and nylon 6,6
☐ predict the type of polymerisation reaction for a given monomer or pair of monomers

☐ deduce the repeat unit of a polymer obtained from a given monomer or pair of monomers
☐ deduce the type of polymerisation reaction which produces a given section of a polymer molecule
☐ identify the monomer(s) present in a given section of a polymer molecule.

27.1 Types of polymerisation

Addition polymerisation

You have already learned about monomers, polymers, and addition polymerisation in Chapter 14 (page 224). You saw how the polymer poly(ethene) is made when thousands of ethene monomers react together in addition polymerisation:

Remember that the section of the polymer shown inside the brackets is called its repeat unit.

Addition polymerisation is characterised by:
- monomers which are unsaturated, e.g. contain a C=C double bond
- the polymer being the only product of the reaction.

Figure 27.1 Polymers make the plastics we use in everyday life.

Condensation polymerisation

Another type of polymerisation reaction was mentioned in Chapter 26 (page 395). Remember that amino acids can react together to form peptides and proteins. The reaction is called a condensation reaction. We can think of it as an addition reaction (which joins reactant molecules together), followed by an elimination reaction (which releases a small molecule). For example, the following equation shows how three amino acids can react to make a tripeptide:

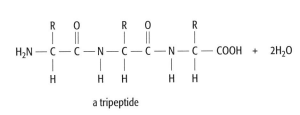

a tripeptide

A large protein molecule, formed by condensation polymerisation, can contain thousands of amino acid monomers. As each amino acid monomer joins the chain a peptide link forms, and an H_2O molecule is also produced (see page 395).
- Condensation polymerisation is characterised by monomers which contain two different functional

groups capable of reacting with each other. This occurs in two ways:

- the two different functional groups are found within the same molecule, as in amino acids; each amino acid monomer molecule has an $-NH_2$ functional group and a $-COOH$ functional group
- the two different functional groups are found in two different molecules; for example, nylon 6,6 is made from two different monomers – one monomer has two $-NH_2$ functional groups and the other monomer has two $-COOH$ functional groups.
- Condensation polymerisation also leads to the formation of small molecules such as H_2O or HCl.

Check-up

1 a Which of these monomers form addition polymers and which form condensation polymers?
   A $NH_2CH(CH_3)COOH$
   B $CH_2=CHC_6H_5$
   C $CH_2=CHCOOH$
   D NH_2CH_2COOH
   E $CH_3CH(OH)COOH$
  b Explain the basis of your decisions in part **a**.
  c i Write an equation to show the polymerisation reaction between propene molecules.
   ii What type of polymerisation reaction is shown in part **c i**?
   iii What is the repeat unit of poly(propene)?

27.2 Polyamides

Proteins have their monomers bonded to each other via peptide links (also called amide links, see page **395**). This means that polypeptides and proteins are types of **polyamide**.

For the last 80 years, chemists have used condensation polymerisation to make synthetic polyamides. For example, nylon is a polyamide. Nylon can be made from a variety of monomers, but all

nylons are made in reactions between the amine group ($-NH_2$) and a carboxylic acid ($-COOH$) or acyl chloride group ($-COCl$).

For example, 1,6-diaminohexane reacts with hexanedioic acid to make nylon 6,6:

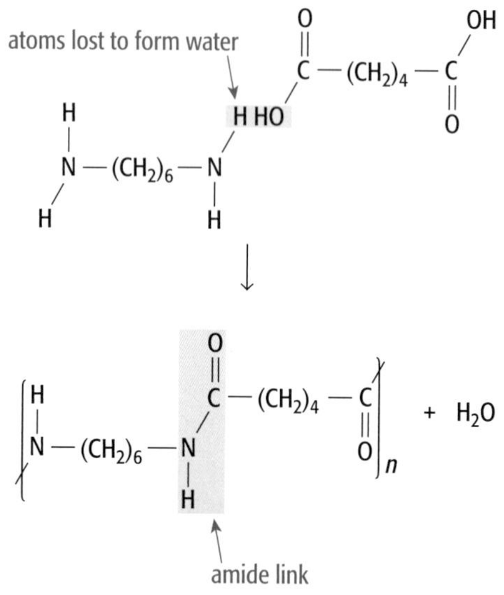

amide link

6,6 refers to the number of carbon atoms from each monomer unit.

Hexanedioyl dichloride, $ClOC(CH_2)_4COCl$, can be used as a more reactive, but more expensive, monomer than hexanedioic acid.

Nylon 6 is the only example of a nylon polymer that is not formed by a condensation reaction; instead it is made from the compound caprolactam which is a cyclic amide. When heated in an atmosphere of nitrogen the ring breaks open at the amide group. The resulting chains join together to make nylon 6 (Figure 27.2).

Note that caprolactam is made from 6-aminohexanoic acid with its $-NH_2$ group and $-COOH$ group, at either end of the molecule. They react with each other in a condensation reaction, releasing water. It is easier to visualise the formation of nylon 6 as the condensation

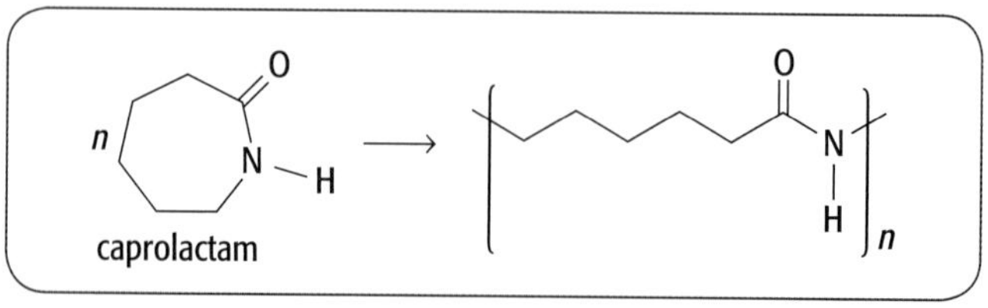

caprolactam

Figure 27.2 Nylon 6 is not formed by condensation polymerisation as no small molecule is given off. The reaction is called 'ring-opening' polymerisation.

polymerisation of 6-aminohexanoic acid (which would follow the usual pattern of condensation polymerisation to form a polyamide).

Nylon's low density, its strength and its elasticity make it a very useful fibre in the clothing industry. These properties also make it ideal for climbing ropes (Figure 27.3).

Figure 27.3 During the manufacturing process, the nylon is forced out of nozzles and pulled into long fibres. This is called 'cold drawing'. It lines up the nylon polymer chains along the length of the fibre. Strong hydrogen bonds form between neighbouring chains, accounting for nylon's high tensile strength and elasticity. Climbers rely on these properties to minimise the effects of a fall.

Fact file

Wallace Carothers invented nylon in 1935. Its name is a trademark of Du Pont Chemicals. Nylon was used to make parachutes in World War II. Parachutes were made out of silk up until then. However, Japan, one of the main suppliers of silk, became involved in the conflict so nylon became a cheaper and stronger alternative.

Carothers was prone to depression. He committed suicide in 1937 by swallowing cyanide from a phial he carried around with him at all times.

Check-up

2   Different types of nylon are identified by the number of carbon atoms in each of its monomers, with the diamine quoted first, followed by the dicarboxylic acid.

   a   Draw the skeletal formula of each monomer used to make nylon 6,10.

   b   Use the skeletal formulae in part **a** to draw an equation showing the condensation polymerisation to make nylon 6,10 from a diamine and a dicarboxylic acid.

   c   i   Draw the skeletal formula of an alternative monomer to the dicarboxylic acid drawn in part **a** to make nylon 6,10.

      ii   What would be the other product of the polymerisation reaction using the alternative monomer?

27.3 Polyesters

Polyesters are another type of condensation polymer. As you learned in Chapter 16 (page 241), esters are made by reacting carboxylic acids with alcohols:

carboxylic acid + alcohol → ester + water

Therefore, polyesters can be made by reacting dicarboxylic acids with diols, e.g. propanedioic acid and ethane-1,2-diol. The most common polyester fibre is Terylene®. Terylene is made from benzene-1,4-dicarboxylic acid and ethane-1,2-diol. The conditions required are a catalyst such as antimony(III) oxide at a temperature of about 280 °C:

Poly(lactic acid), PLA, is another polyester. However, PLA is made using just one monomer, lactic acid. Its systematic name is 2-hydroxypropanoic acid. The monomer contains the carboxylic acid and alcohol groups within each molecule:

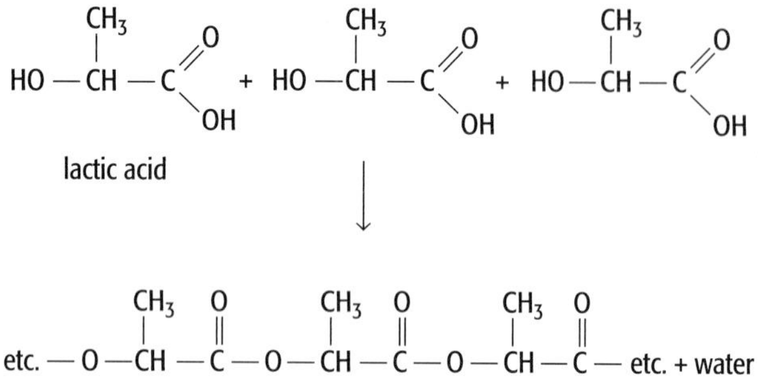

lactic acid

poly(lactic acid)

Check-up

3 a Draw the repeat unit of the polyester, PLA (shown above).
b Draw the repeat unit of Terylene.

Fact file

- Terylene was invented in the 1950s and was the fibre used to make the first non-crease fabrics (the traditional name for benzene-1,4-dicarboxylic acid was terephthalic acid).
- Benzene-1,4-dicarboxylic acid is also used to make the polymer PET for plastic recyclable bottles.
- The polyester PLA, whose raw material is starch from crops such as corn, is now being used as a biodegradable alternative to oil-based plastics.

27.4 Polymer deductions

In your exam, you can be given a variety of different problems about polymers to solve:

1 predict the type of polymerisation reaction for a given monomer or pair of monomers
2 deduce the repeat unit of a polymer obtained from a given monomer or pair of monomers
3 deduce the type of polymerisation reaction which produces a given section of a polymer molecule
4 identify the monomer(s) present in a given section of a polymer molecule.

Predicting the type of polymerisation reaction for given monomer(s).

Addition polymers

Given a monomer which contains the $C=C$ double bond, it will undergo addition polymerisation. Many addition polymers are made using one type of monomer, e.g. poly(propene) from propene monomers. However, co-polymers can also be produced by using more than one type of unsaturated monomer, e.g. $CH_2=CH_2$ and $CH_2=CHCOOH$.

Condensation polymers

When identifying monomers used in condensation polymerisation, look out for the presence of two functional groups that will react with each other, giving off a small molecule in the reaction. These two functional groups can be in the same molecule, as in the case of poly(lactic acid) on the next page, or at either end of two different monomers, as in nylon 6,6 on page 400. The functional groups involved in condensation polymerisation are usually:

- amines ($-NH_2$) and carboxylic acids ($-COOH$) producing a polyamide and H_2O
- amines ($-NH_2$) and acyl chlorides ($-COCl$) producing a polyamide and HCl
- carboxylic acids ($-COOH$) and alcohols ($-OH$) producing a polyester and H_2O.

Deducing the repeat unit of a polymer for given monomer(s)

Addition polymers

Given a monomer with a $C=C$ bond, simply turn the double bond into a $C-C$ single bond and show the bonds either side of the two C atoms that would continue the chain:

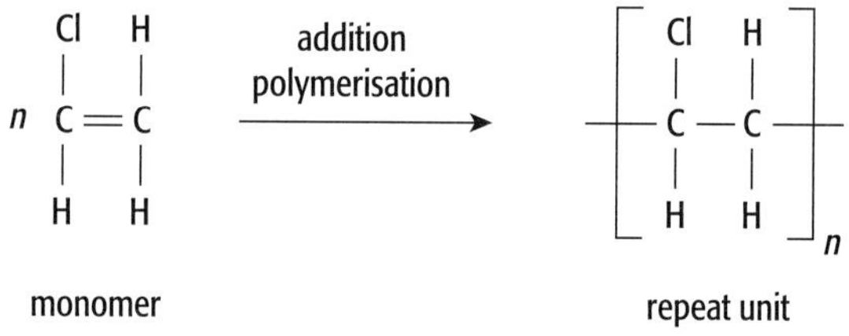

monomer   repeat unit

Condensation polymers

Given monomers with two reactive functional groups, draw the product formed when two monomers react together. Then take off the atoms at both ends that would be lost if another two monomers were to react with those groups.

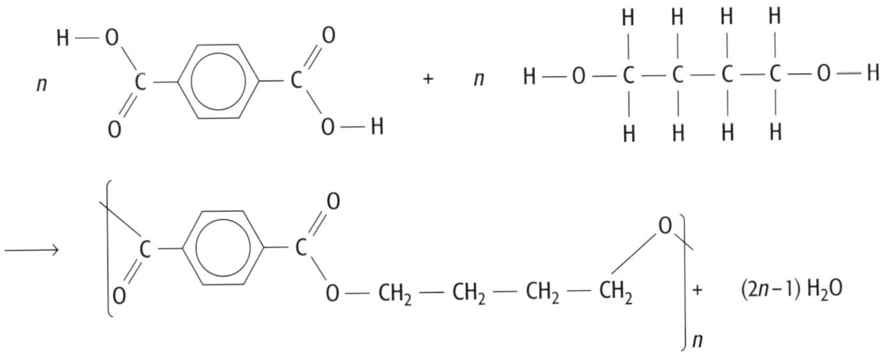

n HOOC—C$_6$H$_4$—COOH $+$ n HO—CH$_2$—CH$_2$—CH$_2$—CH$_2$—OH

$\longrightarrow$ [—OC—C$_6$H$_4$—CO—O—CH$_2$—CH$_2$—CH$_2$—CH$_2$—O—]$_n$ $+$ $(2n-1)$ H$_2$O

Deducing the type of polymerisation reaction for a given section of a polymer molecule

Addition polymers

Polymers resulting from addition polymerisation will have repeat units with no functional groups in the actual chain of carbon atoms that forms the 'backbone' of the polymer. Poly(phenylethene) is an example:

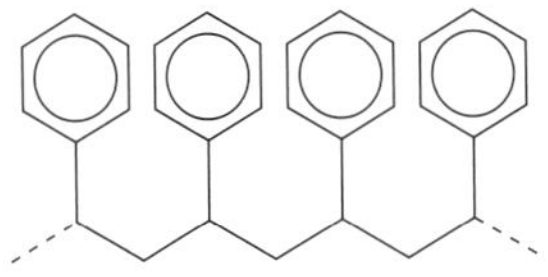

poly(phenylethene)

Note that functional groups may be present on the side-chains, such as the nitrile group, —CN. However, the 'backbone' in addition polymers usually consists of a chain of carbon atoms.

Condensation polymers

Polymers resulting from condensation polymerisation will have amide links (—CONH—) or ester links (—COO—) in the 'backbone' of the polymer chain. For example:

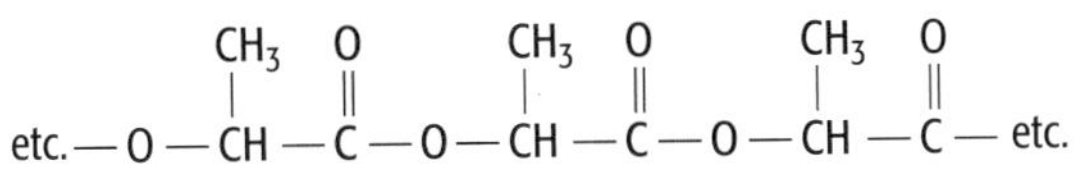

etc.—O—CH(CH$_3$)—C(=O)—O—CH(CH$_3$)—C(=O)—O—CH(CH$_3$)—C(=O)—etc.

Identifying the monomer(s) present in a given section of a polymer molecule

This is an extension of the approach above. Having decided whether the polymer was made in an addition or a condensation polymerisation, you can then split the polymer chain into its repeat units.

Addition polymers

With an addition polymer, you need to put the C=C double bond back into the monomer:

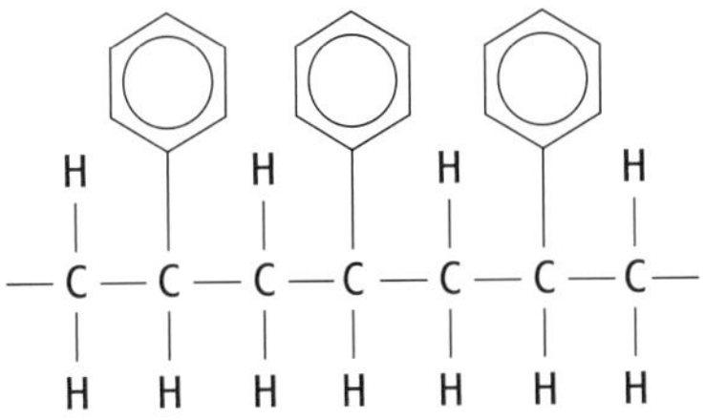

part of addition polymer

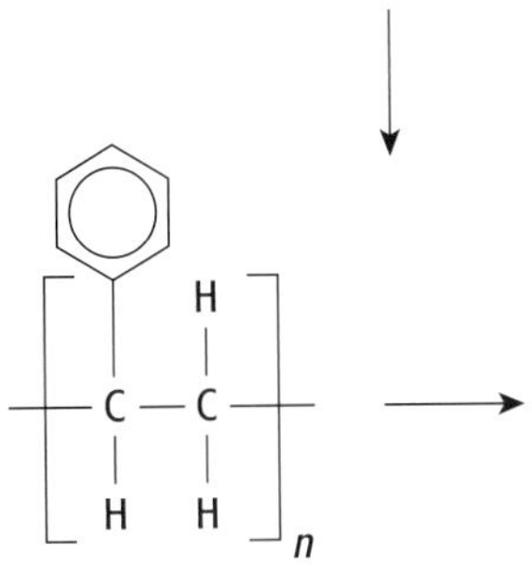

repeat unit 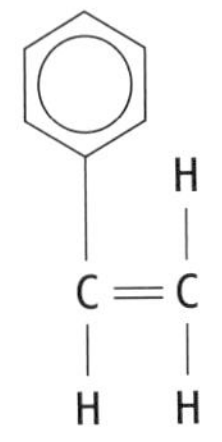 → monomer

Condensation polymers

With condensation polymers, you need to identify the atoms from the small molecules given off in the polymerisation reaction and replace them on the reactive functional groups in the monomers.

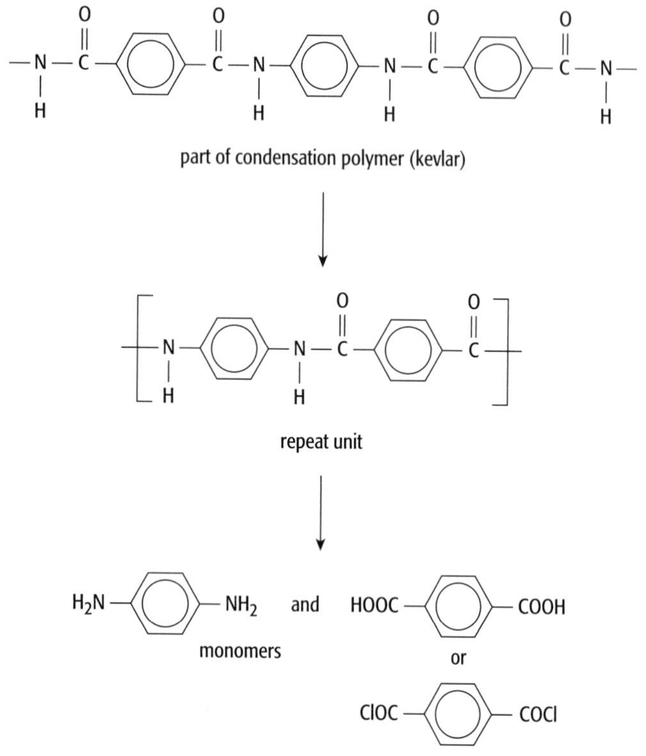

part of condensation polymer (kevlar)

repeat unit

H₂N— ⬡ —NH₂   and   HOOC— ⬡ —COOH

monomers

or

ClOC— ⬡ —COCl

Check-up

4 a Name the monomer used to make this polymer:

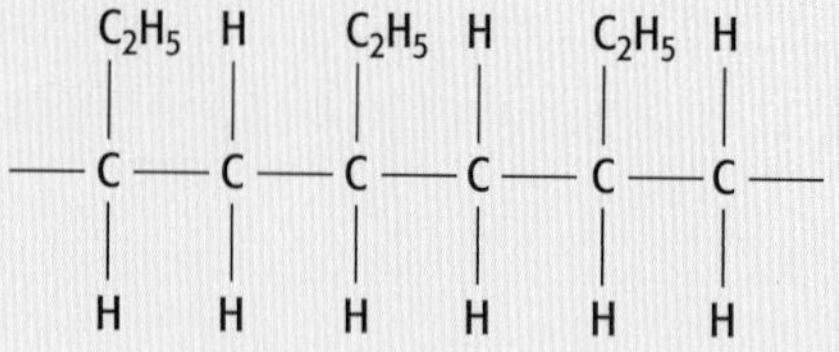

   b i What type of polymerisation reaction formed the polymer shown below?

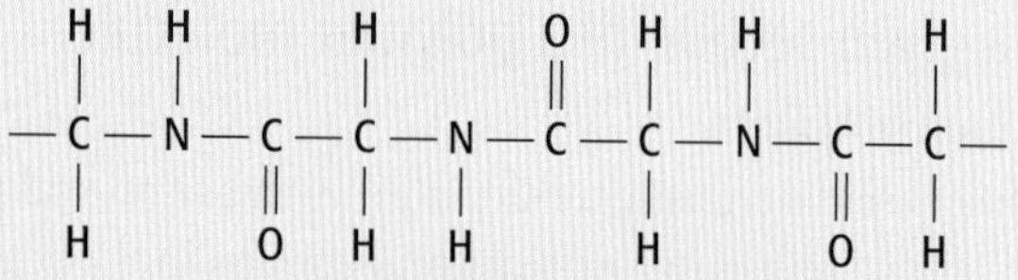

      ii Draw the displayed formula of the single monomer used to make the polymer shown in part **b i**.

Summary

☐ Polymers are very large molecules that are built up from a very large number of small molecules known as monomers.

☐ Addition polymerisation occurs when an unsaturated monomer, such as an alkene, bonds to itself in an addition reaction. Poly(ethene), poly(chloroethene) and poly(phenylethene) are all addition polymers.

☐ Condensation polymerisation involves the loss of a small molecule (usually water) in the reaction between two monomer molecules. Both polyesters and polyamides are formed by condensation polymerisation.

☐ Polyamides are formed by condensation polymerisation between an amine group and a carboxylic acid group. These groups may be in the same monomer or on different monomers. Nylon 6,6 is formed in a condensation polymerisation between 1,6-diaminohexane and hexanedioic acid. Nylon 6 is formed by heating caprolactam, which is produced from 6-aminohexanoic acid in a condensation reaction. The numbers in the name of a particular nylon refer to the number of carbon atoms in the monomers.

☐ Condensation polymerisation between the amino and carboxylic acid groups in amino acids produces a polypeptide or protein. The amide links in these polymers are known as peptide links.

☐ The polyester called Terylene® is formed by condensation polymerisation of benzene-1,4-dicarboxylic acid with ethane-1,2-diol. H_2O is also produced in the reaction.

End-of-chapter questions

1 a Explain the term **condensation polymer**.   [2]
   b Kevlar is a condensation polymer which is used for making bullet-proof vests. Here are two
      monomers that could be used for making Kevlar:

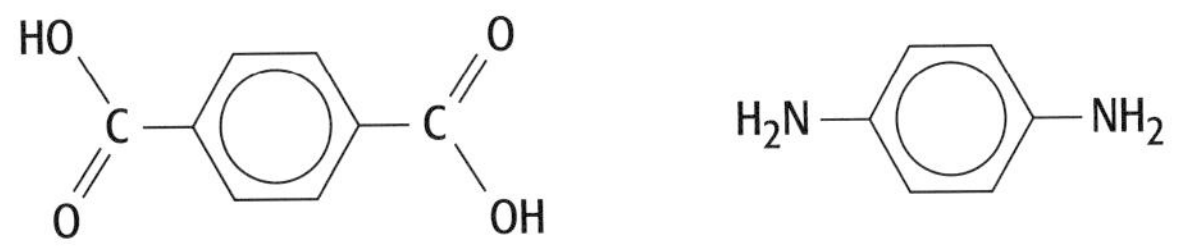

      i   Explain the term **monomer**.   [1]
      ii Give the structure of Kevlar, showing the repeat unit.   [2]
      iii What type of condensation polymer is Kevlar?   [1]
   c Explain how the chains of Kevlar are held together to make such a strong material.   [3]
                                                                                             Total = 9

2 a Polyesters are condensation polymers. Give the structures of two monomers that could be used
      to give a polyester.   [2]
   b Give the structure of the polyester formed from these two monomers.   [2]
                                                                                             Total = 4

3 a Glycine is an amino acid with the formula H_2NCH_2COOH.
      i   Give the systematic name for glycine.   [1]
      ii Give the structure of the polymer that could be formed from glycine showing at least two
          repeat units.   [2]
      iii Name the linkage between the repeat units.   [1]
      iv What type of attractive force forms between the chains of poly(glycine)?   [1]
   b 3-hydroxypropanoic acid is capable of forming polymers.
      i   Give the structure of 3-hydroxypropanoic acid.   [1]
      ii Give the structure of the polymer formed from this acid, showing at least two repeat units.   [2]
      iii Name the linkage present in the polymer.   [1]
      iv What type of attractive force forms between chains of poly(3-hydroxypropanoic acid)?   [1]
                                                                                             Total = 10

4 Sections of some polymers are shown below. For each polymer:
      i   identify the repeat unit
      ii give the structures of the monomers used to make the polymer.

   a   [3]

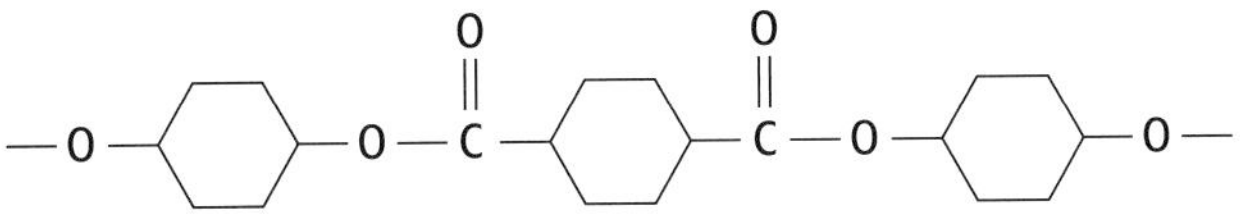

   b   [3]

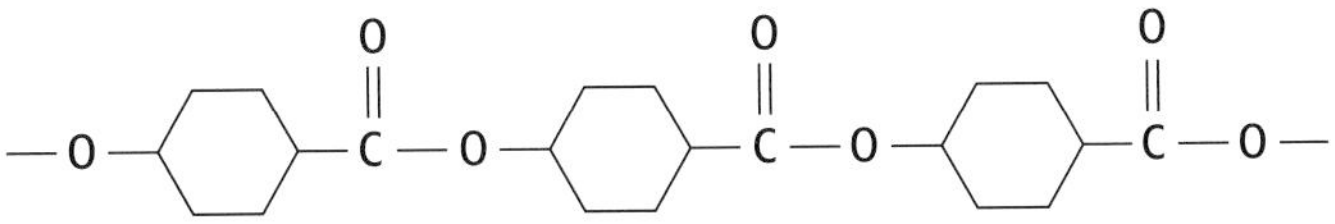

c 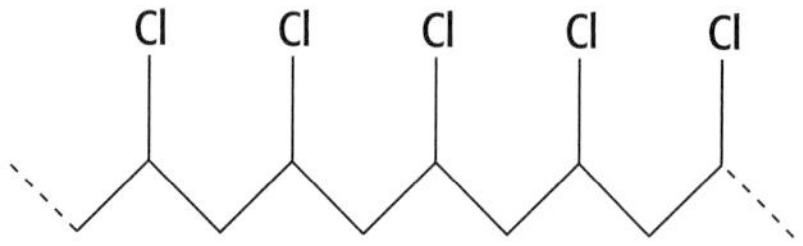
[2]

d 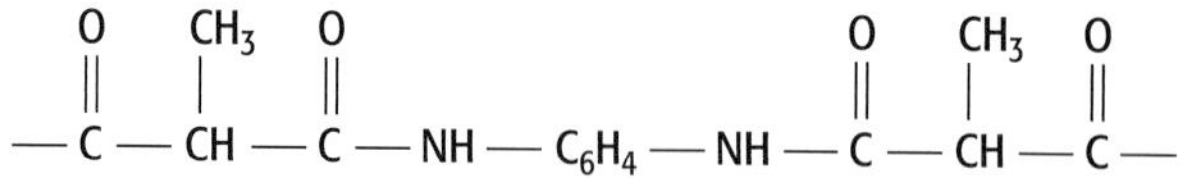
[3]

e 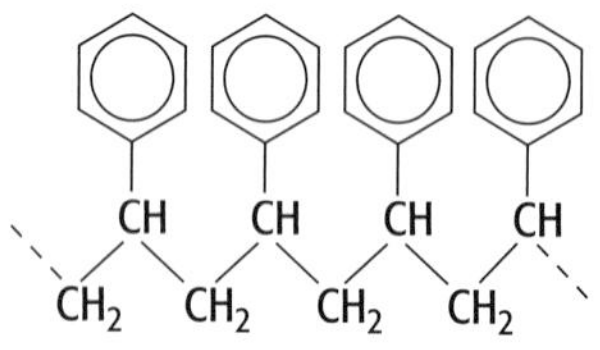
[2]

Total = 13

5　Give the structures of the polymers formed from the monomers given below, showing at least two repeat units. For each polymer identify the following:

  i　the repeat unit

  ii　the type of linkage present

  iii　the attractive force between the polymer chains.

a 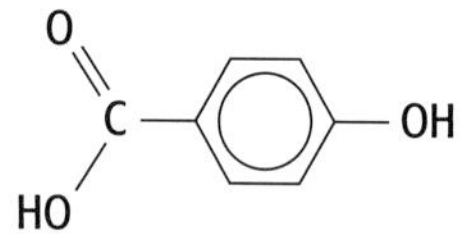
[3]

b 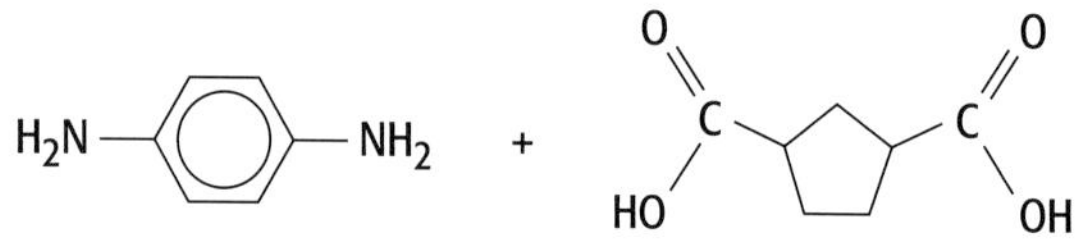
[3]

Total = 6

28 The chemistry of life

Learning outcomes

Candidates should be able to:

☐ recall that proteins are condensation polymers formed from amino acid monomers

☐ recognise and describe the generalised structure of amino acids

☐ explain the importance of amino acid sequence (primary structure) in determining the properties of proteins

☐ distinguish between primary, secondary and tertiary structure of proteins

☐ explain the stabilisation of secondary and tertiary structure using chemistry learned in the core syllabus (hydrogen bonding, ionic bonding and van der Waals' forces)

☐ describe and explain the characteristics of enzyme catalysis including

  – specificity (using a simple lock and key model) and the idea of competitive inhibition

  – structural integrity in relation to denaturation and non-competitive inhibition

☐ use core chemistry to explain how small molecules interact with proteins and how they can modify the structure and functions of biological systems, for example

  – as enzyme inhibitors or cofactors

  – disrupting protein–protein interactions

  – blocking ion channels

☐ describe the double helical structure of DNA in terms of a sugar–phosphate backbone and attached bases

☐ explain the significance of hydrogen bonding in the pairing of bases in DNA in relation to the replication of genetic information

☐ explain in outline how DNA encodes for the amino acid sequence of proteins with reference to mRNA, tRNA and the ribosome in transcription and translation

☐ explain the chemistry of DNA mutation from provided data

☐ discuss the genetic basis of disease (for example sickle-cell anaemia) in terms of altered protein structure and function

☐ explain how modification to protein/enzyme primary structure can result in new structure and/or function

☐ outline, in terms of the hydrolysis of ATP to ADP + P_i, the provision of energy for the cell

☐ understand why some metals are essential to life and, given information, be able to explain the chemistry involved, e.g. iron in haemoglobin, sodium and potassium in the transmission of nerve impulses, zinc as an enzyme cofactor

☐ recognise that some metals are toxic and discuss, in chemical terms, the problems associated with heavy metals in the environment entering the food chain, for example mercury.

28.1 Introduction

Many animal cells have a similar basic structure. Figure 28.2 shows the general features of an animal cell. Each part of a cell has a particular job.

- **Cell membrane:** controls the passage of ions, molecules and water into and out of the cell. The nucleus and mitochondria are also surrounded by membranes.
- **Cytoplasm:** many enzyme-catalysed reactions occur here.
- **Mitochondria:** the site of many of the redox reactions taking place in respiration. The energy transfer molecule, ATP, is synthesised here (see page 432).
- **Nucleus:** contains the genetic material, DNA.
- **Ribosomes:** structures found in the cytoplasm that are the site of protein synthesis.

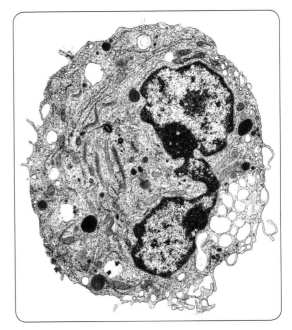

Figure 28.1 Animal cells are complex structures containing a nucleus, cytoplasm, mitochondria and ribosomes.

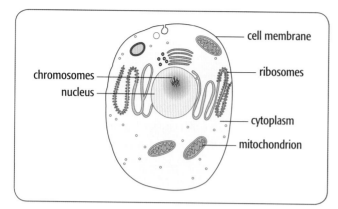

Figure 28.2 The basic structure of an animal cell.

The sequence of linked chemical reactions that take place in the cell is called **metabolism**. The individual chemicals involved in these sequences of reactions are called metabolites.

28.2 Reintroducing amino acids and proteins

The structure of amino acids

In Chapter 26 (page 394) you studied the chemistry of amino acids. The amino acids found in proteins are α-amino acids (Figure 28.3). The names of the amino acids found in proteins can be written in a shorthand form containing three letters. For example Ala is alanine, Try is tryptophan and Gln is glutamine. Proline (Pro) is different from the other amino acids in that it is a secondary amino acid.

The 20 different amino acids that cells use to build proteins are distinguished by their side-chains (R groups). The side-chains can be classified as non-polar, polar or electrically charged (acidic or basic). Table 28.1 shows some examples.

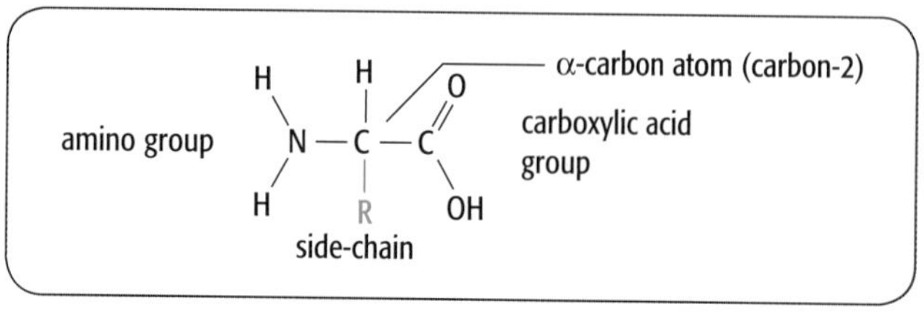

Figure 28.3 The generalised structure of an amino acid, highlighting the key features.

Type of side-chain	Example	Structure
non-polar	alanine (Ala)	$NH_2 - C - COOH$ with H above and CH_3 below
	valine (Val)	$NH_2 - C - COOH$ with H above and CH below, branching to CH_3 CH_3
polar	serine (Ser)	$NH_2 - C - COOH$ with H above and CH_2OH below
electrically charged (acidic or basic)	aspartic acid (Asp)	$NH_2 - C - COOH$ with H above and CH_2COOH below
	lysine (Lys)	$NH_2 - C - COOH$ with H above and $(CH_2)_4NH_2$ below

Table 28.1 Examples of the three different classes of side-chains (in red) in the amino acids found in proteins.

Fact file

Proline (Figure 28.4), one of the amino acids found in proteins, is a secondary amino acid. Its cyclic side-chain is bonded to both the nitrogen and α carbon atom of the amino group. Strictly speaking it is an imino acid.

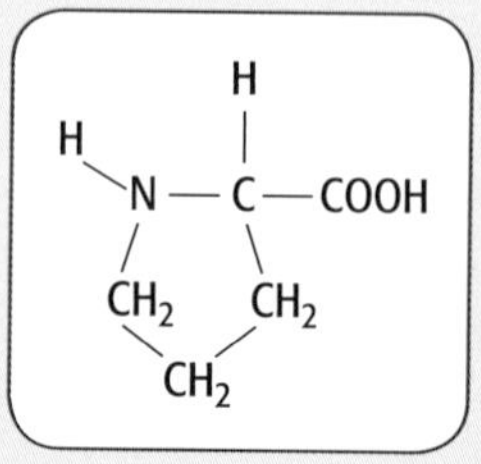

Figure 28.4 The structure of proline.

Proline plays an important part in protein structure. It is often found at the bends linking α-helical or β-pleated sheet sections of proteins (see page 411).

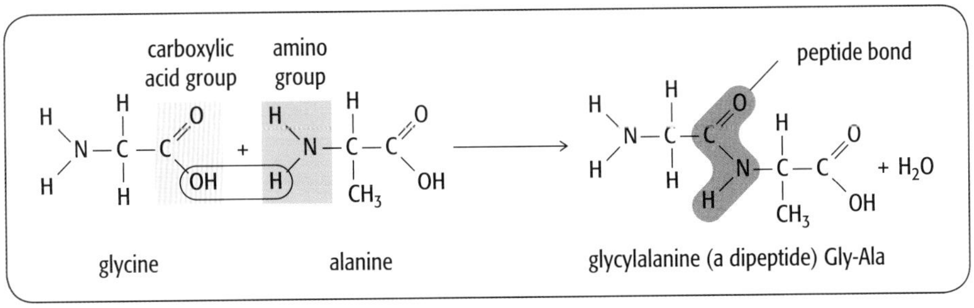

Figure 28.5 The formation of a Gly-Ala dipeptide.

Amino acids are amphoteric – they show both acidic and basic properties, depending on conditions. The pH of many body tissues is near pH 7. At this pH both the $-NH_2$ and the $-COOH$ groups of the amino acid are ionised. So at pH 7 an amino acid, e.g. glycine, exists in a charged form in which the + and – charges are balanced:

$$^+NH_3CH_2COO^-$$

- in acidic conditions amino acids become positively charged
- in alkaline conditions amino acids become negatively charged.

Proteins are condensation polymers

On page **395** you learnt that the $-NH_2$ group of one amino acid can react with the $-COOH$ of another amino acid to form a dipeptide by a condensation reaction. The bond formed is called a peptide bond (amide link). Figure **28.5** shows the formation of a dipeptide from glycine and alanine.

Additional amino acids can then react to form a tripeptide, a tetrapeptide and so on. Eventually a **polypeptide**, containing many **peptide bonds**, is formed.

The four atoms in the peptide bond are all in the same plane, with all bonds angles of approximately 120° (Figure **28.6**). There is no rotation around the C–N bond in a peptide group.

Make sure that you can do the Check-up questions here before continuing with this chapter. Refer back to Chapter **26** (page **394**) if you need some help.

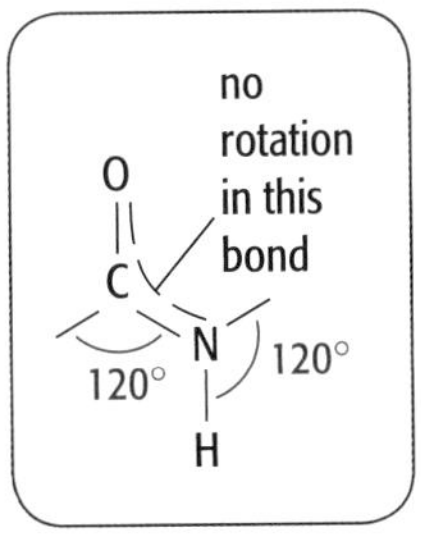

Figure 28.6 The structure of a peptide bond.

Check-up

1 a Name and give the formulae of the two functional groups present in all amino acids.
   b Which of the 20 amino acids found in proteins is a secondary amino acid and what is distinctive about its structure?
   c Name an example of the following types of amino acid:
      i   an amino acid with a non-polar side-chain
      ii an amino acid with a $-COOH$ group on its side-chain.
   d Draw the formula for the dipeptide leucyl alanine (Leu-Ala) using these formulae:

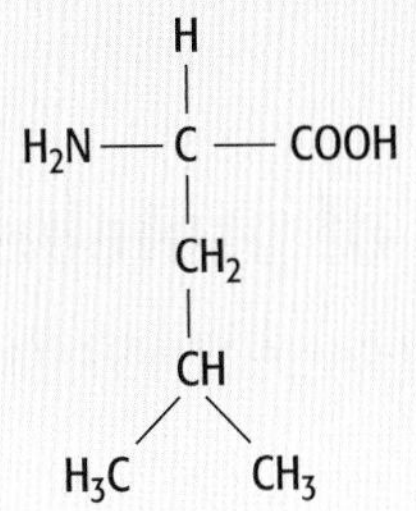

leucine 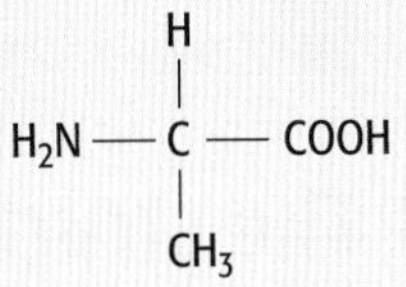   alanine

   e The formula of glutamic acid is:

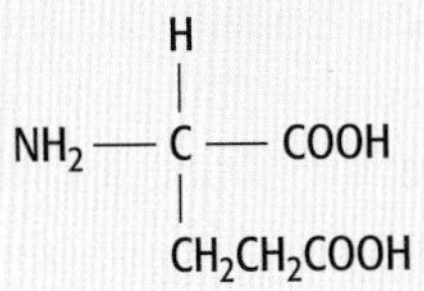

Draw the structural formula of the ion formed when glutamic acid is dissolved in alkali.

A polypeptide chain may contain 50 to 2000 amino acids. An amino acid unit within a polypeptide chain is called an **amino acid residue**. We draw the amino acid

Protein(s)	Function	Where found
myosin/actin	muscle contraction	muscle tissue
pepsin	digestive enzyme	stomach
collagen	structural protein	skin/ tendon
insulin	hormone	blood
haemoglobin	oxygen transport	red blood cells
immunoglobins	antibodies	blood plasma

Table 28.2 Some important proteins.

sequence in a polypeptide starting from the end which has a free $-NH_2$ group (the N-terminal end).

$$NH_2-\square-CONH-\ldots-\square-CONH-\square-COOH$$

Proteins may contain one or more polypeptide chains. Some important facts about proteins are:
- proteins are formed by condensation polymerisation
- the polypeptide chain in proteins is unbranched
- each protein has a unique sequence of amino acids
- the sequence of amino acids is determined by DNA (see page 427)
- each protein has a particular biological function.

The names and functions of some important proteins are given in Table 28.2.

28.3 The structure of proteins

The structure of a protein molecule is described in three parts, or levels.
- **Primary structure**: the sequence of amino acids in the polypeptide chain.
- **Secondary structure**: a regular structural arrangement stabilised by hydrogen bonding between the —NH group of one peptide bond and the —CO group of another peptide bond.
- **Tertiary structure**: the further folding of the polypeptide chain into a 3-dimensional shape. This 3-D shape is stabilised by attractive forces and bonding between the amino acid side-chains (R groups).

Each protein has its own, unique, function because each protein has its own, unique, 3-dimensional shape.

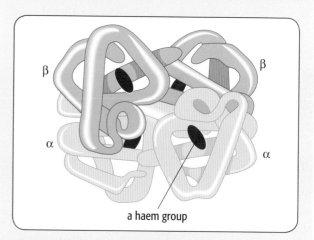
Primary structure

The primary structure is the order in which the amino acids are linked together. The primary structure of one of the polypeptide chains of insulin is shown in Figure 28.8. The primary structure of a protein
- is written with the amino acids numbered from the N-terminal end
- determines the way that the protein can fold to form its secondary and tertiary structure
- is held together by covalent bonds. These bonds are found within amino acid residues, and between the residues as peptide linkages.

(In Figure 28.8 there are —S—S—links (disulfide bridges) between two amino acid residues. These help maintain the *tertiary* structure.)

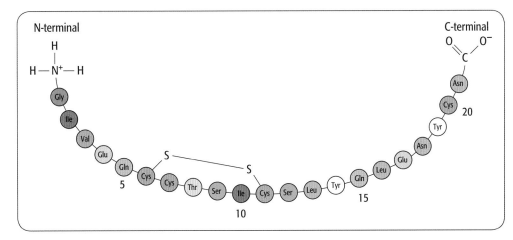

Figure 28.8 The primary sequence of the insulin A chain, a short polypeptide of 21 amino acids.

Secondary structure

Secondary structure describes regions of the polypeptide chain where there is a particular arrangement of the amino acid residues. The structure is stabilised by hydrogen bonding between the —NH group of one peptide bond and the —CO group of another peptide bond. The side-chains of the amino acids are not involved. Two types of secondary structure are:
- the α-helix (alpha-helix)
- β-pleated sheet (beta-pleated sheet).

The α-helix

Each polypeptide chain has a 'backbone' of atoms (—C—C—N—C—C—N—) which runs along the chain. Some points on the chain are flexible and allow free rotation around the bonds (Figure 28.9).

In the α-helix the backbone twists round in a spiral so that a rod-like structure is formed. All the —NH and —CO groups of each peptide bond are involved in hydrogen bond formation. The hydrogen bonds lie parallel with the long axis of the helix with each —NH group forming a weak intermolecular link to a —CO group four amino acid residues further along the backbone (Figure 28.10). The large number of hydrogen bonds in the same direction stabilises the structure. The side-chains of the amino acid residues stick out on the outside of the helix.

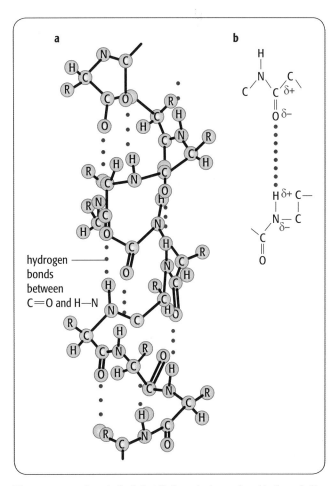

Figure 28.10 a An α-helix. b Detail of one hydrogen bond in the α-helix.

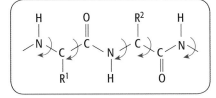

Figure 28.9 There is free rotation around the bonds either side of the peptide group. R^1 and R^2 represent the amino acid side-chains.

The β-pleated sheet

In a β-pleated sheet, hydrogen bonds are formed between —NH and —CO groups in different polypeptide chains or different areas of the same polypeptide chain. Figure 28.11 shows the β-pleated sheet in the structural protein, silk. A fairly flat sheet-like structure is formed.

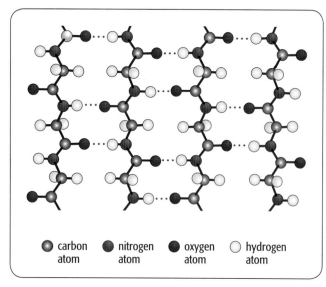

Figure 28.11 A β-pleated sheet in silk. The hydrogen bonds are formed between separate polypeptide chains.

Proteins may have a mixture of secondary structures

Regions of regular secondary structure occur in many proteins. Figure 28.12 shows a computer graphic of pepsin, a digestive enzyme found in the stomach. The structure of pepsin has:

- α-helical regions (represented by the cylindrical rods)
- β-pleated regions (represented by arrows).

Between the regions of secondary structure there are bends (β turns) and apparently randomly coiled regions.

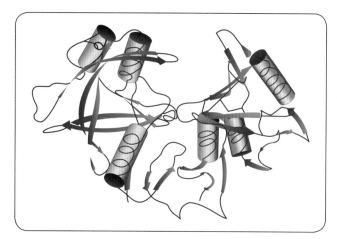

Figure 28.12 A computer graphic model of the structure of pepsin.

Fact file

A third type of secondary structure is found in collagen (an important structural protein found in skin, bones, hair, etc.). Collagen consists of a triple-stranded helix. About one-third of the amino acid residues in each strand are glycine. There is also a considerable amount of proline.

Tertiary structure

The tertiary structure involves further folding of the polypeptide chain. The complex 3-dimensional shape is stabilised by:

- **disulfide bridges** – these are covalent (—S—S—) bonds
- weak van der Waals' forces
- relatively weak hydrogen bonds
- ionic bonds (salt bridges).

Disulfide bridges are usually found in proteins which function outside the body cells; for example, digestive enzymes. The bonds are formed by oxidation of two cysteine residues.

Disulfide bridges can be formed within the same polypeptide chain or between different polypeptide chains. The disulfide bridges help maintain the tertiary structure by 'locking' the polypeptide chains in place.

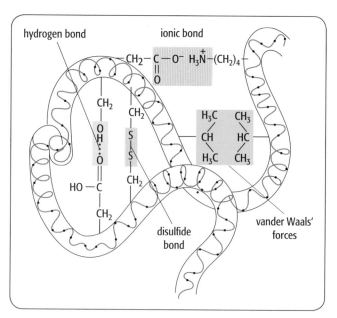

Figure 28.13 A diagram illustrating the nature of the interactions responsible for protein tertiary structure. The forces and bonds stabilising the tertiary structure have been shown in exaggerated size.

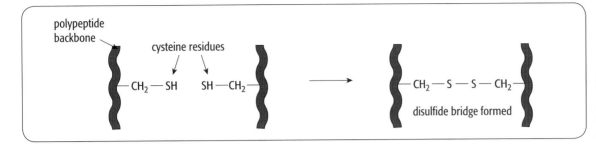

Figure 28.14
The formation of a disulfide bridge from two cysteine residues.

Dipole–induced dipole forces (van der Waals' forces) are formed when non-polar amino acid residues are close to one another. A large proportion of the amino acid residues in the 'centre' of many proteins are non-polar. So, although van der Waals' forces are weak, the stabilisation of tertiary structure due to total van der Waals' forces may be considerable.

Hydrogen bonds are formed between polar side-chains having hydrogen atoms attached to the highly electronegative atoms nitrogen or oxygen. Figure 28.15 shows hydrogen bonds formed between serine and threonine residues.

Ionic bonds are formed between ionised acidic side-chains and ionised basic side-chains. Figure 28.16 shows

the ionic bonds that form between the negatively charged aspartate side-chain and the positively charged lysyl side-chain.

The formation of ionic bonds depends on the pH of the environment in which the residues exist (see page 395).

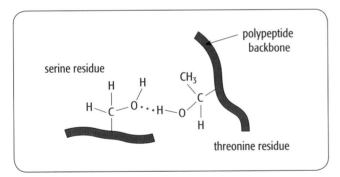

Figure 28.15 A hydrogen bond (shown by three red dots) formed between serine and threonine residues.

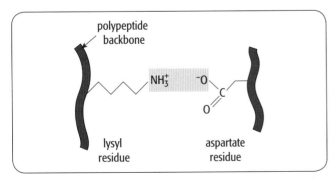

Figure 28.16 An ionic bond formed between an aspartate residue and a lysyl residue (from lysine).

Check-up

2 a A polypeptide is said to have direction. How are the two ends of the chain described?
  b What type of chemical bonding is responsible for maintaining the primary structure of a protein?
  c What is meant by the term **amino acid residue**?
  d Draw a diagram to show how a hydrogen bond may be formed between two peptide bonds in a polypeptide chain.
  e List the different types of interaction responsible for stabilising the tertiary structure of a protein.
  f What is the major difference in the position of the hydrogen bonds in the secondary and tertiary structures of a protein?
  g i Name the amino acid which gives rise to a disulfide bridge.
   ii What part do disulfide bridges play in stabilising the structure of a protein?

28.4 Enzymes

Most of the chemical reactions which take place within living organisms are catalysed by **enzymes**. In common with inorganic catalysts they
• speed up a reaction without being used up
• provide an alternative reaction pathway with lower activation energy.

Enzyme catalysis has some specific features:
- enzymes are all large protein molecules
- enzymes are more efficient than inorganic catalysts; the reaction rate is often increased by a factor of 10^6 to 10^{12}
- enzymes are very specific; they usually only catalyse one particular reaction
- as a consequence of this specificity, enzymes do not produce side products
- enzymes work under very mild conditions; for example 35 °C, pH 7, atmospheric pressure
- the amount of enzyme present in a cell can be regulated according to need.

The specific substance (metabolite) that fits on the enzyme surface and is converted to product(s) is called a **substrate**. For example: the enzyme urease catalyses the reaction:

$$(NH_2)_2CO + H_2O \rightarrow 2NH_3 + CO_2$$
urea

Urea is the substrate in this reaction because it fits onto the surface of the enzyme. Water reacts with the urea, but only when the urea is bound to the enzyme surface.

The catalytic activity of enzymes is measured in two ways:
- **enzyme activity:** the number of moles of substrate converted to product per minute
- **turnover number:** the number of substrate molecules reacted per enzyme per minute.

Enzyme specificity

The complicated folding of the polypeptide chain of the enzyme gives rise to a 'pocket' on the surface of the enzyme called the **active site**. The active site is where the substrate binds to the enzyme and where catalysis takes place. The active site takes up only a small area of the molecule. The active site has several specific amino acid side-chains which form weak bonds with the substrate. This keeps the substrate in place so that other molecules can react with it in the correct orientation.

A simple model, called the **lock and key model**, can be used to explain the specificity of enzymes. In order to undergo reaction, the substrate (the 'key') must fit the shape of the enzyme active site (the 'lock'). We say that the substrate has a complementary shape to the active site (Figure **28.17**)

The substrate must have the correct shape and size to fit the active site of the enzyme. It must also have the necessary functional groups to form weak bonds with the amino acid side-chains lining the active site. This is due to the distribution of electric charge in the substrate and in the active site. For example, when the substrate molecule fits into the active site:
- if a non-polar part of the substrate molecule is next to a non-polar part of the enzyme, van der Waals' forces will be present
- if a slightly positively charged part of the substrate molecule is next to a slightly negatively charged part of the enzyme, dipolar forces will be present.

The sequence of reactions is:
- the substrate diffuses to the active site
- the substrate binds to the active site, forming an enzyme–substrate complex
- amino acid side-chains (and other small molecules or ions) at the active site catalyse the reaction; in this process certain amino acid residues may act as proton donors/acceptors or nucleophiles
- the products diffuse away from the active site.

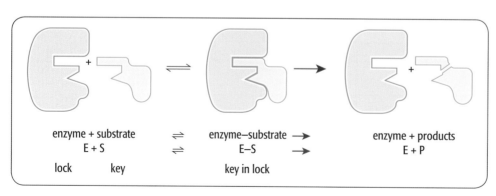

enzyme + substrate	⇌	enzyme–substrate	→	enzyme + products
E + S	⇌	E–S	→	E + P
lock	key	key in lock		

Figure 28.17 The 'lock and key' mechanism.

Fact file

When a substrate binds to an enzyme the active site actually changes shape. Although the lock and key model can account for the specificity of enzymes, it does not take this change in shape into account. A better model is the 'induced fit' model. When the substrate bonds to the enzyme surface, there is a small change in the 3-dimensional structure of the enzyme. This results in specific amino acid side-chains involved in catalysis being brought nearer to the substrate molecule.

An example of enzyme catalysis is provided by the enzyme trypsin. Trypsin is a digestive enzyme which hydrolyses peptides derived from proteins in our food. Trypsin is very specific. It only breaks peptide bonds next to lysine and arginine residues in peptides. The structure of the active site of trypsin is shown in Figure 28.18.

The 'pocket' at the active site only allows amino acid side-chains of a certain size and charge to enter. The $-NH_3^+$ group, which forms when the side-chain of lysine (or arginine) accepts a proton, can form weak bonds with the aspartate residue at the active site. The rest of the pocket is lined with non-polar amino acid residues. These form weak intermolecular attractions with the hydrocarbon part of the lysine (or arginine) side-chains. When the lysine binds to the active site, other groups are brought up which catalyse the bond-breaking reaction. The products then diffuse away.

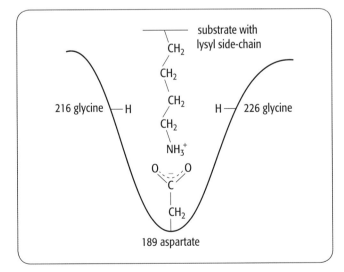

Figure 28.18 The active site of trypsin will only bind amino acid side-chains which are relatively long and have a positively charged NH_3^+ group. The numbers show the position of the amino acid residues in the polypeptide chain.

Check-up

3 a Draw an energy profile diagram to show a typical uncatalysed and enzyme-catalysed reaction. On your diagram show:

    i the activation energy for the catalysed and uncatalysed reaction

    ii the enzyme, substrate and product and the enzyme–substrate complex.

  b Explain the terms:

    i active site

    ii lock and key mechanism.

  c Chymotrypsin is an enzyme that catalyses the hydrolysis of peptide chains next to the amino acid tyrosine. Figure 28.19 shows a tyrosine residue bound to the active site of chymotrypsin.

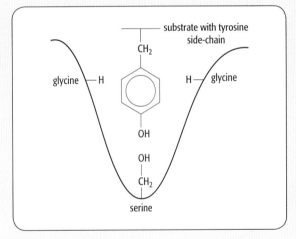

Figure 28.19 A tyrosine residue bound to the active site of chymotrypsin.

    i What features of the active site help to bind tyrosine?

    ii The structure of an alanine side-chain is shown below.

    Suggest why the alanine residue does not bind to the chymotrypsin active site.

Inhibition of enzyme activity

The inhibition of enzymes by naturally occurring small molecules can serve as a control mechanism in the cell. Many other small molecules or ions not generally found in cells can also inhibit enzyme activity. Inhibition can be reversible or non-reversible, according to the type of interaction formed between the inhibitor and the protein.

Competitive inhibition

A **competitive inhibitor** imitates the natural substrate. It can bind to the enzyme in the same way that the substrate does.

• The inhibitor has a similar shape and distribution of charge to the normal substrate.
• The inhibitor binds to the active site (by weak intermolecular attractive forces) but does not take part in the enzyme-catalysed reaction.
• When present in the active site the inhibitor prevents the normal substrate from binding.
• The effect of the inhibitor is overcome by increasing the concentration of the normal substrate.

Figure **28.20** shows a model of the action of a competitive inhibitor.

An example of competitive inhibition is the action of malonate on the enzyme succinic dehydrogenase (Figure **28.21**). Malonate cannot be dehydrogenated to form a double bond since it does not have the $-CH_2-CH_2-$ group.

When the reaction is carried out in the presence of malonate, the enzyme activity decreases. Increasing the concentration of malonate decreases the enzyme activity even further. Increasing the concentration of succinate

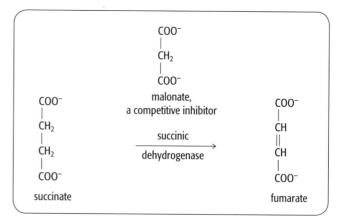

Figure 28.21 Malonate competitively inhibits the conversion of succinate to fumarate.

Fact file

Ethylene glycol (ethane-1,2-diol) is found in antifreeze. Antifreeze is used in cold countries to clear the ice from car windscreens in winter. There are about 60 deaths each year as a result of ethylene glycol poisoning. This is because ethylene glycol is converted to poisonous oxalic acid in the body. Ethanol can be used to treat ethylene glycol poisoning. The ethanol acts as a competitive inhibitor for one of the enzymes in the sequence of reactions which converts ethylene glycol to oxalic acid.

increases the enzyme activity. Malonate is a successful competitive inhibitor because:

• it has two carboxylate groups, just like succinate
• the length of the carbon chain is similar to that of succinate.

Non-competitive inhibition

A **non-competitive inhibitor** also reduces enzyme activity, but does so by a different mechanism. The characteristics of non-competitive inhibition are the following.

• The inhibitor doe not have a similar shape to the normal substrate.
• The inhibitor usually binds at a separate binding site (second site) which is specific for that inhibitor. It does not bind at the active site. The binding involves weak intermolecular attractive forces.
• When the inhibitor binds at the second site, it alters the shape of the enzyme so that the shape of the active site is changed. This shape change means that the normal substrate can no longer bind to the active site.

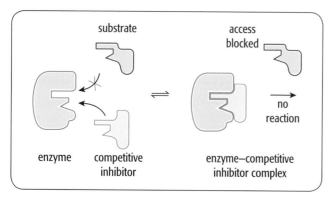

Figure 28.20 A model of action of a competitive inhibitor.

- The inhibitory effect reduces the number of active enzyme molecules available. If there are few inhibitor molecules there are still enough molecules with active sites available to carry out some catalytic activity. If there are many inhibitor molecules, the number of enzyme molecules available to carry out catalysis is low.
- The effect of the inhibitor is not overcome by increasing the concentration of the normal substrate.

Non-competitive inhibition may be reversible or irreversible depending on the nature of the inhibitor and enzyme.

Figure 28.22 shows a model of the action of a non-competitive inhibitor. When the concentration of the inhibitor falls, the enzyme–inhibitor complex falls apart and the shape of the enzyme active site returns to normal.

Non-competitive inhibition helps to control the level of metabolites in the cell by feedback inhibition. An example is the control of haem synthesis. Haem is part of the haemoglobin molecule which is responsible for the transport of oxygen around the body (see page 434). Haem is made by a sequence of enzyme-catalysed reactions. The enzyme which catalyses the first step in this sequence (ALA synthetase) is inhibited non-competitively by haem.

$$\underset{\text{glycine + succinyl CoA}}{\text{reactants}} \xrightarrow{\text{ALA synthetase}} \text{product (ALA)} \xrightarrow{} \xrightarrow{} \xrightarrow{\text{several steps}} \text{haem}$$

When the concentration of haem in the body rises:
- haem binds to the second site on the ALA synthetase
- this changes the shape of the active site so that no more product is formed
- the concentration of haem in the body falls.

Check-up

4 Use the example of the control of haem synthesis above to answer the following questions.
  a Explain what happens when the concentration of haem in the cell is low. Your answer should explain the steps leading first of all to a higher haem concentration, and finally to the haem concentration becoming low again.
  b The synthesis of ALA is the rate-determining step.
    i What is the meaning of **rate-determining step**?
    ii What advantage is there to the cell that the first step in this reaction is the rate-determining step?

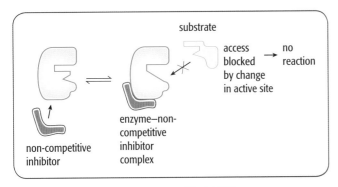

Figure 28.22 A scheme for non-competitive inhibition.

Some small molecules inhibit enzyme activity non-competitively by bonding covalently to specific amino acid side-chains at the active site. The active site may be blocked or an amino acid side-chain needed for catalysis may be modified. This inhibition is non-reversible.

For example, certain fluorophosphate compounds react irreversibly with serine residues that are responsible for binding or catalysis at the active site (Figure 28.23).

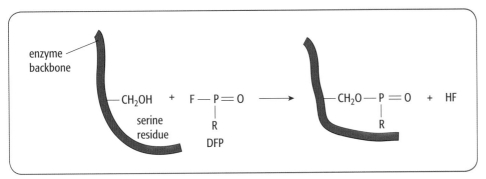

Figure 28.23 DFP (di-(1-methylethyl) fluorophosphate) forms a covalent bond with a serine residue at an enzyme active site.

Heavy metals, such as Ag^+ ions and Hg^+ ions, react with one or more —SH (sulfhydryl) groups, replacing the hydrogen atom with a metal ion (Figure 28.24). In some enzymes, the —SH group of a cysteine amino acid residue plays an important part in catalysis. Heavy metals can therefore acts as inhibitors of enzyme activity.

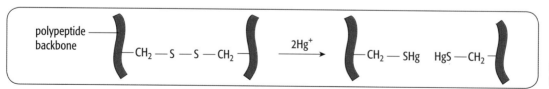

Figure 28.24 The reaction between silver ions and a sulfhydryl group.

Hg^+ ions can also inhibit enzyme activity by breaking disulfide bridges. The tertiary structure of the protein is altered because the disulfide bridges no longer play a part in holding the polypeptide chains in the correct position (Figure 28.25).

These reactions can often be reversed by atmospheric oxidation.

Check-up

5 **a** Describe three differences between a competitive inhibitor and a non-competitive inhibitor.

   b The structures of proline and azetidine-2-carboxylic acid are shown here.

continued ⋯→

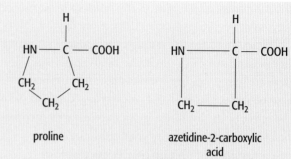

proline   azetidine-2-carboxylic acid

   i Azetidine-2-carboxylic acid (A2C) can act as a competitive inhibitor of proline. What features of azetidine-2-carboxylic acid make it a good competitive inhibitor of proline?

   ii An enzyme uses proline as a substrate. The data in the table shows the effect of different mixtures of proline and azetidine-2-carboxylic acid (A2C) on the rate of reaction.

Experiment	1	2	3	4	5
[proline] / $mol\,dm^{-3}$	3×10^{-4}	3×10^{-4}	3×10^{-4}	6×10^{-4}	9×10^{-4}
[A2C] / $mol\,dm^{-3}$	0	3×10^{-4}	6×10^{-4}	3×10^{-4}	3×10^{-4}
Relative rate of reaction	5.2	4.8	4.4	5.0	5.1

   How does this data show that A2C is a competitive inhibitor of proline?

   c Thallium is a heavy metal.

   i Write an equation to show the reaction of thallium(I) ions, Tl^+, with the sulfhydryl group in a cysteine residue.

   ii What type of inhibitors are thallium(I) ions? Explain your answer.

polypeptide backbone

Figure 28.25 Hg^+ ions can break disulfide bridges.

28.5 Factors affecting enzyme activity

Enzyme catalysis depends on the weak forces of attraction which give rise to the tertiary structure of the enzyme. Small changes in pH and temperature modify the tertiary structure so that the precise geometry of the active site is altered. This leads to loss of enzyme activity. Enzymes are also inactivated by chemicals that cause considerable change to their tertiary structure. Strong acids, strong alkalis and detergents act like this.

Effect of temperature

Figure **28.26** shows how enzyme activity changes with temperature.

At temperatures between 0 °C and about 40 °C the rate of enzyme activity increases in a similar way to other chemical reactions. As temperature increases:
- the molecules move faster causing a greater frequency of collisions
- a greater proportion of the molecules collide with energy equal to or greater than the activation energy.

Enzyme activity decreases markedly above 40 °C. As the temperature increases further:

- the increased thermal motion of the polypeptide chain disrupts the intermolecular forces which maintain the enzyme tertiary structure
- the enzyme starts to lose its tertiary structure
- the shape of the active site changes so that it can no longer bind the substrate
- the enzyme loses its catalytic activity.

At temperatures above about 65 °C, the protein loses its tertiary structure altogether and even starts losing secondary structure. When a protein has lost its precise 3-dimensional structure, we say that it is **denatured**.

Fact file

Some bacteria can live in hot springs at very high temperatures. A bacterium found in hot springs in Yellowstone Park, USA grows best at 105 °C! Enzymes which have unusually high optimum temperatures can be useful. For example, an enzyme called Taq polymerase can be used at about 80 °C to increase the amount of DNA available for DNA fingerprinting to help solve crimes. Fungi often have enzymes that can tolerate very high temperatures without denaturing. Laboratories find that higher sterilisation temperatures are needed to kill all fungi than are needed to kill all bacteria.

Effect of pH

Extremes of pH denature enzymes by disrupting their tertiary structure. Low pH will protonate $-COO^-$ side-chains and high pH will deprotonate $-NH_3^+$ side-chains. This disrupts ionic bonds that help to maintain the tertiary structure.

Small changes in pH can also affect the ionisation of particular amino acid side-chains at the active site (and sometimes the substrate itself). The activity of some enzymes depends on particular amino acid residues at the active site being charged, or not being charged. In these cases, a shift of pH by even 1 unit can change the enzyme activity significantly. Figure **28.27** shows this effect.

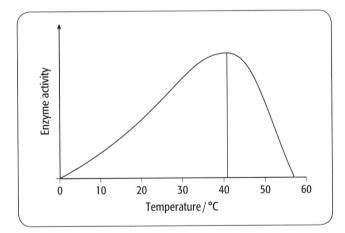

Figure 28.26 A profile of enzyme activity with temperature.

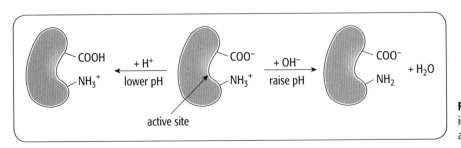

Figure 28.27 How pH changes can affect the ionisation of particular amino acid residues at the active site.

Most enzymes are active over a fairly narrow pH range. Although the optimum (ideal) pH for most enzymes that work within cells is near pH 7, many enzymes which function outside cells, such as the digestive enzymes in the stomach and intestines, have optimum pHs which reflect the pH of the medium in which they work (Figure **28.28**). For example:

- pepsin hydrolyses proteins to peptides in the very acidic conditions of the stomach
- amylase hydrolyses starch in the very slightly alkaline conditions produced by the saliva in the mouth
- trypsin hydrolyses peptides in the mildly alkaline conditions in the small intestine.

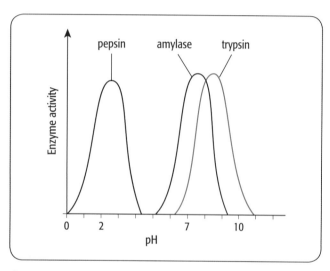

Figure 28.28 Curves showing pH optima for several enzymes.

Check-up

6 a Sketch a graph to show how the activity of a typical enzyme varies with temperature.

b Explain the graph you drew in part **a** in terms of the kinetic theory and the effect of temperature on enzyme structure.

c Look at the shape of the pH/activity curve for pepsin in Figure **28.28**. The activity of pepsin depends on two aspartic acid resides at its active site. One of these is ionised, the other is not. Use this information to explain the pH activity curve of pepsin.

continued ⋯⟶

d Glutamate tRNA ligase is a typical enzyme found in the cytoplasm of the cell. It has a pH optimum of pH 6.7. Sketch a graph to show a pH/enzyme activity curve for this enzyme.

Chemical denaturation

Enzymes extracted from a tissue can be denatured by specific chemicals or by salts, especially the salts of heavy metals such as mercury or lead.

- High salt concentrations can disrupt ionic interactions between different regions of the polypeptide chain and alter the tertiary structure of a protein. Salts such as ammonium chloride, however, do not affect proteins permanently and have been used to purify enzymes.
- Urea denatures proteins by disrupting hydrogen bonds that maintain the tertiary structure.

Cofactors: prosthetic groups and coenzymes

Many enzymes need a non-protein group called a **cofactor** in order to function as catalysts. Without the cofactor, these enzymes cannot function as catalysts. Two types of cofactor are prosthetic groups and coenzymes.

Prosthetic groups are ions or molecules that are permanently bound to a particular enzyme. For example, the enzyme carbonic anhydrase, which catalyses the reaction

$$CO_2 + H_2O \rightarrow HCO_3^- + H^+$$

always has a Zn^{2+} ion bound to its surface.

Fairly large molecules such as haem (see page **434**) are also found bonded to proteins. Two examples of proteins containing haem are:

- haemoglobin, which is involved in transport of oxygen around the body
- cytochrome oxidase, which is involved in redox reactions during respiration.

Coenzymes are complex molecules, often synthesised from vitamins, which are not permanently bound to an enzyme. They work together with the enzyme to bring about the required reaction. They bind temporarily to the active site of the enzyme and function as a co-substrate. The coenzymes NAD^+, $NADP^+$ and FAD are involved

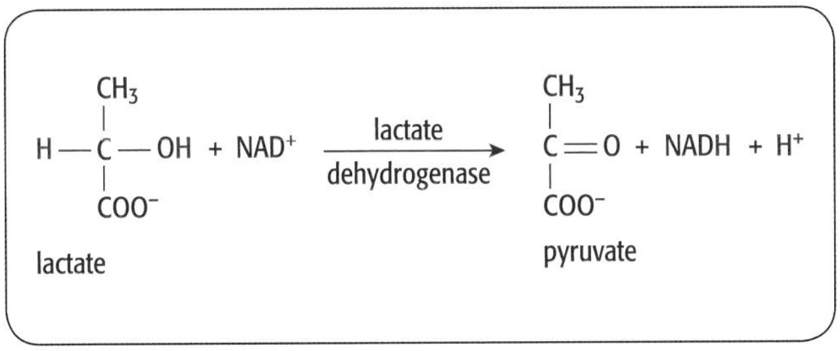

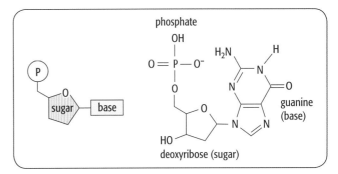

Figure 28.29 NAD⁺ (nicotinamide adenine dinucleotide) acts as an oxidising agent when lactate is converted to pyruvate. Lactate builds up in muscles when we exercise in a limited amount of oxygen. We convert the lactate to pyruvate when we have a plentiful supply of oxygen again.

Figure 28.30 The three components that make up a nucleotide.

in electron and hydrogen ion transfer reactions whilst coenzyme-A is involved in transfer of CH_3CO^- groups. The conversion of lactate (produced during anaerobic respiration in muscles) to pyruvate provides an example of the role of NAD⁺ as a coenzyme involved in redox reactions (Figure **28.29**).

Coenzymes are also modified slightly during the reactions. They are changed back to the original form by other reactions taking place in the cell. For example NADH⁺ is changed back to NAD⁺ by oxidation reactions taking place elsewhere in the cell.

28.6 Nucleic acids

Nucleic acids play an essential role in passing on genetic information from generation to generation. This genetic information determines the structure of living things and the nature of the chemical reactions which go on inside them. The two main types of nucleic acid are deoxyribonucleic acid (DNA) and ribonucleic acid (RNA). The structure of DNA contains a genetic code that determines the specific amino acid sequence for all the proteins in the body. Both DNA and RNA are polynucleotides, They are made by condensation polymerisation of units called **nucleotides**.

The structure of DNA

Deoxyribonucleic acid (**DNA**) has two important functions in living organisms.
- DNA can make copies of itself so that the genetic information can be passed on from generation to generation.
- DNA contains a sequence of bases which form a genetic code used to synthesise proteins.

The nucleotides in DNA are made up of three components (Figure **28.30**). These are:

- a sugar called deoxyribose (which has a five-membered ring)
- a phosphate group (attached by a phosphoester link to deoxyribose)
- a nitrogen-containing base (of which there are four types).

The nitrogen-containing bases (with their abbreviations) are:
- adenine (A)
- guanine (G)
- thymine (T)
- cytosine (C)

Adenine and guanine have a planar structure with two rings; thymine and cytosine have a planar structure with a single ring.

The DNA molecule consists of a double helix made up of two strands which are kept in place by hydrogen bonding between pairs of bases (Figure **28.31**).

The main points about the structure of DNA are:
- each strand has a backbone of alternating sugar and phosphate units; this is on the outside of the structure
- the two strands run in opposite directions to each other (compare the 3′ and 5′ positions of the deoxyribose sugar units in the two chains in Figure **28.31b**)
- the two strands are twisted to form a double helix
- the nitrogen-containing bases link the two strands
- the bases are positioned at right angles to the long axis of the helix (rather like a pile of coins)
- the bases are linked by hydrogen bonds.

The base pairs fit into the space between the two backbones so that the helix has a regular shape. In order to do this the bases pair up so that:
- A always pairs with T (forming two hydrogen bonds between them)
- G always pairs with C (forming three hydrogen bonds between them).

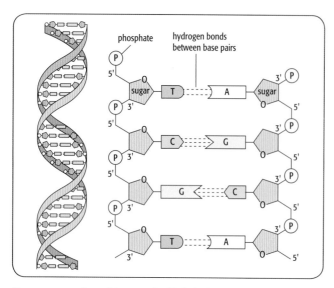

Figure 28.31 a Part of the DNA double helix. **b** An outline structure of DNA, showing base pairing. The chain has been 'straightened out' to make the base pairing clearer.

The bases on one strand always link to a particular base on the other strand. We say they form **complementary base pairs**.

You do not have to know the detailed structure of the bases. They can be represented by blocks, as in Figure **28.31**.

The structure of DNA is kept stable by
• hydrogen bonds between the base pairs
• van der Waals' attractive forces between one base pair and the next.

Fact file

Figure **28.32** shows the hydrogen bonding between the base pairs in DNA in more detail. You can see that the hydrogen bonding is not as regular as indicated in Figure **28.31**. In reality, the bases pairs on each strand are not completely in line with each other; rather they are slightly twisted out of line. This allows the DNA double helix to be able to bend, rather than being a straight rod-like structure.

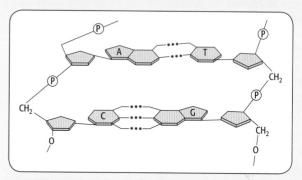

Figure 28.32 The detailed structure of part of a DNA molecule, showing the hydrogen bonding between the base pairs.

Check-up

7 The diagram below represents the basic chemical unit from which DNA is formed.

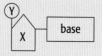

a State the name of:
  i the whole unit
  ii X
  iii Y
b Name the four nitrogen-containing bases present in DNA.

8 a Representing the nitrogen-containing bases by 'B', sugars by 'S' and phosphate groups by 'P', show how these are linked in a short length of double-stranded DNA. Use full lines (———) to show covalent bonds and dots (•••) to show hydrogen bonds.
  b i How do the two backbones in DNA differ?
    ii State how this difference is shown on diagrams of DNA.

How DNA replicates

The chromosomes in the cell nucleus contain DNA. The DNA in almost every cell in our body is identical. When a cell divides, both the new cells need a complete copy of all of this DNA because DNA contains the information for all the cell's activities. The information is provided by the sequence of bases in DNA. The process of copying DNA during cell division is called **replication**.

Replication is a complex process requiring a number of different enzymes and other compounds. A simplified model of replication is shown in Figure **28.33**.

- The hydrogen bonds and van der Waals' forces between the base pairs in part of a DNA molecule are broken.
- This part of the double helix unwinds.
- Nucleotide triphosphates are brought up one by one to the separated part of the chain.
- Enzymes catalyse the polymerisation reaction. During this process the nucleotide triphosphates are converted to nucleotides (and pyrophosphate). The nucleotides pair up with the complementary bases on the original strand. DNA polymerase is one of the enzymes involved in this reaction.

Each new strand contains a sequence of bases that is complementary to the original strand. So if the order of bases in part of the original strand is

–A T G C C G T T A A G T–

then the complementary sequence on the new strand is

–T A C G G C A A T T C A–

The two double helices formed are identical. Each strand contains one strand from the old DNA and one newly synthesised strand. This is called semi-conservative replication (Figure **28.34**).

Fact file

The replication of DNA involves several enzymes. DNA polymerase can only synthesise a complementary DNA backbone in the 5′ to 3′ direction. Since the DNA strands run in opposite directions, different enzymes have to be used to synthesise the complementary strand which runs in a 3′ to 5′ direction. This is made in several short sections working backwards. These short sections are then joined together using a DNA ligase enzyme.

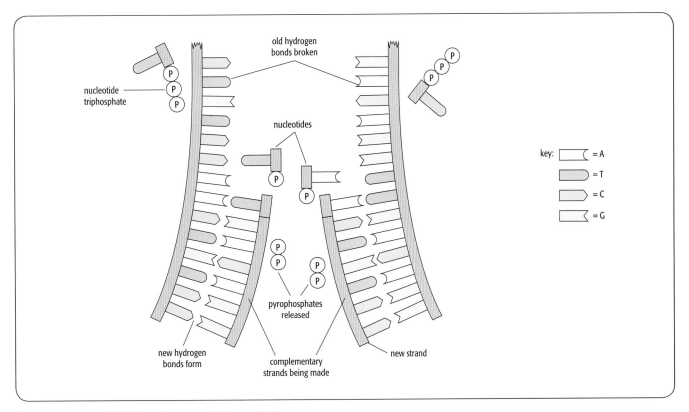

Figure 28.33 A strand of DNA acting as template for replication.

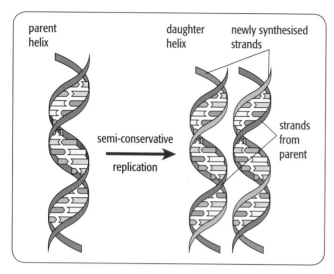

Figure 28.34 Semi-conservative replication.

The structure of RNA

Ribonucleic acids (**RNA**) are polynucleotides which are involved in protein synthesis. There are three main forms of RNA.

- **Messenger RNA** (mRNA): this is copied from the base sequence of DNA (see Section **28.7**). mRNA contains a sequence of bases which codes for a particular polypeptide chain in a protein.
- **Transfer RNA** (tRNA): each tRNA carries a specific amino acid to the ribosomes, where protein synthesis occurs.
- **Ribosomal RNA** (rRNA): this forms part of the structure of the ribosomes. rRNA binds ribosomal proteins which take part in the various reactions at the ribosome and helps binds mRNA.

There are three main structural differences between RNA and DNA.

- The sugar in RNA is ribose (in DNA it is deoxyribose).
- In RNA, uracil (U) replaces thymine as a base. Uracil has a single planar ring and forms complementary base pairs with adenine.
- Most RNAs are single stranded (not double stranded like DNA).

The shape of RNA molecules is complex. For example, tRNA has a 'clover leaf structure' which bends back on itself to form loops. The structure is stabilised by hydrogen bonding (Figure **28.35**). rRNA has a structure with many loops, also stabilised by hydrogen bonding.

Check-up

9 a An analysis of the bases in a sample of double-stranded DNA gave the partial result: adenine 23 mol % and guanine 27 mol %. What would you expect the rest of the analysis to show? Explain your answer.

  b What role do hydrogen bonds play in the accurate replication of DNA?

  c DNA is replicated semi-conservatively. Explain the meaning of **semi-conservatively**.

  d The base sequence in part of the 5′ to 3′ parent strand of DNA is

  –TAGAAAGCTCAG–

  What is the DNA sequence in the corresponding part of the new strand made during replication?

Check-up

10 a State **three** ways in which the structure of RNA differs from DNA.

  b Describe the structure of tRNA.

  c Describe the role of rRNA in protein synthesis.

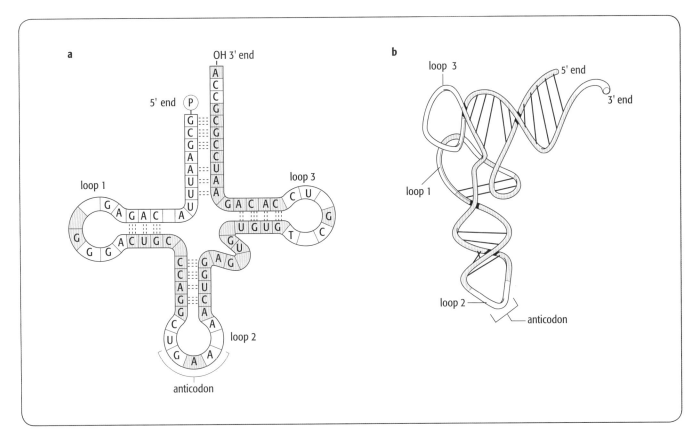

Figure 28.35 The cloverleaf structure of tRNA molecules.

28.7 Protein synthesis

An overview of protein synthesis

The complete sequence of bases in DNA carries a code for synthesising all the proteins and nucleic acids in our body. There are also regions of DNA (called junk DNA) which seem to have no function. A sequence of bases which codes for a specific polypeptide chain or protein is called a **gene**. Different genes have different sequences of bases and so code for different proteins. The sequence of bases that make up a gene is written in the 5′ to 3′ direction (see Figure **28.31**, page **422**). For example:

$$\underset{\text{direction of reading the bases}}{5' - \text{ATGCCGTTAGACCGT} - 3' \longrightarrow}$$

Protein synthesis is a complex process. Figure **28.36** shows a summary of the process.

Transcribing the message from DNA

Within its sequence of bases, DNA contains the instructions for the synthesis of proteins. How does a sequence of bases along a strand of DNA lead to the correct sequence of amino acids in a protein? The first stage in this sequence is the synthesis of mRNA using a strand of DNA as a template. Using the DNA strand 'as a template' means that the nucleotide sequence of the mRNA is complementary to the sequence on the DNA. This process is called **transcription** (which means 'writing across').

In transcription:
- part of the DNA double helix unwinds
- a mRNA copy of the gene is made on a template strand of DNA using the appropriate nucleotides and an enzyme called RNA polymerase (Figure **28.37**)
- the mRNA diffuses away from the DNA and the DNA forms a double helix again.

Note:
- the base U in mRNA is complementary to A in DNA
- the mRNA is synthesised on only one of the DNA strands (the template strand)

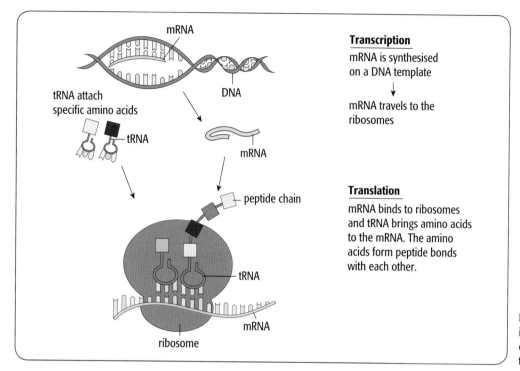

Transcription
mRNA is synthesised on a DNA template

↓

mRNA travels to the ribosomes

Translation
mRNA binds to ribosomes and tRNA brings amino acids to the mRNA. The amino acids form peptide bonds with each other.

Figure 28.36 Protein synthesis involves transcribing the genetic code into mRNA and then translating the message to form proteins.

- the mRNA is synthesised from the 5′ to 3′ end (this is also the direction in which the message is subsequently translated at the ribosome)
- only a small part of the DNA unwinds.

The mRNA copy is complementary to the part of the DNA (the gene) from which it was derived.

If the order of bases in part of the template strand of DNA is

–C C G T T A A G T T A C–

then the complementary sequence on the mRNA is

5′ –G G C A A U U C A A U G– 3′

The genetic code

The sequence of bases on a molecule of mRNA, which is complementary to the sequence of bases in a section of DNA, specifies the sequence of amino acids in the protein that is to be synthesised.

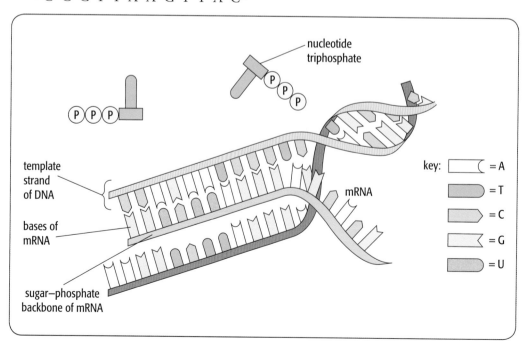

Figure 28.37 A diagram of the transcription process.

The mechanism by which the mRNA base sequence specifies an amino acid sequence is called the **genetic code**. The main points about the code are:

- a sequence of three bases (a triplet) codes for specific amino acids; for example CCA codes for proline, GCA codes for alanine
- a set of three successive bases is called a **codon**
- the coding is continuous – each codon follows directly from the one before; for example:

--- CCA GCA UUU CAU ---
codon for   Pro   Ala   Phe   His

- the sequence of triplet codons determines the order in which the amino acids join together in the polypeptide chain
- most amino acids are coded for by more than one codon; for example, the code for tyrosine can be UAU or UAC
- the sequence of the codons is read in the 5′ to 3′ direction
- the sequence of bases in the mRNA is complementary to the sequence of bases in the DNA.

Figure **28.38** shows the code for the 20 amino acids found in proteins. Note that the code is read out from the centre (5′ to 3′). Using the example of tryptophan (Trp) (Figure **28.39a**), we can see that UGG is the code for tryptophan. This means that the base sequence UGG

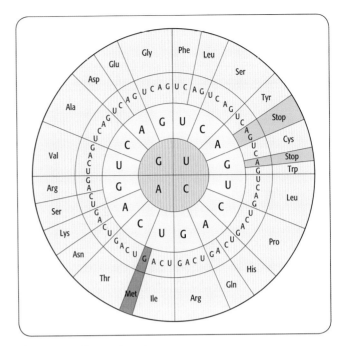

Figure 28.38 The genetic code.

on the mRNA causes the amino acid tryptophan to be incorporated into the protein when it is synthesised.

Using the same 'wheel' in Figure **28.39b**, you can see that arginine (Arg) has more than one possible code. The code can start with A (in the centre) and both AGG and AGA code for arginine. The code for arginine can also start with C (in the centre). If you look carefully at the diagram you can see that there are four possible codes for arginine beginning with C; these are CGG, CGA, CGC and CGU.

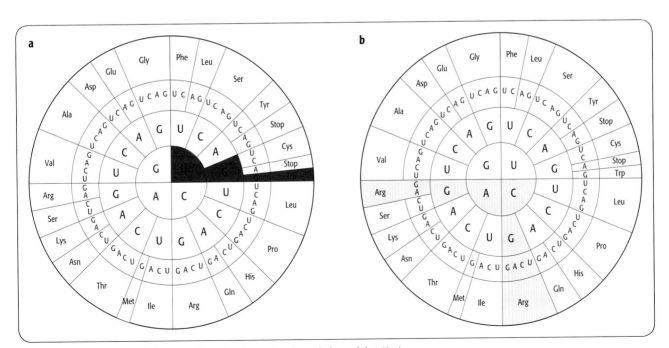

Figure 28.39 **a** Reading the code for tryptophan (Trp). **b** Reading the code for arginine (Arg).

All polypeptide chains have a defined length. So there must be a codon for the first amino acid in the chain (the N-terminal end). This start signal at the 5′ end is provided by the codon AUG for methionine. Although methionine will be the amino acid at the N-terminal end when the polypeptide chain is first synthesised, it is later removed from particular proteins. The start signal ensures that the triplet code is read in the correct groups of three.

There are also several codons for the last amino acid in the chain to show when assembly of the polypeptide is complete. For example, UAG is a 'stop' codon.

Fact file

Some plants contain amino acids which are toxic to other organisms. These amino acids mimic some of the reactions of normal protein amino acids. So the enzymes which join amino acids to tRNA in these plants have active sites which can distinguish between the normal protein amino acid and the toxic pretender. If they could not distinguish between the two, proteins could be made which have an altered tertiary structure and reduced or no activity.

Figure 28.40 The flame tree (*Delonix regia*) found in India and tropical Africa contains a toxic amino acid (azetidine-2-carboxylic acid) which is similar in structure to proline. The enzyme which attaches proline to tRNA has a specially modified active site which allows proline but not azetidine-2-carboxylic acid to be attached to tRNA.

Translating the message at the ribosomes

Proteins are assembled from amino acids at the ribosomes. Here, the code in the mRNA is translated into the amino acid sequence of the polypeptide with the aid of tRNA molecules.

Before they get to the ribosomes, tRNA molecules bind individual amino acids with the aid of enzymes which are specific for particular amino acids and tRNA molecules.

A tRNA molecule forms an ester link with a specific amino acid at one end. The other end of the tRNA has a set of three bases called an anticodon (see Figure **28.35**). The bases in the anticodon are complementary to specific codons on mRNA. So if the codon on mRNA is ACG (Thr), the anticodon on tRNA is UGC. The tRNA with anticodon UGC binds to a threonine molecule at one end. This means that where the codon on the mRNA is ACG, the amino acid added to the protein is always threonine.

Translation from triplet codons on the mRNA to the synthesis of a complete polypeptide chain involves three steps: initiation, elongation and termination (Figure **28.41**).

Initiation

- The start codon (AUG) of the mRNA binds to the ribosome.
- The tRNA with the correct anticodon pairs with the start codon on mRNA.

Elongation

- Further tRNA molecules with their amino acids are brought up to the ribosome. Each tRNA anticodon binds to the correct codon on mRNA in the correct 5′ to 3′ sequence.
- As the ribosome moves along the mRNA, the bond between the tRNA and amino acid breaks and the new amino acid is bonded to the growing polypeptide chain by a peptide link (Figure **28.42**).

Termination

- When the stop codon on the mRNA is reached, the mRNA detaches itself from the ribosome and the peptide chain folds up spontaneously.

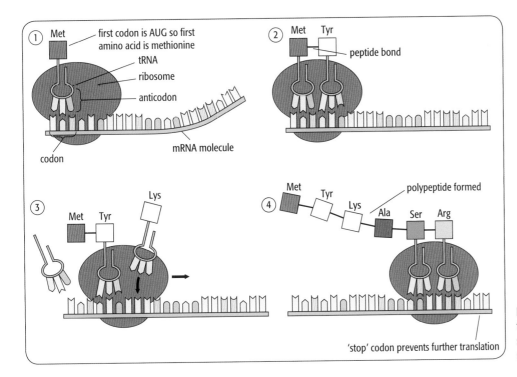

Figure 28.41 The process of translation. Stage 1 represents initiation, stages 2 and 3 represent elongation and stage 4 represents termination.

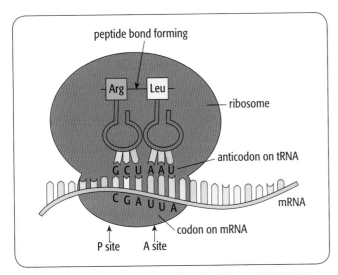

Figure 28.42 Complementary base pairing at the ribosome. Note that there are two sites on the ribosome, one where the incoming tRNA binds and one where the peptide chain lengthens.

Check-up

12 a Outline the role of mRNA and tRNA in protein synthesis.

b The peptide fragment

  –Tyr–Ser–Ala–Ala–Glu–Gly–Q–R–

  is coded somewhere inside the fragment of mRNA with the base sequence shown below.

  5′–GUUACUCUGCUGCGGAAGGAGCCGUAC–3′

  i Use Figure **28.39** to identify the codons in the mRNA fragment that code for the named amino acids.
  ii Use the mRNA fragment and Figure **28.39** to identify the amino acids Q and R in the peptide fragment.
  iii Give the base sequence matching the codon for tyrosine in the DNA from which the RNA was transcribed, indicating the direction of the bases in the DNA strand.

c Why is it important that there is a 'stop' codon in the mRNA?

d Explain how the codons on the mRNA are translated into the amino acid sequence in a polypeptide chain.

continued ⋯▷

28.8 Genetic mutations

A **mutation** is a change in the original DNA sequence. Mutations can arise naturally from errors in DNA replication. These are generally corrected by the cell's own mechanisms. Mutations may also arise through exposure to particular chemicals (e.g. some dyes and organic chemicals such as benzene and the chemicals in cigarette smoke). They may also be caused by ultraviolet light, X-rays, gamma rays, and alpha and beta radiation.

Because DNA is the template for mRNA, which carries the information for the primary structure of a protein, changes to the base sequence in DNA can cause a change in the primary structure of a protein.

Explaining genetic mutations

In some cases the change in the DNA is very small. A single change in a base (for example C to T) is not uncommon and it will not always cause a change in protein structure and function. The fact that there is more than one codon for many amino acids is beneficial. If a mutation occurs and one of the bases is altered, there is still the possibility that the correct amino acid will be incorporated into the protein. For example, if UCU is changed to UCG, serine will still be incorporated in its correct place in the polypeptide chain.

If the change results in a different amino acid being incorporated into protein there is still a chance that the effect will be small. It will only alter protein structure and function if an amino acid essential for protein function is altered: for example an amino acid at the active site of an enzyme. However, mutations which result in a change in a stop or start codon are more serious. A crucial protein may not be produced or may be so changed so that it cannot function properly.

The deletion of a base is a more serious matter. It alters the way the message is read and produces a different sequence of amino acids in the protein chain. For example, if the correct sequence in DNA is

– ATA CGC TAG CAT G–

then the mRNA will be

–UAU GCG AUC GUA C–

which codes for

Tyr   Ala   Ile   Val …

However, if the second A is deleted, then the DNA will be

–ATC GCT AGC ATG–

the new mRNA will be

–UAG CGA UCG UAC–

which codes for

stop Arg Ser Tyr

Alterations or deletions to bases in DNA may result in a genetically based condition such as sickle-cell anaemia or cystic fibrosis.

Check-up

13 a i Explain why the sequence –AGC ATG ATC ACT– in the template strand of DNA making RNA codes for Ser Tyr stop stop
ii Use the information in part **i** to determine a possible base sequence on the anticodons of Ser-tRNA and Tyr-tRNA. Use Figure **28.39** to help you.
b Use the information in Figure **28.39** to suggest the amino acid sequence corresponding to the following sequence of bases in DNA which form a template strand for mRNA.

–TAC TGC TTT AAG CCT ATG–

c The final T in the DNA sequence in part **b** is changed to a C.
i What affect will this have on the amino acid sequence that is coded for?
ii What do we call a change like this when it occurs in nature?

Sickle-cell anaemia

The red blood cells of patients with sickle-cell anaemia have a crescent (sickle) shape rather than the normal disc shape. Sickle cells cannot bend as easily as normal red blood cells in order to get through small blood vessels. The small blood vessels get blocked and oxygen transport to various organs can be reduced. This can lead to severe pain and damage to the organs. The disease arises from a single mutation in the DNA coding for the β polypeptide chain in haemoglobin (see page 434). A single amino acid at the 6th position of the polypeptide chain is altered.

Normal β chain   Val His Leu Thr Pro **Glu** Glu
Sickle-cell β chain   Val His Leu Thr Pro **Val** Glu

The abnormal haemoglobin sticks together to form rods inside the red blood cells, which become sickle-shaped.

Cystic fibrosis

Cystic fibrosis is a condition that affects the lungs, pancreas and sweat glands. Instead of normal watery fluid (mucus) coming out from the cell a thick sticky mucus is produced.

- The thick mucus stops digestive enzymes from the pancreas getting to the digestive system, so that nutrients cannot be absorbed into the bloodstream.
- The thick mucus blocks the lungs, so sufferers (especially young children) are more likely to get chest infections.

In healthy cells a protein (called CFTR protein) in the cell membrane controls the movement of Cl⁻ ions into and out of the cells. In a normal cell, Cl⁻ ions are pumped into the cells from the blood and are pumped out through protein channels in the cell membrane. This is part of the process for keeping a runny layer of watery mucus on the surface of the cells.

In patients with cystic fibrosis:

- there is a mutant gene for the CFTR protein, which has a sequence of three bases deleted; these bases would normally code for phenylalanine (Phe), the

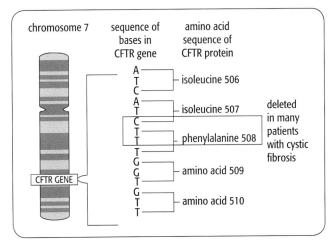

Figure 28.44 The site of the commonest mutation that causes cystic fibrosis.

508th amino acid in the structure of the protein (Figure 28.44)

- the CFTR protein is therefore missing or, if present, does not work properly
- Cl⁻ ions are still pumped into the cells but are not pumped out
- this causes the Cl⁻ ion concentration to build up in the cells
- water moves into the cells by osmosis to try to equalise its concentration inside and outside the cells
- as a result, the mucus on the outside of the cell becomes thick and sticky.

Modifying protein structure

The tertiary structure of an enzyme is essential to its function. Several diseases such as Creutzfeldt–Jacobs disease have been linked to incorrect folding of a particular protein. The failure of proteins to fold correctly leads to the formation of toxic prions (short for **pro**teinaceous infec**tion**). Much work is being done at present to try to modify the DNA of these proteins and produce 'new' proteins which have an improved tertiary structure. Several proteins have been 'improved' by modifying the DNA.

A successful example of making a 'new' enzyme has grown out of the increasing demand for biofuels for cars. Biofuels can be made from woody plants. But the woody material (lignin) prevents the easy extraction of the materials from plant cells. Scientists in the United States have altered plant DNA to produce a modified enzyme which decreases the amount of lignin in the plant. This

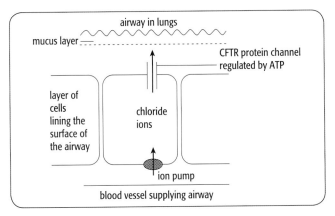

Figure 28.43 The movement of ions across cell membranes in the lungs.

makes the cell walls of the plant easier to break down. They first identified several possible amino acid sites in the enzyme which could be altered to produce a 'less active' enzyme. They then identified and altered two sites on the DNA gene which codes for the lignin-producing enzyme. As a result of this they made the plant produce the 'new' enzyme.

A procedure like this, that deliberately alters the sequence of bases in DNA, is known as **genetic engineering**.

Check-up

14 a Mutation of the mRNA of a T4 bacteriophage leads to the deletion of one base near the beginning of the sequence of 15 bases shown below.

  5′ –AGUCCAUCACUUAUU– 3′
          ↑
  this base deleted

  i Write down the base sequence of the mutant mRNA.

  ii Use the genetic code in Figure 28.39 to translate each of these base sequences into amino acid sequences in the normal and mutant protein. The first codon starts with the A at the 5′ end.

b Write down the sequence of bases in the piece of DNA which would produce the normal mRNA sequence after transcription.

c The normal amino acid sequence is part of the enzyme lysozyme. Explain how the mutation may affect the activity of the enzyme.

28.9 Energy transfers in biochemical reactions

Living things require a continuous supply of energy for:
• mechanical work such as muscle contraction
• the transport of molecules and ions through cell membranes into and out of cells
• the synthesis of molecules such as proteins, starch, fats, vitamins and coenzymes.

In animals, this energy comes from the oxidation of food, especially carbohydrates and fats. This process is called respiration. Oxygen is required to fully oxidise foods to carbon dioxide and water.

The metabolic pathway of respiration is complex. The first part takes place in the cytoplasm of the cell. The second, and most significant, part involves a series of redox reactions which take place in the mitochondria. In the mitochondria a nucleotide triphosphate called adenosine triphosphate (ATP) is synthesised. This molecule has an important role to play in energy transfers in the cell.

ATP and ADP

Figure **28.45** shows the structure of ATP.
ATP consists of:
• three linked phosphate groups (a single inorganic phosphate group is often abbreviated P_i)
• the sugar ribose
• the base adenine.
The active form of ATP in cells is usually a complex of ATP with Mg^{2+} ions.

ATP can be hydrolysed to adenosine diphosphate (ADP). This hydrolysis is an exothermic process, releasing energy. This is because:
• the release of the end phosphate group is favoured by the repulsion between the negatively charged O atoms on adjacent phosphate groups
• ADP and P_i are more stable due to a greater delocalisation of charge on their ions compared with ATP.
Figure **28.46** shows an equation for this reaction.

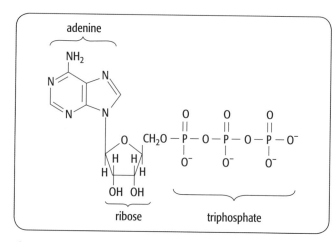

Figure 28.45 The structure of ATP.

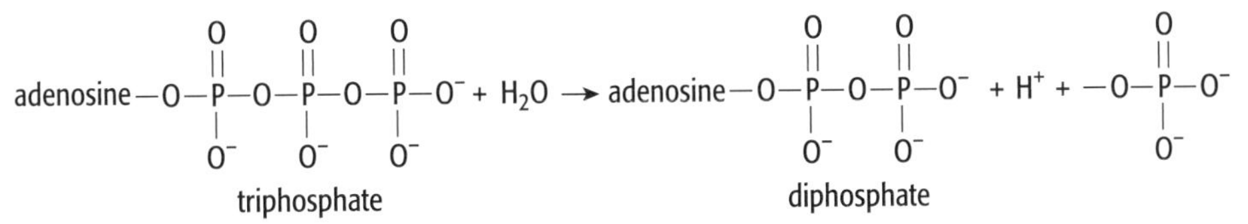

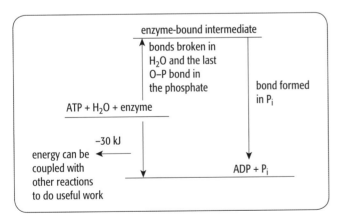

$$\text{ATP} + H_2O \rightleftharpoons \text{ADP} + P_i \qquad \Delta H = -30 \text{ kJ mol}^{-1}$$

Figure 28.46 The hydrolysis of ATP releases 30 kJ of energy per mole of ATP.

ATP is produced during the oxidation of food. When ATP is hydrolysed, energy is released. This energy must be released in a controlled manner so that it is available for cellular processes. In order to achieve this control, ATP is usually hydrolysed in the presence of enzymes. Hydrolysis does not occur in the cell in the absence of enzymes because the reaction has a very high activation energy.

The role of ATP in energy transfers

In the cell, metabolic pathways build up complex substances from simpler ones. Most of these pathways require energy – they are endothermic. The energy released when ATP is hydrolysed in the presence of enzymes is not wasted as heat. It is linked to energetically unfavourable reactions in the cell. Enough energy is provided by the hydrolysis of ATP to 'drive' reactions which require an input of energy (Figure 28.47).

the mitochondria. In the mitochondria $\text{ADP} + P_i$ is converted to ATP. This synthesis is linked to a series of redox reactions involving cytochromes, coenzymes (such as $NADH^+$) and oxygen (from the air we breathe in). This process of making ATP is called oxidative phosphorylation. This series of reactions will only carry on in the presence of oxygen. As long as aerobic respiration (respiration in the presence of oxygen) is occurring, the ATP production in the cell is kept fairly constant. The maximum amount of ATP produced from the oxidation of 1 mole of glucose is 38 moles of ATP.

Figure 28.48 shows the relationship between these processes of ATP formation and hydrolysis.

Figure 28.47 ATP hydrolysis drives unfavourable reactions in the cell.

If ATP is continually being hydrolysed to ADP, ATP would soon run out and ADP would accumulate – unless there is a way of making more ATP from ADP. Fortunately, there is a way. Most ATP is made in

Check-up

15 a What class of compound does ATP belong to?
   b List the **three** main components of an ATP molecule.
   c i Give the full name of ADP.
     ii How does ADP differ from ATP?
   d Where in the cell is ATP mainly synthesised?
   e Explain how ATP is used in the cell to drive unfavourable reactions.

16 a What is the name of the metabolic process in which glucose is oxidised to carbon dioxide and water?
   b What conditions are needed for the synthesis of ATP in the mitochondrion?
   c What does the term **oxidative phosphorylation** mean in relation to ATP?

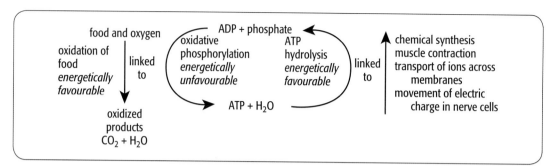

Figure 28.48 The role of ATP in metabolism.

28.10 Metals in biological systems

Some metals are essential to life

Many metal ions play vital roles in metabolism. Some are found naturally in our bodies and are essential for health.

- Iron(II) ions, Fe^{2+}, are a component of haemoglobin (see below). Iron is also involved in the function of cytochromes, which are linked to ATP production in oxidative phosphorylation.
- Zinc ions, Zn^{2+}, act as cofactors in many enzyme-catalysed reactions.
- Sodium and potassium ions are involved in maintaining electrolyte balance in our cells and in generating nerve impulses.

Iron and haemoglobin

Haemoglobin is an oxygen-carrying protein present in red blood cells. Haemoglobin consists of two pairs of polypeptide subunits (α and β). A haem group,

which contains Fe^{2+} ions, is bonded to each subunit (Figure 28.49).

Each haem group can bind one oxygen molecule. Each of the four haem groups can bind one oxygen molecule at the same time. So the overall reaction for a complete molecule of haemoglobin (Hb) is:

$$Hb + 4O_2 \rightleftharpoons \underset{\text{oxyhaemoglobin}}{HbO_8}$$

Each Fe^{2+} ion acts as the centre of a complex ion. The ligands are the four N atoms of the haem, the N atom of an amino acid (histidine) side-chain on the polypeptide and an oxygen molecule (Figure 28.50).

As the equation $Hb + 4O_2 \rightleftharpoons HbO_8$ shows, the binding of oxygen to haemoglobin is an equilibrium process. In places where oxygen concentration is high (e.g. in the lungs) the position of equilibrium moves to the right, so oxygen is bound to haemoglobin. In places where oxygen concentration is low (e.g. in respiring tissues) the position of equilibrium moves to the left, so oxygen is released.

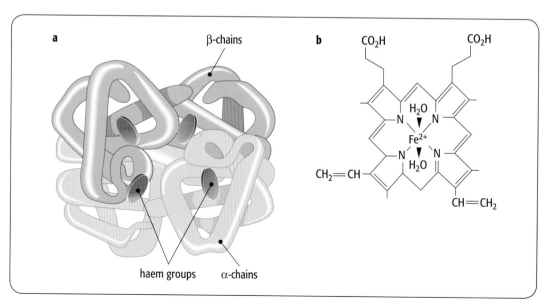

Figure 28.49 a The structure of haemoglobin showing the α and β chains. **b** The structure of haem when not bound to a protein.

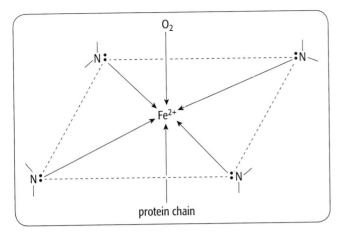

Figure 28.50 The complex ion in haemoglobin.

The oxygen is less strongly bound to the Fe^{2+} ion than the other ligands. It is removed when the red blood cells reach the tissues where oxygen is required. The oxygen ligand can be replaced by another ligand that binds more strongly to the Fe^{2+} ion.

Carbon monoxide molecules will also bind to haemoglobin, occupying the site normally occupied by oxygen. Carbon monoxide molecules are bound 200 times more strongly than oxygen in an irreversible reaction. That is why carbon monoxide is so poisonous – haemoglobin loses its oxygen-carrying function.

Zinc as an enzyme cofactor

Carbonic anhydrase is the enzyme present in red blood cells which is responsible for removing carbon dioxide from the blood. It accelerates the rate of the reaction by a factor of about 1 million.

$$CO_2 + H_2O \rightleftharpoons HCO_3^- + H^+$$
hydrogencarbonate ion

The enzyme contains Zn^{2+} as a prosthetic group at the active site. The Zn^{2+} is bound to the enzyme as part of a complex using N atoms from amino acid side-chains as ligands. Figure 28.52 shows how the Zn^{2+} ion helps provide a nucleophile in this reaction.

Fact file

When haemoglobin combines with oxygen, an iron atom moves into the plane of one of the haem rings by a tiny distance (Figure 28.51). This is sufficient to change the protein conformation and cause the other haem groups in the haemoglobin to bind oxygen as well.

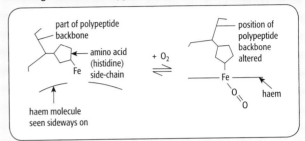

Figure 28.51 A slight movement of one iron atom is all that is needed to alter the shape of the haemoglobin molecule.

The mechanism of this reaction is:
- the high charge density on the Zn^{2+} ion assists the breakdown of a water molecule to form OH^- and H^+
- the OH^- ion is a nucleophile; it attacks the CO_2 molecule
- HCO_3^- is produced ($CO_2 + OH^- \rightarrow HCO_3^-$)
- the HCO_3^- ion is released and a further water molecule binds to the zinc.

Check-up

17 Haem is an important prosthetic group which contains iron at its centre.
   a Prosthetic groups and coenzymes are both cofactors. What is the difference between a prosthetic group and a coenzyme?
   b Give **two** important features about the attachment of oxygen to each haemoglobin molecule.

continued ⋯⟶

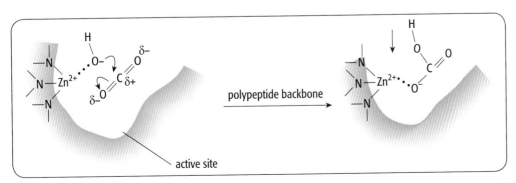

active site

Figure 28.52 How Zn^{2+} ions help catalyse the conversion of carbon dioxide to hydrogencarbonate ions.

c Name another important group of proteins that contain the haem group. Where are these proteins located in the cell?

18 The enzyme carbonic anhydrase converts carbon dioxide to hydrogencarbonate ions.
a Which metal is the prosthetic group in carbonic anhydrase?
b Write the equation for the reaction catalysed by carbonic anhydrase.
c The metal present induces the ionisation of a water molecule to produce a hydroxide ion. This attacks the carbon dioxide to form the hydrogencarbonate ion.
i What type of reagent is the hydroxide ion acting as in this reaction?
ii Use a 'curly arrow' to suggest the mechanism for the formation of the hydrogencarbonate ion.

Sodium and potassium ion transfer

The role of Na⁺ and K⁺ in ion transfer across cell membranes

The Na^+ ion concentration within most animal cells is lower than in the tissue fluid surrounding the cells. The K^+ ion concentration within most animal cells is higher than in the tissue fluid surrounding the cells. These differences in concentration are maintained by a Na^+, K^+ ion pump situated in the cell membrane (Figure **28.53**). The movement of ions through the cell membrane can only occur in the presence of ATP. The ion pump consists of a number of proteins, some of which can hydrolyse ATP. We say that the protein has ATPase activity.

This ion pump is an example of **active transport**. The term 'active transport' is used because the ions are being moved against a concentration gradient. 'Against a concentration gradient' means that the ions are being pumped from a place where they are in a lower concentration to a place where they are in higher concentration. Active transport always requires energy. Here, the energy is provided by ATP $\rightarrow$ ADP + P_i.

The pump works in the following way:
- three Na^+ ions and ATP bind to the inner surface of the protein
- when ATP is hydrolysed (to ADP + P_i), the protein changes shape so that Na^+ ions can move out of the cell
- as the Na^+ ions are released two K^+ ions outside the cell attach to the protein
- the K^+ ions move inwards and are released inside the cell when a new ATP molecule binds to the inner surface of the protein
- the cycle then repeats itself.

Fact file

When we are resting, about a third of the ATP we make in our bodies is used for pumping ions into and out of our cells.

Some plant steroids inhibit the Na⁺, K⁺ ion pump

Plant steroids such as ouabain and digitoxigenin inhibit the transport of Na^+ and K^+ ions through cell membranes. They are non-competitive inhibitors. They act by inhibiting the reaction of the ATPase protein which hydrolyses the ATP. The steroids bind on the outside of the inner protein subunits. This changes the structure of these subunits so that the ATPase activity is inhibited.

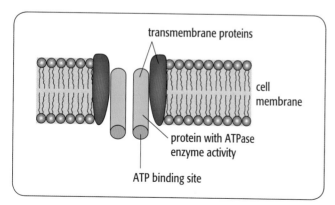

Figure 28.53 The Na^+, K^+ ion pump in the cell membrane helps maintain the concentration of these ions constant.

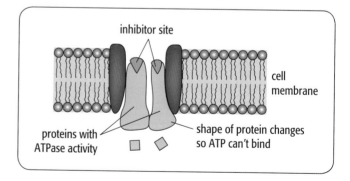

Figure 28.54 Particular plant steroids inhibit the transport of Na^+ and K^+ ions across cell membranes by binding to the outside of the protein. The protein changes shape thus inhibiting the ATPase activity on the inside of the cell.

Vanadate(V) ions, VO_4^{3-}, also inhibit the action of the Na^+, K^+ ATPase, but they do this from the inner side of the membrane.

A knowledge of how these ion pumps work is important to our understanding of how cells function in health and disease. Diabetes and certain diseases of the nervous system, muscles and heart can all be related to incorrect functioning of the protein channels which pump ions and water in through the cell membranes.

Ion transport across a membrane depends on the size and hydration of the ion

Ions do not simply diffuse through ion channels – interactions with the proteins which line the channel are necessary. The ability of an ion to pass through the ion channels depends on the charge and size of the ion. Ions in aqueous solution are usually hydrated (see page 264). So their overall size depends on their hydrated radius. The charge and the nature of the groups on the protein walls of the ion channel may also play a part. The protein walls of the ion channel contain some negatively charged amino acid side-chains. The relatively narrow width of the sodium channel between the proteins in the cell membrane makes it more permeable to the smaller hydrated sodium ion that the larger hydrated potassium ion (Figure 28.55a).

How do potassium ions get through the potassium ion channels? The potassium ions lose their hydration layer and bind to the negatively charged amino acid side-chains. (The energy required to remove the hydration shell is compensated for by the formation of new bonds with the amino acid side-chains.) The potassium ions regain their water of hydration when they reach the other side of the membrane. Sodium ions do not go through

the potassium ion channel because they are too small to form complexes with the amino acid side-chains and be pushed through (Figure 28.55b).

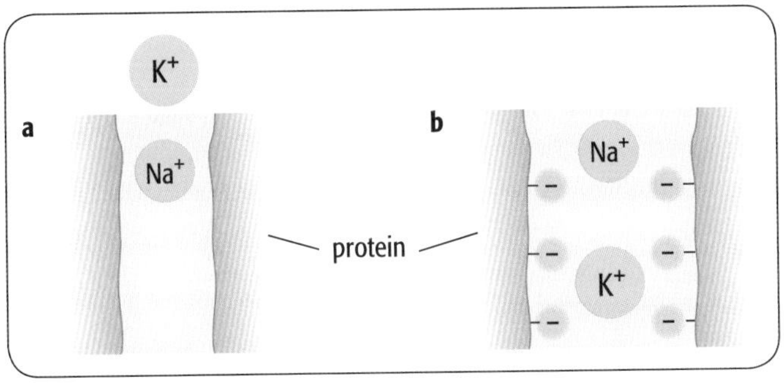

The role of Na^+ and K^+ ions in nerve impulses

A nervous impulse is an electrical signal produced by a flow of ions across the nerve cell membrane. Differences in the flow of K^+ and Na^+ ions into and out of the cell membranes give rise to an electric potential. The energy for the flow of ions comes from the hydrolysis of ATP by the ATPase enzyme.

This is what happens:

- before a nerve is stimulated, the potential across its cell membrane is called the resting potential
- the resting potential exists because the concentration of potassium ions is higher inside the nerve cell, and the concentration of sodium ions is higher outside the nerve cell
- when the nerve is stimulated, Na^+ ions move into the cell
- this increases the electrical potential across the membrane and more and more sodium channels are opened
- eventually an equilibrium is reached
- the Na^+ channels close and K^+ ion channels open
- K^+ ions flow outwards
- after the nerve signal has passed, the Na^+, K^+ ion pump then pumps the Na^+ ions out of the cell, and it pumps the K^+ ions back into the cell
- these processes return the membrane potential to its original value, which is the resting potential.

Figure 28.56 shows these changes.

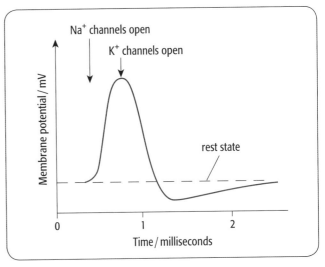

Figure 28.56 The change in electrical potential when a nerve is stimulated.

Figure 28.55 a The size of the hydrated ion affects the ability of positively charged ions to move through the sodium ion channel. **b** The ease of complex formation with amino acid side-chains affects the ability of ions to move through the potassium ion channel.

19 a Which ions are involved in the transmission of a nervous impulse?

b How do the concentrations of these ions in the nerve cell change during the transmission of a nervous impulse?

c Name the enzyme involved in the transport of these ions across the cell membrane.

d What is the position of this enzyme in the cell?

e Where does the energy come from to drive the transport of ions across the cell membrane?

20 Ion-specific channels are important in maintaining the correct balance of ions in cells. The K^+ ion channels depend on the hydrated potassium ions losing their hydration shell in order for transport to take place. The Na^+ ion channels depend on the hydrated ions keeping their hydration shells.

a Is the loss of the hydration layer exothermic or endothermic? Explain your answer.

b What interactions of the K^+ ions replace those with water?

c Why are Na^+ ions not able to use the same channel as the K^+ ions?

d i Explain why Li^+ ions do not move through the Na^+ ion channel as rapidly as Na^+ ions.

ii Explain why K^+ ions do not move through the Na^+ ion channel.

Toxic metals

Some metals, especially heavy metals such as mercury and lead, can have serious effects even though they occur at low concentrations in the environment. Heavy metals or their ions can accumulate in the food chain as one organism feeds on another (Figure 28.57). For example:

plankton ⟶ shrimps ⟶ fish ⟶ man
(microscopic organisms in the sea)

⟶
increasing concentration
of heavy metal in the organism

Eventually the metal ions build up to toxic levels in organisms higher up the food chain. Methods are now being developed to address the problems of identifying particular toxic substances in the environment (see Chapter 29, page 472).

Figure 28.57 Shellfish concentrate mercury and other heavy metal ions from seawater.

Fact file

Research in the Far East has shown that shellfish such as oysters and scallops are particularly good at accumulating mercury. Oysters can concentrate the mercury so that it is 100 000 times the concentration in the surrounding seawater. Scallops can concentrate cadmium up to 2 million times its concentration in seawater!

Living organisms can concentrate metals by:
- precipitating insoluble salts of the metal in their bodies
- concentrating ions, especially organometallic ions, e.g. CH_3Hg^+; many of these are soluble in fats and are easily absorbed by organisms higher up the food chain.

On page **418** you saw that metal ions can interfere with enzyme function by disrupting —SH or —S—S— groups involved in maintaining the tertiary structure of proteins. Metal ions such as Li^+, Ca^{2+}, Pb^{2+} and Hg^+ can also disrupt van der Waals' forces. In extreme cases this can result in loss of protein tertiary structure and loss of enzyme function.

The way in which heavy metals accumulate in the environment varies from metal to metal. Two examples are given here.

Mercury

Symptoms of mercury poisoning include loss of muscle coordination and mental functions.

Mercury can enter the food chain by a number of routes.
- Waste water from factories using mercury in industrial processes, e.g. old processes for making sodium hydroxide.
- Mercury-based fungicides used to spray crops wash off into rivers.
- Mercury compounds used to treat wood wash off into rivers.

Some micro-organisms can convert mercury salts into organomercury compounds which are taken up by organisms in the water and eventually finish up in humans.

Lead

The uptake of lead by humans has harmful effects on the nervous system, including the brain (particularly in children).

Lead can enter the environment in a number of ways.
- Lead used in old water pipes can be taken into the body when water is used for drinking.
- Lead compounds in some paints can get into the air we breathe.
- Lead compounds from car exhausts can settle on fruit and vegetables and be taken in when they are eaten. Pollution levels from this source are falling as the use of lead-free petrol increases.

Fact file

Heavy metal ions have been responsible for several thousand cases of poisoning in the area around Minamata Bay in Japan. Waste water from a chemical factory that processed various heavy metals was released into the bay between 1932 and 1968. The heavy metals accumulated in shellfish and fish living in the bay. These were eaten by the local population. Many people developed muscle pains, lack of feeling and damage to eyes, hearing and speech. Many died. It was not until 1956 that scientists realised that the cause of these symptoms was soluble mercury compounds from the factory.

Check-up

21 a How do heavy metal ions affect the structure and function of enzymes?

b Write an equation to show the reaction of Hg^+ ions with an —S—S— bridge in a polypeptide chain.

22 a Explain how traces of a heavy metal such as mercury can accumulate progressively up the food chain.

b State **two** ways by which mercury can enter the environment.

Summary

- [ ] Proteins are condensation polymers formed from amino acid monomers. The amino acid monomers are linked by peptide bonds to form a polypeptide chain.
- [ ] There are 20 different amino acids used by cells to build proteins.
- [ ] The amino acids found in proteins contain a carboxylic acid, an amino group and a side-chain (represented by R) all attached to the same carbon atom. They have the general formula $NH_2CH(R)COOH$.
- [ ] The R groups may be classified as polar or non-polar, and as acidic, basic or neutral.
- [ ] The primary structure of a protein chain is the sequence of amino acids in the chain.
- [ ] The secondary structure of a protein arises from the folding of the polypeptide backbone into α-helices or β-pleated sheets and their stabilisation by hydrogen bonding between N—H and C=O groups in different peptide bonds.
- [ ] The tertiary structure of a protein arises from further folding of the secondary structure and its stabilisation by bonds and intermolecular forces between the R groups (disulfide bonds, ionic bonds, hydrogen bonds and van der Waals' forces).
- [ ] The functioning of proteins depends on their three-dimensional structure (which is determined by its amino acid sequence).
- [ ] Enzymes are biological (protein) catalysts that provide an alternative reaction pathway of lower activation energy.
- [ ] Each enzyme reacts with a substrate (a specific molecule or class of molecules) and converts it into product(s).
- [ ] The active site is a specific region on the surface of an enzyme which recognises a particular substrate. Catalysis takes place at the active site.
- [ ] The recognition of the shape and charge distribution as well as the binding of a substrate by the active site is called a 'lock-and-key' mechanism.
- [ ] Enzyme-catalysed reactions generally exhibit their maximum activity within a narrow range of temperature and pH. They are very sensitive to changes in temperature and pH.
- [ ] Denaturation is a process by which the 3-dimensional structure of the protein or other biological macromolecule is changed, often irreversibly.
- [ ] Two common types of inhibition of enzymes are competitive and non-competitive inhibition.
  - In competitive inhibition, the substrate has a similar shape and charge to the substrate and competes with it to bind at the active site.
  - In non-competitive inhibition, a substance binds to the enzyme at a place away from the active site of the enzyme. The binding alters the shape of the enzyme sufficiently to prevent the catalysed reaction from taking place. The structure of the inhibitor usually bears no relationship to that of the substrate.
- [ ] Ion channels in cell membranes consist of enzyme-like proteins with properties that allow the selective transport of ions across the membrane.
- [ ] Small molecules or ions can modify the structure and function of enzymes, disrupt protein–protein interactions or block ion channels.
- [ ] Deoxyribonucleic acid (DNA) is a condensation polymer consisting of:
  - two chains of sugar–phosphate backbone (the sugar is deoxyribose)
  - nitrogen-containing bases attached to each sugar; the bases are adenine (A), guanine (G), cytosine (C) and thymine (T).
- [ ] The two sugar–phosphate chains run in opposite directions (they are anti-parallel) with the two chains twisted round each other to form a double helix.
- [ ] Pairs of bases (complementary pairs) are stacked at right angles to the long axis of the helix. A always pairs with T and C always pairs with G by hydrogen bonding. This helps stabilise the helix.
- [ ] Ribonucleic acids (RNA) are condensation polymers consisting of:
  - single chains of sugar–phosphate backbone, the chain sometimes being looped round to form helical regions
  - the sugar is ribose
  - nitrogen-containing bases attached to each sugar; the bases are the same as in DNA except that uracil (U) replaces thymine.
- [ ] DNA produces new copies of itself during cell division. This is called replication.
- [ ] When DNA replicates itself identical copies of the base sequence are produced. After cell division the new DNA molecules consist of one parent DNA strand and one 'new' strand.
- [ ] Complementary base pairing is the molecular basis for DNA replication.

- DNA carries the genetic information for the production of proteins. Each gene stores the information for a polypeptide chain.
- The synthesis of proteins involves messenger RNA (mRNA), transfer RNA (tRNA) and ribosomal RNA (rRNA).
- The process by which the stored information for a protein is copied from DNA to form a strand of mRNA is called transcription.
- The process by which the genetic information is transferred from mRNA to make a polypeptide chain is called translation. It involves tRNA and rRNA as well as specific proteins.
- mRNA contains a triplet code in which three bases in the RNA sequence (a codon) code for one amino acid in the polypeptide chain. The way in which each base triplet codes for a specific amino acid is called the 'genetic code'.
- tRNA molecules bring specific amino acids to the ribosomes and bind to specific codons in the mRNA. Protein synthesis then takes place by the process involving initiation, elongation and termination of the polypeptide chain.
- Mutations can arise from the alteration or deletion of one or more bases in DNA. This may lead to an altered protein structure.
- Altered protein structure is responsible for diseases such as sickle-cell anaemia.
- Modification to the primary structure of a protein can result in modified structure and/or function of that protein.
- Adenosine triphosphate (ATP) is a molecule involved in energy transfer reactions in the cells of the body.
- The energy required for metabolic reactions is provided when ATP is hydrolysed to ADP and inorganic phosphate, P_i.
- Some metals have important roles in biological systems. These include:
  - iron in haemoglobin (the blood pigment that transports oxygen in the body)
  - sodium and potassium in the transmission of nerve impulses
  - zinc as an enzyme cofactor.
- Some metals (for example heavy metals such as mercury) are toxic because they interfere with the tertiary structure of proteins.
- Organisms can be poisoned because heavy metals in the environment enter the body of organisms during feeding and are then concentrated in the food chain.

End-of-chapter questions

1   Adenosine triphosphate (ATP) plays an important part in energy transfers in metabolism.
   a Describe the **three** main components of ATP. [3]
   b State **three** different types of cellular activity which depend on ATP. [3]
   c Explain, with the aid of a simplified equation, how the hydrolysis of ATP can be used to make energetically unfavourable reactions take place in the cell. [3]
   d The nucleotide triphosphates ATP, GTP, CTP and TTP are involved in the replication of DNA. Describe the process of replication of DNA. [6]
                                   Total = 15

2   Ribonuclease is an enzyme which hydrolyses ribonucleic acids. Its secondary structure contains both α-helices and β-pleated sheets.
   a i Describe the structure of a typical α-helix. [5]
      ii Describe the structure of a typical β-pleated sheet. [4]
   b The single polypeptide chain of ribonuclease contains four disulfide bridges.
      i Draw the structure of a disulfide bridge. [1]
      ii How are disulfide bridges formed? [2]
   c Ribonuclease is an enzyme which can be denatured by treating it with urea and β-mercapotoethanol.
      i What is the meaning of the term **denatured**? [2]
      ii The β-mercapotoethanol breaks the disulfide bridges. How does the urea denature ribonuclease? [1]
                                   Total = 15

3 mRNA is formed by transcription from DNA.
  a Describe **three** differences between DNA and mRNA. [3]
  b Write the full name of mRNA. [1]
  c Write the names of the bases A, C and U. [2]
  d Explain how the order of the bases on a particular mRNA codes for a specific protein. [4]
  e Changes in the bases in DNA can cause mutations.
    i Describe **two** things that can cause a mutation other than natural errors in the
      replication process. [2]
    ii Two bases are changed in the gene in DNA which codes for a particular enzyme.
       This may or may not affect enzyme activity. Explain why. [4]

Total = 16

4 Three levels of protein structure are primary, secondary and tertiary.
  a Describe the primary structure of a typical protein containing one polypeptide chain.
    Name the type of chemical bonding involved in the primary structure of a protein. [4]
  b Name **two** types of protein secondary structure. For each type give a named example. For one
    of your examples state where it is found in the cell. Describe the bonding that stabilises these
    secondary structures as fully as you can. [7]
  c The tertiary structure of a protein is stabilised by interactions between the side-chains of particular
    amino acids. Describe **four** different types of interactions which maintain the tertiary structure of
    a protein. For each type of interaction give an explanation of how the attractive forces arise. [8]

Total = 19

5 Some metals are essential to life, whilst others are toxic.
  a Explain the role of iron in red blood cells and describe any chemical reactions involved. [3]
  b Zinc is a cofactor for the enzyme carbonic anhydrase.
    i What does the term **cofactor** mean? [2]
    ii What is the function of carbonic anhydrase in the body? [1]
    iii Describe the chemical role of zinc in the reaction catalysed by carbonic anhydrase. [3]
  c Mercury is a toxic metal.
    i Give one possible source of mercury in the environment. [1]
    ii Explain why eating fish caught from seawater polluted with mercury can lead to poisoning
       even though the concentration of mercury in seawater is too low to cause direct harm. [2]
  d Mercury(I) ions, Hg^+, can inactivate enzymes containing disulfide bridges. Describe with the aid
    of an equation why Hg^+ ions inactivate these enzymes. [3]

Total = 15

6 DNA is a self-replicating molecule which passes on genetic information from one generation to another.

    a Write the full name for DNA. [1]

    b The diagram below shows part of one strand of DNA. Copy the diagram then draw the complementary strand made when DNA replicates itself. On your diagram label:
- the components of the strand you drew
- the bonds formed with the original strand [3]

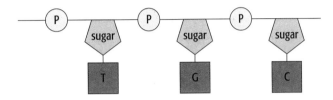

    c Describe the roles of each of the following in protein synthesis:

      i tRNA [3]

      ii the ribosomes. [3]

    d The first stage in protein synthesis is transcription. Describe the process of transcription, including the name and structure of the RNA that is formed during this process. [7]

                                                        Total = 17

7 Enzymes are condensation polymers of amino acids.

    a What is the meaning of the term **condensation polymer**? [2]

    b The structures of two amino acids are shown below.

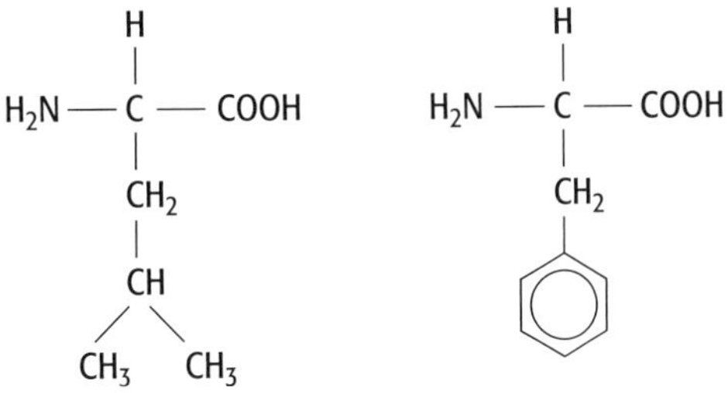

$$H_2N - \underset{\underset{\underset{\underset{CH_3 \quad CH_3}{\diagup \diagdown}}{CH}}{\overset{\overset{H}{|}}{\underset{|}{C}}} - COOH \qquad H_2N - \underset{\underset{\bigcirc}{CH_2}}{\overset{\overset{H}{|}}{\underset{|}{C}}} - COOH$$

               leucine   phenylalanine

    Draw the displayed formula of the structure of the dipeptide Phe-Leu formed by condensation polymerisation. [2]

c In plants the enzyme urease catalyses the hydrolysis of urea to form ammonia. The structure of urea is shown below.

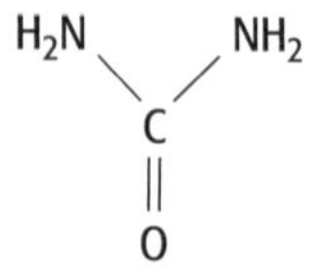

The effect of pH on this catalysis is shown in the graph below.

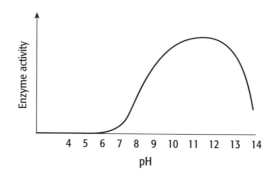

i   How does this graph differ from the pH curve expected for a typical enzyme within a cell? [2]
ii What advantage is there in urease having a pH curve as shown in the diagram? [3]
iii Use your knowledge of the ionisation of amino acid side-chains to suggest why urease shows hardly any catalytic activity at pH 4. [2]

d Ethanehydroxamic acid is a competitive inhibitor of urease.

i   The data in the table shows the effect of different mixtures of urea and ethanehydroxamic acid (EHA) on the rate of reaction.

Experiment	1	2	3	4	5
[Urea] / mol dm^{-3}	4×10^{-2}	4×10^{-2}	4×10^{-2}	7×10^{-2}	1×10^{-1}
[EHA] / mol dm^{-3}	0	2×10^{-2}	4×10^{-2}	4×10^{-2}	4×10^{-2}
Rate of reaction / mol dm^{-3} (NH$_3$) min^{-1}	6.0×10^{-3}	5.2×10^{-3}	4.4×10^{-3}	4.9×10^{-3}	5.4×10^{-3}

How does this data show that EHA is a competitive inhibitor of urease? [2]

ii The structure of ethanehydroxamic acid is:

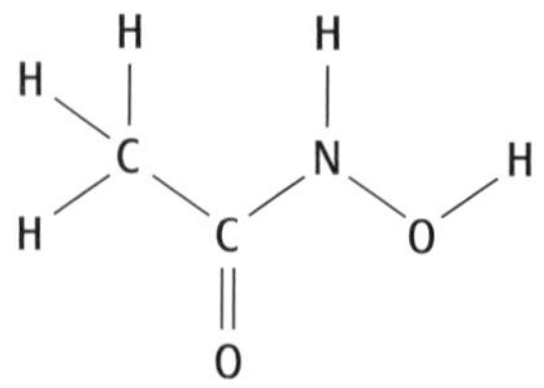

What structural features make ethanehydroxamic acid a suitable competitive inhibitor of the urease-catalysed reaction? [2]

Total = 15

8 Haemoglobin is an iron-containing protein.
  a Where is haemoglobin found in the body? [1]
  b Haem is the prosthetic group in haemoglobin. State the meaning of the term **prosthetic group**. [2]
  c Haemoglobin contains four polypeptide subunits, each of which contains a haem molecule.
    Each haem molecule contains one Fe^{2+} ion which can bond reversibly to an oxygen molecule.
    Write the overall equation for the reaction of one haemoglobin molecule with oxygen. Use the
    symbol Hb for haemoglobin. [2]
  d Describe the type of force or bond that holds the haem group to the polypeptide chain in a subunit
    of haemoglobin. [1]
  e By referring to the structure of haem, explain why carbon monoxide is so poisonous. [2]
  f The first step in the metabolic pathway of haem synthesis involves an enzyme which is inhibited
    by haem. The inhibition is non-competitive. Describe how a non-competitive inhibitor works. [4]

  Total = 12

9 **a** The diagram shows a section of mRNA.

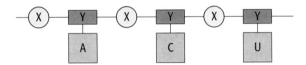

  i Identify the blocks labelled **X** and **Y**. [2]
  ii State the names of each of the three bases represented by the letters A, C and U. [2]
  b The table shows the base codes used by mRNA.

Codon	Amino acid	Codon	Amino acid	Codon	Amino acid	Codon	Amino acid
AUU	Ile	ACU	Thr	AAU	Asn	AGU	Ser
AUC	Ile	ACC	Thr	AAC	Asn	AGC	Ser
AUA	Ile	ACA	Thr	AAA	Lys	AGA	Arg
AUG	Met/start	ACG	Thr	AAG	Lys	AGG	Arg
CUU	Leu	CCU	Pro	CAU	His	CGU	Arg
CUC	Leu	CCC	Pro	CAC	His	CGC	Arg
CUA	Leu	CCA	Pro	CAA	Gln	CGA	Arg
CUG	Leu	CCG	Pro	CAG	Gln	CGG	Arg
GUU	Val	GCU	Ala	GAU	Asp	GGU	Gly
GUC	Val	GCC	Ala	GAC	Asp	GGC	Gly
GUA	Val	GCA	Ala	GAA	Glu	GGA	Gly
GUG	Val	GCG	Ala	GAG	Glu	GGG	Gly
UUU	Phe	UCU	Ser	UAU	Tyr	UGU	Cys
UUC	Phe	UCC	Ser	UAC	Tyr	UGC	Cys
UUA	Leu	UCA	Ser	UAA	stop	UGA	stop
UUG	Leu	UCG	Ser	UAG	stop	UGG	Trp

i The following sequence of bases in mRNA codes for part of a polypeptide chain of an enzyme. What amino acid sequence would this sequence produce? [2]

   –GGGAAUUACCAAUAA–
      3   5

ii Give **two** reasons why the codon UAA is important. [2]

iii What would be the effect, if any, on the enzyme activity if a mutation caused the base numbered 3 to be replaced by one of the other bases, A, C or U? Explain your answer. [2]

iv What would be the effect, if any, on the enzyme activity if a mutation caused the base numbered 5 to be replaced by U? Explain your answer. [3]

c Cystic fibrosis is a genetic disease. Explain how the genetic defect brings about cystic fibrosis. [3]

Total = 16

10 Cell membranes contain Na^+ and K^+ ion channels which regulate the concentration of ions in the cell.

a Compare the relative concentrations of Na^+ and K^+ ions inside the cells and in the tissue fluid just outside the cells. [2]

b The diagram shows the structure of an ion channel.

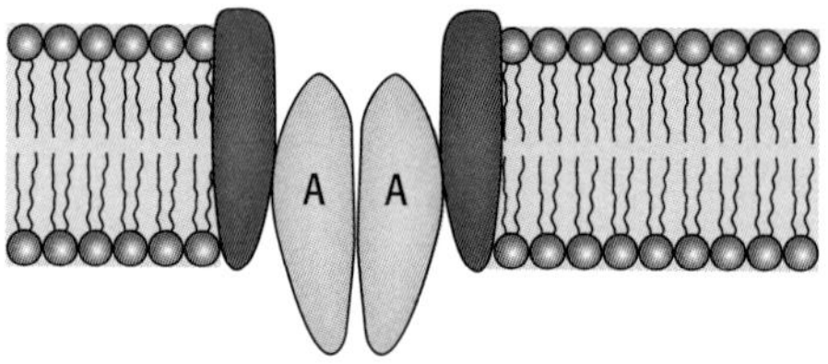

   membrane

What is **A**? [1]

c Na^+ and K^+ ions are only pumped through the cell membrane when ATP is hydrolysed.

   i What is the full name of ATP? [1]

   ii State the name of a substance that can inhibit the transport of ions across the cell membrane and describe how it does this. [4]

d Ion pumps are responsible for the conduction of nervous impulses. Explain how. [4]

e Explain why the sodium ion channel is more permeable to sodium ions than potassium ions. [3]

Total = 15

Learning outcomes

Candidates should be able to:

- describe simply the process of electrophoresis and the effect of pH, using peptides and amino acids as examples (see also Chapter **28**, page **409**)
- explain, in simple terms, the technique of DNA fingerprinting and its applications in forensic science, archaeology and medicine
- describe the importance to modern medicine, and the challenges, of separating and characterising the proteins in cells (see also Chapter **28**, page **410**)
- outline in simple terms the principles of nuclear magnetic resonance in ^{1}H and be able to interpret simple NMR spectra
- show awareness of the use of NMR and X-ray crystallography in determining the structure of macromolecules and in understanding their function (see also Chapter **28**, page **410**)

- state what is meant by **partition coefficient** and calculate a partition coefficient for a system in which the solute is in the same molecular state in the two solvents
- understand qualitatively paper, high-performance liquid, thin-layer and gas/liquid chromatography in terms of adsorption and/or partition and be able to interpret data from these techniques
- explain the concept of mass spectroscopy, deduce the number of carbon atoms in a compound using the $M+1$ peak and the presence of bromine and chlorine atoms using the $M+2$ peak and suggest the identity of molecules formed by simple fragmentation in a given mass spectrum
- draw conclusions given appropriate information and data from environmental monitoring (for example, PCBs in the atmosphere, isotopic ratios in ice cores).

29.1 Electrophoresis

How electrophoresis works

The analytical technique of **electrophoresis** is based on separating ions placed in an electric field. If a sample is placed between two electrodes, positively charged ions will move towards a negatively charged electrode. Negatively charged ions will move towards a positively charged electrode (Figure **29.1**).

The sample is placed on absorbent paper or on a gel supported on a solid base such as a glass plate. A buffer solution carries the ions along. The rate at which the ions move towards the oppositely charged electrode depends, amongst other things, on the size and charge on the ions: larger ions will move more slowly; highly charged ions will move more quickly. Therefore the ions are separated as the electric field is applied. You get a series of lines or bands on the paper or gel once a chemical is applied. Sometimes ultraviolet light is used to show the bands up. The series of bands is called an **electropherogram** (Figure **29.2**).

Electrophoresis is used extensively in biochemical analysis. It can be used to separate, identify and purify proteins and nucleic acids (see page **421**). We can use it with amino acids and peptides obtained when a protein is hydrolysed.

Here is a simple example of how a mixture of three amino acids undergoes separation. Amino acid A could have a side-chain that is positively charged in a certain buffer solution, amino acid B could be neutral and amino acid C could be negatively charged (Figure **29.3**).

At a pH of 7, the amino acid species present in samples of A, B and C are shown in Figure **29.4**.

In Figure **29.1** you will notice the use of a buffer solution in the electrophoresis apparatus. The chemical structures in Figure **29.4** show why we need to control the pH in electrophoresis. On page **395** we saw how amino acids react in acidic and alkaline conditions to form ions. The charge on the ions depends on the pH.

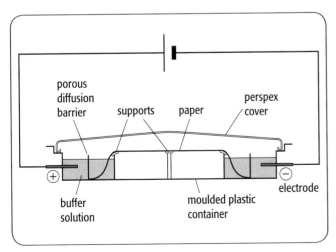

Figure 29.1 This apparatus shows how paper electrophoresis is carried out.

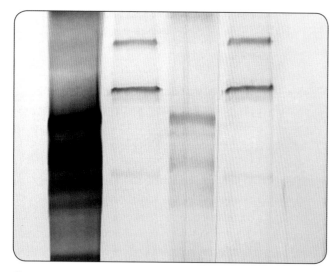

Figure 29.2 Comparing electropherograms.

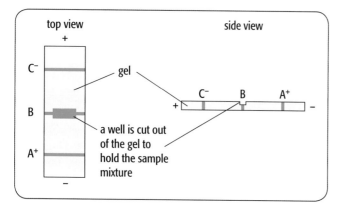

Figure 29.3 The principle of gel electrophoresis.

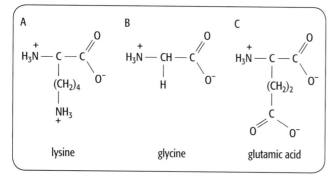

Figure 29.4 The charge on amino acids depends on the pH of the solution.

Therefore pH will affect the movement of ions during electrophoresis.

When separating a mixture of proteins, they are usually first treated with a chemical that makes them all negatively charged. A dye can also be added. All the proteins then migrate in the same direction, towards the positive electrode, but larger proteins move more slowly.

1 A mixture of three amino aids is separated by gel electrophoresis.
The three amino acids are glycine, valine and phenylalanine (Figure 29.5).

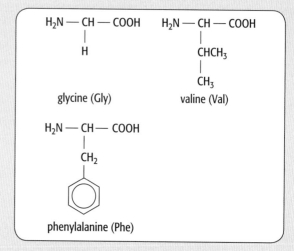

Figure 29.5 Three amino acids to be separated by electrophoresis.

  a The electrophoresis is carried out in a buffer solution of pH 10. Draw the ions present in these alkaline conditions.
  b i Draw a sketch of the electropherogram you would expect (viewed from above), labelling the amino acids as Gly, Val and Phe.
    ii Explain your answer to part b i.

Uses of DNA fingerprinting/profiling

Forensic science

The DNA of each person is basically similar in its chemical structure. The two strands in the double helix of DNA are held in place via hydrogen bonds between base pairs. The DNA stores the information – called the genes – that provide the genetic blueprints for making proteins (see page 425). However, there are segments along the DNA molecules which do not seem to carry the instructions needed to make proteins. These bits of DNA are repeated along the DNA molecule. They are called 'minisatellites'. The number and sequence of these is unique to each person (except identical twins).

Genetic fingerprinting (also called DNA fingerprinting) is based on matching these minisatellite regions of DNA. We inherit half from our mother and half from our father. Figure 29.6 shows the steps in making a genetic fingerprint.

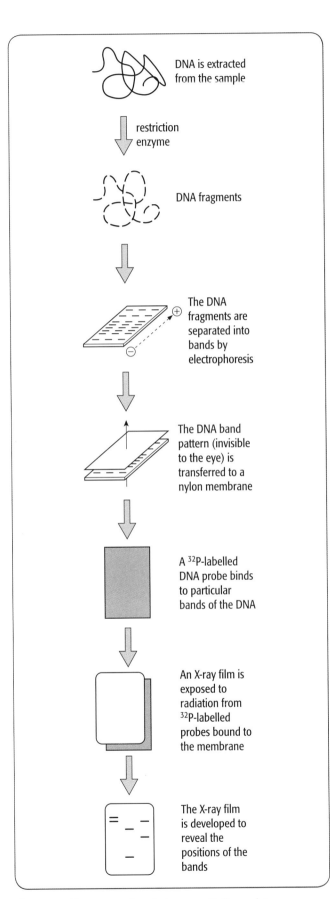

The DNA is extracted from the sample

restriction enzyme

DNA fragments

The DNA fragments are separated into bands by electrophoresis

The DNA band pattern (invisible to the eye) is transferred to a nylon membrane

A ^{32}P-labelled DNA probe binds to particular bands of the DNA

An X-ray film is exposed to radiation from ^{32}P-labelled probes bound to the membrane

The X-ray film is developed to reveal the positions of the bands

Figure 29.6 The process of producing a genetic fingerprint.

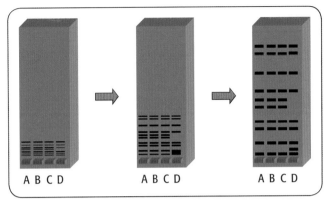

A B C D   A B C D   A B C D

Figure 29.7 When a house was burgled, the police found four samples containing DNA: some hair, A, some skin flakes, B, an eyelash, C, and some blood on a door handle, D. DNA was extracted from the four samples and analysed by genetic fingerprinting. The DNA in samples A, B and C match the homeowners' DNA, but sample D does not. Therefore forensic scientists can check Sample D against the DNA database or match it against a suspect's DNA.

In the first step, restriction enzymes are used to 'cut' the DNA molecule at specific places where the same sequences occur, making smaller fragments for analysis.

DNA fragments are all negatively charged because of the phosphate groups present. Therefore they will all move towards the positive electrode in gel electrophoresis. The fragments move at different rates because they have different sizes. Larger fragments find it harder to get through the matrix formed by the gel than smaller fragments, so larger fragments do not travel as far in a given time (Figure 29.7).

The bands are made visible by radioactive labelling of the bands with the phosphorus-32 isotope, which causes photographic film to fog. Alternatively, a probe can be used that makes the bands fluoresce in ultraviolet light.

However, this technique does need a relatively large sample of DNA to work. At a crime scene the samples can be very small so a technique called **short tandem repeat (STR) analysis** has been developed. This can be used to make a genetic profile from a sample as small as 1×10^{-9} g. This means that the DNA from a single cell is sufficient to obtain evidence! The technique works by multiplying the short sequences of bases that occur on chromosomes that make up genes. It uses the enzyme DNA polymerase to copy selected sequences over a million times so we have enough to separate and detect using electrophoresis. People differ in the number of these short sequences their DNA contains. This affects the distance the bands travel in electrophoresis, which produces different genetic fingerprints.

The FBI in America has selected 13 sites on the DNA molecule to test in order to standardise STR analysis.

This will create a national STR database. The chances of two people having identical sequences at all 13 sites on their DNA are smaller than 1 in a billion. In one crime in Texas a detective had read that the new STR technique could get sufficient DNA for a conviction from a few skin cells on a rope or cord that had been used to strangle someone. The detective was called to a rape scene where the rapist had used a telephone cord around the victim's neck. Unfortunately the rapist had used gloves and had afterwards worn a condom. At first there appeared to be no biological evidence to collect. However, the detective insisted the cord undergo microscopic examination. The forensic scientists found a trace of saliva on the cord. The saliva had been left on the cord as the rapist held it in his mouth as the victim struggled. The rapist was soon arrested and convicted.

DNA profiling is being used more frequently to solve 'cold cases' (unsolved crimes). Biological samples, if stored correctly, can survive for decades. STR analysis means that samples too small to test at the time of the crime can now lead to a conviction. Criminals who thought they had literally got away with murder are now in prison. The technique has also rectified miscarriages of justice. Prisoners who have been falsely imprisoned have now been released using DNA evidence.

More techniques, such as mitochondrial DNA analysis, are still being developed and refined. Mitochondrial DNA can be extracted from samples lacking cells with nuclei, such as hair shafts, teeth and bones, that have been stored or buried for many years.

Familial searching is used when a DNA match is not found on the database. Other DNA profiles offering a close match of the type come from members of the same family. It was first used in 2002, in Wales, to solve the murders of three girls in 1973. The murderer's DNA was not on the national database but 100 close matches, linked with other evidence, eventually led police to a local man who had since died. On exhuming his body he was found to be the guilty man.

As DNA techniques become more sophisticated and more sensitive, police and forensic scientists must take extra care not to contaminate evidence when collecting, testing or storing it. The slightest impurity could affect the separation and position of bands on an electropherogram. Defence lawyers will often turn to sample contamination as a way to question DNA evidence offered against their clients. This can be a real issue. In a case in Germany, a woman suspected of six murders on DNA evidence

turned out to be a worker at a factory supplying the forensic science department with cotton wool swabs. She had accidentally contaminated the swabs so her DNA profile was identified at about 40 different crime scenes. She was completely innocent – of the crimes at least!

Check-up

2 Figure 29.8 shows four DNA fingerprints used in a paternity suit. The father of the child could have been F1 or F2. The mother's profile is labelled M and the child's is C.

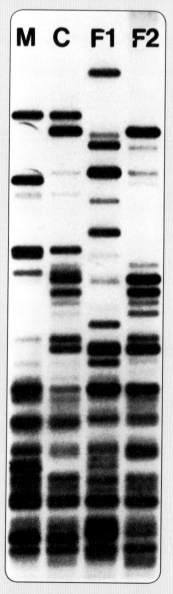

Figure 29.8 Genetic profiles used in a paternity suit.

continued ⋯⫶

a Who is the child's father?

b What is the role of electrophoresis in genetic profiling?

c What problems arise for a police force from the development of a new profiling techniques such as short tandem repeat (STR) analysis?

Archaeology

Sometimes the work of archaeologists and forensic scientists can be similar. A major battle at Fromelle, in France, took place in 1916 during the First World War. Almost 2000 Australian soldiers and 500 British soldiers died. A memorial was erected on the battlefield but individual headstones could not be used because many bodies had never been recovered. In 2009 the remains of 250 soldiers were found, buried in pits dug after the battle. Painstaking work was carried out to piece together the remains and belongings of the soldiers and then DNA analysis was used to try to identify the soldiers (Figure **29.9**).

The researchers found that DNA taken from teeth was in better condition than DNA from bones. The enamel on the teeth provided protection against decomposers in the soil. For identification they used Y chromosome and mitochondrial analysis to match with samples from ancestors of the soldiers. The Y chromosome is inherited on the male side of a family and the mitochondrial DNA on the female side. Both these are used in cold-case forensic science when DNA samples are in poor condition. The remains of the soldiers will be re-buried once DNA analysis has taken place and their headstones will be marked with their name once identification is completed. The researchers estimate that this task might take four or five years.

Research on more ancient problems often leads to controversy. Scientists argue over the validity of evidence from ancient DNA samples and the interpretation of the findings. One example involves the ancient Egyptian pharaoh Tutankhamun and how he died. Dr Zahi Hawass, the head of Egypt's Supreme Council of Antiquities, has led a team that carried out partial Y-chromosome analysis to find out more about the pharaoh's family tree (Figure **29.10**). They also found the DNA of a mosquito in the king's remains and speculate that malaria could have played a role in his death at 19 years old. Others working in the field insist that DNA over 3000 years old can never produce a definitive answer as to which of the young pharaoh's illnesses ultimately killed him.

Medical applications

In 2001 the Human Genome project published the complete sequence of nucleotide bases – adenine, guanine, cytosine and thymine – in human DNA for the first time. Since then research into the role genes play in disease has greatly increased. Quicker and cheaper ways have been developed to analyse the sequence in parts of DNA. Researchers are looking for links between certain genes and particular diseases. This information can lead

Figure 29.9 Forensic archaeologists, in 2009, digging up remains at the site of the Battle of Fromelle, France.

Figure 29.10 Archaeologists test the remains of a 3000-year-old Egyptian mummy.

to early recognition of a person's risk of contracting a particular disease. A person with an increased risk is said to have a predisposition to that disease. At present, companies can analyse your DNA and give you a report on your predisposition to almost 100 different diseases. These include the risk of heart attack, arthritis, macular degeneration (an eye disease), breast cancer, colorectal cancer, prostate cancer, multiple sclerosis, obesity and diabetes. Personalising medical diagnosis using DNA analysis will become more common as genetic reseach makes more advances.

The genes responsible for genetic diseases such as sickle-cell anaemia, Huntington's disease, Duchenne muscular dystrophy and cystic fibrosis can be identified using DNA analysis. People who carry the defective gene can have tests to show if the disease is present in the embryo of an unborn child. This is called genetic screening. Treatment, called gene therapy, is now possible. The replacement of a defective gene by a 'normal' gene is the most common form of gene therapy at present.

Eventually it is hoped that genes responsible for certain non-genetic diseases, once identified, will be able to be modified. This will mean that a genetic predisposition to certain diseases can be eliminated before the disease strikes. The economic and social implications of such advances are difficult to predict.

An existing, specific use of DNA fingerprinting is in the treatment of leukaemia by a bone marrow transplant. After the operation, the patient's blood, and the donor's blood, both undergo DNA analysis. If the bands on the two electropherograms coincide, then the patient's blood cells, and the DNA in them, have come from the transplanted bone marrow. This means that the transplant has been successful.

Check-up

3 a The Dead Sea Scrolls are 2000-year-old documents. Each scroll was written on skin, taken from one sheep or goat. The scrolls are in poor condition and many were found in pieces (Figure **29.11**). For example, one cave contained 15 000 fragments from 500 different scrolls. Suggest how forensic archaeology could be used to help reconstruct the scrolls.

continued ···⇢

b Why is mitochondrial analysis a useful technique in DNA profiling?

Figure 29.11 Part of a Dead Sea scroll.

29.2 Nuclear magnetic resonance (NMR)

How NMR works

Nuclear magnetic resonance (**NMR**) spectroscopy is a widely used analytical technique for organic compounds. NMR is based on the fact that the nucleus of each hydrogen atom in an organic molecule behaves like a tiny magnet. The nucleus of a hydrogen atom consists of a single proton. This proton can spin. This movement of the positively charged proton causes a very small magnetic field to be set up.

In NMR we put the sample to be analysed in a magnetic field. The hydrogen nuclei (protons) either line up with the field or, by spinning in the opposite direction, line up against it (Figure **29.12**).

There is a tiny difference in energy between the oppositely spinning ^{1}H nuclei. This difference corresponds to the energy carried by waves in the radiowave range of the electromagnetic radiation spectrum. In NMR spectroscopy the nuclei 'flip' between the two energy levels (Figure **29.13**). Only atoms whose mass number is an odd number, e.g. ^{1}H or ^{13}C, absorb energy in the range of frequencies that are analysed.

The size of the gap between the nuclear energy levels varies slightly, depending on the other atoms in the molecule (the molecular environment). Therefore, NMR

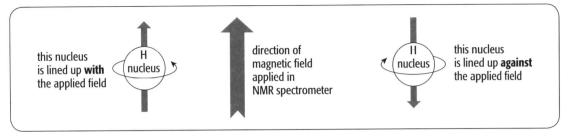

Figure 29.12
Hydrogen (^{1}H) nuclei will line up with or against an applied magnetic field.

can be used to identify ^{1}H atoms in different parts of a molecule. This is easier to visualise by looking at an example. If we look at a molecule of methanol, CH_3OH, we can see that there are ^{1}H atoms in two different molecular environments. We have the ^{1}H atoms in the —CH_3 group and the ^{1}H atom in the —OH group. The energy absorbed by the —CH_3 ^{1}H atoms is different from the energy absorbed by the ^{1}H atoms in —OH.

In NMR spectroscopy, we vary the magnetic field as that is easier than varying the wavelength of radiowaves. As the magnetic field is varied, the ^{1}H nuclei in different molecular environments flip at different field strengths. The different field strengths are measured relative to a reference compound which is given a value of zero. The standard compound chosen is tetramethylsilane (**TMS**). TMS is an inert, volatile liquid which mixes well with most organic compounds. Its formula is $Si(CH_3)_4$, so all its H atoms are equivalent (i.e. they are all in the same molecular environment). TMS only gives one, sharp absorption, called a peak, and this peak is at a higher frequency than most other protons (Figure 29.14). All other absorptions are measured by their shift away from the TMS line on the NMR spectrum. This is called the chemical shift (δ), and is measured in units of parts per million (ppm).

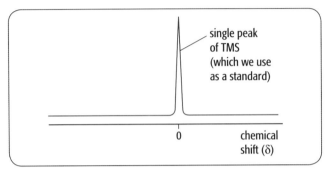

Figure 29.14 The standard TMS peak used as a reference on NMR spectra.

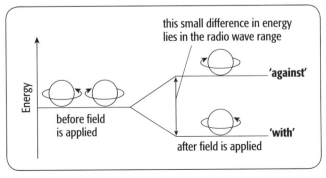

Figure 29.13 Hydrogen (^{1}H) nuclei will absorb energy in the radiowave range when they 'flip' from the lower energy level, lining up with the applied magnetic field, to the higher energy level, lining up against it.

Check-up

4 a Explain why tetramethylsilane (TMS) is used as a standard in NMR spectroscopy.
  b In NMR we use solvents such as tetrachloromethane to prepare samples for the machine (Figure 29.15).

Figure 29.15 Samples dissolved in a solvent in narrow tubes ready for NMR analysis.

  i What is the molecular formula of tetrachloromethane?
  ii Why do you think tetrachloromethane is used as a solvent?

continued ···>

iii Solvents which contain deuterium, D, are also used as solvents in NMR. Deuterium is the isotope ^2H. A substance in which ^1H is replaced by ^2H is said to be deuterated. Why would the deuterated solvent $CDCl_3$ be used instead of $CHCl_3$?

Low-resolution NMR

A low-resolution NMR spectrum shows a single peak for each non-equivalent hydrogen atom; an example is shown in Figure 29.16. Notice how the zero point on the x-axis, chemical shift (δ), is on the right of the spectrum and the shift increases in value going left.

There are three peaks on ethanol's low-resolution NMR spectrum. These correspond to the ^1H atoms in —OH, —CH_2— and —CH_3. Notice how the heights of the peaks vary. The area under each peak tells us the relative number of equivalent ^1H atoms responsible for that particular chemical shift. The largest peak will be from the —CH_3 hydrogen atoms, the middle peak from the —CH_2— hydrogen atoms and the smallest peak from the —OH hydrogen. The relative areas under the peaks are shown on the NMR spectrum by the labels 1H, 2H and 3H (Figure 29.16).

The type of H atom present can be checked against tables of data (Table 29.1) if you are using NMR to identify unknown organic compounds.

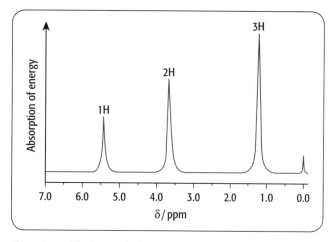

Figure 29.16 The low-resolution NMR spectrum of ethanol, CH_3CH_2OH.

Using Table 29.1 we can see that the peak at about 1.2 ppm is caused by the —CH_3 hydrogen atoms (range 0.7–1.6 ppm), the peak at about 3.7 ppm corresponds to —CH_2— hydrogen atoms (range 3.3–4.3 ppm) and the peak at about 5.4 ppm is due to the —OH hydrogen atom.

Check-up

5 Predict the number of peaks and the relative areas under each peak, where appropriate, on the low-resolution proton NMR spectrum of:
   a methanol, CH_3OH
   b benzene, C_6H_6
   c chloroethane, C_2H_5Cl
   d propan-1-ol
   e propan-2-ol
   f propanone.

High-resolution NMR

As you can see in Table 29.1, the chemical shifts are given over ranges, and the ranges for different types of hydrogen atoms do overlap. In some molecules where there is heavy shielding of the hydrogen nuclei by lots of electrons in surrounding atoms, peaks are shifted beyond their usual range. In such cases high-resolution NMR is useful. High-resolution NMR gives us more information to interpret. Peaks that appear as one 'signal' on a low-resolution NMR spectrum are often revealed to be made up a series of closely grouped peaks. This is because the magnetic fields generated by spinning nuclei interfere slightly with those of neighbouring nuclei. This is called spin–spin coupling. The exact **splitting pattern** of a peak depends on the number of hydrogen atoms on the adjacent carbon atom or atoms.

The number of signals a peak splits into equals **n + 1** where n is the number of ^1H atoms on the adjacent carbon atom.

The high-resolution NMR of ethanol illustrates this n + 1 rule used to interpret splitting patterns (Figure 29.17).

Type of proton	Chemical shift, δ/ppm
R–CH$_3$	0.7–1.6
N–H ⬥ R–OH	1.0–5.5*
R–CH$_2$–R	1.2–1.4
R$_3$CH	1.6–2.0
H$_3$C–C(=O) ⬥ RCH$_2$–C(=O) ⬥ R$_2$CH–C(=O)	2.0–2.9
⬡–CH$_3$ ⬥ ⬡–CH$_2$R ⬥ ⬡–CHR$_2$	2.3–2.7
N–CH$_3$ ⬥ N–CH$_2$R ⬥ N–CHR$_2$	2.3–2.9
O–CH$_3$ ⬥ O–CH$_2$R ⬥ O–CHR$_2$	3.3–4.3
Br or Cl–CH$_3$ ⬥ Br or Cl–CH$_2$R ⬥ Br or Cl–CHR$_2$	3.0–4.2
⬡–OH	4.5–10.0*
–CH=CH–	45.–6.0
–C(=O)NH$_2$ ⬥ –C(=O)HN–	5.0–12.0*
⬡–H	6.5–8.0
–C(=O)H	9.0–10
–C(=O)O–H	11.0–12.0*

Table 29.1 ^{1}H NMR chemical shifts relative to TMS. Chemical shifts are typical values which can vary slightly depending on the solvent, concentration and substituents. * OH and NH chemical shifts are very variable (sometimes outside these limits and are often broad. Signals are not usually seen as split peaks).

- The –CH$_3$ peak is split into three because there are two ^{1}H atoms on the adjacent –CH$_2$– group. $n + 1 = 3$ (as $n = 2$); this is called a triplet.
- The –CH$_2$– peak is split into four because there are three ^{1}H atoms on the adjacent –CH$_3$ group. $n + 1 = 4$ (as $n = 3$); this is called a quartet.

- The –OH peak is not usually split as its ^{1}H atom is constantly being exchanged with the ^{1}H atoms of other ethanol molecules and any water present. This results in one average peak being produced.

Table 29.2 shows the relative intensities and distribution of the splitting patterns you are likely to meet.

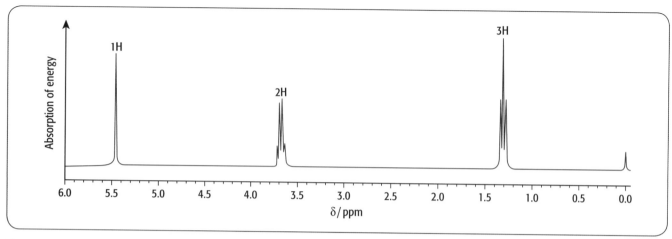

Figure 29.17 The high-resolution NMR spectrum of ethanol, showing the splitting pattern in two of the peaks. The area under each series of peaks still represents the number of equivalent ^{1}H atoms in the molecule, as in low-resolution NMR.

Number of adjacent ^{1}H atoms	Using the $n + 1$ rule, the peak will be split into ...	Relative intensities in the splitting pattern	Observed on the NMR spectrum as ...
0	1 peak, called a singlet	1	
1	2 peaks called a doublet	1:1	
2	3 peaks called a triplet	1:2:1	
3	4 peaks called a quartet	1:3:3:1	

Table 29.2 Splitting patterns in high-resolution NMR spectra.

Figure **29.18** shows another high-resolution NMR spectrum. You should try to interpret it by following these steps:

Step 1 Use δ values to identify the environment of the equivalent protons (^{1}H atoms) present at each peak (remembering the peak at zero is the TMS standard reference peak).

Step 2 Look at the relative areas under each peak to determine how many of each type of non-equivalent protons (^{1}H atoms) are present.

Step 3 Apply the $n + 1$ rule to the splitting patterns to see which protons (^{1}H atoms) are on adjacent carbon atoms in the unknown molecule.

Step 4 Put all this information together to identify the unknown molecule.

Worked example

1 An ester is used as a solvent in a glue. A chemist was given a sample of the ester to analyse. The NMR spectrum of the ester is shown in Figure **29.18**.

continued ⋯⋗

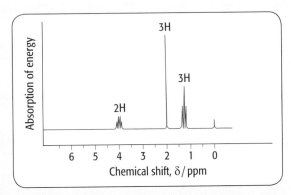

Figure 29.18 The high-resolution NMR spectrum of an unknown ester in a glue.

Step 1 Identify possibilities for the three major peaks that appear at chemical shifts of 1.3, 1.9 and 4.1 ppm. Using Table **29.1**, these could be:

1.3 ppm   R—CH$_3$, R—CH$_2$—R
1.9 ppm   R$_3$CH (possibly H$_3$C—CO—, RCH$_2$CO- or R$_2$CH—CO—)
4.1 ppm   —O—CH$_3$, O—CH$_2$R, O—CHR$_2$

Step 2 Use the relative numbers of each type of proton (^{1}H atom) labelling each major peak to narrow down possibilities.

1.3 ppm   labelled 3H, so could be R-CH$_3$
1.9 ppm   labelled 3H, so could be H$_3$C—CO—
4.1 ppm   labelled 2H, so could be O—CH$_2$R

Step 3 By applying the $n + 1$ rule to the splitting patterns we can see which protons (^{1}H atoms) are on adjacent carbon atoms.

1.3 ppm   labelled 3H and split into triplet, so R—CH$_3$ would be next to a C atom bonded to two ^{1}H atoms (2 + 1 = 3, triplet).
1.9 ppm   labelled 3H and a singlet, so H$_3$C—CO— would be next to a C atom with no ^{1}H atoms attached (0 + 1 = 1, singlet). It could well be next to the C=O, with the carbonyl carbon also bonded to an O atom, as in an ester, i.e. H$_3$C—COOR.
4.1 ppm   labelled 2H and split into quartet, O—CH$_2$R would be next to a C atom bonded to three ^{1}H atoms (3 + 1 = 4, quartet).

Step 4 Putting this information together we get the ester ethyl ethanoate, CH$_3$COOCH$_2$CH$_3$.

Check-up

6 A pathologist was given a sample of white tablet found at the scene of a suicide. In order to complete her report the pathologist received an NMR spectrum of the sample (Figure **29.19**) and information from the police that the tablets involved were either aspirin or paracetamol. The displayed formulae of both drugs are also shown in Figure **29.19**.

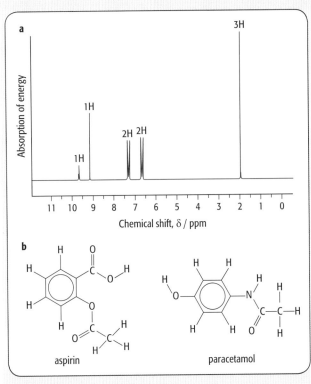

Figure 29.19 **a** NMR analysis of the unknown drug sample. **b** Aspirin and paracetamol.

a Using this information, which drug was in the white tablet? Explain your answer.
b Sketch the NMR spectrum you would expect to see if the other drug had undergone NMR analysis. Label each peak with its relative area and the type of proton that caused it.

Identifying the —OH or —NH— signal in an NMR spectrum

The —OH signal in the high-resolution NMR spectrum of ethanol appears as a single peak. As we have seen on page 455, the peak is not split by the ^{1}H atoms (protons) on the neighbouring —CH$_2$— group. The reason for this is that the —OH proton exchanges very rapidly with protons in any traces of water (or acid) present, as follows:

$$CH_3CH_2OH + H_2O \rightleftharpoons CH_3CH_2OH + HOH$$

The hydrogen atoms involved in this reversible proton exchange have been coloured red and blue. The exchange takes place so rapidly that the signal for the —OH protons becomes a single peak. This exchange also happens in amines and amides which contain the —NH— group.

Table 29.3 shows the chemical shift ranges for the different —OH and —NH— signals.

Different —OH and —NH— protons	Range of chemical shift (δ) / ppm
in alcohols, R—OH protons	1.0–5.5
in phenols, arene—OH protons	6.5–7.0
in carboxylic acids, R—COOH protons	11.0–11.7
in amines, —NH$_2$ / —NH—	1.0–5.5
in aryl amines, arene—NH$_2$	3.0–6.0
in amides, —CONH$_2$, —CONH—	5.0–12.0

Table 29.3 Chemical shift ranges for —OH and —NH— protons in different molecular environments.

As you can see from Table 29.1 (page 455), these ranges overlap with the chemical shifts of other types of proton. The signals can also appear outside the quoted ranges under certain conditions, e.g. choice of solvent or concentration. This makes NMR spectra difficult to interpret. However, there is a technique for positively identifying —OH or —NH— groups in a molecule. Their peaks 'disappear' from the spectra if you add a small amount of deuterium oxide, D$_2$O, to the sample. The deuterium atoms (^{2}H) in D$_2$O, called 'heavy water', exchange reversibly with the protons in the —OH or —NH— groups. For example:

$$-OH + D_2O \rightleftharpoons -OD + HOD$$

$$-NH-CO- + D_2O \rightleftharpoons -ND-CO- + HOD$$

The deuterium atoms do not absorb in the same region of the electromagnetic spectrum as protons (^{1}H atoms). This makes the —OH or —NH— signal disappear from the NMR spectrum. By checking against the peaks in the original NMR spectrum, without D$_2$O, we can tell if the —OH or —NH— groups are present in the sample. The ^{1}H atom in the —OH or —NH— group is referred to as a 'labile' proton.

Check-up

7 **a** Look back to Figure 29.17 on page 456. The high-resolution NMR spectrum shown is from a sample of ethanol containing traces of water. How would the NMR spectrum differ if D$_2$O had been added to the sample of ethanol?

   b Look back to Check-up question **6**. How would repeating the NMR analysis using a solvent of D$_2$O be able to help the pathologist distinguish between aspirin and paracetamol?

Identifying macromolecules

NMR spectroscopy is used extensively in finding out the structures of biological macromolecules such as proteins and nucleic acids. As well as identifying the different types of ^{1}H atoms present, more sophisticated data can yield, for example, the distance between atoms in macromolecules. Large amounts of data are collected and analysed by computer programs to reveal the shape of the molecules under investigation.

Figures 29.20 and 29.21 show images obtained from NMR analysis of two protein molecules made up from over 100 amino acids. These are called ribbon diagrams.

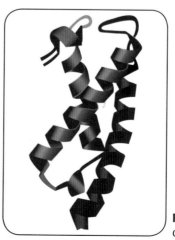

Figure 29.20 A protein made up of 106 amino acid residues.

Figure 29.21 A protein made up of 153 amino acid residues.

This NMR analysis takes place in solution, so it is particularly useful for medical research. Many human proteins exist in solution in the body so we can mimic the interactions that take place in cells or in the bloodstream.

X-ray crystallography

Another technique used to work out structures of complex molecules is **X-ray crystallography**. This has a disadvantage compared with NMR analysis because to get the best results we need to have a very pure crystal of the sample. Fortunately, many large biological molecules can be crystallised from solution.

This technique relies on the diffraction of X-rays as they pass into a crystal. The electrons in the atoms present are responsible for the diffraction pattern obtained in the apparatus shown in Figure 29.22. The larger the atom, the more electrons it contains and the more intense the spot it produces in its diffraction pattern.

The diffraction from each individual atom in the structure is small but the effect is magnified by the regular repeating patterns of atoms or ions in crystals. The crystal is irradiated and the image of the diffraction pattern is recorded. Then the crystal is rotated slightly (about 1°) and the image is recorded again, then another slight rotation takes place and so on. The process is repeated until the crystal has been irradiated from every angle.

At certain angles the waves that make up the X-rays reinforce each other and will produce an intense spot on the detector. At other angles the waves interfere with each other and cancel each other out. Figure 29.23 shows how this happens.

A computer analyses the position and intensity of the series of dots that appear on the X-ray film or other detector (Figure 29.24).

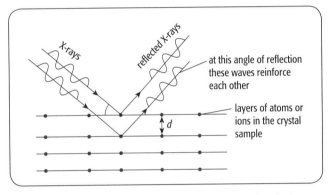

Figure 29.23 X-rays are reflected from layers of atoms or ions in the crystal. An equation, $2d\sin\theta = n\lambda$, tells us the distance between the layers, d, where θ = angle of incidence, λ = wavelength of the X-rays and n = a whole number.

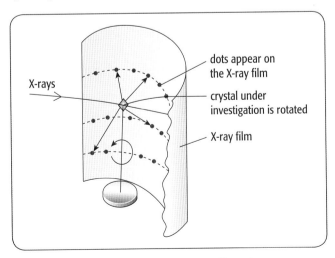

Figure 29.22 The apparatus used in X-ray crystallography.

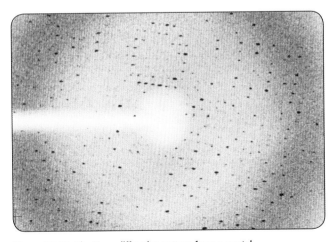

Figure 29.24 The X-ray diffraction pattern from a crystal.

Figure 29.25 The structure of a protein molecule shown using an electron density map.

From this diffraction pattern the distance between the planes of atoms in the crystal are calculated and an electron density map is constructed. This shows the shape of the molecule (Figure 29.25).

From this analysis, the crystallographer can pinpoint the positions of individual atoms in the molecule under investigation. Hydrogen atoms do not show up on an electron density map because they only contain one electron, but their positions can be inferred from the other atoms present. Part of a structure determined by X-ray crystallography is shown in Figure 29.26a and its full ribbon diagram is shown in Figure 29.26b.

Scientists use these structures to speculate about the function of newly isolated protein molecules, by matching their features to proteins whose features and functions are known.

Both NMR and X-ray crystallography have a role to play in finding out more about proteins. X-ray analysis can give very accurate measurements from single crystals and even some information from powders, where the diffraction pattern shows up as concentric circles, not dots. However, NMR can be used to investigate the behaviour of a protein in solution. The solution can be made to match the conditions in the living organism under investigation. NMR can then be used to monitor changes in shape, shedding light on the mechanisms at work in flexible molecules.

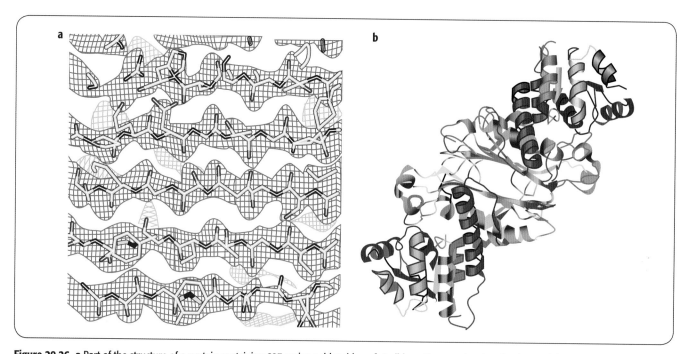

Figure 29.26 a Part of the structure of a protein containing 693 amino acid residues. **b** A ribbon diagram showing the shape of the protein.

8 a Which technique is used to produce an electron density map of a molecule?

b Why don't hydrogen atoms appear on an electron density map?

c What does a 'ribbon diagram' show?

d What are the strengths and weaknesses of using NMR and X-ray crystallography to elucidate the structure and function of proteins?

e Put the following processes used in X-ray crystallography into the correct sequence:

   A construct an atomic model

   B prepare a pure crystalline sample

   C analyse the diffraction pattern

   D construct an electron density map

   E irradiate crystal with X-rays

Medical application of NMR

Besides research into proteins and nucleic acids which will help prevent and cure diseases, NMR is also used to diagnose medical problems. The technique of MRI (magnetic resonance imaging) scanning has been adapted from NMR spectroscopy. The patient is placed inside a body scanner which generates a powerful magnetic field. A computer analyses the radiowaves absorbed by ^1H nuclei in successive 'slices' of the body, combining these to make a 3-D image of organs inside the body. MRI is much safer than high-energy X-ray imaging. As an example of its use, MRI can monitor the success of cancer treatment in reducing the size of tumours.

Much research is now taking place on the function of the brain using MRI. We can monitor brain activity as people perform tasks. Neuroscientists have been looking at the way we form our memories. They believe they have found a way to disrupt memory formation which would help patients avoid post-traumatic stress disorder. By showing traumatic events to volunteers and monitoring their brain activity, they believe that the first 6 hours after the event are crucial in laying down the bad memories.

Sufferers are haunted by flash-backs to the event. However, when half the volunteers played a computer game (Tetris) in that 6-hour period, far fewer flash-backs occurred afterwards. MRI scans were able to show that the computer game sparked activity in many of the same parts of the brain that are responsible for laying down memories.

Manipulating memories will raise ethical issues. Some people think our memories, both good and bad, are part of an individual's unique identity. Others, seeing patients struggling with post-traumatic stress disorder, believe that it is desirable for people to be able to block certain memories if they choose.

29.3 Chromatography

Paper chromatography

You will be familiar with the technique of paper chromatography. It is used to separate mixtures as a solvent moves up a piece of absorbent paper. We call the solvent the **mobile phase** and water trapped between the cellulose fibres of the paper is the **stationary phase**. The substances in the mixture will have different affinities for the solvent and for the water, therefore they move at different rates over the paper (Figure **29.27**).

The R_f values (retardation factors) of substances are calculated as shown in Figure **29.28**. The conditions must be identical to those quoted in the R_f data table, e.g. the same temperature and the same solvent used.

Coloured substances can be seen directly on the paper but others are sprayed with a chemical that forms coloured compounds on the chromatogram. For example, amino acids can be revealed as bluish spots by ninhydrin spray.

Two-way chromatography

Sometimes two or more components in a mixture can have similar R_f values in a particular solvent. This means that their spots on the paper chromatogram will overlap and separation will be poor. This can happen when we hydrolyse a protein and try to identify the amino acid residues present. This is when **two-way chromatography** is useful. In this technique, paper chromatography is carried out as normal but then the chromatogram produced is rotated by 90° and re-run in a different

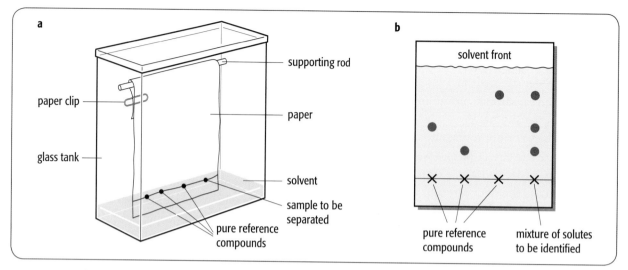

Figure 29.27 a Paper chromatography. **b** The chromatogram produced. Components of the mixture can be identified by comparison with pure reference compounds or by calculating R_f values (see Figure **29.28**) and comparing these values to those in tables of data.

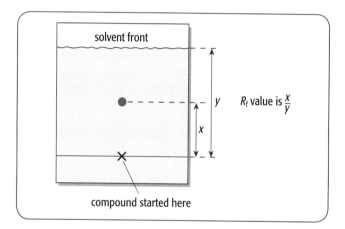

Figure 29.28 How to calculate R_f values, which are then compared with reference values obtained under identical conditions.

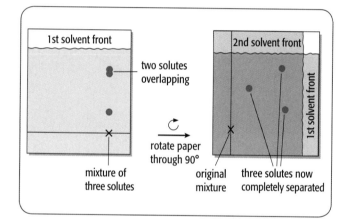

Figure 29.29 Two-way paper chromatography to separate solutes with similar R_f values in a solvent. The technique can also be used with thin-layer chromatography (see page **464**).

solvent. It is unlikely that the R_f values will coincide in two different solvents so separation takes place (Figure **29.29**).

Partition coefficients

The principle of partition of a **solute** between two solvents helps us to understand more fully how the components in a mixture are separated in chromatography. Let us consider ammonia dissolved in two immiscible solvents, i.e. solvents that do not dissolve in each other and so form two separate layers (Figure **29.30**).

A separating funnel is shaken with the organic solvent and an aqueous solution of ammonia. The ammonia is soluble in both solvents so when the mixture is left to settle, a dynamic equilibrium is established. At this point, ammonia molecules are moving from the aqueous layer to the organic layer at the same rate as they are moving from the organic layer to the aqueous layer:

$$NH_3(aq) \rightleftharpoons NH_3(\text{organic solvent})$$

We can calculate a value for the equilibrium constant (see page **135**). We call this the **partition coefficient** (K_{pc}).

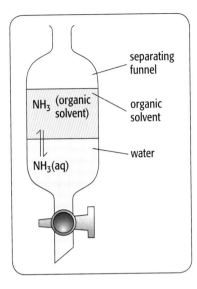

separating funnel

NH₃ (organic solvent)

organic solvent

water

NH₃(aq)

Figure 29.30 Ammonia (the solute) dissolves in both solvents, water and the organic solvent. A state of dynamic equilibrium is established.

Worked example

2   $100 \, cm^3$ of a $0.100 \, mol \, dm^{-3}$ solution of ammonia in water at $20 \, °C$ was shaken with $50 \, cm^3$ of an organic solvent and left in a separating funnel for equilibrium to be established.

A $20.0 \, cm^3$ portion of the aqueous layer was run off and titrated against $0.200 \, mol \, dm^{-3}$ dilute hydrochloric acid. The end-point was found to be $9.40 \, cm^3$ of acid.

What is the partition coefficient of ammonia between these two solvents at $20 \, °C$?

The alkaline ammonia solution is neutralised by dilute hydrochloric acid:

$$NH_3(aq) + HCl(aq) \rightarrow NH_4Cl(aq)$$

1 mole of ammonia reacts with 1 mole of the acid. In the titration we used:

$$\frac{9.40}{1000} \times 0.200 \text{ moles of HCl}$$

$$= 1.88 \times 10^{-3} \text{ moles}$$

This reacts with ammonia in the ratio 1:1 so there must be 1.88×10^{-3} moles of NH_3 in the $20.0 \, cm^3$ portion titrated.

Therefore in the $100 \, cm^3$ aqueous layer there are $1.88 \times 10^{-3} \times \dfrac{100}{20.0}$ mol

$$= 9.40 \times 10^{-3} \text{ mol}$$

continued ⋯⟶

The number of moles of ammonia in the organic layer must be equal to the initial number of moles of ammonia minus the amount left in the aqueous layer at equilibrium

initial number of moles of ammonia

$$= 0.100 \times \frac{100}{1000}$$

$$= 0.0100 \text{ mol}$$

final number of moles of ammonia in organic layer

$$= 0.0100 - 9.40 \times 10^{-3} \text{ mol}$$

$$= 6.00 \times 10^{-4} \text{ mol}$$

Now we need to change the numbers of moles of ammonia in each layer into concentrations (i.e. the number of moles in $1000 \, cm^3$ or $1 \, dm^3$) to substitute into the equilibrium expression for the partition coefficient, K_{pc}.

The concentration of ammonia in $100 \, cm^3$ of the aqueous layer

$$= 9.40 \times 10^{-3} \times \frac{1000}{100}$$

$$= 0.094 \text{ mol dm}^{-3}$$

The concentration of ammonia in $50 \, cm^3$ of the organic solvent

$$= 6.00 \times 10^{-4} \times \frac{1000}{50}$$

$$= 0.012 \text{ mol dm}^{-3}$$

The expression for the partition coefficient, K_{pc} is:

$$K_{pc} = \frac{[NH_3 \text{(organic solvent)}]}{[NH_3 \text{(aq)}]} = \frac{0.012}{0.094}$$

$$= 0.128 \text{ (no units)}$$

This value is less than 1, which shows us that ammonia is more soluble in water than in the organic solvent.

In paper chromatography the different partition coefficients of the components in a mixture correspond to their relative solubilities in the two solvents. In the worked example above the relative solubility of ammonia in water is greater than in the organic solvent. In paper chromatography the mobile phase is the solvent chosen.

The other solvent is the water trapped in the paper's structure, which is the stationary phase. Figure 29.31 shows solute molecules partitioned between the mobile phase and a stationary liquid phase on a solid support.

The solutes in the mixture being separated are partitioned to different extents between the solvents in the mobile and stationary phases. The greater the relative solubility in the mobile phase, the faster the rate of movement as the mobile phase passes over the stationary phase.

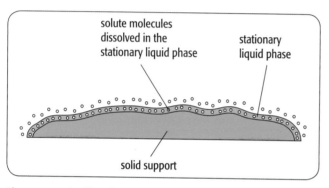

Figure 29.31 Partition chromatography. The mobile phase moves over the stationary liquid phase, carrying solute particles with it. The filter paper is the solid support in paper chromatography.

Check-up

9 Look at this paper chromatogram:

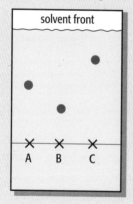

a The solvent used was ethanol. Which sample of ink, A, B, or C, has the greatest relative solubility in ethanol?
b Work out the R_f value of the ink whose partition coefficient in ethanol and water lies between the values of the other two inks.

Thin-layer chromatography (TLC)

In thin-layer chromatography, referred to as **TLC**, the stationary phase is a solid which adsorbs solute molecules onto its surface (Figure 29.32).

The solid stationary phase is usually alumina (Al_2O_3) or silica (SiO_2), which is made into a slurry with water and spread onto a microscope slide. This is then put into an oven where it dries out into a solid white coating on the glass. A chromatogram is then made in a similar way to paper chromatography (Figure 29.33).

Polar molecules have a greater attraction for a polar solid used as the stationary phase and they are adsorbed more strongly onto its surface. Therefore they travel more slowly up the thin layer of alumina or silica and separation occurs. Solutes are located on the chromatogram and identified by comparing with standard known substances or by calculating R_f values.

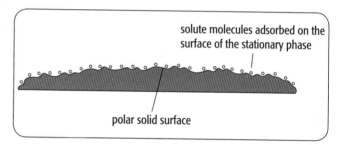

Figure 29.32 Adsorption chromatography. The mobile phase moves over the stationary solid phase.

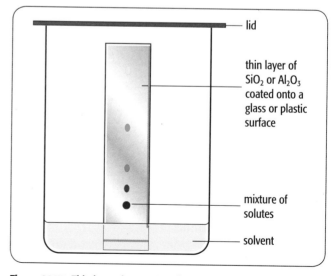

Figure 29.33 Thin-layer chromatography.

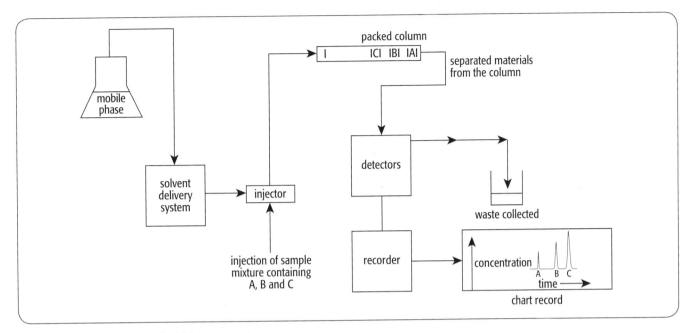

Figure 29.34 High-performance liquid chromatography.

Note that although TLC is normally described as adsorption chromatography, some partitioning does occur if water is present. Both dried alumina and silica can become re-hydrated. When this happens, water also acts as a partitioning stationary phase together with the adsorbing stationary solid phase.

TLC is quicker than paper chromatography and it can be used on smaller samples, making it useful in forensic science where it can be used to identify drugs and explosive residues. For example, TLC is used for the analysis of a substance that is suspected to be cannabis. The stationary phase is silica sprayed with silver nitrate solution which is then dried. The mobile phase is methylbenzene.

High-performance liquid chromatography

High-performance liquid chromatography, referred to as **HPLC**, uses partitioning to separate and identify the components in a mixture. The stationary phase is a non-volatile liquid, such as a long-chain hydrocarbon liquid, bonded onto a solid support, e.g. small particles of silica. This is packed tightly into a column. The solvent chosen for the mobile phase is usually polar, e.g. a methanol/water solvent. This has to be forced under pressure through the densely packed column where separation occurs (Figure **29.34**).

The tiny solid particles in the column have a very large surface area over which partitioning can occur, resulting in excellent separation. The more polar components in the mixture have a greater relative solubility in the polar solvent. Therefore they are carried through the column faster than components whose molecules are more non-polar (which dissolve better in the non-polar stationary phase in the column). The detector records **retention times**, i.e. how long it takes each component to pass through the column. The area under each peak recorded is proportional to the amount of solute emerging from the column (Figure **29.35**).

HPLC is used:

- in medical research to separate peptides and proteins
- to analyse urine samples from athletes for banned substances such as steroids or stimulants
- for monitoring pollutants in the atmosphere and in rivers, e.g. measuring levels of pesticides
- by food standards agencies to check the accuracy of the data on food labels.

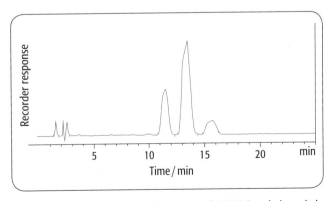

Figure 29.35 The chromatogram from a vitamin E HPLC analysis carried out by a food scientist investigating chilli peppers.

10 Both TLC and HPLC can separate mixtures of components.

   a What do we call the mechanism of separation usually at work in TLC?

   b What do we call the mechanism of separation at work in HPLC?

   c i A mixture of propanone and hexane was separated by HPLC which used a high boiling point hydrocarbon as its stationary phase. The solvent used as the mobile phase was ethanol. Which substance would you expect to leave the column first? Explain why.

   ii Besides identifying the two components in the mixture, what other useful information can HPLC give us?

   iii The same mixture was run in a TLC analysis using alumina as the stationary phase and using methylbenzene as the solvent. Which substance would you expect to rise further up the chromatogram? Explain why.

Gas–liquid chromatography

Gas–liquid chromatography, which is referred to as **GLC**, is similar to HPLC but a gaseous sample enters the column. The column contains the stationary phase and the sample is moved through by an inert carrier gas. This method is used with gases, liquids and volatile solids (as they must be in the form of a vapour). The apparatus is shown in Figure **29.36**.

As in all chromatography, the conditions must be controlled in order to make comparisons with published databases. The chromatogram must be obtained using the same carrier gas, flow rate, stationary phase and temperature that were used when the standard data was obtained. Figure **29.37** shows a chromatogram obtained using GLC.

Analysis by gas–liquid chromatography does have some limitations. For example, similar compounds will have similar retention times and if a newly discovered compound is detected it will not have a match in the computer's database of retention times.

Determination of the percentage composition of a mixture by GLC

For quantitative analysis, the component peaks are first identified and then the area of each is measured. The peaks are roughly triangular in shape so their area is approximately:

$\frac{1}{2} \times$ base $\times$ height (i.e. the area of a triangle)

The GLC machine usually measures the area of the peak automatically and can print the results with the chromatogram. If the peaks are very narrow or have similar base widths, then peak height may be used instead of peak area to estimate the proportion of components in a mixture.

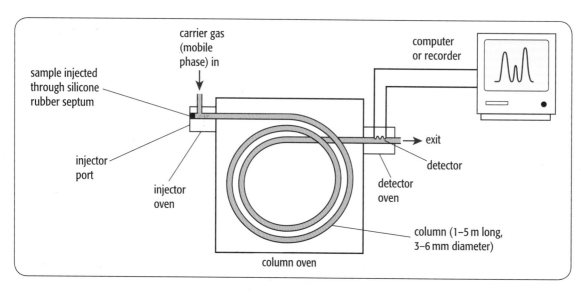

Figure 29.36
Gas–liquid chromatography. The oven maintains a constant temperature, higher than the boiling point of the components in the mixture to be analysed.

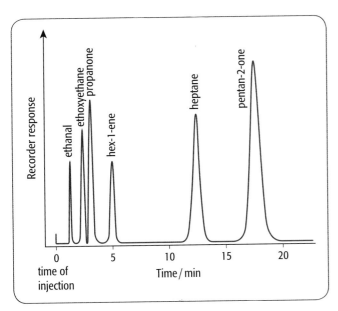

Figure 29.37 A gas chromatogram from a mixture of volatile organic compounds.

For this method:
- the chromatogram must show peaks for all the components in the mixture
- all the components of the mixture must be separated
- the detector must respond equally to the different components so that peak area is directly proportional to the component concentration.

The amount of each component in a mixture is found by expressing it as a percentage of the sum of the areas under all the peaks. For example, for a mixture of three esters A, B and C:

$$\text{(approx.) \% of ester A} = \frac{\text{peak area (or height) of A}}{\text{sum of the areas (or heights) of A, B and C}} \times 100$$

GLC is used in testing for steroids in competing athletes and for testing the fuels used in Formula One motor racing (Figure **29.38**). It is also used for medical diagnosis in analysing blood samples. With GLC it is possible to determine the percentages of dissolved oxygen, nitrogen, carbon dioxide and carbon monoxide in blood samples as small as $1.0\,\text{cm}^3$.

Figure 29.38 GLC is used to check that the components in the fuel used in Grand Prix cars conforms to strict regulations.

Check-up

11 a For GLC separations explain:
   i how retention time is measured
   ii how the areas under the component peaks are used.
   b What can you use as an approximate measure of the proportion of a component in a mixture from a GLC chromatogram which produces sharp peaks?

29.4 Mass spectrometry

You have already seen how a mass spectrometer works (see page 3). The mass spectrum of an element can be used to measure relative isotopic masses and their relative abundances. This information is used to calculate relative atomic masses. However, the main use of mass spectrometry is in the identification of organic compounds. As in other forms of spectroscopy, a substance can be identified by matching its spectrum against the spectra of known substances stored in a database. This technique is known as 'fingerprinting'.

In a mass spectrometer the sample is first vaporised. When vapour from the sample enters the machine it is bombarded by high-energy electrons. This knocks electrons from the molecules and breaks covalent bonds, fragmenting the molecule. Figure **29.39** shows the mass spectrum produced by propanone.

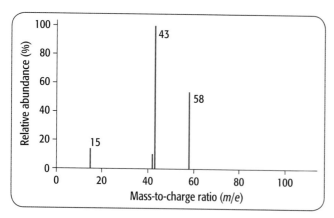

Figure 29.39 The mass spectrum of propanone.

The peak at the highest mass-to-charge ratio is caused by the **molecular ion (M^+)**. This ion is formed by the sample molecule with one electron knocked out. It gives us the relative molecular mass of the sample. We can assume the ions detected carry a single positive charge, so the reading on the horizontal axis gives us the mass. In the case of propanone, CH_3COCH_3, the molecular ion has a relative mass of 58.0. This corresponds to $CH_3COCH_3^+$, with a mass of $(3 \times 12.0) + (1 \times 16.0) + (6 \times 1.0)$.

We also get large peaks at 15 and 43 on the mass spectrum. These peaks are due to fragments that are produced when propanone molecules are broken apart by the electron bombardment. Knowing the structure of propanone we should be able to identify the fragment responsible for each peak (Figure 29.40).

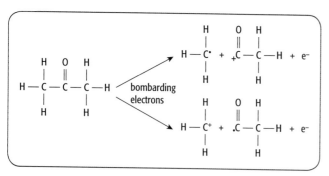

Figure 29.40 The fragmentation of propanone: CH_3^+ causes the peak at 15 and CH_3CO^+ causes the peak at 43.

The electron bombardment has caused the C—C single bonds in the propanone molecules to break. This has resulted in the fragments at m/e 15 and 43 that are observed in Figure 29.37. The breaking of single bonds, such as C—C, C—O or C—N, is the most common cause of **fragmentation**.

Check-up

12 Look at Figure 29.42, which shows the mass spectrum of ethanol, C_2H_5OH. A structural isomer of ethanol is methoxymethane, an ether with the formula CH_3OCH_3.

a Predict the mass-to-charge ratio of a fragment that would appear on the mass spectrum of methoxymethane but does not appear on ethanol's mass spectrum.

b Give the formula of the ion responsible for the peak in your answer to part **a**.

c Look at the mass spectrum of ethanoic acid:

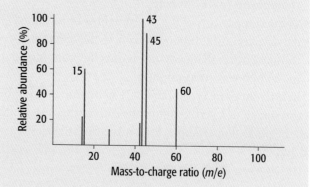

Identify the fragments with mass-to-charge ratios of:

i 15

ii 43

iii 45

iv 60

High-resolution mass spectra

High-resolution mass spectrometers can distinguish between ions that appear to have the same mass on a low-resolution mass spectrum. Table 29.4 shows the accurate relative isotopic masses of the most common atoms found in organic molecules.

Isotope	Relative isotopic mass
^1H	1.0078246
^{12}C	12.0000000 (by definition)
^{14}N	14.0030738
^{16}O	15.9949141

Table 29.4 Accurate masses of isotopes.

These accurate isotopic masses enable us to measure the mass of the molecular ion so accurately that it can only correspond to one possible molecular formula. For example, a molecular ion peak at 45 could be caused by C_2H_7N or CH_3NO. However, a high-resolution mass spectrum would show the $C_2H_7N^+$ peak at 45.057846 and the CH_3NO^+ peak at 45.021462. We can, therefore, be sure which molecule is being analysed.

Using the [M + 1] peak

There will always be a very small peak just beyond the molecular ion peak at a mass of $[M + 1]$. This is caused by molecules in which one of the carbon atoms is the ^{13}C isotope. This is shown in the mass spectrum of ethanol in Figure 29.41.

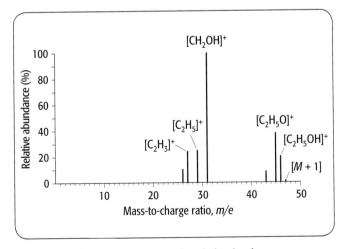

Figure 29.41 The mass spectrum of ethanol, showing the [M + 1] peak.

In any organic compound there will be 1.10% carbon-13. We can use this fact to work out the number of carbon atoms (n) in a molecule. We apply the equation:

$$n = \frac{100}{1.1} \times \frac{\text{abundance of } [M+1]^+ \text{ ion}}{\text{abundance of } M^+ \text{ ion}}$$

Using [M + 2] and [M + 4] peaks

If the sample compound contains chlorine or bromine atoms we also get peaks beyond the molecular ion peak because of isotopes of chlorine and bromine. Chlorine has two isotopes, ^{35}Cl and ^{37}Cl, as does bromine, ^{79}Br and ^{81}Br. Table 29.5 shows the approximate percentage of each isotope in naturally occurring samples.

Isotopes	Approximate %
^{35}Cl	75
^{37}Cl	25
^{79}Br	50
^{81}Br	50

Table 29.5 Naturally occurring isotopes of chlorine and bromine.

One Cl or Br atom per molecule

Imagine a sample of chloromethane, CH_3Cl. We will have molecules of $CH_3{}^{35}Cl$ (75%) and molecules of $CH_3{}^{37}Cl$ (25%). The molecular ion will be $CH_3{}^{35}Cl^+$, and two units beyond that on the mass spectrum will be the peak for $CH_3{}^{37}Cl^+$. The peak for $CH_3{}^{37}Cl^+$ will be one-third the height of the molecular ion. This is the $[M + 2]$ peak.

In the mass spectrum of bromomethane, CH_3Br, we will have two molecular ion peaks of approximately the same height – one for $CH_3{}^{79}Br^+$ and the other for $CH_3{}^{81}Br^+$ (the $[M + 2]$ peak).

You should look out for the relative heights mentioned here when interpreting mass spectra.
- if the $[M + 2]$ peak is one-third the height of the M peak, this suggests the presence of one chlorine atom per molecule
- if the $[M + 2]$ peak is the same as the height of the M peak, this suggests the presence of one bromine atom per molecule.

An example of the $[M + 2]$ peak is shown on the mass spectrum of chlorobenzene (Figure 29.42).

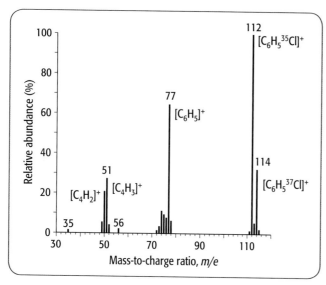

Figure 29.42 The mass spectrum of chlorobenzene, showing the $[M + 2]$ peak. (Notice that there are also tiny $[M + 1]$ and $[M + 3]$ peaks corresponding to ^{13}C in the molecule.)

Two Cl or Br atoms per molecule

The situation is a little more complex with two chlorine atoms in a molecule as there are three possibilities. Consider dichloromethane, CH_2Cl_2, we have:

$^{35}Cl–CH_2–{}^{35}Cl^+$	the M peak
$^{35}Cl–CH_2–{}^{37}Cl^+$	the $[M + 2]$ peak
$^{37}Cl–CH_2–{}^{35}Cl^+$	the $[M + 2]$ peak
$^{37}Cl–CH_2–{}^{37}Cl^+$	the $[M + 4]$ peak

The relative heights of the peaks must take into account the natural abundances: it works out as $9:6:1$ for molecules with two Cl atoms.

The M, $[M + 2]$ and $[M + 4]$ peaks also occur in dibromomethane but the relative height of peaks are easier to work out. Because the ratio $^{79}Br:{}^{81}Br$ is $1:1$, we get the $M:[M + 2]:[M + 4]$ height ratio as $1:2:1$.

Check-up

14 a List the ions responsible for the M, $[M + 2]$ and $[M + 4]$ peaks in a mass spectrum of dibromomethane.

b What would be the mass-to-charge ratio and relative abundances of the major peaks with the highest charge-to-mass ratios in the mass spectrum of chloroethane?

c How many peaks would you see beyond the molecular ion peak in 1,1-dibromoethane? What would be their mass-to-charge ratios and abundances relative to the molecular ion? (Ignore peaks due to ^{13}C.)

Applications of the mass spectrometer

To identify the components in a mixture, we can link gas–liquid chromatography (GLC) or high-performance liquid chromatography (HPLC) apparatus directly to a mass spectrometer.

This combined technique is very sensitive, and any two solutes that can be separated with a time gap of 1 second on a GLC column can be identified almost instantly by the mass spectrometer without the need to be collected. Identification is by comparing the mass spectrum of each solute with the mass spectra of known compounds, using a computer's spectral database. The data generated is complex. There can be many components in a mixture,

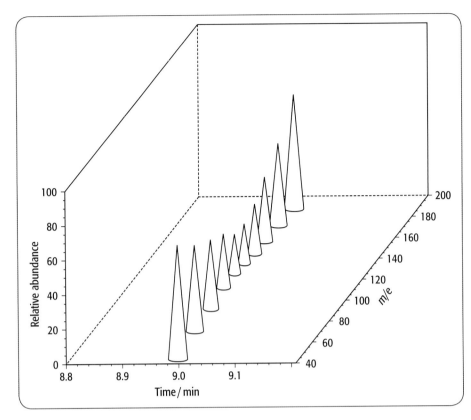

Figure 29.43 The *x*-axis shows retention time, the *y*-axis the amounts and the *z*-axis is the charge/mass ratio of the mass spectra. This 3D data shows the peaks on a mass spectrum for one component in a gas–liquid chromatogram.

each with a peak at its particular retention time on the chromatogram, and each peak will generate its own characteristic series of lines in the mass spectrometer. We can combine the chromatogram and the mass spectra to display the data on a 3-D graph (Figure **29.43**).

Check-up

15 Look at Figure **29.43**.
  a What is the retention time of the compound shown?
  b What is the approximate relative molecular mass of the compound shown?
  c How would the compound be identified?

GLC linked to a mass spectrometer is used for analysing complex mixtures, for example the identification of the hydrocarbons in a sample of crude oil. The combined technique is fast and gives reliable results that can identify trace quantities of pollutants, drugs, biochemical molecules and toxins. This means it is used in:

• forensics
• environmental monitoring of pollutants
• drug testing in sport
• geological and archaeological dating
• airport security.

Mass spectrometry has even been used on space probes to analyse rocks on Mars and in 2005 a mass spectrometer was used to analyse the frozen hydrocarbon surface of Titan, one of Saturn's moons. The technique is also used to analyse the isotopes in the solar wind on board the Solar and Heliospheric Observatory (SOHO) satellite.

As with electrophoresis and NMR spectroscopy, mass spectrometry is also helping in medical research – to both identify and research the amino acid sequences in proteins. It can be used to analyse the whole protein molecule or the peptides left after breaking down the protein with specific enzymes. Figure **29.44** shows the mass spectrum of a pentapeptide that is made into a charged compound by the addition of a proton, hence the $M\mathrm{H}^+$ peak.

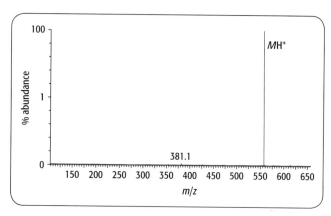

Figure 29.44 The mass spectrum of leucine enkephalin (C₂₈H₃₇N₅O₇), a peptide made up of five amino acids. It has been charged by adding a proton instead of by ionisation by high-energy electrons (which would fragment the molecule). This is known as a 'soft ionisation' method.

Check-up

16 Look at Figure 29.44.
   a Calculate the relative molecular mass of leucine enkephalin ($C_{28}H_{37}N_5O_7$) using relative atomic masses.
   (A_r values C = 12.0, H = 1.0, N = 14.0, O = 16.0)
   b i How is the peptide ionised before detection in the mass spectrometer?
      ii Why is this known as 'soft ionisation'?
   c Why is there a peak at [MH + 1]?
   d An unexpected peak occurs at charge-to-mass ratio 578.1. This is caused by ionisation of the pentapeptide by a metal ion instead of an H⁺ ion. Which metal ion is responsible for this ionisation?

Monitoring the environment

Pollution from the past

Combined GLC and mass spectrometry is used by environmental scientists to:
• separate samples collected from the ground, water or atmosphere into their components
• identify the components of the mixture
• measure the concentration of any pollutants present.
An example is the monitoring of PCBs (polychlorinated biphenyls). Over 200 of these related compounds were used in a variety of industries from the 1930s to the late 1970s. These unreactive compounds found uses in electrical equipment, lubricants, paints, plasticisers and carbonless copy paper. However, the toxic nature of these PCBs was then discovered and their use was banned.

Much of the PCBs produced over the years have found their way into the environment. Discharges from factories have polluted rivers and seas. The PCBs bind to sediment at the bottom of the water, although some remain in suspension in the water itself.

The PCB toxins dissolve in the fatty tissues of organisms. Bioaccumulation takes place and higher mammals such as sea-birds and seals have been affected by PCBs. Human health problems have also been associated with PCBs. These include an acne-like skin condition, called chloracne, in adults. Children can experience neurobehavioural and immunological changes. PCBs are also known to cause cancer in animals.

Although their use has been phased out, they persist in the environment so monitoring is still required. For example, environmental agencies still test:
• breast milk
• foodstuffs
• sewage treatment plants and outfalls
• landfill sites suspected of having received scheduled PCB waste
• wildlife (as biological indicators of pollution at a site).
There are PCB pollution 'hot-spots' where direct discharges took place over many years. An example would be a river next to a paper factory. Environmental scientists will be involved in deciding how to clean up the pollution. For example, dredging the sediment from the bottom of the river, then treating the waste might seem the best way. But will disturbing the river bed cause the PCBs to be spread further downstream because of the clean-up process? Will the PCBs be released into the air when they emerge from beneath the water? Carrying out trial runs and monitoring the effects on a small scale have to be used to decide what action should be taken. Analysis by GLC-MS gives accurate data at very low concentrations and helps inform decisions.

Climate change studies

It took scientists in Greenland 7 years to drill a hollow pipe down through the glacial ice field. On reaching the rock beneath the ice sheet in 2004, they had drilled out a cylinder of ice, called an ice core, over 3 kilometres long.

When light shines on the ice core sample, you see bands of light and dark. The dark bands are from winter snowfall, the light from summer. To check the age of the ice core at different depths the scientists use a mass spectrometer. They measure changes in the ratio of ^{16}O and the much rarer ^{18}O in the water from the ice core. This ratio changes according to the temperature, with less ^{18}O in the H_2O present in winter compared with summer. So the yearly rise and fall in the $^{16}O:^{18}O$ ratio enables scientists to count backwards in time.

Ice core studies can now go back over 750 000 years in time. The ice never melts so a record of each year is preserved in the ice core. This enables us to track changes in temperature and the gases in the atmosphere over time. The ice core has tiny bubbles of air trapped at the time the ice formed which can be analysed in the mass spectrometer. The temperature is monitored by the $^{16}O:^{18}O$ ratio (and $^1H:^2H$ ratio) in the water from the ice. These are standardised against known ratios over recent times when we have temperature records.

Scientists are currently very concerned about climate change. The ice core data can tell us what temperature and CO_2 levels were in the past, and this information can help us make more informed decisions in the present. Figure 29.45 shows how levels of carbon dioxide in the atmosphere and temperatures have varied over the last 800 000 years.

Most people accept that rising levels of carbon dioxide causes increased amounts of global warming.

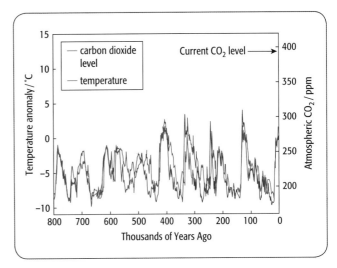

Figure 29.45 The variations in CO_2 and temperature over the last 800 000 years from data taken from ice cores.

A correlation can be seen, as shown in Figure 29.45. However, sometimes there is a time lag between the temperature rise and a rise in levels of CO_2. This suggests that higher temperatures cause higher CO_2 levels, not the other way round. Other factors, such as variations in the Earth's orbit around the Sun and in the solar wind, may also be contributing to the temperature changes.

Summary

☐ Electrophoresis uses an electric field to separate the components in a mixture. It is used extensively to analyse the sequence of amino acids in proteins and in producing DNA fingerprints. It plays an important role in forensic science, archaeology and medicine.

☐ The proton NMR spectrum of a compound provides detailed information about the structure of the compound. In particular, the spectrum for the protons, ^1H, in a compound can provide a complete determination of the compound's structure.

☐ Protons in different chemical environments produce signals at different chemical shifts. The chemical shift provides information about the proton's environment.

☐ Protons on neighbouring carbon atoms cause signals to be split. The splitting pattern establishes which groups of protons are on adjacent carbon atoms. The $n + 1$ rule predicts the splitting pattern.

☐ Protons on —OH and —NH— can be identified by the addition of D_2O to the NMR sample, which collapses the peak due to an —OH or an —NH— proton.

☐ NMR and X-ray crystallography are used in determining the structure of macromolecules such as proteins and nucleic acids.

- Chromatography separates mixtures of substances for identification. In chromatography, the mobile phase moves the components of a mixture through or over the stationary phase. Separation occurs by the transfer of the components to the stationary phase either by:
  - partition between two liquids (due to the different solubility of solutes in the mobile phase and stationary phase),
  - partition between a gas and a liquid or
  - adsorption on a solid surface.
- The stationary phase may be solid or liquid; the mobile phase may be liquid or gas.
- In paper and thin-layer chromatography (TLC) the components of a mixture are identified by their R_f values.
- In gas–liquid chromatography (GLC) and high-performance liquid chromatography (HPLC), the components of a mixture are identified by their retention times; the amount of each component is found by measuring the area of each peak (estimates can be made from peak heights).
- The mass spectrum of a compound enables the relative molecular mass of the compound to be determined using the molecular ion peak. The molecular ion peak, M, is the peak produced by the loss of one electron from a molecule of the compound.
- We can deduce the number of carbon atoms in a compound using the $[M + 1]$ peak and the presence of a single bromine or chlorine atom using the $[M + 2]$ peak (and two Cl or Br atoms by the $[M + 4]$ peak as well).
- We can also use mass spectroscopy to identify unknown organic compounds by 'fingerprinting' (matching the spectrum to other known spectra). The fragmentation peaks give us clues as to the structure of the original molecule.
- Gas–liquid chromatography/mass spectrometry (GLC-MS) provides a more powerful tool for identifying the components in a mixture than GLC alone (compounds can have similar retention times but can be 'fingerprinted' by their unique mass spectra). It is used in airport security checks, food industries and in forensic, environmental and medical testing.

End-of-chapter questions

1   a Identify the fragments that would cause peaks in the mass spectrum of $HOCH_2COCH_3$ with the following m/e values:

    i $m/e = 15$ [1]

    ii $m/e = 17$ [1]

    iii $m/e = 31$ [1]

    iv $m/e = 43$ [1]

    v $m/e = 57$ [1]

    vi $m/e = 59$ [1]

   b At what value for m/e would you find the molecular ion peak?   [1]

Total = 7

2   The gas–liquid chromatogram for a mixture of organic compounds is shown below.

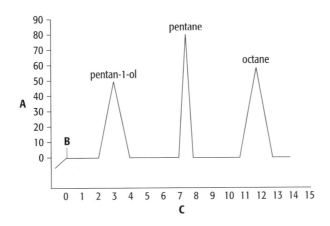

a Give the correct labels for **A**, **B** and **C**.   [3]
b What percentage of the mixture is pentan-1-ol?   [6]
c Give an explanation for the different retention times.   [3]
d i   How would the chromatogram change if the liquid in the stationary phase was much
        more polar?   [1]
   ii Explain your answer.   [2]
e Why is gas–liquid chromatography useful in testing for anabolic steroids in the blood of athletes? [2]
f Explain why the use of gas–liquid chromatography linked to a mass spectrometer is so useful. [2]
g Why is it difficult to separate dyes using gas–liquid chromatography?   [2]

                                                                          Total = 21

3 Paper chromatography was used to separate a mixture of amino acids. The mixture was run in two dimensions using two different solvents. The chromatogram obtained is shown below.

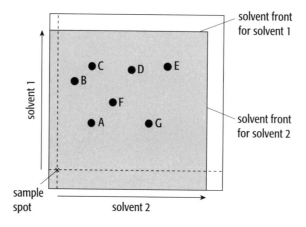

a Explain briefly how the chromatography was carried out. [4]
b Which amino acids were inseparable using solvent 1? (Give just the corresponding letters.) [2]
c How could the amino acids be located? [1]
d Give the R_f value for amino acid C in each solvent. [2]
e Which amino acids would have been inseparable by solvent 2 alone? [1]
f In another experiment, a mixture of radioactively labelled amino acids was separated using paper chromatography. The results obtained are shown below.

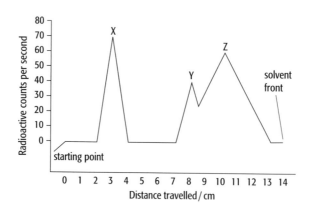

   i Find the R_f values for acids X, Y and Z. Show your working. [3]
   ii Explain how paper chromatography is used to separate the components of a mixture. [4]

Total = 17

When answering questions **4–7**, you will need to use the values in Table **29.1** (page **455**).

4 Compound **B** has the composition 62.1% carbon, 10.3% hydrogen and 27.6% oxygen. Its mass and ^{1}H NMR spectra are shown below.

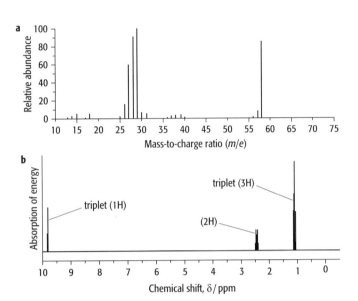

a Mass spectrum for **B**; **b** ^{1}H NMR spectrum for **B**.

   a Calculate the empirical formula of **B**. [2]
   b From the mass spectrum, find the molecular mass of **B** and hence its molecular formula. [2]
   c **i** Draw displayed formulae for the possible isomers of **B** which contain a carbonyl group. [2]
      ii Use the ^{1}H NMR spectrum of **B** to decide which isomer is **B**. [1]
      iii Explain your reasoning. [3]
   d Explain what caused the peak at δ = 1.1 ppm and why it is split into a triplet in the ^{1}H NMR spectrum of **B**. [2]

                                                                 Total = 12

5 Arene **C** has the composition 90.6% carbon and 9.4% hydrogen. Its mass and ¹H NMR spectra are shown below.

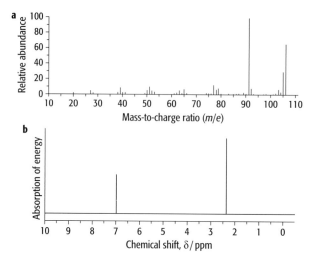

a Mass spectrum for **C**; **b** ¹H NMR spectrum for **C**.

a Calculate the empirical formula of **C**. [2]
b From the mass spectrum, find the molecular mass of **C** and hence its molecular formula. [2]
c i Draw displayed formulae for the possible aromatic isomers of **C**. [4]
ii When **C** is treated with chlorine in the presence of AlCl₃ it undergoes electrophilic aromatic substitution. In this reaction one of the hydrogen atoms bonded directly to the benzene ring is replaced with one chlorine atom, and one single aromatic product is formed. Use this evidence and the NMR spectrum of **C** to decide which isomer is **C**. [5]
d Explain the main features of the ¹H NMR spectrum of **C**. [4]

Total = 17

6 Compound **D** has the composition 77.8% carbon, 7.41% hydrogen and 14.8% oxygen. It mass and ¹H NMR spectra are shown below.

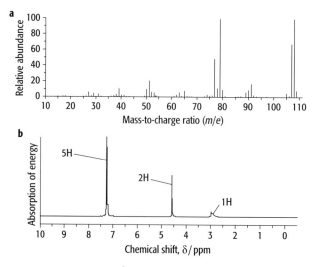

a Mass spectrum for **D**; **b** ¹H NMR spectrum for **D**.

a Calculate the empirical formula of **D**.   [2]

b From the mass spectrum, find the molecular mass of **D** (ignoring the ^{13}C peak) and hence its
molecular formula.   [2]

c i Draw displayed formulae for five possible isomers of **D** that contain a benzene ring.   [5]

  ii Use the ^{1}H NMR spectrum of **D** to decide which isomer is **D**.   [1]

  iii Explain your reasoning.   [3]

d Explain the main features of the NMR spectrum of **D**.   [4]

Total = 17

7   Compound **E** has the composition 69.8% carbon, 11.6% hydrogen and 18.6% oxygen. Its mass and [1]H
NMR spectra are shown below.

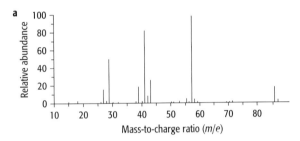

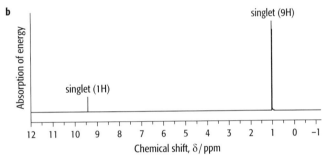

a Mass spectrum for **E**; **b** ^{1}H NMR spectrum for **E**.

a Calculate the empirical formula of **E**.   [2]

b From the mass spectrum, find the molecular mass of **E** (ignoring the ^{13}C peak) and hence
its molecular formula.   [2]

c Compound **E** reacts with 2,4-dinitrophenylhydrazine to give a yellow-orange precipitate.
Draw displayed formulae for the seven possible isomers of **E**.   [7]

d Compound **E** gives a silver mirror with Tollens' reagent. Identify the functional group in **E**. [1]

e Use the ^{1}H NMR spectrum to identify **E**. Explain your reasoning.   [4]

Total = 16

Learning outcomes

Candidates should be able to:

☐ discuss the challenges of drug design and explain in simple terms how molecules may be identified and developed to overcome these problems

☐ discuss the challenges of drug delivery and explain in simple terms how materials may be developed to overcome these problems

☐ discuss the properties and structure of polymers, based on their methods of formation (addition or condensation, link to Chapter 27)

☐ discuss how the presence of side-chains and intermolecular forces affect the properties of polymeric materials (for example, spider silk)

☐ show awareness of nanotechnology and, given information and data, be able to discuss the chemistry involved with reference to the core syllabus

☐ discuss how a knowledge of chemistry can be used to overcome environmental problems (for example, ground water contamination, oil spillage, CFCs)

☐ discuss how a knowledge of chemistry can be used to extend the life of existing resources, to identify alternative resources and to improve the efficiency of energy production and use.

30.1 Designing new medicinal drugs

How do we go about designing new molecules to fight diseases? One way is to identify the structural features the new drug will need to stop particular bacteria or viruses

Figure 30.1 Chemists play a vital role in developing new materials to improve our lives. In this chapter you can find out about their work in medicine, polymers, nanotechnology and environmental issues.

working. The structural features may be associated with the active site on a particular enzyme needed for an essential function of the pathogen. Once these structural features have been identified we can then predict the shape of a molecule that would fit into, and hence block, the active site. The functional groups present would also be crucial to ensure the drug could bind into the active site effectively. The intermolecular bonds formed between the drug and its target molecule could involve:

• hydrogen bonding
• ionic attraction
• dipole–dipole forces or
• instantaneous dipole–induced dipole forces (van der Waals' forces, see Chapter 4, page **63**).

Computers are now used to judge the fit between a potential drug molecule and a receptor site on its target molecule. Such **molecular modelling** has greatly speeded up the process of designing new medicines. The interactions and fit of a potential medicine with a biological receptor molecule can be studied before the medicine is ever made in the lab. Before molecular modelling became available, the synthesis of a new medicine involved far more trial and error. Chemists had to prepare many more possible medicines for testing. With molecular modelling, only those molecules that are definite possibilities are made and tested. Molecular modelling on a computer is now a powerful tool, used when designing medicines and many other compounds (e.g. pesticides and polymers).

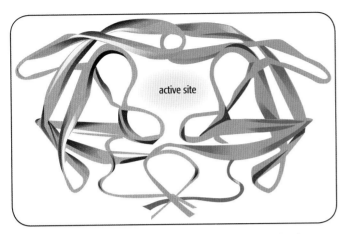

Figure 30.2 A symmetrical HIV protease molecule, with its active site in the centre of the molecule. Knowing its structure made the search for a drug to fight AIDS much quicker and cheaper than traditional trial-and-error methods.

This type of research was used in the fight against AIDS in the late 1980s and 1990s. Scientists using X-ray crystallography (see page **459**) worked out the shape of HIV protease in 1988 (Figure **30.2**). This enzyme plays an important role when the virus becomes infectious. Researchers realised that, if a molecule could be discovered that could block its active site, this might be one step on the route to finding a cure for AIDS. Knowing the molecule that the enzyme worked on (its substrate), researchers were able construct similar molecules on the computer screen to fit the active site.

The first attempts fitted perfectly, but were not water soluble. This meant the drug could not be delivered to its target, the HIV protease. Eventually a soluble molecule that would interfere with the enzyme was found. In less than 8 years pharmaceutical companies had developed three new anti-viral drugs for people with HIV/AIDS. This would have taken about twice as long if the structure of HIV protease had not been determined. Traditional trial-and-error methods involve the testing of many thousands of possible drugs.

The death rate from AIDS dropped significantly. However, the virus developed resistance to the new drugs as it mutated. So scientists now have to model the new drug-resistant strains of the infection and are developing new drugs to inhibit the mutant versions of HIV protease. These inhibitors are one part of a cocktail of drugs that can be used to treat the disease now.

Chirality in pharmaceutical synthesis

The pharmaceutical industry is constantly searching for new drugs. Their research chemists have discovered that most of these drugs contain at least one chiral centre. Remember that a molecule containing a carbon atom bonded to four different atoms or groups of atoms can exist as two non-superimposable mirror images. These two isomers are called enantiomers and they will be optically active. They differ only in their ability to rotate the plane of polarised light to the left or to the right.

Using conventional organic reactions to make the desired product will yield a 50:50 mixture of the two enantiomers. We call this a racemic mixture. Although the physical properties of the enantiomers will be identical, each differs in its 'pharmaceutical activity', i.e. the effect the drug has on the body. For example, naproxen is a drug used to treat the pain caused by arthritis (Figure **30.3**). One enantiomer will ease the pain but the other can cause liver damage.

As another example, one enantiomer of a drug used to treat tuberculosis (TB) is effective whereas the other can cause blindness. Therefore, chemists ideally need a single pure enantiomer to put in their drug product. Note that about 80% of new drugs patented are single enantiomers.

Using pure enantiomers will be beneficial as it:
• reduces the patient's dosage by half as the pure enantiomer is more potent, cutting costs and minimising the risk of side-effects
• protects drugs companies from possible litigation as people will sue for damages when serious side-effects do occur.

There are three ways to prepare pure enantiomers:
• optical resolution
• using optically active starting materials
• using a chiral catalyst.

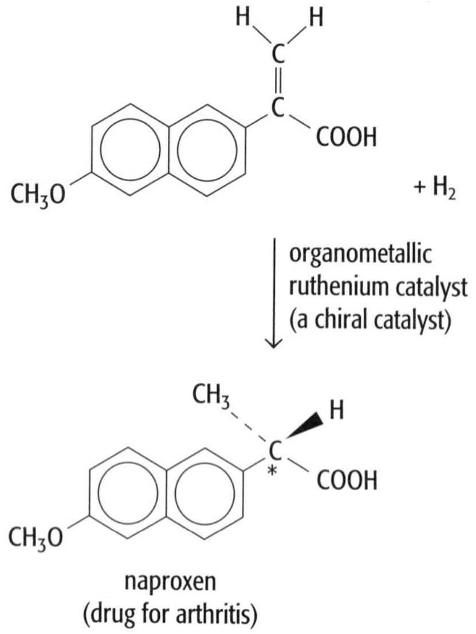

Figure 30.3 The chiral catalyst (an organometallic ruthenium compound) ensures only the desired enantiomer is formed – in this case, naproxen for the treatment of arthritis.

Optical resolution

This method involves the chemists following a traditional synthetic route to make the compound, resulting in a racemic mixture. Then they separate the two enantiomers in a process called **optical resolution**. This involves using a pure enantiomer of another optically active compound (called a chiral auxiliary) that will react with one of the isomers in the mixture. The new product formed will now have different properties and so can be separated by physical means. For example, the solubility in a given solvent will differ so the unwanted enantiomer and the new product can be separated by fractional crystallisation. The new product is then converted back to the desired enantiomer in a simple reaction (e.g. by adding dilute alkali).

The crystallisation is repeated many times to ensure purity. This method is difficult, time-consuming, uses extra reagents and involves the disposal of half the original racemic mixture.

Large volumes of organic solvents (often harmful to the environment) are used in the process. However, chemists are now using supercritical carbon dioxide as a solvent which is much safer. At 31 °C and 73 atmospheres pressure, CO_2 is a suitable non-polar solvent for many drug derivatives in the racemic resolution process. The solubility of the derivatives can be changed, simply by varying the density of the solvent. The solvent, which is non-toxic, is easily removed by reducing the pressure and then recycling it to use in the process again.

We can also use high-performance liquid chromatography (HPLC, see page 465) to separate a racemic mixture, as long as the stationary medium (e.g. the solid that packs the column) is itself optically active.

Using optically active starting materials

This technique uses starting materials that are themselves optically active and in the same orientation as the desired product. These are often naturally occurring compounds such as carbohydrates or L-amino acids. The biochemist will choose from this 'chiral pool'. The synthetic route is designed to keep any intermediates and the final product formed in the same enantiomeric form. As a result, there is no need to carry out the costly separation process needed when a racemic mixture is produced.

Chiral catalysts

Chemists are also developing new chiral catalysts that ensure only one specific enantiomer is formed in a reaction. The benefits of these catalysts are that only small quantities are needed and they can be used over and over again, although the catalyst itself can be expensive. A ruthenium (Ru) organometallic catalyst is used in the production of naproxen (see Figure 30.3).

Often a combination of optical resolution and chiral synthesis is needed in the production of a pharmaceutically active, pure enantiomer.

The pharmaceutical industry can also use enzymes to promote stereoselectivity and produce single-enantiomer products. The specific shape and the nature of the molecular interactions at the active site of an enzyme ensures only one enantiomer will be formed (as in living things). The enzymes are often immobilised (fixed in place) on inert supports. This enables the reactants to be passed over them without the need to separate the product from the enzymes after the reaction.

However, it can be expensive isolating enzymes from living things. Using whole organisms, such as bacteria, can reduce this cost. Nowadays, synthetic enzymes can also be made, designed for a particular synthesis. Therefore a search for a suitable enzyme from the limited pool available from natural sources is not always necessary.

Overall, using an enzyme process might take longer to develop than a conventional synthetic route but in the long run the benefits generally outweigh the disadvantages. There are fewer steps needed in the synthesis route, resulting in a 'greener' process.

Delivery of drugs

In the section on drugs that combat AIDS it was mentioned that a water-insoluble drug could not be delivered effectively to the target molecule, HIV protease. However, the latest techniques being developed use nano-cages of gold to deliver drugs to target sites in the body. (Nanoscientists study particles between 1 and 100 nanometres (nm) in size, where $1\,nm = 1 \times 10^{-9}\,m$.) Researchers have found that the tiny gold particles can be selectively absorbed by tumours. Tumours have thin, leaky blood vessels with holes large enough for the gold to pass into, unlike healthy blood vessels.

When a laser is directed at the tumour the gold nanoparticles absorb energy and are heated up. The temperature of the tumour increases sufficiently to denature its proteins whilst surrounding tissue is barely warmed. This destroys the tumour cells without damaging healthy cells. Not only that, there is potential to use the gold cages to carry cancer-fighting drugs to the tumour at the same time. The gold nano-cages are coated by a polymer called PEG (polyethylene glycol). This stops the body's immune system from attacking the gold particles and ejecting them from the bloodstream. The PEG dissolves in water when it gets hot, releasing the drug from the nano-cage. Smart (or shape-memory) polymers do the same job but they are designed to have a critical temperature at which their molecules change shape. In Figure 30.4 the polymers seal the pores in the gold nano-cage below its critical temperature. Once the nano-cage is warmed by the laser and it reaches its critical

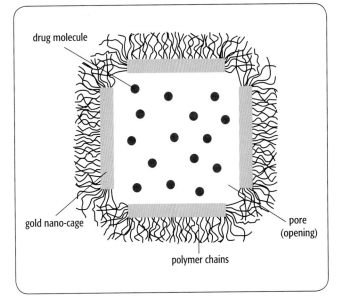

Figure 30.4 Drug delivery by a gold nano-cage. The polymers are shown attached to the surface of the cage. They seal the pores in the cage as it travels in the bloodstream to the tumour. When the laser warms the gold atoms, the cage is effectively opened and the drug is released.

temperature the polymer chains straighten out and the pores are opened to release the drug.

The first clinical use of a nano-particle was drug delivery by liposomes. Liposomes are tiny membrane bubbles, usually made of phospholipids. These molecules have a hydrophilic (water-loving) head and **hydrophobic** (water-hating) tails (Figure 30.5).

Phospholipids line up in two layers, which then wrap around into a sphere. The 'tails' point towards each other, and the 'heads' point outwards towards their aqueous surroundings and inwards like a lining inside the sphere (Figure 30.6).

Liposomes are useful for delivering drugs because a water-soluble drug can be carried in aqueous solution inside the liposome and a drug which dissolves in fat can be transported in the fatty layer of the wall made up of the 'tails' of the molecules. They are also biodegradable and relatively non-toxic. As a drug-delivery system, liposomes can achieve significant benefits for patients, for example, by reducing drug toxicity. This works in cancer treatment in a similar way to the gold nano-cages injected into the bloodstream. The liposomes are similar in size and can get through the loosely packed walls of a tumour's blood vessels, but not through the walls of healthy blood vessels. Again, like gold nano-cages, they can have surface coatings added to avoid attack by the immune system.

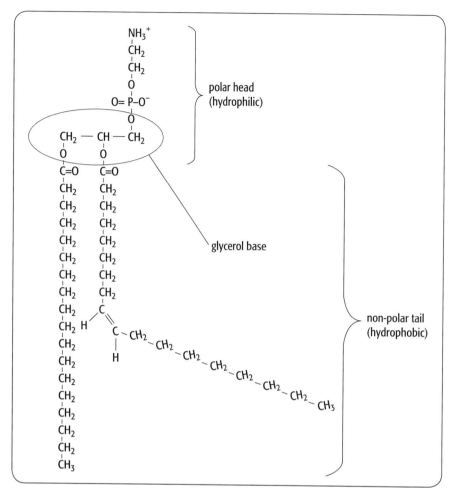

polar head
(hydrophilic)

glycerol base

non-polar tail
(hydrophobic)

Figure 30.5 Phospholipids have a charged 'head' and two non-polar 'tails'.

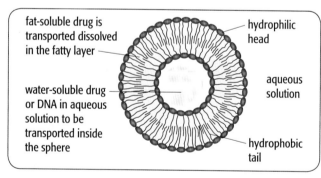

fat-soluble drug is transported dissolved in the fatty layer

water-soluble drug or DNA in aqueous solution to be transported inside the sphere

hydrophilic head

aqueous solution

hydrophobic tail

Figure 30.6 Phospholipids can be made into liposomes for carrying drugs and DNA. They are made in a solution containing the drug or DNA to be transported to the target site.

Liposomes can also fuse with cell membranes which have a similar structure and deliver their contents inside the cell. They are used not only to carry drugs but also to carry DNA for gene therapy. They are also used to deliver the active ingredients of cosmetic agents, such as anti-wrinkle creams, deeper into the skin (Figure 30.7).

Figure 30.7 Liposomes can deliver treatments deeper into the skin than traditional cosmetics. However, some people are worried that the nanoparticle delivery system will mean that some cosmetics will penetrate beyond the skin, with unknown health consequences. Should the new cosmetics be subject to the same stringent tests new drugs must pass which includes monitoring subjects after the drug has been passed for public use?

Check-up

3 a i Look at the structure of a phospholipid in Figure 30.5. Explain why a phospholipid would decolorise bromine water.

  ii Describe how water molecules would interact with the hydrophilic 'head' of the phospholipid molecule shown in Figure 30.5.

  iii Does the structural formula represent the *cis* or *trans* isomer? How would the other isomer differ in its shape?

  iv What type of intermolecular forces would be operating between a drug that is insoluble in water and its liposome carrier?

 b Why can liposomes and gold nano-cages selectively deliver cancer-fighting drugs to the sites of tumours in the body?

 c i Look at the Periodic Table (page 497). Gold and mercury both form a simple 2+ ion. Why is gold (atomic number 79) called a transition metal but mercury (atomic number 80) is not?

  ii Suggest how gold atoms can absorb energy from laser light.

30.2 Designing polymers

We saw in the previous section that a polymer called PEG is used to coat the gold nano-cages and liposomes that can be used in drug delivery. This polymer shows how varying reaction conditions can change the polymer produced. The skeletal formula of PEG is:

$$HO \diagup\diagdown\diagup\diagdown O \diagup\diagdown\diagup\diagdown_n OH$$

PEG is made from monomers of epoxyethane:

$$\begin{array}{c} O \\ \diagup \diagdown \\ H_2C \!-\! CH_2 \end{array}$$

Epoxyethane is a reactive cyclic molecule, written as CH_2CH_2O. It is usually reacted with 1,2-ethanediol to produce PEG. We can represent the polymerisation of epoxyethane by this equation:

$$HOCH_2CH_2OH + n(CH_2CH_2O)$$
$$\rightarrow HO(CH_2CH_2O)_{n+1}H$$

The catalysts used and the ratio of reactants affect the size of the polymer chains. By varying the molecular mass of the polymer, a whole range of products is made. They are often used as liquids or low melting point solids. Their solubility in water, and in many non-polar solvents, is one of their advantages over other polymeric materials (hence their use in drug delivery). Their molecular mass is given after their name, e.g PEG 400 or PEG 10 000.

PEG 200 and PEG 2000 were used to help preserve the timbers of the Mary Rose – a ship that sank about 500 years ago and was raised from the seabed in 1982 (Figure 30.8). Spraying the wood with PEG 200 started in 1994 and the switch to the more waxy PEG 2000 began in 2004. The water in the timbers is replaced by PEG and the remains of the ship can then be slowly dried out without crumbling away.

Figure 30.8 The water in the timbers of the Mary Rose has slowly been replaced by PEG to preserve the timbers.

Check-up

4 a Show the skeletal formula of PEG shown above as a structural formula.

 b Which type of intermolecular forces will PEG form with water?

 c Is PEG an addition or a condensation polymer? Explain your answer.

continued ···▸

d i Explain which will have the higher melting point: PEG 200 or PEG 2000? What will be the strongest type of intermolecular forces between the polymer chains?

ii Given that a sample of PEG was made in this reaction:

$$HOCH_2CH_2OH + n(CH_2CH_2O)$$
$$\rightarrow HO(CH_2CH_2O)_{n+1}H$$

How would you vary the proportion of reactants to produce PEG 200 instead of PEG 2000?

iii Which instrumental technique (mass spectrometry, NMR spectroscopy or X-ray crystallography) would you recommend to check the relative molecular mass of the PEG formed? (see Chapter **29**).

iv How many main peaks would you expect to see in the low-resolution NMR spectrum of ethane-1,2-diol, $HOCH_2CH_2OH$? Explain your answer.

v How would you expect the peaks in part **iv** to be affected if D_2O was used as the solvent to obtain the NMR spectrum?

vi What splitting pattern would you expect the peaks in part **iv** to show in high-resolution NMR?

vii How many main peaks would you expect to see in the low-resolution NMR spectrum of epoxyethane? Explain your answer.

Inspired by natural polymeric materials

From the 1930s, chemists have tried to mimic natural polymers. Finding synthetic substitutes for rubber and silk, for example, offered the chance to produce cheaper materials with improved properties. Neoprene, a synthetic rubber, and nylon, a synthetic polyamide, were both products discovered at that time. Neoprene was made from the polymerisation of the monomer 2-chloro-1,3-butadiene in an addition reaction.

neoprene

The monomer of natural rubber is 2-methyl-1,3-butadiene, which is very similar to the monomer for neoprene. The intermolecular forces between natural rubber polymers are van der Waals' forces. A process called vulcanisation was invented to make rubber tyres more resilient and hardwearing. This links rubber polymer chains by covalent bonds across 'sulfur bridges' (Figure **30.9**).

Nylon was first made by reacting a dicarboxylic acid with a diamine. This condensation reaction, releasing water molecules, is similar to the polymerisation of the amino acid units in natural silk. Silk and nylon are strong materials because of the extensive hydrogen bonding between amide links. Nylon is cold drawn to align the polymer chains, which maximises the hydrogen bonding between chains.

> Note that the —NHCO— link is only called a peptide link in proteins.

Kevlar, discovered in the 1970s, is another example of a synthetic polyamide with strong intermolecular forces (see page **400**). These strong intermolecular forces made Kevlar suitable for use in bullet-proof vests and also in racing leathers for motorbike riders. The strength of Kevlar reflects the strength of one of nature's strongest fibres, the silk spiders use to make webs. Based on weight, spider silk is five times stronger than steel of the same diameter, whereas Kevlar fibres can be nine times as strong as steel.

The spider can spin different types of silk for different functions. The line it spins when moving down from a high place is the strongest. It is made from a protein called fibroin. The main amino acids in its polymers are glycine and alanine. Like nylon, its strength arises from the hydrogen bonds between its polymer chains.

Kevlar polymer chains are linear, with a high degree of alignment between chains. This is possible because the polymer chains are not branched with side-chains. If side-chains are present it is more difficult for the polymers to line up, resulting in weaker intermolecular forces. The role of side-chains is shown in the case of low-density poly(ethene) (LDPE) and high-density poly(ethene)

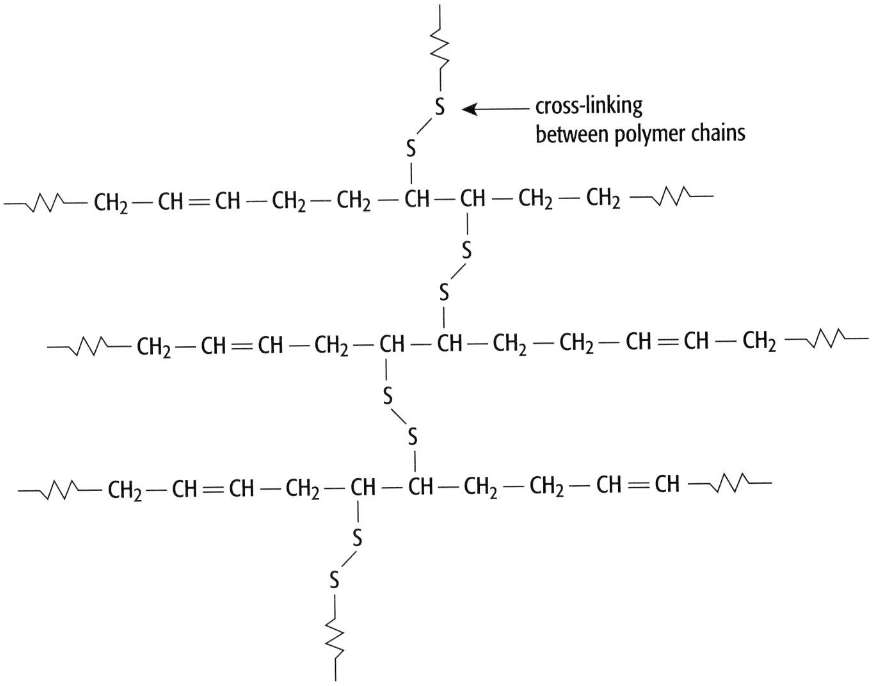

Figure 30.9 The sulfur bridges between polymer chains make rubber more resilient.

(HDPE). In the 1930s, the first form of poly(ethene) to be produced had extensive random branching on its polymer chains. This produced a plastic of low density which softened at a relatively low temperature. It wasn't until the 1950s that HDPE was first manufactured. Carl Zeigler discovered a catalyst that resulted in straight polymer chains. These could pack together more closely, resulting in stronger van der Waals' forces between polymer chains. HDPE is a stronger plastic than LDPE, with a higher softening temperature.

Check-up

5 a The word 'resilient' means to return to the original form or position after being bent, compressed or stretched. Explain why the process of vulcanising makes rubber 'more resilient'.

  b Give an equation to show the polymerisation of 2-methyl-1,3-butadiene to form rubber.

  c Draw a diagram to show a hydrogen bond between two amide links on neighbouring polyamide chains.

continued ⋯⋗

  d Identify one difference between the monomers that make up a nylon and those that form a protein.

  e Using the concept of intermolecular forces, explain why HDPE could be used to make containers that can be sterilised by boiling water but LDPE cannot.

Poly(lactic acid), PLA

Poly(lactic acid), known as PLA, is a polyester (see page 402). This polymer is becoming increasingly popular because the starting material used to produce it comes from plant starch, not from chemicals made from our dwindling supplies of crude oil.

Crops such as corn, wheat, beet and potatoes can all be used as raw materials. PLA also has other advantages, such as its biodegradability. It has also been shown that the life cycle of PLA, starting from the crop and ending at scrapping, reduces greenhouse gas emissions by around 30–50% compared with the manufacture and use of traditional oil-based plastics.

Figure 30.10 summarises the process used to make PLA.

We can think of this as the polymerisation of lactic acid (systematic name, 2-hydroxypropanoic acid), even though in industry the more reactive lactide derivative

30 Design and materials 487

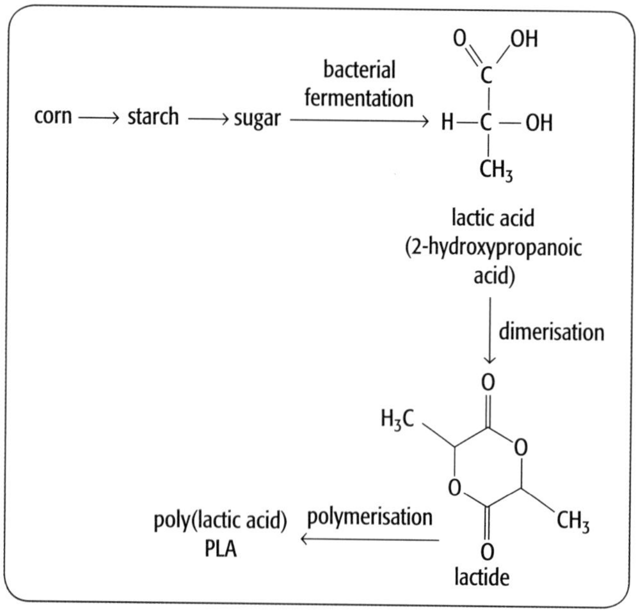

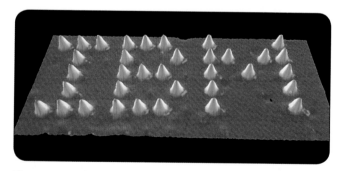

Figure 30.10 The production of poly(lactic acid), PLA.

is used to make PLA. The lactic acid molecules can undergo esterification (a condensation reaction), forming water as well as the polymer. Notice that the lactic acid (2-hydroxypropanoic acid) molecule has an alcohol and a carboxylic acid group within each molecule. Therefore the molecules can react to form ester links between each other:

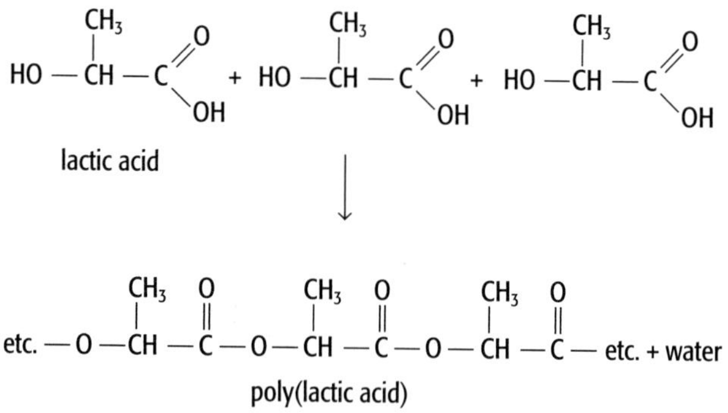

lactic acid

poly(lactic acid)

We can show the repeating unit in the PLA polymer as:

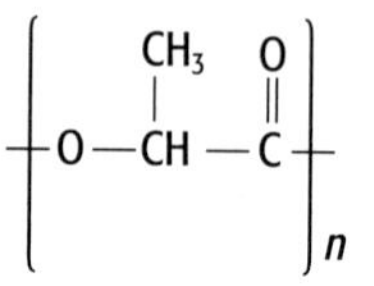

Check-up

6 a Draw the skeletal formula of 2-hydroxypropanoic acid (lactic acid).
  b Draw the repeating unit of PLA in skeletal form.

30.3 Nanotechnology

Nanotechnology is the design and creation of machines that are so small we measure them in nanometres.

It is difficult for us to imagine a nanometre (nm). The nanometre is the unit of measurement used on an atomic level, where $1 \, nm = 10^{-9} \, m$. Therefore, a nanometre is a billionth of a metre; a pinhead is about 1 million nanometres.

Nanotechnologists are now making machines that are less than 100 nm in size. At the moment, research is in its early stages. The tiny machines built so far include 'molecular model kit' rotors, 'robots', motors and circuits.

There are two approaches to making the molecular machines.
• You can sculpt or 'chisel away' at materials until you are left with the molecules or atoms that you want on the surface. Microelectronics at the molecular level uses this technique.
• The latest developments involve building your machine up from individual atoms or molecules. You can do this by physically moving the molecules using atomic force microscopes, as in Figure 30.11, or by chemical reactions in solution. The chemical technique seems to offer the best way forward as physically moving molecules around takes too long.

Figure 30.11 Scientists can manipulate atoms using scanning tunneling microscopes. Scientists at IBM positioned xenon atoms on a nickel platform to write these letters.

Scientists in America have made tiny nickel propellers that sit on top of the enzyme molecule that breaks down ATP in the cells in our bodies. The enzyme acts as the motor and is mounted on a nickel support. When put in a solution containing ATP, the propellers spin round (about 8 times each second).

There are special polymers called conjugate polymers that expand and contract when involved in transferring electrons. Scientists in Sweden and America have made tiny robotic arms by joining the polymer to a film of gold. When the polymer reacts in solution and changes its volume, the arm bends. The scientists have joined strips of their polymer/gold material to create an elbow, wrist and fingers. They have managed to pick up a very small glass bead with their machine. They have also made a molecular box, with a gold/polymer lid. In the right chemicals, the lid will open and shut.

Buckyballs

On page **483** we learned how nano-particles are being used to deliver drugs. The discovery of a form of carbon called buckminsterfullerene first triggered interest in nano-particles and the field of nanoscience. A British chemist, Harry Kroto, was one of three scientists who received the Nobel Prize for Chemistry (1996) for their role in its discovery. Sir Harry was working as a professor in Sussex University at the time. The other two scientists, Robert Curl and Richard Smalley, were from Rice University, Texas.

Radioastronomy had revealed that long chains of carbon atoms existed in outer space. When scientists tried to recreate the conditions that might account for the carbon chains, they found a new molecule formed by chance. The molecule was made of 60 carbon atoms, but it was unclear how the atoms were arranged within each molecule. Analysis showed that all the carbon atoms in the new molecule were equivalent; this meant that there were no carbon atoms stuck at the ends of the molecule. Professor Kroto solved the problem by suggesting a structure of hexagons and pentagons arranged in a sphere – just like the panels that make a football. The structure of C_{60} had been solved (Figure **30.13**).

Since the first discovery, chemists have now identified other similar molecules, called the fullerenes. A close relative is the rugby ball shaped molecule, C_{70}. Other even larger molecules have been made and even 'balls-within-balls', nicknamed bucky-onions. The spherical molecules can be used as 'cages', rather like the gold atoms discussed on page **483**.

'Bucky-tubes' have also been made (Figure **30.14**). These tubes, called nanotubes, consist of a single rolled up sheet of carbon atoms in the graphite structure and are incredibly strong. Fibres of the tubes can reinforce materials, such as those used in bullet-proof vests. If a nanotube is sealed at

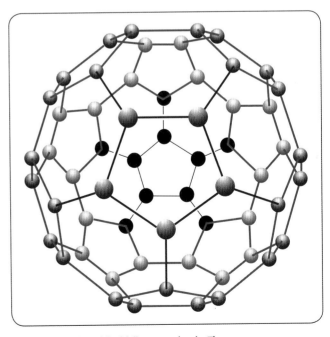

Figure 30.13 The original fullerene molecule. The name buckminsterfullerene was chosen for the molecule after the Canadian architect Buckminster Fuller. He designed a similar shaped building in Montreal in 1967. The name is often abbreviated to 'buckyball'.

Figure 30.12 Sir Harry Kroto is now a professor at Florida State University.

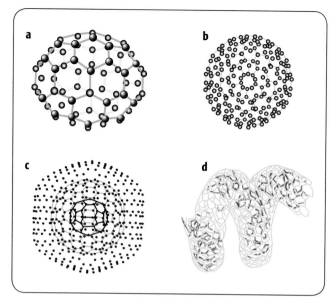

Figure 30.14 Other fullerene molecules, all with potential uses in the field of nanotechnology and nanoscience: **a** C_{70}; **b** C_{240}; **c** a 'bucky onion'; **d** a 'bucky-tube'.

Check-up

7 **a** What is meant by **nanoscale objects**?
   b Buckminsterfullerene is an allotrope of carbon. What is an **allotrope**?
   c One type of nuclear magnetic resonance (NMR) analyses the ^{13}C isotopes in carbon and its compounds. As proton NMR produces peaks for each type of non-equivalent ^{1}H atom, carbon-13 NMR shows peaks for each non-equivalent carbon atom. Predict the number of peaks on the carbon-13 NMR spectrum of buckminsterfullerene.
   d What would you expect to see on a proton NMR spectrum of buckminsterfullerene?
   e Which form of carbon has bonding similar to that found in fullerenes?

one end by exactly half a buckminsterfullerene molecule this gives us a 'bucky test tube' – exactly the same shape as a normal test tube, but much smaller.

The tubes also have free electrons, just like graphite, so they will have uses in electrical equipment. One team of researchers have managed to line glass with the tubes attached at one end. This could eventually replace traditional TV sets with new super-slim models with even better pictures than we have now. Another team have developed tubes that can give out light when stimulated. They suggest that paints of the future could have the tubes mixed in, so that rooms could glow at night, providing 24-hour daylight.

Nanotubes can adsorb hydrogen gas onto their surfaces. The cars of the future are likely to use hydrogen as a fuel. Fuel tanks packed with nanotubes will store more hydrogen than a conventional fuel tank filled with liquid hydrogen.

Other possible applications of nanotechnology and nanoscience range from civil engineering to advanced molecular electronics. One day we could have pocket-sized supercomputers and buildings which can withstand the most powerful hurricanes and earthquakes.

30.4 Fighting pollution

High up in the stratosphere there is a very important layer of ozone gas. Ozone (O_3) absorbs harmful ultraviolet rays from the Sun, protecting the humans and other creatures living on the surface of the Earth. In the 1970s scientists first noticed a problem in our atmosphere, as a hole was discovered in the ozone layer above Antarctica (Figure **30.15**). When actual measurements were taken in 1985 the readings were so low that the scientists thought that their instruments must be faulty.

The problem can be traced back to a group of compounds called CFCs (chlorofluorocarbons). The first of these compounds was made in 1930 by Thomas Midgeley. Its chemical formula was found to be CCl_2F_2.

At first, the CFCs were hailed as new 'wonder compounds'. They were very safe to use because they were so unreactive, which meant they weren't toxic. Because they vaporise easily, industry used them as the coolant in fridges. When aerosols came into fashion, CFCs were the ideal compounds to propel all kinds of droplets into the air.

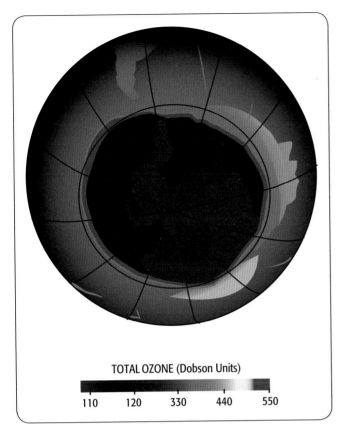

TOTAL OZONE (Dobson Units)

110   120   330   440   550

Figure 30.15 The hole in the ozone layer on September 17th, 2009. The largest hole was recorded on September 24th, 2006.

However, the CFCs are unreactive in normal conditions, but high up in the atmosphere they do react. The CFCs can persist in the atmosphere for about 100 years as they slowly they work their way up to the stratosphere.

In the stratosphere, the ultraviolet light from the Sun breaks up their molecules. A highly reactive chlorine atom splits off, forming a chlorine free radical. This is the initiation step (see page **220**).

Using CCl_2F_2 as an example of a CFC:

$$CCl_2F_2 \xrightarrow{\text{UV light}} \bullet CClF_2 + Cl\bullet$$

The energy from the ultraviolet light is sufficient to break the C—Cl bond but not the stronger C—F bond (see page **232** for information about their bond strength).

These chlorine free radicals then attack ozone molecules, in the propagation steps.

$$Cl\bullet + O_3 \rightarrow ClO\bullet + O_2$$

$$ClO\bullet + O_3 \rightarrow Cl\bullet + 2O_2$$

Adding these two propagation reactions together gives the overall reaction:

$$2O_3 \rightarrow 3O_2$$

with Cl• acting as a catalyst because it is constantly regenerated.

Cl• can also be regenerated by the reaction of the ClO• free radical with an oxygen atom formed when an O_3 molecule is broken down by absorbed UV light.

In the sequence of chain reactions, it has been estimated that each chlorine free radical can destroy 100 000 ozone molecules.

If more UV light reaches the surface we will see more health problems, such as:
• increased risk of sunburn
• faster ageing of our skin
• more skin cancer (it has been predicted that a 1% reduction in the ozone layer could result in 70 000 new cases of skin cancer each year)
• damage to our eyes, such as cataracts
• reduced resistance to some diseases
• disruption of plant photosynthesis (and hence disrupted food chains).

Governments have met to discuss the problem and most industrialised countries have banned the use of CFCs. Chemists have developed new compounds for fridges and aerosols, such as HFCs (hydrofluorocarbons). HFCs break down more quickly than CFCs once released into the air so they don't reach the stratosphere and the ozone layer. Unfortunately, compounds of this type are powerful 'greenhouse gases' and may contribute to global warming. There are plans to phase out the use of these substitutes by 2015 in the EU and by 2030 in the rest of the world. New substitute compounds will need to developed.

The ozone layer is monitored regularly and there are now signs that the ozone layer has stabilised. Some data is shown in Figure **30.16**.

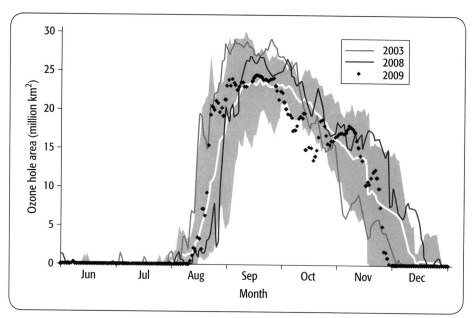

Figure 30.16 The ozone layer is monitored regularly. The grey shaded area gives the range over the period 1990–2001. You can see more at the ozonewatch website run by NASA from the The Goddard Space Flight Center.

Check-up

8 a It says on the previous page that 'Cl• can also be regenerated by the reaction of the ClO• free radical with an oxygen atom formed when an O_3 molecule is broken down by absorbed UV light.'

   Write an equation for this propagation step. (You have learned about initiation, propagation and termination steps on page **220**.)

  b What is a termination step? Write two termination steps for the sequence of propagation steps on the previous page.

  c Look at Figure **30.16**. Comment on the statement 'The hole in the ozone layer was a lot larger in the 1990s and continued getting smaller in the decade starting in 2000.'

30.5 'Green chemistry'

Industrial chemists are becoming increasingly aware of the need to conserve the Earth's resources and to stop the damage that is being caused to the environment. In the past, profits might have been the main consideration in making new materials, but now industrialists have realised their responsibilities to the planet and its inhabitants. 'Green chemistry' enables us to maintain and improve living standards through sustainable development that will safeguard the Earth for future generations.

There are six important principles of a greener chemical industry. These are discussed below, along with an example of each of them.

1 The design of processes to maximise the amount of raw material that is converted into product. Synthetic methods should be chosen to maximise the percentage incorporation of all materials used in the process into the final product. Catalytic reagents that are regenerated help to improve the atom economy of a process.

   An example is the synthesis of ibuprofen, an 'over-the-counter' drug which came into use in the 1980s (Figure **30.17**). At that time the synthetic route used to produce it consisted of six steps, with an overall

Figure 30.17 The production of Ibuprofen has been made more efficient since its introduction in the 1980s.

atom economy of just 40.1%. Atom economy is a measure of the proportion of the mass of atoms in your starting materials that actually end up as useful product. However, in the 1990s the Hoechst Celanese Corporation developed a new three-stage process. This new process improved the atom economy to 77.4%, making more efficient use of the raw materials and creating less waste. This type of innovation relies on the creativity of the research chemists to design new methods and the technologists who can put these into practice on an industrial scale.

2 The use, wherever possible, of raw materials or feedstock that are renewable rather than finite. However, technical and economic factors may make this difficult.

An example is the use of biofuels, such as biodiesel (Figure 30.18) and ethanol, instead of fossil fuels. However, sometimes these initiatives have unforeseen consequences. In 2007 there was a shortage of corn for the food industry in the USA. Farmers who had always grown corn (called maize in the USA) were being encouraged to produce crops for biofuels instead. This drove up the price of corn-based foodstuffs, and made it more difficult for poorer nations to import corn.

3 The use of safe, environmentally friendly solvents or no solvents at all where possible. The use of auxiliary substances (e.g. solvents, separation agents, etc.) should be made unnecessary wherever possible. If there is no way to carry out a process without the use of auxiliary substances, those chosen should be harmless. Wherever practicable, synthetic methods should be designed to use and generate substances that are non-toxic to humans and the environment.

We saw on page 482 that supercritical carbon dioxide can be used as a safer alternative to traditional organic solvents. It is used as a non-polar solvent at 31 °C and 73 atmospheres pressure. The solvent (which is non-toxic) is easily removed by reducing the pressure and recycling the CO_2 to use again.

4 The substances, and the form of the substances, used in a chemical process should be selected to minimise the potential risk of chemical accidents, including emissions, explosions, and fires.

An example is the use of new foam fire-fighting compounds and aerosol sprays that do not rely on halogenated hydrocarbons which end up in the atmosphere, contributing to ozone depletion.

5 The design of energy-efficient processes; the energy requirements of chemical processes should be minimised to reduce their impact on the environment (and should also reduce costs). If possible, synthetic methods should be conducted at ambient temperature and pressure. Wherever possible, the energy that is required should come from a renewable source, such as solar or wind generators, rather than a finite source such as a fossil fuel.

An example is the use of enzyme-catalysed reactions in the biotechnology industry which can operate at much lower temperatures and pressures than traditional industrial processes.

6 The consideration of waste reduction in the production process and at the end of a product's life cycle, aiming not to create waste in the first place. It is more efficient to prevent waste than to treat it or clean it up. Chemical products should be designed so that when finished with they break down into harmless substances.

One example of this is the development of new degradable plastic products that will not take up space in landfill sites and will not persist in the environment for centuries to come (see page 225 and Figure 30.19). Recycling of metals, plastics, paper and glass also helps conserve energy and resources, as well as reducing waste.

Figure 30.18 This oilseed rape is being grown for the production of biodiesel. Biodiesel is a 'carbon-neutral' fuel, in theory, as the carbon dioxide given off when the biodiesel burns had been removed from the air originally as the rape crop photosynthesised.

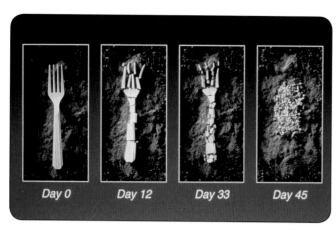

Figure 30.19 Chemists are devising new plastics that can be broken down by bacteria in the soil or by light.

Check-up

9 a Which type of polymer would you expect to degrade more quickly in a landfill site – a polyamide or a poly(alkene)? Explain your answer.

b Copper can be extracted from low-grade ore found in the waste rock in old copper mines. The method, called bioleaching, uses bacteria to make copper salts. Scrap iron can then be used to displace the copper from its salt solution. The traditional method of extraction needs high-grade copper ores which are heated in large smelters. Why is bioleaching a more sustainable way of extracting copper?

Summary

- ☐ Both natural biochemicals and modern medicinal drugs contain chiral molecules. Generally, only one of the enantiomers of a drug is beneficial to living organisms and the other isomer may have undesirable effects. The beneficial isomer has the appropriate shape and pattern of intermolecular forces to interact with a receptor molecule in a living organism.
- ☐ Chemists are now producing drugs containing single enantiomers rather than a racemic mixture of isomers. This enables the dose to be halved, improves pharmacological activity (behaviour of molecule in an organism), reduces side-effects and minimises litigation against manufacturers.
- ☐ Molecular design of a new medicinal drug is made possible with a sound understanding of the structural features that produce beneficial effects. The computerised study of the interactions between molecules and biological receptors has become a powerful tool in the search for new medicines.
- ☐ The delivery of a drug to its target area of the body, e.g. to a cancerous tumour, involves nano-particles, such as liposomes and gold nano-cages.
- ☐ Knowing about addition and condensation polymerisation and intermolecular forces enables chemists to design polymers for specific uses.
- ☐ Nanotechnology and nanoscience are at the cutting edge of chemical research, with new applications that have the potential to change our world.
- ☐ Chemists are at the forefront of initiatives to reduce the threat of pollution to the environment.
- ☐ The design and preparation of new compounds will involve safety and environmental considerations. It involves making decisions on:
  - which raw materials to use
  - the minimum quantities of reagents to use
  - what conditions and route provide the best yield, taking into account any issues of sustainability, such as producing as little waste as possible and reducing energy requirements as far as possible.

End-of-chapter questions

1   A sample of lactic acid ($CH_3CH(OH)COOH$) was extracted from a natural source and found to be optically active. It was then subjected to two reactions, as shown below.

$$CH_3CH(OH)COOH \xrightarrow{\text{step A}} CH_3COCOOH \xrightarrow{\text{step B}} CH_3CH(OH)COOH$$
sample 1   sample 2

Sample 1 was optically active but sample 2 was not optically active.

a i   Give the systematic name for lactic acid.   [1]
   ii The structure of one optical isomer of the lactic acid is:

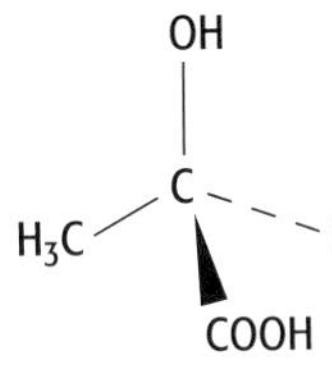

            Draw the other optical isomer.   [1]
   iii Explain why lactic acid can form optical isomers.   [1]
b i   Give the reagents and conditions necessary for step **A**.   [2]
   ii Give the balanced equation for the reaction.   [2]
c i   Give the reagents and conditions necessary for step **B**.   [2]
   ii Give the balanced equation for the reaction.   [2]
d i   Give the mechanism for step **B**. The first step involves nucleophilic attack on the carbon
            of the ketone group by an H^- ion from $NaBH_4$.   [5]
   ii Explain why sample 2 does not show any optical activity – it does not rotate
            plane-polarised light.   [3]

                                                                                          Total = 19

2   Explain how 2-aminopropanoic acid can be prepared from lactic acid in **two** steps. You should
    give the reagents and conditions necessary plus balanced symbol equations for the reactions
    taking place.   [9]
                                                                                          Total = 9

3   Write short notes on the following methods of synthesising chiral molecules:
    a using a chiral auxiliary   [3]
    b use of a chiral pool.   [3]
                                                                                          Total = 6

4   The structure of the compound known as thalidomide is:

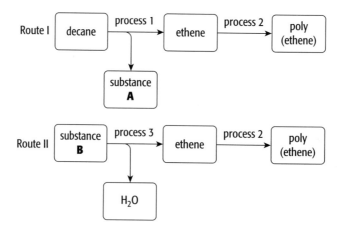

   a Copy the molecule and mark the chiral centre on your drawing.   [1]
   b Explain why the chirality of thalidomide has been such an important issue in the history
      of chemical synthesis.   [3]
                                                                          Total = 4

5   The flowcharts below show how poly(ethene) can be obtained by two different routes.

   a i   Identify substance **A** and give the equation for the reaction taking place in process 1.   [3]
      ii What term is used to describe process 1?   [1]
   b i   Name substance **B** and give the equation for the reaction taking place in process 3.   [3]
      ii What term is used to describe process 3?   [1]
                                                                          Total = 8

6 a Explain the term **biodegradable**.   [2]
   b Explain how the production of biodegradable polymers has lessened the impact of polymers
      on the environment.   [3]
   c Poly(L-lactic acid) is a biodegradable polymer. Give **two** uses of poly(L-lactic acid) and explain
      how its properties make it suitable for each use.   [4]
                                                                          Total = 9

7 a Give **two** reasons why the depletion of the ozone layer is dangerous for the environment.   [2]
   b Using equations, explain how chlorine radicals break down ozone in the stratosphere.   [4]
                                                                          Total = 6

Appendix 1

The Periodic Table

The Periodic Table of the Elements

Key
relative atomic mass
atomic symbol
name
atomic number

Group I	II												III	IV	V	VI	VII	0
						1.0 **H** Hydrogen 1												4.0 **He** Helium 2
6.9 **Li** Lithium 3	9.0 **Be** Beryllium 4												10.8 **B** Boron 5	12.0 **C** Carbon 6	14.0 **N** Nitrogen 7	16.0 **O** Oxygen 8	19.0 **F** Fluorine 9	20.2 **Ne** Neon 10
23.0 **Na** Sodium 11	24.3 **Mg** Magnesium 12												27.0 **Al** Aluminium 13	28.1 **Si** Silicon 14	31.0 **P** Phosphorus 15	32.1 **S** Sulfur 16	35.5 **Cl** Chlorine 17	39.9 **Ar** Argon 18
39.1 **K** Potassium 19	40.1 **Ca** Calcium 20	45.0 **Sc** Scandium 21	47.9 **Ti** Titanium 22	50.9 **V** Vanadium 23	52.0 **Cr** Chromium 24	54.9 **Mn** Manganese 25	55.8 **Fe** Iron 26	58.9 **Co** Cobalt 27	58.7 **Ni** Nickel 28	63.5 **Cu** Copper 29	65.4 **Zn** Zinc 30		69.7 **Ga** Gallium 31	72.6 **Ge** Germanium 32	74.9 **As** Arsenic 33	79.0 **Se** Selenium 34	79.9 **Br** Bromine 35	83.8 **Kr** Krypton 36
85.5 **Rb** Rubidium 37	87.6 **Sr** Strontium 38	88.9 **Y** Yttrium 39	91.2 **Zr** Zirconium 40	92.9 **Nb** Niobium 41	95.9 **Mo** Molybdenum 42	98.9 **Tc** Technetium 43	101 **Ru** Ruthenium 44	103 **Rh** Rhodium 45	106 **Pd** Palladium 46	108 **Ag** Silver 47	112 **Cd** Cadmium 48		115 **In** Indium 49	119 **Sn** Tin 50	122 **Sb** Antimony 51	128 **Te** Tellurium 52	127 **I** Iodine 53	131 **Xe** Xenon 54
133 **Cs** Caesium 55	137 **Ba** Barium 56	139 **La** Lanthanum 57 *	178 **Hf** Hafnium 72	181 **Ta** Tantalum 73	184 **W** Tungsten 74	186 **Re** Rhenium 75	190 **Os** Osmium 76	192 **Ir** Iridium 77	195 **Pt** Platinum 78	197 **Au** Gold 79	201 **Hg** Mercury 80		204 **Tl** Thallium 81	207 **Pb** Lead 82	209 **Bi** Bismuth 83	**Po** Polonium 84	**At** Astatine 85	**Rn** Radon 86
Fr Francium 87	**Ra** Radium 88	**Ac** Actinium 89 *	**Rf** rutherfordium 104	**Db** dubnium 105	**Sg** seaborgium 106	**Bh** bohrium 107	**Hs** hassium 108	**Mt** meitnerium 109	**Uun** ununnilium 110	**Uuu** unununium 111	**Uub** ununbium 112		**Uut** ununtrium 113	**Uuq** ununquadium 114		**Uuh** ununhexium 116		**Uuo** ununoctium 118

lanthanides *

140 **Ce** Cerium 58	141 **Pr** Praseodymium 59	144 **Nd** Neodymium 60	**Pm** Promethium 61	150 **Sm** Samarium 62	152 **Eu** Europium 63	157 **Gd** Gadolinium 64	159 **Tb** Terbium 65	163 **Dy** Dysprosium 66	165 **Ho** Holmium 67	167 **Er** Erbium 68	169 **Tm** Thulium 69	173 **Yb** Ytterbium 70	175 **Lu** Lutetium 71

actinides * *

Th Thorium 90	**Pa** Protactinium 91	**U** Uranium 92	**Np** Neptunium 93	**Pu** Plutonium 94	**Am** Americium 95	**Cm** Curium 96	**Bk** Berkelium 97	**Cf** Californium 98	**Es** Einsteinium 99	**Fm** Fermium 100	**Md** Mendelevium 101	**No** Nobelium 102	**Lr** Lawrencium 103

Appendix 2

Standard electrode potentials

Electrode reaction	$E^{\ominus}/V$
$Ag^+ + e^- \rightleftharpoons Ag$	+0.80
$Br_2 + 2e^- \rightleftharpoons 2Br^-$	+1.07
$Cl_2 + 2e^- \rightleftharpoons 2Cl^-$	+1.36
$Cr^{2+} + 2e^- \rightleftharpoons Cr$	−0.91
$Cr^{3+} + 3e^- \rightleftharpoons Cr$	−0.74
$Cr_2O_7^{2-} + 14H^+ + 6e^- \rightleftharpoons 2Cr^{3+} + 7H_2O$	+1.33
$Cu^+ + e^- \rightleftharpoons Cu$	+0.52
$Cu^{2+} + 2e^- \rightleftharpoons Cu$	+0.34
$Cu^{2+} + e^- \rightleftharpoons Cu^+$	+0.15
$F_2 + 2e^- \rightleftharpoons 2F^-$	+2.87
$Fe^{2+} + 2e^- \rightleftharpoons Fe$	−0.44
$Fe^{3+} + e^- \rightleftharpoons Fe^{2+}$	+0.77
$Fe^{3+} + 3e^- \rightleftharpoons Fe$	−0.04
$2H^+ + 2e^- \rightleftharpoons H_2$	0.00
$I_2 + 2e^- \rightleftharpoons 2I^-$	+0.54
$Mn^{2+} + 2e^- \rightleftharpoons Mn$	−1.18
$MnO_4^- + 8H^+ + 5e^- \rightleftharpoons Mn^{2+} + 4H_2O$	+1.52
$Ni^{2+} + 2e^- \rightleftharpoons Ni$	−0.25
$O_2 + 4H^+ + 4e^- \rightleftharpoons 2H_2O$	+1.23
$O_2 + 2H_2O + 4e^- \rightleftharpoons 4OH^-$	+0.40
$Pb^{2+} + 2e^- \rightleftharpoons Pb$	−0.13
$SO_4^{2-} + 4H^+ + 2e^- \rightleftharpoons SO_2 + 2H_2O$	+0.17
$Sn^{4+} + 2e^- \rightleftharpoons Sn^{2+}$	+0.15
$V^{2+} + 2e^- \rightleftharpoons V$	−1.20
$V^{3+} + e^- \rightleftharpoons V^{2+}$	−0.26
$VO^{2+} + 2H^+ + e^- \rightleftharpoons V^{3+} + H_2O$	+0.34
$VO_2^+ + 2H^+ + e^- \rightleftharpoons VO^{2+} + H_2O$	+1.00
$VO_3^- + 4H^+ + e^- \rightleftharpoons VO^{2+} + 2H_2O$	+1.00
$Zn^{2+} + 2e^- \rightleftharpoons Zn$	−0.76

Check-up answers

Chapter 1

1 **a** 111.1
   b 159.6
   c 132.1
   d 256.3

2 **a** $^{76}_{32}Ge$
   b $\dfrac{(20.6 \times 70)+(27.4 \times 72)+(7.7 \times 73)+(36.7 \times 74)+(7.6 \times 76)}{100} = 72.7$

3 **a** **i** 0.33 mol
      ii 0.25 mol
      iii 0.25 mol
   b moles Cl $= \dfrac{7.10}{35.5} = 0.200\,mol$

   $0.20 \times 6.02 \times 10^{23} = 1.20 \times 10^{23}$ (to 3 significant figures)

4 **a** 8.8 g
   b 5.3 g
   c 449.0 g

5 **a** 46.0 g Na → 78.0 g Na_2O_2
      so 4.6 g Na → 7.8 g Na_2O_2
   b 150.7 g SnO_2 → 24 g C
      so 14.0 g SnO_2 → 2.23 g C

6 $\dfrac{56.2}{28.1} = 2\,mol\,Si$

   $\dfrac{284.0}{71.0} = 4\,mol\,Cl_2$

   $\dfrac{340.2}{170.1} = 2\,mol\,SiCl_4$

   so ratio of $Si : Cl_2 : SiCl_4 = 1 : 2 : 1$

   $Si + 2Cl_2 \rightarrow SiCl_4$

7 $100 \times \dfrac{24}{46} = 52.2\%$ (to 3 significant figures)

8 **a** NH_2
   b C_4H_9
   c CH
   d NH_3

9

Carbon	Hydrogen
$\dfrac{90}{12.0}$	$\dfrac{10}{1.0}$
= 7.5	= 10

   simplest ratio = 3C to 4H
   empirical formula is C_3H_4

10 **A** C_6H_{10}
    B C_2Cl_6
    C C_8H_{16}

11 **i** $Mg(NO_3)_2$
     ii $CaSO_4$
     iii NaI
     iv HBr
     v Na_2S
    b **i** sodium phosphate
       ii ammonium sulfate
       iii aluminium chloride
       iv calcium nitrate

12 **a** $Fe + 2HCl \rightarrow FeCl_2 + H_2$
    b $2Al(OH)_3 \rightarrow Al_2O_3 + 3H_2O$
    c $2C_6H_{14} + 19O_2 \rightarrow 12CO_2 + 14H_2O$

13 **a** $CaCO_3(s) + 2HCl(aq)$
       $\rightarrow CaCl_2(aq) + CO_2(g) + H_2O(l)$
    b $ZnSO_4(aq) + 2NaOH(aq)$
       $\rightarrow Zn(OH)_2(s) + Na_2SO_4(aq)$

14 **a** $H^+(aq) + OH^-(aq) \rightarrow H_2O(l)$
    b $Br_2(aq) + 2I^-(aq) \rightarrow 2Br^-(aq) + I_2(aq)$

15 **a** $Cu^{2+}(aq) + 2OH^-(aq) \rightarrow Cu(OH)_2(s)$
    b $Pb^{2+}(aq) + 2I^-(aq) \rightarrow PbI_2(s)$

16 **a** **i** $\dfrac{2.0}{40.0} \times \dfrac{1000}{50} = 1.0\,mol\,dm^{-3}$

       ii $\dfrac{12.0}{60.0} \times \dfrac{1000}{250} = 0.80\,mol\,dm^{-3}$

    b **i** $0.2 \times \dfrac{40}{1000} = 8 \times 10^{-3}\,mol$

       ii $0.01 \times \dfrac{50}{1000} = 5 \times 10^{-4}\,mol$

17 **a** number of moles of HCl $= 0.100 \times \dfrac{15.00}{1000}$

       $= 1.5 \times 10^{-3}\,mol$
       number of moles of $Sr(OH)_2 = \dfrac{1.5 \times 10^{-3}}{2}$

       $= 7.50 \times 10^{-4}\,mol$
       concentration of $Sr(OH)_2 = 7.50 \times 10^{-4} \times \dfrac{1000}{25}$

       $= 3.00 \times 10^{-2}\,mol\,dm^{-3}$
    b number of moles of NaOH $= 0.400 \times \dfrac{20.0}{1000}$

       $= 8.00 \times 10^{-3}\,mol$
       number of moles of $H_2SO_4 = \dfrac{8.00 \times 10^{-3}}{2}$

       $= 4.00 \times 10^{-3}\,mol$

concentration of $H_2SO_4 = 4.00 \times 10^{-3} \times \dfrac{1000}{25.25}$

$= 1.58 \times 10^{-1} \, mol \, dm^{-3}$ (to 3 significant figures)

18 a $0.0600 \times \dfrac{20.0}{1000} = 1.20 \times 10^{-3} \, mol$

b $0.100 \times \dfrac{24.00}{1000} = 2.40 \times 10^{-3} \, mol$

c 1 mol metal hydroxide : 2 mol hydrochloric acid

d $M(OH)_2 + 2HCl \rightarrow MCl_2 + 2H_2O$

19 a $\dfrac{26.4}{44.0} = 0.60 \, mol$

$0.60 \times 24.0 = 14.4 \, dm^3$

b number of moles He $= \dfrac{120}{24000} = 5.0 \times 10^{-3} \, mol$

mass $= 4.0 \times 5.0 \times 10^{-3} = 2.0 \times 10^{-2} \, g$

20 a 3

b PH_3 (ratio of volumes = ratio of moles)

c $PH_3(g) + 3Cl_2(g) \rightarrow PCl_3(l) + 3HCl(g)$

Chapter 2

1 a i Protons are deflected towards the plate / move towards the plate; because unlike charges are attracted to each other.

ii Neutrons are not deflected; because neutrons have no charge / zero charge / are uncharged.

b Electrons; because for a charged particle it has the least mass / has a lower mass than the proton.

2 a vanadium-51: electrons = 23, neutrons = 28

b strontium-84: electrons = 38, neutrons = 46

c phosphorus-31: electrons = 15, neutrons = 16

3 a i $^{81}_{35}Br$

ii $^{44}_{20}Ca$

iii $^{58}_{26}Fe$

iv $^{110}_{46}Pd$

b i Br: protons = 35; neutrons = 46

ii Ca: protons = 20; neutrons = 24

iii Fe: protons = 26; neutrons = 32

iv Pd: protons = 46; neutrons = 64

4 a 18

b 10

c 10

d 28

Chapter 3

1 a 2, 8, 6

b 2, 8, 2

c 2, 7

d 2, 8, 8, 1

e 2, 4

2 a i $Ca(g) \rightarrow Ca^+(g) + e^-$

ii $K^{2+}(g) \rightarrow K^{3+}(g) + e^-$

iii $Li^+(g) \rightarrow Li^{2+}(g) + e^-$

iv $S^{4+}(g) \rightarrow S^{5+}(g) + e^-$

b Charge on the ion is greater when the third electron is removed than when the second electron is removed. So, it is more difficult to remove the third electron as there is a greater attractive force between the outer electrons and the nucleus.

3 a i Large change between the third and fourth ionisation energies. This suggests that the first three electrons are easier to remove because they are further away from the nucleus and are shielded by the inner electrons from the full nuclear charge. The fourth electron is much more difficult to remove because it is closer to the nucleus and there is no (or little) shielding.

ii Three electrons are easily removed, so are on the outside (in the second shell) and two are very difficult to remove (in the first shell).

b Gradual rise in ΔH_i for first 3 electrons. Large rise between ΔH_{i3} and ΔH_{i4}. Gradual rise in ΔH_i for next 8 electrons. Large rise between ΔH_{i11} and ΔH_{i12}. Gradual rise in ΔH_i for final 2 electrons.

4 a Group 4. Large increase in value of ΔH_i between the removal of the fourth and fifth electrons.

b Small rise between ΔH_i for first 2 electrons. Large rise between ΔH_{i2} and ΔH_{i3}. (Gradual rise in ΔH_i for next electrons.)

5 a s, p, d

b s = 2, p = 6, d = 10

6 a $1s^2 \, 2s^2 \, 2p^6 \, 3s^2 \, 3p^4$

b $1s^2 \, 2s^2 \, 2p^5$

c $1s^2 \, 2s^2 \, 2p^6 \, 3s^2 \, 3p^6 \, 4s^2$

7 a $1s^2 \, 2s^2 \, 2p^6 \, 3s^2 \, 3p^6 \, 3d^3 \, 4s^2$

b $1s^2 \, 2s^2 \, 2p^6 \, 3s^2 \, 3p^6 \, 3d^{10} \, 4s^1$

c $1s^2 \, 2s^2 \, 2p^6 \, 3s^2 \, 3p^6 \, 3d^{10} \, 4s^2 \, 4p^4$

8 a i p block

ii Group VII

iii iodine

b d block

9 **a** $1s^2\,2s^2\,2p^6$
   b $1s^2\,2s^2\,2p^6$
   c $1s^2\,2s^2\,2p^6\,3s^2\,3p^6\,3d^5$
   d $1s^2\,2s^2\,2p^6\,3s^2\,3p^6\,3d^9$
   e $1s^2\,2s^2\,2p^6\,3s^2\,3p^6\,3d^{10}$

10 **a i** From sodium to silicon, the nuclear charge increases.
          The distance between the nucleus and the outer electron
          remains reasonably constant. The shielding by inner
          shells remains reasonably constant. Ionisation energy
          increases to match increase in attraction from the nucleus
          with an increased nuclear charge.
      ii The distance between the nucleus and the outer electrons
          increases from Mg to Al. The shielding by inner shells
          increases. These two factors outweigh the increased
          nuclear charge.
   b The distance between the nucleus and the outer electrons
       increases from F to I. The shielding by inner shells increases.
       These two factors outweigh the increased nuclear charge.

Chapter 4

1 **a**

   b

   c

   d

2 **a**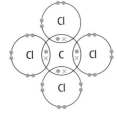

b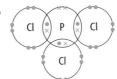

c

d

e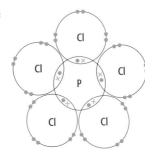

3 **a**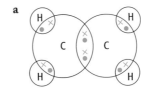

   b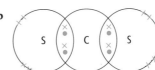

4 **a i**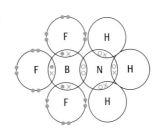

      ii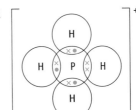

b

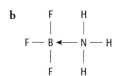

c

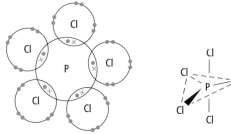

5 a The longer the bond length, the weaker the bond.
   b Going down the halogen group, the atoms are bigger; the attractive force between the bonding electrons and the nucleus gets smaller; so less energy needed to break bond.
   c Allow between 0.09 and 0.11 nm.

6 a i tetrahedral
     ii linear
     iii triangular pyramidal / trigonal pyramidal

   b

> **Examiner's tip**
> The text hasn't told you what the shapes of these molecules are. You have to do something that is common in exams – apply your knowledge. When you have completed each dot and cross diagram look for another molecule with the same number of lone pairs and bond pairs. The shapes, and bond angles, of the H₂S and the PH₃ molecules can be predicted if you think like this.

   i

   ii

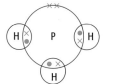

7 a

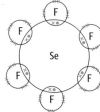

   b octahedron

8

> **Examiner's tip**
> At A-level, questions like this must be answered by referring to the structure and bonding of the materials involved. Here you must focus on the giant metallic bonding involved.

   a Metallic bonding is between metal ions in a sea of delocalised electrons. In aluminium there are more delocalised electrons and the ions have a higher charge compared with sodium. There is a greater force of attraction between the electrons and the ions in aluminium, so it requires more energy to overcome these forces of attraction, leading to a higher melting point.
   b Copper provides better heat transfer because it conducts better than stainless steel. Flow of delocalised electrons is greater in copper than in stainless steel / electrons are held more strongly by iron ions in steel. For a saucepan, you want higher thermal conductivity at the base, so copper is used at the base.
   c Electric current in metals is due to a flow of delocalised electrons. Three electrons are produced when an aluminium ion is formed but only one when a sodium ion is formed. There are more delocalised electrons in aluminium than in sodium.

9 a Cl_2: non-polar; electronegativities are the same.
   b HF: polar; fluorine more electronegative than hydrogen.
   c SCl_2: polar; chlorine more electronegative than sulfur and the V-shape of the molecules means that the electron density is asymmetric / centres of positive and negative charge do not coincide.
   d CH_3Cl: polar; chlorine more electronegative than hydrogen so very small dipoles on C—H bonds can't cancel out the dipoles on the C—Cl bond. Electron density is asymmetric / centres of positive and negative charge do not coincide.
   e CBr_4: non-polar; equal dipoles on each C—Br bond and these cancel each other out since the molecule is symmetrical.

10 a i The trend is for higher boiling points going down Group VII.
      ii Bigger molecules (more protons) have more electrons. Van der Waals' attractive forces are larger with increasing number of electrons. So the van der Waals' forces are greater as the halogen molecules increase in size.

b The trend is for higher boiling points with increasing length of alkane molecules. Longer and bigger molecules have more electrons. There are more contact points with longer molecules. Van der Waals' attractive forces are larger with increasing number of contact points as well as with increasing number of electrons. So the van der Waals' forces are greater as molecules get longer.

11 Bromine is a non-polar molecule so only has van der Waals' forces as intermolecular forces. Iodine monochloride has a permanent dipole since chlorine is more electronegative than iodine. The permanent dipole–dipole force makes for a greater attraction between iodine monochloride molecules compared with the van der Waals' forces between bromine molecules. So it requires relatively more energy to overcome these dipole–dipole forces.

12 a

b

c

13 a The trend is for higher boiling points with increasing size of Group V hydride molecules. Bigger molecules have more electrons. Van der Waals' attractive forces are larger with increasing number of electrons. So the van der Waals' forces are greater as the hydrides of Group V increase in size.

b Atoms of nitrogen are more electronegative than hydrogen. Hydrogen bonding occurs in ammonia since there are hydrogen atoms attached to a very electronegative atom (nitrogen) and a very electronegative atom (nitrogen) with a lone pair of electrons on a neighbouring atom. Hydrogen bonds are stronger than dipole–dipole bonds or van der Waals' forces present in phosphine, so it takes more energy to break the intermolecular forces in ammonia and the boiling point is correspondingly higher.

14 a Aluminium oxide is ionic. There are strong electrostatic forces between the metal ions and the delocalised electrons in the metal structure, so it requires a lot of energy to break these forces. This can only be done at high temperature. Aluminium chloride has a simple molecular structure. The attractive forces between molecules are weak, so it only requires a small amount of energy to break these intermolecular forces.

b Electrical conduction in ionic compounds is due to the movement of ions. In an ionic solid the ions are not free to move because of the strong electrostatic forces keeping them together in the ionic lattice. So, solid magnesium chloride does not conduct. Molten magnesium chloride conducts because its ions are free to move.

c Iron conducts electricity when solid because it has a metallic structure of ions in a sea of mobile electrons. The movement of the mobile electrons is an electric current. Iron chloride does not conduct when solid because the ions are not free to move because of the strong electrostatic forces keeping them together in the ionic lattice. In addition there are no free delocalised electrons to conduct electricity.

d Water molecules are polar so they can form bonds with the sodium and sulfate ions in the solid. The bonds formed allow the sodium and sulfate ions to go into solution. Sulfur is a non-polar solid. It cannot form bonds with water molecules and so cannot go into solution.

e Propanol can form hydrogen bonds with water because both water and propanol have a hydrogen atom attached to a very electronegative (oxygen) atom. Propane does not dissolve in water because it is non-polar.

f Hydrogen chloride reacts with water to form hydrogen ions and chloride ions and these ions allow the solution to conduct electricity.

Chapter 5

1 a Particles in a solid are close together / touching. When a solid changes to a liquid the particles move slightly further apart but many are still touching. In a solid the particles are only vibrating. As the temperature is raised, the particles vibrate more until they can move from place to place by sliding over other particles.

b Particles in a liquid are close together and many are still touching. As the temperature is raised they move faster then escape to form a gas where the particles are much further apart. The particles in a liquid are moving slowly over each other but in a gas they move more rapidly.

2 Helium and neon atoms are non-polar so the only forces between them are van der Waals' forces. There are very few electrons in each atom so the van der Waals' forces here are particularly weak.

3 a i 518 K
   ii 228 K
  b 15×10^3 / 15 000

4 At high temperatures the molecules are moving very fast. They have a lot of kinetic energy. The particles hit the walls of the tube with a considerable force. If the temperature is too high the force of the particle hitting the wall may be great enough to break the tube.

5　**a**　A gas whose volume varies in proportion to the kelvin temperature and is inversely proportionally to the pressure.

　　b　Real gases deviate from the ideal gases at high pressures and low temperatures, because under these conditions the molecules are close enough for intermolecular forces of attraction to pull the molecules towards one another. The volume of the molecules must also be taken into account.

6　**a**　$54\,^{\circ}\mathrm{C} = 54 + 273 = 327\,\mathrm{K}$; $250\,\mathrm{kPa} = 250\,000\,\mathrm{Pa}$

　　　　$$\text{moles of methane} = \frac{272}{16} = 17\,\mathrm{mol}$$

　　　　rearrange the gas equation

　　　　$$pV = nRT \text{ so } V = \frac{nRT}{p}$$

　　　　$$V = \frac{17 \times 8.31 \times 327}{250\,000} = 0.185\,\mathrm{m}^3 \text{ (to 3 significant figures)}$$

　　b　$10\,\mathrm{dm}^3 = \dfrac{10}{1000}\,\mathrm{m}^3 = 0.01\,\mathrm{m}^3$; $120\,\mathrm{kPa} = 120\,000\,\mathrm{Pa}$

　　　　rearrange the gas equation

　　　　$$pV = nRT \text{ so } T = \frac{pV}{nR}$$

　　　　$$T = \frac{120\,000 \times 0.01}{0.25 \times 8.31} = 578\,\mathrm{K} \text{ (to 3 significant figures)}$$

7　$100\,^{\circ}\mathrm{C} = 100 + 273 = 373\,\mathrm{K}$; $23\,\mathrm{cm}^3 = 2.3 \times 10^{-5}\,\mathrm{m}^3$

　　rearrange the gas equation

　　$$pV = \frac{mRT}{M_r} \text{ so } M_r = \frac{mRT}{pV}$$

　　$$M_r = \frac{0.08 \times 8.31 \times 373}{(1.02 \times 10^5) \times (2.3 \times 10^{-5})} = 105.7$$

　　$M_r = 106$ (to 3 significant figures)

8　At first, bromine molecules escape from the surface of the liquid to become vapour. The colour of the vapour above the liquid becomes darker. As more and more molecules escape, the molecules in the vapour become closer together. Eventually the molecules with lower kinetic energy will not be able to overcome the attractive forces of neighbouring molecules. Some of the molecules in the vapour begin to condense, and these bromine molecules return to the liquid. Eventually, bromine molecules return to the liquid at the same rate as bromine molecules escape to the vapour. A position of equilibrium is reached. The colour of the vapour above the liquid remains constant.

9　**a**　Many metals are strong because of the strong forces of attraction between the ions and the delocalised electrons. Ionic solids are brittle because when a force is applied along the planes of ions in the lattice, the ions come to occupy new positions in which ions with the same charge are opposite each other. The repulsion between many ions of the same charge weakens the forces keeping the ions together and the layers break apart.

　　b　In pure copper or pure tin, the layers of metal atoms/ions can slide over each other when a force is applied. New bonds are formed due to the force of attraction between the metal ions and the delocalised electrons. In the alloy, the different sized atoms cause the lattice structure to be disrupted. So the layers of metal ions do not slide over each other as easily.

10　**a**　Although aluminium is not as good an electrical conductor as copper, pure copper is too dense and cannot support its own weight when used in overhead cables. Aluminium has low density but has low tensile strength, so steel (which has high tensile strength) is used to support the aluminium.

　　b　Aluminium is less dense than steel, so the engine block has a lower mass and less energy is used by the car. The lower strength of aluminium compared with steel is not a problem for this application.

　　c　Iron is strong because of the strong metallic bonding between the ions and the mobile electrons in the metallic lattice. Sulfur breaks easily because it has a simple molecular structure. Intermolecular forces/van der Waals' forces between sulfur molecules are weak. The intermolecular forces are easily broken.

Examiner's tip
The question says 'by referring to its structure and bonding', so begin your answer by stating what the structure and bonding is.

11　**a**　Silicon(IV) oxide has a giant covalent structure. It has a high melting point because of the strong covalent bonding throughout the whole structure. A high temperature is needed to break these strong bonds and separate the atoms.

　　b　Silicon(IV) oxide does not conduct electricity because all the electrons are used in bonding, so there are no free electrons available to carry the electric current.

　　c　Silicon(IV) oxide is a crystalline solid because the atoms are in a regular tetrahedral arrangement / the atoms are in a lattice structure.

　　d　Silicon(IV) oxide is hard because it is difficult to break the three-dimensional network of strong covalent bonds by simply scratching the surface.

12

	Giant ionic	Giant molecular	Metallic	Simple molecular
Two examples	e.g. sodium chloride, magnesium oxide	e.g. graphite, silicon(IV) oxide	e.g. copper, iron	e.g. bromine, carbon dioxide
Particles present	ions	atoms	positive ions in sea of electrons	small molecules
Forces keeping particles together	electrostatic attraction between oppositely charged ions	electrons in covalent bonds between atoms	delocalised sea of electrons attracts positive ions	weak intermolecular forces between molecules (but covalent bonds within the molecules)
Physical state at room temperature	solid	solid	solid	solid, liquid or gas
Melting points and boiling points	high	very high	moderately high to high	low
Hardness	hard, brittle	very hard	hard, malleable	soft
Electrical conductivity	conduct when molten or in aqueous solution	non-conductors (except graphite)	conduct when solid or molten	non-conductors
Solubility in water	most are soluble	insoluble	insoluble but some react	usually insoluble but soluble if polar enough to form hydrogen bonds with water

13 a Aluminium oxide and silicon(IV) oxide ceramics have giant molecular structures. They have a three-dimensional network of strong covalent bonds. It takes a lot of energy to break these bonds, so these oxides do not melt in the high temperature of the furnace. They are thermal insulators because they have no free electrons to conduct the heat or ions to move. The heat of the furnace is therefore not transmitted to the outside and the outer wall of the furnace does not melt.

b Aluminium oxide ceramics have giant molecular structure with a three-dimensional network of strong covalent bonds. The bonds will not be broken when a force is applied on them during grinding. Aluminium oxide ceramics are thermal insulators and have high melting points. So the heat produced by friction during grinding does not melt such ceramics.

Chapter 6

1 a exothermic
   b exothermic
   c endothermic
   d exothermic
   e endothermic

2 a

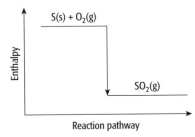

b

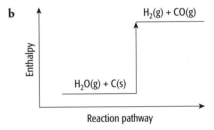

3 a $\Delta H_r^{\ominus}$
   b $\Delta H_f^{\ominus}[CO_2(g)]$ or $\Delta H_c^{\ominus}[C_{(graphite)}]$
   c $\Delta H_r^{\ominus}$
   d $\Delta H_f^{\ominus}[H_2O(l)]$ or $\Delta H_c^{\ominus}[H_2(g)]$

4 a 9718.5 J (9720 J to 3 significant figures)
   b 250.8 J (251 J to 3 significant figures)
   c 6270 J

5 One mole of sulfuric acid reacts with two moles of sodium hydroxide to form two moles of water. The definition of the standard enthalpy change of neutralisation relates to the formation of one mole of water. The enthalpy change for sulfuric acid is twice this.

6 Time taken for sodium to dissolve / energy loss to thermometer or air or calorimeter; assumption that the specific thermal capacity of the solution is the same as that of water.

7 In the experiment there may be: heat losses to the surroundings from the flame and into the calorimeter, thermometer and air; incomplete combustion of the ethanol; evaporation of ethanol so that not all the weight loss is due to burning.

8 a

$$2Al(s) + Fe_2O_3(s) \xrightarrow{\Delta H_r^{\ominus}} 2Fe(s) + Al_2O_3(s)$$

$\Delta H_f^{\ominus}[Fe_2O_3(s)] \diagdown \Delta H_1 \qquad \Delta H_2 \diagup \Delta H_f^{\ominus}[Al_2O_3(s)]$

$$2Al(s) + 2Fe(s) + 1\tfrac{1}{2}O_2(g)$$

b $\Delta H_r + \Delta H_1 = \Delta H_2$

$\Delta H_r + (-824.2) = -1675.7$

$\Delta H_r = -851.5\,\text{kJ}\,\text{mol}^{-1}$

9 a

$$2C(graphite) + 3H_2(g) + 3\tfrac{1}{2}O_2(g) \xrightarrow{\Delta H_f} C_2H_5OH(l) + 3O_2(g)$$

$2\Delta H_c^{\ominus}[C(graphite)] \diagdown \Delta H_1 \qquad \Delta H_2 \diagup \Delta H_c^{\ominus}[C_2H_5OH(l)]$
$+ 3\Delta H_c^{\ominus}[H_2(g)]$

$$2CO_2(g) + 3H_2O(l)$$

b $\Delta H_f + \Delta H_2 = \Delta H_1$

$\Delta H_f + (-1367.3) = 2(-393.5) + 3(285.8)$

$\Delta H_f = -277.1\,\text{kJ}\,\text{mol}^{-1}$

10 It is difficult to know when the salt is just fully hydrated; most of the heat will be lost because of the time taken to do the experiment; it is difficult to measure the temperature of a solid accurately using a standard thermometer.

11 $\Delta H_r = +1663.5\,\text{kJ}\,\text{mol}^{-1}$

There are four C—H bonds in methane, so the average C—H bond energy is $\dfrac{1663.5}{4} = +415.9\,\text{kJ}\,\text{mol}^{-1}$

12 a

b $C_2H_5OH + 3O_2 \xrightarrow{\Delta H_5} 2CO_2 + 3H_2O$

$(C—C) + 5 \times (C—H) + (C—O) + (O—H)$

$+3 \times (O{=}O) \xrightarrow{\Delta H_c} 4 \times (C{=}O) + 6 \times (O—H)$

$347 + 5 \times (410) + (336) + (465) + 3 \times (496)$

$\longrightarrow 4 \times (805) + 6 \times (465)$

$+4686\,\text{kJ} \longrightarrow -6010\,\text{kJ}$

$\Delta H_c = -1324\,\text{kJ}$

c Bond energies used are average bond energies and are based on data from gaseous reactants and products whereas experimental combustion results for ethanol are for ethanol liquid.

Chapter 7

1 a i H_2
  ii CO
  iii Mg
  b i I_2O_5
  ii SO_2
  iii CH_2CH_2

2 a i $Cl_2 + 2e^- \rightarrow 2Cl^-$; reduction
    $2I^- \rightarrow I_2 + 2e^-$; oxidation
  ii $2Mg \rightarrow 2Mg^{2+} + 4e^-$ (or $Mg \rightarrow Mg^{2+} + 2e^-$); oxidation
    $O_2 + 4e^- \rightarrow 2O^{2-}$; reduction
  iii $4Fe \rightarrow 4Fe^{3+} + 12e^-$ (or $Fe \rightarrow Fe^{3+} + 3e^-$); oxidation
    $3O_2 + 12e^- \rightarrow 6O^{2-}$ (or $O_2 + 4e^- \rightarrow 2O^{2-}$); reduction
  b $2IO_3^- + 5Zn + 12H^+ \rightarrow I_2 + 5Zn^{2+} + 6H_2O$

3 a +5
  b +6
  c −2
  d +3
  e −3
  f +3
  g +4

4 a i 0 to −1 = −1; reduction
  ii −3 to 0 = +3; oxidation
  iii +3 to +5 = +2; oxidation
  iv +7 to +2 = −5; reduction
  b i I^-
  ii NH_4^+
  iii As_2O_3
  iv HCl

5 a sodium sulfate(IV)
  b sodium sulfate(VI)
  c iron(II) nitrate(V) or iron(II) nitrate
  d iron(III) nitrate(V) or iron(III) nitrate
  e iron(II) sulfate(VI) or iron(II) sulfate
  f copper(I) oxide
  g sulfuric(IV) acid
  h manganese(VII) oxide

6 a NaClO
  b Fe_2O_3
  c KNO_2
  d PCl_3

7 a $H_2SO_4 + 6HI \rightarrow S + 3I_2 + 4H_2O$
  b $2HBr + H_2SO_4 \rightarrow Br_2 + SO_2 + 2H_2O$
  c $2V^{3+} + I_2 + 2H_2O \rightarrow 2VO^{2+} + 2I^- + 4H^+$

8 a The conduction is due to the movement of ions. The ions must be free to move to the electrodes before electrolysis can occur.
  b It conducts electricity; this is due to the delocalised electrons which can move throughout the layers of graphite. It has a high melting point so does not melt under the high temperatures in the electrolytic cell; this is due to its giant molecular structure of strong covalent bonds.

9 a Cations are positively charged. The cathode is negatively charged. Opposite charges attract.
  b i $Pb^{2+} + 2e^- \rightarrow Pb$
    Lead ions are reduced because electrons are gained. Reduction always occurs at the cathode.
  ii −1 to 0 = +1

10 a To push them further into the electrolyte when the ends have been oxidised by the oxygen. To allow them to be replaced regularly.

> **Examiner's tip**
> For part **b** think of costs. The factory must be near to its raw materials and near to its markets. If you have studied Business Studies you may be able to bring knowledge from that subject to help with this answer.

b Near to a large source of (electrical) energy, e.g. hydroelectric or conventional power station.
Near to a source of the bauxite ore, or near to a port for importing it.
Near to a workforce (preferably with the necessary skills).
Near to a market for the aluminium (e.g. a factory making aircraft or electric cables), or near to a port for exporting it.
Away from environmentally important areas.
Near to good road and rail links.
It is unlikely that an aluminium factory can be built in a site that satisfies all six of these requirements. The actual site will probably have to be a compromise.

c Two reason from: saves energy / electricity; saves transport costs; saves mining costs; waste aluminium not going into landfill.

11 a Reduction – the hydrogen ions gain electrons from the cathode.

b $4OH^- \rightarrow O_2 + 2H_2O + 4e^-$

c i –1

ii +1

12 a i They might be deposited on the cathode and reduce the purity of the copper.

ii Use fresh copper(II) sulfate electrolyte.

b The ions removed at the cathode are replaced by those being formed at the anode from copper atoms: $Cu \rightarrow Cu^{2+} + 2e^-$. The rate of replacement is equal to the rate of removal at the cathode.

Chapter 8

1 a According to the equation, HI decomposes to form equal number of moles of hydrogen and iodine.

b The gas in the vessel starts off colourless and then becomes more and more purple (as more iodine vapour is formed from the decomposition of hydrogen iodide). Eventually the depth of colour does not change (when equilibrium has been reached).

c For every mole of I_2 formed 2 moles of hydrogen iodine are decomposed. To form 0.68 mol of I_2, $2 \times 0.68 = 1.36$ mol of HI must decompose. We started with 10 moles of HI so number of moles of HI present = $10 - 1.36 = 8.64$ mol.

2 a i There is no loss of matter.

ii rate of movement of Na^+ and Cl^- ions from solution to solid = rate of movement from solid to solution

b Initially more bromine molecules evaporate than return to the liquid. So the concentration of the bromine in the vapour increases. So the colour deepens. At equilibrium the concentration of bromine in the vapour is constant. The depth of colour remains the same. This is because the rate of movement of bromine molecules from gas to liquid = rate of movement from liquid to gas.

3 a i moves to left / more ethanoic acid and ethanol formed; reaction moves in direction to oppose the effect of added ethyl ethanoate; so ethyl ethanoate decreases in concentration

ii moves to left / more ethanoic acid and ethanol formed; reaction moves in direction to oppose the removal of ethanol; so more ethanol (and ethanoic acid) formed from ethyl ethanoate and water

b i moves to right / more Ce^{3+} and Fe^{3+} formed; reaction moves in direction to oppose the effect of added Fe^{2+}; so C^{4+} and Fe^{2+} decrease in concentration

ii no effect – the water dilutes all the ions equally, so there is no change in the ratio of reactants to products

4 a i equilibrium shifted to the left as fewer gas molecules on left

ii equilibrium shifted to left as no gas molecules on left but CO_2 on right

b equilibrium shifted to the right as greater number of gas molecules on the right

5 a equilibrium shifts to the right as endothermic reaction favours the products

b endothermic as the forward reaction is favoured by an increase in temperature

6 a $K_c = \dfrac{[CH_3OH]}{[CO][H_2]^2}$; units are $dm^6 mol^{-2}$

b $K_c = \dfrac{[H_2O]^2[Cl_2]^2}{[HCl]^4[O_2]}$; units are $dm^3 mol^{-1}$

7

	$H_2(g)$	+	$CO_2(g)$	$\rightleftharpoons$	$H_2O(g)$	+	$CO(g)$
initial concentrations	10.00		10.00		0		0
equilibrium concentrations	$10.00 - 9.47 = 0.53$		$10.00 - 9.47 = 0.53$		9.47		9.47

$$K_c = \frac{(9.47)^2}{(0.53)^2} = 319$$

8 a Reaction is exothermic – so increase in temperature shifts the equilibrium in the direction of the reactants – so K_c decreases.
  b Position of equilibrium shifts to the right / favours product; oxygen combines with NO to form more NO_2 until K_c returns to original value.

9 a partial pressure of NO
  $= (10.00 \times 10^4) - (4.85 \times 10^4 + 4.85 \times 10^4)$
  $= 0.30 \times 10^4 \, Pa / 3 \times 10^3 \, Pa$

10 a Pa
  b Pa^{-2}
  c no units

11 a total pressure at start = total pressure at equilibrium
  $(7.27 \times 10^6) + (4.22 \times 10^6) = 3.41 \times 10^6 + 7.72 \times 10^6 + p_{I_2}$
  partial pressure of iodine $= 0.36 \times 10^6$

  b $K_p = \dfrac{(7.72 \times 10^6)^2}{(3.41 \times 10^6) \times (0.36 \times 10^6)} = 48.5$

12 a Reaction is exothermic; so the back reaction is favoured with increase in temperature; position of equilibrium moved away from ammonia synthesis by increase in temperature.
  b With increase in pressure, reaction goes in direction of fewer moles of gas; which is the forward reaction; so more ammonia formed.
  c Removal of ammonia shifts equilibrium in direction of forward reaction; this is in favour of increased ammonia production.
  d The ammonia is stored at very low temperatures; there is no catalyst present with the stored ammonia; any decomposition reaction is far too slow to matter.

13 a $KOH(s) + aq \rightarrow K^+(aq) + OH^-(aq)$
  b $HNO_3(l) + aq \rightarrow NO_3^-(aq) + H^+(aq)$
  c i $H^+ + OH^- \rightarrow H_2O$
    ii $H^+ + OH^- \rightarrow H_2O$

14 a NH_4^+ is the acid; H_2O is the base
  b $HClO_2$ is the acid; HCOOH is the base

15 a i $HCOOH_2^+$ is the acid; ClO_2^- is the base
    ii H_3O^+ is the acid; HS^- is the base
  b CH_3NH_2 is the base on the left-hand side, so $CH_3NH_3^+$ is the conjugate acid

16 a A strong acid is (almost) completely ionised in water; weak acid is only slightly ionised in water.
  b $HClO(l) + H_2O(l) \rightleftharpoons ClO^-(aq) + H_3O^+(aq)$
    $HNO_3(l) + H_2O(l) \rightarrow NO_3^-(aq) + H_3O^+(aq)$
  c Chloric(I) acid has a higher pH than nitric acid

    i chloric(I) acid pH 3–5
    ii nitric acid pH 1 (allow pH 2)
  d i $N_2H_4 + H_2O \rightleftharpoons N_2H_5^+ + OH^-$
    ii N_2H_4 relatively high concentration; $N_2H_5^+$ and OH^- relatively low concentrations

17 a $1.0 \, mol \, dm^{-3}$ ethanoic acid
  b $1.0 \, mol \, dm^{-3}$ sodium hydroxide
  c ions in solution conduct electricity / are charge carriers; ethanoic acid has fewer ions in solution / lower concentration of ions in solution than hydrochloric acid
  d hydrogen ions react with magnesium; ethanoic acid has fewer ions in solution / lower concentration of ions in solution than hydrochloric acid, therefore lower rate of reaction.

Chapter 9

1 a

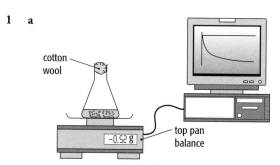

cotton wool
top pan balance

  b i The minimum energy required for a reaction to occur when reactant particles collide.
    ii A substance that speeds up a reaction by providing an alternative route with a lower activation energy. A catalyst also remains chemically unchanged at the end of the reaction.
  c By increasing the proportion of particles with energy greater than the activation energy.
  d Increasing the surface area will expose more particles to attack by reactant particles, resulting in more frequent collisions, thereby increasing the rate of reaction.

2 a $10 \, cm^3$ of $1.0 \, mol \, dm^{-3}$
  b The more concentrated the acid, the greater the number of hydrogen ions dissolved in given volume of solution, resulting in an increased frequency in collisions between the hydrogen ions and the calcium carbonate. The volume of acid will not affect the initial rate of the reaction.

3 a Need a graph showing the distribution of energies of the particles in a sample at a given temperature.
  b At the higher temperature the particles are moving around more quickly. This increases the rate of the reaction for two reasons: it increases the frequency of collisions; the proportion of successful/effective collisions increases as the proportion of particles exceeding the activation energy increases. The second factor is more important.

4 a i iron (with traces of other metal oxides)

 ii vanadium(V) oxide

 b Enzymes usually catalyse specific reactions; this can reduce the level of unwanted reactions that produce unwanted products. Enzymes work best under conditions that are close to room temperature and pressure. This reduces energy costs. Generating high temperatures and pressures for traditional chemical processes results in pollution, so this is also reduced.

Chapter 10

1 a bromine

 b If they are put in atomic mass order tellurium (Te) and iodine (I) do not line up with similar elements in the same groups. Mendeleev reversed their order.

 c The s-block elements all have electronic configurations with the outermost electrons in an 's' sub-shell (s^1 in Group I or s^2 in Group II). The Group VII elements have electronic configurations with the outermost electrons in a 'p' sub-shell (they are all p^5).

2 a A lithium atom is larger than a fluorine atom. A fluorine atom has six more electrons than a lithium atom and these occupy the same principal quantum shell as lithium's single outer electron. This means that the shielding effect is approximately the same in both atoms but the nuclear charge of a fluorine atom (9+) is greater than that of lithium (3+) which pulls fluorine's outermost electrons closer to the nucleus than lithium's.

 b i A lithium atom is larger than a Li^+ ion. The positively charged Li^+ ion has lost its outer shell electron (effectively removing the second principal quantum shell) from the Li atom so Li^+ ions are much smaller than Li atoms.

 ii An oxygen atom is smaller than an O^{2-} ion. The O^{2-} ions have gained two extra electrons into their third principal quantum shell whilst keeping the same nuclear charge. The third shell in an oxygen atom contains six electrons which repel each other. In an O^{2-} ion the third shell contains eight electrons, so there is more repulsion, increasing the radius. Therefore O^{2-} ions are larger than O atoms.

 iii A nitride ion, N^{3-}, is larger than a fluoride ion, F^-. An N^{3-} ion has a smaller positive nuclear charge (7+) than an F^- ion (9+). As the outermost electrons are in the same principal quantum shell in both anions, they are not held as tightly in a N^{3-} ion making it larger than an F^- ion.

3 a Sulfur has a simple molecular structure with relatively weak van der Waals' forces between its S_8 molecules whereas silicon has a giant molecular structure with a giant lattice of silicon atoms bonded throughout its structure by strong covalent bonds. Therefore it takes a lot less energy to overcome van der Waals' forces between sulfur molecules than it does to break covalent bonds between silicon atoms.

 b S_8 molecules contain more electrons than Cl_2 molecules so there are greater van der Waals' forces between S_8 molecules than there are between Cl_2 molecules.

c i Magnesium has free delocalised electrons which can carry electrical charge through its giant metallic structure. Phosphorus has a simple molecular structure, each molecule has no overall electrical charge and the electrons are unable to move from molecule to molecule.

 ii Each magnesium atom donates two electrons into the 'sea' of delocalised electrons whereas each sodium atom only donates one electron, making more electrons available to carry the charge through the metal in magnesium.

4 a In general, the first ionisation energies increase across Period 3.

 b Although aluminium has a greater nuclear charge than magnesium, the outer electron lost in its first ionisation is removed from a 3p orbital which is slightly further away from the nucleus than the 3s orbital from which magnesium loses its first electron. Therefore the first electron removed is not held as strongly in aluminium compared with magnesium.

 c Although sulfur has a greater nuclear charge than phosphorus, the first electron it loses comes from a 3p orbital that is occupied by a pair of electrons whereas phosphorus loses its first electron from a singly occupied 3p orbital. It is the mutual repulsion between the 3p electron pair in sulfur that makes it slightly easier to remove than the first electron from phosphorus.

 d A value lower than $966 \, kJ \, mol^{-1}$ but higher than $800 \, kJ \, mol^{-1}$ (actual value is $941 \, kJ \, mol^{-1}$).

5 a i $4Li(s) + O_2(g) \rightarrow 2Li_2O(s)$

 ii $2Li(s) + Cl_2(g) \rightarrow 2LiCl(s)$

 b i $Ca(s) + 2H_2O(l) \rightarrow Ca(OH)_2(aq) + H_2(g)$

 ii Calcium hydroxide is more soluble in water than magnesium hydroxide, therefore more hydroxide ions per unit volume are in the solution formed from calcium.

6 a i Covalent bonding and giant molecular structure (or giant covalent structure).

 ii $GeO_2(s) + 2NaOH(aq) \rightarrow Na_2GeO_3(aq) + H_2O(l)$

 iii no reaction / remains unchanged / does not dissolve

 b i $K_2O(s) + H_2O(l) \rightarrow 2KOH(aq)$

 ii $K_2O(s) + 2HNO_3(aq) \rightarrow 2KNO_3(aq) + H_2O(l)$

 iii ionic bonding and giant ionic structure

7 a i Group V

 ii hydrolysis

 iii hydrogen chloride gas

 b Group I

Chapter 11

1 a i The melting points decrease down the group.

 ii Mg

 b A new shell of electrons is occupied with each new period.

 c Smaller, as the outer shell has been removed.

d i about 700 °C (below 714 °C)
  ii about $4.5\,\text{g cm}^{-3}$ (above $3.5\,\text{g cm}^{-3}$)
  iii 2.18–2.19 nm

2 a i $2Sr(s) + O_2(g) \rightarrow 2SrO(s)$
  ii $SrO(s) + H_2O(l) \rightarrow Sr(OH)_2(aq)$
b i $Ba(s) + 2H_2O(l) \rightarrow Ba(OH)_2(aq) + H_2(g)$
  ii pH 11–14
c i Ra^{2+}
  ii RaO; $Ra(OH)_2$
  iii 450–$480\,\text{kJ mol}^{-1}$
  iv more reactive than Ba

3 a i calcium carbonate
  ii magnesium nitrate
b i $SrCO_3(s) \xrightarrow{\text{heat}} SrO(s) + CO_2(g)$
  ii $2Ba(NO_3)_2(s) \xrightarrow{\text{heat}} 2BaO(s) + 4NO_2(g) + O_2(g)$

4 a roasted / heated to a high temperature in a kiln
b concrete and mortar
c Calcium carbonate decomposes on heating whereas magnesium oxide has a very high melting point and does not decompose on heating.
d $Ca(OH)_2(s) + 2HNO_3(aq) \rightarrow Ca(NO_3)_2 + H_2O(l)$

5 a The volatility of the halogens decreases down Group VII.
b Fluorine is a gas; chlorine is a gas; bromine is a liquid; iodine is a solid.
c The atomic radii increase down the group as one more shell of electrons is occupied as each new period is started.
d i solid
  ii black / dark grey
  iii about 0.15 nm

6 a $Cl_2(aq) + 2KI(aq) \rightarrow 2KCl(aq) + I_2(aq)$
b $Cl_2(aq) + 2I^-(aq) \rightarrow 2Cl^-(aq) + I_2(aq)$
c purple

7 a i $H_2(g) + At_2(g) \rightleftharpoons 2HAt(g)$
  ii slow reaction
  iii HAt decomposes easily on heating
b Oxidation is loss of electrons. Chlorine atoms have a smaller atomic radius than bromine atoms. Therefore, an incoming electron will experience greater attraction from the nuclear charge of a chlorine atom, which is also less shielded by complete inner shells of electrons.

8 a Dissolve the compound in dilute nitric acid and add silver nitrate solution. A cream precipitate should form which is insoluble in dilute ammonia solution but will dissolve in concentrated ammonia solution.
b i purple vapour given off, yellow solid produced
  ii $KI(s) + H_2SO_4(l) \rightarrow KHSO_4(s) + HI(g)$
followed by oxidation of HI(g):

$2HI(g) + H_2SO_4(l) \rightarrow I_2(g) + SO_2(g) + 2H_2O(l)$
and:
$6HI(g) + H_2SO_4(l) \rightarrow 3I_2(g) + S(s) + 4H_2O(l)$
and:
$8HI(g) + H_2SO_4(l) \rightarrow 4I_2(g) + H_2S(g) + 4H_2O(l)$

9 a disproportionation
b $3Cl_2(aq) + 6OH^-(aq) \rightarrow 5Cl^-(aq) + ClO_3^-(aq) + 3H_2O(l)$
c $2\tfrac{1}{2}Cl_2 + 5e^- \rightarrow 5Cl^-$
d $\tfrac{1}{2}Cl_2 + 6OH^- \rightarrow ClO_3^- + 3H_2O + 5e^-$
e The chlorine gets reduced to chloride ions at the same times as it is also oxidised to chlorate(V) ions.
f sodium chlorate(V)

Chapter 12

1 a Nitrogen, N_2, is such an unreactive gas because of the high bond energy of its triple bond.
b $NH_3(aq) + HNO_3(aq) \rightarrow NH_4NO_3(aq)$
c $(NH_4)_2SO_4(s) + 2NaOH(s)$
$\rightarrow Na_2SO_4(s) + 2H_2O(l) + 2NH_3(g)$

2 a The Haber process is operated at 450 °C. This is called a 'compromise' because a lower temperature causes a higher yield of ammonia but decreases the rate of reaction, while a higher temperature causes a lower yield but increases the rate of reaction.
b $2NH_3(aq) + H_2SO_4(aq) \rightarrow (NH_4)_2SO_4(aq)$
c 35%

3 a Nitrogen is essential for plant growth. Crops remove nitrogen from the soil when they are harvested. Ammonia is used to make fertilisers that replace the nitrogen.
b eutrophication; blue baby syndrome
c $SO_2(g) + NO_2(g) \rightarrow SO_3(g) + NO(g)$
Then NO_2 is regenerated as NO reacts with oxygen in the air:
$NO(g) + \tfrac{1}{2}O_2(g) \rightarrow NO_2(g)$
NO_2 can then go on to oxidise more sulfur dioxide, and so on, acting as a catalyst for the oxidation of SO_2 to SO_3.
d $2CO(g) + 2NO(g) \rightarrow 2CO_2(g) + N_2(g)$
   +2   +2   +4   0
The oxidation number of oxygen is –2 throughout.
Carbon is oxidised as it changes from carbon monoxide (ox. no. = +2) to carbon dioxide (in which its ox. no. has increased to +4). Nitrogen in NO (ox. no. = +2) is reduced to nitrogen gas (in which its ox. no has been reduced to 0).

4 a $SO_3(g) + H_2O(l) \rightarrow H_2SO_4(l)$
b Kills or damages plants (especially trees); kills aquatic animals in rivers, streams and lakes; chemically attacks limestone in buildings/statues and metal structures.

5 a Although the formation of SO_3 is favoured by a low temperature the reaction is carried out at 450 °C in order to increase the rate of reaction.

b High pressure is expensive. For economic reasons it is not worth compressing the gases to high pressures when an excellent yield can be obtained at atmospheric pressure.

c vanadium(V) oxide, V_2O_5

d It has no effect on the equilibrium yield of SO_3.

Chapter 13

1 $C_2H_4O_2$

2 a

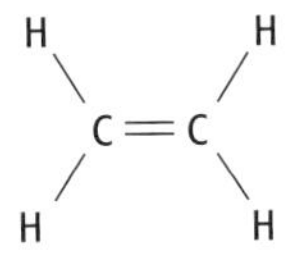

$$\begin{array}{cc} H & H \\ \backslash & / \\ C = C \\ / & \backslash \\ H & H \end{array}$$

b

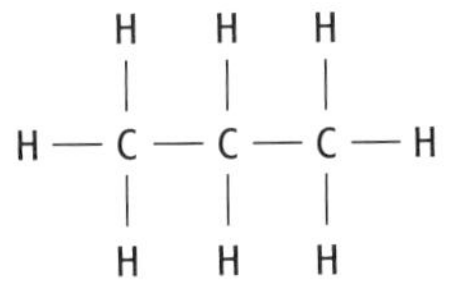

$$H - \overset{\displaystyle H}{\underset{\displaystyle H}{C}} - \overset{\displaystyle H}{\underset{\displaystyle H}{C}} - \overset{\displaystyle H}{\underset{\displaystyle H}{C}} - H$$

3 a (zig-zag skeletal structure)

b octane = $CH_3CH_2CH_2CH_2CH_2CH_2CH_2CH_3$

2,2,4-trimethylpentane = $CH_3C(CH_3)_2CH_2CH(CH_3)CH_3$

cyclohexane =

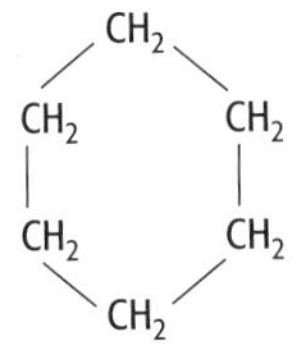

$$\begin{array}{c} CH_2 \\ CH_2 \quad CH_2 \\ CH_2 \quad CH_2 \\ CH_2 \end{array}$$

4 a i

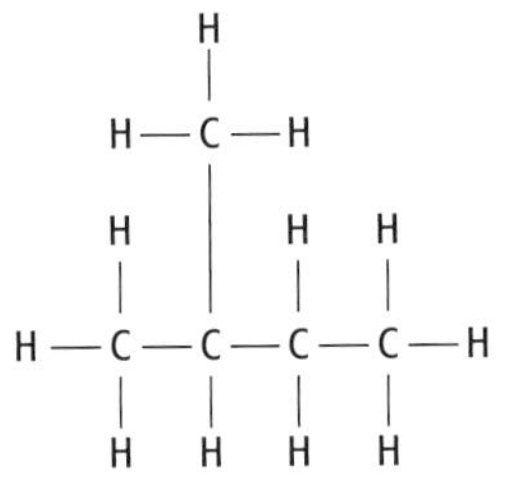

(branched structure: central carbon chain of 4 carbons with a $-CH_3$ branch)

ii

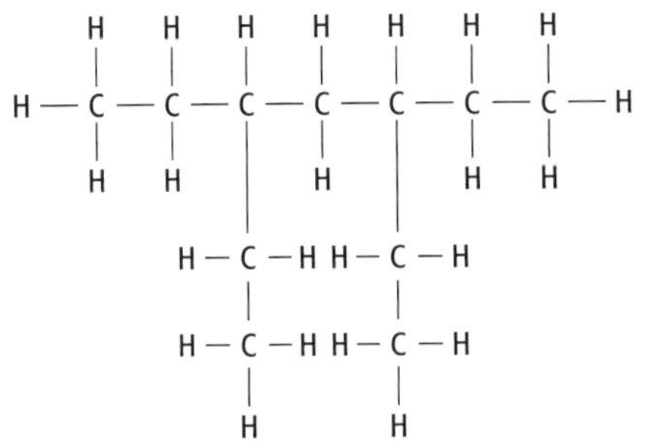

(7-carbon chain with two ethyl-type branches)

iii

(8-carbon chain with three $-CH_3$ branches)

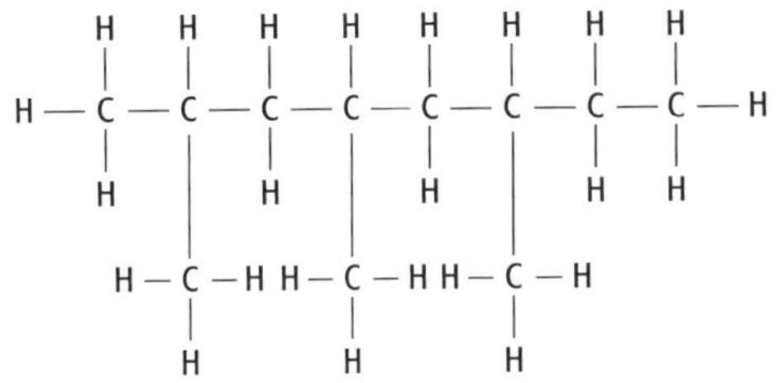

b 3-ethyl-3-methylhexane

5 a

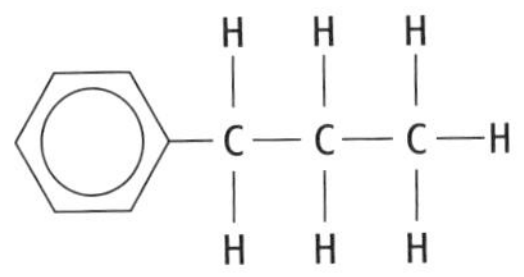

(benzene ring attached to a propyl chain)

b

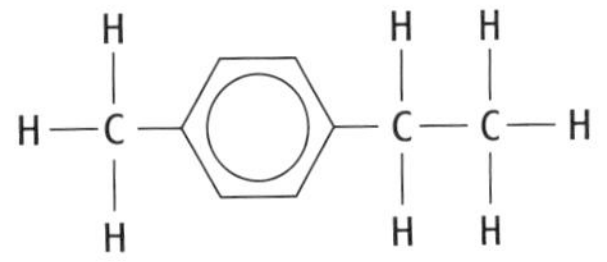

(methyl group and ethyl group on para positions of benzene ring)

c

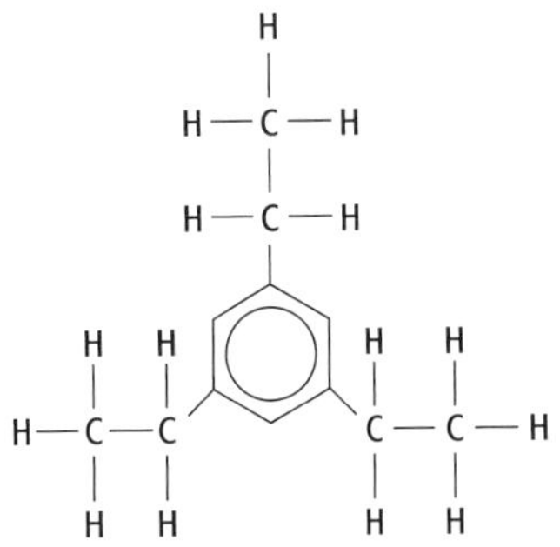

(1,3,5-trisubstituted benzene ring)

6

(3D structure with wedge/dash bonds)

(alkene with a wedge/dash CH_3 group)

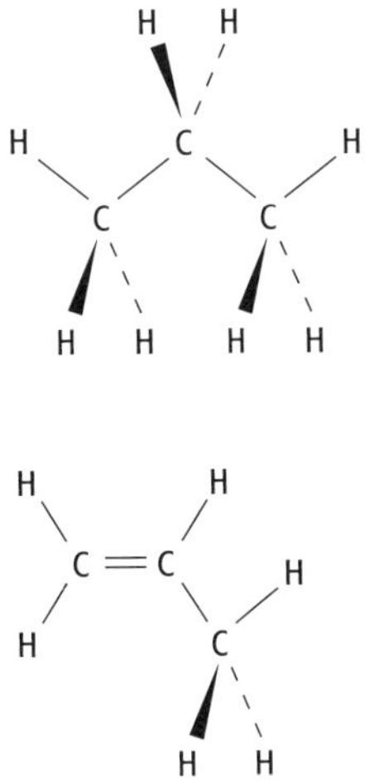

7 a

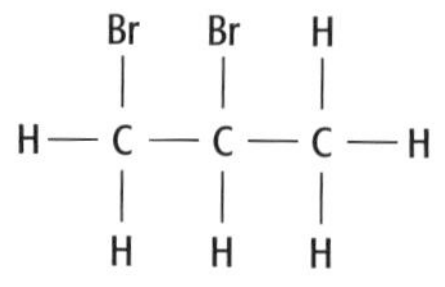

1,2-dibromopropane

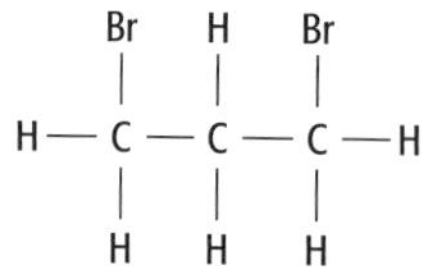

1,3-dibromopropane

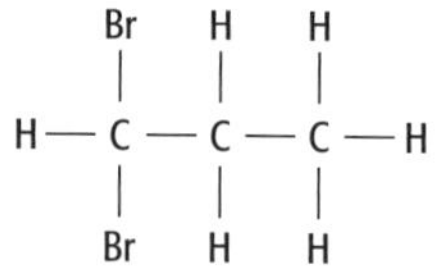

1,1-dibromopropane

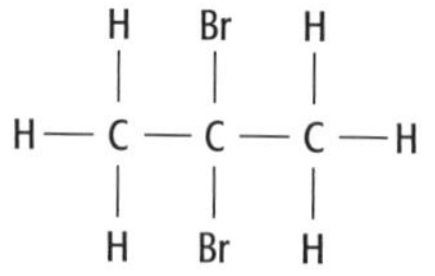

2,2-dibromopropane

b

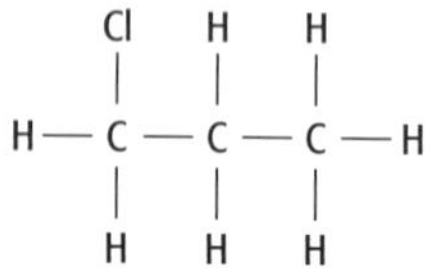

1-chloropropane

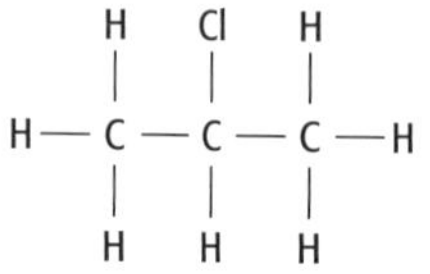

2-chloropropane

8 a i

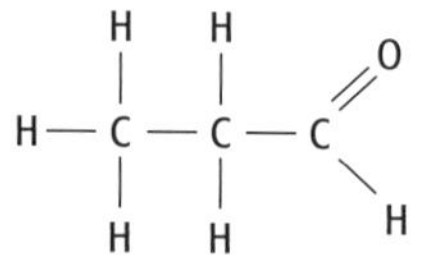

propanal

ii

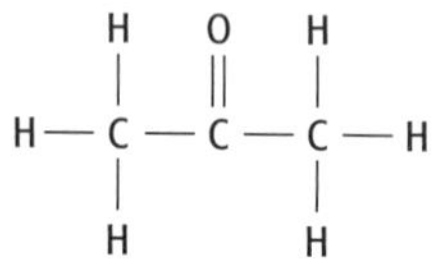

propanone

b

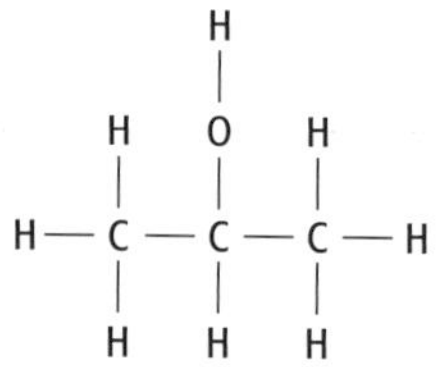

propan-2-ol

9

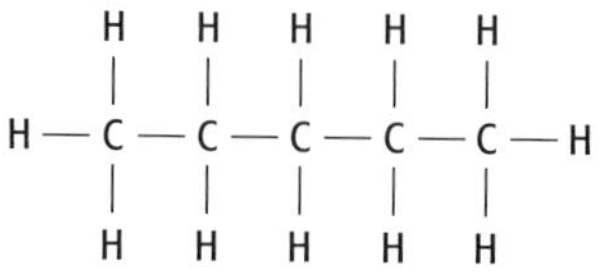

pentane

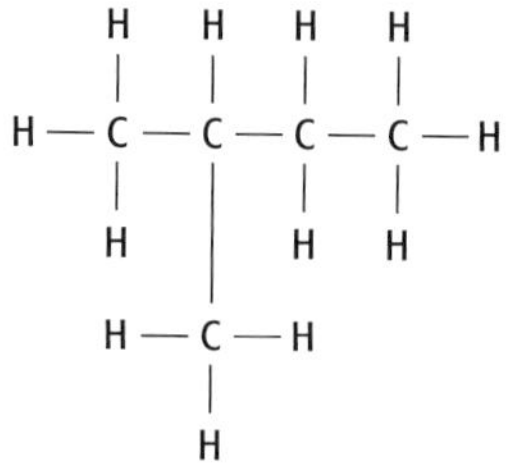

methylbutane

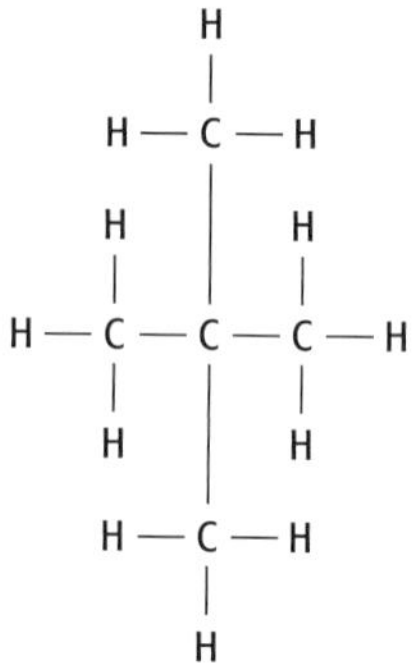

dimethylpropane

10

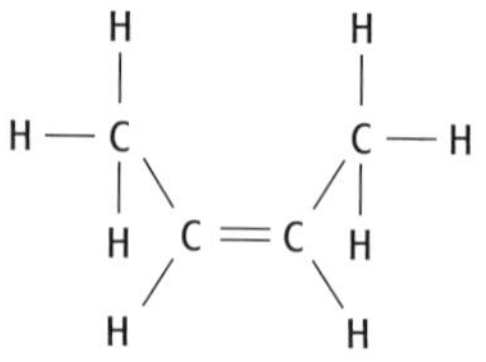

cis-but-2-ene

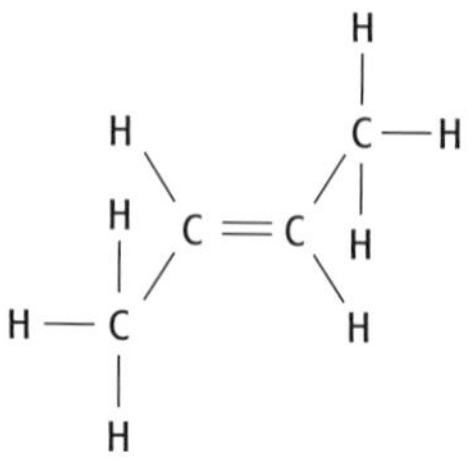

trans-but-2-ene

11

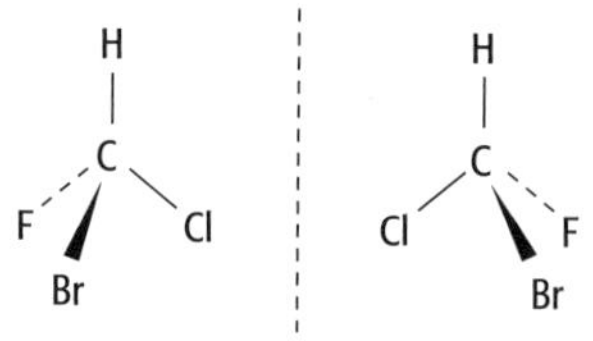

12 $Cl_2 \rightarrow Cl\bullet + Cl\bullet$
or $Cl_2 \rightarrow 2Cl\bullet$

13 a

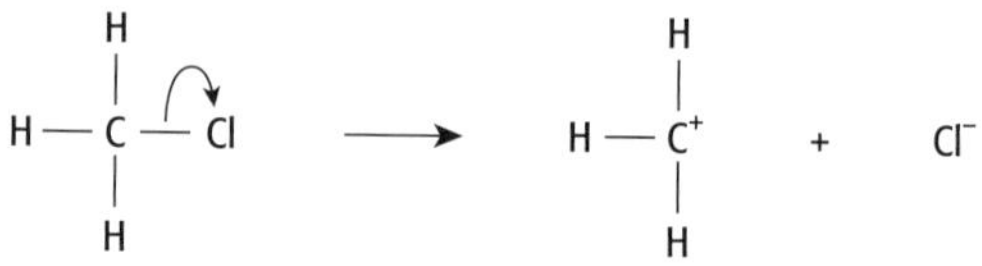

b OH⁻

c OH⁻ has lone pairs of electrons on its oxygen atom whereas H_2 and H⁺ have no available lone pairs of electrons.

d H⁺

e H⁺ can accept a pair of electrons whereas H_2 and OH⁻ cannot.

14 a hydrolysis
    b reduction
    c elimination
    d addition
    e substitution (free-radical)

Chapter 14

1 a $C_{20}H_{42}$
   b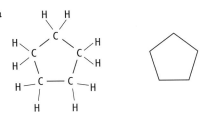

2 a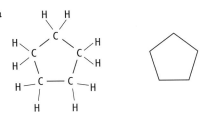
   b C_nH_{2n}
   c Two from: cyclopentane is a cyclic molecule whereas
      pentane is a straight-chain molecule; pentane molecules
      have two more hydrogen atoms than those of cyclopentane;
      pentane molecules have two CH_3 groups while cyclopentane
      molecules have only CH_2 groups.
   d decane

3 a No change
   b The non-polar alkane would not react with the charged ions
      in sodium hydroxide solution (nor with the polar water
      molecules).

4 a $C_7H_{16} + 11O_2 \rightarrow 7CO_2 + 8H_2O$
   b $C_9H_{20} + 9\frac{1}{2}O_2 \rightarrow 9CO + 10H_2O$
      or
      $2C_9H_{20} + 19O_2 \rightarrow 18CO + 20H_2O$
   c $CH_4 + 1\frac{1}{2}O_2 \rightarrow CO + 2H_2O$
      or
      $2CH_4 + 3O_2 \rightarrow 2CO + 4H_2O$

5 a carbon monoxide and unburnt hydrocarbons
   b nitrogen oxides
   c carbon dioxide; enhanced greenhouse effect / global warming

6 a sunlight / ultraviolet light
   b (free-radical) substitution
   c $C_2H_6 + Br_2 \rightarrow C_2H_5Br + HBr$
   d A mixture of bromo-substituted compounds are formed, not
      pure bromoethane, so it would need to be separated from the
      mixture.
   e i   initiation, propagation and termination
      ii $Br_2 \rightarrow 2Br\bullet$
      iii homolytic bond breaking

7 a ethene
   b $C_{18}H_{36}$
   c decane $\rightarrow$ 2-methylpentane + but-1-ene
   d $C_9H_{20} \rightarrow C_7H_{16} + C_2H_4$

8 a nickel catalyst (finely divided), $140\,°C$
   b 1,2-dichloropropane
   c Steam and ethene, in the presence of concentrated
      phosphoric acid catalyst, are reacted at a temperature of
      $330\,°C$ and a pressure of $6\,MPa$.
   d 2-chloropropane and 1-chloropropane

9 a A species that accepts a pair of electrons.
   b When a chlorine molecule approaches an ethene molecule,
      the area of high electron density around the C=C bond
      tends to repel the bonding pair of electrons in the Cl—Cl
      bond away from the nearer Cl atom. This makes the nearer
      Cl atom slightly positive and the further Cl atom slightly
      negative. The chlorine atom with the partial positive charge is
      deficient in electrons and is now ready to accept an electron
      pair from the C=C bond.
   c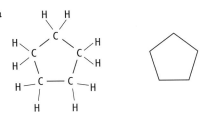

10 a poly(tetrafluoroethene)
    b addition polymerisation
    c $nC_2F_4 \rightarrow -[C_2F_4]_n-$, where n = a very large number
    d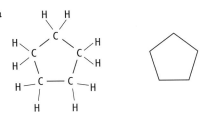

11 a The poly(alkene)s could be burned in power stations to
       generate electricity instead of using coal-, oil- or gas-fired
       power stations.
    b Carbon dioxide would still be produced by burning
       poly(alkene)s, although not as much as is produced by a coal-
       fired power station.
    c carbon monoxide

12 a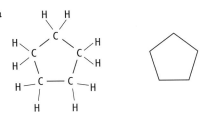

       propane-1,2-diol

    b

       butane-2,3-diol

13 a i It breaks the C=C bonds and oxidises the product molecules to give a mixture of oxidation products (carboxylic acids, ketones and carbon dioxide).

ii Chemists can identify the oxidation products and deduce the position of the C=C bond in an alkene.

b But-1-ene (as there must be two hydrogen atoms on one of the C=C carbon atoms for CO_2 to be produced, corresponding to CH_2=CHCH$_2$CH$_3$).

c i

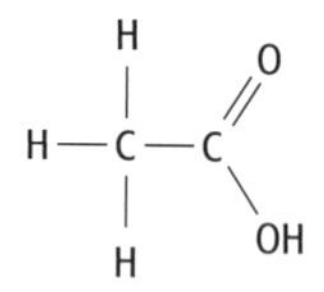

ethanoic acid 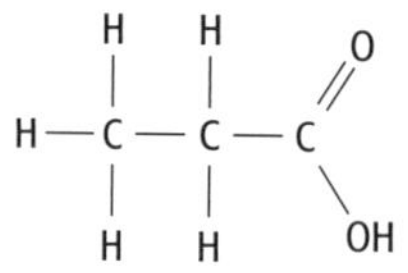   propanoic acid

ii $C_5H_{10} + 4[O] \rightarrow CH_3COOH + CH_3CH_2COOH$

d i

propanone 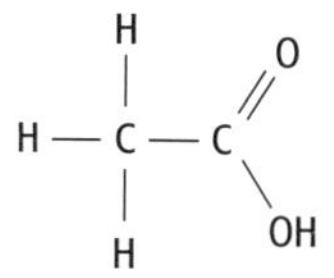   ethanoic acid

ii $(CH_3)_2C=CHCH_3 + 3[O]$
$\rightarrow (CH_3)_2C=O + CH_3COOH$

Chapter 15

1 a OH⁻ ions are negatively charged so are attracted more strongly than neutral water molecules to the partially positively charged carbon atoms in halogenoalkanes.

b The hydrolysis of halogenoalkanes produces halide ions; the rate of their formation can be monitored by using silver nitrate solution. The silver halide precipitates make the reaction mixture cloudy. The ionic equations for the formation of the precipitates are:

$Ag^+(aq) + Cl^-(aq) \rightarrow AgCl(s)$
$Ag^+(aq) + Br^-(aq) \rightarrow AgBr(s)$
$Ag^+(aq) + I^-(aq) \rightarrow AgI(s)$

2 Both ammonia and amines contain a nitrogen atom with a lone pair of electrons that is available to donate.

3

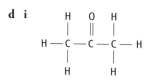

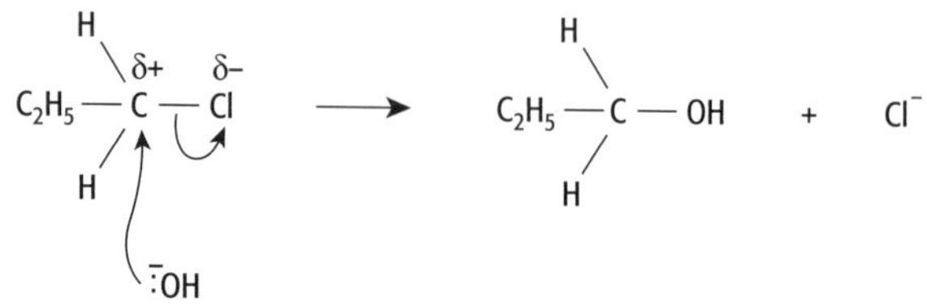

4 a

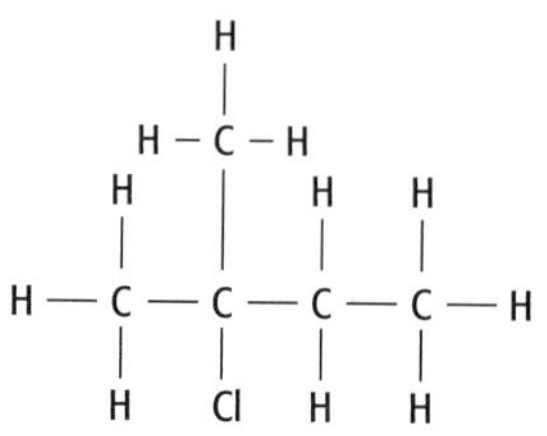

b

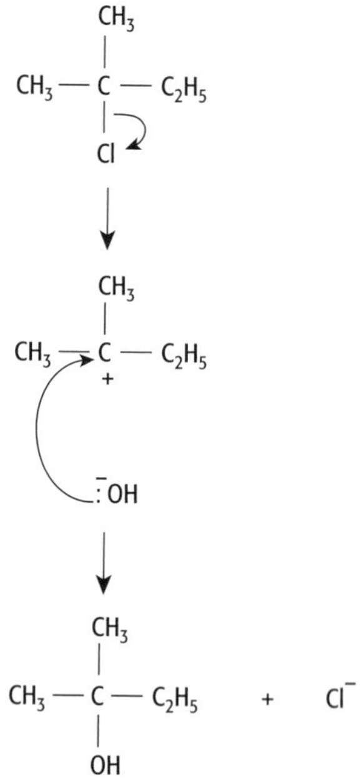

5 $CH_3CH_2Br + NaOH(ethanol)$
$\rightarrow CH_2$=$CH_2 + H_2O + NaBr$

6 The ultraviolet light from the Sun breaks the C—Cl bonds in the CFC molecules in the upper atmosphere. This releases highly reactive chlorine free radicals.

Chapter 16

1 a i The strongly electronegative oxygen atom in the —OH group has two lone pairs and carries a partial negative charge, and the less electronegative hydrogen atom carries a partial positive charge. Therefore the oxygen atom in ethanol molecules will attract hydrogen atoms in neighbouring molecules, forming hydrogen bonds.

ii When mixed with water, the partially positive hydrogen atoms in H_2O are strongly attracted to the partially negative oxygen atom in ethanol molecules, forming hydrogen bonds.

b Hexan-1-ol has a longer non-polar hydrocarbon chain than ethanol, which disrupts hydrogen bonding between water and the alcohol.

2 a i $C_3H_7OH + 4\frac{1}{2}O_2 \rightarrow 3CO_2 + 4H_2O$
  ii $C_4H_9OH + 6O_2 \rightarrow 4CO_2 + 5H_2O$
  b ethanol and carbon dioxide

3 a $\quad\quad\quad I + HBr \rightarrow CH_3CH_2Br + H_2O$
  b Et_____lium bromide and concentrated sulfuric acid are heated _____der reflux.
  c nucleophilic substitution

4 a Bubbles of gas given off from the lithium, which gets smaller and smaller until it disappears.
  b lithium propoxide and hydrogen
  c the fizzing would be more vigorous

5 a i butyl ethanoate
    ii ethyl hexanoate
    iii pentyl methanoate
  b i $CH_3COOCH_2CH_2CH_2CH_3$
    ii $CH_3CH_2CH_2CH_2CH_2COOCH_2CH_3$
    iii $HCOOCH_2CH_2CH_2CH_2CH_3$

6 a $C_2H_5OH \xrightarrow{\text{conc. } H_2SO_4} CH_2{=}CH_2 + H_2O$
  b propene

7 a Propan-1-ol should be heated gently with acidified dichromate(VI), the propanal should be distilled out immediately.
  b $CH_3CH_2CH_2OH + [O] \rightarrow CH_3CH_2CHO + H_2O$
  c Propan-1-ol should be refluxed with acidified dichromate(VI), the propanoic acid should be distilled out after at least 15 minutes refluxing.
  d $CH_3CH_2CH_2OH + 2[O]$
    $\rightarrow CH_3CH_2COOH + H_2O$
    alternatively:
    $CH_3CH_2CH_2OH + [O] \rightarrow CH_3CH_2CHO + H_2O$
    followed by:
    $CH_3CH_2CHO + [O] \rightarrow CH_3CH_2COOH$

Chapter 17

1 a i hexanal
    ii octan-4-one

  b i

   ii

   iii

  c i

   ii

2 a i $CH_3CH_2OH + [O] \rightarrow CH_3CHO + H_2O$
    ii Add a solution of potassium dichromate(VI), acidified with dilute sulfuric acid, one drop at a time to warm ethanol in a flask. Distil off and collect the ethanal as it forms.
  b i $CH_3CH(OH)CH_2CH_3 + [O]$
    $\rightarrow CH_3COCH_2CH_3 + H_2O$
    ii The reaction mixture turns from orange to green.

3 a $CH_3CH_2CHO + 2[H] \rightarrow CH_3CH_2CH_2OH$
  b pentan-3-ol

4 a i 2-hydroxypropanenitrile
    ii 2-hydroxymethylpropanenitrile

  b

5 a Deep orange precipitate is formed.
  b i The unknown compound could be butanal or propanone.
    ii butanal
    iii Butanal can be oxidised by the silver ions in warm Tollens' reagent, to form butanoate ions. In the process the silver ions are reduced to silver atoms which form a silver mirror effect on the inside surface of the reaction vessel. However, butanone cannot be oxidised easily so no change is observed when it is warmed with Tollens' reagent – the mixture remains colourless.
  c $Ag^+ + e^- \rightarrow Ag$
  d $Cu^{2+} + e^- \rightarrow Cu^+$

Chapter 18

1 **a** standard temperature = 298 K; standard pressure
= 1×10^5 Pa / 100 kPa

b **i** $Mg^{2+}(g) + O^{2-}(g) \rightarrow MgO(s)$
ii $K^+(g) + Br^-(g) \rightarrow KBr(s)$
iii $2Na^+(g) + S^{2-}(g) \rightarrow Na_2S(s)$

2 **a** The bond energy for chlorine is the enthalpy change
$Cl_2(g) \rightarrow 2Cl(g)$. The enthalpy change of atomisation is
$\frac{1}{2}Cl_2(g) \rightarrow Cl(g)$. The enthalpy change of atomisation is
$+244/2 = +122\,kJ\,mol^{-1}$.

b **i** $\frac{1}{2}O_2(g) \rightarrow O(g)$

ii $Ba(s) \rightarrow Ba(g)$
iii $\frac{1}{2}Br_2(l) \rightarrow Br(g)$

c $0\,kJ\,mol^{-1}$; helium exists naturally as single gaseous atoms, so
no change is involved in the process $He(g) \rightarrow He(g)$

3 **a** There must be an input of energy to overcome the repulsive
forces between the (negative) electron and the negative ion.
b $+440\,kJ\,mol^{-1}$
c **i** $I(g) + e^- \rightarrow I^-(g)$
ii $S^-(g) + e^- \rightarrow S^{2-}(g)$

4 **a** **i** $Cs(g) \rightarrow Cs^+(g) + e^-$
ii $Al^{2+}(g) \rightarrow Al^{3+}(g) + e^-$
iii $Ca(s) + \frac{1}{2}O_2(g) \rightarrow CaO(s)$

iv $Fe(s) + 1\frac{1}{2}Cl_2(g) \rightarrow FeCl_3(s)$

b $\Delta H^\ominus_{1\text{att}} = \Delta H^\ominus_f - \{\Delta H^\ominus_{at}[Na] + \Delta H^\ominus_{ion1}[Na]$
$\qquad\qquad\qquad\qquad + \Delta H^\ominus_{at}[\frac{1}{2}Cl_2(g)] + \Delta H^\ominus_{ea1}[Cl]\}$
$\Delta H^\ominus_{1\text{att}} = (-411) - \{(+107) + (+496) + (+122) + (-348)\}$
$\Delta H^\ominus_{1\text{att}} = (-411) - (+377) = -788\,kJ\,mol^{-1}$

5 **a**

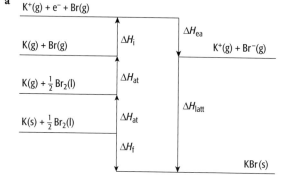

b **i** enthalpy change of atomisation of iodine
ii first electron affinity of nitrogen
iii enthalpy change of formation of strontium chloride
iv lattice energy of cadmium chloride

6 **a**

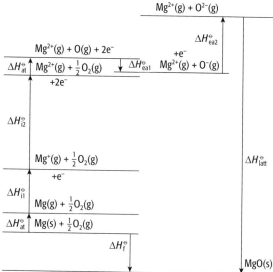

b

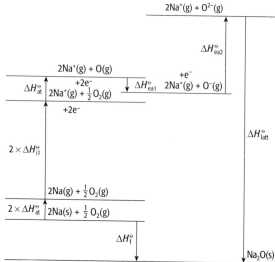

7 **a**

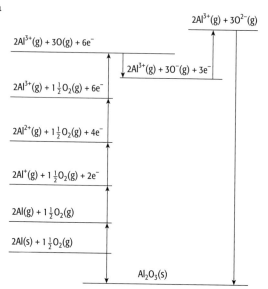

b $\Delta H^\ominus_{latt} = \Delta H^\ominus_f - \{2\Delta H^\ominus_{at}[Al] + 2\Delta H^\ominus_{ion1+2+3}[Al] + 3\Delta H^\ominus_{at}[\frac{1}{2}O_2(g)]$
$+ 3\Delta H^\ominus_{ea1+2}[O]\}$
$\Delta H^\ominus_{latt} = (-1676) - \{2\times(+326) + 2\times(+577 + 1820 + 2740)$
$+ 3\times(+249) + 3\times(-141) + 3\times(+798)\}$
$\Delta H^\ominus_{latt} = (-1676) - (+13644) = -15320\,\text{kJ}\,\text{mol}^{-1}$

8 a i BaO
ii MgI_2
iii CaO
b RbCl < LiF < MgO
Lattice energy gets more exothermic the greater the charge on the ions, so MgO > LiF and RbCl.
Lattice energy gets more exothermic the smaller the ions, so LiF > RbCl.

9 a For magnesium oxide $Q_1 \times Q_2$ is 4, for lithium fluoride $Q_1 \times Q_2$ is 1. Because ionic radii are (almost) unchanged, r^2 will be very similar. The force between the particles, which is proportional to $\frac{Q_1 \times Q_2}{r^2}$, will be four times greater for MgO than it is for LiF, accounting for the greater lattice energy.
b The ionic charges are the same so $Q_1 \times Q_2$ is 1 for both compounds. However r, the separation of the centres of the ions, is much greater for KBr than it is for LiF. Therefore $\frac{Q_1 \times Q_2}{r^2}$ is much greater for LiF than it is for KBr, so the attractive force between the particles is greater for LiF than it is for KBr, accounting for the greater lattice energy.

10 a The charge is spread out over a smaller volume so the charge density is higher.
b Li^+, because it has the smallest ionic radius and therefore has the highest charge density.
c I^-, because it has the largest ionic radius.

11 The nitrate ion is an ion with a large ionic radius so is easily polarised by a small highly charged cation. Mg^{2+} has a smaller ionic radius than Ba^{2+}. Magnesium ions are better polarisers of nitrate ions than barium ions. The greater the polarisation, the lower the thermal stability (the more likely the nitrate is to decompose).

12 a i $K_2SO_4(s) + aq \rightarrow K_2SO_4(aq)$
or $K_2SO_4(s) + aq \rightarrow 2K^+(aq) + SO_4^{2-}(aq)$
ii $ZnCl_2(s) + aq \rightarrow ZnCl_2(aq)$
or $ZnCl_2(s) + aq \rightarrow Zn^{2+}(aq) + 2Cl^-(aq)$
b Sodium chloride and sodium bromide are soluble in water (they have values of $\Delta H^\ominus_{sol}$ which are negative or slightly positive). Silver chloride and silver bromide are insoluble (they have large positive values of $\Delta H^\ominus_{sol}$). The data suggests that silver bromide is less soluble than silver chloride because its value of $\Delta H^\ominus_{sol}$ is more endothermic. The data suggests that sodium chloride is less soluble than sodium bromide because its value of $\Delta H^\ominus_{sol}$ is slightly positive, whereas the $\Delta H^\ominus_{sol}$ of silver bromide is slightly negative.

13 a Bond formation is always exothermic. Ion–dipole bonds are being formed between the gaseous ions and the water molecules.
b i $Na^+(g) + aq \rightarrow Na^+(aq)$
ii $Cl^-(g) + aq \rightarrow Cl^-(aq)$
c

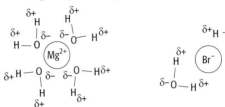

d Magnesium has a 2+ ion but potassium has only a 1+ ion. The magnesium ion also has a smaller radius than the potassium ion. So the magnesium ion has a greater charge density than a potassium ion. The greater the charge density, the greater the attractive force between the ion and the polar water molecules and the greater the value of $\Delta H^\ominus_{hyd}$.

14 a The enthalpy change of solution of KBr.
b The enthalpy change of hydration of K^+.
c The lattice energy of KBr.
d The enthalpy change of hydration of Br^-.

15 a

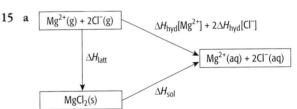

b $\Delta H^\ominus_{latt} + \Delta H^\ominus_{sol} = \Delta H^\ominus_{hyd}[Mg^{2+}] + 2\Delta H^\ominus_{hyd}[Cl^-]$
$\Delta H^\ominus_{hyd}[Mg^{2+}] = \Delta H^\ominus_{latt} + \Delta H^\ominus_{sol} - 2\Delta H^\ominus_{hyd}[Cl^-]$
$\Delta H^\ominus_{hyd}[Mg^{2+}] = (-2592) + (-55) - 2\times(-364)$
$\Delta H^\ominus_{hyd}[Mg^{2+}] = -2592 + 673$
$\Delta H^\ominus_{hyd}[Mg^{2+}] = -1919\,\text{kJ}\,\text{mol}^{-1}$

16 a

$Ba^{2+}(g) + SO_4^{2-}(g)$

$\Delta H^\ominus_{hyd}[Ba^{2+}] + \Delta H^\ominus_{hyd}[SO_4^{2-}]$

$\Delta H^\ominus_{latt}[BaSO_4]$

$BaSO_4(aq)$

$\Delta H^\ominus_{sol}[BaSO_4]$

$BaSO_4(s)$

b The lattice energy and enthalpy change of hydration of magnesium sulfate are more exothermic than those of barium sulfate, but the difference is more marked for the enthalpy change of hydration than for lattice energy. It is the enthalpy change of hydration of the cations which plays the greatest part in determining the value of $\Delta H^\ominus_{sol}$. Because magnesium has a smaller ion than barium, the enthalpy change of hydration is more exothermic than for barium.

Overall, the enthalpy change of solution is less endothermic for magnesium sulfate than for barium sulfate. This means that magnesium sulfate is more soluble because value of $\Delta H^{\ominus}_{sol}$ is less endothermic (than for barium sulfate).

Chapter 19

1 a i Cu^{2+} (in $CuCl_2$)
      ii Fe
      iii Cu^{2+} (in $CuCl_2$)
      iv Fe
   b i Br_2
      ii Cu
      iii Br_2
      iv Cu
   c i PbO_2
      ii SO_2
      iii PbO_2
      iv SO_2
   In part **c**, lead goes from an oxidation state of +4 in PbO_2 to +2 in $PbSO_4$; it gains electrons. S goes from an oxidation state of +4 in SO_2 to +6 in $PbSO_4$; it loses electrons.

2 a $2I^- + H_2O_2 + 2H^+ \rightarrow I_2 + 2H_2O$
   b $2Cl^- + MnO_2 + 4H^+ \rightarrow Cl_2 + Mn^{2+} + 2H_2O$
   c $5Fe^{2+} + MnO_4^- + 8H^+ \rightarrow 5Fe^{3+} + Mn^{2+} + 4H_2O$

3 a Zn
   b Zn^{2+}
   c Zn
   d Ag^+

4 a Ag^+ ions react with Cl^- ions in the $ZnCl_2$ and form a precipitate of silver chloride.
   b i $Cr^{3+} + e^- \rightarrow Cr^{2+}$
      ii $Br_2 + 2e^- \rightarrow Br^-$
      iii $O_2 + 2H_2O + 4e^- \rightarrow 4OH^-$
      iv $VO_2^+ + 2H^+ + e^- \rightarrow VO^{2+} + H_2O$

5 For the Fe^{2+}/Fe half-cell:
   a $Fe^{2+} + 2e^- \rightarrow Fe$
   b $-0.44V$
   c Fe^{2+}: $1.00\,mol\,dm^{-3}$
   For the Cr^{2+}/Cr half-cell
   a $Cr^{2+} + 2e^- \rightarrow Cr$
   b $-0.91V$
   c Cr^{2+}: $1.00\,mol\,dm^{-3}$
   For the Ag^+/Ag half-cell
   a $Ag^+ + e^- \rightarrow Ag$
   b $+0.80V$
   c Ag^+: $1.00\,mol\,dm^{-3}$

In all three cells the temperature must be 298 K; standard hydrogen electrodes with H^+ concentration $1.00\,mol\,dm^{-3}$, hydrogen gas pressure 1 atmosphere (101 kPa) and the electrical contact made by platinum (coated with platinum black).

6 a $S + 2e^- \rightleftharpoons S^{2-}$
   b $+0.51V$

7

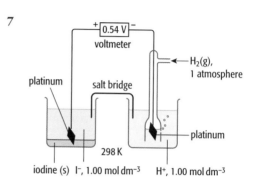

8 $+1.52V$

9 Platinum is an inert electrode. It does not take part in reactions.

10

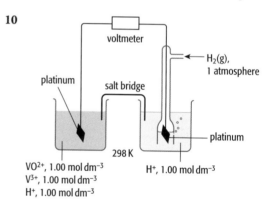

11 a

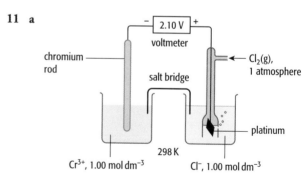

   b $1.36 - (-0.74) = +2.10V$
   c Cl_2/Cl^- half-cell

12 a

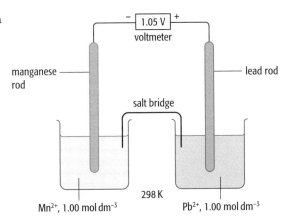

b $(-0.13) - (-1.18) = 1.05\,V$

c lead half-cell

13 a F_2/F^- is the + pole and Mn^{2+}/Mn is the – pole, so electron flow is Mn^{2+}/Mn to F_2/F^-

b I_2/I^- is the + pole and Sn^{4+}/Sn^{2+} is the – pole, so electron flow is Sn^{4+}/Sn^{2+} to I_2/I^-

c $Cr_2O_7^{2-}/2Cr^{3+}$ is the + pole and Cu^{2+}/Cu is the – pole, so electron flow is Cu^{2+}/Cu to $Cr_2O_7^{2-}/2Cr^{3+}$

d Ni^{2+}/Ni is the – pole and Fe^{3+}/Fe is the + pole, so electron flow is Ni^{2+}/Ni to Fe^{3+}/Fe.

14 a Yes
$5Cl^- + MnO_4^- + 8H^+ \rightarrow 2\frac{1}{2}Cl_2 + Mn^{2+} + 4H_2O$
$MnO_4^- + 8H^+ + 5e^- \rightleftharpoons Mn^{2+} + 4H_2O$ has a more positive $E^\ominus$ value so will proceed in the forward direction. The reaction $Cl_2 + 2e^- \rightleftharpoons 2Cl^-$ proceeds in the reverse direction.

b No
$MnO_4^- + 8H^+ + 5e^- \rightleftharpoons Mn^{2+} + 4H_2O$ has a less positive $E^\ominus$ value so cannot proceed in the forward direction while $F_2 + 2e^- \rightleftharpoons 2F^-$ proceeds in the back direction.

c Yes
$V^{2+} + H^+ \rightarrow V^{3+} + \frac{1}{2}H_2$
$2H^+ + 2e^- \rightleftharpoons H_2$ has a more positive $E^\ominus$ value so will proceed in the forward direction. The reaction $V^{3+} + e^- \rightleftharpoons V^{2+}$ proceeds in the reverse direction.

d No
$2H^+ + 2e^- \rightleftharpoons H_2$ has a less positive $E^\ominus$ value so cannot proceed in the forward direction while $Fe^{3+} + e^- \rightleftharpoons Fe^{2+}$ proceeds in the reverse direction.

15 a $E^\ominus$ value must be more negative than $-0.76\,V$ so Cr or V (on the right-hand side) will do this.

b $E^\ominus$ value must be more positive than $+1.07\,V$ so Cl_2/acidified $Cr_2O_7^{2-}/F_2$/acidified MnO_4^-/acidified O_2 will do this.

c $E^\ominus$ value must be less positive than $+0.17\,V$. Any of the species on the right-hand side with a half equation showing a negative value or less positive value than $+0.17\,V$ will do this.

d $E^\ominus$ value must be more positive than $+1.36\,V$ so F_2, or acidified MnO_4^-, for example, will do this.

16 a voltage = 1.52 – 1.36 = +0.16V, therefore yes

b voltage = 1.52 – 2.87 = –1.35V, therefore no

c voltage = 0.00 – (–0.26) = 0.26V, therefore yes

d voltage = 0.00 – 0.77 = –0.77V, therefore no

17 a The $E^\ominus$ value for $\frac{1}{2}Br_2 + e^- \rightleftharpoons Br^-$ has a more positive $E^\ominus$ value than $\frac{1}{2}I_2 + e^- \rightleftharpoons I^-$. So $\frac{1}{2}Br_2 + e^- \rightleftharpoons Br^-$ accepts electrons more readily and will proceed in the forward direction while $\frac{1}{2}I_2 + e^- \rightleftharpoons I^-$ proceeds in the reverse direction. Bromine will oxidise iodide ions to iodine.

b The $E^\ominus$ value for $\frac{1}{2}Br_2 + e^- \rightleftharpoons Br^-$ has a less positive $E^\ominus$ value than $\frac{1}{2}Cl_2 + e^- \rightleftharpoons Cl^-$. So $\frac{1}{2}Br_2 + e^- \rightleftharpoons Br^-$ accepts electrons less readily and cannot proceed in a forward direction while $\frac{1}{2}Cl_2 + e^- \rightleftharpoons Cl^-$ proceeds in the reverse direction. Bromine will not oxidise chloride ions to chlorine.

18 a Cr^{2+}

b Ag

19 a i E value more than 1.33 V

ii E value less than 1.33 V

iii E value less than 1.33 V

b i stronger oxidising agent

ii weaker oxidising agent

iii weaker oxidising agent

c high concentration of $Cr_2O_7^{2-}$, high concentration of H^+, low concentration of Cr^{3+}

d Increasing the concentration of reactants moves the equilibrium to the right in order to reduce these concentrations. So E goes up (becomes more positive) and the $Cr_2O_7^{2-}/H^+$ solution becomes a stronger oxidising agent.

20 Add a catalyst; increase the temperature; increase the concentration of dissolved reactants; increase the pressure of gaseous reactants; increase the surface area of solid reactants/solid catalyst.

21 $E^\ominus$ values relate to standard conditions, but lab and/or industry conditions are not usually standard. However, if the $E^\ominus$ values differ by more than 0.30V, predictions based on $E^\ominus$ values are usually correct.
 The rate of reaction may be very slow even though $E^\ominus$ values indicate that a reaction is feasible.

22 a $NiO_2 + 2H_2O + 2e^- \rightarrow Ni(OH)_2 + 2OH^-$ has a more positive $E^\ominus$ value so proceeds in the forward direction.

b 1.30V

c $Cd + NiO_2 + 2H_2O \rightarrow Ni(OH)_2 + Cd(OH)_2$

d $Ni(OH)_2 + Cd(OH)_2 \rightarrow Cd + NiO_2 + 2H_2O$

23 a Its half-equation has a very negative $E^\ominus$ value because it is a very reactive metal. Therefore it releases electrons very readily.

b i 0.54 – (–3.04) = 3.58V

ii The concentration of electrolytes are not $1.00\,mol\,dm^{-3}$/ not the standard concentrations.

c Small; lightweight; has a relatively high voltage; has a long shelf life; maintains a constant voltage.

24
  a $40 \times 5 \times 10^7 = 2 \times 10^9\,J$
  b $2 \times 10^9 \times 0.4 = 8 \times 10^8\,J$
  c $\dfrac{8 \times 10^8}{1 \times 10^6} = 800\,km$

25
  a $400 \times 143\,000 = 5.72 \times 10^7\,J$
  b $5.72 \times 10^7 \times 0.6 = 3.42 \times 10^7\,J$
  c $\dfrac{3.43 \times 10^7}{1 \times 10^6} = 34.3\,km$

26 The range of the fuel cell vehicle between refuelling stops is much lower than a petrol engine vehicle.

27
  a Hydrogen is below sodium in the discharge series. The H^+/H_2 system has a more positive $E^\ominus$ value than the Na^+/Na system so hydrogen ions accept electrons more readily than sodium ions.
  b $4OH^- \rightarrow O_2 + 2H_2O + 4e^-$

28
  a anode: iodine; cathode: aluminium
  b anode: chlorine; cathode: hydrogen
  c anode: bromine; cathode: hydrogen
  d anode: oxygen; cathode: zinc

29
  a **i** $2H^+ + 2e^- \rightarrow H_2$
  　　ii $2Cl^- \rightarrow Cl_2 + 2e^-$
  b A mixture of oxygen and chlorine may be formed. The proportion of oxygen will increase as the solution becomes more dilute. In a concentrated solution of HCl, the chloride ions fall below OH^- ions in the discharge series because they are present in such high concentrations. Oxygen, rather than chlorine, is formed at the anode in very dilute solutions because the relatively lower concentration of Cl^- ions allows OH^- ions to fall below Cl^- ions in the discharge series.

30 $Q = It$ (charge = current × time in seconds)
  charge $= 1.80 \times 45.0 \times 60 = 4860\,C$
  for $Ag^+ + e^- \rightarrow Ag$;
  1 mol of silver (108 g) is deposited by 96 500 C
  so 4860 C deposits $\dfrac{4860}{96\,500} \times 108 = 5.44\,g$

31 $2H^+ + 2e^- \rightarrow H_2$
  2 moles of electrons are required to produce 1 mole of hydrogen gas
  so $2 \times 96\,500\,C = 193\,000\,C$ are required to produce 1 mol of hydrogen gas
  $Q = It$
  charge $= 1.40 \times 15.0 \times 60 = 1260\,C$
  1 mol hydrogen gas occupies $24\,dm^3$ at r.t.p.
  volume of hydrogen produced $= \dfrac{1260}{193\,000} \times 24 = 0.157\,dm^3$

32 When aqueous sodium sulfate is electrolysed, oxygen is produced at the anode from OH^- ions.
  $4OH^-(aq) \rightarrow O_2(g) + 2H_2O(l) + 4e^-$
  4 moles of electrons are released per mole of O_2 formed
  $= 4F = 4 \times 96\,500 = 386\,000\,C\,mol^{-1}$
  $Q = It = 0.70 \times 55 \times 60 = 2310\,C$
  $386\,000\,C$ produces 1 mole $O_2 = 24\,dm^3\,O_2$
  so 2310 C produces $\dfrac{2310}{386\,000} \times 24.0 = 0.144\,dm^3\,O_2$ at r.t.p.

33 quantity of charge passed $Q = It = 0.15 \times 45 \times 60 = 405\,C$
  to deposit 0.45 g of silver requires 405 C
  the equation for the electrolysis shows that 1 mole of electrons is needed to produce 1 mole of silver:
  $Ag^+ + e^- \rightarrow Ag$
  so to deposit 1 mole of silver (108 g) requires $\dfrac{108}{0.45} \times 405\,C$
  $= 97\,200\,C$

  $= \dfrac{97\,200}{1.6 \times 10^{-19}} = 6.1 \times 10^{23}\,mol^{-1}$

34 $L = \dfrac{\text{charge on 1 mole of electrons } (F)}{\text{charge on one electron}}$

  $L = \dfrac{96\,485}{1.6022 \times 10^{-19}} = 6.0220 \times 10^{23}\,mol^{-1}$ (to

  5 significant figures)

Chapter 20

1
  a 3.5 (using $pH = -\log[H^+]$)
  b 2.0
  c 7.4
  d 11.3
  e 9.1

2
  a $1.26 \times 10^{-3}\,mol\,dm^{-3}$ (using $[H^+] = 10^{-pH}$)
  b $2.00 \times 10^{-4}\,mol\,dm^{-3}$
  c $6.31 \times 10^{-12}\,mol\,dm^{-3}$
  d $3.98 \times 10^{-6}\,mol\,dm^{-3}$
  e $1.26 \times 10^{-13}\,mol\,dm^{-3}$

3
  a pH = 0 (the acid is completely ionised so $[HNO_3] = [H^+]$)
  b pH = 0.32 (the acid is completely ionised)
  c The aqueous solution contains 3.00 g of hydrogen chloride per dm^3. To find the pH we need the hydrogen ion concentration in $mol\,dm^{-3}$. The relative formula mass of HCl is 36.5 (1.0 +35.5).
  concentration of hydrogen ions $= \dfrac{3.00}{36.5} = 0.0822\,mol\,dm^{-3}$
  HCl is completely ionised so $[H^+] = 0.0822\,mol\,dm^{-3}$
  $pH = -\log[H^+] = -\log_{10}(0.0822) = 1.09$

d KOH dissociates completely in solution, so $0.001\,00\,mol$ of KOH produces $0.001\,00\,mol$ of OH^- ions.
Using $K_w = [H^+][OH^-] = 1.00 \times 10^{-14}\,mol^2\,dm^{-6}$

$$[H^+] = \frac{K_w}{[OH^-]}$$

$$[H^+] = \frac{1.00 \times 10^{-14}}{0.00\,100} = 1.00 \times 10^{-11}\,mol\,dm^{-3}$$

pH = 11.0

e We first have to convert grams of NaOH to moles dm^{-3} of NaOH. M_r [NaOH] = 40.0

so moles NaOH $= \dfrac{0.200}{40} = 5.00 \times 10^{-3}\,mol\,dm^{-3}$

We have $1\,dm^3$ of solution, so the concentration of NaOH is $5.00 \times 10^{-3}\,mol\,dm^{-3}$
NaOH dissociates completely in solution, so the concentration of hydroxide ions is the same as the concentration of sodium hydroxide, which is $5.00 \times 10^{-3}\,mol\,dm^{-3}$
Using $K_w = [H^+][OH^-] = 1.00 \times 10^{-14}\,mol^2\,dm^{-6}$

$$[H^+] = \frac{K_w}{[OH^-]}$$

$$[H^+] = \frac{1.00 \times 10^{-14}}{5.00 \times 10^{-3}} = 2.00 \times 10^{-12}\,mol\,dm^{-3}$$

pH = 11.7

4 a i $K_a = \dfrac{[H^+(aq)][C_6H_5COO^-(aq)]}{[C_6H_5COOH(aq)]}$

ii $K_a = \dfrac{[H^+(aq)][CO_3^{2-}(aq)]}{[HCO_3^-(aq)]}$

iii $K_a = \dfrac{[H^+(aq)][NH_3(aq)]}{[NH_4^+(aq)]}$

b i acid $= [Fe(H_2O)_6]^{3+}$ base $= [Fe(H_2O)_5OH]^{2+}$
ii acid $= HNO_2$ base $= NO_2^-$
iii acid $= CO_2 + H_2O$ base $= HCO_3^-$
iv acid $= HSiO_3^-$ base $= SiO_3^{2-}$
(a hydrogen ion has been removed to form the base which is conjugate to the acid)

5 In each case we first find the hydrogen ion concentration, then use the general equilibrium expression, $K_a = \dfrac{[H^+][A^-]}{[HA]}$; since

$[H^+] = [A^-]$ we can write this as $K_a = \dfrac{[H^+]^2}{[HA]}$

a i $[H^+] = 5.01 \times 10^{-5}\,mol\,dm^{-3}$

$K_a = \dfrac{(5.01 \times 10^{-5})^2}{0.02} = 1.26 \times 10^{-7}\,mol\,dm^{-3}$

ii $[H^+] = 7.94 \times 10^{-4}\,mol\,dm^{-3}$

$K_a = \dfrac{(7.94 \times 10^{-4})^2}{0.05} = 1.26 \times 10^{-5}\,mol\,dm^{-3}$

iii $[H^+] = 7.94 \times 10^{-5}\,mol\,dm^{-3}$

$K_a = \dfrac{(7.94 \times 10^{-5})^2}{0.100} = 6.31 \times 10^{-8}\,mol\,dm^{-3}$

b in each case, $pK_a = -\log_{10} K_a$
i $-\log_{10} 1.26 \times 10^{-7} = 6.90$
ii $-\log_{10} 1.26 \times 10^{-5} = 4.90$
iii $-\log_{10} 6.31 \times 10^{-8} = 7.20$

6 a $K_a = \dfrac{[H^+]^2}{[\text{benzoic acid}]}$

$[H^+]^2 = K_a \times [\text{benzoic acid}]$
$= (6.3 \times 10^{-5}) \times (0.0200)$
$[H^+] = \sqrt{(6.3 \times 10^{-5}) \times (0.0200)}$
$= 1.12 \times 10^{-3}\,mol\,dm^{-3}$
pH $= -\log_{10}(1.12 \times 10^{-3}) = 2.95$

b $K_a = \dfrac{[H^+]^2}{[Al(H_2O)_6^{3+}(aq)]}$

$[H^+]^2 = K_a \times [Al(H_2O)_6^{3+}(aq)]$
$= (1.0 \times 10^{-5}) \times (0.010)$
$[H^+] = \sqrt{(1.0 \times 10^{-5}) \times (0.010)}$

$= 3.16 \times 10^{-4}\,mol\,dm^{-3}$
pH $= -\log_{10}(3.16 \times 10^{-4}) = 3.5$

c $K_a = \dfrac{[H^+]^2}{[\text{methanoic acid}]}$

$[H^+]^2 = K_a \times [\text{methanoic acid}]$
$= (1.6 \times 10^{-4}) \times (0.10)$
$[H^+] = \sqrt{(1.6 \times 10^{-4}) \times (0.10)}$
$= 4.0 \times 10^{-3}\,mol\,dm^{-3}$
pH $= -\log_{10}(4.0 \times 10^{-3}) = 2.4$

7 a The slope of the graph is steep between pH 3.5 and 10.5. Any indicator with a colour change range between these values is suitable: bromocresyl green, methyl red, bromothymol blue or phenylphthalein. Methyl yellow, methyl orange and bromophenol blue would not be first choice indicators. Although the midpoint of their colour range is just within the range of the steep slope, their full range is outside the lower limit of 3.5.
b Methyl violet, methyl yellow and alizarin yellow have midpoints in their colour ranges at pH values which do not correspond with the steepest point of the pH/volume curve.

8 a i Nitric acid is a strong acid and aqueous ammonia is a weak base. The steepest part of the pH curve is in the region of 7.5 to 3.5. So any indicator which has its colour change range within this region would be suitable, e.g. methyl red or bromothymol blue.

ii Sulfuric acid is a strong acid and sodium hydroxide is a strong base. The steepest part of the pH curve is in the region of 10.5 to 3.5. So any indicator which has its colour change range within this region would be suitable, e.g. methyl red or bromothymol blue, phenolphthalein.

iii Butanoic acid is a weak acid and potassium hydroxide is a strong base. The steepest part of the pH curve is in the region of 11 to 7.5. So any indicator which has its colour change range within this region would be suitable, e.g. phenolphthalein.

b The titration of a strong acid with a weak base has a steep pH change only in acidic regions and not alkaline regions, for example, between pH 3 and pH 9. Phenolphthalein has a midpoint in its colour range above pH 9. This is a pH value which does not correspond with the steepest point of the pH/volume curve.

9 a The equilibrium mixture is:

$$NH_3(aq) + H_2O \rightleftharpoons NH_4^+(aq) + OH^-(aq)$$

When hydrochloric acid is added, the additional H^+ ions combine with the OH^- ions in the equilibrium mixture (forming water). The position of equilibrium shifts to the right. Because there are relatively high concentrations of ammonia (base) and ammonium ions (conjugate acid) present compared with the concentration of added H^+ ions, the pH does not change very much.

When sodium hydroxide is added, the additional OH^- ions shift the position of equilibrium to the left. More ammonia and water is formed. Because there are relatively high concentrations of ammonia and ammonium ions present compared with the concentration of added OH^- ions, the pH does not change very much.

b Ammonia is a weak base. The equilibrium lies well over to the left. So there are not enough NH_4^+ ions in the equilibrium mixture to remove added OH^- ions.

10 a i The equilibrium expression for this weak acid in the presence of its conjugate base is:

$$K_a = \frac{[H^+][HCOO^-]}{[HCOOH]}$$

Rearrange the equilibrium expression to make $[H^+]$ the subject:

$$[H^+] = K_a \times \frac{[HCOOH]}{[HCOO^-]}$$

$$[H^+] = 1.6 \times 10^{-4} \times \frac{(0.0500)}{(0.100)} = 8.00 \times 10^{-5}\, mol\, dm^{-3}$$

$$pH = -\log_{10}[H^+] = -\log_{10}(8.00 \times 10^{-5}) = 4.10$$

ii Using the same method as in part **a i**:

$$[H^+] = 6.3 \times 10^{-5} \times \frac{(0.0100)}{(0.0400)} = 1.58 \times 10^{-5}\, mol\, dm^{-3}$$

$$pH = -\log_{10}[H^+] = -\log_{10}(1.58 \times 10^{-5}) = 4.80$$

b Here we have to rearrange the equilibrium expression to make the conjugate base (sodium ethanoate) the subject.

$$K_a = \frac{[H^+][CH_3COO^-]}{[CH_3COOH]}$$

$$[CH_3COO^-] = K_a \times \frac{[CH_3COOH]}{[H^+]}$$

$pH = -\log_{10}[H^+]$ so $[H^+] = 1.26 \times 10^{-5}\, mol\, dm^{-3}$

$$[CH_3COO^-] = 1.74 \times 10^{-5} \times \frac{0.100}{1.26 \times 10^{-5}}$$

$[CH_3COO^-] = 0.138\, mol\, dm^{-3}$
number of moles = concentration × volume in dm^3
= 0.138 × 1.00 = 0.138 mol

11 a i The acid will have one more proton than the base which is conjugate with it. So the acid is $H_2PO_4^-$ and the base is HPO_4^{2-}.

ii $H_2PO_4^- \rightleftharpoons HPO_4^{2-} + H^+$

b The addition of hydrogen ions shifts the position of equilibrium to the left. Pr^- (the deprotonated form of the protein) combines with the extra hydrogen ions to form HPr (the protonated form of the protein) until equilibrium is re-established. If there are still fairly high concentrations of proteins present then the pH will not change very much.

12 a i $K_{sp} = [Fe^{2+}][OH^-]^2$
ii $K_{sp} = [Fe^{3+}]^2[S^{2-}]^3$
iii $K_{sp} = [Al^{3+}][OH^-]^3$

b i $mol\, dm^{-3} \times (mol\, dm^{-3})^2 = mol^3\, dm^{-9}$
ii $(mol\, dm^{-3})^2 \times (mol\, dm^{-3})^3 = mol^5\, dm^{-15}$
iii $mol\, dm^{-3} \times (mol\, dm^{-3})^3 = mol^4\, dm^{-12}$

13 a i the concentrations of Cd^{2+} and S^{2-} ions are both $1.46 \times 10^{-11}\, mol\, dm^{-3}$
$K_{sp} = [Cd^{2+}][S^{2-}]$
$K_{sp} = (1.46 \times 10^{-11}) \times (1.46 \times 10^{-11})$
$= 2.13 \times 10^{-22}\, mol^2\, dm^{-6}$

ii We first have to calculate the concentration of the ions in $mol\, dm^{-3}$
$M_r(CaF_2) = 40.1 + (2 \times 19.0) = 78.1$
concentration in $mol\, dm^{-3} = \dfrac{0.0168}{78.1}$

$= 2.15 \times 10^{-4}\, mol\, dm^{-3}$
for every formula unit of CaF_2 that dissolves, one Ca^{2+} ion and two F^- ions are formed
$[Ca^{2+}] = 2.15 \times 10^{-4}\, mol\, dm^{-3}$
$[F^-] = 2 \times (2.15 \times 10^{-4})\, mol\, dm^{-3}$
$= 4.30 \times 10^{-4}\, mol\, dm^{-3}$
$K_{sp} = [Ca^{2+}][F^-]^2$
$K_{sp} = (2.15 \times 10^{-4}) \times (4.30 \times 10^{-4})^2$
$= 3.98 \times 10^{-11}\, mol^3 dm^{-9}$

b $K_{sp} = [Zn^{2+}][S^{2-}]$

since the concentration of Zn^{2+} and S^{2-} ions are the same, we can write the equilibrium expression:

$K_{sp} = [Zn^{2+}]^2$

$1.6 \times 10^{-23} = [Zn^{2+}]^2$

so $[Zn^{2+}] = \sqrt{1.6 \times 10^{-23}}$

$= 4.0 \times 10^{-12} \, mol \, dm^{-3}$

(this is also the solubility of zinc sulfide since one formula unit of ZnS contains one Zn^{2+} ion)

c The equilibrium equation is:

$Ag_2CO_3(s) \rightleftharpoons 2Ag^+(aq) + CO_3^{2-}(aq)$

if the solubility of Ag_2CO_3 is $y \, mol \, dm^{-3}$, then:

$[Ag^+] = 2y$ (because there are two silver ions in each formula unit of Ag_2CO_3)

$[CO_3^{2-}] = y$ (because there is one carbonate ion in each formula unit of Ag_2CO_3)

The equilibrium expression is:

$K_{sp} = [Ag^+]^2[CO_3^{2-}]$

$6.3 \times 10^{-12} = [Ag^+]^2[CO_3^{2-}]$

substituting the values for y:

$6.3 \times 10^{-12} = (2y)^2(y) = 2y \times 2y \times y = 4y^3$

$6.3 \times 10^{-12} = 4y^3$

$y = \sqrt[3]{\dfrac{6.3 \times 10^{-12}}{4}}$

$= 1.2 \times 10^{-4} \, mol \, dm^{-3}$

(since $y = [CO_3^{2-}]$ and there is one mole of CO_3^{2-} in one mole of Ag_2CO_3, this is also the solubility of silver carbonate)

14 a This can be explained by the common ion effect. The equilibrium equation and the expression for the solubility product are:

$TlCl(s) \rightleftharpoons Tl^+ + Cl^-$

$K_{sp} = [Tl^+][Cl^-]$

The chloride ion is common to both hydrochloric acid and thallium chloride, so the added chloride ions shift the position of equilibrium to the left and thallium chloride is precipitated because the solubility product $[Tl^+] \times [Cl^-]$ is exceeded.

b i Equal volumes of each solution are combined, so each solution has diluted the other by 2.

The concentration of each solution is $\dfrac{0.001\,00}{2}$

$= 5.0 \times 10^{-4} \, mol \, dm^{-3}$

$[Ca^{2+}] = [SO_4^{2-}] = 5 \times 10^{-4} \, mol \, dm^{-3}$

ii A precipitate will form if the solubility product of calcium sulfate is exceeded. The equilibrium expression for the solubility product of calcium sulfate is:

$K_{sp} = [Ca^{2+}][SO_4^{2-}] = 2.0 \times 10^{-5} \, mol^2 \, dm^{-6}$

$[Ca^{2+}][SO_4^{2-}] = (5.00 \times 10^{-4}) \times (5.00 \times 10^{-4})$

$= 2.50 \times 10^{-7} \, mol^2 \, dm^{-6}$

This value is below the value of the solubility product for calcium sulfate, so no precipitate will form.

Chapter 21

1 a $0.254 \, g \, I_2 = \dfrac{0.254}{2 \times 127} = 1.00 \times 10^{-3} \, mol$; this is the change in number of moles in 1 hour.

volume = $1 \, dm^3$ so the change in concentration is $1.00 \times 10^{-3} \, mol \, dm^{-3}$ in 1 hour

1 hour = 3600 seconds, so rate $= \dfrac{1.00 \times 10^{-3} \, mol \, dm^{-3}}{3600 \, s}$

$= 2.78 \times 10^{-7} \, mol \, dm^{-3} \, s^{-1}$

b $0.044 \, g \, CH_3COOC_2H_5 = \dfrac{0.0440}{88.0}$

$= 5.00 \times 10^{-4} \, mol$; this is the change in number of moles in 1 minute.

volume = $400 \, cm^3$, so the change in concentration is

$5.00 \times 10^{-4} \times \dfrac{1000}{400} = 1.25 \times 10^{-4} \, mol \, dm^{-3}$ in 1 minute

1 minute = 60 seconds, so rate $= \dfrac{1.25 \times 10^{-4} \, mol \, dm^{-3}}{60 \, s}$

$= 2.08 \times 10^{-5} \, mol \, dm^{-3} \, s^{-1}$

2 a i Measure the decrease in electrical conductivity. As the reaction proceeds, the iodide and hydrogen ions (which are charge carriers in aqueous solution) are converted to molecules (which do not carry charge).

or

Measure the increase in colour of the solution by colorimetry. The reactants are colourless but the iodine produced is brown.

or

Sample the solution and titrate the sample with sodium thiosulfate.

ii Titrate small samples with standard strong alkali using a suitable acid/base indicator. As the reaction proceeds, the amount of methanoic acid formed increases.

iii Measure the volume of oxygen gas produced. This increases with time.

iv Measure the decrease in electrical conductivity. As the reaction proceeds the bromate, bromide and hydrogen ions (which are charge carriers in aqueous solution) are converted to molecules (which do not carry charge).

or

Measure the increase in colour of the solution by colorimetry. The reactants are colourless but the bromine produced is reddish-brown.

b Change in temperature changes the reaction rate markedly. An increase in temperature increases the value of the rate constant.

3 a i

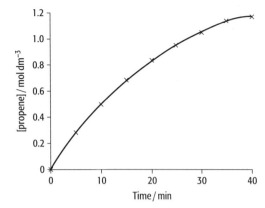

ii $6.68 \times 10^{-4} \, \text{mol dm}^{-3} \text{s}^{-1}$

b initial rate: rate = $9.98 \times 10^{-4} \, \text{mol dm}^{-3} \text{s}^{-1}$
at $0.30 \, \text{mol dm}^{-3}$: rate = $8.00 \times 10^{-4} \, \text{mol dm}^{-3} \text{s}^{-1}$
at $0.90 \, \text{mol dm}^{-3}$: rate = $4.00 \times 10^{-4} \, \text{mol dm}^{-3} \text{s}^{-1}$

c i when [propene] = 0.00,
[cyclopropane] = 1.50 – 0.0 = $1.50 \, \text{mol dm}^{-3}$
when [propene] = 0.30,
[cyclopropane] = 1.50 – 0.30 = $1.20 \, \text{mol dm}^{-3}$
when [propene] = 0.50,
[cyclopropane] = 1.50 – 0.50 = $1.00 \, \text{mol dm}^{-3}$
when [propene] = 0.90,
[cyclopropane] = 1.5 – 0.90 = $0.60 \, \text{mol dm}^{-3}$

ii

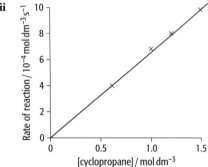

4 a rate = $k[\text{cyclopropane}]$
b rate = $k[\text{HI}]^2$
c rate = $k[\text{C}_{12}\text{H}_{22}\text{O}_{11}][\text{H}^+]$
d rate = $k[[\text{HgCl}_2][\text{K}_2\text{C}_2\text{O}_4]^2$
e rate = $k[\text{CH}_3\text{COCH}_3][\text{H}^+]$

5 a rate = $k[\text{cyclopropane}]$:
  i 1st order with respect to cyclopropane
  ii 1st order overall
b rate = $k[\text{HI}]^2$
  i 2nd order with respect to HI
  ii 2nd order overall
c rate = $k[\text{C}_{12}\text{H}_{22}\text{O}_{11}][\text{H}^+]$
  i 1st order with respect to $\text{C}_{12}\text{H}_{22}\text{O}_{11}$; 1st order with respect to H^+
  ii 2nd order overall

d rate = $k[\text{HgCl}_2][\text{K}_2\text{C}_2\text{O}_4]^2$
  i 1st order with respect to HgCl₂; 2nd order with respect to $\text{K}_2\text{C}_2\text{O}_4$
  ii 3rd order overall
e rate = $k[\text{CH}_3\text{COCH}_3][\text{H}^+]$
  i 1st order with respect to CH_3COCH_3 and H^+; 0 order with respect to I_2
  ii 2nd order overall

6 a rearrange the equation in terms of k

$$k = \frac{\text{rate}}{[\text{NO}_2]^2}$$

substitute the units

$$k = \frac{\text{mol dm}^{-3} \, \text{s}^{-1}}{(\text{mol dm}^{-3}) \times (\text{mol dm}^{-3})}$$

cancel mol dm^{-3}

$$k = \frac{\cancel{\text{mol dm}^{-3}} \, \text{s}^{-1}}{(\cancel{\text{mol dm}^{-3}}) \times (\text{mol dm}^{-3})}$$

units of $k = \text{s}^{-1} \text{mol}^{-1} \text{dm}^3 = \text{dm}^3 \text{mol}^{-1} \text{s}^{-1}$

b rearrange the equation in terms of k

$$k = \frac{\text{rate}}{[\text{NH}_3]^0}$$

substitute the units

$$k = \frac{\text{mol dm}^{-3} \, \text{s}^{-1}}{1}$$

units of $k = \text{mol dm}^{-3} \text{s}^{-1}$

c rearrange the equation in terms of k

$$k = \frac{\text{rate}}{[\text{BrO}_3^-][\text{Br}^-][\text{H}^+]^2}$$

substitute the units

$$k = \frac{\text{mol dm}^{-3} \, \text{s}^{-1}}{(\text{mol dm}^{-3}) \times (\text{mol dm}^{-3}) \times (\text{mol dm}^{-3})^2}$$

cancel mol dm^{-3}

$$k = \frac{\cancel{\text{mol dm}^{-3}} \, \text{s}^{-1}}{(\cancel{\text{mol dm}^{-3}}) \times (\text{mol dm}^{-3}) \times (\text{mol dm}^{-3})^2}$$

units of $k = \text{s}^{-1} \text{mol}^{-3} \text{dm}^9 = \text{dm}^9 \text{mol}^{-3} \text{s}^{-1}$

d rearrange the equation in terms of k

$$k = \frac{\text{rate}}{[\text{cyclopropane}]}$$

substitute the units

$$k = \frac{\text{mol dm}^{-3} \, \text{s}^{-1}}{(\text{mol dm}^{-3})}$$

cancel mol dm^{-3}

$$k = \frac{\cancel{\text{mol dm}^{-3}} \, \text{s}^{-1}}{(\cancel{\text{mol dm}^{-3}})}$$

units of $k = \text{s}^{-1}$

7 a 2nd order reaction, so there is an upward curve (see red line in Figure **21.9**, page **330**)

b zero order reaction, so there is a horizontal straight line

c 1st order reaction so there is a straight line through (0,0) showing direct proportionality (see blue line in Figure **21.9**, page **330**)

8 a there is a steep curve which then levels out

b there is a straight line in constant decline (see black line in Figure **21.10**, page **331**)

c there is a shallow curve (see blue line in Figure **21.10**, page **331**)

9 a By measuring the increase in pressure with time in a closed system where the reaction is taking place or by measuring the volume of nitrogen gas given off with time using a gas syringe.

b Graph is a smooth downward curve levelling off gradually, so seems to be first order with respect to benzenediazonium chloride.

c 1st half-life from $0.58 \times 10^{-4}\,\text{mol}\,\text{dm}^{-3}$ to $0.29 \times 10^{-4}\,\text{mol}\,\text{dm}^{-3}$ = 470 s
2nd half-life from $0.29 \times 10^{-4}\,\text{mol}\,\text{dm}^{-3}$ to $0.145 \times 10^{-4}\,\text{mol}\,\text{dm}^{-3}$ = 450 s

d first order reaction because successive half-lives are more or less the same (within experimental error).

10 a rate = $k[\text{H}_2\text{O}_2][\text{I}^-]$

so $k = \dfrac{\text{rate}}{[\text{H}_2\text{O}_2][\text{I}^-]}$

for experiment 2:

rate = $\dfrac{5.30 \times 10^{-6}}{(0.0300) \times (0.0100)} = 0.0177\,\text{dm}^3\,\text{mol}^{-1}\,\text{s}^{-1}$

for experiment 3:

rate = $\dfrac{1.75 \times 10^{-6}}{(0.0050) \times (0.0200)} = 0.0175\,\text{dm}^3\,\text{mol}^{-1}\,\text{s}^{-1}$

b $k = \dfrac{0.693}{480} = 1.44 \times 10^{-3}\,\text{s}^{-1}$

c $t_{\frac{1}{2}} = \dfrac{0.693}{k}$; $k = 9.63 \times 10^{-5}\,\text{s}^{-1}$

$t_{\frac{1}{2}} = \dfrac{0.693}{9.63 \times 10^{-5}} = 7200\,\text{s}$ (to 3 significant figures)

11 The temperature must remain constant throughout the experiment. The experiment should be designed to study the effect of changing the concentration of only one reactant at a time. The best approach is to ensure that a large excess of methanol is used. The concentration of methanol is then assumed to be constant since it is much higher than that of hydrochloric acid and we can monitor the concentration of HCl. This allows the order of reaction with respect to HCl to be deduced.

12 a There is only one molecule in the rate equation so the reaction is first order

b rate = $k[\text{NO}_2]$

$k = \dfrac{\text{rate}}{[\text{NO}_2]} = \dfrac{3.15 \times 10^{-5}}{3.00} = 1.05 \times 10^{-5}\,\text{s}^{-1}$

[did you spot the '10^{-5}' in the heading of column 2?]

13 a rate = $k[\text{CH}_3\text{COCH}_3][\text{H}^+][\text{I}_2]^0$ or
rate = $k[\text{CH}_3\text{COCH}_3][\text{H}^+]$

b rearranging the rate equation then substituting the data:

$k = \dfrac{\text{rate}}{[\text{CH}_3\text{COCH}_3][\text{H}^+]}$

$k = \dfrac{10.9 \times 10^{-6}}{(0.5 \times 10^{-3}) \times (1.25)} = 1.74 \times 10^{-2}\,\text{dm}^3\,\text{mol}^{-1}\,\text{s}^{-1}$

14 The rate-determining step is the slow step. This involves the reaction of H_2O_2 with I^- ions. These are the only two species which appear in the rate equation. The hydrogen ions do not appear in the rate equation because they are involved in a fast step which takes place after the rate-determining step.

15 a Mn^{3+} and Mn^{2+} (**ii**) and Ce^{4+} and Ce^{3+} (**iii**). These are the only pairs which have $E^\ominus$ values between those of the $\text{S}_2\text{O}_8^{2-}/\text{SO}_4^{2-}$ and I^-/I_2 pairs.

b i

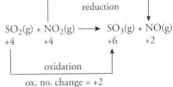

ii

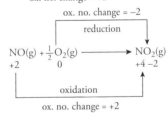

16 a Desorption is the releasing of product molecules from the surface of a catalyst.

b The ethene and hydrogen are adsorbed onto the surface of the nickel. In this process weak bonds are formed between the ethene and the surface of the nickel and between hydrogen and the surface of the nickel.

The bonds between the hydrogen atoms are weakened and the π bond of the ethene is also weakened. Adsorbed hydrogen atoms close to the adsorbed ethene then react to form ethane.

The bonds between the ethane and the surface of the nickel weaken and the ethane moves away from the surface of the catalyst.

c i bonds weakening

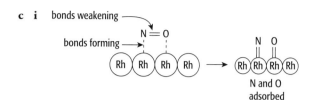

bonds forming

N and O
adsorbed

ii

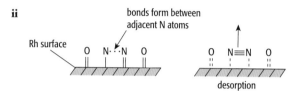

bonds form between
adjacent N atoms

Rh surface

desorption

Chapter 22

1 a $150 \, kJ \, mol^{-1}$ (values between 130 and 170 are acceptable). The bond energies decrease as the atoms become larger.

b Iron ions are smaller than tin or lead ions so the charge density of iron ions is higher. The charge is spread out over a larger volume in the tin and lead ions (lower charge density), so the force of attraction between tin (and lead) ions and the delocalised electrons is lower compared with iron ions.

c All the four outer electrons on each carbon atom are used in bonding. No electrons are free to move and act as charge carriers.

2 a They have simple molecular structures. The forces keeping the molecules together are weak van der Waals' forces. (The dipoles in the molecules cancel out so there is no net dipole.) It does not require much energy to overcome the weak attractive forces keeping the molecules together, so the boiling points are low.

b i $GeCl_4(l) + 2H_2O(l) \rightarrow GeO_2(s) + 4HCl(g)$

ii $PbCl_4(l) \rightarrow PbCl_2(s) + Cl_2(g)$

c

Cl
|
Cl — Sn — Cl
109.5° Cl

For a revision of bond angles see Chapter 4.

3 a Successive ionisation energies get increasingly larger. The huge amounts of energy required to ionise the atoms to form 4+ ions is far too high to be compensated for by the lattice energy (assuming that the compounds are ionic).

b The oxides get more ionic and less covalent descending the group from CO to PbO.

c $2SiO(s) \rightarrow SiO_2(s) + Si(s)$

d Disproportionation. Some silicon atoms are oxidised from +2 to +4, some are reduced from +2 to 0.

4 a i $CO_2 + 2NaOH \rightarrow Na_2CO_3 + H_2O$

ii $PbO_2 + 4HCl \rightarrow PbCl_4 + 2H_2O$

iii Both PbO_2 and $PbCl_4$ are thermally unstable.

b An oxide which reacts with both acids and bases.

c i They get more basic descending the group.

ii Very weakly acidic (it should be less acidic than SiO_2 since the oxides in oxidation state +2 are slightly less acidic than the corresponding oxide in oxidation state +4).

5 a i doesn't react

ii Sn^{4+}; $Sn^{4+} + H_2S \rightarrow Sn^{2+} + S + 2H^+$

iii PbO_2 (+4H$^+$); $PbO_2 + H_2S + 2H^+ \rightarrow Pb^{2+} + S + 2H_2O$

b i Pb^{4+}

ii Sn

6 a SiO_2 has a giant covalent structure with a network of very strong bonds. It takes a lot of energy to break these bonds, so it will not melt in the high temperature of the oven.

b The outer electrons of the silicon atoms in SiO_2 are all used in bonding. The outer electrons of the oxygen atoms in SiO_2 are either used in bonding or are localised in lone pairs. There are no electrons free to move. (It has a giant covalent structure so it does not have ions that are free to move either.)

Chapter 23

1 a i Ti $\quad 1s^2 2s^2 2p^6 3s^2 3p^6 3d^2 4s^2$

ii Cr $\quad 1s^2 2s^2 2p^6 3s^2 3p^6 3d^5 4s^1$

iii Co $\quad 1s^2 2s^2 2p^6 3s^2 3p^6 3d^7 4s^2$

iv Fe^{3+} $\quad 1s^2 2s^2 2p^6 3s^2 3p^6 3d^5 4s^0$

v Ni^{2+} $\quad 1s^2 2s^2 2p^6 3s^2 3p^6 3d^8 4s^0$

vi Cu^+ $\quad 1s^2 2s^2 2p^6 3s^2 3p^6 3d^{10} 4s^0$

b For scandium the only observed oxidation state is +3, so the electronic configuration of Sc^{3+} is $1s^2 2s^2 2p^6 3s^2 3p^6 4s^0$. This ion has no d electrons, so does not satisfy the definition of a transition element. The only ion of zinc is Zn^{2+}, with the electronic configuration $1s^2 2s^2 2p^6 3s^2 3p^6 3d^{10} 4s^0$. This ion has a completely filled, not a partially filled d sub-shell – so zinc is also not a transition element.

c The +7 oxidation state involves all of the 3d and 4s electrons in manganese.

d a (vanadium metal) is 0; b (V^{2+}) is +2; c (V^{3+}) is +3; d (VO^{2+}) is +4; e (VO_2^+) is +5.

e i +4, as this involves all the 4d and 5s electrons, leaving the noble gas electronic configuration of krypton.

ii ZrO_2

2 a The outer electron in calcium is further from the attractive force of the nucleus than in cobalt (atomic radius decreases across a period) and cobalt has a higher nuclear charge (nuclear charge increases across a period).

b density $= \dfrac{m}{V}$. Nickel atoms have a higher A_r and a lower volume than calcium atoms, so the density of nickel is higher.

3 a $Fe^{2+}(aq) \rightarrow Fe^{3+}(aq) + e^-$

$Cr_2O_7^{2-}(aq) + 14H^+(aq) + 6e^- \rightarrow 2Cr^{3+}(aq) + 7H_2O(l)$

b $6Fe^{2+}(aq) \rightarrow 6Fe^{3+} + \cancel{6e^-}(aq)$

$Cr_2O_7^{2-}(aq) + 14H^+(aq) + \cancel{6e^-} \rightarrow 2Cr^{3+}(aq) + 7H_2O(l)$

$Cr_2O_7^{2-}(aq) + 6Fe^{2+}(aq) + 14H^+(aq)$
$\rightarrow 2Cr^{3+}(aq) + 6Fe^{3+} + 7H_2O(l)$

c $E^{\ominus} = +1.33V + (-0.77V) = +0.56V$

The positive value indicates that the reaction as written is feasible and its relatively large value suggests the reaction is likely to occur (although values of $E^{\ominus}$ tell us nothing about the rate of a reaction).

d 6

e **i** $\dfrac{15.30}{1000} \times 0.001\,00 = 0.000\,015\,3$ mol potassium dichromate(VI)

ii $0.000\,015\,3 \times 6 = 0.000\,091\,8$ mol Fe^{2+}

iii $0.000\,091\,8 \times \dfrac{1000}{25.0} = 0.003\,67\,mol\,dm^{-3}$

4 **a** **i** +3

ii +2

iii +3

iv +3

v +2

b $[Ni(EDTA)]^{2-}$

c ethanedioate ion (ox) and ethane-1,2-diamine (en)

5 **a** +2

b $[CoCl_4]^{2-}(aq) + 6H_2O(l) \rightarrow [Co(H_2O)_6]^{2+}(aq) + 4Cl^-(aq)$

6 **a** Orbitals at the same energy level.

b The ligands in a complex cause the d orbitals to split, forming two sets of non-degenerate orbitals. The difference in the energy (ΔE) between the non-degenerate d orbitals corresponds to the energy of part of the visible spectrum of light. When light travels through a solution or a solid containing the complex, an electron from one of the three lower non-degenerate orbitals absorbs that amount of energy (ΔE) and jumps into one of the two higher non-degenerate orbitals. This leaves the transmitted light coloured.

c
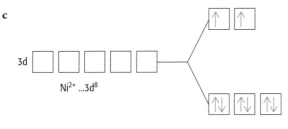

7 **a** Sc^{3+} ions have electronic configuration $(Ar)3d^0 4s^0$. If d-orbital splitting were to occur in a complex ion containing Sc^{3+} there would be no electrons in the three 3d orbitals of lower energy, so visible light would not be absorbed in promoting an electron from a lower energy 3d orbital to a higher energy 3d orbital.

b Zn^{2+} ions have electronic configuration $(Ar)3d^{10}4s^0$. If d-orbital splitting were to occur in a complex ion containing Zn^{2+} each of the 3d orbitals would contain two electrons, and would therefore be fully occupied. Visible light could not be absorbed in promoting an electron from a lower energy 3d orbital to a higher energy 3d orbital.

Chapter 24

1 **a** 6 electrons

b p (2p) orbitals

c Electrons which are free to move around the molecule in the π bonding system above and below the plane of the carbon atoms in the benzene ring.

d In benzene the six electrons in the π bonding system are no longer associated with any particular carbon atoms in the molecule whereas in hex-3-ene the two electrons in the π bond in the centre of the molecule are only found above or below the central two carbon atoms.

2 **a** **i**

ii

b **i** 2-methylphenol

ii 1-bromo-2,3-dichlorobenzene

3 **a**

b electrophilic substitution

c
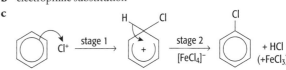

d

e The hydrogen atoms in the —CH_3 side-chain would be all or partially replaced by Br atoms.

f free-radical substitution

4 **a** **i** $C_6H_4(NO_2)CH_3 + H^+$

ii $C_6H_4(NO_2)CH_3 + H_2O$

iii 1-methyl-2-nitrobenzene and 1-methyl-4-nitrobenzene

iv

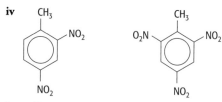

b i sulfur atom
ii $C_6H_6 + SO_3 \rightarrow C_6H_5SO_3H$

5 a HCl, CH_3COOH, C_6H_5OH, H_2O, C_3H_7OH
b Methanol is less acidic than phenol because methanol has an electron-donating methyl group attached to the oxygen atom in the methoxide ion which is formed on dissociation. This has the effect of concentrating more negative charge on this oxygen atom which more readily accepts an H^+ ion, re-forming undissociated methanol. On the other hand, the phenoxide ion, $C_6H_5O^-$(aq), has its negative charge spread over the whole ion as the benzene ring draws in electrons from the oxygen atom, reducing the attraction of this ion for H^+ ions.

6 a C_6H_5OH, $C_6H_5CH_3$, C_6H_6, C_6H_5COOH (remember —COOH is a deactivating group)
b i

OH $\;\;$ + 3Br$_2$ $\longrightarrow$ OH (2,4,6-tribromophenol with Br at positions) + 3HBr

ii A catalyst of anhydrous $FeCl_3$/Fe or $AlCl_3$/Fe would be needed.

Chapter 25

1 a CH_3CCl_2COOH, $CH_3CHClCOOH$, CH_3CH_2COOH
b The electron-withdrawing carbonyl group in the ethanoic acid molecule weakens the O—H bond in the —COOH group, making it more likely for an ethanoic acid molecule to lose an H^+ ion than it is for an ethanol molecule. Secondly, delocalisation of electrons around the —COO^- group stabilises the ethanoate ion. This is not possible in the ethoxide anion formed when ethanol loses an H^+ ion.
c Methanoic acid would be the stronger acid as ethanoic acid has an electron-donating methyl group next to the —COOH group, which does not aid the breaking of the O—H bond. Also, once the ethanoate anion is formed the methyl group tends to increase the concentration of the negative charge on the —COO^- end of the ion, making it more attractive to H^+ ions than a methanoate anion. Therefore ethanoic acid molecules are more likely to exist in the undissociated form whereas methanoic acid molecules are less likely to exist in the undissociated form.

2 a i $CH_3CH_2COOH + SOCl_2$
$\rightarrow CH_3CH_2COCl + SO_2 + HCl$
ii $3HCOOH + PCl_3 \rightarrow 3HCOCl + H_3PO_3$
iii $CH_3CH_2CH_2COOH + PCl_5$
$\rightarrow CH_3CH_2CH_2COCl + POCl_3 + HCl$
b Reaction ii (with PCl_3) – heat is required.
c The carbonyl carbon in an acyl chloride carries a greater partial positive charge than the carbon atom bonded to the oxygen atom in an alcohol. This is because it has two strongly electronegative atoms (oxygen and chlorine) attached to the carbonyl carbon, compared with just the oxygen atom in an alcohol.

3 a propanoic acid and hydrogen chloride
b i CH_3CH_2COCl, $CH_3CH_2CH_2Cl$, C_6H_5Cl
ii The hydrolysis of CH_3CH_2COCl is far more vigorous than the hydrolysis of $CH_3CH_2CH_2Cl$. The hydrolysis of $CH_3CH_2CH_2Cl$ needs a strong alkali and heating under reflux to bring about a reaction. The nucleophile is the negatively charged hydroxide ion, OH^-, as opposed to the neutral water molecule which is sufficient to hydrolyse CH_3CH_2COCl quickly at room temperature. That is because the carbon bonded to the chlorine atom in a $CH_3CH_2CH_2Cl$ molecule is not as electron deficient as the carbon atom in CH_3CH_2COCl. In CH_3CH_2COCl the carbon bonded to a chlorine atom is also attached to an oxygen atom. It has two strongly electronegative atoms pulling electrons away from it. Therefore the attack by the nucleophile is much more rapid. On the other hand, C_6H_5Cl, an aryl chloride, will not undergo hydrolysis. The p-orbitals from the Cl atom overlap with the delocalised π electrons in the benzene ring. This causes the C—Cl bond to have some double bond character, making it stronger and more resistant to hydrolysis.
iii steamy fumes (of HCl)

4 a i ethanoyl chloride and ethanol
ii butanoyl chloride and methanol
iii benzoyl chloride and phenol
b $CH_3CH_2COCl + CH_3CH_2CH_2NH_2$
$\rightarrow CH_3CH_2CONHCH_2CH_2CH_3 + HCl$

5 a i tri-iodomethane

H — C — I with I above, I below, I to the right (CHI$_3$)

ii Step 1: CH_3COCl_3; step 2: $CH_3COO^-Na^+ + CHI_3$
b The ethanol is first oxidised by the alkaline iodine solution to give ethanal, CH_3CHO. Ethanal has a methyl group adjacent to the carbonyl carbon so will give a positive tri-iodomethane test. In step 1 of the test we get tri-iodoethanal. Then in step 2 we get tri-iodomethane and sodium methanoate.
c Only i, iv and v will give tri-iodomethane.

Chapter 26

1 a i pentylamine
      ii dipropylamine
      iii ethylammonium chloride
   b Diethylamine is a stronger base than ethylamine because it has two ethyl groups each releasing electrons to its N atom, making the lone pair more readily available to bond with an H^+ ion than it is in ethylamine which only has one electron-donating ethyl group.

2 a i The vapour of butanenitrile and hydrogen gas are passed over a nickel catalyst or alternatively sodium and ethanol are used to reduce the butanenitrile.
      ii 1-bromopropane
   b i 2-aminophenol, $C_6H_5NH_2$
      ii reduction

3 a i Phenylamine, because of the greater electron density around the benzene ring because the lone pair of the nitrogen atom is delocalised into the π-bonding electron system.
      ii

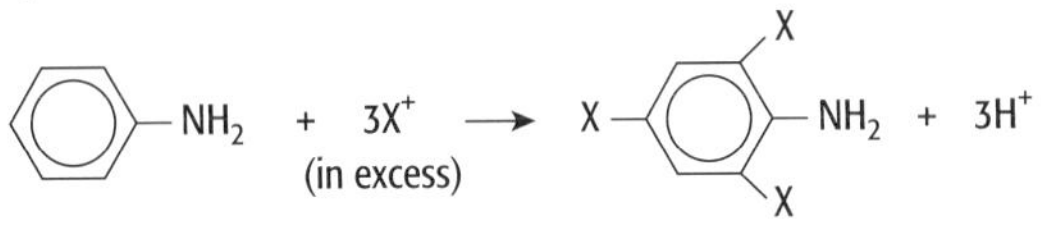

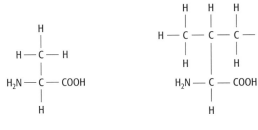

   b i The benzenediazonium ion will decompose, giving off nitrogen gas, above 10 °C. The nitrous acid used as a reactant also decomposes above 10 °C.
      ii $NaNO_2 + HCl \rightarrow HNO_2 + NaCl$
      iii Step 1

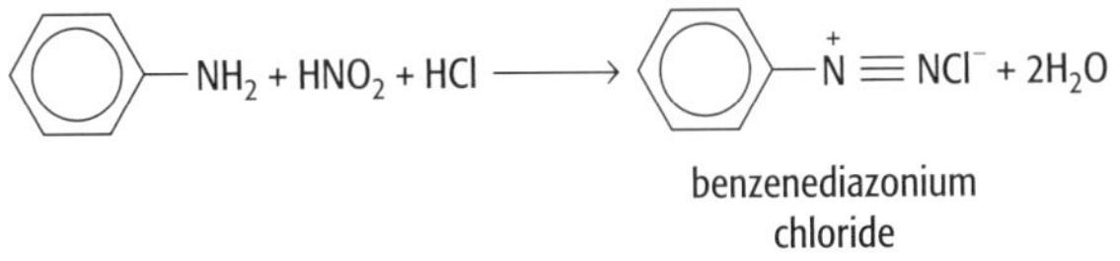

Step 2

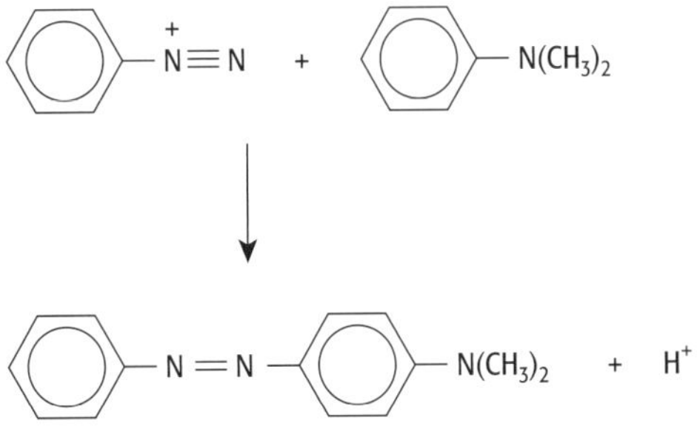

4 a i $CH_3CH_2COCl + NH_3 \rightarrow CH_3CH_2CONH_2 + HCl$
      ii $C_2H_5COCl + C_2H_5NH_2 \rightarrow C_2H_5CONHC_2H_5 + HCl$

b i $C_3H_7CONH_2 + H_2O \xrightarrow{H^+} C_3H_7COOH + NH_3$
      (Note that NH_3 will react with excess HCl to give $NH_4^+Cl^-$)
   ii $C_3H_7CONHC_2H_5 + NaOH$
      $\rightarrow C_3H_7COO^-Na^+ + C_2H_5NH_2$

5 a i $RCH(NH_2)COOH$
      ii They have relatively high melting points for organic compounds of their molecular mass because of the strong electrostatic forces of attraction between the oppositely charged parts of the zwitterions formed.
   b i

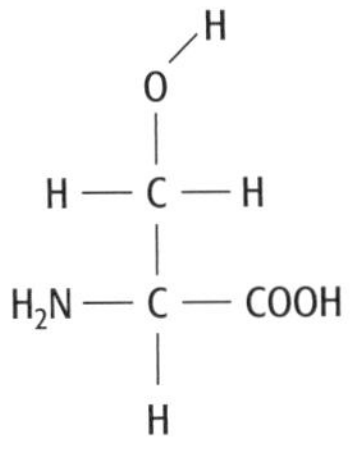

      ii

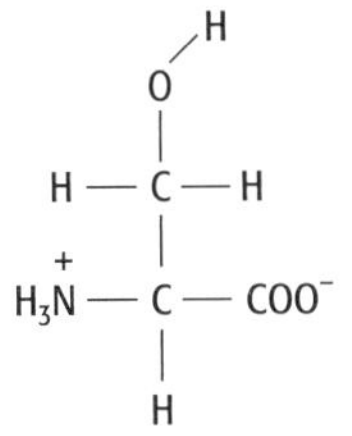

      iii

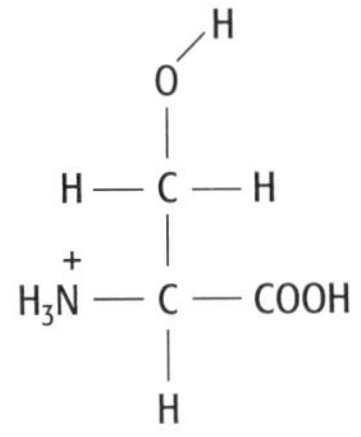

      iv

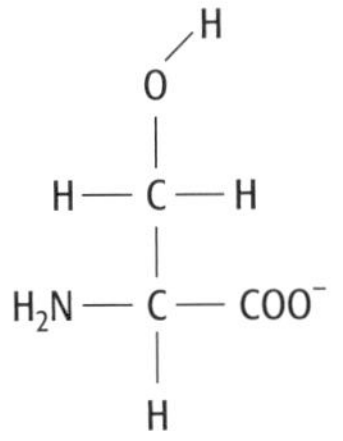

6 a

alanine   valine

b

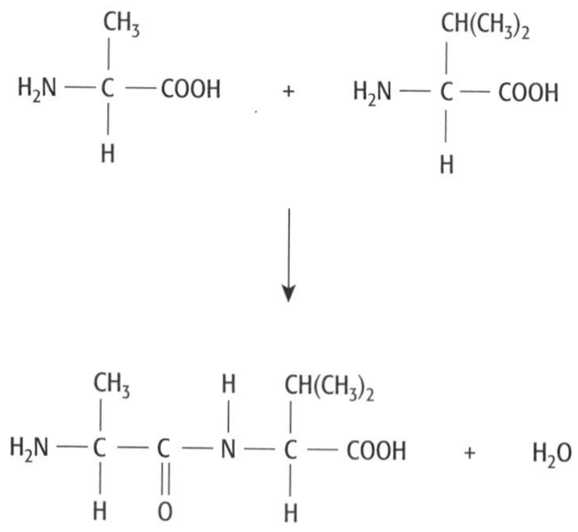

c the sodium salts of alanine and valine

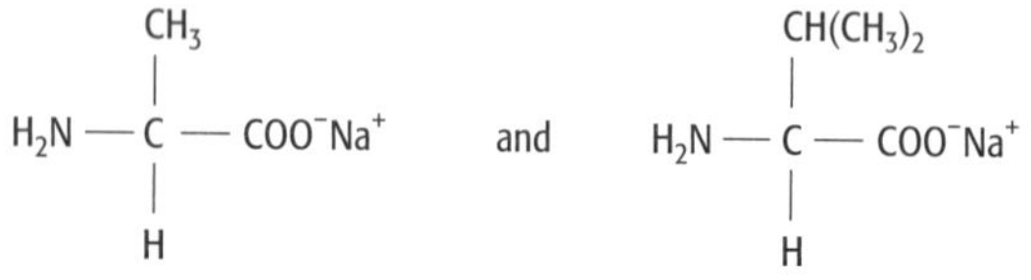

d hydrolysis

Chapter 27

1 **a** Addition polymers from B and C; condensation polymers from A, D and E

b Addition polymers have monomers that are alkenes; condensation polymers have monomers that are not alkenes, but that have two functional groups per molecule. A and D both have an
—NH_2 group and a —COOH group. E has an
—OH group and a —COOH group.

c **i**

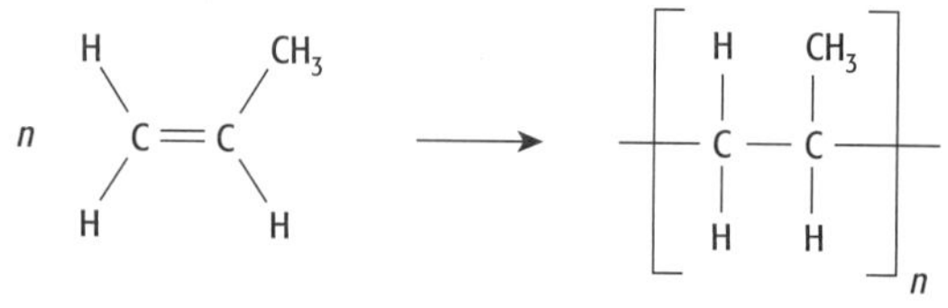

ii addition polymerisation

iii

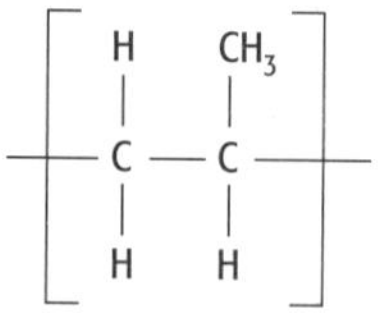

2 **a**

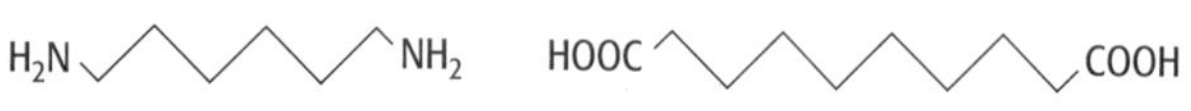

1,6 – diaminohexane　　decanedioic acid

b

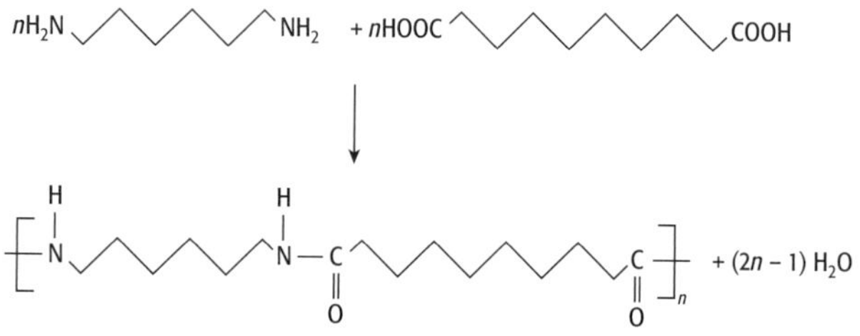

c **i** 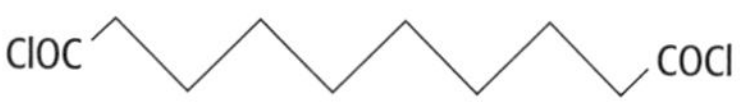

ii hydrogen chloride, HCl

3 **a**

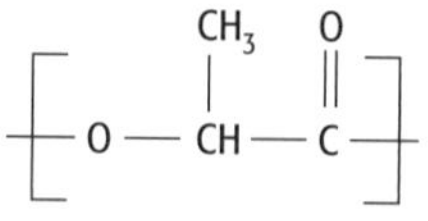

b

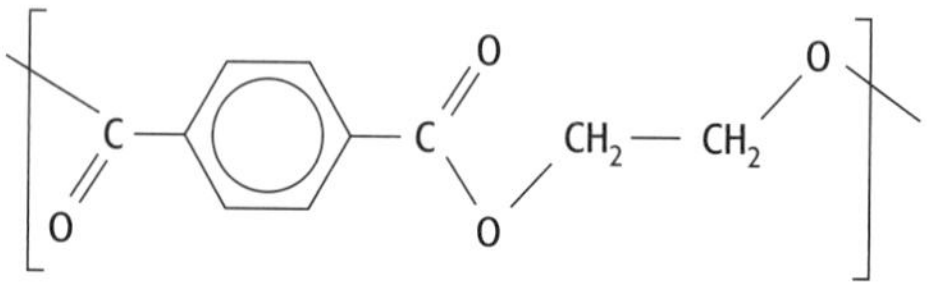

4 **a** but-1-ene

b **i** condensation polymerisation

ii

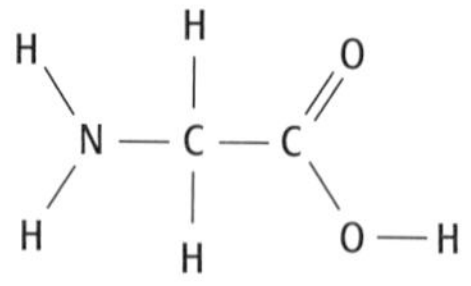

Chapter 28

1 **a** amine/amino group, —NH_2; carboxylic acid group, —COOH.

b proline/Pro; it is a secondary amino acid/imino acid; this is because it contains an —NH group rather than an —NH_2 group.

c **i** any amino acid which has a hydrocarbon side-chain, e.g. alanine, valine, leucine, isoleucine, phenylalanine. Glycine, the simplest amino acid, has a non-polar side chain.

ii There are two found in proteins – aspartic acid and glutamic acid.

d

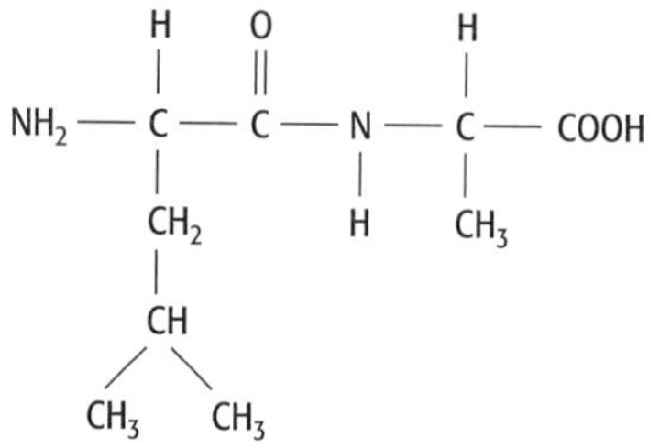

Note: the N-terminal end is placed on the left and the first amino acid in the dipeptide is the left one of the pair.

e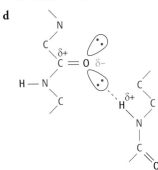

H_2N — CH — COO^-
           |
        $CH_2CH_2COO^-$

Both carboxylic acid groups will be deprotonated ($-COOH$ + OH^- → $-COO^-$ + H_2O) and the amino group will remain as $-NH_2$.

2 a N-terminal, which is always written on the left, and C-terminal, which is always written on the right.

b covalent bonding

c An amino acid when it is part of a peptide chain. 'Residue' means what is left after something has been removed. In this case it is water which has been removed by the condensation of the amino acids.

d

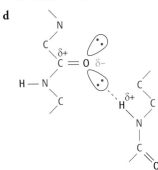

e Sulfhydryl (disulfide) bridges (strong covalent bonding); hydrogen bonding (weak); van der Waals' forces (very weak); ionic bonding/salt link (not as strong as ionic bonding in solids since the + and – charges are usually further apart than in ionic solids).

f In the secondary structure hydrogen bonds are formed between the $-NH$ of one peptide group and the $C=O$ of another peptide group. In tertiary structure, the hydrogen bonds are formed between appropriate groups on the amino acid side-chains, e.g. $-NH_2$, $-OH$, $-COOH$.

g i cysteine

ii Disulfide groups bridge across different parts of the same polypeptide chain or different polypeptide chains to help keep them in the correct position. Disulfide bridges are covalent bonds, this means that they are stronger than the other forces that stabilise the tertiary structure of a protein.

3 a

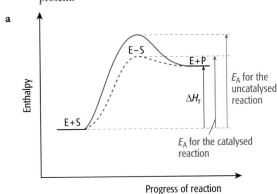

b i The pocket on the enzyme surface where a substrate (and cofactors) bind and where catalysis takes place.

ii The substrate is complementary in shape to the active site. It binds to the enzyme specifically because of the match in shape, and because of the positions of polar and non-polar regions of the substrate and the active site (distribution of charge). The substrate is said to be like a key in the lock, with the active site of the enzyme being the lock.

c i Hydrogen bonding between the $-OH$ of the tyrosine and the $-OH$ at the bottom of pocket of the active site. The small glycine side-chains on the protein allow the large tyrosine molecules to fit into the active site where it is also held by van der Waals' forces.

ii The $-CH_3$ group on the alanine side-chain is quite small, so it does not get near enough to the polypeptide chain at the active site to be stabilised by van der Waals' forces. It does not fit far enough into the pocket to be stabilised by any other amino acid residues.

4 a 1: When the concentration of haem is low, there is less haem to bind to enzyme molecules. 2: This means that fewer enzyme molecules are inhibited, and more enzyme molecules are active. 3: The active enzyme molecules catalyse the ALA synthesis, more haem is synthesised. 4: Haem concentrations become high, there is more haem to bind to enzyme molecules. 5: As a result, more enzyme molecules are inhibited, and fewer enzyme molecules are active. 6: There are few active enzyme molecules to catalyse the ALA synthesis, less haem is synthesised. 7: The concentration of haem becomes low again, and so on (back to step 1).

b i The rate-determining step is the slowest step in a reaction/reaction pathway.

ii If the first step is slow it prevents waste of biochemical materials. If the rate-determining step were one of the middle steps, then the previous steps would lead to a build-up of metabolites which may be harmful and certainly wasteful.

5 a With a competitive inhibitor the inhibition can be overcome by increasing the normal substrate concentration. With a non-competitive inhibitor, increasing the normal substrate concentration has no effect.

Competitive inhibitors act at the active site of the enzyme. Non-competitive inhibitors usually act at a second site on the enzyme.

Competitive inhibitors have a similar shape and similar charge distribution characteristics to the normal substrate. Non-competitive inhibitors do not.

b i A2C is a secondary amine, as is proline, with one lone pair on the nitrogen. A2C has one $-COOH$ group in a similar position to that of proline. The size of the ring in A2C is not significantly different from that of proline.

ii When we compare the data from experiments 1, 2 and 3, we see that increasing the concentration of A2C decreases the rate of the reaction, therefore A2C is an inhibitor.

When we compare the data from experiments 2, 4 and 5, we see that the inhibitory effect of A2C is lessened by increasing the concentration of normal substrate. The greater the concentration of substrate present, the less the inhibitory effect. Therefore A2C is a competitive inhibitor.

c **i** $RCH_2SH + Tl^+ \rightarrow RCH_2STl + H^+$

ii Tl^+ is a non-competitive inhibitor because it forms a covalent bond with the sulfur atom. This can only be reversed by reaction with a compound containing —SH groups. (Competitive inhibitors only form weak intermolecular forces at the active site.)

6 **a**

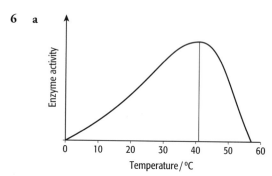

The graph shows an increase in activity, doubling for approximately every 10 °C up to about 30 °C. Activity peaks at about 40 °C then sharply declines.

b Below about 35–40 °C enzyme activity increases with temperature in a similar fashion to inorganic reactions. The reactants (substrate and cofactors) are colliding with more energy, so more reactants possess the activation energy and there are more successful collisions. Collisions occur with greater frequency (on the enzyme surface). Above 40 °C the increased vibration of the polypeptide chain disrupts intermolecular bonding (hydrogen bonds, van der Waals' forces, etc.) which keeps the tertiary structure in place. The tertiary structure begins to alter, thus changing the shape of the active site so that efficient catalysis cannot occur. At even higher temperatures, e.g. 60 °C, the polypeptide chain unfolds and the enzyme becomes denatured.

c The pH curve shows an optimum at pH 2 and loss of enzyme activity either side of this. The two aspartic acid residues could be ionised (—COO⁻) or un-ionised (—COOH). At the optimum pH one is ionised and the other is not. As the pH decreases below pH 2, the ionised group becomes protonated (—COO⁻ + H⁺ → —COOH) and enzyme activity is lost. As the pH increases above pH 2, the —COOH group become deprotonated and enzyme activity reduces. It may seem strange that at such a low pH, the —COO⁻ group is in an ionised form but you must remember that the groups at the active site and elsewhere in the protein may be 'protected' by the presence of cofactors or other amino acid residues.

d

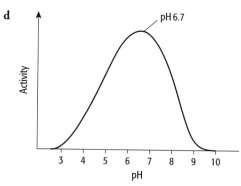

This is a pH curve with a maximum at 6.7 and curving off at either side.

7 **a** **i** nucleotide
ii deoxyribose (a 5-ringed sugar)
iii phosphate group
b adeneine, thymine, cytosine, guanine

8 **a**

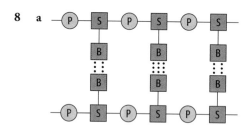

b **i** The chains run in opposite directions. Related to the position of the sugars, one runs from the 5′ to the 3′ position and the other runs from 3′ to 5′.
ii By numbering the positions of the sugars, 3′ and 5′ (these numbers can be put on the ends of the individual chains in simplified diagrams).

9 **a** Thymine 23 mol% and cytosine 27 mol%. This is because adenine is complementary to thymine and guanine is always complementary to cytosine.
b The hydrogen bonds are formed between the base pairs. The bases will line up so that the hydrogen bonding is maximised. There will be three hydrogen bonds between cytosine and guanine and two hydrogen bonds between adenine and thymine.
c A new strand of DNA is formed from each original strand. After replication, each of the two new DNA molecules contains one old strand and one new strand.
d A is complementary to T and C is complementary to G. So the complementary strand is 3′–ATCTTTCGAGTC–5′.

10 **a** RNA has ribose sugar whereas DNA has deoxyribose sugar. RNA has uracil as a base which is complementary to adenine whereas the complementary base to adenine in DNA is thymine. RNA is single stranded but DNA is double stranded.

b A tRNA molecule is a polynucleotide. The polymer backbone consists of alternating ribose and phosphate groups, with an organic base (G, C, A, or U) joined to each ribose. The three-dimensional structure of a tRNA molecule is a cloverleaf structure of loops, which are folded over and stabilised by hydrogen bonding. At one end of the tRNA is a sequence of three bases called an anticodon; the other end of the tRNA binds an amino acid.

c The rRNA forms the skeleton for the structure of the ribosome. It allows the attachment of mRNA to it. The rRNA 'skeleton' allows ribosomal proteins to bind to it to catalyse the various reactions occurring during protein synthesis.

11 a Phe: UUU, UUC
b Pro: CCG, CCA, CCC, CCU
c Lys: AAG, AAA
d Ile: AUA, AUC, AUU

12 a mRNA transfers the coded message for the primary structure of a protein from the DNA, by the process of transcription. The code is a series of triplet bases (codons). mRNA transfers the coded message to make a specific polypeptide sequence to the ribosomes. At the ribosomes the message is translated from the mRNA to form the protein. tRNA binds specific amino acids in the cytoplasm and takes them to the ribosomes where it binds to specific triplets in the mRNA by its triplet anticodon. It then releases the amino acid to the growing polypeptide chain.

b i UAC is Tyr; UCU is Ser; GCU is Ala; GCG is Ala; GAA is Glu; GGA is Gly
ii Q is Ala (the codon is GCC); R is Val (the codon is GUA)
iii The mRNA codon for Tyr used here is UAC. U in RNA is complementary to A; A is complementary to T in DNA (there is no U in DNA); C is complementary to G. So the DNA template for Tyr is ATG.

c The stop codon gives information that the polypeptide chain and the mRNA should be released from the ribosome. If there were no signal for this, another mRNA would not be able to bind to the ribosome. Without a stop codon more tRNAs would bind to the mRNA, adding more amino acids to the growing polypeptide chain, making an incorrect protein.

d mRNA contains a set of consecutive codons. Each codon in mRNA contains a set of three bases. Each codon codes for a particular amino acid. Each tRNA carries a specific amino acid and contains a particular anticodon. The tRNA anticodon can only link to the codon on the mRNA which is complementary to it. So the tRNAs carrying a specific amino acid can only be brought up to the mRNA in the sequence specified by the code on the mRNA. The sequence of codons in the mRNA produces the sequence of the amino acids in the polypeptide chain.

13 a i The template strand of DNA must be translated to the complementary sequence in mRNA.
template strand of DNA
    –AGC   ATG   ATC   ACT–
mRNA sequence
    –UCG   UAC   UAG   UGA–
amino acid coded for by mRNA
        Ser   Tyr   stop   stop
ii tRNA anticodons are complementary to codons on mRNA. Ser = AGC; Tyr = AUG
(U replaces T in RNA molecules)

b
template strand of DNA
    –TAC   TGC   TTT   AAG   CCT   ATG–
mRNA sequence
    –AUG   ACG   AAA   UUC   GGA   UAC–
amino acids coded for by mRNA
        Met Thr Lys Phe Gly Tyr
final amino acid sequence
        Thr-Lys-Phe-Gly-Tyr, as the methionine coded for by the 'start' codon AUG is removed.

c i The final ATG changes to ACG on the DNA. This causes the final UAC to change to UGC on the mRNA. UGC codes for cysteine. The final amino acid sequence will be changed to Thr-Lys-Phe-Gly-Cys.
ii mutation

14 a i –AUC CAU CAC UUA UU–
ii normal is Ser-Pro-Ser-Leu-Ile
mutant is Ile-His-His-Leu (the fifth amino acid could be either Phe or Leu)
b –TCA GGT AGT GAA TAA–
c The amino acid sequence is considerably different. Amino acids with different types of side chain are in equivalent positions. So the protein will not fold up in the correct way for catalysis and the amino acid residues in the active site will not be correct. The enzyme is unlikely to function at all.

15 a nucleotide triphosphate
b nitrogen-containing base (adenine); ribose/5-carbon sugar; triphosphate/3 linked phosphate groups
c i adenosine diphosphate
ii ADP has one phosphate group less than ATP
d the mitochondrion
e Energy is released on hydrolysis of ATP (exothermic). When linked to chemical reactions which are endothermic, the energy released on hydrolysis can be used to drive these reactions in the forward direction. The reactions take place in the presence of enzymes.

16 a (aerobic) respiration
b Oxygen must be present to drive a series of redox reactions. ADP and inorganic phosphate are the substrates required. (Reduced forms of coenzymes must also be present so that they can be oxidised by atmospheric oxygen.)
c Oxidative phosphorylation is the production of ATP from ADP and P_i in the presence of oxidising conditions/oxygen.

17 a Prosthetic groups are bound firmly to the enzyme. Coenzymes are only bound weakly to the enzyme.

b The oxygen is attached to an Fe^{2+} ion at the centre of a haem group. The oxygen is a ligand (in the sixth coordination position of the haem complex). The bonding of oxygen to the Fe^{2+} ion is strong enough for it not to be displaced very easily but weak enough for it to be released. All four oxygen molecules bind to the four subunits in haemoglobin at the same time.

c Cytochromes in the mitochondria / myoglobin in muscle tissue

18 a zinc

b $CO_2 + H_2O \rightarrow HCO_3^- + H^+$

c i nucleophile

ii

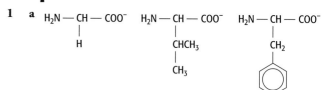

The OH^- ion attacks the $\delta+$ carbon atom of carbon dioxide to form the HCO_3^- ion.

19 a Na^+ and K^+

b When the nerve is stimulated the Na^+ concentration within the cell increases (by ions moving inwards from the outside). When there is equilibrium between the Na^+ and K^+ ions, sodium ions stop moving inwards and K^+ ions move out, therefore the K^+ concentration within the cell decreases.

c ATPase

d On the inner side of a protein (which is part of an ion channel) positioned across the cell membrane.

e the hydrolysis of ATP

20 a Endothermic. It needs an input of energy to break the attractive ion–dipole forces between the ions and the water molecules.

b The K^+ ions are attracted to the negatively charged $-COO^-$ groups in the proteins walls of the ion channels.

c Na^+ ions are smaller than K^+ ions. They are further away from the negatively charged walls of the ion channel so the forces of attraction are not as great.

d i A hydrated Li^+ ion is much smaller than a hydrated Na^+ ion. So, compared with Na^+ it does not form as strong an attraction with the negatively charged amino acid side-chains in the walls of the ion channel.

ii Hydrated K^+ ions are much larger than hydrated Na^+ ions so do not easily fit into the ion channel.

21 a Heavy metal ions react with $-SH$ groups in enzymes and they react with ionic groups. This may result in loss of tertiary structure of the enzyme (denaturation). The active site is no longer in the correct shape to accept the substrate and the enzyme will not function. They act as non-competitive inhibitors. Some may bind directly to an $-SH$ group at the active site and thereby inhibit the enzyme directly. Heavy metal ions such as Hg^+ break disulfide bridges, which keep the polypeptide chain in the correct position and therefore cause enzyme denaturation.

b $R-S-S-R + 2Hg^+ \rightarrow R-S-Hg + Hg-S-R$ (where R represents one or more polypeptide chains)

22 a Mercury in low concentrations in seawater is concentrated by small microscopic sea creatures (plankton) or directly by shellfish. It is further concentrated by other organisms when they feed off the first consumers in the food chain. For example shrimps or fish feed off plankton. Humans might eat the shellfish or fish and concentrate the mercury even more. In each case the mercury is not got rid of from the body. It accumulates in organs especially in fats.

b Mercury can enter water from industrial processes such as making sodium hydroxide, from fungicides sprayed on crops 'running off' the land into streams or from chemicals used to treat timber.

Chapter 29

1 a

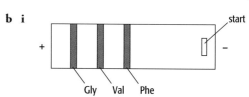

b i

ii The molecules are separated according to size, with the smallest (glycine) moving furthest, and the largest (phenylalanine) moving the shortest distance. Each of the ions will have a –1 charge at pH 10, so the size of the ions is the only factor involved in their separation.

2 a F2

b separating DNA fragments

c A new database has to be started. The genetic profiles of suspects can then be matched against this database.

3 a The DNA from each animal skin scroll will be unique. Therefore, following DNA analysis, pieces of the same scroll can be identified and then matched together.

b Mitochondrial analysis is useful in forensic science or archaeology when DNA samples are in poor condition.

4 a Its formula is $Si(CH_3)_4$ so all its H atoms are equivalent (i.e. they are all in the same molecular environment) so it only gives one, sharp absorption. It is also inert (it does not react with samples being tested), volatile (easily removed from the sample after NMR analysis) and mixes well with most organic compounds.

b i CCl$_4$

ii It has no hydrogen atoms so it won't produce a peak in the NMR spectrum.

iii Deuterium nuclei do not absorb radiowaves in the range we use for NMR so there will be no peaks to interfere with the sample's NMR spectrum.

5 a two peaks, with areas in the ratio 1:3
b single peak (as all the H atoms are equivalent)
c two peaks, with areas in the ratio 2:3
d four peaks, with areas in the ratio 1:2:2:3
e three peaks, with areas in the ratio 1:1:6
f single peak (as all the H atoms are equivalent)

6 a Paracetamol. There are two peaks from single protons with relatively high chemical shifts, corresponding to the —OH and —NH protons in paracetamol (whereas you would expect aspirin to have one peak between 11 and 12 ppm at the high end of the spectrum from its —COOH proton.)

b

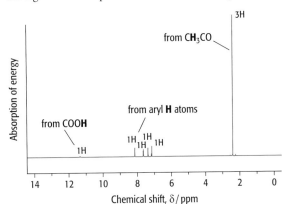

7 a The single —OH peak would disappear from the NMR spectrum.
b Two peaks (from the —OH and —NH protons) would disappear from the NMR spectrum of paracetamol but only one peak would disappear from aspirin's spectrum (from the —COOH peak).

8 a X-ray crystallography (X-ray diffraction)
b As H atoms have only one electron the electron density is not high enough to appear.
c The shape of a macromolecule.
d X-ray analysis can give very accurate measurements from single crystals. However, a very pure sample of the crystal has to be prepared. NMR is not as precise in its measurements but can be used to investigate what happens to proteins in solution, where it can monitor flexible molecules, so NMR can give information on how proteins function.
e B prepare a pure crystalline sample
  E irradiate crystal with X-rays
  C analyse the diffraction pattern
  D construct an electron density map
  A construct an atomic model

9 a C
b $0.57 / \dfrac{145 \text{ mm}}{26 \text{ mm}}$

10 a adsorption
b partition
c i Propanone, which has polar molecules, would leave the column first. The non-polar hydrocarbon stationary phase would have a stronger affinity for the non-polar hexane molecules than for the polar propanone molecules. The polar solvent, ethanol, would have a stronger affinity for the polar propanone molecules than for hexane molecules.
  ii The relative proportions of each component in the mixture.
  iii Hexane would rise furthest on the alumina as it has a greater affinity for non-polar methylbenzene than for the polar alumina stationary phase. Polar propanone has the greater affinity for the polar alumina than hexane does and is less soluble in methylbenzene so does not move as far as hexane over the alumina in a given time.

11 a i the time it takes for a substance to travel through the stationary phase and be detected
  ii the areas under the peaks give the relative proportions of each component of the mixture
b the height of the peaks

12 a 31
b the CH_3O^+ ion
c i CH_3^+
  ii CH_3CO^+
  iii $COOH^+$
  iv CH_3COOH^+ (the molecular ion)

13 a 6
b C_6H_{12}
c cyclohexane

14 a $M = CH_2{}^{79}Br{}^{79}Br^+$
  $[M + 2] = CH_2{}^{79}Br{}^{81}Br^+$
  $[M + 4] = CH_2{}^{81}Br{}^{81}Br^+$
b 64 (from $C_2H_5{}^{35}Cl^+$) and 66 (from $C_2H_5{}^{37}Cl^+$), relative abundances 3:1
c Two peaks beyond the M^+ ion: one at m/e of 188 (twice as abundant as the M^+ ion) and one at 190 (with the same abundance as the M^+ ion).

15 a 9 minutes
b 180–190
c By matching its mass spectrum 'fingerprint' to a database of spectra from known compounds.

16 a 555.0
b i it has an H^+ ion added to its molecules
  ii the molecule is not fragmented
c Because of the presence of some ^{13}C atoms.
d sodium ion, Na^+

Chapter 30

1 **a** X-ray crystallography

  b NMR spectroscopy

  c protein

  d The drug blocked the active site on the enzyme.

2 **a** **i** Less dosage required; reduces risk of side-effects as the unwanted enantiomer might present a health hazard.

  ii Reduces the chances of litigation against the drug company as a result of side-effects caused by the unwanted enantiomer; possibly cheaper as don't waste the unwanted enantiomer.

  b Points to include:
  - racemic mixture produced in traditional synthetic routes
  - this results in the need to separate the mixture of enantiomers
  - this can use large volumes of organic solvents which have to be disposed of, along with the unwanted enantiomer
  - the process will also use more chemicals which require natural resources
  - enzymes are stereospecific
  - whole organisms can be used (without having to isolate enzymes)
  - fewer steps in process resulting in more efficiency

  c Thalidomide was prescribed to pregnant women as a sedative during the early 1960s. It was for a time the preferred sedative during pregnancy as the alternatives, such as valium, were addictive. Unfortunately, one of the two optical isomers of thalidomide proved to have disastrous side-effects, causing babies to be born with congenital deformities (teratogenicity). Not surprisingly, thalidomide was quickly withdrawn from use and law suits were filed against the manufacturers to compensate those affected and to help finance their care. If the optical isomer that had therapeutic effects, without side-effects, had been purified and given as a medicine, this still wouldn't have solved the problem. The 'good' optical isomer is converted into the 'bad' optical isomer in the body, with the same outcome.

3 **a** **i** it contains a C=C double bond/it is unsaturated

  ii The hydrogen atoms in water, with their partial positive charge, would be attracted to the negative charged oxygen in the phosphate group. The oxygen atoms in water, with their partial negative charge, are attracted to the positively charged nitrogen atom in the alkyl ammonium group.

  iii It is the *cis* isomer. The *trans* isomer would have a straighter hydrocarbon 'tail'.

  iv van der Waals' forces

  b The cells in the walls of the blood vessels in a tumour are not as tightly packed as in healthy blood vessels. Therefore the nano-particle delivering the drug can pass into a tumour but can't get through the blood vessels of healthy organs.

c **i** Gold will form ions with a partially filled d sub-shell ($\dots 5d^9$ for Au^{2+}) but mercury only forms an Hg^{2+} ion with a complete d sub-shell ($\dots 5d^{10}$).

  ii Electrons jump into higher unoccupied orbitals.

4 **a** $HOCH_2\text{---}(CH_2OCH_2)_n\text{---}CH_2OH$

  b hydrogen bonds

  c An addition polymer because the polymer is the only product of the reaction (no small molecule is released). (Note: it is an unusual addition polymer as its monomer is not an alkene.)

  d **i** PEG 2000 will have the higher melting point. The strongest forces between the polymer chains will be permanent dipole–dipole attractions.

  ii Increase the concentration of $HOCH_2CH_2OH$ (as this terminates the chains).

  iii mass spectrometry

  iv Two peaks, one for the two equivalent —OH protons and one for the four equivalent protons in the two —CH_2— groups.

  v The —OH peak would disappear.

  vi The —OH peak would not be split but the —CH_2— peak would be a triplet.

  vii One peak as all four protons (^1H atoms) in epoxyethane are equivalent.

5 **a** The cross-linking sulfur atoms form strong covalent bonds between the flexible polymer chains ensuring they return to their original positions following distortion.

  b

  c

  d In nylon, the amine and carboxylic acid (or acyl chloride) groups are in different monomer molecules whereas in proteins the amino acids have both functional groups in the same molecule. (Note: nylon is sometimes made from a single monomer molecule which has both functional groups, e.g. $HOOC(CH_2)_5NH_2$.)

In nylon, the two amine groups and the two carboxylic acid (or acyl chloride) groups are usually separated by several carbon atoms within each monomer molecule. In the natural amino acids that form proteins, the amine group and the carboxyilic acid group are always separated by one carbon atom.

e HDPE has stronger van der Waals' forces between its polymer chains, as they have fewer side-branches so can pack closer together, than those in the highly branched LDPE polymer chains. These stronger van der Waals' forces cause HDPE to have a higher softening temperature, so it can withstand a temperature of 100 °C without losing its shape.

6 a

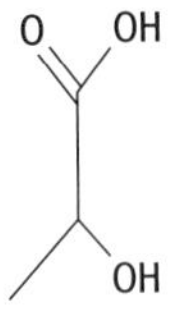

or

b

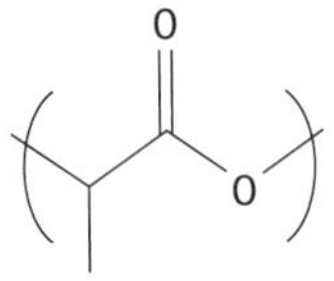

or

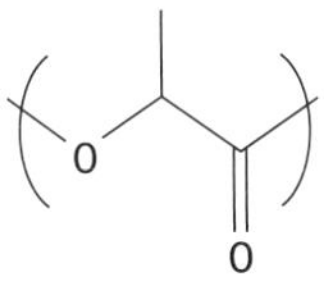

7 a objects whose size ranges from 1×10^{-9} to 1×10^{-7} metres, i.e. from 1 to 100 nanometres.

b Allotropes are two forms of the same element in the same physical state.

c A single peak as all the carbon atoms in C_{60} are equivalent.

d No peaks (as there are no hydrogen atoms present).

e graphite

8 a $ClO\bullet + O \rightarrow Cl\bullet + O_2$

b A termination step ends a series of propagation steps as two free radicals react to make a molecule. Examples are:
$Cl\bullet + ClO\bullet \rightarrow Cl_2 + O$
$Cl\bullet + Cl\bullet \rightarrow Cl_2$
$ClO\bullet + ClO\bullet \rightarrow Cl_2 + O_2$

c The data do not support the statement as the data from 2000 onwards largely lies within the range of the 1990–2001 data.

9 a A polyamide will degrade more quickly because the amide link can undergo hydrolysis and the polymer chain will break down. The unreactive non-polar saturated hydrocarbon polymer chains in poly(alkenes) only have C—C and C—H bonds, which will not undergo hydrolysis.

b Bioleaching uses much less energy than smelting and can use low-grade waste as its raw material instead of depleting our limited supplies of high-grade copper ores (which are taken from open-cast mines that scar the landscape).

Glossary

acid dissociation constant, K_a the equilibrium constant for a weak acid: $K_a = \dfrac{[H^+][A^-]}{[HA]}$

acid a proton (hydrogen ion) donor.

acid–base indicator a substance which changes colour over a narrow range of pH values.

activation energy the minimum energy that colliding particles must possess for a successful collision that results in a reaction to take place.

active site (of an enzyme) the 'pocket' on an enzyme surface where the substrate binds and undergoes catalytic reaction.

active transport the movement of a substance against a concentration gradient.

acyl chloride a reactive organic compound related to a carboxylic acid, with the $-OH$ group in the acid replaced by a $-Cl$ atom, for example ethanoyl chloride, CH_3COCl.

addition reaction an organic reaction in which two reactant molecules combine to give a single product molecule.

addition polymerisation the reaction in which monomers containing carbon-to-carbon double bonds react together to form long-chain molecules called polymers.

adsorption (in catalysis) the first stage in heterogeneous catalysis – molecules of reactants (usually gases) form bonds with atoms on the surface of the catalyst.

alkali a base which is soluble in water.

alkaline earth metals the elements in Group II of the Periodic Table.

alkanes saturated hydrocarbons with the general formula C_nH_{2n+2}.

alkenes unsaturated hydrocarbons with a carbon–carbon double bond. Their general formula is C_nH_{2n}.

allotrope different crystalline or molecular forms of the same element. Graphite and diamond are allotropes of carbon.

alloy a mixture of two or more metals or a metal with a non-metal.

amino acid residue an amino acid unit within a polypeptide chain.

amphoteric able to behave as both an acid and a base. Aluminium oxide is amphoteric.

anion a negatively charged ion.

anode the positive electrode.

arenes hydrocarbons containing one or more benzene rings.

atomic orbitals regions of space outside the nucleus which can be occupied by one or, at most, two electrons. Orbitals are named s, p, d and f. They have different shapes.

ATP (adenosine triphosphate) a molecule involved in energy transfers in cells. The hydrolysis of ATP releases energy which can be used to do useful work, e.g. provide energy for enzyme-catalysed reactions, for muscle contraction or to drive molecules through cell membranes against a concentration gradient.

average bond energy a general bond energy value used for a particular bond, e.g. a $C-H$, when the exact bond energy is not required. Average bond energies are often used because the strength of a bond between two particular types of atom is slightly different in different compounds.

Avogadro constant the number of atoms (or ions, molecules or electrons) in a mole of atoms (or ions, molecules or electrons): its numerical value is 6.02×10^{23}.

azo dyes coloured compounds formed on the addition of phenol (or another aryl compound) to a solution containing a diazonium ion. They contain the $-N=N-$ group.

base a proton (hydrogen ion) acceptor.

bidentate ligands which can form two co-ordinate bonds from each ion or molecule to the central transition metal ion.

biofuels renewable fuels, sourced from plant or animal materials.

boiling point the temperature at which the vapour pressure is equal to the atmospheric pressure.

Boltzmann distribution a graph showing the distribution of energies of the particles in a sample at a given temperature.

bond energy/bond enthalpy the energy needed to break 1 mole of a particular bond in 1 mole of gaseous molecules.

Born–Haber cycle a type of enthalpy cycle used to calculate lattice energy.

Brønsted–Lowry theory of acids acids are proton donors and bases are proton acceptors.

buffer solution a solution that minimises changes in pH when moderate amounts of acid or base are added. Common forms of buffer consist of either a weak acid and its conjugate base or a weak base and its conjugate acid.

carbocation an alkyl group carrying a single positive charge on one of its carbon atoms, e.g. $^+CH_2CH_3$

catalyst a substance that increases the rate of a reaction but remains chemically unchanged itself at the end of the reaction.

cathode the negative electrode.

cation a positively charged ion.

cell membrane a membrane surrounding each cell which controls the entry and exit of particular biological molecules and ions.

ceramic an inorganic non-metallic solid which is prepared by heating a substance or mixture of substances to a high temperature.

chiral centre a carbon atom with four different groups attached, creating the possibility of optical isomers.

closed system a system in which matter or energy is not lost or gained, e.g. gases in a closed vessel.

codon a set of three successive bases in mRNA which codes for a specific amino acid in protein synthesis.

cofactor a small molecule which is not a substrate but which is essential for an enzyme-catalysed reaction.

common ion effect the reduction in the solubility of a dissolved salt by adding a compound which has an ion in common with the dissolved salt. This often results in precipitation of the salt.

competitive inhibition enzyme inhibition by molecules that bind to the active site, preventing the normal substrate from reacting. They have a structure similar to the substrate molecule. The inhibition is reversible.

complementary base pairing In nucleic acids, bases are said to be complementary to each other if they form specific hydrogen-bonded pairs. In DNA adenine (A) always pairs with thymine (T) and cytosine (C) always pairs with guanine (G).

complex a central transition metal ion surrounded by ligands.

compound a substance made up of two or more elements bonded (chemically joined) together.

condensation the change in state when a vapour changes to a liquid.

condensation reaction a reaction in which two organic molecules join together and in the process eliminate a small molecule, such as water or hydrogen chloride.

conjugate pair (acid/base) an acid and base on each side of an equilibrium equation that are related to each other by the difference of a proton; e.g. the acid in the forward reaction and the base in the reverse reaction or the base in the forward reaction and the acid in the reverse reaction.

co-ordinate bond a covalent bond where both electrons in the bond come from the same atom.

co-ordination number the number of co-ordinate (dative) bonds formed by ligands to the central transition metal ion in a complex.

coupling reaction when a diazonium ion reacts with an alkaline solution of phenol (or similar compound) to make an azo-dye.

covalent bond a bond formed by the sharing of pairs of electrons between two atoms.

cracking the process in which large, less useful hydrocarbon molecules are broken down into smaller, more useful molecules.

dative covalent bond another name for a co-ordinate bond.

degenerate orbitals atomic orbitals at the same energy level.

dehydration a reaction in which a water molecule is removed from a molecule, e.g. in the dehydration of an alcohol to give an alkene.

delocalised electrons electrons which are not associated with a particular atom – they can move between three or more adjacent atoms.

denaturation the process by which the three-dimensional structure of a protein or other biological macromolecule is changed, often irreversibly. Relatively high temperatures, extremes of pH and organic solvents often cause denaturation.

desorption the last stage in heterogeneous catalysis. The bonds holding the molecule(s) of product(s) to the surface of the catalyst are broken and the product molecules diffuse away from the surface of the catalyst.

diazotisation the reaction between phenylamine and nitrous acid (nitric(III) acid), HNO_2, to give a diazonium salt in the first step in making an azo dye.

dipeptide the product formed when two amino acids react together.

dipole a separation of charge in a molecule. One end of the molecule is permanently positively charged and the other is negatively charged.

discharge(d) the conversion of ions to atoms or molecules at electrodes during electrolysis, for example, during the electrolysis of concentrated sodium chloride solution, chlorine is discharged at the anode by the conversion of Cl^- ions to Cl atoms which then combine to form Cl_2 molecules.

displayed formula a drawing of a molecule that shows all the atoms and bonds within the molecule.

disproportionation the simultaneous reduction and oxidation of the same species in a chemical reaction.

dissociation the break-up of a molecule into ions, for example, when HCl molecules dissolve in aqueous solution, they dissociate completely into H^+ and Cl^- ions.

disulfide bridge an S—S bond formed when the —SH groups on the side-chain of two cysteine residues in a protein combine. Disulfide bridges help maintain the tertiary structure of some proteins.

DNA (deoxyribonucleic acid) a polymer with a double helical structure containing two sugar–phosphate chains with nitrogenous bases attached to them. The sequence of bases forms a code which is used to form more DNA by replication or to encode mRNA (transcription).

dot-and-cross diagram a diagram showing the arrangement of the outer-shell electrons in an ionic or covalent element or compound. The electrons are shown as dots or crosses to show their origin.

double covalent bond two shared pairs of electrons bonding two atoms together.

dynamic (equilibrium) in an equilibrium mixture, molecules of reactants are being converted to products at the same rate as products are being converted to reactants.

electrochemical cell two half-cells in separate compartments joined by a salt bridge. When the poles of the half-cells are joined by a wire, electrons travel in the external circuit from the half-cell with the more negative $E^\ominus$ value to the half-cell with the more positive $E^\ominus$ value.

electrode potential the voltage measured for a half-cell compared with another half-cell.

electrode a rod of metal or carbon (graphite) which conducts electricity to or from an electrolyte.

electrolysis the decomposition of a compound into its elements by an electric current.

electrolyte a molten ionic compound or an aqueous solution of ions that is decomposed during electrolysis.

electron affinity (first electron affinity) $\Delta H^\ominus_{ea1}$; the enthalpy change when 1 mole of electrons is added to 1 mole of gaseous atoms to form 1 mole of gaseous 1– ions under standard conditions.

electron affinity (second electron affinity) $\Delta H^\ominus_{ea2}$; the enthalpy change when 1 mole of electrons is added to 1 mole of gaseous 1– ions to form 1 mole of gaseous 2– ions under standard conditions.

electron tiny subatomic particles found in orbitals around the nucleus. They have a negative charge but have negligible mass.

electronegativity the ability of an atom to attract the bonding electrons in a covalent bond.

electronic configuration a way of representing the arrangement of the electrons in atoms showing the principal quantum shells, the sub-shells and the number of electrons present, e.g. $1s^2 2s^2 2p^3$. The electrons may also be shown in boxes.

electropherogram the physical results of electrophoresis.

electrophile a species which can act as an acceptor of a pair of electrons in an organic mechanism.

electrophoresis the separation of charged particles by their different rates of movement in an electric field.

electrovalent bond another name for an ionic bond.

element a substance made of only one type of atom.

elimination a reaction in which a small molecule, such as H_2O or HCl, is removed from an organic molecule.

empirical formula the formula that tells us the simplest ratio of the different atoms present in a molecule.

endothermic term used to describe a reaction where energy is absorbed from the surroundings: the enthalpy change is positive.

energy levels (of electrons) the regions at various distances from the nucleus where electrons have a particular amount of energy. Electrons further from the nucleus have more energy. See principal quantum shells.

enhanced global warming the increase in average temperatures around the world as a consequence of the huge increase in the amounts of CO_2 and other greenhouse gases produced by human activity.

enthalpy change of atomisation $\Delta H^\ominus_{at}$; the enthalpy change when 1 mole of gaseous atoms is formed from its element under standard conditions.

enthalpy change of hydration $\Delta H^\ominus_{hyd}$; the enthalpy change when 1 mole of a specified gaseous ion dissolves in sufficient water to form a very dilute solution.

enthalpy change of solution $\Delta H^\ominus_{sol}$; the energy absorbed or released when 1 mole of an ionic solid dissolves in sufficient water to form a very dilute solution.

enthalpy change the energy transferred in a chemical reaction (symbol ΔH).

enthalpy cycle a diagram showing alternative routes between reactants and products that allows the determination of one enthalpy change from other known enthalpy changes by using Hess's law.

enthalpy profile diagram a diagram showing the enthalpy change from reactants to products along the reaction pathway.

enzyme activity a measure of the rate at which substrate is converted to product in an enzyme-catalysed reaction.

enzyme a protein molecule that is a biological catalyst. Most act on a specific substrate.

equilibrium constant a constant calculated from the equilibrium expression for a reaction.

equilibrium expression a simple relationship that links K_c to the equilibrium concentrations of reactants and products and the stoichiometric equation.

equilibrium reaction a reaction that does not go to completion and in which reactants and products are present in fixed concentration ratios.

esterification the reaction between an alcohol and a carboxylic acid (or acyl chloride) to produce an ester and water.

eutrophication an environmental problem caused by fertilisers leached from fields into rivers and lakes. The fertiliser then promotes the growth of algae on the surface of water. When the algae die, bacteria thrive and use up the dissolved oxygen in the water, killing aquatic life.

exothermic the term used to describe a reaction where energy is released to the surroundings: the enthalpy change is negative.

Faraday constant the charge carried by 1 mole of electrons (or 1 mole of singly charged ions). It has a value of 96 500 coulombs per mol ($C\,mol^{-1}$).

Faraday's laws first law: the mass of a substance produced at an electrode during electrolysis is proportional to the quantity of electricity passed in coulombs. Second law: the number of Faradays needed to discharge 1 mole of an ion at an electrode equals the number of charges on the ion.

feasibility (of reaction) the likelihood or not of a reaction occurring when reactants are mixed. We can use $E^{\ominus}$ values to assess the feasibility of a reaction.

Fehling's solution an alkaline solution containing copper(II) ions used to distinguish between aldehydes and ketones. A positive test is one in which the clear blue solution gives a red/orange precipitate when warmed with aldehydes, but no change is observed with ketones.

fragmentation the breaking up of a molecule into smaller parts by the breaking of covalent bonds in a mass spectrometer.

free radical very reactive atom or molecule which has a single unpaired electron.

free-radical substitution the reaction in which halogen atoms substitute for hydrogen atoms in alkanes. The mechanism involves steps in which reactive free-radicals are produced (initiation), regenerated (propagation) and consumed (termination).

fuel cell a source of electrical energy which comes directly from the energy stored in the chemicals in the cell, one of which is oxygen (which may come from the air).

functional group an atom or group of atoms in an organic molecule that determine the characteristic reactions of a homologous series.

gene a length of DNA that carries a code for making a particular protein.

general formula a formula that represents a homologous series of compounds using letters and numbers; e.g. the general formula for the alkanes is C_nH_{2n+2}. By substituting a number for n in the general formula you get the molecular formula of a particular compound in that homologous series.

general gas equation an equation relating the volume of a gas to the temperature, pressure and number of moles of gas. Also called the ideal gas equation.
$$pV = nRT$$

genetic code a code made up of sets of three consecutive nitrogenous bases that provides the information to make specific proteins.

genetic engineering the deliberate alteration of one or more bases in the DNA of an organism, leading to an altered protein with improved properties. Scientists hope to be able to use genetic engineering to eliminate genetic diseases which are caused by mutations in DNA.

genetic fingerprinting a technique based on matching the minisatellite regions of a person's DNA to a database of reference samples.

giant molecular structure/giant covalent structure structures having a three-dimensional network of covalent bonds throughout the whole structure.

GLC gas–liquid chromatography.

GLC/MS a technique in which a mass spectrometer is connected directly to a gas–liquid chromatograph to identify the components in a mixture.

haemoglobin the iron-containing protein found in red blood cells which transports oxygen around the body.

half-cell half of an electrochemical cell. The half-cell with the more negative $E^{\ominus}$ value supplies electrons. The half-cell with the more positive $E^{\ominus}$ value receives electrons.

half-equation in a redox reaction, an equation showing either an oxidation or a reduction.

half-life the time taken for the amount (or concentration) of the limiting reactant in a reaction to decrease to half its value.

halogens Group VII elements.

Hess's law the total enthalpy change for a chemical reaction is independent of the route by which the reaction takes place.

heterogeneous catalysis the type of catalysis in which the catalyst is in a different phase from the reactants. For example, iron in the Haber process.

homogeneous catalysis the type of catalysis in which the catalyst and reactants are in the same phase. For example, sulfuric acid catalysing the formation of an ester from an alcohol and carboxylic acid.

HPLC high-performance liquid chromatography.

hydrocarbon a compound made up of carbon and hydrogen only.

hydrogen bond the strongest type of intermolecular force – it is formed between molecules having a hydrogen atom bonded to one of the most electronegative elements (F, O or N).

hydrolysis the breakdown of a compound by water, which is often speeded up by reacting with acid or alkali.

hydrophobic the non-polar part of a molecule that has no attraction for water molecules ('water hating').

hydroxynitrile an organic compound containing both an —OH and a —CN group, e.g. 2-hydroxypropanenitrile, $CH_3CH(OH)CN$.

ideal gas a gas whose volume varies in proportion to the temperature and in inverse proportion to the pressure. Noble gases such as helium and neon approach ideal behaviour because of their low intermolecular forces.

initiation step the first step in the mechanism of free-radical substitution of alkanes by halogens. It involves the breaking of the halogen–halogen bond by UV light from the Sun.

intermolecular forces the weak forces between molecules.

ion polarisation the distortion of the electron cloud on an anion by a neighbouring cation. The distortion is greatest when the cation is small and highly charged.

ionic bond the electrostatic attraction between oppositely charged ions.

ionic product of water, K_w The equilibrium constant for the ionisation of water.

$$K_w = [H^+][OH^-]$$

ionisation energy, ΔH_i the energy needed to remove 1 mole of electrons from 1 mole of atoms of an element in the gaseous state to form 1 mole of gaseous ions.

isotopes atoms of an element with the same number of protons but different numbers of neutrons.

kinetic theory the theory that particles in gases and liquids are in constant movement. The kinetic theory can be used to explain the effect of temperature and pressure on the volume of a gas as well as rates of chemical reactions.

lattice a regularly repeating arrangement of ions, atoms or molecules in three dimensions.

lattice energy the enthalpy change when 1 mole of an ionic compound is formed from its gaseous ions under standard conditions.

le Chatelier's principle when any of the conditions affecting the position of equilibrium are changed, the position of that equilibrium shifts to minimise the change.

ligand a molecule or ion with one or more lone pairs of electrons available to donate to a transition metal ion.

lock-and-key mechanism a model used to explain why enzymes are so specific in their activity. It is suggested that the active site of the enzyme has a shape into which the substrate fits exactly – rather like a particular key fits a particular lock.

lone pairs (of electrons) pairs of electrons in the outer shell of an atom that are not bonded.

mass number see nucleon number.

mass spectrometer an instrument for finding the relevant isotopic abundance of elements and to help identify unknown organic compounds.

messenger RNA a type of RNA which is synthesised using part of the DNA strand as a template. The sequence of triplet bases along the mRNA codes for the sequence of amino acids in a protein.

metabolism the series of linked chemical reactions taking place in living organisms.

metalloid elements which have a low electrical conductivity at room temperature but whose conductivity increases with increasing temperature. Metalloids are found in a diagonal band running from the top left to nearly the bottom right of the p-block in the Periodic Table.

mobile phase the solvent in the chromatography process, which moves through the column or over the paper or thin layer.

molar mass the mass of a mole of substance in grams.

mole the unit of amount of substance. It is the amount of substance that has the same number of particles (atoms, ions, molecules or electrons) as there are atoms in exactly 12 g of the carbon-12 isotope.

molecular formula the formula that tells us the actual numbers of each type of atom in a molecule.

molecular ion the ion formed by the loss of an electron from the original complete molecule during mass spectrometry and which gives us the relative molecular mass of an unknown compound.

monodendate ligands, such as water and ammonia, which can form only one co-ordinate bond from each ion or molecule to the central transition metal ion.

monomer a small, reactive molecule that reacts to make long-chain molecules called polymers.

mutation a change in the structure of DNA that results in an alteration of the genetic code.

nanotechnology the design and production of machines that are so small we measure them in nanometres (nm), where $1\,nm = 1 \times 10^{-9}$ m.

neutron a subatomic particle found in the nucleus of an atom. It has no charge and has the same mass as a proton.

nitrogenous bases nitrogen-containing bases found in DNA and RNA. In DNA they are adenine (A), guanine (G), thymine (T) and cytosine (C). In RNA uracil (U) replaces thymine.

NMR nuclear magnetic resonance spectroscopy.

non-competitive inhibition a type of enzyme inhibition in which the inhibitor molecule binds to a region of the enzyme surface, often at a region other than the active site. It distorts the shape of the active site or blocks the active site permanently so that the active site no longer functions.

non-degenerate orbitals atomic orbitals that have been split to occupy slightly different energy levels.

non-polar (molecule) a molecule with no separation of charge; it will not be attracted to a positive or negative charge.

nucleon number the total number of protons and neutrons in the nucleus of an atom.

nucleophile species that can act as a donor of a pair of electrons.

nucleophilic addition the mechanism of the reaction in which a nucleophile attacks the carbon atom in a carbonyl group and adds across the $C=O$ bond, e.g. aldehydes or ketones reacting with hydrogen cyanide.

nucleotide a compound consisting of a nitrogenous base, a sugar (ribose or deoxyribose) and a phosphate group. Nucleotides form the basic structural units of DNA and RNA.

nucleus the small dense core at the centre of every atom, containing protons (positively charged) and neutrons (no charge). Nuclei are therefore always positively charged.

open system a system in which matter is lost or gained, e.g. a mixture of solids and gases in an open beaker.

optical resolution the separation of optically active isomers (enantiomers) from a mixture.

order of reaction the power to which the concentration of a reactant is raised in the rate equation. If the concentration does not affect the rate, the reaction is zero order. If the rate is directly proportional to the reactant concentration, the reaction is first order. If the rate is directly proportional to the square of the reactant concentration, the reaction is second order.

oxidation the addition of oxygen, removal of electrons or increase in oxidation number of a substance; in organic chemistry refers to a reaction in which oxygen atoms are added to a molecule and/or hydrogen atoms are removed from a molecule.

oxidation number (oxidation state) a number given to an atom in a compound which describes how oxidised or reduced it is.

oxidising agent a reactant that increases the oxidation number of (or removes electrons from) another reactant.

partial pressure the pressure that an individual gas contributes to the overall pressure in a mixture of gases.

partition coefficient the ratio of the concentrations of a solute in two different immiscible solvents when an equilibrium has been established.

peptide bond the link between the amino acid residues in a polypeptide or protein chain. The link is formed by a condensation reaction between the $-NH_2$ group of one amino acid and the $-COOH$ group of another amino acid.

periodicity the repeating patterns in the physical and chemical properties of the elements across the periods of the Periodic Table.

permanent dipole–dipole forces a type of intermolecular force between molecules which have permanent dipoles.

pH the hydrogen ion concentration expressed as a logarithm to base 10.
$$pH = -\log_{10}[H^+]$$

pi (π) bonds multiple covalent bonds involving the sideways overlap of p atomic orbitals.

pK_a values of K_a expressed as a logarithm to base 10.
$$pK_a = -\log_{10}[H^+]$$

polar (covalent bond) a covalent bond in which the two bonding electrons are not shared equally by the atoms in the bond. The atom with the greater share of the electrons has a partial negative charge, $\delta-$ and the other has a partial positive charge, $\delta+$.

polarising power (of a cation) the ability of a cation to attract electrons and distort an anion.

polyamides polymers whose monomers are bonded to each other via the amide link, $-CONH-$.

polyesters polymers whose monomers are bonded to each other via the ester link, $-COO-$.

polymer a long-chain molecule made up of many repeating units.

polypeptides natural polymers whose monomers are bonded to each other via the amide link, $-CONH-$, and whose monomers are amino acids.

primary alcohol an alcohol in which the carbon atom bonded to the $-OH$ group is attached to one other carbon atom (or alkyl group).

primary structure (of proteins) the sequence of amino acids in a polypeptide chain.

principal quantum shells, n regions at various distances from the nucleus which may contain up to a certain number of electrons. The first quantum shell contains up to 2 electrons, the second up to 8 and the third up to 18.

propagation step a step in a free-radical mechanism in which the radicals formed can then attack reactant molecules generating more free-radicals, and so on.

prosthetic group an ion or molecule that is permanently bound to part of an enzyme, for example, a Zn^{2+} ion is the prosthetic group in the enzyme carbonic anhydrase.

protein condensation polymer formed from amino acids and joined together by peptide bonds. Proteins can be structural (e.g. cartilage), catalysts (enzymes), hormones (e.g. insulin) or antibodies.

proton a positively charged subatomic particle in the nucleus.

rate constant the proportionality constant in the rate equation (see rate equation).

rate equation an equation showing the relationship between the rate constant and the concentrations of those reactants which affect the rate of reaction. The general form of the rate equation is:

$$rate = k[A]^m[B]^n$$

where k is the rate constant, [A] and [B] are the concentrations of those reactants which affect the rate of reaction, m is the order of the reaction with respect to A and n is the order of reaction with respect to B.

rate of reaction a measure of the rate at which reactants are used up or the rate at which products are formed. The units of rate are $mol\,dm^{-3}\,s^{-1}$.

rate-determining step the slowest step in a reaction mechanism.

real gases gases which do not obey the ideal gas law especially at low temperatures and high pressures.

redox reaction a reaction where oxidation and reduction take place at the same time.

reducing agent a reactant that decreases the oxidation number of (or adds electrons to) another reactant.

reduction the removal of oxygen, addition of electrons or decrease in oxidation number of a substance; in organic chemistry it is the removal of oxygen atoms from a molecule and/or the addition of hydrogen atoms to a molecule.

relative atomic mass the weighted average mass of the atoms of an element, taking into account the proportions of naturally occurring isotopes, measured on a scale on which an atom of the carbon-12 isotope has a mass of exactly 12 units.

relative formula mass the mass of one formula unit of a compound measured on a scale on which an atom of the carbon-12 isotope has a mass of exactly 12 units.

relative isotopic mass the mass of a particular isotope of an element on a scale where an atom of the carbon-12 isotope has a mass of exactly 12 units.

relative molecular mass the mass of a molecule measured on a scale on which an atom of the carbon-12 isotope has a mass of exactly 12 units.

replication the process of copying DNA during cell division; it is a complex process requiring a number of different enzymes and other compounds.

residue see amino acid residue.

retention time the time taken for a component in a mixture to travel through the column in GLC or HPLC.

reversible reaction a reaction in which products can be changed back to reactants by reversing the conditions.

R_f value the ratio of the distance a component has travelled compared to the distance travelled by the solvent front during paper chromatography or TLC.

ribosomes small units about 20 nm in diameter present in most cells, on which protein synthesis takes place. They contain rRNA and protein.

RNA (ribonucleic acid) a polynucleotide molecule which, in most organisms, is single stranded. There are several types of RNA including messenger RNA (mRNA), ribosomal RNA (rRNA) and transfer RNA (tRNA).

salt bridge a piece of filter paper soaked in potassium nitrate solution used to make electrical contact between the half-cells in an electrochemical cell.

saturated hydrocarbons compounds of hydrogen and carbon only in which the carbon–carbon bonds are all single covalent bonds, resulting in the maximum number of hydrogen atoms in their molecules.

secondary alcohol an alcohol in which the carbon atom bonded to the —OH group is attached to two other carbon atoms (or alkyl groups).

secondary structure (of proteins) the second level of protein structure. The folding of a polypeptide chain into specific structures (e.g. α-helix and β-pleated sheet) which are stabilised by hydrogen bonds formed between —CO and —NH groups in peptide bonds.

shielding the ability of inner shells of electrons to reduce the effective nuclear charge on electrons in the outer shell.

short tandem repeat (STR) analysis a DNA fingerprinting technique in which the enzyme DNA polymerase is used to copy selected short sequences of bases over a million times. This gives enough sample material to separate and detect using electrophoresis, even if the original sample was very small.

sigma (σ) bonds single covalent bonds, formed by the 'end-on' overlap of atomic orbitals.

single covalent bond a shared pair of electrons bonding two atoms together.

skeletal formula a simplified version of the displayed formula which has all the symbols for carbon and hydrogen atoms removed, as well as the carbon to hydrogen bonds. The carbon to carbon bonds are left in place as are the bonds to other atoms.

S_N1 mechanism the steps in a nucleophilic substitution reaction in which the rate of the reaction (which is determined by the slow step in the mechanism) involves only the organic reactant, e.g. in the hydrolysis of a tertiary halogenoalkane.

S_N2 mechanism the steps in a nucleophilic substitution reaction in which the rate of the reaction (which is determined by the slow step in the mechanism) involves two reacting species, e.g. in the hydrolysis of a primary halogenoalkane.

solubility product, K_{sp} the equilibrium expression showing the product of the concentrations of each ion in a saturated solution of a sparingly soluble salt at 298 K, raised to the power of the relative concentrations:
$$K_{sp} = [C^{y+}(aq)]^a[A^{x-}(aq)]^b$$
where a is the number of C^{y+} ions in one formula unit of the compound and b is the number of A^{x-} ions in one formula unit of the compound.

solute a substance that is dissolved in a solution.

specific most enzymes are described as specific because they will only catalyse one reaction involving one particular molecule or pair of molecules.

spectator ions ions present in a reaction mixture which do not take part in the reaction.

spin pair repulsion electrons repel each other since they have the same charge. Electrons arrange themselves so that they first singly occupy different orbitals in the same sub-level. After that they pair up with their spins opposed to each other.

splitting pattern the pattern of peaks that main signals are divided into in high-resolution NMR.

standard cell potential the difference in standard electrode potential between two half-cells.

standard conditions conditions of temperature and pressure which must be the same in order to compare moles of gases or enthalpy changes accurately. Standard conditions are a pressure of 10^5 pascals (100 kPa) and a temperature of 298 K (25 °C).

standard electrode potential the electrode potential of a half-cell when measured with a standard hydrogen electrode as the other half-cell.

standard enthalpy change an enthalpy change which takes place under the standard conditions of pressure (10^5 Pa) and temperature (298 k).

standard hydrogen electrode a half-cell in which hydrogen gas at a pressure of 1 atmosphere (101 kPa) bubbles into a solution of $1.00 \, mol \, dm^{-3} \, H^+$ ions. This electrode is given a standard electrode potential of 0.00 V. All other standard electrode potentials are measured relative to this value.

state symbol a symbol used in a chemical equation which describes the state of each reactant and product: (s) for solid, (l) for liquid, (g) for gas and (aq) for substances in aqueous solution.

stationary phase the immobile phase in chromatography that the mobile phase passes over or through. Examples are the surface of the thin-layer particles in TLC or the involatile liquid adsorbed onto the column in GLC or HPLC.

stereoisomers compounds whose molecules have the same atoms bonded to each other but with different arrangements of the atoms in space.

stoichiometry the mole ratio of the reactants and products in the balanced equation for a reaction.

strong acid/base an acid or base which is (almost) completely ionised in water.

structural formula the formula that tells us about the atoms bonded to each carbon atom in an organic molecule, e.g. $CH_3CH=CH_2$

structural isomers compounds with the same molecular formula but different structural formulae.

sub-shells regions within the principal quantum shells where electrons have more or less energy depending on their distance from the nucleus. Sub-shells are given the letters s, p, d and f.

substitution a reaction which involves the replacement of one atom, or group of atoms, by another.

substrate a molecule that fits into the active site of an enzyme and reacts.

successive ionisation energy ΔH_{i1}, ΔH_{i2}, etc: the energy required to remove the first, then the second, then the third electrons and so on from a gaseous atom or ion, producing an ion with one more positive charge each time. Measured in kJ per mole of ions produced.

surroundings in enthalpy changes, anything other than the chemical reactants and products, for example the solvent, the test tube in which the reaction takes place, the air around the test tube.

termination step the final step in a free-radical mechanism in which two free radicals react together to form a molecule.

tertiary alcohol an alcohol in which the carbon atom bonded to the —OH group is attached to three other carbon atoms (or alkyl groups).

tertiary structure (of proteins) the third level of protein structure. It involves further folding of the polypeptide chain which is stabilised by interactions between the amino acid side-chains (ionic interactions, hydrogen bonding, van der Waals' forces and disulfide bonds).

titre in a titration, the final burette reading minus the initial burette reading.

TLC thin-layer chromatography.

TMS tetramethylsilane. An inert, volatile liquid used as a reference in NMR, given a chemical shift of zero.

Tollens' reagent an aqueous solution of silver nitrate in excess ammonia solution, sometimes called ammoniacal silver nitrate solution. It is used to distinguish between aldehydes and ketones. It gives a positive 'silver mirror' test when warmed with aldehydes but no change is observed with ketones.

transcription the process by which the genetic message encoded on the template strand of DNA is 'copied' to make a strand of messenger RNA.

transfer RNA a type of RNA which transfers amino acids to a lengthening peptide chain during protein synthesis by interaction with mRNA and the ribosomes.

translation (in protein synthesis) the process by which the genetic message encoded by mRNA is translated at the ribosomes into a sequence of amino acids in the polypeptide chain. mRNA, tRNA and ribosomes are all involved in the process.

triple covalent bond three shared pairs of electrons bonding two atoms together.

turnover number the number of substrate molecules converted to product per minute per enzyme molecule.

two-way chromatography a technique used in paper or thin-layer chromatography in which one spot of a mixture is placed at the corner of a square sheet and is developed in the first solvent as usual. The sheet is then turned through 90° and developed in the second solvent, giving a better separation of components having similar R_f values.

unsaturated hydrocarbons compounds of hydrogen and carbon only whose molecules contain carbon-to-carbon double bonds (or triple bonds).

van der Waals' forces the weak forces of attraction between molecules caused by the formation of temporary dipoles.

vaporisation the change in state when a liquid changes to vapour.

vapour pressure The pressure exerted by a vapour in equilibrium with a liquid.

weak acid/base an acid or base which is only slightly ionised in water.

X-ray crystallography an analytical technique which uses the diffraction pattern of X-rays passed through a solid sample to elucidate its structure.

Index

Acknowledgements

We would like to thank the following for permission to reproduce images:

Cover: Pasieka / SPL

Figure 1.1, Martyn F Chillmaid / SPL; 1.2, Tek Image / SPL; 1.7, SPL; 1.8, Geoscience features; 1.9, Andrew Lambert / SPL; 1.10, Ben Johnson / SPL; 1.12, David Acaster; 1.13, Martyn F Chillmaid; 1.14, © GP Bowater / Alamy; 1.15, David Acaster; 1.16, Jim Varney / SPL; 2.1, NASA / JAXA; 2.2, Prof Peter Fowler / SPL; 2.6, University of Cambridge Cavendish Laboratory; 3.1, Charles D Winters / SPL; 3.3, Don Elbers; 4.1, Tony Camacho / SPL; 4.3, 4.7, 4.27, Charles D Winters / SPL; 4.29, Pasieka / SPL; 4.30, © Natural Visions; 4.37, sciencephoto / Alamy; 4.44, Steve Allen / SPL; 4.45, Andrew Lambert / SPL; 5.1l, © foodfolio / Alamy; 5.1c, © Modern Images Ltd / SPL; 5.1r, © D. Hurst / Alamy; 5.7, Natural History Museum; 5.14, Roberto de Gugliemo / SPL; 5.16, Burke / Triolo Productions; 6.1, Peter Menzel / SPL; 6.2, © David R Frazier Photolibrary. Inc / Alamy; 7.1, NASA; 7.2, © Mar Photographics / Alamy; 7.3, Charles D Winters / SPL; 7.7, ICI; 8.1, © Mike Goldwater / Alamy; 8.2, David Acaster; 8.7, © Images of Africa Photobank / Alamy; 8.11a, Andrew Lambert / SPL; 8.11b, © Linda Kennedy / Alamy; 8.14, © mediablitzimages; 9.1t, Cephas Picture Library; 9.1b, Seila Terry / SPL; 10.1, Serge Lachinov; 10.2, Gordon Woods, 3 Peterboro' Av. LE15 6EB; 10.9, 10.10, 10.11, Andrew Lambert / SPL; 10.12, David R Frazier Photolibrary, Inc. / Alamy; 10.15, Andrew Lambert / SPL; 11.1, © arnoenzerink.com; 11.5, Andrew Lambert / SPL; 11.6, LCpl. Andrew Z. Williams, United States Marine Corps; 11.7, 11.8, Andrew Lambert / SPL; 11.9, Dirk Wiersma / SPL; 11.10, Moirenc / hemis.fr; 11.11, 11.12, 11.13, Andrew Lambert / SPL; 11.15, © Ron Bull / Alamy; 12.1, © Tor Eigeland / Alamy; 12.3, Keith Kent / SPL; 12.6, GrowHow UK Ltd; 12.10, Nigel Cattlin; 12.11, geophotos / Alamy; 12.12, Cordelia Molloy / SPL; 12.13, Steve Taylor / SPL; 13.1, © Paul Springett / Alamy; 14.1, Stephane Compoint / eyevine; 14.5, Andrew Lambert / SPL; 14.6, dbimages / Alamy; 14.7, © Tina Manley / Alamy; 14.8, © National Geographic Image Collection / Alamy; 14.9, © Document General Motors / Reuter R / Corbis Sygma; 14.11a, Paul Rapson / SPL; 14.13, © Realimage / Alamy; 14.17, © Marcelo / Rudini / Alamy; 14.19, © Ashley Cooper / Alamy; 15.1, © Caro / Alamy; 15.8, © By Ian Miles-Flashpoint Pictures / Alamy; 15.9, Nasa / SPL; 16.2, AFP / Getty Images; 16.3, Bjorn Svensson / SPL; 16.4, 16.5, Andrew Lambert / SPL; 16.6, © Graphest / Alamy; 16.8, Andrew Lambert / SPL; 17.1t, © funkyfood London – Paul Williams / Alamy; 17.1b, © Art Directors & TRIP / Alamy; 17.3, 17.4, 17.5, Andrew Lambert / SPL; 18.1, © Scott Camazine / Alamy; 19.1 a–f, 19.4, 19.17, 19.19, 19.20, 19.22, Andrew Lambert / SPL; 19.23, © Michael Klinec / Alamy; 20.1, Bjorn Svensson; 20.2, Martin Shields / SPL; 20.3, Scientific Identity; 20.4, © Gordon Mills / Alamy; 20.5, Jerry Mason / SPL; 20.12, CNRI / SPL; 20.13, Barry Slaven / The Medical File; 20.15, Douglas Faulkner; 21.1, Jack Finch / SPL; 21.2, Martyn F Chillmaid; 21.3, Andrew Lambert / SPL; 21.16, Roger Norris; 21.20, Elenac / BASF; 22.1a, Erich Schrempp / SPL ; 22.1b, Paskieka / SPL and Albert Copley Visuals Ltd; 22.3l, © Phototake Inc. / Alamy; 22.3r, © Phototake Inc. / Alamy; 22.6, Wendy Meester; 23.1, Andrew Lambert / SPL; 23.2l, © Stock Connection Blue / Alamy; 23.2c, © Clair Dunn / Alamy; 23.2r, © Moodboard / Alamy; 23.3, 23.8, 23.9, Andrew Lambert / SPL; 24.1, © blickwimkel / Alamy; 24.5, 24.6, Andrew Lambert / SPL; 25.1, Michael Rosenfeld; 25.3, Andrew Lambert / SPL; 26.1, © Jake Lyell / Alamy; 26.6, 26.7, Andrew Lambert / SPL; 26.10, © imagebroker / Alamy; 26.11, © Images of Africa Photobank / Alamy; 27.1, Charles D Winters / SPL; 27.3, Corbis RF / Alamy; 28.1, Thomas Deerinck. Ncmir / SPL; 28.40, © Danita Delimont / Alamy; 28.57, © Imagebroker / Alamy; 29.2, R.A Longuehaye / SPL; 29.8, Cellmark Diagnostics;; 29.9, Tim Loveless, Oxford Archaeology; 29.10, Barry Iverson / DCI; 29.11, Donald Nausbaum; 29.15, Colin Cuthbert / SPL; 29.24, Philippe Plailly / Eurelios / SPL; 29.25, Lawrence Berkeley National Laboratory/ SPL; 29.38, © speedpix / Alamy; 30.1, © Bill Varie / Alamy; 30.7, © blickwinkel / Alamy; 30.8, The Mary Rose Trust; 30.11, IBM; 30.12, Trevor J. Simmons; 30.17, © Kristoffer Tripplaar / Alamy; 30.18, © Guenter Rossenbach / Corbis; 30.19, Roger Ressmeyer / Corbis

While every effort has been made, it has not always been possible to identify the sources of all images used, or to trace all copyright holders. If any omissions are brought to our attention we will be happy to include the appropriate acknowledgement on reprinting.

b = bottom; c = centre, l = left; r = right; t = top; SPL = Science Photo Library